MW00815256

Dinah Zike's
Photographic Reference Guide
to Kinesthetic Graphic Organizers

Foldables®, Notebook Foldables®, and VKVs® for Spelling and Vocabulary:

Test Prep, Academic Vocabulary, and ESL Strategies

Intermediate to Advanced
4th - 12th Grades

Dinah-Might Adventures, LP
P.O. Box 690328
San Antonio, Texas 78269
Phone (210) 698-0123
Fax (210) 698-0095
1-800-99-DINAH
Visit our website: **www.dinah.com**

Copyright © 2009 Dinah Zike
1st Edition 2009
2nd Edition 2010
Published by Dinah-Might Adventures, LP, San Antonio, Texas
www.dinah.com   1-800-99DINAH

ISBN-13: 978-1-882796-28-1
ISBN-10: 1-882796-28-4

Editors
Jan Manzanero, Senior Editor
Assistant Editors: Rhonda Meyer, Judi Youngers, Jami Humphrey, Sara Potter,
Carma Ward, Barbara Meyer, Jackie Petty, Ignacio Salas-Humara

Book Design and Layout
Dinah Zike

Photography
Ignacio Salas-Humara
All photos copyright ©2009 Dinah-Might Adventures, LP

Dedication:
To Dr. Judith Youngers, Founding Director of Dinah Zike Academy:
Thank you for helping me make my dream of a teacher academy come true.
Your professionalism, dedication to education, endless energy, tireless work ethic,
and love of language and literature are an inspiration to all who know you. I am thankful you
are part of my education family, neighborhood, and circle of friends. dz

Thank You!
Thank you to the many teachers and students who contributed Foldables® to this book.
A special thanks to the Dinah Zike Academy attendees and after-school groups.

The words and pictures used in these lessons as *real world print* (RWP) came from numerous
newspapers, magazines, flyers, and advertisements from across the U.S.—all valuable teaching
tools. The vast majority of the words and phrases used on the Foldables® and VKVs® were found in
the following publications, or supplements to these publications:
USA Today, San Antonio Express-News, Austin American-Statesman.

Dinah Zike's
Photographic Reference Guide
to Kinesthetic Graphic Organizers

Foldables®, Notebook Foldables®, and VKVs® for Spelling and Vocabulary:

Test Prep, Academic Vocabulary, and ESL Strategies

**Intermediate to Advanced
4th - 12th Grades**

Please contact DMA for permission to use parts of this book
in workshops, classes, or presentations.

Table of Contents

Table of Contents

Table of Contents

Keys to the Words

A Key to the Word Lists

*	Test-Prep Type Words
Sp	spelling demon
H	heteronym
	homograph
	homophone
Cl	clipped word
Int	interjection
SL	silent letter

Keys

Parts of Speech

adj.	adjective
adv.	adverb
conj.	conjunction
int.	interjection
n.	noun
prep.	preposition
pron.	pronoun
v.	verb

* Test-Prep Type Words

I have compiled the word lists in this book over a period of 20 years. Through the years, the lists have been transferred from my original 1980's computer—which had a dual floppy drive DOS program—through at least five other operating systems.

As I continued to add words from reading programs, worksheets, seminars, literacy guidelines, test preparation books, and words found on copies of old tests, I began to realize that many of the same words or various forms of the words were used on advanced tests year after year.

In my word lists, I coded words I considered "test-prep type words" with an asterisk, which indicated that I had found the words on, or on materials related to, advanced tests such as state exit exams, SAT/ACT tests, or test-prep study guides. Since testing methods and tests constantly change, by no means does an asterisk next to a word mean that the word will be found on any given test; instead, it indicates an advanced word that might be found in some form on tests, or that by knowing the etymology of the word students will be able to analyze and determine the meaning of related words when encountered on a test.

Etymological Abbreviations

Brit	British, Britain
E	English
F	French
Gk	Greek
It	Italian
Japn	Japanese
L	Latin
ME	Middle English
OE	Old English
OF	Old French
Span	Spanish

Other Abbreviations

VKV	Visual Kinesthetic Vocabulary
RWP	real world print
f.	feminine
m.	masculine

Dear Friends and Educators,

I am frequently asked, "When did you invent *Foldables?*" and "How did you become the 'hamburger' and 'hotdog' lady?" I enjoy sharing my story with teachers and students, and I'd like to share it with you to provide a historic reference for the 3-D instructional strategies presented in this book.

I first started designing and using paper-based manipulatives when I was in sixth grade. Originally, I used them as study aids to help organize my own notes in junior high, and later in high school and college. I discovered they also worked as study aids for the students who needed a little extra help whom I tutored throughout HS. Later, to make money for college, I worked with students with severe learning disabilities. I continued to design paper-based study aids, or manipulatives, and invented names for the folds I was using to make the manipulatives. *Hamburger, hotdog, taco, burrito,* and *shutterfold* were some of my first terms because they were easy for my "students" to remember. I adopted, or borrowed, the terms *mountain* and *valley* from origami books and programs.

Sometimes I got ideas for new manipulatives from greeting card folds or folded advertisements; but most of the time, I would just take paper and fold it to illustrate something I needed to remember or something I needed to teach others. That was the beginning of *Foldables,* even though they were not known by that name at the time. And since I started Junior High School in 1966 and graduated from high school in 1970, you can do the math: I've been designing, using, and teaching others to use my three-dimensional graphic organizers for over 40 years.

After graduating from college, I became a teacher. I taught school during the week and presented workshops and continuing education sessions for schools and conferences on the weekends. With the help of excited, creative teachers who attended my presentations, my three-dimensional graphic organizers began to spread across the U.S.; and I remember how thrilling it was to receive my first letters from teachers who were using my manipulatives in other countries, too.

In the 1970s and early 1980s, my folds and manipulatives were met with resounding approval in my teacher workshops; but when I presented my ideas for 3-D manipulatives to major publishing companies, I experienced rejection. I was told that the strategies were too time consuming, they were too dependent upon student production and writing, they were too artsy-craftsy for upper level students, and innumerable other negative critiques. For several years I sent query letters to publishers, trying to find someone who would print books with instructions on how to make and use my three-dimensional graphic organizers. This was over thirty years ago, and the world of education was paper based, but the paper was used to produce "ditto sheets" or duplicated worksheets, not 3-D study aids. To put this time in perspective, it was before most of the brain research was published, before cooperative learning was an accepted practice, and years before two-dimensional graphic organizers began to appear in nearly every educational publication—supplemental and required—as duplicable sheets. And the duplicated worksheets we used at this time were made on a crank machine that used a powerful fluid to copy information imbedded on purple masters.

Thoroughly frustrated, and with a file drawer full of rejections, I withdrew all the money I had accrued in my teacher retirement fund; and with a loan from my community bank in Anderson, Texas, I started my own publishing company in my garage in 1984. My first publications were not based upon my folds, even though I was still inventing new folds and using both the old and new manipulatives in my classroom, in my graduate work, and in my staff development training sessions. I began by publishing the thematic units I used in my classroom and taught in my staff development sessions, and I also published social studies materials I had developed to teach the history of my home state of Texas. I knew that those teaching aids were needed and were easily understood, and they would generate the revenue I needed to publish my book of 3-D manipulatives. (Looking back, I believe I lacked the confidence to put what little money I had into a book based solely on my folds because my folding activities had received so many rejections from so many successful companies!)

In 1986, after two years of garage publishing, I wrote my first book consisting entirely of my folds and 3-D graphic organizers. It was entitled *Dinah Zike's Big Book of Books and Activities*; and, like my other self-published books, it consisted of photocopied pages bound with notebook rings or brads. I often gave away parts of it as a handout at my workshops. In 1991, my company published the official, copyrighted, bound version of this award-winning book and included black-line illustrations to accompany the fold instructions, along with black-and-white photographs. It was one of the first (if not the first) supplemental educational books to use more photographs than black-line art.

Over the years I continued to design, publish, and teach others by using my three-dimensional graphic organizers, which continued to grow in popularity because teachers who used them successfully shared them with others. My folds were spreading across the country, and It was rewarding to see my ideas and hear my terms used by students, teachers, and professors. While presenting the Mary C. McCurdy lecture at the National Science Teachers Association Conference in 2000, Glencoe McGraw-Hill approached me to include my 3-D graphic organizers in their textbooks. Michael Oster, my dear friend with McGraw-Hill, coined the term *Foldables*, and today my *Foldables* are an exclusive feature of McGraw-Hill School Solutions. They appear as a study aid in nearly every K-12 McGraw-Hill textbook and many McGraw-Hill ancillaries.

Two-dimensional graphic organizers have been in use for decades, and I am certainly not the first person to fold paper to teach a skill or concept; but I started and popularized the practice of using innumerable three-dimensional graphic organizers as teaching aids and developing them into a supplemental program based upon proven, research-based skills and strategies. When I take Venn diagrams, concept maps, KWL lists, comparing and contrasting activities, and other research-based graphic organizers and make them as *Foldables*, they have tabs or layers so main ideas can be written and viewed clearly on the top plane and supporting facts, definitions, and notes can be recorded on underlying planes, or under the tabs. (See Appendix Two, Research Citations, page 420.)

You will see my *Foldables* used in other people's presentations and publications, but as the originator of *Foldables* and *VKVs* (*Visual Kinesthetic Vocabulary* manipulatives introduced in this book), I present this photographic reference guide to you as a compilation of 40 years of my experience inventing 3-D graphic organizers. Many of you know and use my many content-specific *Foldable* publications, but this is my first book published specifically for 4th-12th grade vocabulary and spelling. In it, you will find hundreds of ideas on ways you can use *Foldables* and *VKVs* (*Visual Kinesthetic Vocabluary Flashcards*) with your students to create a print-rich environment.

Have fun and be creative as you use and adapt the *Foldables* and *VKVs* in this book!

Before

During

After
With Husband Ignacio Salas-Humara

Please support breast cancer research and awareness programs.
Tell those you love to get mammograms.

Introducing Visual Kinesthetic Vocabulary

P.S. My Pre-K-3rd VKV book and this, the second book in the series, present my VKVs (Visual Kinesthetic Vocabulary) for the first time in print! I have used them in workshops for many years, and we teach them at the Dinah Zike Academy; but this is my first publication demonstrating my VKVs for 4th-12th test prep and ESL/ELL classes.

What are VKVs? In my years of teaching, I have made hundreds, probably thousands, of flashcards—confusing word cards, root word cards, parts of speech cards, vocabulary cards. I tried different organizational methods to help me retrieve the appropriate cards when needed, but still had to deal with hundreds of cards.

While learning K-12 reading strategies, I discovered sets of stapled word family cards that I loved to use because one "card" made numerous words, and the cards were kinesthetic. Who knows when these stapled card sets were first used in classrooms? I don't remember using them myself as a student in the '50s, but I did use them as a teacher in the '70s. These cards inspired me to invent other kinesthetic methods for manipulating and forming words. (See pages 367-393.)

Twenty years ago, I began designing VKVs with three goals in mind:

1. I wanted two-dimensional words to become three-dimensional, allowing one or more parts of the word—initial or final consonant, medial vowel/vowels, root word, blend, prefix, suffix—to be manipulated and changed to form numerous words.

The flashcards focused student attention on the part of the word being manipulated as well as the stationary part of the word. My goal, by placing visual and kinesthetic "importance" on a movable portion of a word, and by having students encounter the word base several times while manipulating the VKV, was to foster students' ability to transfer what they learned during the experience to similar words found in print.

2. I wanted to find a way to decrease the number of word cards I had to organize and store, and yet maintain or increase the number of words presented for student interaction and immersion; so I tried to design flashcards where each card presented two or more words. My mission was to invent folds that would kinesthetically present as many words as possible, based on a commonality. When I designed one VKV flashcard that presented 14 words, I was ecstatic and students loved it! (See page 300.)

VKV® Three-Word Example: Irregular Verb Conjugation

3. I designed the flashcards using only one sheet of paper, or one strip of paper, that was neither glued nor stapled. You will see a few exceptions to this rule where I use glue, but the majority of my VKVs are neither glued nor stapled unless they are placed within a composition book or a spiral notebook.

The VKV forming the words spring, sprang, and sprung is typical—one sheet of paper used to form three words without using glue or staples. The VKV below uses one sheet of paper to form five words, but it is an exception in that it works better if the sections are glued together. See page 392.

VKV® Five-Word Example: Prefix and Root Analysis

Double VKV® Flashcard Example: Contractions

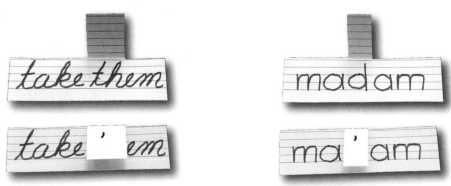

This personal challenge resulted in the VKVs you will find in this book and other books in this series. The more experienced I became as a teacher in the early '80s, the more I realized the need for 3-D graphic organizers to enhance the teaching of phonics, spelling, vocabulary, grammar, and cognates in all grade levels. Older students responded as positively to the kinesthetic aspect of the VKVs as did elementary students. I used these folds when I taught first graders to read, tutored middle school and high school students with learning disabilities, helped ESL and ELL students learn English, and experimented with strategies to prepare HS students for GED, SAT, and ACT testing.

Today you will find my *Foldables* and VKVs used to teach a wide range of skills, from pre-Kindergarten picture words to college preparatory vocabulary. This book focuses on 4th to 12th grades. Other books available in this series feature activities and word lists for Pre-K to 3rd grades and English-Spanish Cognates.

Please take the time to read the rest of the introduction for ideas on how to make, store, organize, and use *Foldables* and VKVs. Have fun and be creative,

DZ

A Summary of VKVs®
Visual Kinesthetic Vocabulary

VKVs kinesthetically focus on words and their structure, use, and meaning. VKVs are also referred to as *interactive or kinesthetic flashcards*.

1. VKVs make two-dimensional words three-dimensional, allowing one or more parts of each word to be manipulated and changed to form numerous words with a common part.

2. VKVs present two, three, four, six, or more words on each flashcard.

3. VKVs are usually made using one sheet or section of paper that is neither glued nor stapled, but shaped in a manner that allows strategically designed tabs to be folded or unfolded to form words.

Single VKV® Flashcard Example (below): Double suffix example forms three words.

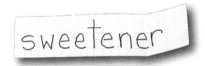  

Double VKV® Flashcard Example (below): Adding affixes to a word to form multiple words.

Triple VKV® Flashcard Example (below): Adding two different suffixes to the same word.

How to Make Classroom VKVs®

Instructions for making VKVs can be found in Appendix One and throughout this book. Photographs illustrate how to fold them, and photographs of finished VKVs are also featured throughout.

What Size Do I Make Classroom VKVs®?

Most classroom VKVs are teacher-made and based upon a single sheet of paper folded into thirds along the short, or horizontal, axis. I usually use 8½" x 11" regular photocopy paper or index weight paper (80#). I refer to the basic shapes of VKV Flashcards as either single, double, or triple, depending on how or whether they are cut.

1. **Single VKV Flashcard**: A sheet of 8½" x 11" paper folded into thirds along the horizontal axis, and cut to form three Single Flashcards.

1.

2. **Double VKV Flashcard**: A sheet of 8½" x 11" paper folded into thirds along the horizontal axis, and cut to form a Single and a Double Flashcard.

2.

3. **Triple VKV Flashcard**: A sheet of 8½" x 11" paper folded into thirds along the horizontal axis. All three sections are used.

3.

Classroom VKVs® Are All the Same Size: Even though VKVs have many different shapes and tab configurations, when folded, they are all the same height if they were made from the same size paper. As illustrated below, a single sheet of 8½" x 11" heavy-weight paper (80# to 110#) can be cut to form the following:

     a) three Single VKV Flashcards
     b) one Double and one Single VKV Flashcard
     c) one Triple VKV Flashcard

a.   b.   c.

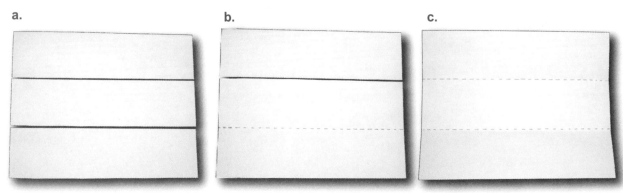

Supersize the VKVs® (right): If you have a large group of students and feel you need to make your classroom VKVs as large as possible for easier reading, consider making them out of 11" x 17" heavyweight paper (80# to 110#). **Note**: To introduce four new words based upon the same Latin root to a group of college biology students in a theater-style classroom, I used a VKV made from posterboard. I was pleasantly surprised when 50% of the class came forward to manipulate the VKV at the end of the period.

One Flashcard, Four Terms:
abolish
abolition
abolitionist
abolitionist movement

11" x 17"

abolitionist movement (1831–1860)

abolish

abolition

abolitionist (1831–1860)

Dual-Cut Scissors (above and below): I found that the tabs on VKVs or Foldables made for classroom use were easier and faster to open if there was space between them. I created this space by making two cuts—one on each side of a fold line—every time I made a classroom VKV or a Foldable. This technique works fine, but it is time consuming. My company now offers Dual-Cut Scissors that cut two lines at the same time to form this space. www.dinah.com

Declarative Imperative

Exclamatory ...EVERYDAY!

Interrogative What types of jobs can we get for $819 billion?

THE BEST! CHOICE!

VKV® Flashcard Box (below): Throughout a semester, I would make different VKV Flashcards and store them in a VKV Box so I could retrieve them for review at a future date or assign them as homework for a student who missed class. Once again, if all of the teacher-made demo VKVs are made using 8½" x 11" paper, they can be stored and organized using the lid of a 5000-sheet/10-ream paper box. Dividers can be made by cutting posterboard into 4" x 10½" sections and labeling them along a long edge. VKV Flashcards can also be stored in recycled cereal boxes (see page 36) or in labeled plastic bags.

Two Vowels
Abbreviations
Vocabulary
Prefixes
Consonants: Double
Antonyms graphs
Alphabetizing

V-K-Vs

Visual Kinesthetic Vocabulary

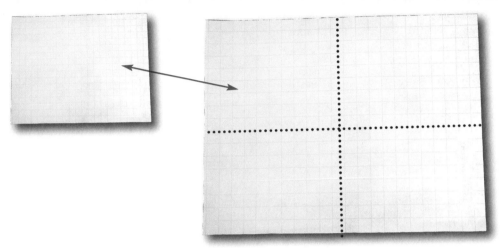

What Size VKVs® Do Students Make?

Student VKVs are commonly made using quarter sheets of paper. One sheet of notebook paper, grid paper, or photocopy paper yields four flashcards. Each quarter section is folded into thirds along the short axis to form three long sections.

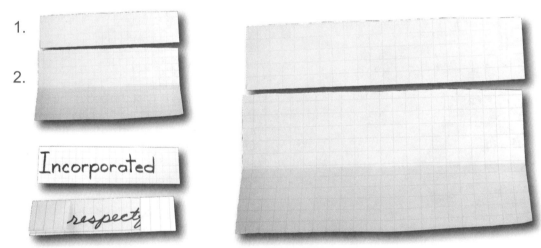

1. **Single VKV® Flashcard:** One-third of a quarter sheet of paper.
2. **Double VKV® Flashcard:** Two-thirds of a quarter sheet of paper.
3. **Triple VKV® Flashcard:** All three sections of a quarter sheet of paper.

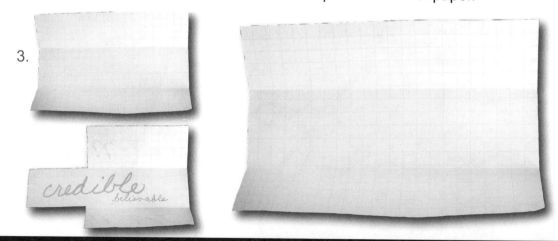

Shrink the VKVs® (below): Compare the VKV (below left) made using a quarter sheet (4½" x 5½") of paper with a classroom-sized VKV made using 8½" x 11" paper (below right).

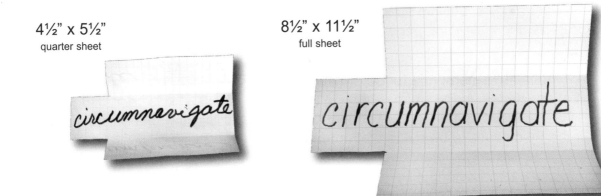

4½" x 5½"
quarter sheet

8½" x 11½"
full sheet

Single-, Double-, or Triple VKV® Flashcards (below) can be made using large index cards, small legal paper tablets, handwriting tablets, or colorful note cards.

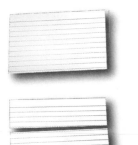

Other VKV® Materials (above): Single and Double VKV Flashcards can be made from small index cards, as illustrated in the photo above.

White or Colored Paper? The majority of Foldables, and nearly all VKVs, are made using plain white paper or binder paper due to cost, availability, and readability. It is much easier to read a word written on a white flashcard than to read a word on a colored card. Colors also provide clues that students could become dependent on. I frequently use colored paper to make Foldables or VKVs to collect words cut from *real world print (RWP)*, or commercial print. I justify using the more expensive colored paper if it is to be used by a large group of students or an entire class.

How to Make Foldables®:

Instructions for making my most commonly used Foldables can be found at the back of this book in Appendix Two, pages 395 to 419. When Foldables are featured in photographs, instructional strategies, bulletin boards, teacher- or student-made activities, and class or group projects, the instruction page for the Foldable will be noted in the photo caption.

What Size Do I Make Foldables®?

The following is my general rule for determining paper sizes when making Foldables:

If every student in the class is making a Foldable, use 8½" x 11" photocopy paper, notebook paper, or grid paper. Colored paper is great, but seldom available.

If the Foldable is to be made by the teacher and used by all students to collect words and sentences, use 11" x 17" index-weight (80#) or cover-stock paper (100#), found in office supply stores.

If the Foldable is for class use, and if large pictures or lots of quarter-sheet sized student writing cards will be glued onto the front tabs or under the tabs, use posterboard, chart paper, or sections of butcher paper.

Pocket Chart with Word Strip (below): Use posterboard to make this wall Pocket Chart. VKVs and Foldables are stored in the large pocket and displayed in the bottom strip formed by folding and stapling a 1" tab.

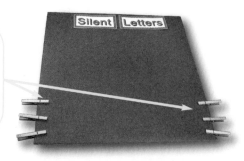

Use clothespins or binder clips to hold the pocket closed until the glue dries.

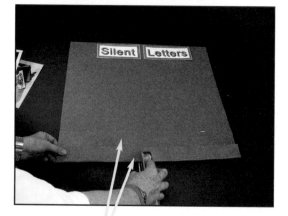

Fold the pocket 1" deeper than needed to store VKV Flashcards and quarter-sheet note cards. Fold a second pocket 1" deep and staple along the thick bottom fold.

Notebook Foldables®: Notebooking is used across the United States in all content areas. It is an easy way for students to keep track of notes and daily work assignments, and it results in a cumulative view of a period of instruction. Several problems were encountered when Foldables were glued into composition books and spirals:

- Most of the time, Foldables were too big to fit on a page in a composition book.
- When Foldables were glued to the page, paper was wasted because neither the backs of the Foldables, nor the paper in the notebook that was under the Foldables, could be used.
- Notebooks that included Foldables were exceedingly thick and difficult to use because of the added paper.

I've adapted my Foldables to be used with notebooks, and I've developed a CD of templates that are exactly the size needed for notebooks. They also allow teachers and students to individualize each Foldable. In this book you will see examples of both my original Independent Foldables and the newer Notebook Foldables:

Independent Foldables stand alone as daily work, note-taking devices, assessment tools, and projects. They can be glued inside larger Foldables to form a cumulative project and/or study guide. **Dependent Foldables**, or **Notebook Foldables**, are designed to form the front tabs of a Foldable with a notebook page forming the back. Notebook Foldables usually use half the paper needed for Independent Foldables. These Foldables are *dependent* upon another piece of paper.

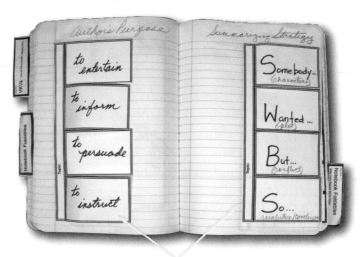

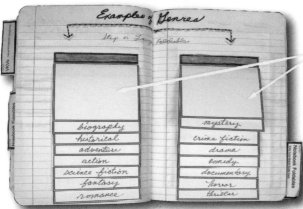

Above: Four-Tab Notebook Foldables were printed using a *Notebook Foldables* CD template, and then labeled by hand. The CD also allows the option of labeling the tabs using a computer.

Left: Fourteen genres of literature can be defined, and information collected on each, using this Notebook Foldable version of a Layered Foldable.

Dinah Zike's
Notebook Foldables® for Spirals, Binders, & Composition Books
www.dinah.com
1-800-99dinah

What Goes Under Foldable® Tabs?

1. Information obtained from a dictionary:
   a. definitions
   b. pronunciation guides
   c. parts of speech
   d. etymologies of roots, prefixes, and/or suffixes
   www.dictionary.reference.com
2. A phrase, sentence, or short paragraph using the word in a manner that illustrates its meaning
3. Students can write related words or include related words from RWP (real world print):
   a. words with the same root
   b. words with the same prefix or suffix
   c. words with the same consonant or vowel cluster
   d. words with the same phonogram
   e. conjugations of verbs (Example: swim, swam, swum)
   f. degrees of comparison of adjectives (Example: cold, colder, coldest)
   g. confusing spelling variations of words (Example: bath, bathe)
   www.wordnavigator.com
   www.morewords.com
4. Information obtained from a thesaurus:
   antonyms for the term/s
   synonyms for the term/s
   www.thesaurus.com
5. Idioms that use the featured word or its root
   www.idioms.thefreedictionary.com
   www.idiomsite.com
   www.idiomconnection.com
6. Related abbreviations, acronymns, or initializations
   www.abbreviations.com
7. Compound words that include the term/s as part of the word
   closed compound words
   open compound words
   hyphenated compound words
8. Homographs or homophones related to a term
9. Translations into other languages
   www.dictionary.reverso.net
   Spanish - English; English - Spanish
   French - English; English - French
   German - English; English - German
   Portuguese - English; English - Portuguese

Make an Original and Photocopy for Individual Use (below right): Use one sheet of 8½" x 11" paper to make a Foldable or VKV to be used by the class, and then photocopy it for individual student use. Photocopy one side (usually the side with the most print) and have students fold, cut, and label the other side to make their individual Foldables. Students continue to add RWP words and write their own words, sentences, definitions, and more on these study aids.

Too Easy, Too Hard, Just Right: You can take advantage of the fact that students find words of varying levels of difficulty in RWP, literature, and content text-books. The various word levels can be used to individualize student work. On a photocopied Foldable, have students use a highlighter to mark words they need to study for spelling tests, words they should be prepared to use in vocabulary drills or while reading, or words they are to use in a written assignment. Different marker colors can be used to differentiate between different assignments.

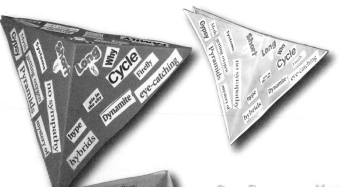

One Becomes Many:
Photocopy one side of a class- or group-made Foldable, and have students finish the Foldable to make their own personal study guide.
Above left: photocopied Pyramid
Above right: photocopied Shutterfold
Left: photocopied Four-Door Display.
Right: photocopied Twelve-Tab Foldable.

ESL/ELL Multi-Tab Example (right): In this example, the outside word list (words on the front of the tabs) was photocopied. Students folded the 11" x 17" photocopied sheet in half like a *hotdog* with the words to the outside. Students cut between the photocopied words (being careful not to cut through the back of the folded sheet) to form a Twelve-Tab Foldable. Students continued to place names of the months and abbreviations for the months on the front tabs, and to write about things that happen in each month under the tabs. Information on holidays, birthdays, special family events, and school functions can be included.

Design Projects to Grow: Continue to immerse students in previously learned skills and previously written print by "growing" Foldables. The "old" skills on the first Foldables glued into a project become easier with students' continued use and exposure. When skills begin to seem easy, students gain confidence. Students take an amazing amount of pride in personal and class projects that grow into scrapbook-like collections of their learning and progress. Foldable projects are great study and assessment aids.

Puzzle Pieces: Foldables made using 8½" x 11" paper can be used like puzzle pieces within student projects. Project Foldables are made using 11" x 17" or 12" bx 18" paper or posterboard. The type of fold and the size of paper used to make each Foldable example glued onto the projects pictured below has been written on the front of each.

See project example, pages 64-65.

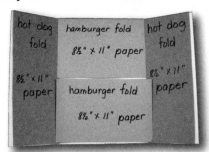

Hotdog Puzzle Pieces: *Hotdog*-shaped Foldables (above) or two quarter-sheet-sized Foldables (below) made using 8½" x 11" paper will fit on the sides of an 11" x 17" Shutterfold Project. Students can plan their projects as if the Foldables were puzzle pieces.

Posterboard Shutterfold Projects (below):

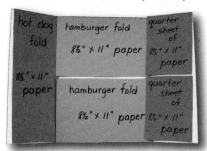

Hamburger and Quarter-Sheet Puzzle Pieces: Foldable *hamburger* folds (above) made using 8½" x 11" paper fit on the inside sections of an 11" x 17" Shutterfold Project. Two quarter-sheet-sized Foldables (below) also fit in the *hamburger*-sized space.

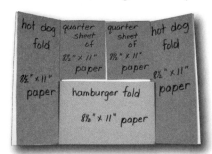

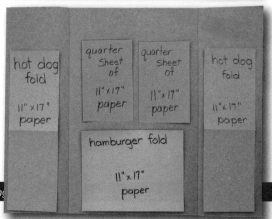

Content Project Foldables®: Small Foldables can be glued into larger Foldables to make skills-based projects. Some Foldable projects might grow over a week, a six-week period, or the entire school year. Other Project Foldables might be used to collect unit- or skills-based work and information. Skills-based Project Foldables are perfect for content subjects. The example on this page shows how posterboard can be used to make a large science Foldable that can become the "home" for smaller Foldables and quarter sheets or half sheets of paper.

Right: Two sheets of posterboard were used to make the Layered Foldable entitled *Angiosperms*. The three sections of the Foldable were labeled with the three main ideas that students need to focus on during this study.

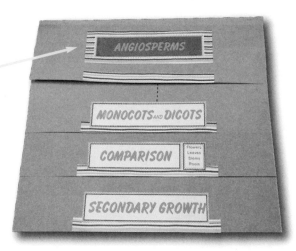

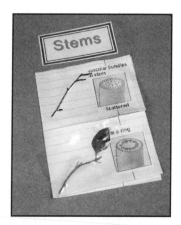

Above: A full sheet of notebook paper, folded like a *hamburger* and cut to form a Two-Tab Foldable, was used to compare and contrast monocot and dicot root systems.
Below: Examples of monocot and dicot flowers were taped to the front tabs of the Foldable to illustrate how monocot flowers usually have petals in multiples of three and dicot petals are usually in fours or fives.

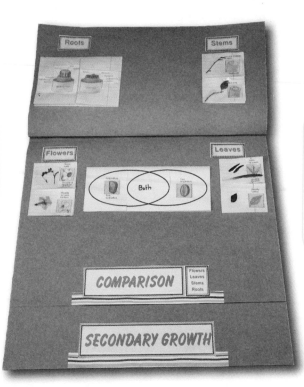

Above: A half sheet of notebook paper was used to make a small Two-Tab Foldable. It was used to record information about the differences between monocot and dicot stems.
Below: The same Foldable was used to compare and contrast monocot and dicot leaf structures. Note the shape and vein patterns of the leaves on the diagrams and the specimens taped to the tabs.

Clear Tape Laminate: Clear 2" tape was used to adhere examples of monocot and dicot flowers, leaves, stems, and seeds to the small Foldables on this large project.

Foldables® Foldables® Within Foldables®

Foldables® in Large Foldable® Projects: Place Foldables made from 8½" x 11" paper or 11" x 17" paper and VKVs of any size inside the Social Studies Bound Book Dictionary made from sheet posterboard (below left) or the Cognates Dictionary made from a half sheet of posterboard (right and below right). See page 401.

Three-Column Chart Foldable: See page 415.

Half-Book Foldable: See page 395.

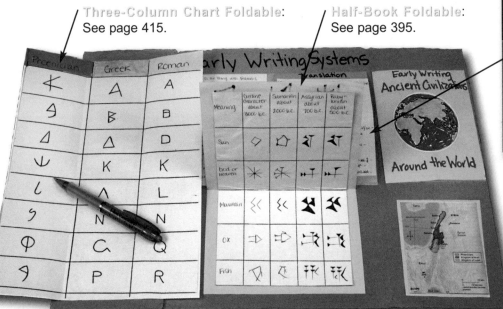

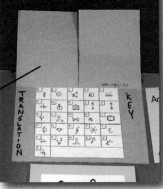

Two-Tab Foldable: See page 396.

A **Shutterfold Project** (left) can be made using 11" x 17" or 12" x 18" paper. **See project, pages 64-65.**

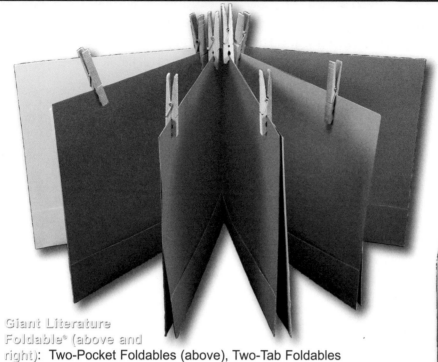

Giant Literature Foldable® (above and right): Two-Pocket Foldables (above), Two-Tab Foldables (right), and large Half-Book Foldables can be made using posterboard and glued side by side to form giant Foldables with pockets, tabs, and/or inside sections that become individual or collective class projects.

Add a Spine (right): Use a strip of posterboard to make a book spine. Label the spine and glue it to cover the ends of the Foldables. Instructions for the spine fold and photographs are on page 394.

One Per Class: One giant Foldable can be made per class, per cooperative learning group, or per period and glued together to make a collective multi-page book that documents student activities during a unit of study.

Make Really Big Projects: Students get creative as they determine how smaller Foldables can be glued into larger ones to make a project or study aid. Individual student projects and group projects become 3-D experiences when any of the following Foldables are included:

- Pop-ups
- Accordion Foldables
- Foldable Bound Journals
- Foldable Tables and/or Charts
- Layered Foldables
- Tabbed Foldables
- Dimensional Foldables: Pyramid Dioramas, Four-Door Dioramas, Display Cubes, and more.

Side By Side: Two-Tab, Four-Tab, Six-Tab, or Eight-Tab Foldables can be folded in half and glued together (side by side) to form a larger book with multiple pages. See pages 328 and 329 for other examples of side by side Pocketbooks.

1.

Make a Four-Tab Foldable. The example above was made using 11" x 17" paper.

2.

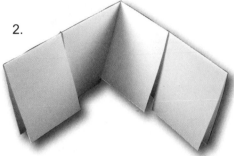

Fold in half with the tabs to the inside.

3.

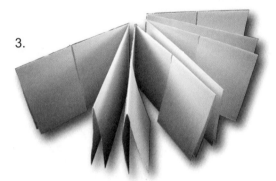

Glue multiple Four-Tab Foldables together (side by side) to make as many tabbed sections as needed.

4.

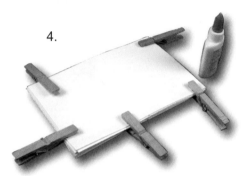

Glue together with the help of clothespins or binder clips.

5.

Write words and/or glue examples of RWP related to specific skills, vocabulary terms, questions, names of characters, titles of locations, names of events, etc., on the front tabs. Have students write sentences, definitions, antonyms, homographs, pronunciation guides, and more under the tabs.
See page 22, *What Goes Under the Tabs?*
See page 245, Word Study guide.

6.

Make a spine for the book, decorate it, and write a title. (See page 394 for photographs showing how to fold a spine.)

Side By Side: Make Foldables "grow" by gluing them side by side to form multi-page booklets. Most Foldables can be glued together, though Two-Pocket, Two-Tab, Four-Tab, and Six-Tab Foldables are the easiest to use in this way. With a spine or a cover, these side-by-side Foldables comprise a meaningful collection of student work and progress. Students are proud of these special individual or class books. They "read" them frequently and use them as study guides and reference books.

Side-by-side projects are more interesting than flat posterboard projects. During a school year, teacher-made and student-made side-by-side Foldable booklets can become part of the classroom reference materials.

Examples of Foldable side-by-side projects can be seen throughout this book. See pages 181 and 323.

Six Four-Tab Foldables® (below) glued side by side make this 12-page heteronyms book.

Eight Two-Tab Foldables® (above) glued side by side make this 16-page homophones book.

Sentence Strip Holder
Bulletin Board
Displaying Matchbook
Adopted Word Cards
(right): These sentence strip displays were made using 8½" x 11" paper. Each sentence strip was cut in half to form two small sections, and then glued onto a sheet of black foam board. See page 413.

Matchbook Flashcards (left): Sheets of 8½" x 11" paper were made into matchbooks and cut in half to form study cards. Students found examples in RWP of French words that are commonly used in English, and they glued them on the front of the cards. Definitions and sentences featuring the words have been written under the tabs. Note the French flag on the front and the map of France on the back of each card. Visual immersion promotes memory and cultural literacy. See page 400.

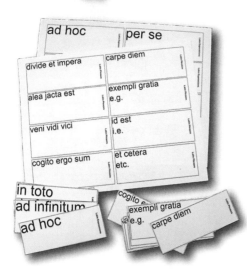

Pocket Chart with Word Strip (above): Use posterboard to make large storage pockets. The deep pocket is used for storing VKVs and Foldables—see flashcards protruding from the deep pocket, above—and the stapled strip along the bottom provides a space to display featured flashcards and/or sentence strips. See page 416.

The Importance of Using Print: The use of print from magazines, newspapers, advertisements, menus, and other materials is called many things—*life print*, *commercial print*, and *environmental print*, to name a few. I started calling it *Real World Print*, or *RWP*, in 1985, and that term continues to work well. MS/HS students get excited upon seeing photos of something they recognize. I've heard them say, "That's where I played ball when I was a kid," or "I've eaten at that restaurant," or "My grandmother was in that hospital." Some students use their cell phones to take photos of print that relates to something they are studying, and they e-mail the photos to the classroom computer.

Collecting RWP for Foldables® and VKVs®: Instead of having stacks of newspapers and magazines in my classroom, I do what I call a "Paper Cut."

Quickly cut headlines, captions, titles, diagrams, graphs, and/or other labeled graphics from newspapers and magazines. While cutting, censor titles that you consider inappropriate for the maturity level of your students. Teachers should review all print before student use.

Serving trays purchased at garage sales are perfect for storing, sorting, and carrying the print to work areas and/or desks. Trays can usually be stacked for storage. You will see some of the print in the tray shown to the right used in Foldables and VKVs pictured in this book.

Quarter- and Eighth-Sheet Flashcards: Students use hundreds of these small cards during a semester. The cards fit in Foldable pockets, Notebook Foldable pockets, Envelope Foldables, Academic Vocabulary Pocketbooks, and more.

Hint: Label flashcards with a code to designate when they were studied and with which piece of literature, chapter, lesson, or unit. Designate the label location on cards so they will be uniform and easy to find.

Content Example: Ch.10, p.245

Literature Example: <u>DF</u>, p. 79;

DF stands for *Dream Factory,* by Brad Barkley.

Why Use Multiple Examples of the Same Word? I'm asked this question frequently. I've found that ELL/ESL students tend to become dependent upon one type of font for word identification. This is especially true for students whose primary language alphabet differs from English. When they see a word they learned in one font written in a different font, they can stumble or fail to identify the word. My RWP flashcards and Foldables are filled with the same word in many different fonts, sizes, colors, and letter combinations: capitals and lowercase, all capitals, all lowercase, and with or without affixes.

Guidelines

Find and place a featured word ...

... written in all lowercase letters.

... written in all lowercase letters, but in a different font.

... written with an initial capital letter and lowercase letters.

... written with an initial capital letter and lowercase letters, but in a different font.

... written in all capital letters.

... written in all capital letters of a different font.

... written in a different or unusual color.

... written with a prefix and/or suffix.

... written as a possessive.

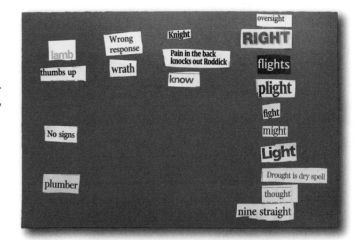

First Word Sort (below): RWP is collected and sorted into labeled letter envelopes, sorting boxes, file folder pockets, or some other container suitable for storing RWP for future projects. When the time comes to use the collected words, empty them from the collection container onto a piece of bright posterboard. Flip all print to the side that relates to the skill being studied. For example, the words below were in a "Silent Letters" envelope at the Dinah Zike Academy, and all RWP sections below feature a silent letter.

Second Word Sort (above): Organize and align RWP words into more specific categories. The silent letter words (below left) have been sorted into the following:

- silent *b* words
- silent *gh* words
- silent *k* words
- silent *w* words

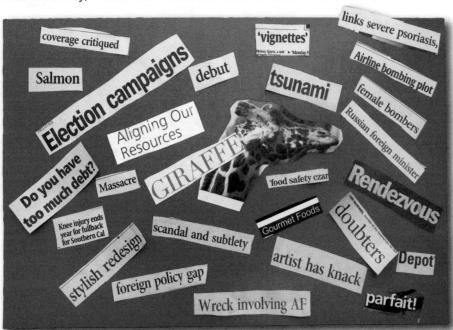

Above: Quarter-sheet flashcards and a Triple VKV.

Photographs of Signs: Take photographs of print found on signs and labels that are an everyday part of the students' world. Signs and billboards that illustrate skills being taught and/or reviewed in language arts and reading classes are frequently found in neighborhoods, communities, service locations, and state and national sites. Take photographs of these frequently observed signs or objects to illustrate skills being studied.

Example: Students living in Fort Davis, Texas, will see it abbreviated on road signs as *Ft. Davis*, and a sign near Fort Davis indicates that Fort Stockton (*Ft. Stockton*) is 98 miles away.

Photographs of Students in Action: Take photographs of ELL/ESL students in action to illustrate vocabulary terms or words that help teach a skill or concept. For example, when teaching *-ing* words, take photos of students talk<u>ing</u>, writ<u>ing</u>, study<u>ing</u>, and read<u>ing</u>.

Photographs of Familiar Objects and People: Integrate photographs of familiar objects and people into picture-word and initial-reading activities for ELL/ESL students.

Free Photos:
Search the internet for copyright-free photographs and other graphics that you can download and use for objects, locations, or concepts that cannot be photographed locally.

Film

Digital

Film (above left): When I first began collecting photographs for what I called "sign language," we used a 35 mm camera and had the film developed. This was expensive, but it gave me a beautiful color photo for the class book, and I photocopied the photographs for student use in Foldables.

Digital (above right): With today's digital cameras and cell phone cameras, it is easy to take photographs and use them immediately. Nine photos arranged on a page result in flashcards that are close to the same size as eighth-sheet flashcards. A combination of photos and word cards provides an interesting vocabulary study aid. The photos and word cards can be stored in Pocket Foldables, Notebook Foldable Pockets, and Pocket Charts; and they can be used in Four-Door Display Cases.

Four-Door Display (above): Made from a sheet of posterboard, this display can be used both with and without a sentence strip holder. Quarter-sheet Idiom cards can be sorted and displayed on the sentence strip.

Below: Pockets can be glued onto the back of the display and used to sort the quarter-sheet or eighth-sheet flashcards. See page 38.

Picture and Word Files (above): Manila file folders can be used to sort and store RWP, photographs, and pictures from magazines.

Envelope RWP Files: Envelopes of any size can be used as files for sorting RWP. Seal an envelope and cut off one of the long edges to form a pocket.

RWP Sorting Boxes (below): Fourth graders made the eight Foldable display boxes pictured here. Glue eight boxes together to make two rows of four boxes. Glue the two rows of boxes together with the ends of the ribbon between them to form a rectangle of eight boxes with a ribbon handle. Use clothespins to hold the rows and ribbon in place until the glue dries. See page 411.

Glue Sponge (below): Take a damp (not wet) sponge that has a heavy mesh scrubbing side, cut it to size, and place it inside a sealable plastic container. With the sponge side down, saturate the mesh with glue and allow it to soak into the sponge below. Continue until the sponge is completely soaked with glue. Place RWP on the mesh, word side up, press lightly, and glue the RWP onto paper. Re-wet the sponge with glue and thin it with drops of water as necessary.

Smashed Glue Stick: Remove the glue from a glue stick and "smash" the glue into the bottom of a small, sealable plastic container. In the example below, we used a colored glue stick that dries clear. Use a drop of water as needed to remoisten the glue glob.

Two-Sided Tape For a Fast Fix: For easy, quick RWP mounting, use small pieces of two-sided (double-stick) tape placed on poster-boards, charts, or the front of Foldables. Over time, students place words on the tape as they collect them. Often the RWP is larger than the piece of tape, and, at a future date, students can glue the extended edges of the RWP as needed to finish the Foldable. Completed Foldables can be laminated to prevent any exposed tape from adhering to other teaching aids when stored.

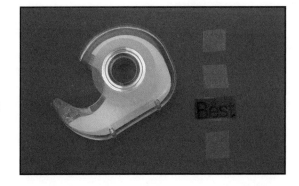

Foldable® and VKV® Files
Cereal boxes can be used to collect and store student- and teacher-made examples of Foldables and VKVs. These box files are perfect for keeping examples of previously made activities at one's fingertips for review and continued immersion throughout the school year. The teacher selects student-made Foldables that would be useful for future review, and stores them in the "library."

The cereal box library above was made for the Dinah Zike Academy using sponge brushes to paint cereal boxes with water-based enamel paint. Labels were made using a font style with outlines and shadows, and the labels were colored and glued onto colored paper before gluing them onto the ends of the boxes. These boxes were made to last for many years, so we put time and effort into their construction. You can greatly reduce production time by covering the boxes with wrapping paper or contact paper and writing on the box ends with permanent marker.

Powder and Paint: Painted boxes tend to stick together. To prevent this, dust the sides of the boxes with baby powder or talc after the paint has dried thoroughly. This usually helps to prevent sticking.

Foldable® Book Boxes:
This Foldable Book Box featuring the book *The Giver* was made using two cereal boxes. Instructions for Dinah Zike's Box Foldables, Envelope Foldables, and Top Tab Foldables are featured in a book to be released in the summer of 2010.

Thank You!
This beautiful Foldable Book Box was made by Robert Stremme, a graduate of Dinah Zike Academy, State Level Certification, and co-author of *Book of Lists II*, Scholastic, 2007.

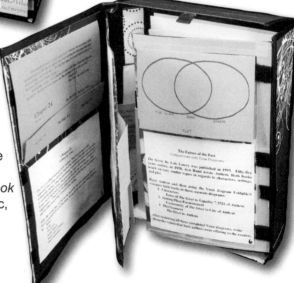

Supplies to use with Foldables® and VKVs®

Construction Supplies:

- sharp scissors to be used by teacher
- Dinah Zike's Dual-Cut Scissors for cutting along fold lines
- liquid, water-based glue
- stapler and staples
- large paper clips
- water-based markers (for use on lightweight paper)
- permanent markers (for use on posterboard and heavy paper)
- crayons and/or colored pencils
- pastels and/or paints for giant Foldable bulletin boards
- clothespins for securing glued edges

Decorative Supplies: Frequently, MS and HS students will bring the following items to use when making their VKVs or Foldables. I don't mind the use of these aids, but I stress that **time and effort should go into content and not "color."**

- stamps
- stencils
- stickers
- borders
- templates
- special design scissors
- scrapbooking materials
- glitter pens
- decorative hole punches, and more.

Publishing Center Paper:

- quarter and half sheets of photocopy paper
- quarter and half sheets of grid paper and notebook paper
- quarter and half sheets of continent maps, picture frames, clocks, blank time lines, other publishing aids
- 8½" x 11" photocopy (20#) and index-weight (80#) paper
- 11" x 17" photocopy (20#) and index-weight (80#) paper

Organize Publishing Center Quarter and Half Sheets Using:
- napkin holders
- desk organizers
- cake mix boxes

Collect Paper Scraps: Make a paper scraps box and allow students to access it so they can use the scraps to make small Foldables, VKV strips, book spines, and more. Scraps can also be used as background frames for titles or important words. Note the *Scrap Paper Box* and the *Scratch Paper* box in the publishing center, above left. The posterboard display featured on page 34 illustrates how a computer-generated title such as *Idioms* can be framed with scrap paper.

Top: Language Arts publishing center aids are stored in a letter holder (top left) and a napkin holder (top right). Publishing center quarter sheets were used in the Four-Door Foldable pictured above. See page 401.

Computer-Generated Publishing Center Aids: I use a small personal computer in the classroom for teacher-generated quarter- and half-sheet publishing aids like those pictured above. Titles might include the following: genre, setting, author, synopsis, book review, conflict/resolution, spelling demons, and more.

Envelopes and Pockets: Use envelopes and CD sleeves within Foldables and notebooks, or use scrap paper to make pockets.

Coin envelopes (above), 2½" x 4¼", are inexpensive and can be purchased at office supply stores. Seal an envelope and cut off one of the long edges to make a pocket for eighth-sheet flashcards.

CD sleeves can also be used to store worksheets or computer printouts that have been folded into fourths. See Worksheet/Folded Book, page 395.

How Do I Grade This? I am frequently asked how Foldables are graded. Keep in mind that Foldables and VKVs can be used successfully as instructional strategies for concept and skills introduction, demonstration, practice, drill, reinforcement, and review without grades being taken. However, the majority of teachers using Foldables and VKVs will also use them as a grading tool. Using Foldables and VKVs does not suggest or require a particular assessment strategy. Foldables can be assessed in many ways, including teacher observation with anecdotal notes, student observations and comments on personal strengths and weaknesses, point assignment for a given number of correct responses, and simple to complex rubrics.

Foldable® Assessment and a Simple Skills Rubric: The internet is filled with samples of rubrics that can be adapted and used with Foldables. Most school districts have established their own rubrics. In this book and in my workshops, I mention only a few ways that rubrics might be used, to give you ideas on how to write your own and/or adapt those used by your district.

A very simple, straightforward rubric might include the following:
1. the skill/s upon which an activity is based
2. the student action required for the activity
3. the level/s of action to be assessed within the activity
4. the outcome of the students' actions and performance.

For example, on a Foldable activity over a period of four days, students might be asked to find or recall, and list, ten *portmanteau* words they have used, heard, or discovered in RWP (real world print). They will be required to read the ten words on their list, explain the formation of each word, and use each word in writing to illustrate its meaning. If students find, list, read, and explain ten words, they receive an A+, or 100%. If students get seven words, they receive a B, or 85%, and if they get five words they receive a C, or 75%. However, students who find only two or three words would receive a D, or 65%.

This rubric provides a curve that differs from the more traditional grading method where ten items would be worth ten points each. With this more traditional method, a student would make a C- (70) if they missed three, instead of a B (85) as outlined above. Why give a curve? When using Foldables and VKVs, the level of student responsibility for and involvement in their own learning process is high compared to the low level of student responsibility and involvement when completing fill-in-the-blank worksheets and workbook pages. For example, students might complete a worksheet on *portmanteau words* and mark them or match them to word pairs. This example requires a very low level of performance (recognition), as the *portmanteau* words are provided on the worksheet, or word combinations are provided that give major clues as to what the words might be. In these types of activities, there is little space for student production. Worksheets can be completed in minutes, and students have very little time to feel "ownership" of their work. Foldables are completed over hours, days, or weeks, and students are very involved with their production and completion.

Rubric Assessment for Foldables® and VKV® Flashcards

I = *Introduction*, *P* = Practice, *M* = Mastery

Dinah's Graduated Skills Rubric: I have designed and used simple rubrics for Foldables that reflect the level of instruction as well as the level of student performance, and I have found them to be very fair during the learning process. For example, the rubric pictured to the right is used to assess student understanding of root words.

When the concept is first introduced, I do not grade as strictly as I do after time has been given for mastery. A student who misses two of ten root words during the introduction level of the rubric would receive a 90. Once mastery is expected, the same student who missed two would receive an 80. This rubric gives students a given amount of time to learn, practice, and apply skills. Students are told, and/or help to determine, when the rubric grading will move to the next level:

I = *introduction*, *P* = *practice*, *M* = *mastery*.
Number of items to be assessed – 10.
Number of items student attempted <u>correctly</u> – 6.

Student: Lesson: Skill: Date:		Introduction I 5pts. each	Practice P 7 pts. each	Mastery M 10 pts. each
Number Required:	10	100	100	100
Number Correct:	9	95	93	90
Number Correct:	8	90	86	80
Number Correct:	7	85	79	70
Number Correct:	6	80	72	60
Number Correct:	5	75	65	50
Number Correct:	4	70	58	40
Number Correct:	3	65	51	30
Number Correct:	2	60	44	20
Number Correct:	1	55	37	10
Observations and Comments:				

c 2007, Dinah Zike Academy, www.dinah.com

Student: Lesson: Skill: Date:		Introduction I 10 pts. each	Practice P 15 pts. each	Mastery M 20 pts. each
Number Required:	5	100	100	100
Number Correct:	4	90	85	80
Number Correct:	3	80	70	70
Number Correct:	2	70	55	60
Number Correct:	1	60	40	50
Observations and Comments:				

c 2007, Dinah Zike Academy, www.dinah.com

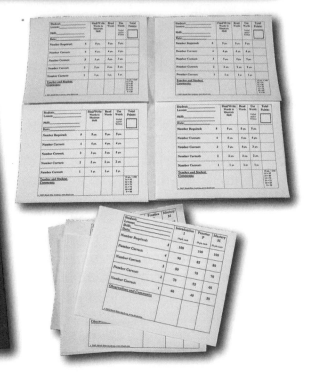

Post It (above): Post a large rubric so all students can see what is required of them and the level at which they will be graded. This rubric allows more advanced students to be scored on a different level than ESL/ELL students who might be new to the skill being studied. Small, quarter-sheet rubrics can be stapled to student work and used by the teacher and/or student to assess work.

Example of a Student-and-Teacher-Made Rubric: Allow students to help design rubrics to assess their work. For example, students might be asked to make a Two-Tab Foldable that has the labels *Silent Consonant Spelling Demons* on one tab and *Silent Vowel Spelling Demons* on the other. In this example (and frequently when using Foldables) the **skill** is stated by the teacher and determined by student needs and district curriculum requirements.

Ask students what they should be required to do (student action) on this Foldable. How they respond to this question will depend on what you have been modeling as the teacher. If you have asked them to find a given number of examples, list them on the front tabs beneath the tab titles, and use a given number of the words in sentences under the tabs, it is likely that students will say something close to what you have asked them to do in the past. Remember to vary what you ask students to do.

Student:_____ Lesson:_____ Skill:_____ Date:_____	Numbers Assigned Numbers Achieved	Points Asssigned Points Earned	Grade
Assigned Silent Consonants:	4 (5 pts. each)	20	
Number Found:			
Assigned Silent Vowels:	6 (5 pts. each)	30	
Number Found:			
Oral Sentences Using Each of the Ten Words:	10 (2 pts. each)	20	
Number Spoken:			
Paragraphs Under Tabs:	2 (5 pts. each)	10	
Number Written:			
Internal Punctuation:		10	
External Punctuation:		10	
Capitalization:		10	
Teacher and Student Comments:			Final Grade

c 2007, Dinah Zike Academy, www.dinah.com

Next, get students to help you determine the levels of action to be assessed within the activity. Students might think it is harder to spell words with silent vowels than silent consonants, so they feel they should find four silent vowels and six silent consonants. Students decide that they will each have a partner and read their words to their partner. The partner will mark a check on the Foldable in front of words spelled correctly and a minus in front of words spelled incorrectly. Students think they should be asked to use each word in a sentence orally after reading it, and that the partners should put a check or minus after the word to indicate if this is done correctly. Students suggest they write a simple paragraph under each tab using three of the words listed on the front. Ten points are given just for writing the two paragraphs, regardless of structure and content. Since the class has been reviewing internal and external punctuation rules, students determine that these will be evaluated as part of their paragraph writing grade and will be awarded 30 points.

—Example of a Student-and-Teacher-Made Rubric (continued):

Once students have helped set the levels of action, they help assign value to the work. In this example, students determined that the entire project was worth 100 points:

20 points	- 5 points for each of the four silent vowel words found, recorded, read
30 points	- 5 points for each of the six silent consonant words found, recorded, read
10 points	- 1 point for each word spelled correctly
10 points	- 5 points for each paragraph written using three words with silent letters
10 points	- proper internal punctuation
10 points	- proper external punctuation
10 points	- proper capitalization
‾‾‾‾‾‾‾	
100 points	Total points on a Two-Tab Foldable

One Foldable® Can Provide Multiple Grades: Since students are doing lots of production when using a Foldable, Foldables take much longer to complete than a worksheet. The above example will take several days to complete. The teacher might suggest to students that three separate grades be taken on this exercise. The first grade might be given for the finding and listing of four silent vowel words and six silent consonant words, where 50 points would equal 100%. The second grade could be taken on the

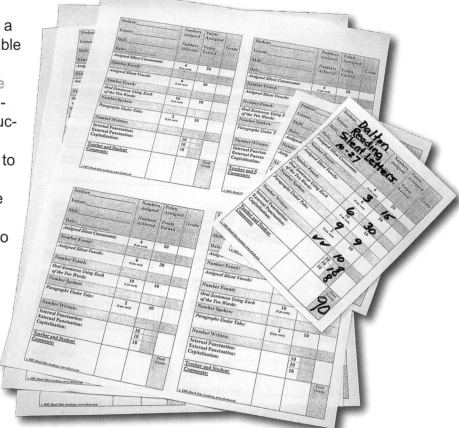

spelling of the ten words and the use of each in a written format: 10 points for each word (5 for spelling and 5 for use in writing), with 100 points available. The final grade could be taken on the writing of the simple paragraphs using six of the words under the tabs, where 50 points would equal 100%. In this example, the teacher and students have determined that the entire Foldable is worth 200 points. Three grades—one each for spelling, writing, and vocabulary—were collected from this activity.

Staple to Student Work: Reduce rubrics so four will fit on one sheet of photocopy paper. Make multiple small rubrics. Staple scored rubrics to Foldables so students and parents can see and discuss the evaluation of student performance.

Abbreviations

Abbreviations—Keep In Mind:

1. "When in doubt, spell it out." Abbreviations should not be used in formal writing.

2. Some words have several abbreviated forms.
Use the dictionary to confirm the spelling of the most common form of an abbreviation.
Select the abbreviation to be used in a document, and then use it consistently.
Do not switch abbreviations within a document.

3. If a word can be shortened by using either an abbreviation or a contraction,
use the abbreviated form of the word. Example: Use *cont.* instead of *cont'd*.

4. If an abbreviation is only a few letters or keystrokes shorter than the word,
the abbreviation should not be used.

Bold signs can be glued into a notebook and might also appear in the classroom to remind students of what is expected in their classroom writing and their writing on a test.

Large magazine **picture tab** with tabbed examples of abbreviations in RWP underneath.

Index cards can be used to make Two-Tab Notebook Foldables (shown open and closed).

Abbreviations VKVs

Many words in the English language have abbreviations. Some abbreviations are so commonly used that students might not link them to the words they represent.

1. Write. 2. Fold. 3. Period.

1. Write. 2. Fold. 3. Period.

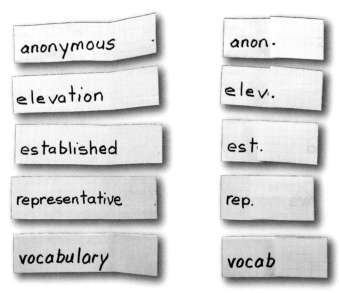

Single VKV® Flashcards (above and right):
Large abbreviation VKV Flashcards can be made using 1/3 of a sheet of copy paper, as pictured to the right. Small flashcards are made using 1/3 of a quarter sheet of paper. See Introduction, page 18.

Large cards are made and used by cooperative learning groups or an entire class. Small flashcards are used by individual students and are glued into a notebook or placed in pockets.

1. Glue. 2. Write.
3. Fold so period shows.

SAN PEDRO AVE. NUE

SAN PEDRO AVE.

1. Write.
2. Multiple folds.
3. Period.

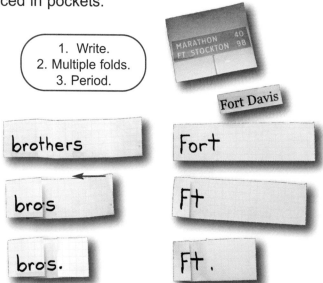

1. Write.
2. Multiple folds.
3. Period.

h

hdquarters

hdqrs

See page 53 for other examples.

Below: Note the photograph of a sign with the abbreviation for the word *headquarters*. Once students begin to look for specific things in RWP, they will be surprised at what they find. Cell phone cameras are great for recording everyday experiences with print.

hdqrs

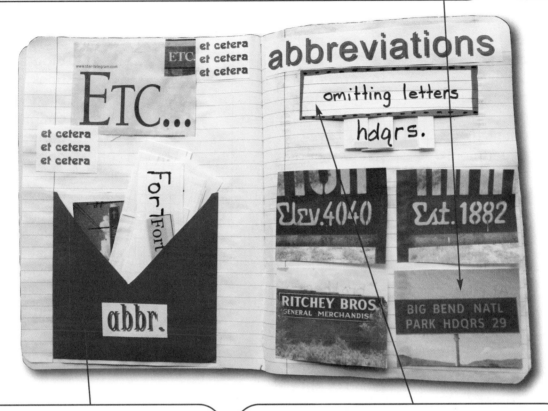

Computer disk sleeves glued in composition books make deep pockets for holding flashcards, folded worksheets, information sheets, terms collected from RWP, and more.

Three edges (top, left, and right) of half an **index card** were glued into the composition book. The bottom edge was left open, allowing students to slip folded Single VKV Flashcards underneath for viewing and sharing with others. Have each student fold one abbreviation card and pass it around for others to manipulate and record in their notebooks. See page 53 for an independent Foldable version of this activity.

Photographs taken by teachers and students can be used as 1/8 flashcards (page 33). Four photographs were used on this page. (Photographs are usually printed in black and white.)

When placing photos on the right page of a notebook, glue the left edge or top edge of each photo to form tabs. Write the abbreviated word under the tab and use the word in a sentence.

Remember, items glued on the left page of a notebook are usually glued along the right edge or along the top.

Abbreviations

General

acct.	**account**
act.	**active**
add.	**add**endum
ans.	**ans**wer
assn.	**ass**ociation
b.	**born**
bro.	**brother** (also br.)
constr.	**constr**uction
d.	**died**
	daughter
dept.	**dep**artment
dist.	**dist**rict
div.	**div**ision
ea.	**each**
etc.	**et** cetera
ex.	**ex**ample
fig.	**fig**ure
fr.	**from**

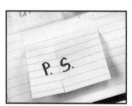

Above: A Two-Tab Foldable made using a Sticky Note™.

inc.	**inc**orporated
instr.	**instr**ument
l.	left
m.	**m**arried
	male
	measure
mgr.	**manager**
neg.	**neg**ative
no.	number + **o**
p.	page
perf.	**perf**ect
pers.	**pers**onal
pkg.	**package**
r.	right
re.	**re**garding
repr.	**repr**int
	reprinted
rev.	**rev**iew
	revised
	revision
sec.	**sec**tion
ser.	**ser**ies
supp.	**supp**lement
treas.	**treas**urer
vs.	**v**er**s**e
	versu**s**

Language Arts

anon.	**anon**ymous
ant.	**ant**onymn
app.	**app**endix
art.	**art**icle
bib.	**bib**liography
biog.	**biog**raphy
bk.	**b**oo**k**
ca.	**circa** about
chap.	**chap**ter
cons.	**cons**onant
cont.	**cont**inued
dict.	**dict**ionary
ed.	**ed**itor
	edition
encyc.	**encyc**lopedia
illus.	**illus**tration
intro.	**intro**duction
introd.	**introd**uction
jour.	**jour**nal
mag.	**mag**azine
p.	page
par.	**par**agraph
pl.	**pl**ural
P.S.	**p**o**s**tscript
ref.	**ref**erence
sing.	**sing**ular,
sg.	**s**in**g**ular
st.	**st**anza
subj.	**subj**ect
syn.	**syn**onym
vocab.	**vocab**ulary

See common dictionary abbreviations on page 51.

Abbreviations for States and Provinces
Abbreviations for states and provinces begin with a capital letter, end with a period, and are only used on maps and charts and in lists and addresses. Any abbreviations can be used in informal writing, but never in formal writing. Exceptions: *U.S.A.* and *Washington, D.C.*

Avoid abbreviations for states, provinces, and countries in formal writing. The exceptions are the abbreviations for the relatively long names *U.S., U.S.A., U.S.S.R.,* and *C.I.S.* These abbreviations may be used at any time.

Postal Abbreviations
The two-letter U.S. Postal Service abbreviations are written in all capitals with no periods, and they do not have to be set apart from the name of the city by commas. These abbreviations are used only on letters and packages being mailed or shipped.

Abbreviations

States of the United States

Alabama	Ala.	**AL**		New Hampshire	N.H.	**NH**
Alaska	Alaska	**AK**		New Jersey	N.J.	**NJ**
Arizona	Ariz.	**AZ**		New Mexico	N. Mex.	**NM**
Arkansas	Ark.	**AR**		New York	N.Y.	**NY**
California	Calif.	**CA**		North Carolina	N.C.	**NC**
Colorado	Colo.	**CO**		North Dakota	N.D.	**ND**
Connecticut	Conn.	**CT**		Ohio	Ohio	**OH**
Delaware	Del.	**DE**		Oklahoma	Okla.	**OK**
Florida	Fla.	**FL**		Oregon	Ore./Oreg.	**OR**
Georgia	Ga.	**GA**		Pennsylvania	Pa.	**PA**
Hawaii	Hawaii	**HI**		Rhode Island	R.I.	**RI**
Idaho	Idaho	**ID**		South Carolina	S.C.	**SC**
Illinois	Ill.	**IL**		South Dakota	S.D./S. Dak.	**SD**
Indiana	Ind.	**IN**		Tennessee	Tenn.	**TN**
Iowa	Iowa	**IA**		Texas	Tex.	**TX**
Kansas	Kans.	**KS**		Utah	Utah/Ut.	**UT**
Kentucky	Ky.	**KY**		Vermont	Vt.	**VT**
Louisiana	La.	**LA**		Virginia	Va.	**VA**
Maine	Me./Maine	**ME**		Washington	Wash.	**WA**
Maryland	Md.	**MD**		West Virginia	W. Va.	**WV**
Massachusetts	Mass.	**MA**		Wisconsin	Wis./Wisc.	**WI**
Michigan	Mich.	**MI**		Wyoming	Wyo.	**WY**
Minnesota	Minn.	**MN**				
Mississippi	Miss.	**MS**				
Missouri	Mo.	**MO**		**District and Territories**		
Montana	Mont.	**MT**		District of Columbia	D.C.	**DC**
Nebraska	Neb./Nebr.	**NE**		Puerto Rico	P.R.	**PR**
Nevada	Nev.	**NV**		Virgin Islands	V.I.	**VI**

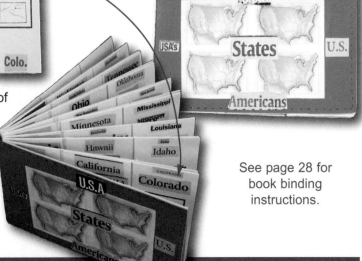

U.S.A. Side-by-Side Bound Book: Nine sheets of 11" x 17" paper were used to make this book. Each sheet was folded in half like a *hotdog*, then folded in half like a *hamburger*; and then six tabs were cut. Nine sections of Six-Tab Foldables were glued side by side. The names of the 50 states were written in alphabetical order on the tabs, and information on each state was collected under the tabs. Note abbreviations on front tabs.

See page 28 for book binding instructions.

Abbreviations

Addresses

Abbreviations for geographical terms used before or after a proper noun begin with a capital letter and end with a period. Use only in addresses, lists, charts, and maps.

Ave.	**Avenue**
Bldg.	**Building**
Blvd.	**Boulevard**
Co.	**Company**
Corp.	**Corporation**
Ct.	**Court**
Dept.	**Department**
Dr.	**Drive**
Ft.	**Fort**
Frwy.	**Freeway**
Govt.	**Government**
Hdqrs.	**Headquarters**
Hwy.	**Highway**
Inc.	**Incorporated**
Ln., La.	**Lane, Lane**
Mt.	**Mount**
Pkwy.	**Parkway**
Pl.	**Place**
Pt.	**Point**
Prt.	**Port**
Rd.	**Road**
Rte.	**Route**
Sq.	**Square**
St.	**Street**
Terr.	**Terrace**
Univ.	**University**

Titles

Abbreviations for titles of position and rank are used only before a person's full name— first and last:
Incorrect: Adm. Jones
Correct: Adm. John Jones, Admiral Jones
But *Dr.* can be used with the last name only: Dr. Smith.

Adm.	**Admiral**
Asst.	**Assistant**
Atty.	**Attorney**
Capt.	**Captain**
Col.	**Colonel**
Dent.	**Dentist**
Dir.	**Director**
Dr.	**Doctor**
Esq.	**Esquire**
Gen.	**General**
Gov.	**Governor**
Hon.	**Honorable**
H.R.H.	**His (Her) Royal Highness**
Jr.	**Junior**
Lt.	**Lieutenant** Sp
Maj.	**Major**
Mgr.	**Manager**
Mr.	**Mister**
Miss	an unmarried woman
Mrs.	a married woman
Ms.	a married/unmarried woman
Pres.	**President**
Prof.	**Professor**
Rep.	**Representative**
Rev.	**Reverend**
Secy.	**Secretary**
Sen.	**Senator**
Sgt.	**Sergeant** Sp
Sr.	**Senior, Sister** (Latin *Soror*)
St.	**Saint**
Supt.	**Superintendent** Sp
V.P.	**Vice President**

Word Study: *et al.*

Et al. is an abbreviation of the Latin phrase *et alia*. It means *and others*, and is a more formal version of **etc.** Notice that there is a period after **al.** since it is the abbreviation for *alia*, but not after *et* since it is not abbreviated.

Word Study: *etc.*

Etc. is an abbreviation for the Latin phrase *et cetera*, meaning *and others* or *and so forth*. Do not pronounce it with an "x" in the first syllable; instead, say the first "t" in *et* clearly. Do not use a redundant *and* before **etc.**

Reading Abbreviations

The following abbreviations are frequently used in writing. When encountered in print, they are read as the word, not as the abbreviation: *volume*, not *vol*.

biol.	**biology**
dB	**decibel**
hp	**horsepower**
Hz	**hertz**
K	**Kelvin**
kn	**knot (nautical)**
kW	**kilowatt**
kWh	**kilowatt-hour**
lt-yr	**light-year**
neg.	**negative**
pos.	**positive**
sci.	**science**
temp.	**temperature**
vol.	**volume**
w.	**watt**

Initializations are Abbreviations

The following abbreviations are referred to as Initializations. See pages 56-59. Initializations are read or spoken letter by letter. For example, one might say that a car's gas rating is 45 "m-p-g" or a battery is "D-C."

a.c./AC	**alternating current**
AU	**astronomical unit**
bp	**boiling point**
d.c./DC	**direct current**
HDL	**high-density lipoprotein**
LDL	**low-density lipoprotein**
MP, mp	**melting point**
MPG, mpg	**miles per gallon**
MPH, mph	**miles per hour**

Chemical Elements

Chemical elements are abbreviated using one, two, or three letters. These abbreviations become the *symbols* for the elements. Never use periods with these abbreviations.

Notice that some abbreviations do not use the letters of the element's name. Some examples are Pb symbolizing lead and Fe representing iron.

aluminum	**Al**
calcium	**Ca**
carbon	**C**
copper	**Cu**
gold	**Au**
helium	**He**
hydrogen	**H**
iron	**Fe**
lead	**Pb**
magnesium	**Mg**
nickel	**Ni**
nitrogen	**N**
oxygen	**O**
phosphorus	**P**
potassium	**K**
silicon	**Si**
silver	**Ag**
sodium	**Na**
sulfur	**S**
tin	**Sn**
zinc	**Zn**

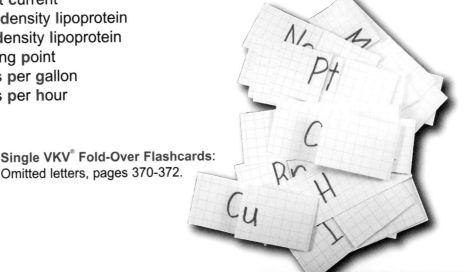

Single VKV® Fold-Over Flashcards:
Omitted letters, pages 370-372.

Mathematics: Measurement and Time

Abbreviations for most units of measurement use lowercase letters followed by periods.
Exceptions include temperature abbreviations because they are derived from proper nouns.
Abbreviations for metric units, including temperatures (Kelvin or Celsius), do not end with periods.
Non-metric units containing *per* (such as *miles per hour*) usually do not have periods.

a.	acre
A.M., a.m.	*ante meridiem* (Latin, before noon)
C	Celsius
	Centigrade
c.	cup
cc	cubic centimeter
cm	centimeter
cu	cubic
d.	day
deg.	degree
diam.	diameter
div.	division
doz.	dozen
ea.	each
eq.	equation
F	Fahrenheit
fig.	figure
ft.	foot, feet
g	gram
gal.	gallon
gm	gram
hr.	hour
hrs.	hours
ht.	height
in.	inch
K	Kelvin
kg	kilogram
kL	kiloliter
l	liter
lb.	pound
lg.	large
m	meter
math.	mathematics
med.	medium
mg	milligram
mi.	mile
min.	minute

mL	milliliter
mm	millimeter
mo.	month
mos.	months
neg.	negative
mph	miles per hour
no.	number + o
oz.	ounce + z
P.M., p.m.	*post meridiem* (Latin, after noon)
pos.	positive
pk.	peck
pt.	pint
qt.	quart
sec.	second
sm.	small
T.	tablespoon
tbsp.	tablespoon
t.	teaspoon
tsp.	teaspoon
vol.	volume
w. or W	watt
wk.	week
wt.	weight Sp
yd.	yard
yr.	year

Year

A.D.	Anno Domini (in the year of the/Our Lord)
B.C.	Before Christ
B.C.E.	Before Common Era
	Before Christian Era

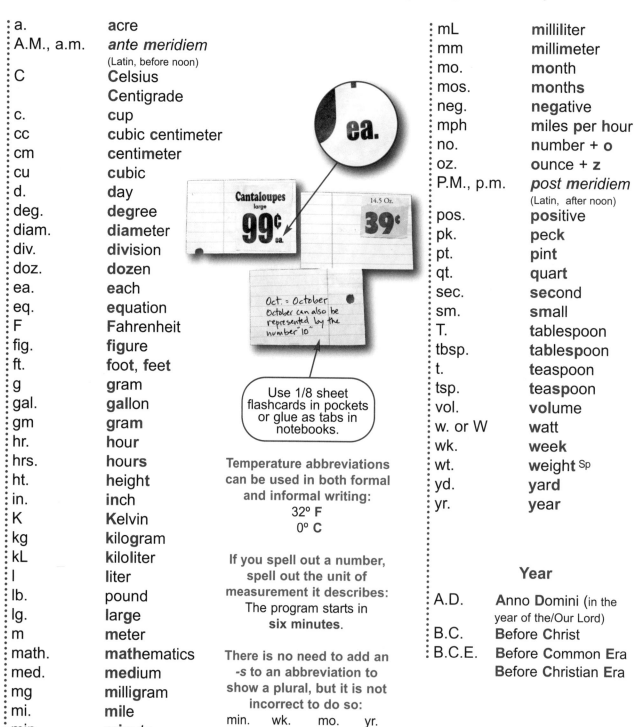

Oct. = October
October can also be represented by the number "10"

Use 1/8 sheet flashcards in pockets or glue as tabs in notebooks.

Temperature abbreviations can be used in both formal and informal writing:
32° F
0° C

If you spell out a number, spell out the unit of measurement it describes:
The program starts in **six minutes**.

There is no need to add an *-s* to an abbreviation to show a plural, but it is not incorrect to do so:

min.	wk.	mo.	yr.
mins.	wks.	mos.	yrs.

Abbreviations

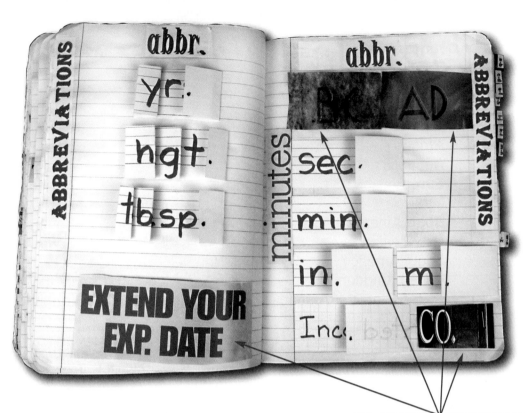

Abbreviations Frequently Used in Dictionaries

abbr.	**abbr**eviation
adj.	**adj**ective
adv.	**adv**erb
art.	**art**icle
comb.	**comb**ination
conj.	**conj**unction
contr.	**contr**action
exclam.	**exclam**ation
fem.	**fem**inine
interj.	**interj**ection
mas.	**mas**culine
n.	**n**oun
part.	**part**iciple
pl.	**pl**ural
prep.	**prep**osition
pron., pn.	**pron**oun
pronunc.	**pronunc**iation
sing./sg.	**sing**ular, **s**in**g**ular
usu.	**usu**ally
v.	**v**erb, **v**erse

RWP Tabs: Abbreviations found in magazines have been used as tabs in this composition book. The arrows indicate the edges that were glued to form the tabs. Students explain the abbreviations underneath.

Geography and Social Sciences

Names of Countries

The names of countries and continents are nearly always spelled out. They are sometimes abbreviated when used in small text spaces, on small maps, in Olympic nomenclature, and in postal abbreviations.

Af.	**Africa**
Aus.	**Australia**
Eur.	**Europe**
Mex.	**Mexico**
N.A.	**North America**
N.Z.	**New Zealand**
S.A.	**South America**
U.K.	**United Kingdom**
U.S.A.	**United States of America**

Directions and Coordinates

N, No.	**north**
S, So.	**south**
E	**east**
W	**west**
N.E.	**Northeast**
N.W.	**Northwest**
S.E.	**Southeast**
S.W.	**Southwest**
lat.	**latitude**
long.	**longitude**

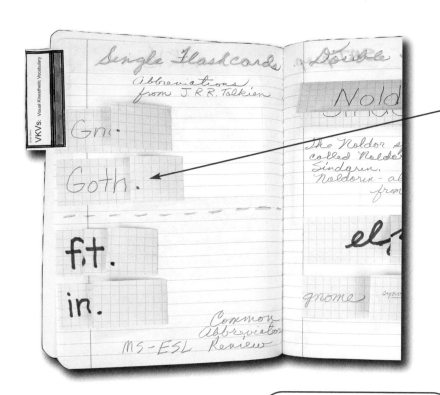

Abbreviations Used by J.R.R. Tolkien:

M-e	Middle-earth
Gn.	Gnome
Goth.	Gothic
H	The Hobbit
HoMe	History of Middle-earth
LR	Lord of the Rings
FR	Fellowship of the Rings

Using 1/8 sheet flashcards, write or glue an abbreviation on the front. Have students write the word/s being abbreviated on the back, as well as any alternate abbreviations.
See the front of the S.C. card (left), and the writing on the back (right).

Abbreviations

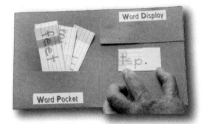
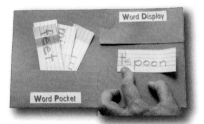
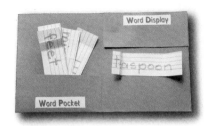

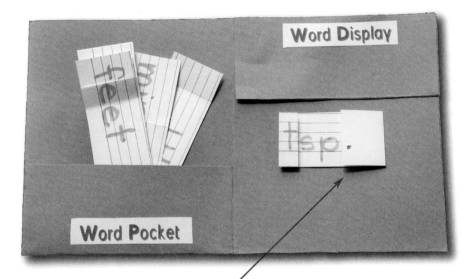

Pocket Foldable® Variation
1. Make a Two-Pocket Foldable.
2. Cut off the right pocket tab and glue or staple it above its original position, or to the top right inner edge.
3. Store abbreviation Single VKV Flashcards in the left pocket, and display them under the right flap.
See a variation of this tab in the composition notebook pictured on page 45.

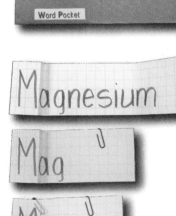

Chemical Element Symbols:
Some chemical element symbols are written with letters that are not sequential. Use this fold-over omission techinique to demonstrate how these symbols are formed.

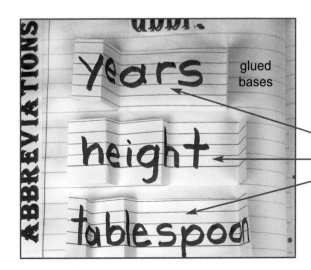

glued bases

Notebook Foldables®
version of the pocket abbreviation activity pictured above and on page 45.
1. Fold the word to form the abbreviation.
2. Look at the back of the folded flashcard.
3. Place glue on the part of the card that is not folded.
4. Glue this "base" into a notebook. The tabs can still be folded to form the abbreviation, illustrating which letters can be deleted.

The practice of abbreviating words in text messages began because many cell phone systems limited the number of characters per text message. The goal was to get as much said, as clearly as possible, in as few characters as possible.

1. Leave out as many letters or words as you can. Vowels are often the easiest to omit.
2. Use abbreviations that have become standardized over the years by frequent text-message use.
3. Note that people from different interest groups may be using their own abbreviations for the same words.
4. Just as languages change over time, abbreviations used for texting are fluid and subject to rapid change.

Can you read this?
I plj alejns 2 th flg of th U S of A, n 2 th rpbc 4 whch it stnds; 1 ntn, undr God, ndvsble, wth lbrty n jstc 4 all.

abt2	about to		XLNT	excellent
addy/ADR	address		X-I-10	exciting
ADIP	another day in paradise		Xme, EM?	excuse me
ADN	any day now		Xpect	expect
afair	as far as I remember		F2F	face to face
aisi	as I see it		fwiw	for what it's worth
AMBW	all my best wishes		4evr	forever
aml	all my love		GOI	get over it
ATB	all the best		gf	girlfriend
ans	answer		gonna bl8	going to be late
ru@___	are you at ___		g2g/GTG	got to go
RUF2T	are you free to talk?		gr8	great
RUOK	are you OK? (uok?)		grrr	growling
RUT	are you there?		hbtu	happy birthday to you
AAMOF	as a matter of fact		HRU	how are you
ASAP	as soon as possible		hru2d	how are you today
atm	at the moment		HB	hurry back
@wrk	at work		IDGI	I don't get it
bbl	be back later		idk	I dont know
brb	be right back		IG2R	I got to run
BCNU	be seeing you		404	I have no clue/lost
bf	best friend/boyfriend		IKT	I knew that
bff	best friends forever		143/ILU	I love you
bol	best of luck		14324*7	I love you 24hrs/day, 7 days/week
bday	birthday		J/C	just checking
btw	by the way		JIC	just in case
CX	cancelled		J/J	just joking
cla$	class		J/K	just kidding
craZ	crazy		J4F	just for fun
d8	date		JOOC	just out of curiosity
def	definitely		JTLYK	just to let you know
DYK	did you know		KMP	keep me posted
DIY	do it yourself		l8r	later
DHAC 1	doesn't have a clue		LMHO	laughing my head off
EZ	easy		LOL	laughing out loud
EOM	end of message		LMK	let me know
NUFF, enuf	enough/enough said		LFTI	looking forward to it
NTR	enter		MMD	made my day
ETA	estimated time of arrival		MYOB	mind your own business

Abbreviations Text Messaging Abbreviations

NRN	no reply necessary
NoTY	no thank you
ntm	not that much
omg	oh my gosh
on9	on line
POV	point of view
plz/PLS	please
QstN	question
QL	quit laughing
rcvd	received
RnR	rest and relaxation
RN	right now
rotfl	rolling on the floor laughing
S2U	same to you
STW	search the web
C2it	see to it
cu	see you
srsly	seriously
sete	smiling ear to ear
s%n	soon
*vin	starving
SIT	stay in touch
ttyl	talk to you later
txt	texting
ty	thank you
tnx/THX	thanks
T+	think positive
TTTT	to tell the truth
2day	today
2moro	tomorrow
2nite	tonight
TMI	too much information
upd8	update
w8	wait
w84M	wait for me
w8U	wait up
WTG	way to go
WU?	what's up
WRU?	where are you
WWY?	where were you
w/ w/o	with/without
yr	yeah, right
yoyo	you're on your own
YW	you're welcome
ZZ	boring, sleepy, tired

Two **index cards** were used to make Multi-Tabbed Notebook Foldables.®

Large **rubber band** used to keep notebook closed and tabs flat.

Text Messaging
Text Messaging
wHr r Ur car kEz?
I nEd 2 mEt ^ wit
my fRnds
RUF2T
ETA
brb
noob
IDGI
gr8
F2F
g2g
S'up
Examples: Text Messages

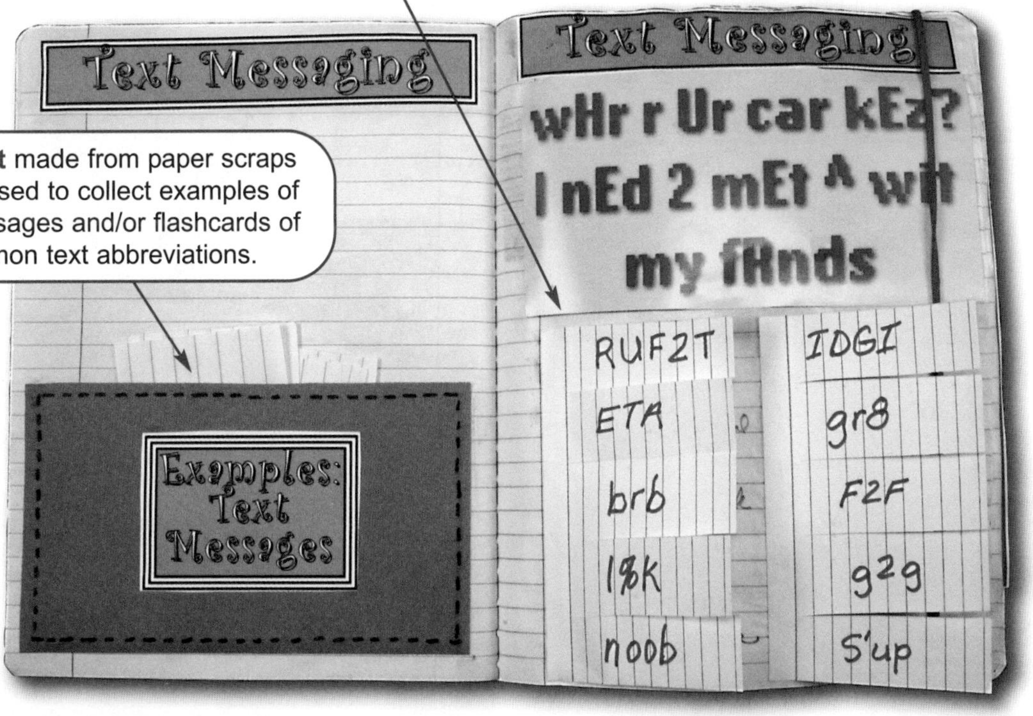

A **pocket** made from paper scraps can be used to collect examples of text messages and/or flashcards of common text abbreviations.

Acronyms and Initializations

Acronyms and initializations are forms of abbreviations. They are often used to name groups, including government agencies, companies, organizations, unions, and associations. They are formed by using the first letters of the words in the names of organizations or titles. Periods are usually not used when writing acronyms and initializations. The initialization *RWP* that is used throughout this book stands for *Real World Print*, or print from publications.

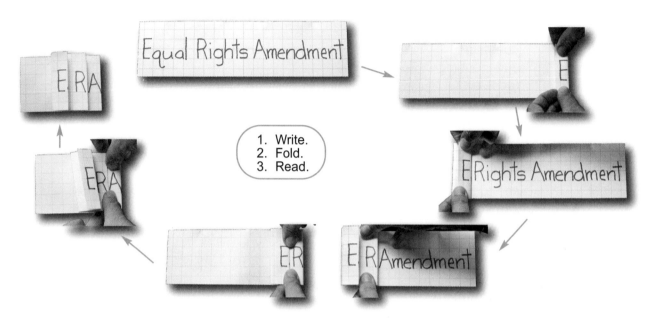

1. Write.
2. Fold.
3. Read.

Large Pocket Poster and Large Pocket Charts (below): Use a sheet of 12" x 18" paper or a sheet of posterboard to make a giant pocket or Pocket Chart for collecting quarter- or eighth-sheet flashcards made by a class or multiple periods of students. Generate a computer list of the examples collected and share them with all students as a study guide. Select a given number of acronyms and initializations for students to define and include in a writing and/or spelling assessment activity.

One **giant pocket** can be used to collect examples from RWP, folded worksheets, and quarter-sheet flashcards.

This **Two-Pocket Foldable Chart** is filled with quarter-sheet grid paper flashcards.

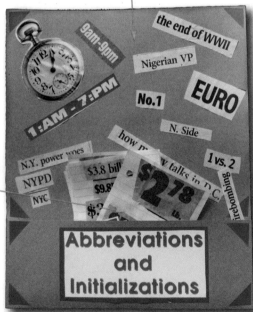

Triple VKV® Flashcard: With the flashcard closed, see if students can identify the words represented by the letters. Open the inside bottom tabs to self-check by viewing all or part of the title. Write a sentence using the title and/or its initialization in the middle of the Triple VKV Flashcard. See page 385.

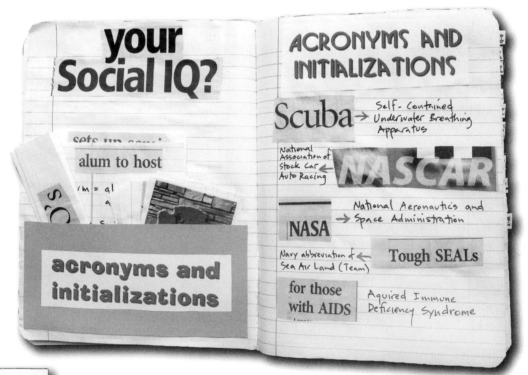

Left: This Six-Tab Foldable was made from a sheet of photocopy paper for use in an Economics class.

GDP Gross Domestic Product
GNP Gross National Product
NNP Net National Product
NI   National Income
PI   Personal Income
DI   Disposable Personal Income

Use **quarter sheets** to collect examples from RWP. Store cards in a pocket like the one pictured above.

Acronyms and Initializations

Acronyms

The letters forming an acronym are read as *a word*.

AIDS	**a**cquired **i**mmune **d**eficiency **s**yndrome; **a**cquired **i**mmuno**d**eficiency **s**yndrome
AWOL	**a**bsent **w**ithout **l**eave; **a**bsent **w**ithout **o**fficial **l**eave
BASIC	**B**eginner's **A**ll-purpose **S**ymbolic **I**nstruction **C**ode (programming language)
COOL	**c**ountry-**o**f-**o**rigin **l**abeling
EPCOT	**E**xperimental **P**rototype **C**ommunity **o**f **T**omorrow
FAX	**fac**simile
MADD	**M**others **A**gainst **D**runk **D**riving
NASA	**N**ational **A**eronautics and **S**pace **A**dministration
NASCAR	**N**ational **A**ssociation for **S**tock **C**ar **A**uto **R**acing
NATO	**N**orth **A**tlantic **T**reaty **O**rganization
OPEC	**O**rganization of **P**etroleum **E**xporting **C**ountries
OSHA	**O**ccupational **S**afety and **H**ealth **A**dministration
POTUS	**P**resident **o**f the **U**nited **S**tates
RADAR	**ra**dio **d**etecting **a**nd **r**anging
SCUBA	**s**elf-**c**ontained **u**nderwater **b**reathing **a**pparatus
SONAR	**so**und **n**avigation **a**nd **r**anging
SWAT	**S**pecial **W**eapons **a**nd **T**actics
TEFLON	**t**e**t**ra**fluo**ro**e**thyle**n**e resin
UNESCO	**U**nited **N**ations **E**ducational, **S**cientific, and **C**ultural **O**rganization
UNICEF	**U**nited **N**ations **I**nternational **C**hildren's **E**mergency **F**und
WAC	**W**omen's **A**rmy **C**orps
WASP	**w**hite **A**nglo-**S**axon **P**rotestant
ZIP	**Z**one **I**mprovement **P**lan

Trifold Pocket: Use a sheet of 12" x 18" art paper folded into thirds to make the Pocketbook pictured right and below. Use it to store VKVs and to collect RWP. This Trifold Pocketbook can be used for any skill; and folded worksheets, internet-generated print, Foldables, and more can be stored within. "Write Less, Say More" is a good title for booklets or charts relating to the study of abbreviations, acronyms and initializations. See page 399.

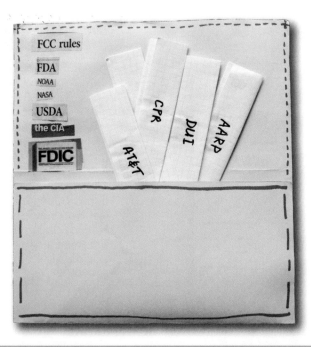

Acronyms and Initializations

Initializations

The letters forming an initialization are read *individually*.

AARP	American Assoc. of Retired Persons	MO	modus operandi
ABC	American Broadcasting Company	NAACP	National Association for the Advancement of Colored People
AFL	American Football League		
AKA	also known as	NASA	National Aeronautics and Space Administration
ASAP	as soon as possible	NATO	North Atlantic Treaty Organization
AT&T	American Telephone and Telegraph	NBC	National Broadcasting Company
ATM	automated teller machine	NFL	National Football League
BLT	bacon, lettuce, tomato	NPS	National Park Service
CBS	Columbia Broadcasting System	OPEC	Organization of Petroleum Exporting Countries
CD	compact disk	PB&J	peanut butter and jelly
CEO	chief executive officer	PC	personal computer
COD	cash on delivery	PE	physical education
CPR	cardiopulmonary resuscitation	POW	prisoner of war
CSI	crime scene investigation	PR	public relations
DJ	disk jockey	PTO	parent-teacher organization
DOA	dead on arrival	RIP	rest in peace
DUI	driving under the influence	RSVP	répondez s'il vous plaît (French: "please reply")
DVD	digital video disk	RV	recreational vehicle
EPA	Environmental Protection Agency	S&L	savings and loan
ER	emergency room	SASE	self-addressed, stamped envelope
ERA	Equal Rights Amendment	SAT	Scholastic Aptitude Test
ESL	English as a second language	SOS	save our ship
EU	European Union	SUV	sport utility vehicle
FEMA	Fed. Emergency Management Agency	TBA	to be arranged; to be announced
FTC	Federal Trade Commission	TLC	tender loving care
FYI	for your information	TSA	Transportation Security Administration
GOP	Grand Old Party	UFO	unidentified flying object
GPA	grade point average	UN	United Nations
GPS	global positioning system	USA	United States of America
HD	high definition	UV	ultraviolet
HIV	human immunodeficiency virus	VCR	video cassette recorder
IOU	I owe you	VIP	very important person
IQ	intelligence quotient	WB	World Bank
IRS	Internal Revenue Service	WHO	World Health Organization
MIA	missing in action		

This Trifold VKV Flashcard is found in the Trifold Pocket Foldable pictured at the bottom of the previous page. See page 385.

Adopted Words and Phrases

An *adopted word*, a *borrowing*, or a *loanword* is adopted directly into one language from another language with little or no change. Wikipedia has a list of loanwords by country or language of origin. Have students use an internet site such as Dictionary.com to check the etymologies of the words in the lists.

Afrikaans
aardvark
Afrikaans
apartheid
banana
banjo
chimpanzee
commandeer
gnu
goober
gumbo
impala
kalimba
Kwanzaa
meerkat
mumbo jumbo
okapi
okra
trek
voodoo
yam
zebra
zombie

Australian Aboriginal
barramundi
dingo
kangaroo
koala
kookaburra
numbat
wallaby
wombat

Chinese
chop-chop
chopsticks
chop suey
chow
chow mein
Confucianism
feng shui
ginkgo
ginseng
gung-ho
ketchup
kowtow
kumquat
cumquat
kung fu
lo mein
loquat
lychee
mu shu
tangram
wok

Celtic: Irish, Scottish
banshee
bard *
blarney
bog
brogue
galore
leprechaun
loch
phony, phoney
shamrock

Czech
howitzer
kolache or kolacky
pilsner
pistol
polka
robot

Dutch
aloof
beaker
boss
bow (ship)
brawl
bulwark
bumpkin
bundle
caboose
cockatoo
coleslaw
cookie
cruise
decoy
dike
easel
etch
freight
frolic
furlough
golf
hankering
holster
iceberg Sp
knapsack
landscape
morass
offal
patroon
pickle
quack
scone
shoal
skate
sketch
sled
snack
tattoo
tickle
trek
tulip
waffle
wagon
walrus

Above: These Bound Books were made with 8½" x 11" paper folded like a *hotdog* and folded in half like a *hamburger*. These sections were glued side by side to form multi-page booklets. See page 28 for book binding instructions.

Adopted Words and Phrases

Spanish/Portuguese

adios	junta
adobe	key (land form)
afficionado	lariat
alfalfa	lasso
alligator	loco
amigo	macho
armada	maize
armadillo	margarita
arroyo	mesa
barrio	mosquito
blanco	mustang
breeze	nacho
bronco	oregano
buffalo	palmetto
burrito	pampa
burro	papaya
cabana	patio
cafeteria	peccadillo *
caldera	peon
canary	pimento
canyon	platinum
cargo	plaza
chaparral	pueblo
charro	ranch
cigar	renegade
cilantro	rodeo
cockroach	salsa
corral	savvy
crusade	siesta
desperado	sombrero
embargo	tabasco
fiesta	taco
filibuster *	tapas
flamenco	tapioca
galleon *	tobacco
guerrilla	tornado
hacienda	tortilla
hammock	vanilla
iguana	vigilante
incommunicado	wrangler
jaguar	
jalapeno	

Yiddish

bagel
blintz
chutzpah
glitch
kibitz
klutz
kosher
latke
lox
oy!
schlep
schlock
schnook
schnoz
shtick
tush

Hawaiian

aa or a'a
aloha
hula
lei
luau
mahalo
mahi-mahi
mu'umu'u
(mumu)
pahoehoe
poi
ukulele
wiki
(*wikiwiki* means
quick; a *wiki* is also
a collaborative
website)

Hindi

bandanna
(also bandana)
bangle
bazaar Sp
brahmin
bungalow
chai
cheetah
cot
guru
jungle
jute
karma
loot
pundit
pyjama
shampoo
swami
swastika
thug
yoga

Italian

a capella
alto
balcony
ballerina
broccoli
calzone
cameo
campanile
cantaloupe
cantata
canto
cartoon
colonnade
corridor
crescendo
dilettante
fiasco
fresco
gallery
gazette
gelatin
gelato
gondola
graffiti
maestro
magenta
maraschino
mascara
model
mosaic
pergola
pizza
regatta
replica
salami
scenario
sequin
serenade
spaghetti
squadron
tariff
umbrella
virtuoso

G racias!

CANTINA

MERCADO

PUEBLO

CALIENTE
Spanish-speaking town
Say "Si"
Words & Phrases Borrowed
From Spanish *

Above: This booklet was made with a four-tabs-per-page spread. See page 28 for book binding instructions.

Adopted Words and Phrases

Japanese
bonsai
edamame
futon
ginkgo
haiku
hibachi
jujutsu
kamikaze
karaoke
karate
kimono
koi
origami
ramen
rickshaw
samurai
sashimi
shogun
soy
sumo
sushi
tempura
teriyaki
tofu
tsunami
tycoon
wasabi

Nahuatl
via **Spanish**
avocado
cacao, cocoa
chile, chili
chocolate
coyote
guacamole
mesquite
mole (sauce)
ocelot
quetzal
tamale
tomato

Native American
caribou
chipmunk
hickory
hogan
hominy
husky
igloo
moccasin Sp
moose
muckluck
muskrat
opossum
(also possum)
papoose
pecan
persimmon
podunk
powwow
raccoon
sequoia
skunk
squash
succotash
tepee (teepee, tipi)
toboggan
tomahawk
totem
wapiti
wigwam
woodchuck

German
angst
blitz
bratwurst (brat)
delicatessen
ersatz
frankfurter
gneiss
kindergarten
kitschy
kohlrabi
lager
landau
poltergeist
pretzel
pumpernickel
quartz
sauerkraut
schnapps
smug
smuggle
spritzer
verboten
wanderlust
wiener
wurst
yodel
zwieback

French

Some French word endings have a silent *t*, as in *debut* and *ballet*. Other French words with silent endings include *corps* Sp, *coup*, and *rendezvous* Sp. The *u* is effectively silent after *q* and *c* in some words, such as *quarter* and *biscuit*.

a la carte
a la mode
adieu
analogue *
archives *
au gratin
au revoir
avalanche
avant-garde *
ballet
banal *
barrage *
bastion *
beau
beaucoup
beret *
bistro
bon appetit
bonbon
bonhomie
bon mot
bon vivant
bon voyage
boudoir
bouquet
buffet
bureaucracy *
cabaret
camaraderie *
camouflage
caprice *
casserole
chalet
champagne
charade
chartreuse
chauffeur Sp

chauvinism *
chauvinist *
chez
chic
chicanery *
clairvoyant *
cliche *
clientele *
collage *
concierge
connoisseur *
corps Sp
coterie *
coup
couture
creme brulee
crepe
crochet
cul de sac
debonair
debut
deja vu
depot
dossier
effigy *
encore
entrepreneurs
epaulet *
facade *
faux
fracas *
fusillade *
gaucherie *
genre *
gourmet
grille
haute
hors d'oeuvre(s)

levee *
matte
melange
melee *
menagerie *
milieu *
mon ami
mortgage Sp
motifs
mousse
niche
nom de plume
nuance
panache
passe
persiflage *
pirouette *
potpourri
praline
protege *
questionnaire Sp
raconteur *
rendezvous Sp
repartee *
reservoir
restaurateur
resume
rouge
sabotage
salon
savoir-faire
soiree
touche
trousseau
valet
venue
vignette *
voila

Adopted Words and Phrases

Below: A classroom book of French words collected from RWP. Students write definitions under the tabs and continue to add to the book throughout the school year. See French word list, left.

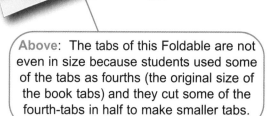

Above: The tabs of this Foldable are not even in size because students used some of the tabs as fourths (the original size of the book tabs) and they cut some of the fourth-tabs in half to make smaller tabs.

Grid Paper Four-Tab Notebook Foldable®: Students glue RWP examples or write adopted words on the front tabs of Single VKV Flashcards or Notebook Foldables. Under the tabs, they can write sentences using each word, give the etymology of the word, provide a pronunciation guide, and/or write phrases or advertising slogans using the words.

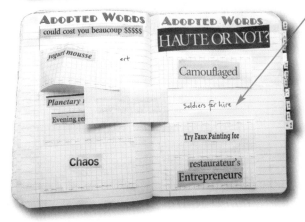

Adopted Words Foldable® Project

Shutterfold Project: A sheet of 12" x 18" art paper or a sheet of 11" x 17" photocopy paper can be used to make a large Shutterfold Project like the one featured on these two pages. Other Foldables can be displayed and stored on the inside. Information sheets, vocabulary lists, maps, or tables can be glued to the back.
See pages 24 and 400.

Multi-Tab Vocabulary Foldable®: Notebook paper can be cut to form multi-tabbed vocabulary books. This Foldable can be used independently or glued into a project as illustrated below. See page 415.

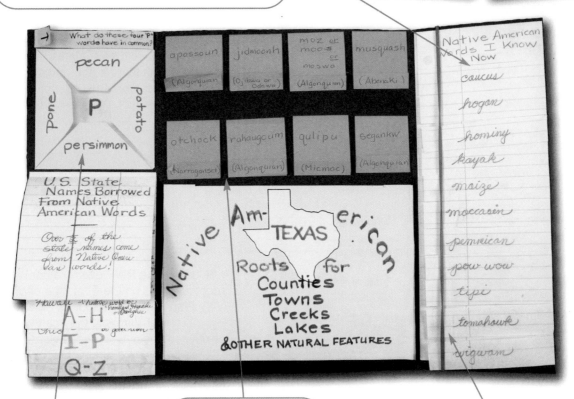

Envelope Foldable®: Made from a half sheet of photocopy paper, an Envelope Foldable can be used on the side panels of a project. See page 404 for folding instructions.

Small Matchbook Foldables®: These small Matchbook Foldables, made from 1/8th pieces of photocopy paper, are used for featuring important or unusual terms or facts. Definitions are under the tabs. Makes a great self-checking activity.

Fold to Fold: If you know beforehand that a Foldable is to be glued into a project, plan for the fold of the Foldable to be glued into the fold of the project. This will prevent some of the crumpling that can occur when the project is opened and closed frequently. Large rubber bands are a great Foldable Project aid, too.

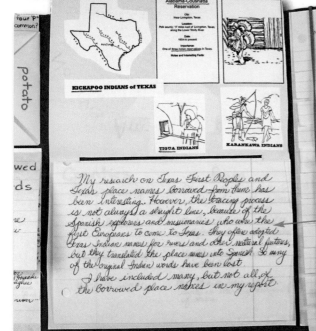

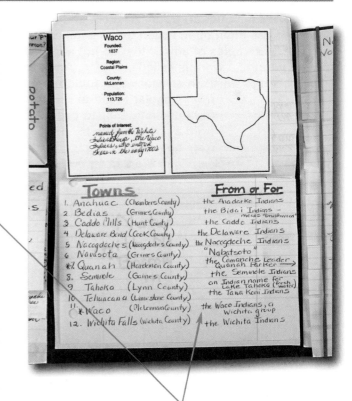

Foldable® Bound Book Journal:
Two sheets of notebook paper and one sheet of copy paper were used to bind this journal. The sheets of copy paper within the journal were used for graphics, and the notebook paper for student research, notes, and reports. See page 401.

Layered Foldable®: Two sheets of notebook paper were cut in half along the long axis (*hotdog*) and used to make this Foldable. This size fits perfectly along the side panels of a Shutterfold Project.

Foldable® Puzzle Pieces: Any Foldable based on a *hamburger* fold (like the journal above) can be displayed in the middle of a Shutterfold Project, and any Foldable based on a *hotdog* fold (like the twelve-word vocabulary activity on the opposite page) can be displayed along the sides. Quarter sheets of paper and quarter-sheet sized Foldables also fit nicely along the sides. See Shutterfold Project layout suggestions on page 24.

An *affix* is a letter or group of letters added to the beginning or end of a base word to form a new word. Affixes are most often added to the beginning or end of a base word, usually adding a syllable to the word. (Examples of affixes that do not add syllables: call, calls; walk, walked.) An affix added to the beginning of a word is called a *prefix*. An affix added to the end of a word is called a *suffix*. Affixes can change words in several ways, including the following:

- from singular to plural
- from present tense to past or future tense
- from a noun to a verb
- from an adjective to an adverb

See pages 225-243 on prefixes and pages 270-299 on suffixes.

Content Vocabulary: Make VKVs for words with affixes and/or combining forms encountered in math, science, social studies, and health.

Examples: *sub*zero, *sub*merge, *sub*marine   *deci*meter, *deci*mal, *deci*bel
            *micro*phone, *micro*wave, *micro*scope   *trans*port, *trans*atlantic, *trans*cribe

1. Write or glue a term with affixes in the middle of a Single VKV Flashcard.

2. Fold the left and/or right edge/s of the flashcard over to cover the affix/es.

3. Open and close the tabs, and read the base word with and without the affix/es.

Procedure (above): With the right and left tabs closed, view the stem word. Open the left tab and read the stem with a prefix. Close the left tab. Open the right tab and read the stem with a suffix. Open both tabs and read the word formed—*cultural, multicultural, multiculturalism*.

Binding Single Fold-Over VKV Flashcards to Make Books (right): After classroom flashcards are no longer needed as individual cards, they can be bound into a booklet and kept for future skill review. See page 368 for binding instructions.

1. Write a term on the inside bottom section of a Double VKV Flashcard.

2. Make a cut in the top strip between the affix/es and the base word. See page 378.

3. Opening and closing the tabs, read the base word with and without the affix/es. Students write the meaning of the affix and the base word under the words or on the back of the flashcard, and explain how the affix changes or enhances the meaning of the word.

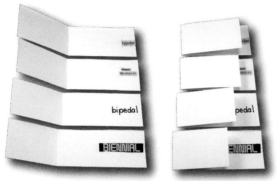

Single VKV Flashcards (above and right): Prefixes and/or suffixes can be added to and deleted from words by using Fold-Over Cover-Ups. See page 370.

Two-Column Pocket Chart Foldable® (left): Use a sheet of 11" x 17" paper or posterboard to make a two-column Pocket Chart Foldable, and use it to collect examples of words with prefixes and suffixes. Students write examples of words or collect examples from RWP and place them on quarter sheets or Single VKV Flashcards. Encourage students to made affix-based VKV Flashcards that can be used by the class to enhance vocabulary skills. See page 416.

VKVs® Glued To Chart: VKV Flashcards can be glued onto charts or bulletin boards, as seen in the example above. Note that other VKV cards are stored in the pockets of the affix chart pictured.

Anagrams Word Play

An *anagram* is a word or phrase that contains all the letters of
another word or phrase, but arranged in a different order.
Examples: *listen - silent; astronomers - no more stars*

One-Syllable Words

Easy

act	cat
arm	ram
beak	bake
boss	sobs
case	aces
ear	are
face	cafe
fast	fats
grin	ring
how	who
idea	aide
lips	slip
meat	team
meats	steam
night	thing
note	tone
now	won
pan	nap
pay	yap
run	urn
saw	was
skin	sink
sour	ours
spin	pins
spot	pots, tops
tap	pat
tea	eat
use	sue
war	raw

Harder

blot	bolt
bowl	blow
cape	pace
cola	coal
dairy	diary
death	hated
dense	needs
dice	iced
dimple	limped
finger	fringe
fried	fired
grab	brag
hams	mash, sham
heart	earth
knee	keen
lamp	palm
leap	pale, peal
lemon	melon
list	slit
march	charm
mean	mane
moist	omits
much	chum
none	neon
nude	dune
parks	spark
pear	reap
plum	lump
pools	spool
races	cares
rinse	siren
room	moor
sales	seals
sport	ports
stick	ticks
stops	posts
votes	stove
what	thaw

1. Write words that will be used to form anagrams on Single VKV Flashcards. Example: antler

2. Cut the letters apart and reassemble them to form a new word. Record both words. Example: antler, rental

Production Note:
Students made a miniature Pocket Chart with a sentence strip to store and display the whole and cut word cards. See instructions on page 416.

Anagrams Word Play

Animals

ant	tan
antler	rental
ape	pea
bat	tab
beak	bake
bear	bare
cat	act
clam	calm
cod	doc
coral	carol
dog	god
eel	lee
fowl	flow, wolf
lamb	balm
lion	loin
mare	ream
owl	low
ram	arm, mar
rat	art, tar
rats	arts, star
snail	nails
trout	tutor
wolf	flow, fowl
wasp	paws, swap

Science

amp	map
earth	heart
death	hated
heavy rain	hire a navy
Mars	rams, arms
salt	last, slat
soil	oils
star	arts, rats
the eyes	they see
weather	wreathe

Geography

Africa lion	California
African oil	California
amp	map
avenge	Geneva
big mule	Belgium
coal odor	Colorado
counts	Tucson
diagnose	San Diego
domains	Madison
dottier	Detroit
hasten	Athens
hating snow	Washington
hogs want in	Washington
hot on us	Houston
looted, tooled	Toledo
meals	Salem
more	Rome
nerved	Denver
pairs	Paris
panels	Naples
rock	Cork
salvages	Las Vegas
solo	Oslo
taxes	Texas
studies at ten	United States
ultra Asia	Australia

Math

add	dad
a decimal point	I'm a dot in place
eleven plus two	twelve plus one
inch	chin

Social Sciences

senator	treason
west	stew
Fourth of July	joyful fourth
the Morse Code	here come dots
old England	golden land
Statue of Liberty	built to stay free
dynamite	may end it

Sentence Strip Holder (above): This example was made using a sheet of 11" x 17" paper folded like a *hotdog*. See folding instructions, page 413.

1.

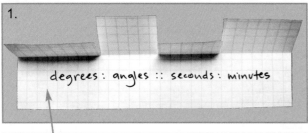

degrees : angles :: seconds : minutes

1.

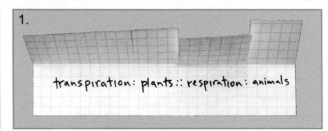

transpiration: plants :: respiration : animals

2.

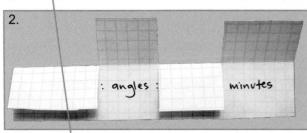

: angles :   minutes

2.

: plants :   animals

3.

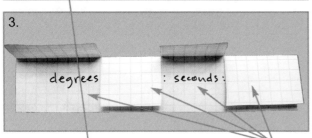

degrees   : seconds :

3.

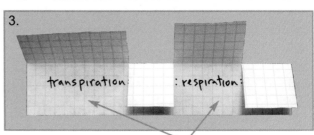

transpiration: : respiration :

1. Write an analogy under the tab of a Double Flashcard.

2. Cut the top tab so that each of the four sections of the analogy can be viewed separately.

3. Raise and lower the tabs to view what the two sides have in common. Could other terms be used? See page 383.

1.

celcius : 0° :: Farenheit : 32°

1.

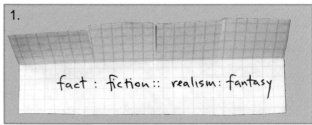

fact : fiction :: realism: fantasy

2.

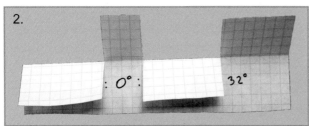

: 0° :   32°

2.

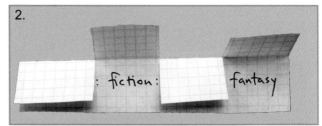

: fiction :   fantasy

3.

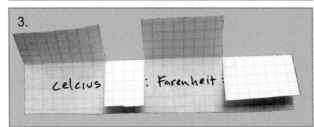

celcius   : Farenheit :

3.

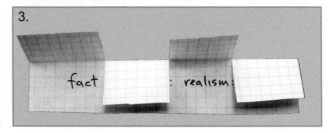

fact   : realism :

Analogies VKVs®

The word *analogy* comes from the Greek work *analogia*, which means *ratio* or *proportion*. Analogies show relationships between two ordered pairs and are usually written in the Aristotelian format of

____:____::____:____. This is read as ____ *is to*____ *as*____ *is to*____.

Read *bird:air::fish:water* as *Bird is to air as fish is to water*.

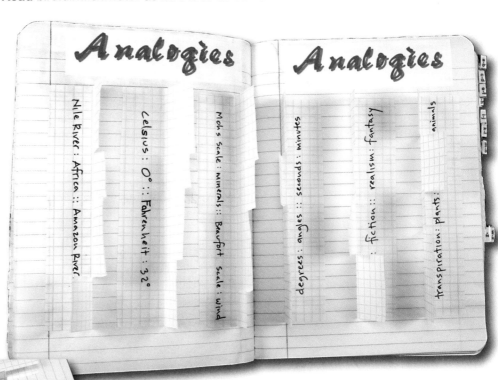

Content Application: Help students write analogies for literature, science, math, and social studies concepts. Examples of content analogies are included in the lists on pages 72-75.

Predicting Ordered Pairs:
Open the first and third tabs. Study the concepts under the tabs and analyze the relationship/s between them. Close these tabs, open the second and fourth tabs, and analyze the relationship/s between these two. Now open the tabs to show the first ordered pair and try to predict the second ordered pair. Open the tabs to check answers.

Compare and Contrast: Analogies compare two ideas or events that are similar or have something in common. Open the first two tabs—Nile River: Africa. Open the third tab. Students are to think about what would relate to the Amazon River the way Africa relates to the Nile River. Students raise the fourth tab to see if they have the correct solution. (South America is the only correct answer because the Amazon is found on only one continent.)

Analogies

Technology

CD:music::DVD:video
computer:monitor::TV:screen

Math Content

one:two::single:double
one:first::three:third
four:six::eight:ten
5:10::6:12
2:4:6::3:6:9
second:minute::minute:hour::day:year
five:twenty-five::six:thirty-six::seven:forty-nine...
add:subtract::multiply:divide
circle:sphere::square:cube
length:weight::inches:pounds
inches::yard::centimeters:meter
Celsius:0 degrees::Fahrenheit:32 degrees
degrees:angles::seconds:minutes

Language Arts

fact:fiction::drama:comedy (antonyms)
cold:frigid::hot:steamy (synonyms)
is not:isn't::will not:won't (contractions)
run:ran::sit:sat (verb tense)
she:hers::he:his (pronouns)
goose:geese::cow:cattle (noun plurals)
girl:girls::boy:boys (noun plurals)
girl:woman::boy:man
watch:watching::look:looking (affixes)
wind:blows::dog:barks (noun/action verb)
work:worker::build:builder (verb + er = "one who" noun)
hard:labor::difficult:job (adjective/noun)
silk:smooth::sandpaper:rough

Geography

Austin:Texas::Baton Rouge:Louisiana
Washington, D.C.:U.S.A.::Paris:France::London:England
Canada:United States::United States:Mexico
Nile River:Africa::Amazon River:South America
Antarctica:South Pole::Arctic Ice Sheet:North Pole
Ellis Island:East Coast immigration::Angel Island:West Coast immigration
longitude:vertical::latitude:horizontal
saltwater:ocean::freshwater:river
Hawaii:Pacific::Iceland:Atlantic::Ceylon:Indian
Andes Mountains:South America::Himalaya Mountains:Asia

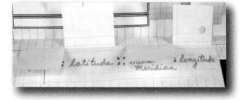

Analogies

Science Content

Earth

ocean:hydrosphere::land:lithosphere

rain:precipitation::steam:evaporation

moon:earth::earth:sun

temperature:thermometer::humidity:hygrometer *or* temperature:humidity::thermometer:hygrometer

tsunami:ocean::earthquake:land

Mohs scale:minerals::Beaufort scale:wind

Newton:gravity::Einstein:relativity

tyrannosaurus rex:Cretaceous::triceratops:Jurassic

core:earth::yolk:egg

fertilizer:soil::vitamins:body

weathering:breakdown::erosion:movement

sedimentary:limestone::igneous:granite::metamorphic:marble

gravity:earth::zero gravity:space

carbon dioxide:greenhouse effect::oil spills:ocean pollution

ichnite:footprint::coprolite:feces

hurricane:ocean::tornado:land

deposition:lake::delta:river

particulates:air::sediment:water

Life

ear:hear::tongue:taste

foot:hoof::nose:snout

cell:tissue::organ:system

microscope:biologist::telescope:astronomer *or*

microscope:telescope::biologist:astronomer

inhale:respiration::ingest:digestion

corn:monocot::bean:dicot

meat-eater:plant-eater::carnivore:herbivore (antonyms and synonyms)

cold-blooded:reptiles::warm-blooded:mammals

bee:hive::wasp:nest

insecticides:herbicides::insects:weeds

seed:flower::spore:fern

lion:antelope::predator:prey

fox:bird::bird:insect::insect:plant

transpiration:plants::respiration:animals

neuron:nervous system::bone cell:skeletal system

Physical

opaque:transparent::cloudy:clear (antonyms)

atoms:molecules::elements:matter

ice:solid::water:liquid::steam:gas

bronze:copper and tin::brass:copper and zinc::steel:iron and carbon (alloys)

212° F:water::675° F:mercury

screw:inclined plane::lever:pulley

heat:rising::cold:sinking

hydrogen and oxygen:water::sodium and chloride:salt

solute:solvent::sugar:water

hypotonic:hypertonic::low concentration:high concentration

Analogies

Social Studies Content

mayor:city::governor:state::president:country
city:state::state:nation
Senator:Congress::soldier:army
Federalist:Antifederalist::Democrat:Republican (U.S.A.)
conservative:liberal::right:left (politics)
Union Army:North::Confederate Army:South (U.S. Civil War)
Native American:America::Aborigine:Australia (world)
Columbus:Spain::Cabot:England
Cortez:Aztec::Pizarro:Inca::Puritans:John Winthrop::Quakers:William Penn
loyalists:king::patriots:independence
Treaty of Paris:Revolutionary War::Treaty of Ghent:War of 1812::Treaty of Versailles:WWI
U.S.S. *Maine*:Spanish-American War::Pearl Harbor:WWII
Richard Nixon:Watergate::Jimmy Carter:Iran Hostage Crisis
Emancipation Proclamation:President Abraham Lincoln::*I Have a Dream*:Dr. Martin Luther King, Jr.
Angel Island:West Coast::Ellis Island:East Coast

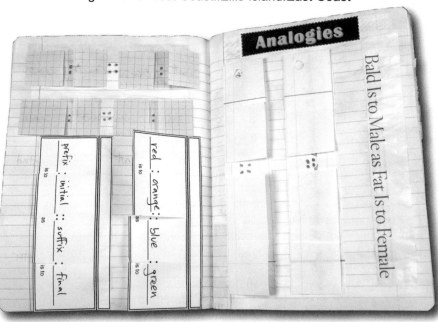

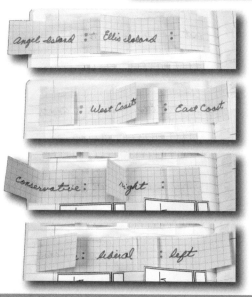

Two Analogy Formats

Half-and-Half VKV (left):
Use Single VKV Flashcards to make two *shutterfolds* and glue them ½" apart. See page 372.

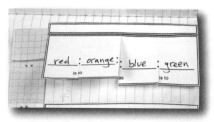

Four-Tab Foldable (right):
Can be independent or a Notebook Foldable like the one pictured right.

Sequencing

morning:noon::afternoon:evening
breakfast:lunch::lunch:dinner
12 PM:3 PM::5 PM:8 PM
go:depart::arrive:leave
plant:harvest::cook:eat
serve:food::pour:drink
first:last::beginning:ending
preface:book::introduction:speech
private:sergeant::colonel:general
Revolutionary War:War of 1812::Civil War:Spanish American War
Ford:Nixon::Reagan:Carter::Clinton:George H. W. Bush

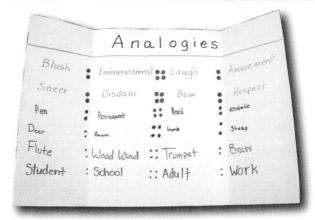

Three-Tab Foldable® (above): Fold a sheet of paper like a *hotdog*. Cut a ½" tab in the center of the top section, forming three tabs—a large tab to the left and right of the small central tab. Write the "as" symbol on the front. Under the large tabs, write the first and second half of an analogy. Students open one tab at a time and attempt to complete the analogies. Alternate analogy suggestions can be written on the top tabs, or on the back. See page 397.

Shutterfold (above): Fold a sheet of notebook paper or copy paper into a Shutterfold. Leave a ½" space between the two front tabs. Use the two sections to the inside left of the space to write the first two parts of the analogy and the two sections to the inside right for the last two parts. The middle symbol for "as" is visible when the Shutterfold is closed, and the symbols for "is to" are written in the *valleys* of the left and right sides. (See illustration.) Students can use this Shutterfold to record numerous examples of analogies. They can open either the left or the right side to try to finish the analogy. Tabs can be cut through the left and right tabs to separate the analogies. See page 400.

Antonyms

An *antonym* is a word that means the opposite or nearly the opposite of another word.
For example, a synonym for *offense* is *crime*, and an antonym would be *obedience*.
Another synonym for *offense* might be *attack*, and the antonym would be *defense*.
Or *offense* might indicate hurt feelings, and the antonym would be *kindness*.

Teach students how to use a thesaurus by making and using your own.
Use a Foldable® Bound Book, page 401, to make a giant classroom thesaurus.

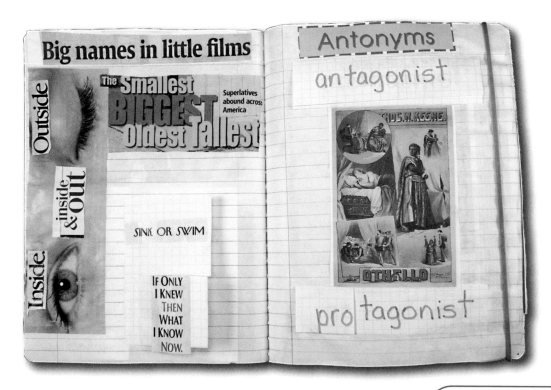

Triple VKV Flashcard (right):
Write and read the definition of
antagonist. Flip both tabs up.
Write and read the definition
of *protagonist*. See page 385.

Open all tabs and write a
sentence using both terms
in the middle of the Triple
VKV Flashcard.

A Two-Tab Foldable was
made using a quarter
sheet of grid paper.
Students were instructed to
find two common sayings,
phrases, or idioms that
include antonyms.

Sink or Swim:
To Fail or Succeed

If Only I Knew Then
What I Know Now

This Triple VKV Flashcard is the same as the one pictured below. It flips to define each term separately (*bust*, *boom*) and then opens to show them used together as antonyms. See page 385.

Double VKV Flashcard with two tabs for analyzing the meanings of the antonyms used in the phrase.

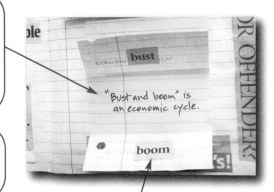

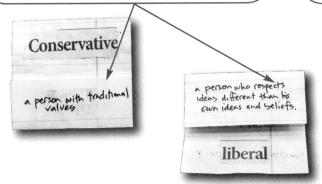

Triple VKV Flashcard (below): Write/read the definition of *conservative*. Flip both tabs down. Write/read the definition of *liberal*. See page 385.

Open all tabs and write a sentence using both terms in the middle of the Triple VKV Flashcard.

Antonyms VKVs

Finding and using *antonyms* strengthens vocabulary development and the ability to analyze words to determine levels of meaning. The study of antonyms is generally confined to nouns, verbs, and adjectives. Common antonym prefixes include *anti-, de-, dis-, il-, im-, ir-, mis-, non-, un-,* and others.

Easy test questions require *a general knowledge of terms.* More *advanced* test questions require *a detailed understanding of terms* to differentiate between nuances in meaning. When taking an antonym test, try to find the term that is the <u>most nearly opposite</u>.

Flip-Flop VKVs® (below): Antonyms are written or illustrated on opposite ends of a Single VKV Flashcard folded into thirds. See page 376. Sentences using the antonyms and/or definitions are written in the middle section. When the tabs are opened and closed, students relate the antonyms.

Content Antonyms: In content subjects, specific terms are frequently used as antonyms: interior, exterior; East, West; organic, inorganic; positive, negative.

Above: The center back section of the Flip-Flop Single VKV Flashcard is glued into a notebook, allowing students to flip the tabs up and down to compare and contrast the antonyms.

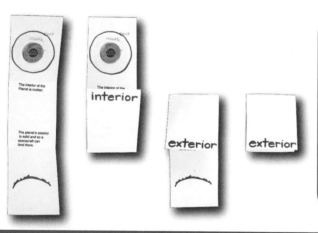

If each student makes one flashcard using different antonyms and cards are exchanged between students, the class will experience a varied collection of antonyms.

Fold a 1" tab to the left of a large Single VKV Flashcard. Fold the remaining portion of the flashcard in half.

Write antonyms on each side of the center fold.

Flip the flashcard and write definitions for the antonyms on the back of the card.

Staple the 1" tabs together to make an antonyms "booklet" that can be read forward or backward. Either way, students look at the word on the half of the card that is visible and provide an antonym. When applicable, multiple antonyms can be given and added to the flashcard.

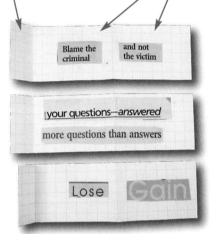

Above and Right: Make the antonym VKV Flashcards described above, and use them to collect examples of antonyms found in RWP—from newspapers, magazines, advertisements, catalogs, and other print sources.

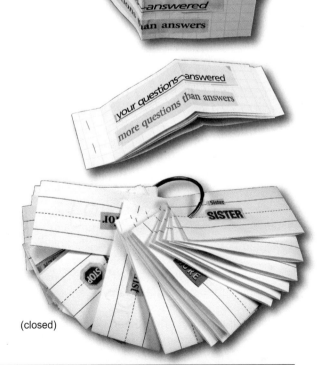

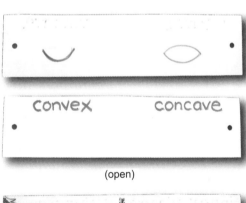

(open)

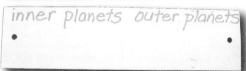

Variation (above and right): Follow the same procedure for VKV Rings. See page 368.

(closed)

Antonyms

-less and -ful (below): Use a Triple Flashcard to make a three-word VKV antonym card.

everything is OLD NEW again

From Loathing to Loving

THE WINNERS, THE LOSERS, AND EVERYBODY IN BETWEEN

Forming Antonyms with -less and -ful (above left):

fear<u>less</u>   fear<u>ful</u>
help<u>less</u>   help<u>ful</u>
hope<u>less</u>   hope<u>ful</u>
joy<u>less</u>   joy<u>ful</u>
tear<u>less</u>   tear<u>ful</u>
thought<u>less</u>   thought<u>ful</u>

Negating Prefixes in-, dis-, non-, un-:

in-	dis-	un-
accessible	able	faithful
accurate	content	fair
adequate	interested	likeable
discrete ᴴ	like	resolved
direct	own	responsive
voluntary	respectful	willing

non- (not)
Usually refers to the absense of something rather than its opposite.
nonaggression
nonprofessional
nonviolent

Analogies and Antonyms:
Write analogies that are antonyms and see if students can complete them. Examples: macro-:micro-::large:small
ascend:descend::rise:fall

Definitions Using Antonyms:
Define a word by using its antonym in the same sentence:
    She was upset because her pants were *tight* and she
        wanted them to be *loose*.
    If you don't know the *answer*, ask a *question* instead.
    I was *ill* most of last year, but I am *healthy* this year.

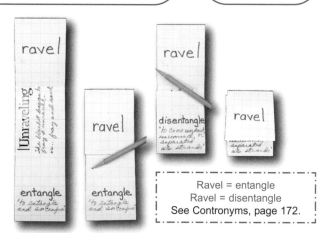

Ravel = entangle
Ravel = disentangle
See Contronyms, page 172.

More Than One Meaning:
Many words have more than one meaning. Help students understand that an antonym is the opposite for only one meaning of the word. Analyze the etymology of the word *antonym*: ant- means *against*, -nym means *name*.

For example, if a synonym for *tired* is *sleepy*, then an antonym might be *energetic*. But using another meaning, a synonym for *tired* might be *overused*, and the antonym would then be *fresh* or *new*.

Alternate the use of printed and electronic thesauruses with students. Have students make their own thesauruses using a Foldable Bound Book. See page 401.

Antonyms

Two-Tab Matching Foldable® (right and below):
Use this Foldable as a matching activity
for any of the following:

- antonyms and/or synonyms
- terms and definitions
- homophones, homographs
- idioms and their meanings
- important people and events
- authors and their works
- characters from literature
- and others

See page 396 for instructions.

Above & Left:
See list of geography
antonyms on page 88.

Word Study:
The terms *fat chance*
and *slim chance* sound
like antonyms, but they
are synonyms.

Forward and back

Two-Tab Foldables® (right):
Two-Tab Foldables made using
11" x 17" or 12" x 18" paper can be used by
students working in groups, or can be glued
together side by side to form a class book.
See page 28 for book binding instructions.

Test Prep

When taking an antonym test, determine the part of speech of the word in question.
All correct answer choices will be the same part of speech as the word; answer choices
that are different parts of speech can be eliminated. However, if the word in question can be more
than one part of speech, use the answer choices in the test to figure out which part of speech you
should use to define the word, and then use that definition
to determine the correct antonym.

Word	Part of speech	Antonyms
abbreviate *	v.	enlarge, increase, lengthen
abridge *	v.	add, enlarge, lengthen
abstain *	v.	indulge, vote, take action
accidentally * Sp	adj.	purposefully, intentionally
adequate *	adj.	inadequate, unfit, unqualified
adjacent *	adj.	disconnected, separate, nonadjacent
advantage	n.	disadvantage, drawback, handicap
agreement	n.	disagreement, dispute
amicable *	adj.	hostile, unfriendly
ancient	adj.	modern, new
antagonist	n.	protagonist, ally, supporter
antisocial	adj.	friendly, sociable
approval	n.	disapproval, rejection
arid *	adj.	wet, humid
assiduous *	adj.	lazy, neglectful, lax
balance	n.	disproportion, imbalance, instability
benevolent *	adj.	greedy, unkind, uncharitable
compile	v.	disassemble, disperse, separate, scatter
conformist *	n.	nonconformist
conscious Sp	adj.	impassive, senseless, unaware, unconscious
considerate	adj.	disrespectful, impatient, inconsiderate
controversial	adj.	agreeable, undisputable, unquestionable
convergence *	n.	divergence
deleterious *	adj.	assisting, helpful, harmless
diligent *	adj.	indifferent, lethargic, negligent
discredit *	v.	commend, credit, honor
enervate * Sp	v.	activate, energize, strengthen
ephemeral *	adj.	enduring, eternal, lasting
exasperate *	v.	calm, comfort, ease, placate
exemplary *	adj.	erring, incorrect, lacking
fortuitous *	adj.	calculated, deliberate, intentional, unlucky
frugal *	adj.	generous, wasteful, lavish
haughty *	adj.	humble, meek, shy
hypothesis *	n.	measurement, proof, truth
impetuous *	adj.	calm, circumspect, cautious
incompatible *	adj.	compatible, harmonious, well-matched

Test Prep

Frequently, antonym tests will include one or more synonyms as answer choices. Remind students to be alert for this confusing situation. Without thinking, test takers can easily shift to marking synonyms instead of antonyms.

inconsequential *	adj.	consequential, important, significant
inevitable *	adj.	avoidable, doubtful
intrepid *	adj.	cowardly, meek, fearful
magnanimous	adj.	petty, stingy, suspicious
moribund	adj.	living, vivacious
mundane *	adj.	exciting, imaginative, extraordinary
nonchalant *	adj.	intense, excited
novice *	n.	expert, professional
nuisance	n.	delight, pleasure
opulent *	adj.	poor, destitute, meager
ostentatious *	adj.	modest, unpretentious, plain
parched *	adj.	wet, moist, saturated
perfidious *	adj.	loyal, faithful, reliable
prosaic *	adj.	creative, imaginative, interesting
prosperous *	adj.	failing, poor, unsuccessful
provocative *	adj.	repressive, unexciting, unstimulating
prudent *	adj.	imprudent, careless, unwise
querulous *	adj.	cheerful, happy, uncomplaining
rancor *	n.	kindness, good will, sympathy
recluse *	n.	extrovert
reluctant	adj.	anxious, eager, willing
renovate *	v.	demolish, ruin
restrained *	adj.	assured, outgoing, uncontrolled, unrestricted
reverence *	n.	disdain, disregard, disrespect, irreverence
spurious *	adj.	genuine, authentic, real
submissive *	adj.	disobedient, domineering, authoritarian
substantiate *	v.	break, disprove
superficial *	adj.	deep, profound, genuine
superfluous *	adj.	important, necessary, needed
superior	adj.	below, inferior, minor
surreptitious *	adj.	authorized, open, public
tactful *	adj.	indiscreet, undiplomatic, impolite
tenacious *	adj.	docile, weak, yielding
transient *	adj.	enduring, permanent, lasting
venerable *	adj.	disrespected
virulent	adj.	harmless, healthy, benign
wise	adj.	foolish, ignorant, unwise

Test-Taking Strategy: Say the test word, mentally define the word, and then think of possible antonyms. Mentally say the antonyms while reviewing the answer choices to prevent a mind-switch to synonyms. If you do not see an appropriate antonym, reconsider the definition of the test word. Could it have a different meaning? If so, begin the process again.

Antonyms

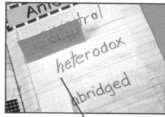

Below: Double VKV Flashcards can be cut so the root or base word is visible and the prefix that imparts an opposite meaning is covered. One set of antonyms is formed per flashcard. See page 379.

sinistral	dextral
orthodox	heterodox
	unorthodox
abridged	unabridged
decelerate	accelerate

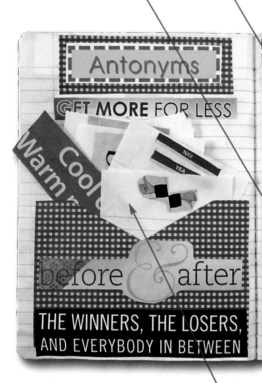

Quarter-Sheet Antonym Flashcards: Students use quarter sheets of notebook paper to make antonym flashcards. Cards are collected and used for matching activities. This is a good activity for academic vocabulary enrichment.

Above: Two-Tab Foldables and VKV Flashcards can be stored in notebook pockets.
Right: Look at the tabs of a Two-Tab antonym Foldable—*cold* and *copy*. Under the tabs, the antonyms for each term are written, illustrated, and used in sentences.

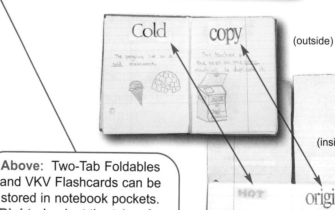

(outside)

(inside)

Antonyms   (ant- = against, -nym = name)

Review: An *antonym* is a word that means the opposite or nearly the opposite of another word.
For example, a synonym for *offense* is *crime*, and an antonym would be *obedience*.
Another synonym for *offense* might be *attack*, and the antonym would be *defense*.
Or *offense* might indicate hurt feelings, and the antonym would be *kindness*.

Students can learn to use a thesaurus by making their own.
Use a Foldable® Bound Book, page 401, to make a giant classroom thesaurus.

Frequently Used Antonyms

absent	present H	feast	famine	offense	defense
accept	refuse	fiction	nonfiction	often	seldom
achieve	fail	finish	begin, start	partial	whole H
active	passive	flimsy	solid	pass	fail
adult	child	follow	lead H	quick	slow
advance	retreat	following	preceding	quiet	loud
agree	disagree	forget	remember	remember	forget
alike	different	fresh	stale	sad	cheerful, happy
always	never	friend	foe, enemy	sharp	dull
appear	vanish	generous	miserly, stingy	single	multiple
arrive	depart	graceful	clumsy	straight	crooked
ascend	descend	guilty	innocent	stranger	friend
behind	ahead	include	omit	stay	go, leave
bland	spicy	increase	decrease	sweet	bitter, sour
brave	cowardly	joy	grief	tender	tough
busy	idle H	kind	cruel	thaw	freeze H
change H	persist, stay	left	right H	ugly	pretty
common	rare	lose	find H	unique	common
complex H	simple	many	few	vertical	horizontal
create	destroy	minimum	maximum	wake H	sleep
dead	alive	multiply	divide	weak H	strong
deep	shallow	narrow	broad	wide	narrow
difficult	easy	new H	used	winding	straight
dull	shiny	nice	naughty	winter	summer
evil	good	no one	everyone	yell	whisper
expensive	inexpensive	nothing	everything		
exterior	interior				

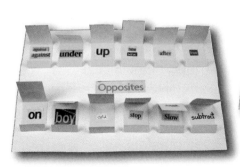

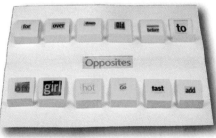

Matchbook Antonyms (left): Use small strips of paper to make tiny matchbooks. Write or paste words on the front tabs of the matchbooks, and antonyms under the tabs. See if students can name an antonym for a selected word before raising the tab. Write alternate antonyms for the words under the tabs on the top (not glued) section. See page 400.

Antonyms

Science

above	below (water, ground, crust)	explosion	implosion
accelerate	decelerate	extinction	survival
acid	base H	fertile	infertile, barren
active	passive	filter	emit
active	dormant (volcano)	fission	fusion
aerobic	anaerobic	flight	flightless (ratites like ostriches)
angiosperms	gymnosperms	forestation	deforestation
annual Sp	perennial	freeze H	melt, thaw
ascend	descend	freezing point	boiling point
attract	repel	fresh	stagnant, stale
audible	inaudible	freshwater	saltwater
balanced	unbalanced	full	empty
benign	malignant	gain electrons	lose electrons
biodegradable	non-biodegradable	gravity	zero gravity
bipedal	quadrupedal	hard	soft (minerals)
birth H	death	heavy	light
capture	release	herbivore	carnivore
cause	effect	high H	low (density, frequency, humidity, pressure, temperature, viscosity)
cloudy, overcast	clear		
color	colorless (gas)	homogeneous	heterogeneous (mixtures)
combustible	noncombustible	humid	dry
complex	simple (eyes)	hydrate	dehydrate
conductor	insulator	hydrosphere	lithosphere
conservation	depletion	hypo-	hyper-
convex	concave	hypotonic	hypertonic
core H	crust	ignite	extinguish
day	night H SL	inhale	exhale
decay	preservation	inner	outer
deep	shallow	interior	exterior
deposition	sublimation	intrusive	extrusive
diurnal	nocturnal	kinetic energy	potential energy
dominant	recessive	light zone	dark zone (ocean, cave)
drought	flood	macro-	micro-
dusk	dawn	magnetic	nonmagnetic
dwarfs	supergiants (galaxies)	mature	immature
dye H SL	bleach	moist	dry
dynamic	static	learned	inborn, instinctive
earth	sky, space	living	nonliving
element	compound	male H	female
endothermic	exothermic	metallic	nonmetallic
expand	contract	metals	nonmetals

Antonyms

Science

melting point	freezing point	sterile	fertile
migratory	stationary	stimulant	tranquilizer
natural	synthetic, artificial	strong	weak [H] (forces)
nearsighted	farsighted	subduction	uplifting
noise, sound	silence	sunrise	sunset
nutrition	malnutrition	suspension	solution
odor	odorless (hydrogen gas)	taste	tasteless (gas)
opaque	transparent	threatened	protected
open circuit	closed circuit	trench	ridge (ocean floor)
organic	inorganic	vacuum	air molecules
outer	inner (planets, ear)	variable	constant
oxidation (lose electrons)	reduction (gain electrons)	vertebrate	invertebrate
pasteurized	unpasteurized	visible	invisible
permeable	impermeable	warm-blooded	cold-blooded
poisonous	nonpoisonous	warm front	cold front (weather)
polymer	monomer	weak [H]	strong, powerful
positive	negative (poles, charges, tropisms)	wild	tame
pure, clean	polluted	wilderness	development
push	pull	windward	leeward
rain forest	desert [H]	windy	still [H]
random	specific	young	old (living organisms, mountains)
rear	front		
reflection	refraction (waves)		
renewable	nonrenewable		
retain	lose		
rough	smooth		
salination	desalination		
saturated	unsaturated (solution)		
shrink	expand		
single celled	multi-celled		
sink [H]	float		
solid	liquid		
soluble	insoluble		
sour	sweet		
surface	floor (ocean)		
surface	core (planet, satellite)		
stable equilibrium	unstable equilibrium		
stalactites	stalagmites		

Right: Two-Tab Foldable with student writing, examples of RWP, and photographs from the community. This antonym activity on "right" and "wrong" became a phonics and spelling review, too.

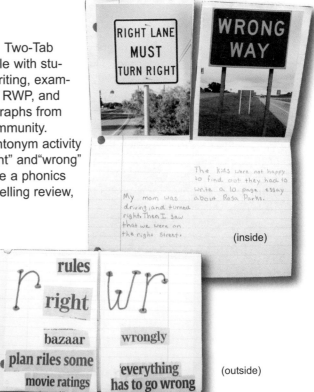

Antonyms

Geography

Arctic Circle	Antarctic Circle
coastline	inland
east	west
highest	lowest
hill	valley
land H	water
largest	smallest
longest	shortest
mountain	valley
north	south
North Korea	South Korea
North Pole	South Pole
Northern Hemisphere	Southern Hemisphere
plains	plateaus, mountains
tallest	deepest
tropics	poles

Social Sciences

active	passive
advance	retreat
ally	enemy
ancient	modern
approve	veto
attack	defend
Axis powers	Allied powers
civilian	military
communism	democracy
divide	unite
emancipate	enslave
federalist	antifederalist
friend	foe, enemy
imperialism	isolationism
import	export
individual	group
innocent	guilty
kingdom	republic
lawful	unlawful, illegal
left-wing	right-wing
liberal	conservative
loyalist	patriot
majority	minority
monotheism	polytheism
native	alien
offensive	defensive
palace	hut, shack, hovel
past H	future
poverty	wealth
pros	cons
rural	urban
secular	nonsecular
segregate	integrate
slavery	freedom
victory	defeat
war	peace H

Extension for the Double VKV Flashcards (below):
Have students use a thesaurus to write synonyms for the two antonyms on the inside top tabs of the Double Flashcards. (The following synonyms come from www.thesaurus.com.)

Above *conservative*, students might write *conventional*, *constant*, *bourgeois*, and *inflexible*.

Above *liberal,* students might write *flexible*, *progressive*, *avant-garde*, *loose*, and *lenient*.

Have students determine which term from one side best matches one from the other side. For example, *constant* on the conservative side would be a good antonym for *lenient* or *loose* on the liberal side.

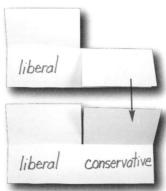

> **Left:** Open one tab at a time, either left or right, and say the antonym of the word viewed before looking under the other tab. If each student makes one VKV Flashcard and exchanges it with classmates, students will be exposed to multiple antonyms that can be added to their notebooks or study guides.

Antonyms

Math

acute	obtuse
add [H]	subtract
adjacent	nonadjacent
approximate	exact
cluster graph	scatter graph
combine	separate [Sp]
empty	full
equal	unequal
equality	inequality
finite	infinite
greater than	less than
height	depth
increase	decrease
interior	exterior
less	more
long [H]	short
many	few
most	least
multiply	divide
none [H]	all [H]
odd	even
part	whole [H]
positive	negative
profit	loss
prove	disprove
reduce	increase
short	long
straight [H] [SL]	curved
vacant, null	full
vertical	horizontal
whole numbers	fractions

Language Arts

antagonist	protagonist
antonym	synonym
applaud	deride, boo
censure	condone
climax	anticlimax
comedy	tragedy
drama	fantasy
fact	opinion
factual	fictional
fiction	nonfiction
imaginary	real
literal	figurative
or [H]	nor
original [Sp]	copy
past [H]	future
prefix	suffix
question	answer
single	plural
strength	weakness (of a character)
tragedy	comedy
villain	hero

Foldable® Charts: Make a Foldable Pocket Chart and use it to collect examples of antonyms found in RWP. Fill the pockets with quarter sheets of student writing featuring antonyms, VKV Flashcards, and other Foldables that can be used by students who need vocabulary practice. Note that at the bottom of the pocket an extra fold was stapled and used to display terms, phrases, idioms, and other related print. See pages 415 and 416.

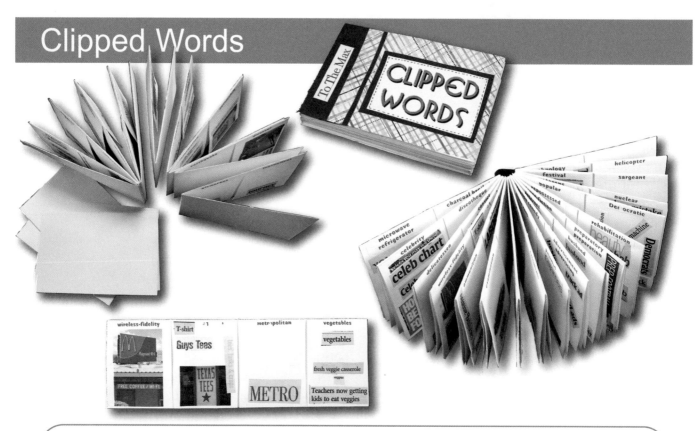

Four-Tab Foldables® (above): Four-Tab Foldables can be made from 11" x 17" or 12" x 18" paper by individual students or students working in groups. The Foldables can also be glued together side by side to form a class book. See page 28 for book binding instructions and page 394 for instructions on folding a book spine. As discussed in the Introduction, these Foldables incorporate photographs of common clipped words found on signs within the community.

Above: Students take photos of signs that include clipped words. Nine photos can be printed on a sheet, cut apart, and used as tabs within notebooks.

Variation: Use printed photos as flashcards.

Note: Photos are usually printed in black and white.

Above: Single VKV Flashcards
1. Write. 2. Fold.
3. Read clipped word and full word.

Clipped Words

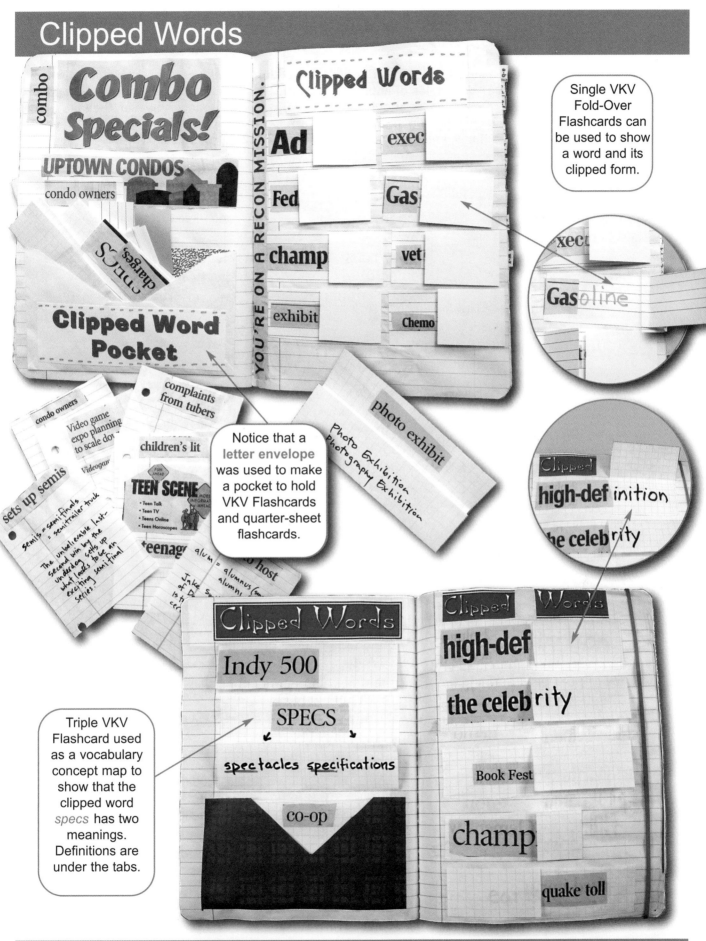

Single VKV Fold-Over Flashcards can be used to show a word and its clipped form.

Notice that a **letter envelope** was used to make a pocket to hold VKV Flashcards and quarter-sheet flashcards.

Triple VKV Flashcard used as a vocabulary concept map to show that the clipped word *specs* has two meanings. Definitions are under the tabs.

When a word is shortened for efficiency in writing or speech it is called a *clipped*, *abbreviated*, or *shortcut* word (Sitton, 1995). Examples of abbreviated words include *memo* for memorandum and *intro* for introduction. Clipped words should not be used in formal writing; however, they are frequently used when space is limited on signs, on business cards, in advertisements, in newspaper or magazine headlines, and in pamphlets. See page 222, Portmanteau Words.

Above: The clipped word *sub* can mean three things—a substitute, a submarine, or a type of sandwich. A Triple VKV Flashcard was used to show the three different meanings of "Send in the subs."

Medial and Final

- air**plane**
- al**chemist**
- a**mend**
- ano**nym**ous
- barbec(q)ue
- baseball **mitt**en
- bi**cyc**list
- cara**van**
- coat**tails**
- dis**port**
- dis**till** (n., a distillery)
- ice **box** (refrigerator)
- cara**van**
- chrysanthe**mum**
- engine **revolution**
- escape+goat
- earth**quake**
- flat**iron** (clothes)
- good**bye**
- ham**burger**
- heli**copter**
- inner **tube**
- inter**net**
- live**stock**
- motor**cycle**
- neck**tie**
- neighbor**hood**
- news**paper**
- omni**bus**
- peri**wig**
- rac**coon**
- refri**ge**rator + d (fridge)

A *d* is added to *frige* to keep the short sound of *i* in the clipped word.

- super**market**
- tele**phone**
- turn**pike**
- violon**cello**

Word Study: Clipped -vv- Words

American English words do not double the consonant *v*. **Clipped Word Exceptions:**

civvy	**civ**ilian + -**vy**
divvy	**div**ide (up) + -**vy**
revved	**rev** (up) + -**ved**

(rev is short for revolution of an engine or the like)

savvy Spanish loanword

In American English, words do not end with the letter *v*. A final *v* sound is spelled with -*ve*, no matter what the preceding vowel sound may be. **Examples:**

con**nive**   con**trive**   ha**ve**
kna**ve**   reprie**ve**   slee**ve**

A few clipped words and abbreviations end in *v* and are exceptions, but it is not acceptable to use them in formal writing:

civ.   div.   gov.   abbreviations

rev   clipped word

Collect clipped words found in RWP.

Types of Elision: Omission of Sounds

Aphesis, loss of one or more sounds from the beginning of a word.
Apocope, loss of one or more sounds from the end of a word.
Syncope, loss of one or more sounds from the middle of a word.

abdominal
advertisement
alumni
ammunition + o
automobile
biography
biological
burst
buttock
cabriolet
camouflage
Canterbury gallop
celebrity
cellular
cellular phone
centum
chimpanzee
champion
charcoal broiled
chemotherapy
cleric + k
combinations + o
coeducational
condominium
confidence artist
convict
copper (British)
crocodile
cucumber + ke
curiosity
debutante
decoration
delicatessen
Democrats
demonstration
dinosaur
discotheque
doctor
dormitory
drapery

electronic mail
examination
ex-convict
executive
exposition
fabulous
facsimile + x
fanatic
Federal + s
festival
frankfurter
gabble
gasoline
gentleman
glamorous
gobbet
government
governor
graduate
gymnasium
hackney
hippopotamus
home runs
husband + bby
hyperactive
I D entification
influenza
information
intercommunication
introduction
jet aircraft
knickerbockers
laboratory
limousine
literature
lithograph
lubricate
luncheon
market
mathematics
mayonnaise

medicines
memorandum
metropolitan
microscopic
miniature Sp
mistress
modern
morning
moving picture + e
muttonhead
normal
nuclear + ke
oleomargarine
operations
opportunity
options
pajamas
pantaloons
passion + h
penitentiary
pepper
percolate + k
petroleum
photograph
pianoforte
popular
post-operation
premature + ie
pre-operation
preparatory
professional
professional-amateur
professor Sp
promenade
promotional
proofread
propeller
quasi-stellar
reconnaissance
referee
refrigerator + d (fridge)
rehabilitation
repossessed

representative
rhinoceros
sergeant Sp + a (sarge)
science fiction
scramble
semifinals
situation comedy
Special Operations
spectacles
spotlight
squadron
staphylococcus
statistics
stenography pad
stereophonic
submarine
subterranean way
summarize
superintendent Sp
synchronization
taxicab
technician
technology
teenager
temporary Sp
tournament + ey
trigonometry
triumph
tuxedo
two-by-four
typographical error
university + a (varsity)
vegetables + gies
vegetarian
vegetate
veteran
veterinarian
vocabulary
wireless-fidelity
wizard + h (whiz)
zoological gardens

Cognates are words that are descended from the same ancestral roots; i.e., they can be traced to a common etymological origin. These often similar-sounding words can be found in different languages today (and sometimes within the same language). Sometimes, but not always, cognates have comparable meanings to one another. For example, the word for *education* in English is *educacion* in Spanish.

False cognates are words and expressions that people use incorrectly because they look similar to English counterparts that may or may not have the same etymology. For example, the Spanish word *ropa* means *clothes*, not *rope*.

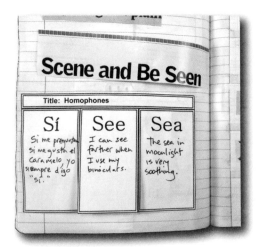

False Cognates (above): The Spanish word *si* is not a cognate of the English words *see* and *sea*. The pronunciation is the same, but the meaning differs. These are examples of Spanish/English homophones.

Important:
The following word lists include true cognates (words descended from the same ancestral root), as well as words that appear similar in both languages but might not be cognates by strict definition, and words of modern origin that different languages have adopted, like *glasnost*.

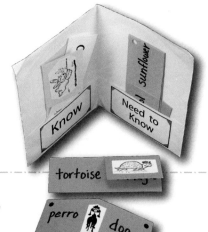

Studies show that . . .
- Vocabulary is the single most encountered obstacle for students learning the English language.
- Vocabulary is the single strongest predictor of academic success for second language students (Kinsella, 2005).
- Vocabulary is also the primary determinant of future reading comprehension.
- Vocabulary knowledge is virtually indistinguishable from reading comprehension on quantitative tests.
- Graphic organizers helped at least 80 percent of students to master key vocabulary skills (Brookbank et. al., 1999).

- Students need to learn English through the content area. Teachers need to be skilled in modifying mainstream instruction and lessons that will scaffold learning subject matter through another language. Language-integrated approaches to instruction should present opportunities for both content and language acquisition (Whelan Ariza, 2006).

- Because language acquisition takes place in contexts where language is used for genuine communicative purposes, effective programs feature instructional designs that place students in proximity to each other and demand that they interact to complete meaningful tasks. English language development is best achieved when it is integrated with content instruction, rather than being taught in isolation (Davies, Samway & McKeon, 1999).

- For ELL's who speak Romance languages like Spanish or French, it is important to teach cognates as a connection to academic English.

- Using cognates increases vocabulary for Spanish speakers. 10-15,000 words in Spanish are easily transferred to English (J Cummins, 2002).

Compiled by Dr. Judith Youngers for Dinah Zike Academy, ESL/ELL Academy Session

Geography

See Social Studies, Pages 109 to 111 .

English	Spanish	English	Spanish
acid deposition	deposición ácida	clan	clan
agriculture	agricultura	climate	clima
alluvial	aluvial	collective	colectiva
altitude	altitud	commerce	comercio
American	Americano	commercial	comercial
animal	animal	commune	comuna
aquaculture	acuacultura	communism	comunismo
aquifer	acuífero	conquistador	conquistador
arable	arable	conservation	conservación
archipelago	archipiélago	consumer	consumo
artesian	artesiana	continent	continente
atmosphere	atmósfera	continental	continental
atoll	atolón	cooperative	cooperativa
autocracy	autocracia	coral	coral
avalanche	avalancha	cordillera	cordillera
		cultivation	cultivación
bazaar Sp	bazar	cultural diffusion	difusión cultural
bedouin	beduino	culture H	cultura
bifurcation	bifurcación	culture region	región cultural
bilingual	bilingüe	cuneiform	cuneiforme
biologist	biólogo	current H	corriente
biomass	biomasa	cycle	ciclo
biosphere	biosfera	cyclone	ciclón
Bolsheviks	Bolcheviques	czar	zar
boomerang	bumerang		
		deciduous	deciduo
cabinet	gabinete	deficit	déficit
calligraphy	caligrafía	deforestation	deforestación
capitalism	capitalismo	delta	delta
cartography	cartografía	democracy	democracia
cataract	catarata	desalination	desalinización
caudillo	caudillo	desertification	desertificación
center	centro	dharma	dharmaj
cereal H	cereal	dialect	dialecto
chaparral	chaparral	diatoms	diátomo
chinook	chinuco	dikes	diques
		dissident	disidente
		distribution	distribución
		domesticate	domesticar
		dominion	dominio
		double	doble
		duplication	duplicación
		dynasty	dinastía

Triple VKV Flashcard (above): Notice the fold-over tab to the right. By opening or closing this tab, either the English suffix *-tion* or the Spanish suffix *-cion* shows. See page 385.

Geography
See Social Studies, Pages 109 to 111 .

English	Spanish	English	Spanish
economic sanctions	sanciones económicas	habitat	habitat
economy	economía	hemisphere	hemisferio
ecosystem	ecosistema	homogeneous	homogéneo/a
ecotourism	ecoturismo	human	humano/a
elevation	elevación	human geography	geografía humana
El Niño	El Niño	hurricane	huracán
embargo	embargo	hydroelectric	hidroeléctrico/a
endemic	endémico	hydrosphere	hidrosfera
energy	energía	hypothesis	hipótesis
English	Inglés		
equinox	equinoccio	icon	icono
erosion	erosión	iconographic	iconográfico/a
escarpment	escarpa	ideogram	ideograma
estuary	estuario	immigration	inmigración
ethnic group	grupo étnico	impressionism	impresionismo
European Union	Unión Europea	indigenous	indígena
eutrophication	eutroficación	industrial	industrial
evaporation	evaporación	industrial capitalism	capitalismo industrial
extinction	extinción	industrialization	industrialización
		industry	industria
family	familia	infrastructure	infraestructura
fault [H]	falla	insular	insular
fauna	fauna	intellectual	intelectual
federal	federal	interaction	interacción
federal system	systema federal	interdependent	interdependiente
feudalism	feudalismo	introduced species	especies introducidas
fjord	fiordo	island	isla
flora	flora	isle [H]	isla
formal region	región formal	isthmus	istmo
functional region	funcional		

English	Spanish
gasoline	gasolina
gaucho	gaucho
generation	generación
genetically modified	modificado genéticamente
geography	geografía
glacial	glacial
glacier	glaciar
glasnost	glasnost
global	global
globe	globo
glyph	glifo
group	grupo
guru	gurú

Shutterfold Project With and Without Tabs
(below and on next page): See page 400.

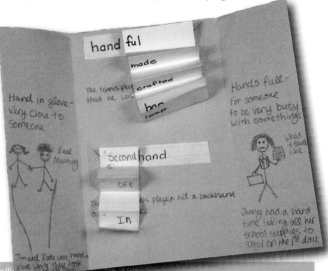

Geography
See Social Studies, Pages 109 to 111 .

English	Spanish	English	Spanish
lagoon	laguna	oasis	oasis
latitude	latitud	oligarchy	oligarquía
lichen H	líquene	organic	orgánico/a
liquid	liquido/a	ozone	ozono
lithosphere	litosfera		
location	locación	pagoda	pagoda
loess	loes	pampas	pampa
longitude	longitud	pastoralism	pastoreo
		patriarch	patriarca
magma	magma	patriotism	patriotismo
malnutrition	malnutrición	peninsula	península
mantle H Sp	manto	perceptual region	región perceptual
mantra	mantra	pesticide	pesticida
maritime	marítimo	petrochemical	petroquímico
material	material	phosphate	fosfato
megalopolis	megalópolis	physical geography	geografía fisíca
merchant marine	marina mercante	plain H	plano
meteorology	meteorología	plate tectonics	placa tectónica
metropolitan area	área metropolitana	polar	polar
mica	mica	pollution	polución
migration	migración	population	población
mixed economy	economía mixto	population density	densidad de población
mobile	móvil	port H	puerto
mobility	mobilidad	post-industrial	postindustrial
monopoly	monopolio	precipitation	precipitación
monotheism	monoteísmo	privatization	privatización
monsoon	monzón	product	producto
moraine	morena	proliferation	proliferación
mountain	montaña		
movable	movible	quiet	quieto
movement	movimiento		
mural	mural		
nation	nación		
nationalism	nacionalismo		
nationalities	nacionalidades		
nationalize	nacionalizar		
Native American	Nativo Americano		
natural	natural		
natural resource	recurso natural		
natural vegetation	vegetación natural		
navigable	navegable		
nuclear	nuclear		
nuclear proliferation	proliferación nuclear		

Geography

See Social Studies, Pages 109 to 111 .

English	Spanish	English	Spanish
race H	raza	tariff	tarifa
radioactive	radioactivo	temperature	temperatura
realism	realismo	territory	territorio
reforestation	reforestación	time H	tiempo
reform	reforma	tradition	tradición
refuge	refugio	tsunami	tsunami
refugee	refugiado	tundra	tundra
region	región	typhoon	tifón
reincarnated	reencarnado		
relative	relativo	unitary system	sistema unitario
relief H Sp (maps)	relieve Sp	universal	universal
reparations	reparaciones	universal sufferage	sufragio universal
republic	republica	urbanization	urbanización
revolution	revolución		
rotation	rotación	valley	valle
		wadi	wadi
sanctions	sanciones	zone	zona
sanitation	sanidad		
satellite Sp	satélite		
savanna	sabana		
sedentary	sedenteria		
service	servicio		
service industry	industria de servicios		
shamanism	shamanismo		
sirocco	siroco		
smog	smog		
socialism	socialismo		
socialist realism	realismo socialista		
socioeconomic	socioeconomico/a		
solstice	solsticio		
species	especies		
state H	estado		
steppe H	estepa		
subcontinent	subcontinente		
subsistence	subsistencia		
subterranean	subterráneo		
suburbs	suburbios		
supercells	superceldas		
sustainable	sostenible		
syncretism	sincretismo		
system	sistema		

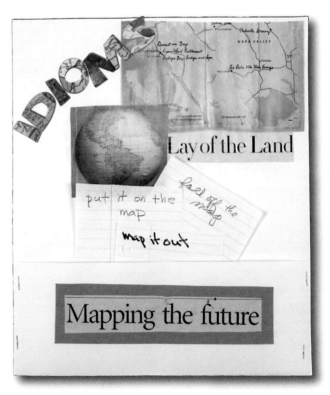

Pocket Full of Idioms (above): Idioms can be very confusing for ESL/ELL students. Use a sheet of 11" x 17" 80# paper or half a sheet of posterboard to make a pocket to collect examples of idioms found in RWP, literature, and speech. See page 416.

Math

English	Spanish	English	Spanish
abscissa	abscisa	center	centro
absolute	absoluto	center of rotation	centro de rotación
absolute value	valor absoluto	central	central
acute angle	ángulo agudo	central angle	ángulo central
acute triangle	triángulo acutángulo	circle	círculo
addition	adición	circle graph	gráfica circular
additive	aditivo	circular	circular
additive identity	identidad aditiva	circumference	circunferencia
additive inverse	inverso aditivo	coefficient	coeficiente
adjacent	adyacente	column	columna
adjacent angles	ángulos adyacentes	combination	combinación
algebraic	algebraica	commission	comisión
algebraic expression	expresión algebraica	common	común
alternate	alterno	common difference	diferencia común
analysis	análisis	common ration	razón común
analytic	analítico	compatible	compatible
analytic geometry	la geometría analítica	compatible numbers	números compatibles
angle	ángulo	complex	complejo/a
angle of rotation	ángulo de rotación	complex figure	figura compleja
antiderivative	antiderivada	complex solid	solido complejo
antidifferentiation	antidiferenciación	complimentary [H]	complimentario
area	área	complimentary angles	ángulos complimentarios
arithmetic	aritmética	complimentary events	eventos complimentarios
arithmetic sequence	suseción aritmética	cone	cono
axis [H]	eje	congruent	congruente
		congruent polygons	polígonos congruentes
bar notation	notación de barras	conjecture	conjetura
base [H]	base	consequence	consecuencia
binary numbers	números binarios	constant	constante
binomial	binomio	coordinate	coordenada
		coordinate plane [H]	plano de coordenadas
		corresponding	correspondiente
		corresponding angles	ángulos correspondientes
		corresponding parts	partes correspondientes
		cosine [H]	cosino
		count [H]	contar
		counter	contra
		counterexample	contraejemplo
		cubic	cúbico/a
		cubic function	función cúbica
		cylinder	cilindro

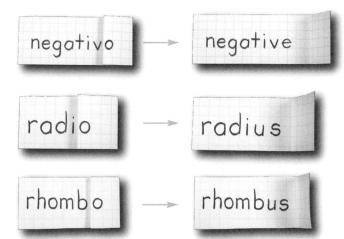

negativo → negative

radio → radius

rhombo → rhombus

Single VKV Fold-Over Flashcards
(left): See page 370.

Cognates English/Spanish

Math

English	Spanish	English	Spanish
decimal	decimal	factor	factor
define	definir	factorial	factorial
defining a variable	definir una variable	figure [H]	figuro/a
dependent	dependiente	formula	fórmula
dependent events	eventos dependientes	fraction	fracción
dependent variable	variable dependiente	function	función
diagonal	diagonal	function table	tabla de funciones
diagram	diagrama	fundamental	fundamental
diameter	diámetro		
difference	diferencia	geometric	geometrico
digit	digito	geometry	geometría
digital	digital		
dilation	dilatación	hemisphere	hemisferio
dimensional	dimensional	histogram	histograma
dimensional analysis	análisis dimensional	hypotenuse	hipotenusa
dimensions	dimensiones		
discount	descuento	independent	independiente
divide	dividir	independent events	eventos independientes
division	división	independent variable	variable independiente
domain	dominio	indirect	indirecto/a
double	doble	inform	informar
dozen	docena	information	información
		integers	enteros
element	elemento	interest [H]	interés
elimination	eliminación	interior	interior
equal	igual	internal	interno/a
equation	ecuación	interquartile	intercuartílica
equiangular	equiangular	inverse	inverso
equilateral	equilátero	inverse operations	operaciones inversas
equilateral triangle	triángulo equilátero	irrational	irracional
equivalent	equivalente	irrational numbers	números irracionales
equivalent expressions	expresiones equivalentes	isosceles	isósceles
error	error	isosceles triangle	triángulo isósceles
evaluate	evaluar		
event	evento	lateral	lateral
example	ejemplo	lateral area	área lateral
experimental	experimental	line	línea
experimental probability	probabilidad experimental	lineal	lineal
exponent	exponente	linear function	función lineal
expression	expresión	line graph	gráfica lineal
exterior	exterior	line of reflection	línea de reflexión
external	externo/a	line symmetry	simetría lineal
		logic	lógico

Math

English	Spanish	English	Spanish
mathematics	matemáticas	polynomial	polinomio
matrix	matiz	positive	positivo
median	mediana	precision	precisión
mode [H]	moda	price	precio
monomial	monomio	principal [H Sp]	principal
multiplication	multiplicación	prism	prisma
multiplicative inverse	inverso multiplicativo	probability	probabilidad
multiply	multiplicar	products	productos
mutually exclusive	mutuamente exclusivo	property	propiedad
		proportion	proporción
negative	negativo	pyramid	pirámide
negative number	número negativo	Pythagorean Theorem	Teorema de Pitágoras
nonlinear function	función no lineal	Pythagorean triple	triplete pitagórico
notation	notación		
number	número	quadrants	cuadrantes
numerical	numérico/a	quadratic	cuadratico/a
numerical expression	expresión numérica	quadrilateral	cuadrilátero
		quartiles	cuartiles
obtuse	obtuso	quaternion	cuaternión
obtuse angle	ángulo obtuso	quotient	cociente
obtuse triangle	triángulo obtuso		
operations	operaciones	radical	radical
opposites	opuestos	radical sign	signo radical
order [H]	orden	radius	radio
ordered pair	par ordenado	rational	racional
order of operations	orden de operaciones	rational number	número racional
ordinate	ordenada	real [H]	real
origin	origen	real number	número real
		reciprocal	recíproco/a
pair [H]	par	rectangle	rectángulo
parallel	paralelo/a	reflection	reflexión
parallelogram	paralelogramo	regular	regular
part [H]	parte	regular polygon	polígono regular
percent	por ciento	result	resultado
percentage	porcentaje	rhombus	rombo
percent equation	ecuación percentual	right angle	ángulo recto
perfect	perfecto	rotation	rotación
permutation	permutación	rotational symmetry	simetría rotacional
perpendicular	perpendicular		
perspective	perspectiva		
pi [H]	pi		
plane [H]	plano		
point [H]	punto		
polygon	polígono		
polyhedron	poliedro		

 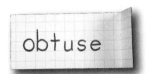

Single VKV Fold-Over Flashcards
(above): See page 370.

Language Arts

English	Spanish
abbreviate	abreviar
abbreviation	abreviación
academy	academia
accommodate Sp	acomodar
acronym	acrónimo
act	acto
action	acción
actor	actor
activity	actividad
actress	actriz
adaptation	adaptación
adjective	adjetivo
adventure	adventura
adverb	adverbio m.
article	artículo
artist	artista
assume	assumir
audience	audiencia
authentic	auténtico
author	autor
auxiliary	auxiliar
bilingual	bilingüe
biography	biografía
calligraphy	caligrafía
cause	causa
cause and effect	causa y efecto
class H	clase
classical	clasico
collective	colectiva
column	columna
combine	combinar
common	común
completely	completamente
complimentary H	complimentario
conflict	conflicto
conjecture	conjetura
consequence	consecuencia
continue (to)	continuar
copy	copia
correct	correcto
create	crear
culture	cultura
curious	curioso/a
current	corriente

Triple VKV Flashcards: See page 389.

English	Spanish
debate	debate
decisive	decisivo
declare	declarar
dedicate	dedicar
define	definir
describe (to)	describir
description	descripción
diagram	diagrama
dictate	dictar
direct	directo
direction	dirección
discuss (to)	discutir
duplication	duplicación
education	educación
effect	efecto
elimination	eliminación
English	Inglés
episode	episodio
error	error
essential	esencial
evaluate	evaluar
exaggerate	exagerar
examine (to)	examinar
example	ejemplo
exclaim	exclamar
exclamation	exclamación
exhibit	exhibir
expression	expresión
fabricate	fabricar
favorite	favorito/a
fiction	ficción
figure H	figuro/a
genuine	genuino
gesture	gesto
gradual	gradual
graph	gráfica
group	grupo
guide	guía
hour H	hora
human	humano/a
hypothesis	hipótesis

Language Arts

English	Spanish	English	Spanish
icon	icono	object [H]	objeto
iconographic	iconográfico/a	objective	objetivo
idea	idea	observe	observar
ideal	ideal		
identification	identificación	paper	papel
illuminate	iluminar	part	parte
image	imagen	passive	pasivo
imaginary	imaginario	past [H]	pasado
indirect	indirecto/a	perfect	perfecto/a
infer	inferis	period [H]	periodo
interrupt (to)	interrumpir	prepare (to)	preparar
introduce (to)	introducir	present [H] (to)	presentar
irregular	irregular	problem	problema
		program	programa
jargon	jerga	project [H]	proyecto
jazz	jazz		
		realism	realismo
lesson [H]	lección	realist	realista
limit	limitar	reason v.	razonar
line	línea	recite	recitar
list	lista	reference	referencia
literature	literatura	regular	regular
logic	lógico		
		series	serie
major [H]	mayor	study (to)	estudiar
malice	malicia		
manner [H]	manera	theater	teatro
mantra	mantra	theme	tema
manual	manual	thesis	tesis
manuscript	manuscrito	time [H]	tiempo
map	mapa	tone	tono
margin	margen	tradition	tradición
memory	memoria	traditional	tradicional
mention	mención	tragedy	tragedia
multilingual	multilingüe	typical	típico
multinational	multinacionál		
		ulterior	ulterior
narrate	narrar	ultimate	ultimo
necessary [Sp]	necesario	urgent	urgente
notation	notación		
note	notar	vague	vago
notice	noticia	verb	verbo
novel	novela	version	versión
number	número		

Collect RWP (below):
See page 31.

ATENCIÓN
DEPORTACIÓN
Aumente su protección en la vía
INMIGRACIÓN

Science

English	Spanish	English	Spanish
absolute	absoluta	cerebellum	cerebelo
absolute magnitude	magnitude absoluta	cerebrum	cerebro
acceleration	aceleración	chemical	químico/a
acid	ácido/a	chemical digestion	digestión química
acid precipitation	precipitación ácida	chemical equation	ecuación química
activation energy	energía de activación	chemical formula	fórmula química
active	activo/a	chemical reaction	reacción química
active immunity	immunidad activa	chemotherapy	quimioterapia
activity	actividad	chromosphere	cromosfera
adaptation	adaptación	chyme	quimo
aerosol	aerosol	circular	circular
air [H]	aire	circulation	circulación
air mass	masa de aire	climate	clima
allergen	alérgeno	cloning	clonación
allergy	alergia	cochlea	cóclea
amino acids	aminoácidos	comet	cometa
antigen	antígeno	concentration	concentración
apparent magnitude	magnitud aparente	condensation	condensación
Archimedes' principle [H Sp]	principio de Arquímedes	coniferous	coníferas
artery	arteria	conservation	conservación
asexual reproduction	reproducción asexual	constant	constante
asteroid	asteroide	constellation	constelación
atmosphere	atmósfera	contagious	contagiosa
atom	átomo	contaminant	contaminante
atomic	atómico/a	control	control
atomic number	numero atómico	controlled experiment	experimento controlado
atrium	atrio	Coriolis effect	efecto Coriolis
axon	axón	corona [H]	corona
		coronary	coronario/a
balance	balanza	coronary circulation	circulación coronaria
Bernoulli's principle [H Sp]	principio de Bernoulli	coronary thrombosis	trombosis coronaria
biodiversity	biodiversidad	covalent	covalente
biological	biológico/a	critical	critico/a
biological vector	vector biológico	crude	crudo
biology	biología	cycle	ciclo
capillary	capilar	deforestation	deforestación
carbohydrates	carbohidratos	dendrite	dendrita
cardiac	cardíaco/a	density	densidad
cartilage	cartílago	depletion	depleción
catalyst	catalizador	dermis	dermis
cause	causa	diagram	diagrama
cause and effect	causa y efecto	digestion	digestión
cell [H]	célula	disintegration	disintegración
cellular	celular	DNA	DNA
central	central	dominant	dominante

Science

English	Spanish	English	Spanish
effect	efecto	habitat	hábitat
elastic	elástico	habitat restoration	restauración de hábitats
electromagnetic	electromagnético	hemoglobin	hemoglobina
electron	electrón	heredity	herencia
electronic	electrónico/a	hibernation	hibernación
element	elemento	homeostasis	homeostasis
ellipse	elipse	hominid	homínido
El Niño	El Niño	homologous	homólogo
embryo	embrión	Homo sapiens	Homo sapiens
embryology	embriología	humidity	humedad
endothermic	endotérmica	hurricane	huracán
endothermic reaction	reacción endotérmica	hydraulic	hidráulico
energy	energía	hydraulic system	sistema hidráulico
enzyme	enzima	hydroelectric	hidroeléctrico/a
epidermis	epidermis	hypothesis	hipótesis
equation	ecuación		
equilibrium	equilibrio	iceberg Sp	iceberg
equinox	equinoccio	illuminate	illuminar
erosion	erosión	immunity	immunidad
event	evento	impact	impacto
evolution	evolución	inertia	inercia
exothermic	exotérmica	infection	infección
exothermic reaction	reacción exotérmica	infer	inferir
experiment	experimento	inform	informar
explosion	explosión	information	información
extinct	extinto/a	inhibitor	inhibidor
extinction	extinción	instantaneous	instantánea
extinct species	especie extinta	introduced	introducida
extinguish	extinguido/a	introduced species	especie introducida
		involuntary	involuntario
fluid	fluido	involuntary muscle	músculo involuntario
force	fuerza	ion	ion
form	forma	ionic	iónico
formula	fórmula	isotope	isótopo
fossil	fósile		
		jade	jade
galaxy	galaxia	Jupiter	Júpiter
gene	gene		
genetics	genética	krill	krill
geothermal	geotérmico/a		
geothermal energy	energía geotérmico		
giant	gigante		
global	global		
gradualism	gradualismo		
group	grupo		

Double VKV Flashcard (left): Use with cognates that are the same except for final letters.

átomo

átom

Science

English	Spanish	English	Spanish
law	ley	net force	fuerza neta
ligament	ligamento	neuron	neurona
lunar	lunar	neutron	neutrón
lunar eclipse	eclipse lunar	nitrate	nitrato
lunar phase	fase lunar	nonmetal	no metal
lymph	linfa	nonrenewable no	renovable
lymphatic system	sistema linfático	nuclear	nuclear
lymphocyte	linfocito	nuclear energy	energía nuclear
		number	número
magnitude	magnitude	nutrients	nutrientes
maize H	maiz		
major H	mayor	observatory	observatorio
maria	mares	olfactory	olfativo/a
Mars	Marte	olfactory cell	célula olfativa
marsupial	marsupial	orbit	órbita
mass H	masa	ozone	ozono
mass number	número de masa		
mechanical	mecánico/a	papyrus	papiro
mechanical digestion	digestión mecánica	Pascal's principal H Sp	principio de Pascal
medium H	medio/a	passive immunity	immunidad pasiva
meiosis	meiosis	pasteurization	pasteurización
melanin	melanina	period H	período
Mercury	Mercurio	periosteum	periósteo
metal H	metal	peripheral	periférico/a
metalloid	metaloide	peristalsis	peristalsis
meteor	meteoro	pesticide	pesticida
mineral	mineral	petroleum	petróleo
mitosis	mitosis	phase H	fase
model	modelo	phosphate	fosfato
modification	modificación	photosphere	fotosfera
modify	modificar	physical	fisico/a
molecule	molécula	physical science	ciencias fisicas
momentum	momento	physical therapy	fisioterapia
monsoon	monzón	plate tectonics	tectónica de placas
moraine	morena	Pluto	Plutón
muscle	músculo	polar	polar
mutation	mutación	polar zones	zonas polar
		potash	potasa
natural	natural	precious	precioso
natural resources	recursos natural		
natural selection	selección natural		
nebula	nebulosa		
Neptune	Neptuno		
nervous	nervioso		
net	neto/a		

Double VKV®
Flashcard (right):
Use with cognates
that are the same
except for final letters.

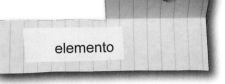

elemento

element

Science

English	Spanish	English	Spanish
precipitation	precipitación	satellite	satélite
pressure	presión	Saturn	Saturno
primates	primates	science	ciencia
product	producto	scientific law	ley cientifica
program	programa	scientific theory	teoría cientifica
project [H]	proyecto	season [H]	estación
Project Apollo	Proyecto Apolo	sedimentary	sedimentaria
Project Gemini	Proyecto Géminis	semiconductor	semiconductor
Project Mercury	Proyecto Mercurio	sex cells	células sexuales
protein	proteína	sexual reproduction	reproducción sexual
proton	protón	skeleton	esqueleto
pulmonary	pulmonar	sodium	sodio
pure	puro	sodium nitrate	nitrato de sodio
purification	purificación	solar	solar
purify	purificar	solar eclipse	eclipse solar
		solar system	sistema solar
quiet	quieto	solstice	solsticio
		space [H]	espacio
radio	radio	space station	estación espacial
radioactive	radioactivo/a	species	especies
radioactive element	elemento radioactivo	spectrum	espectro
radioactivity	radioactividad	sphere	esfera
radio telescope	radiotelescopio	station	estación
reactant	reactivo	structure	estructura
reaction	reacción	supergiant	supergigante
recycling	reciclaje	synapse	sinapsis
reflect	reflectar, reflejar	synthetic	sintético
reflecting telescope	telescopio reflector	synthetic elements	elementos sintéticos
reflex	reflejo	system	sistema
refract	refractar	systemic circulation	circulacion sistémica
refracting telescope	telescopio refractor		
reintroduce	reintroducir		
renewable	renovable		
renewable resources	recursos renovables		
repair	reparar		
reproduction	reproducción		
residual	residual		
residue	residuo		
resources	recursos		
retina	retina		
revolution	revolución		
revolve	revolver		
rock [H]	roca		
rotation	rotación		

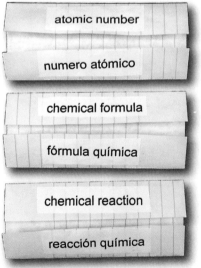

Quarter-Sheet Shutterfold VKVs: Use this VKV to compare and contrast words or phrases in two languages. Students write sentences using the words or phrases under the tabs. Sentences should provide clues as to word meaning. This VKV is larger than the usual quarter sheet. Fold it in half to store in a VKV box.

Science

English	Spanish	English	Spanish
technology	tecnología	Uranus	Urano
telescope	telescopio		
temperate	templado/a	vaccination	vacunación
temperate zone	zona templada	vapor	vapor
temperature	temperatura	vaporization	vaporización
tendon	tendón	variable	variable
terminal	terminal	variation	variación
terminal velocity	velocidad terminal	vector	vector
terrestrial	terrestre	vein H	vena
theory	teoría	velocity	velocidad
thrombosis	trombosis	ventricle	ventrícolo
tornado	tornado	Venus	Venus
transition	transición	vestigial	vestigial
transition element	elemento de transición	virus	virus
transmit	transmitir	vitamin	vitamina
tropical	tropical	voluntary muscle	músculo voluntario
tropics	trópicos		
troposphere	troposfera		
tsunami	tsunami		
typhoon	tifón		
typical	típico		

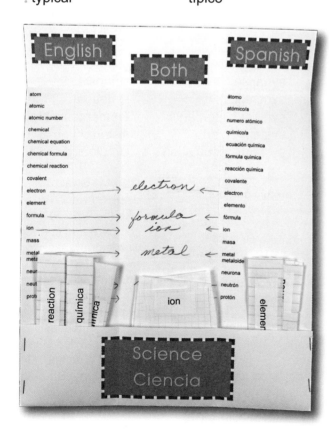

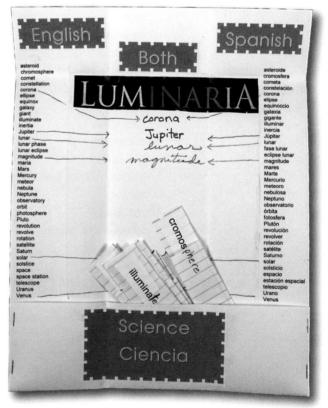

Trifold Pocket Charts (left and above): The left and right columns of these charts were used to list words from two different languages, and the middle section was used to record words that were the same in both. See pages 399 and 416.

Social Sciences
See Geography, Pages 95 to 98 .

English	Spanish	English	Spanish
aborigine	aborigen	consul	consúl
absolute monarchy	monarquía absoluta	consume	consumar
adobe	adobe	consumer	consumo
alliance	alianza	contiguous	contiguas
alluvial	aluvial	convent	convento
altiplano	altiplano	cooperative	cooperativa
amend	enmendar	Crusades	Cruzadas
apartheid	apartheid	cultural	cultural
apparent	aparente	cultural diffusion	difusión cultural
apprentice	aprendiz	culture	cultura
aquifer	acuifero	cuneiform	cuneiforme
archipelago	archipiélago	custom	costumbre
atheism	ateísmo		
atoll	atolón	delta	delta
autobahn	autobahn	democracy	democracia
autonomy	autonomía	depletion	depleción
		Diaspora	diáspora
bar graph	gráfica de barras	dictator	dictador
bauxite	bauxita	dictatorship	dictadura
Bedouin	beduino	dike	dique
bilingual	bilingüe	disciple	discípulo
Boer	bóer	diversity	diversidad
		divine	divino
calligraphy	caligrafía	dominant	dominante
campesino	campesino	dominion	dominio
canyon	cañón	dynasty	dinastia
caste H	casta		
center	centro	education	educación
central	central	elimination	eliminación
centrism	centrismo	embalm	embalsamar
circle graph	gráfica de círculo	embargo	embargo
civil	civil	emperor	emperador
civilization	civilización	empire	imperio
clan	clan	enclave	enclave
class H	clase	estancia	estancia
classical	clasico	ethnic	étnico/a
coalition	coalición	ethnic group	grupo étnico
cocoa	cocao	ethnocentrism	etnocentrismo
colony	colonia	Eurasia	Eurasia
common	común	Eurodollar	eurodólar
company H	compañía	European Union	Unión Europea
concentration	concentración	exercise	ejercicio
conservation	conservación	exile	exilio
constitution	constitución	extinction	extinción
constitutional monarchy	monarquía constitucional		

Social Sciences

See Geography, Pages 95 to 98 .

English	Spanish	English	Spanish
family	familia	market	mercado
federal	federal	medium H	medio/a
federal government	gobierno federal	Messiah	Mesías
federal republic	republica federal	mestizo	mestizo
feudalism	feudalismo	migrate	migrar
fiction	ficción	minister	ministro
		minority	minoria
generation	generación	missionary	misionario
genocide	genocidio	monarchy	monarquía
geographic	geográfico/a	monastery	monasterio
geography	geografía	monotheism	monoteísmo
geothermal energy	energia geotérmica	multilingual	multilingüe
geyser	géiser	multinational	multinacionál
glasnost	glasnost	municipal	municipal
globalization	globalización	mural	mural
government	gobierno		
group	grupo	nation	nación
		national	nacional
habitat	habitat	neutral	neutral
hacienda	hacienda	neutrality	neutralidad
hieroglyphics	jeroglíficos	nomad	nómada
Holocaust	Holocausto		
		Parliament	Parlamento
immigrant H	inmigrante	pharoah	faraón
imperialism	imperialismo	philosophy	filosofía
indigenous	indigeno	pictograph	pictograma
indulgences	indulgencias	plantation	plantación
industrialize	industrializar	plaza	plaza
industry	industria	political system	sistema politico
influence	influencia	polytheistic	politeísta
information	información	pope	papa
intensive	intensivo	population	población
interdependence	interdependencia	power	poder
invest	invertir	prime minister	primer ministro
irrigation	irrigación	prince	principe
		principality	principado
jazz	jazz	principle H Sp	principio
jute	yute	product	producto
		program	programa
kibbutz	kibutz	prophet H	profeta
		Protestant	protestante
limited government	gobierno limitado	province	provincia
		pueblo	pueblo
maize H	maiz	pyramid	pirámide
majority	mayoria		

Social Sciences
See Geography, Pages 95 to 98 .

English	Spanish	English	Spanish
recycle	reciclar	terrace	terraza
reform	reforma	territory	territorio
Reformation	Reforma	terror	terror
refugee	refugiado	terrorism	terrorismo
region	región	textiles	textiles
reincarnation	reencarnación	theocracy	teocracia
Renaissance Sp	Renacimiento	tropical	tropical
renovation	renovación	tropics	tropicós
representative	representivo/a	tsunami	tsunami
republic	republica	tundra	tundra
resources	recursos	typhoon	tifón
responsibility	responsabilidad	typical	típico
reunification	reunificación		
revolution	revolución	urban	urbano
rural	rural	urbanization	urbanización
samurai	samurai	vaquero	vaquero
satellite nation	nación satélite	vassal	vasallo
sauna	sauna		
savanna	sabana	wadi	uadi
scale H	escala		
secular	secular	yurt	yurt
Senate	senado		
service	servicio	ziggurat	zigurat
service industry	industria de servicio	zone	zona
sex	sexo		
sexual	sexual		
shah	sha		
shogun	shogún		
sisal	sisal		
Slav	eslavo		
smog	smog		
socialism	socialismo		
sociologist	sociólogo		
sorghum	sorgo		
station	estación		
steppe H	estepa		
subcontinent	subcontinente		
subsistence	subsistencia		
suburb	suburbio		
sufferage	sufragio		
superior	superior		
supermarket	supermercado		
syndicate	sindicato		
system	sistema		

Triple VKV Flashcard (above): Notice the fold-over tab to the right. By opening or closing this tab, either the English suffix *-tion* or the Spanish suffix *-cion* shows.

This VKV Flashcard forms six words:
civilization civilización
renovation renovación
revolution revolución

Compound Words

A *compound word* is formed when two words are combined to make a new word. Some compound words mean the same as the two words combined: *blueberry* means the *berry* is *blue* in color. Some compound words do not mean the same as the words they are composed of: *bullheaded*.

Compound words can be open, closed, or hyphenated. *Open compound words* have a space between the two words. *Closed compound words* have no space between the two words. *Hyphenated compound words* have a hyphen between the two words. **Note: Students might be surprised to discover that dictionaries do not always agree about which words are written as compound words.**

Foldable® Charts: Make Foldable Charts out of posterboard or chart paper for classroom use. Use photocopy paper or lined paper to make smaller, individual student charts.
• Make a giant two-column chart to collect *simple* (*into*) and *complex* (*everywhere*) compound words.
• Make a giant three-column Foldable Chart to collect *open*, *closed*, and *hyphenated* compound words.
• Make a chart of compound words that *are* and *are not* always capitalized. See an example of this type of chart at top right.

Foldable® Chart (below): Fold a sheet of posterboard into fifths vertically and horizontally to form 25 equal sections. (See page 415.) Write a letter of the alphabet in each section, placing x and y in the same square. Write compound words encountered during reading, and/or collect examples of compound words found in RWP.

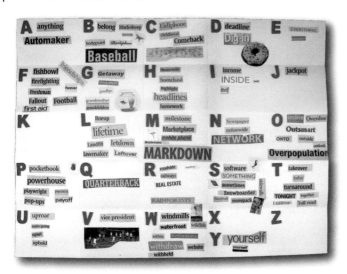

Foldable® Pocket Chart Bulletin Board (right): Use one sheet of posterboard to make this large bulletin board Pocket Chart and use it to collect compound word Foldables, VKV Flashcards, and other compound word study aids. Teacher-generated print providing information on compound words is featured on the pocket of this poster.

Compound Words

Some *compound words* cannot be taken literally. For example, a flea market is not where fleas are sold; a crowbar is not a bar where crows are served; an eggplant does not grow eggs; there is no ham in a hamburger; and there are neither apples nor pine in a pineapple. Other Examples Include: brainstorm, horsefly, horseradish, pigtail, softhearted, strawberry, and sweetheart.

Four-Door Foldable® (below): Use a dictionary to look up four of the following words, and list at least four compound words for each: *air*, *back*, *ball*, *black*, *blue*, *butter*, *grand*, *out*, *over*, *sea*, and *sun*.

Alternative (below): Collect examples of compound words that begin or end with any of the words listed above. Write or glue the compound words across the fold of each of the four sections to reinforce the idea that two separate words have been joined to form the compound words displayed.

Other words that could be used on the front tabs of the Four-Door Foldables® (left) include the following:			
air H	butter	grand	play H
any	check	half	rain H
back	day	head	school H
ball	door	home	sea H
bath	down H	house	side H
bed	earth	land H	sky
bird	every	life	snow
birth H	eye H	light	some H
black	fire	line	under
blood	foot	name	water
book	for H	news	wood H
	good	out	work

Lots of Compound Words: Open, closed, and hyphenated compound words are very common in math, social sciences, sports, and cooking. Make classroom dictionaries for collecting compound words for these subjects like the Shutterfold project pictured below.

Stressed or Not?

The first word of a compound word is usually stressed. If the first word is a preposition, the second word may take the stress:
for*give*   over*a*bundance   under*e*stimate

A compound verb often has equal stress on the two words that comprise it:
n. - a *pickup* (truck) - stress the first word (*pick*)
v. - *Pick up* the toys. - stress both words (*pick, up*)
n. - a hostile *takeover* - stress the first word (*take*)
v. - I'll *take over* now. - stress both words (*take, over*)

Compound Words

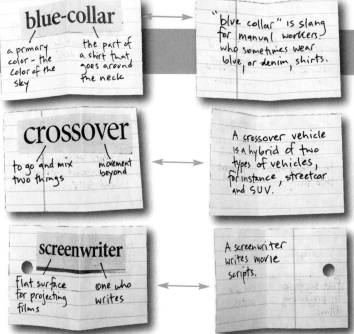

blue-collar
- a primary color – the color of the sky
- the part of a shirt that goes around the neck

"blue collar" is slang for manual workers, who sometimes wear blue, or denim, shirts.

crossover
- to go and mix two things
- movement beyond

A crossover vehicle is a hybrid of two types of vehicles, for instance, streetcar and SUV.

screenwriter
- flat surface for projecting films
- one who writes

A screenwriter writes movie scripts.

Right and Below: Write or glue compound words found in RWP into a notebook or onto a sheet of paper. Underline each of the two words with a different color of marker. Underline the entire word with a third color of marker. Green, orange, and blue were used in the example below.

Say and spell each word separately. Say and spell the compound word.

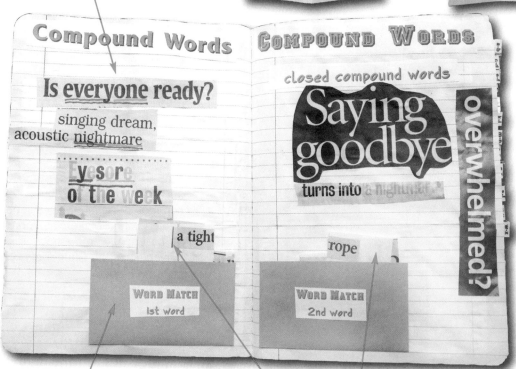

Compound Words

COMPOUND WORDS

Is everyone ready?

singing dream, acoustic nightmare

Eyesore of the week

closed compound words

Saying goodbye turns into a nightmare.

overwhelmed?

a tight   rope

WORD MATCH
1st word

WORD MATCH
2nd word

Coin envelopes used as pockets. See page 38.

Matching Activity: Write compound words on 1/8th flashcards. Fold the cards in half like a *hamburger*, and write or glue the first half of a compound word to the left and the second half to the right of the fold. Define each term on the appropriate side, and write a sentence using the word on the back of the flashcard. Cut the cards in half, store in envelopes as illustrated, and use them to form words.

a tight rope

Dealing with the two opposing sides during the negotiations was like walking a tightrope.

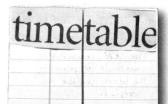

time table

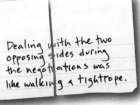

The SEAL commander's timetable for securing the beach had the team worried.

Compound Words

Use a quarter sheet of notebook paper to make a Triple VKV Flashcard with tabs to the right. Form these compound words: *foreshadow*, *foregoing*, and *foreground*. Glue in notebook. See page 386 for instructions.

Numerous compound words begin with the word after. Use a Triple VKV Flashcard with four tabs to the right to illustrate four of these words: aftermath, aftershock, aftereffect, afterward. Glue in a composition book or spiral notebook, or store in a pocket. See page 388 for instructions.

Compound Words

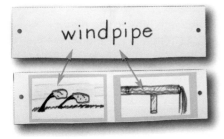

VKV Rings for Compound Words and/or Picture Words (left and below right): Make Single VKV Flashcards with a compound word written on the middle of the front and pictures representing the two words forming the compound on the back.

Fold each card so the words are to the inside. Read the words represented by the pictures, and read the pictures as compound words.

Reverse all VKV Flashcards so the words show. Read the words individually, then together as a compound word.

Compound Word Examples (right):
a. Use a sheet of 11" x 17" paper to make a large Sentence Strip Holder, and display picture cards that form a compound word.

b. Write *table* on one card and *spoon* on another card. Place the cards on a large holder that has been cut in half.

c. When the holders are pushed together, they form the word *tablespoon*.

Extension: Ask students to define each word. Write the definitions on the backs of the word cards. Display the definitions on the sentence strips, read them, and see if students can determine the meanings of the compound words they represent.

Compound Words

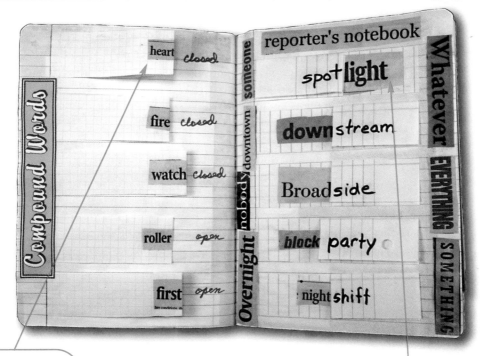

Fold-Back Single VKVs show the two words that form a compound word, separate and together. See page 373.

heartbreaking
firefighter
watchdog
roller coaster
first aid

Double VKV Flashcards are cut to show the two words that form the compound word, separate and together. See page 378.

blue, berries, blueberries
sugar, coating, sugarcoating
court, house, courthouse
head, quartered, headquartered

Three compound words are formed by each of the Triple VKV Flashcards pictured above. See page 386.

spotlight, starlight, limelight
downstream, downsize, download
broadside, Broadway, broadband
block party, blockbuster, blockade (suffix)
nightshift, nighttime, nightmare

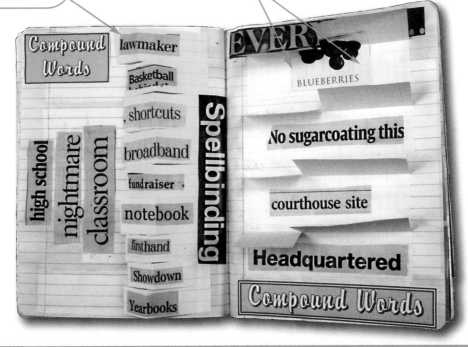

Compound Words VKVs®

Left: Under the two tabs of the Double VKV, students write about the etymology of each word part and explain how these formulate the meaning of the compound word.

Stereotype: "a conventional, formulaic, and oversimplified conception, opinion, or image."

Large and Small Compound Word VKV® Flashcards: Use quarter sheets of paper to make VKVs for notebooks (above left) and 8 1/2" x 11" sheets to make the large flashcards pictured on this page.

Above and Below: Use Double VKV Flashcards for the activities featured on this page. Write the two words that form the open, closed, or hyphenated compound word under the tabs. When applicable, have students illustrate each of the words on the front tabs of the VKV. Open and close the tabs to view the words separately or as an open, closed, or hyphenated compound word. Use the compound words in sentences on the backs of the flashcards. See page 378.

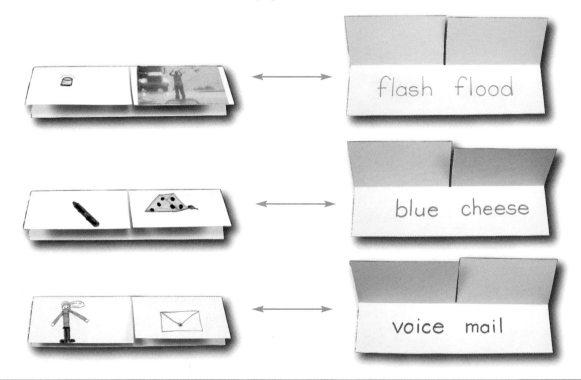

Compound Words VKVs®

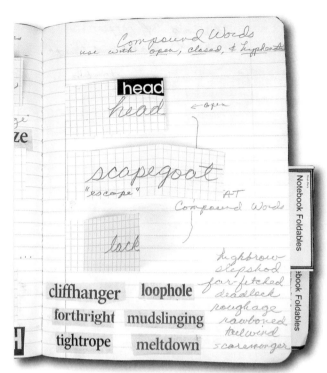

Fold-Back VKVs® (left): Glue the left edge of a Single VKV Flashcard to the right side of a notebook page. Write a compound word. Fold the tab under so that only half of the compound word is visible. Open and close the tab to read the multiple words formed. Note which word is accented. See page 373.

Adverbs and Pronouns (right): Make an accordion VKV Flashcard to form five words based upon the same initial or final word. See the compound word lists in this section for ideas, and see page 392 for instructions.

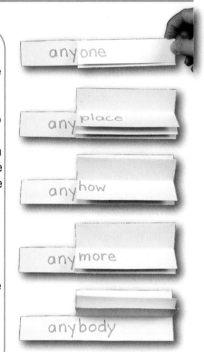

Below: Each of the three VKV Flashcards pictured below form three compound words that begin with the same word. Use the dictionary to determine if there are more than three compound words that begin with the featured word. If so, write the other words on the back of the flashcard. This VKV can be used for all three types of compound words.

bathroom → bathrobe → bathtub

sundown → sunflower → sunshine

bluejay → blueberry → bluebird

Compound Words

Some compound words are used more frequently than others. Add high-frequency compound words to spelling lists and work toward mastery in student writing projects. Select from the examples listed below, and add your own words.

Common Compound Words

another	comeback	forgive	lookout	someday	understand
anybody	everlasting	goodbye	maybe	somehow	undertake
anyhow	evermore	herself	meanwhile	someone	upset
anymore	everybody	himself	myself	something	whatsoever
anyone	everyday	holdup	nobody	sometime	whenever
anyplace	everyone	however	ourselves	sometimes	wherever
anything	everything	inside	outside	somewhere	whoever
anyway	everywhere	into	outstanding	themselves	without
anywhere	forever	itself	overlook	today	yourself
cannot	forget	leftover	somebody	tryout	

Matchbook Concentration: Write the first or last word of several common compound words under each matchbook tab. Players open two tabs at a time, remembering the words exposed. Students get a point for opening two tabs that form common compound words. For example, the words listed under the 12 matchbooks pictured will form the following compound words:

anything	inside	before
anyone	into	beside
someone	everyone	maybe
something	everything	therefore

Easy or Difficult: Students can open tabs in any order to form the compound words, or students must form the words in the order in which the tabs were opened.

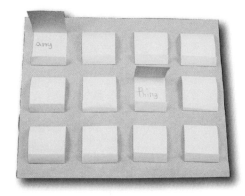

Multi-Tab Vocabulary Foldable® (right and bottom left of next page): Make a Four-, Six-, Eight-, or Ten-Tab Foldable, and use it to collect compound words found in RWP or encountered during reading. See page 415.

Write any of the following under the tabs: sentences using the compound words, quotes from literature in which the words are used, definitions of the compound words and definitions of their individual words, or idioms that contain the compound words.

Compound Words

All Levels of Difficulty: Foldables and VKVs can be used by all levels of students at the same time. While some students might be collecting SAT prep words like those featured to the right, ESL/ELL students might be using a Multi-Tab Foldable or VKVs (like those pictured below) to familiarize themselves with the spelling and use of compound words.

Looking At the Same Thing in Different Ways: Some students need to see the same word or concept presented in several different formats before learning takes place. If one VKV or Foldable doesn't work, try another Foldable format or change the size from large to small or small to large.

SAT-Type Compound Words

brainstorm *
broad-minded *
double-dealing *
dumbfound *
farfetched *
(also far-fetched)
foresee *
foretell *
foretoken *
headstrong *
highbrow *
lackluster *
merrymaking *
overstatement *
pigeonhole *
scapegoat *
slipshod *
typecast *
withdrawn *

Compound Words With Double Letters

When two words are combined and the first ends with the same letter with which the last begins, include both letters.

arrowwood
barroom
bathhouse
beachhead
birddog
bookkeeper Sp
cannot
cattail
coattail
cutthroat
dumbbell Sp
earring
filmmaker
fishhook
glowworm
granddaughter
headdress
highhanded
hitchhike
holddown
jackknife
knickknack
lamppost
nighttime
overrate
overreach
overreact
override
overripe
overrule
overrun Sp
roommate
roughhouse
sleuthhound
teammate
underrate
withheld
withhold Sp

Compound Words

Open Compound Words

Dictionaries do not always agree about which words are written as compound words.

air conditioning
air mattress
ancient history
answering machine
apartment building
apple green
armed forces
art deco
baby teeth
bad manners
ball game
bank account
bay window
bean sprout
black hole
black pepper
black tie
blank check
blind alley
blood test
blue cheese
blue jeans
board game
body language
booby trap
breaking point
brown bread
brown rice
car wash
cell phone
coast guard
cold war
comic book
cosmic ray
cow town
crew cut
curtain call
dead end
dew point
dill pickle

dirt bike
diving board
dollar sign
domino effect
double dribble
drag race
drop cloth
dune buggy
dung beetle
dust storm
ear lobe
earth science
egg white
eighth note
ejection seat
electric chair
electric eel
energy bar
field house
field trip
fire station
first aid
first class
flash flood
form letter
foul ball
free world
frozen food
fund raiser
funny bone
fur seal
future tense
garage sale
general store
ghost town
giant panda
good will
grade school
graham cracker
grand jury
grass snake
green bean
green light

green pepper
grizzly bear
ground floor
ground hog
guinea pig
half note
half time
hay fever
health food
heat wave
high school
home base
home page
home run
hook shot
horse sense
hot cake
hot spring
human being
hurry up
ice cream
ice skate
ice storm
ice water
ill will
inclined plane
index finger
inner ear
ivory tower
jet stream
joy ride
juke box
jump rope
June bug
junior high
killer whale
living room
main course
map key
memory stick
middle school

milk shake
Milky Way
mountain bike
mountain lion
mud puppy
mung beans
music box
note paper
nucleic acid
nursery rhyme
nursery school
nursing home
olive oil
outer space
pampas grass
paper clip
paper cutter
parking garage
peat moss
pilot light
ping pong
pit bull
place kick
post office
proper noun
quarter note
real estate
red cross
remote control
rocking chair
safety pin
sea gull
second hand
second wind
secret service
sheep dog
skim milk
square root
straight angle
super size
sweet potato
tape measure

tape record
test tube
theme park
tidal wave
time to time
tin foil
touch pad
trap door
trick or treat
trundle bed
turn down
turn off
turn on
upper hand
upside down
vampire bat
vanilla bean
vice president
video game
virtual reality
vocal cords
voice box
voice mail
(also voicemail)
waiting room
walking stick
water buffalo
water clock
water lily
water polo
wax bean
wear out
weather vane
Web site
whole note
whole number
wild boar
window box
wisdom teeth
word processor
working class
wrap up
zoom lens

Compound Words

Instructions for the Fold-Over Omission VKVs pictured below can be found on page 372.

Compound words formed with the word *all* drop one *l*.

all + like = alike
all + lone = alone
all + mighty = almighty
all + most = almost
all + ready = already
all + so = also
all + together = altogether
all + though = although

Note: *All right* **is an open compound word**
all-around, *all-round*, **and** *all-star* **are hyphenated compound words.**

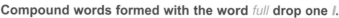

Compound words formed with the word *full* drop one *l*.

arm + full = armful
care + full = careful
flavor + full = flavorful
force + full = forceful
full + fill = fulfill Sp
harm + full = harmful
hate + full = hateful
lap + full = lapful
play + full = playful
taste + full = tasteful
will + full = willful

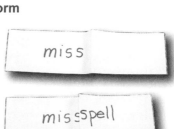

Compound words formed with *miss* drop one *s* when adding another word to form a compound word.

miss + behave = misbehave
miss + count = miscount
miss + lay = mislay
miss + read = misread
miss + shape = misshape
miss + spell = misspell
miss + step = misstep
miss + take = mistake
miss + treat = mistreat
miss + trust = mistrust
miss + understand = misunderstand

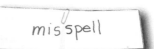

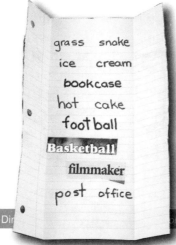

grass snake
ice cream
bookcase
hot cake
football
Basketball
filmmaker
post office

Foldable® Compound Word Review (left):
Have each student collect examples of open, closed, or hyphenated compound words collected from RWP. Cut the words in half and glue the first word under the left side and and second word under the right side of a Shutterfold.

Alternative: Cut the front tabs so they can be opened and closed to form word strips. Students manipulate the tabs to read the words individually or as compound words.

Compound Words

Closed Compound Words

Dictionaries do not always agree about which words are written as compound words.

aboveground	basketball	buttermilk	driveway	goodhearted
addend	bathrobe	butterscotch	dropout	grandchild
afternoon	bathroom	buttonhole	drugstore	grandfather
aircondition	bathtub	campfire	drumstick	grandmother
aircraft	battleground	campground	dugout	grandparent
aircrew	beachfront	cardboard	earphone	grapefruit
airflow	bedroom	carpool	earring	grasshopper
airline	bedspread	carport	earthquake	grasslands
airplane	bedtime	catfish	earthworm	graveyard
airport	benchmark *	chalkboard	edgewise	greenhouse
airtight	bighead	checkmate	eggnog	greyhound
anteater	bigmouth	checkup	eggplant	groundwater
armrest	billboard	cheeseburger	eggshell	guardrail
audiotape	birdbath	classroom	elsewhere	guideword
backache	birdhouse	clipboard	evergreen	hairbrush
backbone	birdseed	cobweb	eyeball	haircut
backdrop	birthday	cockpit	eyebrow	hairdresser
background	birthplace	cockroach	fingernail	hamburger
backyard	birthstone	cookbook	firecracker	handbook
baldheaded	blackbird	cookout	firefly	handcuff
ballpark	blackboard	copyright	fireplace	handmade
ballroom	blacktop	cowboy	fireplug	handsome
bankcard	blindfold	cowhand	fireproof	handwork
barbwire	bloodhound	crosscheck	flashlight	hardback
barefoot	bloodstream	crossroad	floorboard	hardhead
barnyard	bluebell	crosswalk	folklore	hardware
baseball	blueberry	crowbar	folktale	hardwood
	bluebird	crybaby	football	headache
	bodyguard	cupcake	footnote	headboard
	bodysurf	daydream	footstep	headlight
	bookcase	daylight	forearm	headquarters
	bookmark	daytime	freestanding	headset
	bookshelf	deadbolt	freeway	headstrong *
	bookstore	dishwasher	freshman	heartache
	bottleneck	dodgeball	freshwater	heartbeat
	boyfriend	doorbell	frostbite	heartburn
	breakfast	doorknob	fruitcake	hidebound *
	bridegroom	doormat	fullback	highchair
	broomstick	downstairs	gateway	highlights
	bulldog	downtown	gentlemen	highway
	bulldozer	dreadlocks	gingerbread	homemade
	bullfrog	dragonfly	girlfriend	homesick
	butterfly		goldfish	homework

Compound Words

Closed Compound Words

Dictionaries do not always agree about which words are written as compound words.

horsefly
horseradish
hourglass
housework
iceberg ᔆᵖ
icebox
icefall
indoor
infield
jailbreak
jellyfish
junkyard
keyboard
keyhole
keynote
kickoff
kinship *
kneepad
knockout
lackluster *
ladybug
landfall
landlady
landlord
letterhead
letterpress
lifeboat
lifeguard
lifelike
lifetime
lipstick
loudspeaker
lowlands
mailbox
mainland
midair
midnight
moonlight
moonwalk
motorboat
motorcycle
mountaintop
mouthwash

mushroom
network
newscast
newspaper
nighttime
noontime
northeast
northwest
notebook
notepaper
noteworthy
oatmeal
outcome
outfield
outfit
outlaw
outline
outlive
overcoat
overnight
overpass
overwrought *
pancake
paperback
parkway
peanut
peppermint
pigtail
pinball
playbill
playground
playpen
popcorn
postcard
pushcart
pushover *
quicksand
railroad
rainbow
raincoat
rainfall
rattlesnake
redwood

riverboat
rosebud
rowboat
runaway
sailboat
salesperson
sandbox
sandpaper
scapegoat *
seacoast
seagull
seashell
seaweed
seesaw
shipwreck
sidewalk
silverfish
silverware
skateboard
skyscraper
skywriting
slipcover
snowball
snowflake
snowman
snowstorm
softball
softhearted
songbird
soothsayer *
southeast
southwest
spotlight
starfish
steadfast *
steamship
stopwatch
strawberry
streetcar
sweatpants
sweatshirt
sweetheart
sunburn

sundial
sundown
sunflower
sunlight
sunrise
sunset
sunshine
suntan
tablecloth
tablespoon
teaspoon
textbook
thanksgiving
(capitalize the holiday, Thanksgiving Day)
thunderstorm
timberline
toenail
toothbrush
toothpick
touchdown
turncoat *
turnpike
typewriter
underground
undermined *
underscore
understand
undertake
underwater
uproot

upset
uptown
videotape
vineyard
volleyball
washcloth
wastebasket
watercolor
waterfall
waterfront
watermelon
wavelength
weekend
wetlands
wheelchair
whirlpool
wholesale
windmill
windpipe
windshield
woodland
woodpecker
woodwork
worksheet
workshop
wristwatch
yardstick
yearbook
yearlong

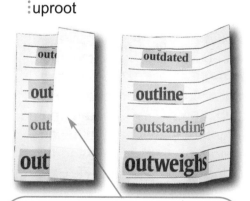

Fold-Over VKVs®: Glue words or write words so the first half of the word is visible when the right tab is closed.

Compound Words

Hyphenated Compound Words

Always be aware of the parts of speech and grammatical functions of words that comprise hyphenated compounds. Some of the word combinations on this page are not always hyphenated and do not always function as compound words. See examples below.

Run can function as a verb, and *in* as a preposition: Please don't *run in* the halls.
But *run-in* is a noun meaning an argument: The neighbors had a *run-in* over the barking dog.
To do can function as a verb: What are you going *to do*?
But *to-do* can function as a noun: They made a big *to-do* over the baby.

Compound adjectives like *larger-than-life* are only hyphenated when preceding the word/s they modify: It was a *larger-than-life* portrait.
But if the compound adjective is in the predicate—after the verb—hyphens are not used:
The portrait was *larger than life*.

absent-minded	double-decker	hide-and-seek	part-time	tip-off
after-hours	double-space	high-tech	pigeon-toed	to-and-fro
arm-twisting	down-to-earth	hit-and-run	pinch-hit	to-do
armor-plated	drive-in	jack-in-the-box	play-off	top-hat
avant-garde *	drop-off	jack-o-lantern	portal-to-portal	top-heavy
baby-faced	empty-handed	jump-start	quick-witted	top-notch
bell-shaped	father-in-law	knee-deep	ready-to-wear	top-secret
big-hearted	fail-safe	know-how	right-hand	topsy-turvy
black-and-blue	fair-minded	know-it-all	right-handed	track-and-field
black-tie	floor-length	larger-than-life	rough-and-ready	two-by-four
blow-by-blow	fly-by-night	law-abiding	rose-colored	two-dimensional
blow-dry	follow-through	lead-up	run-down	two-faced
brother-in-law	follow-up	leave-taking	run-in	two-handed
built-in	for-profit	left-handed	runner-up	two-way
built-up	four-footed	life-size	self-service	U-turn
bull's-eye	four-star	long-range	sharp-eyed	up-to-date
button-down	four-wheel	low-key	short-term	walk-in
by-pass	frame-up	merry-go-round	sister-in-law	warm-blooded
by-product	full-blown	middle-aged	skin-deep	warm-up
call-in	full-length	moth-eaten	sky-high	way-out
cave-in	full-scale	mother-in-law	smoke-filled	well-being
clean-cut	get-together	mother-of-pearl	snail-paced	well-done
close-up	go-between	nitty-gritty	strong-minded	well-known
crow's-foot	good-hearted	not-for-profit	take-over, takeover	well-to-do
cut-in	good-humored	old-fashioned	thin-skinned	wide-awake
daughter-in-law	good-looking	old-timer	third-class	world-class
day-to-day	give-and-take	old-world	third-rate	would-be
derring-do*	half-life	one-sided	three-decker	wrap-up
dog-eat-dog	hard-boiled	open-minded	three-dimensional	write-off
door-to-door	head-on	out-and-out	three-quarter	year-round
double-cross				

Confusing Words

Common Confusing Words

a lot	allot	good	well [H]	said	told
affect	effect	hear [H]	listen	see [H]	watch [H]
all ready	already	its [H]	it's [H]	sit	set
all right	alright (non-standard; do not use in formal writing)	know [H] [SL]	no [H]	so [H]	such
all together	altogether	lay [H]	lie [H]	some [H]	any
a part	apart	lay down	lie down	take care	take care of
been	gone	less than	fewer than	there [H] their [H]	they're [H]
beside	besides	me	I [H]	threw [H]	through [H] [SL]
by [H]	until	most	the most	what	which [H]
chief	chef	not [H]	knot [H] [SL]	who	that
every day	everyday	raise [H]	rise	who	whom
		road [H] rode [H]	rowed [H]	your [H]	you're [H]

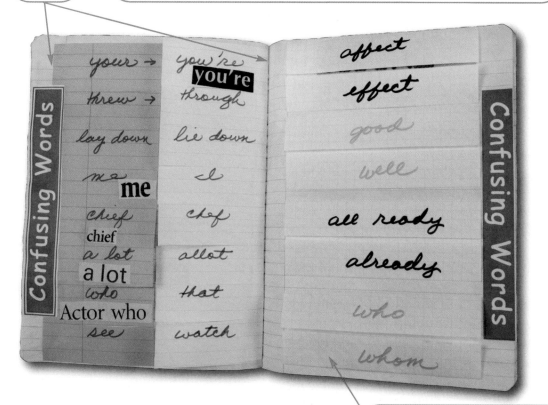

Glue along these edges.

Two Eight-Tab Notebook Foldables were glued into the composition book with their tabs in opposing positions. Students can open and close the tabs to compare and contrast the usage and meaning of these confusing words.

Four VKV Shutterfolds were made using quarter sheets of grid paper. Four pairs of confusing words were written on the front tabs and explained or used in sentences or phrases underneath. See page 384.

accept	except
access	excess
adolescents	adolescence
adopt	adapt
advice	advise
allude	elude
allusion	illusion
alone	lonely
ambivalent	ambiguous
amiable	amicable
among	between
amoral	immoral
anecdote	antidote
angel Sp	angle Sp
appraise	apprise
apt	likely
assent	ascent
biennial	biannual
bizarre Sp	bazaar Sp
blatant	flagrant
breath	breathe
canvas	canvass
censure	censor H
chef	chief
chose	choose
climactic	climatic
clothes H	cloths
compliment H	complement H
confident	confidant
conscious Sp	conscience Sp
counsel H	council H
credible	creditable
criterion	criteria
decent	descent
denotes	connotes
devise	device
disassemble	dissemble
discreet	discrete
eager	anxious
farther	further
gorilla H	guerilla H
historical	historic
horde H	hoard H
incidence	incidents

Mnemonics

Lie on the couch and I'll lay a blanket on top of you.

No knows how to grow by adding k and w.

U can have four or fourteen pieces of candy, but not forty.

Here you must use your *ear* to hear.

Cold weather affected the game and had the effect of making the ball slippery.

affect ... action
effect ... result

Word Study: Mnemonics

Mnemonics, or memory aids, can be helpful when learning to use and spell confusing words.

Encourage students to make up their own mnemonics for any words they have difficulty with.

Note that the letter *m* in the word *mnemonics* is silent. See Silent Letters, page 258.

---

incipient	insipid
incite	indict
incredulous	incredible
indeterminate	indeterminable
infer	imply
inflicted	afflicted
ingenuous	ingenious
intensely	intently
lightening SL	lightning SL
loose	lose
martial H Sp	marital
martial H Sp	marshal Sp
moot	mute
nugget	nougat
omission	oversight
opaque	transparent
peasant	pheasant
perimeter	parameter
personnel Sp	personal
precedent	president
predominantly	predominately
presidents	precedence
proceed	precede
proscribe	prescribe
purpose	propose
raise H	rear
reluctant	reticent
resent	recent
respectfully	respectively
reverence	reference
revile	revel
rises	raises
salacious	salutary
secret	secrete
simple	simplistic
skimp	scrimp
solitary	solitaire
statute	statue
taunt taut H	taught H
torturous	tortuous
turgid	turbid
well	good
whether H	weather H
wonder	wander

Consonants are speech sounds made by varying degrees of obstruction in the mouth of the air from the lungs. This obstruction causes friction that results in different sounds.
(Vowels are speech sounds made without obstruction or friction of the air flow. See page 334.)
Games like Wheel of Fortune® and Scrabble® clearly illustrate that some consonants
are more commonly used to spell words than others.
The following consonant graphemes are listed from most commonly used to least commonly used:
r, t, n, s, l, c, d, p, m, b, f, v, g, h, k, w, th, sh, ng, ch, x, z, j, qu, wh, y.

Have you ever seen this word?
ghearniti
Pronounce the gh- as in tough.
Pronounce the -earn as in learn.
Pronounce the -i as in igloo.
Pronounce the -ti as in nation.
Put these sounds together, and you get the word *furnish*.

A variation of this word play is attributed to Irish playwright George Bernard Shaw (1856-1950), who pointed out how confusing English spelling can be. Though there are many exceptions, English spelling does follow general rules. If we follow these rules, the spelling *ghearniti* cannot be pronounced as *furnish* because gh- never represents the sound of /f/ at the beginning of an English word and -*ti*- never represents the sound of /sh/ at the end of an English word. Familiarity with some basic English spelling rules can eliminate unnecessary errors.

In this section on consonants, and in the sections of this book on phonograms (pages 203 to 209) and vowels (pages 334 to 366), rules and information for strengthening spelling skills are presented. I stress that students need "*familiarization*, not *memorization*" when it comes to rules.

RULES
You do not need to *memorize*
but rather *familiarize* yourself
through use and observation.

Dinah Zike

Three-Tab Foldable:
A Foldable can be partially completed by a student or group of students, photocopied on one side only (photo far right), and distributed to the class. Students then fold, cut and complete the Foldable for a grade.

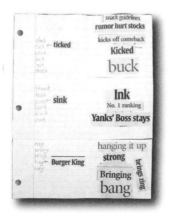

Consonant Observations to Prevent Spelling Errors:

Consonants only

Only one common word is spelled with all consonants and no vowels.

nth   the nth degree
the nth power

Double Consonants (other than blends or digraphs) at the beginnings of words

Many of these words have been adopted from other languages. One consonant—usually the first—is often silent.

czar
gnu
mnemonic
psalm
pterodactyl
rhythm
tsunami

/ch/ but no *h* after *c*

Italian loanwords.

cello
concerto

No *d* before *g*

pigeon

No *p* after *m*

hamster

n before *m*

enmity
environment
government

Right: This three-word VKV was made using a quarter sheet of paper. Consonant prefixes and suffixes are very common.

Sub- is an example of a consonant prefix. See page 233 for a list of words beginning with the prefix *sub-*.

No *c* after *s*

silent

-tach not *-atch*

Only two common words, which happen to be antonyms.

attach
detach

One or two consonants?

discus
discuss

blizzard
hazard
wizard

Vowel and consonant alteration

Many words have a repeated vowel-consonant pattern, or a repeated consonant-vowel pattern.

Geography Terms:

Alabama
Amazon
Arizona
Colorado
Delaware
Idaho
Oregon
Nevada
Texas
Utah
United Arab Emirates

Common Words:

banana Sp
overimaginative
pajama
regenerate

Don't forget the *p*

When pronouncing the *-mpt* portion of these words, the *p* can blend into the other sounds, making it difficult to hear and spell.

assumption
attempt
consumption
comptroller

(pronounced *kuhn*-**troh**-ler)

contempt
emptied
exempt
gumption
humpty
impromptu
preempt
prompt
scrumptious
sumptuous
symptom
temptation
unkempt

Don't forget *t*

bankruptcy

Don't forget *r*

February

Don't forget *s*

asterisk

Consonant Observations to Prevent Spelling Errors:

No *d*
The *-ege* ending can be misspelled as *-edge*.

all**ege**

coll**ege**

li**ege**

privil**ege** Sp

sacril**ege**

The *-age* ending can be misspelled as *-adge*.

salv**age**

selv**age**

No *d*
pigeon

Don't forget the *d*
The spelling *-(e)dge* is more common than *-ege*.

acknowle**dge**

blu**dge**on

curmu**dge**on

dre**dge**

e**dge**

fle**dge**

he**dge**

knowle**dge**

le**dge**

ple**dge**

sle**dge**

smi**dge**n   smidgin, smidgeon

we**dge**

Ending in *-mt*
Only one common word.

drea**mt**

Ending in *-gry*
There are only two words (not three, despite what a popular but frustrating internet puzzle says) that end in *-gry*:

an**gry**

hun**gry**

Ending in *-shion*
Only two common words.

cu**shion**

fa**shion**

Ending in *-cion*
Only two common words.

coer**cion**

suspi**cion**

Ending in *-bt*
Only two common words.

de**bt**

dou**bt**

Ending in *-sede*
Only one common word.

super**sede** Sp

Ending in *-igy*
Only two common words.

eff**igy**

prod**igy**

Ending in *-cay*
Only one common noun.

de**cay**

An unusual *-ay* word.

c**ay**

a low island pronounced as *key*; also spelled as *key*: Example: Florida Keys.

Ending in *-nen*
Only one common word.

li**nen**

Ending in *-ln*
Only one common noun.

ki**ln**

Linco**ln**   proper noun

Ends in *-ch*, not *-tch*
/ch/ is usually spelled *-tch* after a short vowel sound. Exception:

sandwi**ch**

Common consonant prefixes
A consonant prefix begins with a consonant:

bi-, circum-, com-, con-, de-, for-, fore-, non-, pre-, pro-, re-, sub-, syn-

Common Consonant Suffixes:
A consonant suffix begins with a consonant:

-ble, -dom, -ful, -fold, -less, -ly, -ment, -ness, -ship, -ster, -tor, -tion, -ward, -wise

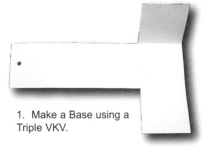

1. Make a Base using a Triple VKV.

2. Write a letter/letter combination on the front of the bottom tab.

3. Write a letter/letter combination on the front of the top tab.

VKV Spelling Rings (above and below): Make a set of Spelling Ring VKV flashcards featuring words that end in difficult spellings. Students flip the cards on the ring, and select the final letter/s to spell the words correctly. For self-checking, correct spellings should be written on the back of each flashcard. Use this activity with any of the spellings featured in the Consonant Review section at the bottom of this page.
Variation: Reverse the position of the tabs on the base VKV, and punch holes along the left edge for Spelling Rings featuring words that begin with letter combinations that can be difficult to spell. See another Spelling Ring variation on page 152. See instructions on page 381.

4. Cut VKV cards to fit on top of the base. See the card above.

5. Write words on the top cards omitting the final letter/letters.

Word Study: Consonant Review
Use VKVs, Two- or Three-Tab Foldables, Two- or Three-Column Charts, or Pocket Foldables to review the following:

/r/ right	and	/r/ spelled wr- (wrist)
/t/ tenor	and	/t/ spelled -ed (hooked)
/n/ nocturnal	and	/n/ spelled -en (frozen) and /n/ spelled kn- (knock)
/z/ zoo	and	/z/ spelled -s (his)
/l/ lesson	and	/l/ spelled -le (able)
/f/ faithful	and	/f/ spelled ph- (phone)
/j/ justify	and	/j/ spelled g- (gymnasium)
hard c /k/ carrot	and	soft c /s/ circus
hard g /g/ grate [H], great [H]	and	soft g /j/ giraffe

/k/ spelled as *k*, as hard *c, ck, cc, ch, ic*
y as a consonant and *y* as a vowel

(closed)

(open)

Top Pocket Foldable: The ESL/ELL activity above investigates *sp-* words that students might encounter in RWP in their community and during reading. It was made using a sheet of 8½" x 11" paper, which makes it a perfect size for collecting quarter-sheet flashcards. Notice the two tabs with featured vocabulary terms on each side of the central pocket. See page 417.

Two-Pocket Foldable® and Consonant Cards: Make 11 Two-Pocket Foldables and glue them side by side to form a 22-page Pocket Book. In alphabetical order, write one consonant on each pocket, and use them to collect examples of words with initial, medial, or final consonants or consonant combinations that might be difficult to spell. This is also a good activity for collecting and sorting content vocabulary terms. Make 13 Two-Pocket Foldables to make a 26-page Pocket Book.

Foldable Bound Book Classroom Vocabulary Dictionary (below): Made using eight half-sheets of posterboard folded like *hamburgers*. See instructions for binding on page 401.

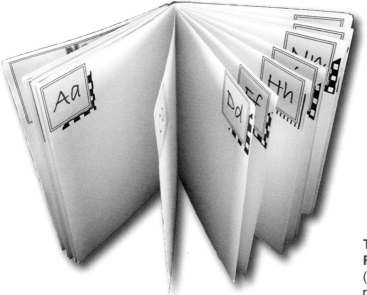

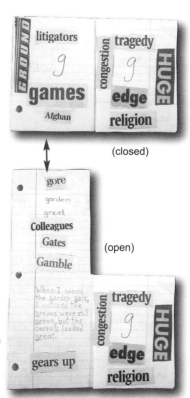

(closed)

(open)

Two-Tab Foldable (right): See page 396.

Notebook Foldables and VKV Flashcards for /k/ and /s/ Spelled as *c*

Left /s/: A Triple VKV Flashcard made using a quarter sheet of notebook paper was used to form three words that begin with the soft sound of *c*.

Note: If students glue the left edge of a finished VKV Flashcard into their notebooks, the rest of the card can be raised and lowered as a tab to allow students to write sentences using the words, idioms that contain the words, or definitions of the terms underneath.

Right /s/: A sheet of 8½" x 11" paper was used to make the large Triple VKV Flashcards pictured right.

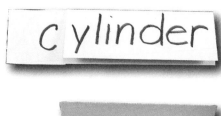

Above: Notice that the letter *c* has the soft sound of /s/ when followed by the vowels *e* and *y*.

Below: Notice that *c* has the hard sound of /k/ when followed by the vowels *a* and *o*.

Left /k/: A Triple VKV Flashcard made using a quarter sheet of notebook paper was used to form three words that begin with the hard sound of *c*.

Note: If students glue the left edge of a finished VKV Flashcard into their notebooks, the rest of the card can be raised and lowered as a tab to allow students to write sentences using the words, idioms that contain the words, or definitions of the terms underneath.

Right /k/: A sheet of 8½" x 11" paper was used to make the large Triple VKV Flashcards pictured to the right.

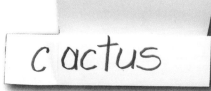

Consonants Spelling /k/ and /s/

Notice that *c* has the hard sound of **/k/** when followed by the vowels *a, o,* and *u.*
The letter *c* usually has the soft sound of **/s/**—and infrequently /ch/, as in *cello* and *concerto*—
if followed by *e, i,* and *y.* The letter *k* is used instead of *c* if /k/ is followed by an *e, i,* or *y.*

Key:
* = test prep
Cl = clipped word
H = heteronym, homograph, homophone
Int = interjection
Sp = spelling demon

c
Sound of */k/* when followed by the vowels *a, o,* and *u.*
<u>c</u>acophony
<u>c</u>ajole *
<u>c</u>aper
<u>c</u>atastrophe
<u>c</u>ollaborative *
<u>c</u>ollate *
<u>c</u>olumn Sp
<u>c</u>ommitted Sp
<u>c</u>ondone *
<u>c</u>onformist *
<u>c</u>ounterfeit *
<u>c</u>overt *
<u>c</u>ower *
<u>c</u>ubi<u>c</u>al
<u>c</u>urtail *

c
c followed by an *e, i,* or *y* is softened from */k/* to */s/* (as in *central*), or occasionally to /ch/ (as in *cello* and *concerto*).
Exception: Celt
<u>c</u>elery
<u>c</u>emetery Sp
<u>c</u>ensor *
<u>c</u>ensorship
<u>c</u>ensure *
<u>c</u>entipede
<u>c</u>enturion *
<u>c</u>entury
<u>c</u>erebral *
<u>c</u>eremony
<u>c</u>ertitude *
<u>c</u>ivilian *
<u>c</u>yberspa<u>c</u>e *

/s/

Sound of */k/*
Celt
Celtic
A people and their language: Irish, Gaels, Welsh, and Bretons.

/k/

Both
/k/ and /s/
<u>c</u>ir<u>c</u>uitous *
<u>c</u>ir<u>c</u>umferen<u>c</u>e
<u>c</u>ir<u>c</u>umscribe *
<u>c</u>ir<u>c</u>umspe<u>c</u>t *
<u>c</u>ir<u>c</u>umvent *
<u>c</u>on<u>c</u>eal
<u>c</u>on<u>c</u>ede
<u>c</u>on<u>c</u>eit
<u>c</u>on<u>c</u>entric
<u>c</u>on<u>c</u>iliatory
<u>c</u>on<u>c</u>ise *
<u>c</u>y<u>c</u>lical *
<u>c</u>ylindri<u>c</u>al *
<u>c</u>yni<u>c</u>al *
e<u>cc</u>entric *
i<u>c</u>i<u>c</u>les

Sound of */s/*
Celtics
A professional basketball team from Boston.

ch
Greek words often have /k/ spelled *ch,* as in *chronic* and *chorus.*
<u>ch</u>ameleon *
<u>ch</u>aos *
<u>ch</u>aracter
<u>ch</u>arisma *
<u>ch</u>asm *
<u>ch</u>olera
<u>ch</u>ord H
<u>ch</u>oreography
<u>ch</u>romatic *
<u>ch</u>romosome
<u>ch</u>ronology *
<u>ch</u>rysalis

k
The */k/* sound at the beginning of a word is spelled *k* if followed by *e* or *i.*
<u>k</u>eel
<u>k</u>elvin
<u>k</u>ennel
<u>k</u>eratin
<u>k</u>ernel H
<u>k</u>eypad
<u>k</u>ibitz
<u>k</u>ickoff
<u>k</u>idney
<u>k</u>ilogram
<u>k</u>indle
<u>k</u>inetic

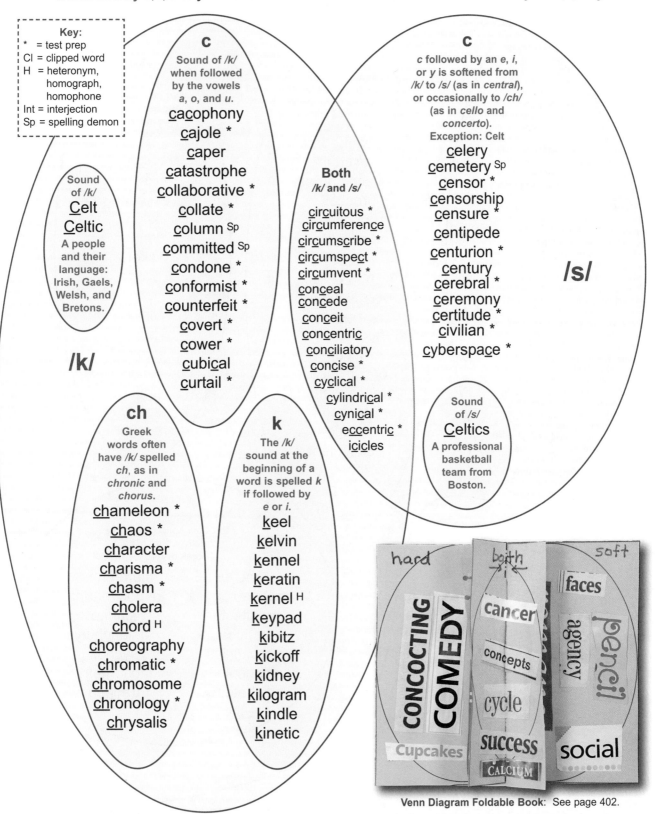

Venn Diagram Foldable Book: See page 402.

Consonants Medial /k/ Spelling

This sound /k/ is nearly always spelled in one of five ways: *c*, *cc*, *k*, *ck*, and occasionally *ch*.
The letter *c* is the most common spelling for /k/. It may be used anywhere in a word.
Sometimes the letter *c* is doubled to *cc* to protect the sound of a short vowel.

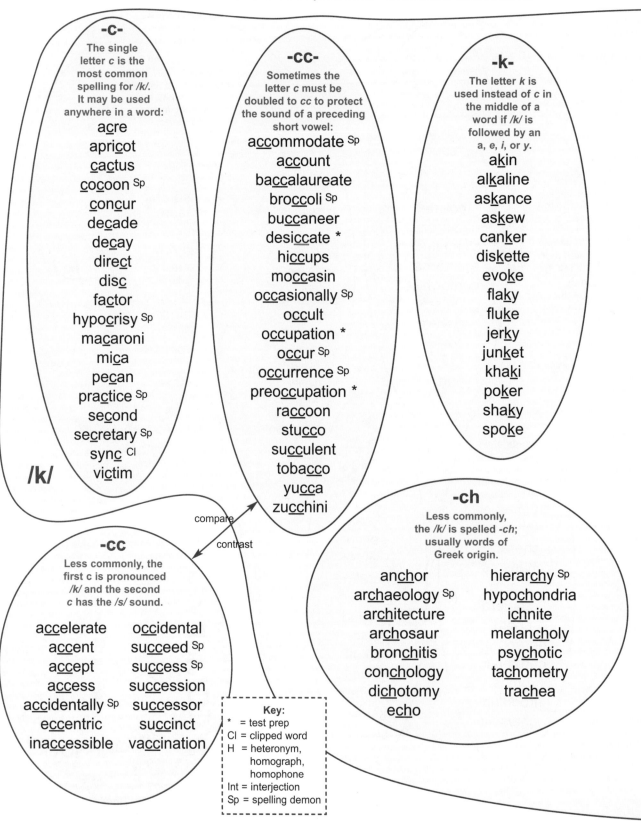

-c-

The single letter *c* is the most common spelling for /k/. It may be used anywhere in a word:

acre
apricot
cactus
cocoon Sp
concur
decade
decay
direct
disc
factor
hypocrisy Sp
macaroni
mica
pecan
practice Sp
second
secretary Sp
sync Cl
victim

/k/

-cc-

Sometimes the letter *c* must be doubled to *cc* to protect the sound of a preceding short vowel:

accommodate Sp
account
baccalaureate
broccoli Sp
buccaneer
desiccate *
hiccups
moccasin
occasionally Sp
occult
occupation *
occur Sp
occurrence Sp
preoccupation *
raccoon
stucco
succulent
tobacco
yucca
zucchini

-k-

The letter *k* is used instead of *c* in the middle of a word if /k/ is followed by an *a*, *e*, *i*, or *y*.

akin
alkaline
askance
askew
canker
diskette
evoke
flaky
fluke
jerky
junket
khaki
poker
shaky
spoke

compare

contrast

-cc

Less commonly, the first c is pronounced /k/ and the second c has the /s/ sound.

accelerate   occidental
accent   succeed Sp
accept   success Sp
access   succession
accidentally Sp successor
eccentric   succinct
inaccessible   vaccination

-ch

Less commonly, the /k/ is spelled -ch; usually words of Greek origin.

anchor   hierarchy Sp
archaeology Sp   hypochondria
architecture   ichnite
archosaur   melancholy
bronchitis   psychotic
conchology   tachometry
dichotomy   trachea
echo

Key:
* = test prep
Cl = clipped word
H = heteronym, homograph, homophone
Int = interjection
Sp = spelling demon

The **/k/** sound at the end of a one-syllable, short-vowel word is usually spelled *-ck*.
The spelling *-ck-* is also used in two-syllable words ending in *-et* and *-le*.

/k/

-ck-

Is found in the middle of a compound word when the first word ends in *-ck*.

ba**ck**pack
bri**ck**layer
che**ck**book
clo**ck**work
cra**ck**pot
de**ck**hand
do**ck**side
du**ck**bill
ja**ck**knife
ja**ck**rabbit
la**ck**luster
lo**ck**box
ne**ck**tie
pi**ck**ax
qui**ck**silver
ro**ck**slide
sho**ck**proof
tra**ck**suit
tru**ck**line

-ck-

/k/ is heard in the middle of a word that ends in *-ck* but has an added suffix.

airsi**ck**ness
atta**ck**ing
ba**ck**handedly
fini**ck**y
froli**ck**ed
hija**ck**ing
homesi**ck**ness
lu**ck**ily
sho**ck**ingly
tri**ck**ster
wi**ck**edness
wi**ck**er
wre**ck**age

-ic becomes -ick

A few words ending in *-ic* add *-k* before adding a suffix (other than *-s*) to maintain a short vowel sound. See page 141.

frol**ic**	frolic**k**ing
mim**ic**	mimic**k**ed
pan**ic**	panic**k**y
picn**ic**	picnic**k**ing ᔆᵖ
traff**ic**	traffic**k**ing

Four-Door Foldable® Display Case and Consonant Cards: Make Foldable display cases to collect student-made or class-made flashcards that feature words that contain specific spellings of consonants. Any applicable spelling rule/s might be written on the inside of the display case as a reminder that students need to become "familiarized" with the rules of language. See page 410.

Above: Note that quarter-sheet flashcards feature *br-*, *pr-*, *cr-*, and *gr-* words in English and Spanish.
Below: A classroom set of consonant flashcards featuring br-, cr-, dr-, fr-, kr-, pr-, tr-, and wr-.

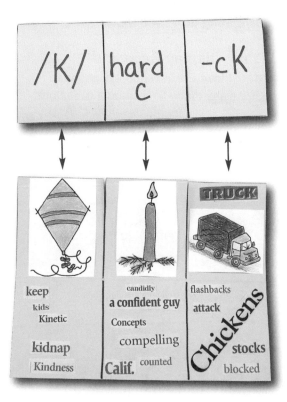

Three-Tab Foldable (left):
A Three-Tab Foldable was made using a sheet of 8½" x 11" paper. Students labeled the front tabs and found example words for each sound, then wrote/glued them under the tabs.

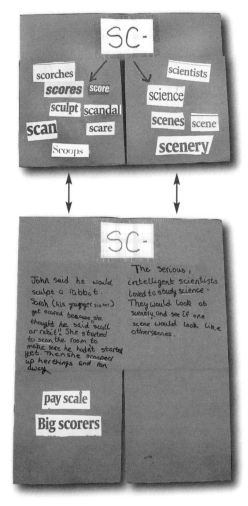

Two-Tab Foldable (right):
A Two-Tab Foldable Concept Map was made with a sheet of 8½" x 11" paper. Students labeled the top tab *sc-* and drew arrows to each of the two tabs. Words illustrating the soft and hard sounds made by *sc-* were written/glued on the front tabs and used in sentences or paragraphs under the tabs.

> The phrase *back to basics* was found in RWP and glued between the two as an example of both spellings.

Pocket Charts (above and right):
Pocket Charts can be made using 11" x 17" copy paper (above) or posterboard (bottom right). These Two-Column Charts each have a pocket for collecting flashcards, information cards, quotes from literature that include words that illustrate the featured sounds, and more. Note that the posterboard chart has an extra stapled strip along the bottom that serves as a display for selected cards. See *-ick* and *-ic* word lists on page 141.

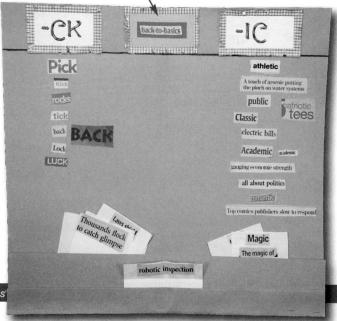

The letters *k* and *ck* are more than substitutes for *c* and *cc*. They are used to spell /k/ at the end of a monosyllable. If there is a letter (vowel or consonant) between the first vowel in a syllable and the /k/ sound, the sound is usually spelled *k* (*bilk*). When there is no letter (besides *c*) between the vowel and the final *k* sound, the sound is spelled *ck*.

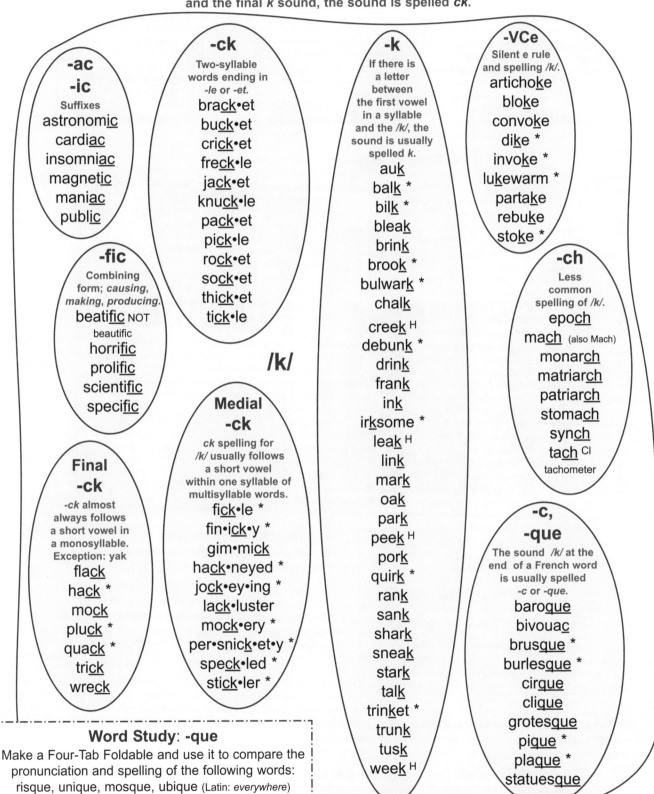

-ac
-ic
Suffixes
astronomic
cardiac
insomniac
magnetic
maniac
public

-fic
Combining form; *causing, making, producing.*
beatific NOT
beautific
horrific
prolific
scientific
specific

Final -ck
-ck almost always follows a short vowel in a monosyllable. Exception: yak
flack
hack *
mock
pluck *
quack *
trick
wreck

-ck
Two-syllable words ending in *-le* or *-et.*
brack•et
buck•et
crick•et
freck•le
jack•et
knuck•le
pack•et
pick•le
rock•et
sock•et
thick•et
tick•le

/k/

Medial -ck
ck spelling for /k/ usually follows a short vowel within one syllable of multisyllable words.
fick•le *
fin•ick•y *
gim•mick
hack•neyed *
jock•ey•ing *
lack•luster
mock•ery *
per•snick•et•y *
speck•led *
stick•ler *

-k
If there is a letter between the first vowel in a syllable and the /k/, the sound is usually spelled k.
auk
balk *
bilk *
bleak
brink
brook *
bulwark *
chalk
creek H
debunk *
drink
frank
ink
irksome *
leak H
link
mark
oak
park
peek H
pork
quirk *
rank
sank
shark
sneak
stark
talk
trinket *
trunk
tusk
week H

-VCe
Silent e rule and spelling /k/.
artichoke
bloke
convoke
dike *
invoke *
lukewarm *
partake
rebuke
stoke *

-ch
Less common spelling of /k/.
epoch
mach (also Mach)
monarch
matriarch
patriarch
stomach
synch
tach CI
tachometer

-c, -que
The sound /k/ at the end of a French word is usually spelled *-c* or *-que.*
baroque
bivouac
brusque *
burlesque *
cirque
clique
grotesque
pique *
plaque *
statuesque

Word Study: -que
Make a Four-Tab Foldable and use it to compare the pronunciation and spelling of the following words: risque, unique, mosque, ubique (Latin: *everywhere*)

Triple VKV (below): A Triple VKV Flashcard was used to make three *-ic* words. The word *fantastic* was glued inside the middle section of the flashcard. The top and bottom sections of the card were cut away to expose only the *-ic* at the end of the word *fantastic*. Two more *-ic* words were found in RWP. The *-ic* was cut off of these words, and the remaining parts of the words were glued onto the top and bottom tabs of the VKV.
NOTE: Students are encouraged to write terms, as well as to find terms in RWP, to use on VKVs.

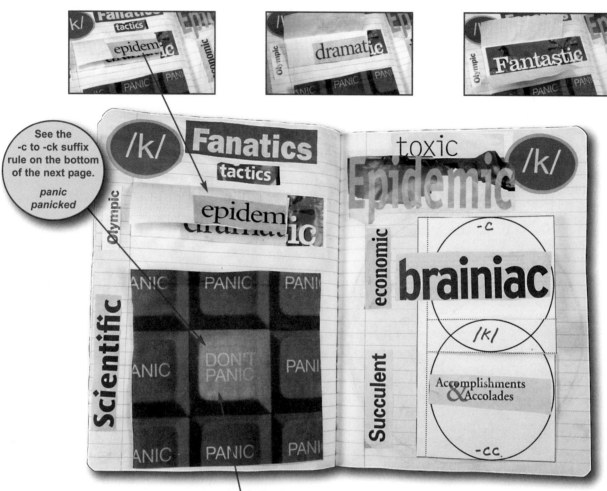

Venn Diagram Template (above):
The template pictured above, showing examples of two spellings of the /k/ sound, is from Dinah Zike's *Notebook Foldables* book and CD. A half sheet of notebook paper can also be used to make a Three-Tab Notebook Foldable. Fold the notebook paper into thirds. Fold a ¼" tab along the left long edge and glue this tab into the notebook. After the tab is secure, cut along the fold lines to form three tabs.

Newspaper Advertisement Tab (above): Since this tab is on the left side of the composition book, it was glued along the right side to prevent it from getting crumpled when the book is closed. Other student-collected examples of *-ic* words can be seen under the newspaper tab. Remember, these words can either be written by students or collected from RWP and glued under tabs. When appropriate, surrounding words, phrases, or paragraphs are cut out to accompany the featured word to give it context.

When a word ends with an /ick/ sound, it will be spelled **-ick** if the word has one syllable (*trick, pick, stick*), and **-ic** if it has two or more syllables (*clinic, sarcastic, panic*). Syllable exceptions are usually compound words. For example: air*sick*, chop*stick*, tooth*pick*. There are a few syllable exceptions that are not compound words, as in *der-rick* and *mav-er-ick*.

ESL/ELL English Pronunciation Guide: Suffixes like *-ic* create a new word, and they change the stress placement within the word. Often it is the first, and sometimes the second, syllable to the left of the *-ic* syllable that receives the stress. Students need to practice this pronunciation enough to familiarize themselves with the pattern of stress placement.

Examples:
a•pol•o•**get**•ic
an•es•**thet**•ic
bi•o•**graph**•i•cal
do•**mes**•tic
e•co•**nom**•ic
en•thu•si•**as**•tic
fan•**tas**•tic
hy•po•**thet**•ic
sys•tem•**at**•ic

-ick

When a word ends with an /ick/ sound and has one syllable, it is spelled *-ick*. If the word has two or more syllables, it is spelled *-ic*.

brick
flick
hick
nick
pick
slick
tick [H]
trick
wick

Exceptions are usually compound words:

chopstick
nitpick

Exceptions other than compound words:

derrick
limerick
maverick *

/ick/

-ic

The *-ic* suffix forms adjectives from other parts of speech: *metal* (n.), *metallic* (adj.). It means *of, relating to, or characterized by*. Most words ending in *-ic* are derived from Latin and Greek: poetic, *poeticus* (L), from *poietikos* (Gk).

academic	graphic
aesthetic *	hectic *
agoraphobic *	hieroglyphic *
altruistic *	historic
anachronistic *	histrionic *
anarchistic *	hygienic
apathetic *	ironic *
aquatic *	laconic *
archaic *	lethargic *
aromatic *	lyric
bibliophilic *	mimic *
caustic *	mosaic
chaotic *	nomadic *
chronic *	nostalgic *
concentric *	pathetic *
cryptic *	pedantic *
cubic	periodic *
didactic *	pragmatic *
dogmatic *	sarcastic *
eccentric *	sardonic *
eclectic *	schematic *
empathetic *	sophomoric * Sp
endemic *	soporific *
energetic *	sporadic *
episodic *	stoic *
erratic *	taxonomic *
esoteric *	therapeutic *
euphoric *	toxic *
extrinsic *	unauthentic *

Word Study:
The *-c* to *-ck* Suffix Rule

Only five common verbs end in the adjective suffix *-ic*, but the ones that do change the *-c* to *-ck* when adding the verb suffixes *-ed* and *-ing*. An *-s* is added without changes (*mimics*), but a *-y* suffix is preceded by *-ck* (*panicky*). See page 138.

frolic n./v.	frolicked	frolicking
mimic n./v.	mimicked	mimicking
panic n./v.	panicked	panicking
		panicky
picnic n./v.	picnicked	picnicking Sp
traffic n./v.	trafficked	trafficking

Key:
* = test prep
Cl = clipped word
H = heteronym, homograph, homophone
Int = interjection
Sp = spelling demon

Consonants Spelling /j/

Note that the letter *j* is never doubled in English, and it always has the soft sound /j/.

initial j

j is usually used at the beginning of a word if followed by an *a*, *o*, or *u* sound.

jaded
jaguar
jargon *
jaundiced *
jocular *
journey
joust
jubilant *
jubilation *
judgment Sp
junction *
jungle
justice
juvenile *
juxtaposition *

/j/
Both Spellings

judge Sp
judging *
judgment * Sp
judgmental *

-dge

If /j/ immediately follows a short vowel sound, it is usually spelled -dge. The *d* in -dge is silent, but it is added to prevent the short vowel from being pronounced as a long vowel. Generally, words that end in -dge are of Middle/Old English origin.

abridge   gadget
badge   grudge
begrudge   hedge
bludgeon *   knowledge
budget   ledge
cadge *   lodge
cartridge   nudge
dodge   pledge
dredge   porridge
drudgery   ridge
edge   smudge
fidget   trudge
fudge H   wedge

/j/

g-

The letter *g* can have the soft sound of /j/ when it is followed by an *e*, *i*, or *y*.

gemologist
gender
genealogy *
general
generate
generic
generous
genius
genre *
genuine
genus *
geode
geometry
germinal *
gestation
gesticulate *
giant
ginger
ginseng
giraffe
gymnasium
gypsy
gyrate
gyroscope

Example of an exception:

gecko

-age

/ij/ Sound
The vowels in these words are in unaccented syllables where they are scarcely pronounced. These are usually words borrowed from Latin, mostly through French into Middle English.

adage
breakage
coinage
coverage
mileage
parsonage
patronage
peerage
shortage
spoilage
voltage

-j-

Less Common:
j instead of *g* used in medial spelling for /j/.

adjective
adjourn
banjo
conjoin
majesty
majority
object
pajamas
perjury
projectile
reject
rejoice
rejoin

g-

g is commonly used in the medial spelling of /j/. Often a *silent e* is added after a *g* to soften the *g*, as in *age*, *page*, and *pigeon*.

algebra
allege Sp
apologize Sp
cagey *
convergence *
digest
energy
legend
origin
oxygen
pigeon
privilege Sp
regent
rigid *
wages

Key:
* = test prep
Cl = clipped word
H = heteronym, homograph, homophone
Int = interjection
Sp = spelling demon

Right: Instructions on page 392.

/j/

The letter g can have the soft sound of /j/ when it is followed by an e, i, or y.

gel
gelatin
gem
gender
generations
genetic
genteel
genus
geode
geology
geranium
gerbil
geriatric
germ
gesture
giant
gymnastics
gymnosperm
gypsum

Both
Soft and Hard Sounds

gadget
gage
garage
garbage
gauge
geography
gigantic
gorge
gorgeous
gouge
grunge

/g/
Hard g Sounds

gaffe
gait
galactic
galant
galaxy
galvanize
garb
gargle
gear
gill
gingko
gizmo
gizzard
goal

Consonant digraph gh- has the hard g sound and a silent h.

aghast
ghastly
gherkin
ghetto
ghost
ghoul
spaghetti

The consonant blends gl- and gr- begin with a hard g sound blended into the second consonant.

glacial
gladiator
glamorize
glisten
glucose
glyph
gracious
granola
gregarious
grouch
grunt

/g/

Sometimes when a hard /g/ sound is followed by an e or i, the g is immediately followed by a silent u.

guess
guide
guile
guilt
guitar

A silent u is also found in some words of French origin.

guarantee
guard

Venn Diagram Bound Book (above):
Follow the instructions on page 402 to make this Venn Diagram Foldable. It features *g* words that have soft sounds, hard sounds, and words that are spelled with both soft and hard sounds. Free Venn diagram template downloads are available at www.dinah.com.

Top Pocket Foldable®

This Foldable was made using a sheet of 8½" x 11" paper. See instructions on page 417. This is a good size for individual student use since quarter-sheet flash-cards, as well as worksheets folded into fourths, can be stored in the pocket.

(closed)

Central Paragraph

The central paragraph was written on a computer by either the teacher, individual students, or cooperative learning groups. Copies were made for all students, and glued into the Foldable as illustrated. Students highlight words that illustrate the skill being studied. Students individualize the Top Pocket by selecting their own words for the six tabs, and they write sentences using the words under the tabs.

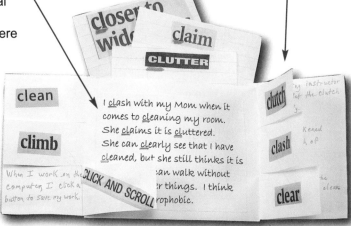

(open)

Word Tabs: Three tabs were cut on each side panel of this Top Pocket to feature six words that begin with the consonant blend *cl-*. This same Foldable can be used for many different activities, including the following:

- prefixes
- suffixes
- root words
- homographs
- homophones
- clipped words
- synonyms
- antonyms

qu
Medial and Final
(/kw / sound)

ac**qu**ire	in**qu**isitive
a**qu**it Sp	li**qu**id
ade**qu**ate *	relin**qu**ish
earth**qu**ake	re**qu**est
elo**qu**ence *	re**qu**ire
e**qu**al	re**qu**isite
e**qu**ation	se**qu**ence
e**qu**ator	se**qu**ester
e**qu**ipment Sp	s**qu**are
e**qu**ivalent	s**qu**ash H
fre**qu**ent	tran**qu**il *
in**qu**est	van**qu**ish
in**qu**ire	

Word Study: Regional Variations

Barbecue comes from the word *barbacoa*, which was borrowed by the Spanish from the Caribbean language of the Taino people. The main dictionary spelling for the word is *barbecue*, but numerous other spellings and abbreviations have become popularized in different regions of the world. There are not as many spellings of the term, though, as there are variations of cooking styles and sauces.

BBQ, B-B-Q, Bar-B-Q Phonetically abbreviated by letter names

bar-b-que

barbeque

'que clipped version of *barbecue*, USA West Coast

barbie Australian term

braai Term used in Southern Africa; rhymes with *cry*

/kw/

The sound /kw/
is always spelled
qu in English.

quack * H
quadrant
quadrilateral
quadrillion
quadruped
quaff *
quagmire *
quail
quaint *
qualify
qualm *
quandary *
quantity
quarantine *
quarrel
quarry *
quartet
quartile
quartz
queasy
quell *
quench
querulous *
query *
questionnaire Sp
queue Sp
quibble *
quill
quilt
quintessential *
quintet
quip
quit
quiver
quixotic *
quiz
quota
quote
quotient

squ-

Consonant
Digraph

squadron
squall
squalor *
squamous *
squander
square
squash
squat
squatter
squaw
squawk
squeak
squeal
squeamish
squeegee
squeeze
squid
squire
squirm

/kw/

Key:
* = test prep
Cl = clipped word
H = heteronym,
   homograph,
   homophone
Int = interjection
Sp = spelling demon

Review and Extension:

Terms found in RWP will include those appropriate for a given grade level, as well as for those above and below. This wide range provides students a chance for growth, review, and extension.

Fold-Over VKV (below):
Use this simple VKV to help students focus on spelling initial sounds. Fold a card, leaving a tab on the left side. Write or glue words so the initial consonant, consonant blend, or prefix of each word is on the exposed tab. The initial letters should be visible when the right side of the card is closed. When the card is open, entire words can be viewed and read. Have students exchange their VKVs with other students.

Two-Column Pocket Chart (below):
Use a sheet of 11" x 17" copy paper or 12" x 18" art paper to make this chart. Students use the chart to write examples of *qu-* and *squ-* words they know and need to know, and they collect words cut out from RWP in the pockets.

Key:
* = test prep
Cl = clipped word
H = heteronym, homograph, homophone
Int = interjection
Sp = spelling demon

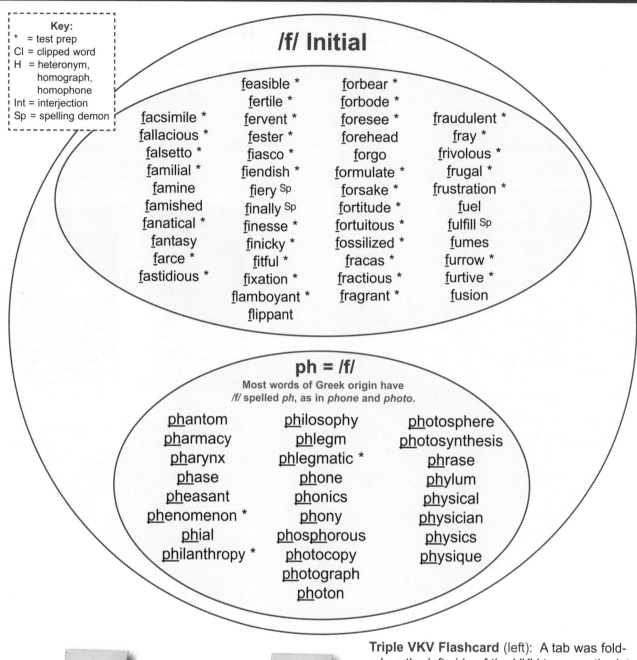

/f/ Initial

facsimile *
fallacious *
falsetto *
familial *
famine
famished
fanatical *
fantasy
farce *
fastidious *

feasible *
fertile *
fervent *
fester *
fiasco *
fiendish *
fiery Sp
finally Sp
finesse *
finicky *
fitful *
fixation *
flamboyant *
flippant

forbear *
forbode *
foresee *
forehead
forgo
formulate *
forsake *
fortitude *
fortuitous *
fossilized *
fracas *
fractious *
fragrant *

fraudulent *
fray *
frivolous *
frugal *
frustration *
fuel
fulfill Sp
fumes
furrow *
furtive *
fusion

ph = /f/
Most words of Greek origin have /f/ spelled *ph*, as in *phone* and *photo*.

phantom
pharmacy
pharynx
phase
pheasant
phenomenon *
phial
philanthropy *

philosophy
phlegm
phlegmatic *
phone
phonics
phony
phosphorous
photocopy
photograph
photon

photosphere
photosynthesis
phrase
phylum
physical
physician
physics
physique

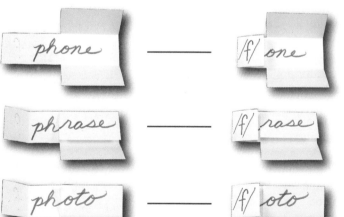

Triple VKV Flashcard (left): A tab was folded on the left side of the VKV to cover the letters *ph*. Notice that /f/ was written on the back of this tab to emphasize the sound made by the letters.

The three words formed on this VKV can be read with and without the /f/ tab. A few words have the /f/ sound spelled by *ph* at both the beginning and middle or end of the word. See page 387.

A similar VKV could be made for these:
phonograph
photograph
phototrophic

Spelling Initial /f/: Use a quarter sheet of paper to make the Triple VKV Flashcard featured in the composition book above. Cut away the top and bottom tabs of the left half of the card. On the inside center section of the Triple Flashcard, write a word that begins with the /f/ sound so that the first letters of the word are exposed when the right tabs are closed. Open and close the right tabs and write the endings of two more words to form three words beginning with the /f/ sound. Fold the left edge of the flashcard over to cover the *ph*, and write the letter *f* or the symbol for the *f sound* on the back of the flashcard.

Word Study Based on Foldable (right):
Analyze Examples and Make Spelling Observations:

/f/ spelled with the letter *f*
    Initial: fortitude
    Medial: reference
    Final: proof

/f/ spelled with the digraph *ph-*
    Initial: phony
    Medial: symphony
    Final: graph

/f/ spelled with the *-gh* digraph
    Initial: Never spells /f/ in initial position.
    Medial: Never spells /f/ in medial position.
    Final: rough

Check word observations and conclusions during reading and word study. Are your observations still correct? Are there exceptions?

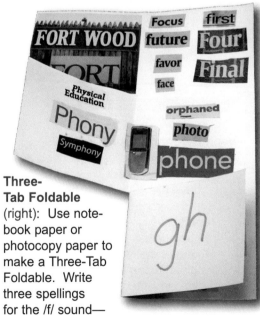

Three-Tab Foldable (right): Use notebook paper or photocopy paper to make a Three-Tab Foldable. Write three spellings for the /f/ sound—f, ph, and gh—on the front tabs. Write or glue examples of words with the /f/ sound spelled with these letters under the tabs.

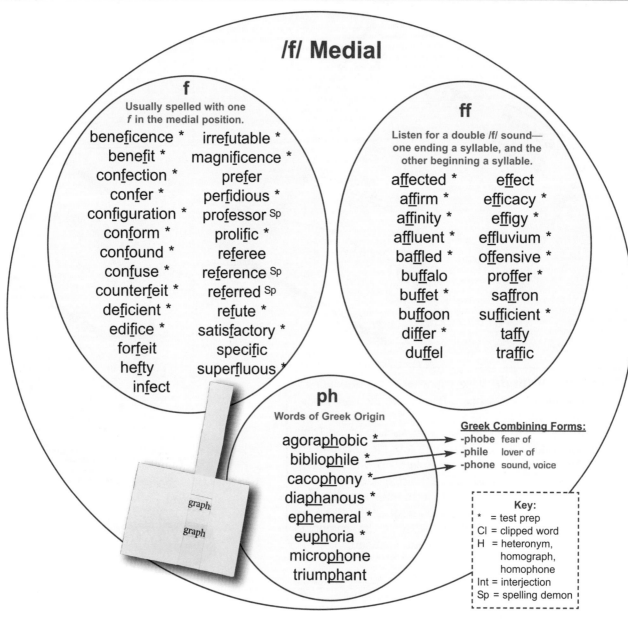

/f/ Medial

f
Usually spelled with one *f* in the medial position.

beneficence *
benefit *
confection *
confer *
configuration *
conform *
confound *
confuse *
counterfeit *
deficient *
edifice *
forfeit
hefty
infect
irrefutable *
magnificence *
prefer
perfidious *
professor Sp
prolific *
referee
reference Sp
referred Sp
refute *
satisfactory *
specific
superfluous *

ff
Listen for a double /f/ sound—one ending a syllable, and the other beginning a syllable.

affected *
affirm *
affinity *
affluent *
baffled *
buffalo
buffet *
buffoon
differ *
duffel
effect
efficacy *
effigy *
effluvium *
offensive *
proffer *
saffron
sufficient *
taffy
traffic

ph
Words of Greek Origin

agoraphobic *
bibliophile *
cacophony *
diaphanous *
ephemeral *
euphoria *
microphone
triumphant

Greek Combining Forms:
-phobe   fear of
-phile   lover of
-phone   sound, voice

Key:
* = test prep
Cl = clipped word
H = heteronym, homograph, homophone
Int = interjection
Sp = spelling demon

graph
graph

Venn Diagram Tabbed Foldable®: A rectangle of blue paper is used to represent the set of all words that have the /f/ sound. The four tabs on the front of the blue sheet represent four ways this sound can be spelled. The blue background and all small white tabs were glued along their left edges. Students can write in the composition book under the large blue tab, and they can write under each of the small white tabs. See lists of words with the final /f/ sound on the next page.

Consonants Final Spelling /f/

/f/ Final

-ph
Most words of Greek origin have /f/ spelled *ph*, as in *graph*.

diagra**ph**
digra**ph**
epita**ph**
gly**ph**
lym**ph**
mor**ph**
nym**ph**

Interjection

um**ph**

-ff
When a single-short-vowel word ends in *f*, *l*, *s*, or *z*, the last letters are doubled to keep the short vowel sound.

bailiff	mastiff	sheriff
buff	midriff	skiff
bluff	miff	sluff
chaff	muff	sniff
cliff	off	staff
cuff	plaintiff	stiff
dandruff	pontiff	stuff
doff	puff	tariff
fluff	quaff	tiff
gaff	rebuff	tuff
gruff	riff	whiff
huff	ruff	
	scoff *	
	scuff	

-gh
Many words of Middle and Old English origin have /f/ spelled *-gh*.

cou**gh**
enou**gh**
lau**gh**
rou**gh**
slou**gh**
tou**gh**
trou**gh**

-f
Most common spelling of /f/.

aloof	golf	ref Cl
aperitif	goof	relief Sp
beef	grief	roof
belief Sp	gulf	scarf
brief	half	self
calf	hoof	sheaf
chef	leaf	shelf
chief	loaf	spoof *
deaf	motif	surf
dwarf	oaf	thief
elf	prof Cl	turf
fief	proof	wolf
	reef	

Key:
* = test prep
Cl = clipped word
H = heteronym, homograph, homophone
Int = interjection
Sp = spelling demon

Other -oug sounds:
- **bough** rhymes with *cow*
- **cough** rhymes with *off*
- **tough** rhymes with *puff*
- **though** rhymes with *go*
- **through** rhymes with *you*

Two-Tab Foldable (right): Students used this Foldable to collect examples of words that have the /f/ spelled as *-f*, *-ff*, or *-ph*.

Which Spelling Looks Correct? (left): Make a set of Spelling Ring VKV flashcards featuring words that end in either a single or double *f*. Students flip the cards and select the correct final letter/s to spell the words correctly. The most common *-f* and *-ff* words are listed above. Instructions on page 381.

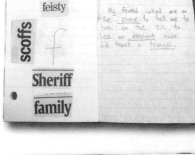

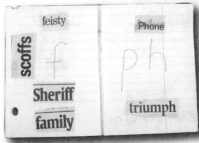

Consonants Final Spelling /ch/

Two-Tab Notebook Foldables
(below): Difficult spelling words and
sounds are featured on the front tabs of
these Foldables. Under the tabs,
students collect examples of words
they need to learn to spell.

Download
templates for the
speech bubble
pictured below at
www.dinah.com.

Spelling Gremlin:
sandwich
ends in *-ch*, not *-tch*.

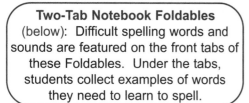

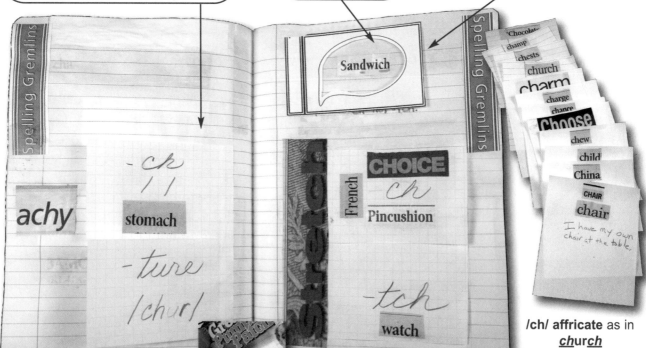

Spelling Gremlins

Sandwich

Spelling Gremlins

-ch
//

achy

stomach

-ture
/chur/

French

CHOICE
ch
Pincushion

-tch

watch

stretch

'Chocolate'
champ
chests
church
charm
charge
chance
Choose
chew
child
China
CHAIR
chair
I have my own
chair at the table.

/ch/ **affricate** as in
chur**ch**

fetch

glitch

stretch

PITCH
The Great
Pumpkin Patch

fetch pitch

pitch

notch

Chalk   /k/   ch   /sh/
         sound   sound

choir &
chorus

chandelier

China
CHAIR
chair
I have my

Chrome
CHOLESTEROL
chameleon

It's Chic, It's Cheap

---

fetch
stretch
sketch

pitch
glitch
stitch

notch
botch
blotch

**Triple VKV
Flashcards**
(above): Use a
quarter sheet of
paper to make the
flashcards featured in
this composition
notebook.
See page 385.

Foldable Pocket Chart (above):
Use a sheet of 11" x 17" paper
to make a two-column chart for
comparing hard and soft sounds.
See page 415.

Consonants Spelling /ch/

The sound */ch/* has two main spellings: *-tch* and *-ch*. Note that *-tch* is usually
used after a short vowel sound and *-ch* after all other sounds.
Exceptions include: *attach*, *bachelor*, *much*, *ostrich*, *sandwich*, *rich*, *such*, *touch*, and *which*.

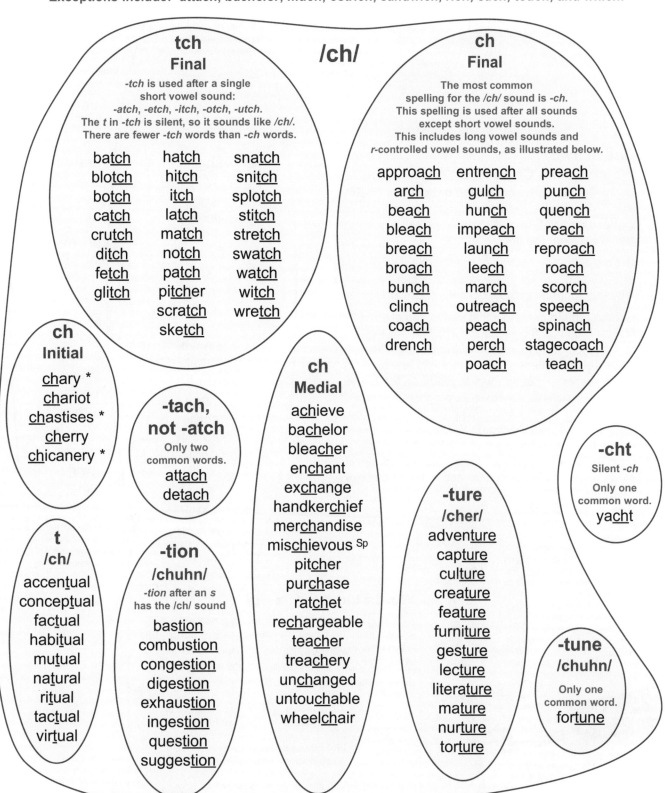

/ch/

tch
Final

-tch is used after a single
short vowel sound:
-atch, -etch, -itch, -otch, -utch.
The *t* in *-tch* is silent, so it sounds like */ch/*.
There are fewer *-tch* words than *-ch* words.

ba**tch**	ha**tch**	sna**tch**
blo**tch**	hi**tch**	sni**tch**
bo**tch**	i**tch**	splo**tch**
ca**tch**	la**tch**	sti**tch**
cru**tch**	ma**tch**	stre**tch**
di**tch**	no**tch**	swa**tch**
fe**tch**	pa**tch**	wa**tch**
gli**tch**	pi**tch**er	wi**tch**
	scra**tch**	wre**tch**
	ske**tch**	

ch
Final

The most common
spelling for the */ch/* sound is *-ch*.
This spelling is used after all sounds
except short vowel sounds.
This includes long vowel sounds and
r-controlled vowel sounds, as illustrated below.

approa**ch**	entren**ch**	prea**ch**
ar**ch**	gul**ch**	pun**ch**
bea**ch**	hun**ch**	quen**ch**
blea**ch**	impea**ch**	rea**ch**
brea**ch**	laun**ch**	reproa**ch**
broa**ch**	lee**ch**	roa**ch**
bun**ch**	mar**ch**	scor**ch**
clin**ch**	outrea**ch**	spee**ch**
coa**ch**	pea**ch**	spina**ch**
dren**ch**	per**ch**	stagecoa**ch**
	poa**ch**	tea**ch**

ch
Initial

chary *
chariot
chastises *
cherry
chicanery *

-tach, not -atch

Only two
common words.

at**tach**
de**tach**

ch
Medial

a**ch**ieve
ba**ch**elor
blea**ch**er
en**ch**ant
ex**ch**ange
handker**ch**ief
mer**ch**andise
mis**ch**ievous *Sp*
pit**ch**er
pur**ch**ase
rat**ch**et
re**ch**argeable
tea**ch**er
trea**ch**ery
un**ch**anged
untou**ch**able
wheel**ch**air

-ture
/cher/

adven**ture**
cap**ture**
cul**ture**
crea**ture**
fea**ture**
furni**ture**
ges**ture**
lec**ture**
litera**ture**
ma**ture**
nur**ture**
tor**ture**

-cht
Silent *-ch*

Only one
common word.
ya**cht**

t
/ch/

accen**t**ual
concep**t**ual
fac**t**ual
habi**t**ual
mu**t**ual
na**t**ural
ri**t**ual
tac**t**ual
vir**t**ual

-tion
/chuhn/

-tion after an *s*
has the */ch/* sound

bas**tion**
combus**tion**
conges**tion**
diges**tion**
exhaus**tion**
inges**tion**
ques**tion**
sugges**tion**

-tune
/chuhn/

Only one
common word.

for**tune**

One or Two?
Which Looks Correct to You? (above):

Use a Double Flashcard for the back of this Spelling Ring VKV. On the inside bottom section, write a word that ends in the letters -*ll*. Leave a small amount of space between the double letters.

Cut away the top section of the flashcard so only the -*ll* is covered. Keep this section, as it can be used as a template for making the rest of the flashcards.

Cut the top tab in half so that each half covers a letter. Make numerous Single Flashcards that are the length of the discarded top section of the Double Flashcard. Write the first letters of words that end in -*l* or -*ll* on these sections. Staple them together on top of the Double Flashcard. As students progress through the flashcards, they try to determine whether one -*l* or two -*ll*s properly spells the word. Write the correct spelling for each word on the back of the Single Flashcard sections so students can self-check their selections. Have students record the words formed in their notebooks. See page 132 for another variation of Spelling Rings. See instructions on page 381

-ll
When a single short-vowel word ends in *l, f, s,* or *z,* the letters are doubled to keep the short vowel sound.

-all words
ma<u>ll</u>
pa<u>ll</u> *
st<u>all</u> H

-ell words
she<u>ll</u> H
sme<u>ll</u>
sp<u>ell</u>

-ill words
dist<u>ill</u>
fulf<u>ill</u> Sp
kr<u>ill</u>
qu<u>ill</u>
shr<u>ill</u>
tw<u>ill</u>

-oll words
at<u>oll</u>
dr<u>oll</u>
kn<u>oll</u>
scr<u>oll</u>

-ull words
d<u>ull</u>
h<u>ull</u>
n<u>ull</u>
sk<u>ull</u>

-yll words
Only two common words.
chloroph<u>yll</u>
id<u>yll</u>

-l
Words are spelled with one final *l* if it is preceded by a consonant.

atlat<u>l</u>
(spear-thrower)
aw<u>l</u>
bow<u>l</u>
braw<u>l</u>
chur<u>l</u>
craw<u>l</u>
draw<u>l</u>
ear<u>l</u>
fow<u>l</u>
grow<u>l</u>
how<u>l</u>
hur<u>l</u>
ow<u>l</u>
pear<u>l</u>
prow<u>l</u>
scow<u>l</u>
shaw<u>l</u>
snar<u>l</u>
spraw<u>l</u>
swir<u>l</u>
traw<u>l</u>
twir<u>l</u>
viny<u>l</u>
whir<u>l</u>

Exceptions include words with the suffixes -*al* and -*ful*. See next page, 153.

/l/

Word Study: Suffix *-ful*
Use a Three-Tab Foldable to investigate the three meanings of the suffix -ful, and collect word examples for each meaning. Make a Triple VKV Flashcard for each of the three meanings. See Suffixes, page 279.

-**ful** is a suffix meaning *full of, characterized by*
Examples: beautiful, painful

-**ful** means *tending to, able to*
Examples: harmful, wakeful

-**ful** means *as much as will fill*
Examples: cupful, bowlful, spoonful

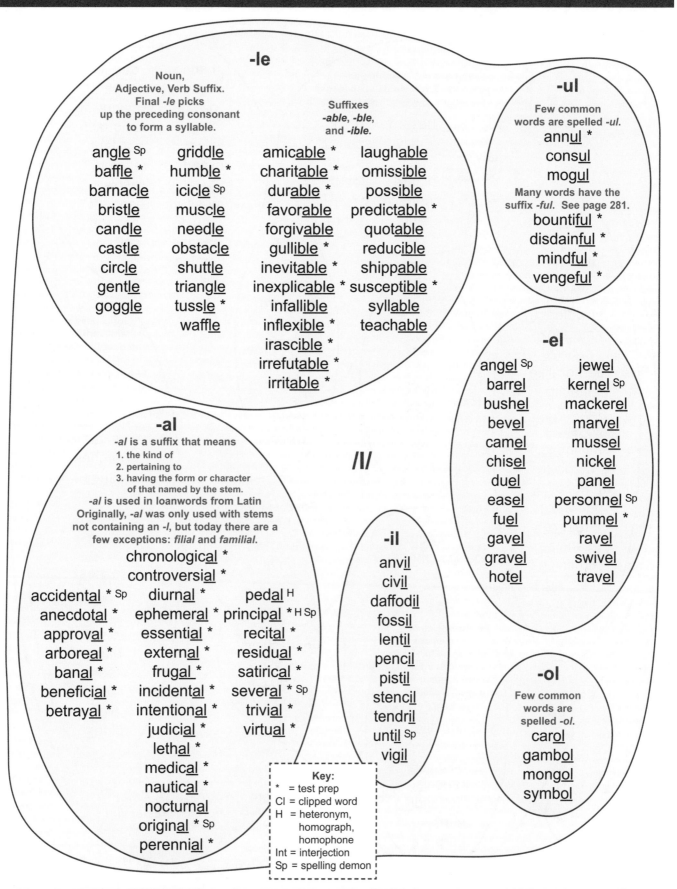

-le

Noun, Adjective, Verb Suffix. Final *-le* picks up the preceding consonant to form a syllable.

Suffixes *-able*, *-ble*, and *-ible*.

angle Sp	griddle
baffle *	humble *
barnacle	icicle Sp
bristle	muscle
candle	needle
castle	obstacle
circle	shuttle
gentle	triangle
goggle	tussle *
	waffle

amicable *	laughable
charitable *	omissible
durable *	possible
favorable	predictable *
forgivable	quotable
gullible *	reducible
inevitable *	shippable
inexplicable *	susceptible *
infallible	syllable
inflexible *	teachable
irascible *	
irrefutable *	
irritable *	

-ul

Few common words are spelled *-ul*.

annul *
consul
mogul

Many words have the suffix *-ful*. See page 281.

bountiful *
disdainful *
mindful *
vengeful *

-al

-al is a suffix that means
1. the kind of
2. pertaining to
3. having the form or character of that named by the stem.
-al is used in loanwords from Latin Originally, *-al* was only used with stems not containing an *-l*, but today there are a few exceptions: *filial* and *familial*.

chronological *
controversial *

accidental * Sp	diurnal *	pedal H
anecdotal *	ephemeral *	principal * H Sp
approval *	essential *	recital *
arboreal *	external *	residual *
banal *	frugal *	satirical *
beneficial *	incidental *	several * Sp
betrayal *	intentional *	trivial *
	judicial *	virtual *
	lethal *	
	medical *	
	nautical *	
	nocturnal	
	original * Sp	
	perennial *	

-el

angel Sp	jewel
barrel	kernel Sp
bushel	mackerel
bevel	marvel
camel	mussel
chisel	nickel
duel	panel
easel	personnel Sp
fuel	pummel *
gavel	ravel
gravel	swivel
hotel	travel

-il

anvil
civil
daffodil
fossil
lentil
pencil
pistil
stencil
tendril
until Sp
vigil

-ol

Few common words are spelled *-ol*.

carol
gambol
mongol
symbol

Key:
* = test prep
Cl = clipped word
H = heteronym, homograph, homophone
Int = interjection
Sp = spelling demon

/l/

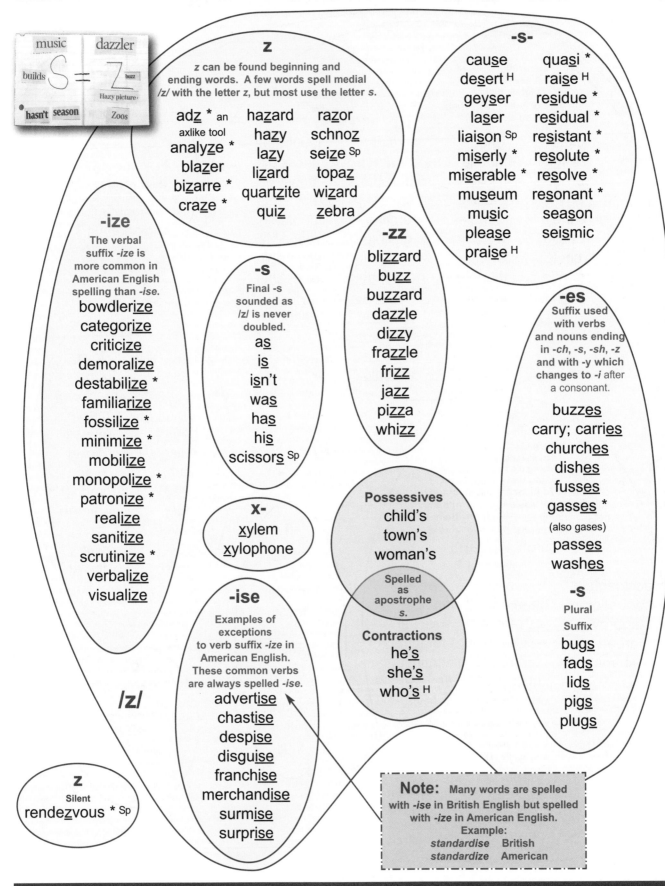

z

z can be found beginning and ending words. A few words spell medial /z/ with the letter z, but most use the letter s.

adz * an axlike tool
analyze *
blazer
bizarre *
craze *
hazard
hazy
lazy
lizard
quartzite
quiz
razor
schnoz
seize Sp
topaz
wizard
zebra

-s-

cause
desert H
geyser
laser
liaison Sp
miserly *
miserable *
museum
music
please
praise H
quasi *
raise H
residue *
residual *
resistant *
resolute *
resolve *
resonant *
season
seismic

-ize

The verbal suffix -ize is more common in American English spelling than -ise.

bowdlerize
categorize
criticize
demoralize
destabilize *
familiarize
fossilize *
minimize *
mobilize
monopolize *
patronize *
realize
sanitize
scrutinize *
verbalize
visualize

-s

Final -s sounded as /z/ is never doubled.

as
is
isn't
was
has
his
scissors Sp

-zz

blizzard
buzz
buzzard
dazzle
dizzy
frazzle
frizz
jazz
pizza
whizz

-es

Suffix used with verbs and nouns ending in -ch, -s, -sh, -z and with -y which changes to -i after a consonant.

buzzes
carry; carries
churches
dishes
fusses
gasses *
(also gases)
passes
washes

-s

Plural Suffix

bugs
fads
lids
pigs
plugs

X-

xylem
xylophone

Possessives

child's
town's
woman's

Spelled as apostrophe s.

Contractions

he's
she's
who's H

-ise

Examples of exceptions to verb suffix -ize in American English. These common verbs are always spelled -ise.

advertise
chastise
despise
disguise
franchise
merchandise
surmise
surprise

/z/

z

Silent

rendezvous * Sp

Note: Many words are spelled with -ise in British English but spelled with -ize in American English.
Example:
standardise British
standardize American

Consonants Spelling /s/

The letter *s* makes the /s/ sound after an unvoiced consonant; otherwise, /z/.

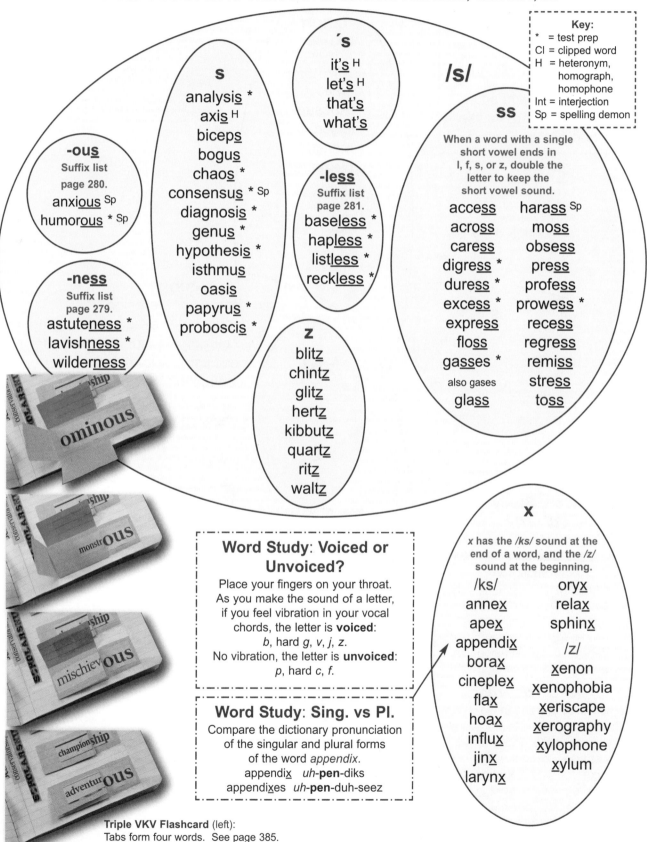

´s
it'<u>s</u> H
let'<u>s</u> H
that'<u>s</u>
what'<u>s</u>

s
analysi<u>s</u> *
axi<u>s</u> H
bicep<u>s</u>
bogu<u>s</u>
chao<u>s</u> *
consensu<u>s</u> * Sp
diagnosi<u>s</u> *
genu<u>s</u> *
hypothesi<u>s</u> *
isthmu<u>s</u>
oasi<u>s</u>
papyru<u>s</u> *
probosci<u>s</u> *

/s/

Key:
* = test prep
Cl = clipped word
H = heteronym, homograph, homophone
Int = interjection
Sp = spelling demon

ss
When a word with a single short vowel ends in l, f, s, or z, double the letter to keep the short vowel sound.

acce<u>ss</u>   hara<u>ss</u> Sp
acro<u>ss</u>   mo<u>ss</u>
care<u>ss</u>   obse<u>ss</u>
digre<u>ss</u> *   pre<u>ss</u>
dure<u>ss</u> *   profe<u>ss</u>
exce<u>ss</u> *   prowe<u>ss</u> *
expre<u>ss</u>   rece<u>ss</u>
flo<u>ss</u>   regre<u>ss</u>
ga<u>ss</u>es *   remi<u>ss</u>
also gases   stre<u>ss</u>
gla<u>ss</u>   to<u>ss</u>

-ous
Suffix list page 280.
anxi<u>ous</u> Sp
humor<u>ous</u> * Sp

-ness
Suffix list page 279.
astute<u>ness</u> *
lavish<u>ness</u> *
wilder<u>ness</u>

-less
Suffix list page 281.
base<u>less</u> *
hap<u>less</u> *
list<u>less</u> *
reck<u>less</u> *

z
blit<u>z</u>
chint<u>z</u>
glit<u>z</u>
hert<u>z</u>
kibbut<u>z</u>
quart<u>z</u>
rit<u>z</u>
walt<u>z</u>

x
x has the /ks/ sound at the end of a word, and the /z/ sound at the beginning.

/ks/   ory<u>x</u>
anne<u>x</u>   rela<u>x</u>
ape<u>x</u>   sphin<u>x</u>
appendi<u>x</u>
bora<u>x</u>   /z/
cineple<u>x</u>
fla<u>x</u>   <u>x</u>enon
hoa<u>x</u>   <u>x</u>enophobia
influ<u>x</u>   <u>x</u>eriscape
jin<u>x</u>   <u>x</u>erography
laryn<u>x</u>   <u>x</u>ylophone
     <u>x</u>ylum

Word Study: Voiced or Unvoiced?
Place your fingers on your throat. As you make the sound of a letter, if you feel vibration in your vocal chords, the letter is **voiced**: *b, hard g, v, j, z.*
No vibration, the letter is **unvoiced**: *p, hard c, f.*

Word Study: Sing. vs Pl.
Compare the dictionary pronunciation of the singular and plural forms of the word *appendix.*
appendi<u>x</u> *uh-**pen**-diks*
appendi<u>x</u>es *uh-**pen**-duh-seez*

Triple VKV Flashcard (left):
Tabs form four words. See page 385.

/zh/

A consonant sound created by allowing only a small amount of air to leave the mouth, often resulting in a hissing sound (unvoiced) or a buzzing sound (voiced).

Listen for the /zh/ sound at the beginning, middle, or end of these words.

Key:
* = test prep
Cl = clipped word
H = heteronym, homograph, homophone
Int = interjection
Sp = spelling demon

Only one common word begins with the /zh/ sound.
ge<u>n</u>re

/zher/

Spelled -sure.

clo<u>sure</u>
compo<u>sure</u>
expo<u>sure</u>
lei<u>sure</u> Sp
mea<u>sure</u>
plea<u>sure</u>
trea<u>sure</u>

Only two words spelled *-zure.*

a<u>zure</u>
sei<u>zure</u> Sp

-sion

abra<u>sion</u>   ero<u>sion</u>
adhe<u>sion</u>   eva<u>sion</u>   occa<u>sion</u> Sp
colli<u>sion</u>   excur<u>sion</u>   persua<u>sion</u>
conclu<u>sion</u>   expan<u>sion</u>   preci<u>sion</u>
confu<u>sion</u>   fu<u>sion</u>   seclu<u>sion</u>
corro<u>sion</u>   illu<u>sion</u>   televi<u>sion</u>
deci<u>sion</u>   inver<u>sion</u>   ver<u>sion</u>
delu<u>sion</u>   le<u>sion</u>   vi<u>sion</u>
divi<u>sion</u>

s

amne<u>s</u>ia   kinesthe<u>s</u>ia
anesthe<u>s</u>ia   u<u>s</u>ual
ca<u>s</u>ual   vi<u>s</u>ual
esthe<u>s</u>ia

/zh/

g

Many words that spell the /zh/ sound with the letter g are of French origin.

bei<u>g</u>e
camoufla<u>g</u>e
colla<u>g</u>e
corsa<u>g</u>e
entoura<u>g</u>e
espiona<u>g</u>e
gara<u>g</u>e
<u>g</u>enre
massa<u>g</u>e
mira<u>g</u>e
monta<u>g</u>e
presti<u>g</u>e
sabota<u>g</u>e

Word Study
/d/ : /zh/

Some verbs that end in *-de* change the *-de* to *-s* before adding the noun suffix *-ion*.

allu<u>de</u> /d/	allu•<u>sion</u> /zh/
corro<u>de</u> /d/	corro•<u>sion</u> /zh/
deci<u>de</u> /d/	deci•<u>sion</u> /zh/
divi<u>de</u> /d/	divi•<u>sion</u> /zh/
deri<u>de</u> /d/	deri•<u>sion</u> /zh/
eva<u>de</u> /d/	eva•<u>sion</u> /zh/

/s/ or /z/ : /zh/

Some words that end in *-se* change the /z/ or /s/ sound to /zh/ sound when the suffix *-ion* is added.

confu<u>se</u> /z/	confu•<u>sion</u> /zh/
fu<u>se</u> /z/	fu•<u>sion</u> /zh/
inver<u>se</u> /s/	inver•<u>sion</u> /zh/
preci<u>se</u> /s/	preci•<u>sion</u> /zh/

/uhs/

-us
abacus
alumnus
apatosaurus
bacillus
bonus
bronchus
bus
cactus
campus
census
chorus
circus
cirrus
colossus
consensus Sp
cumulus
discus
exodus
fetus
focus
fungus
genus
hiatus
hippopotamus
impetus
minus
nautilus
nucleus
radius
rhombus
sinus
stimulus
stratus
stylus
thymus
versus
virus
walrus

Both
mucus
noun
mucous
adjective

-ous
anonymous *
cantankerous *
circuitous *
credulous *
duplicitous *
fortuitous *
frivolous *
herbivorous *
humorous Sp
languorous *
ludicrous *
luminous *
malodorous *
meticulous *
mischievous Sp
numerous *
poisonous *
pompous *
preposterous *
querulous *
rancorous *
rapturous *
raucous *
ravenous *
ridiculous *
rigorous *
scrupulous *
venomous *
viscous *
vociferous *

/uhs/
spelled -ous

-ious
capricious *
conscientious * Sp
copious *
devious *
egregious *
fractious *
gregarious *
harmonious *
inharmonious *
luxurious *
mischievous Sp
noxious *
perfidious *
precocious *
pretentious *
pugnacious *
rapacious *
rebellious *
sagacious *
seditious *
surreptitious *
tedious *
tenacious *
unpretentious *
vivacious *
voracious *

-eous
erroneous *
heterogeneous *
igneous
miscellaneous *
outrageous * Sp
simultaneous *
spontaneous *

-uous
assiduous *
disingenuous *
impetuous *
incongruous *
sumptuous *
superfluous *
vacuous *

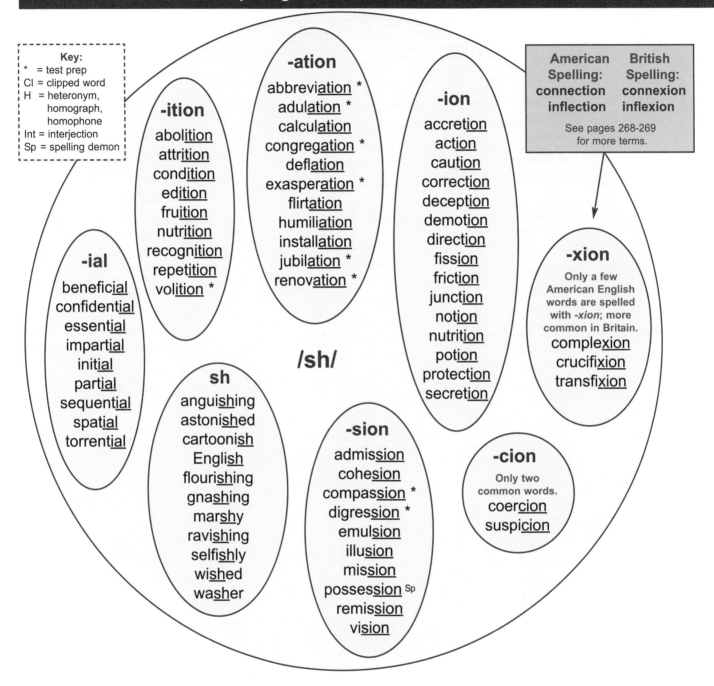

Key:
* = test prep
Cl = clipped word
H = heteronym, homograph, homophone
Int = interjection
Sp = spelling demon

/sh/

-ial
benefic**ial**
confident**ial**
essent**ial**
impart**ial**
init**ial**
part**ial**
sequent**ial**
spat**ial**
torrent**ial**

-ition
abol**ition**
attr**ition**
cond**ition**
ed**ition**
fru**ition**
nutr**ition**
recogn**ition**
repet**ition**
vol**ition** *

-ation
abbrevi**ation** *
adul**ation** *
calcul**ation**
congreg**ation** *
defl**ation**
exasper**ation** *
flirt**ation**
humili**ation**
install**ation**
jubil**ation** *
renov**ation** *

-ion
accre**tion**
ac**tion**
cau**tion**
correc**tion**
decep**tion**
demo**tion**
direc**tion**
fis**sion**
fric**tion**
junc**tion**
no**tion**
nutri**tion**
po**tion**
protec**tion**
secre**tion**

American Spelling: connection / inflection
British Spelling: connexion / inflexion
See pages 268-269 for more terms.

-xion
Only a few American English words are spelled with *-xion*; more common in Britain.
comple**xion**
crucifi**xion**
transfi**xion**

sh
angui**sh**ing
astoni**sh**ed
cartooni**sh**
Engli**sh**
flouri**sh**ing
gna**sh**ing
mar**sh**y
ravi**sh**ing
selfi**sh**ly
wi**sh**ed
wa**sh**er

-sion
admis**sion**
cohe**sion**
compas**sion** *
digres**sion** *
emul**sion**
illu**sion**
mis**sion**
posses**sion** Sp
remis**sion**
vi**sion**

-cion
Only two common words.
coer**cion**
suspi**cion**

ESL/ELL English Pronunciation Note: Suffixes like those featured on this page create a new word instead of forming a plural or verb tense. Often this type of suffix changes the stress placement within the new word. Frequently, the syllable to the left of the *-ion* syllable receives the stress. Students need to practice this enough to familiarize themselves with the pattern of stress placement.

Examples: cre•**a**•tion
ex•pe•**di**•tion
im•**pres**•sion
in•tu•**i**•tion
su•per•**vi**•sion
rep•u•**ta**•tion

/t/

-te
Silent e Rule
acu**te**
ammoni**te**
collabora**te** *
comple**te**
emula**te** *
inocula**te** Sp
invi**te**
ro**te** H
reci**te**
reple**te**
tribu**te**

-ed
Verb and Adjective Suffix
ach**ed**
bak**ed**
cross**ed**
dropp**ed**
look**ed**
stopp**ed**
talk**ed**
walk**ed**

-t
Final
acqui**t** Sp
alphabe**t**
allo**t**, a lo**t** Sp
baske**t**
biscui**t**
chario**t**
chea**t**
col**t**
erup**t**
inhabi**t**
misfi**t**
slee**t**
sui**t**
throa**t**

-t
Final -t After Silent Letters
deb**t**
playwrigh**t** Sp
receip**t** Sp
See page 263.

-ant, -ent
abs**ent**
clairvoy**ant** *
cons**ent**
dilig**ent** *
excell**ent** Sp
independ**ent** Sp
lat**ent**
nonchal**ant** *
opul**ent** *
relev**ant** Sp
torr**ent**

-tt
Not a Common Spelling for /t/
ba**tt**
boyco**tt**
bu**tt** H
mi**tt**
mu**tt**
pu**tt**
wa**tt**

-ed = /t/
See the next page, 160, for examples of other sounds made by the -ed spelling.
/d/
/id/
/jd/
/rd/

Key:
* = test prep
Cl = clipped word
H = heteronym, homograph, homophone
Int = interjection
Sp = spelling demon

Silent Final -t:
Usually found in words of French origin or direct loanwords.

balle**t**	debu**t**
beigne**t**	depo**t**
bere**t**	duve**t**
bouque**t**	fille**t**
buffe**t**	gourme**t**
cabare**t**	parfai**t**
cache**t** *	rappor**t**
chale**t**	sache**t**
croche**t** *	sorbe**t**
croque**t**	vale**t**

Multi-Tab Notebook Foldables Template (right):
See Dinah Zike's *Notebook Foldables* book and CD for templates, or have students make their own using a tabbed piece of paper glued into the notebook and cut to form multiple tabs. The *It's French to Me!* example has words typed on the front tabs of the template and a dictionary pronunciation guide written below each word. Copies were made, distributed to students, and glued into their notebooks. They defined the terms under the tabs and used them in sentences.

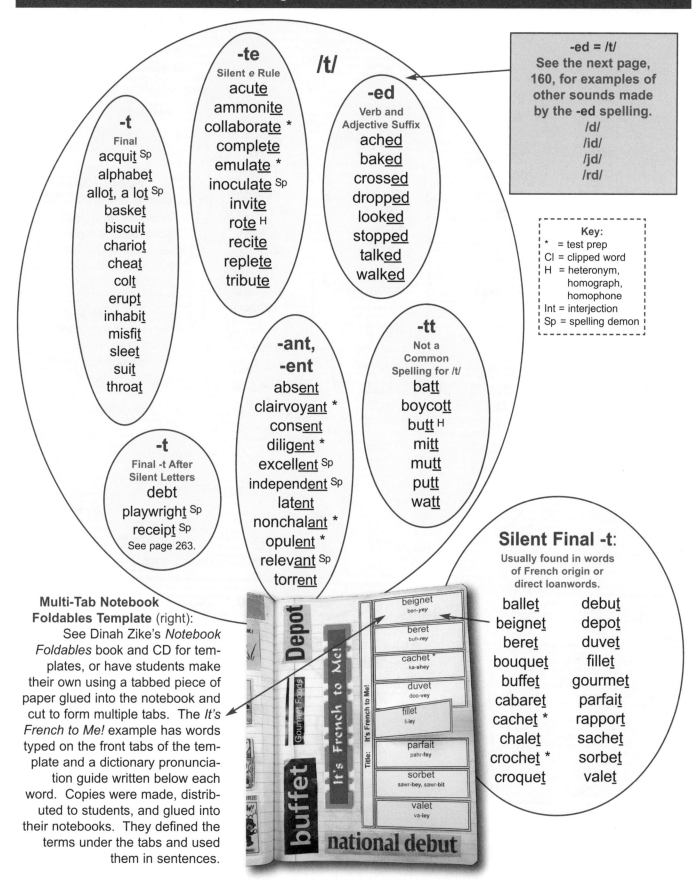

OBLITERATED.

refreshed

PREOWNED

revitalized

Title: Spelling -ed Endings

opinionated

-ed	-ed
Verbs	*Adjectives*
past tense	from Nouns
past participle	
failed, lied	**flawed mantras**

/d/
absolv**ed**
accus**ed**
aw**ed**
betray**ed**
happen**ed**
resum**ed**
ti**ed**

/rd/
acqui**red** Sp
bar**red**
ca**red**
desi**red**
fi**red**
flavo**red**
hi**red**
mi**red**
prepa**red**
occur**red** Sp
refer**red** Sp
sca**red**
sha**red**
ti**red**
wi**red**

/jd/
abrid**ged**
alle**ged**
arran**ged**
ca**ged**
chan**ged**
dama**ged**
enga**ged**
for**ged**
jud**ged**
mer**ged**
pled**ged**
privile**ged** Sp
sta**ged**

/id/
act**ed**
affect**ed**
benefit**ed** Sp
calculat**ed**
dott**ed**
fold**ed**
inflat**ed**
mut**ed**
reject**ed**
vault**ed**
want**ed**
wick**ed**
wilt**ed**

-ed

/t/
cook**ed**
hyp**ed**
lik**ed**
link**ed**
typ**ed**
wip**ed**
work**ed**
zipp**ed**

Two-Tab Notebook Foldables Template (above): See Dinah Zike's *Notebook Foldables* book for templates, or have students make their own using a tabbed piece of paper glued into the notebook and cut to form two tabs.

Key:
* = test prep
Cl = clipped word
H = heteronym, homograph, homophone
Int = interjection
Sp = spelling demon

provoked

British English
dreamt
leant
learnt
spelt

Common in Both:
burned
burnt
kneeled
knelt

American English
dreamed
leaned
learned
spelled

English: American vs. British
See pages 268-269 for more terms.

Word Study: The Suffix -ed

1. **Forms the past tense of regular verbs.**
   Examples: trek, trekk**ed**
   provoke, provok**ed**
   walk, walk**ed**

2. **Forms the past participle of regular verbs.**
   Examples: She had trekk**ed**...
   He had walk**ed** to...

3. **Forms adjectives from nouns.**
   Examples: hood, hood**ed**
   money, moni**ed**
   talent, talent**ed**
   wind, wind**ed**

Consonants y as /ē/ and /ī/

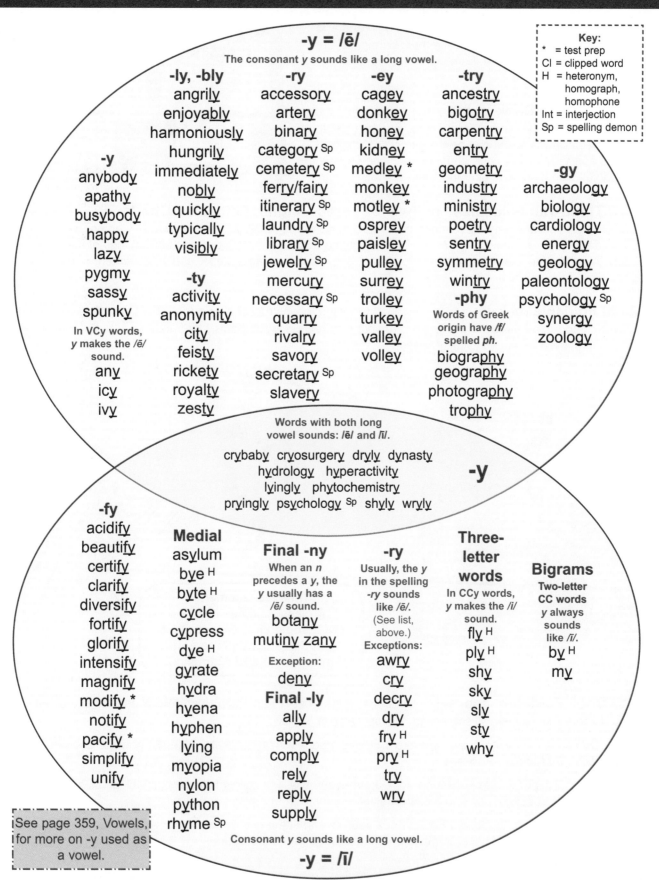

-y = /ē/
The consonant *y* sounds like a long vowel.

Key:
* = test prep
Cl = clipped word
H = heteronym, homograph, homophone
Int = interjection
Sp = spelling demon

-ly, -bly
angrily
enjoyably
harmoniously
hungrily
immediately
nobly
quickly
typically
visibly

-ty
activity
anonymity
city
feisty
rickety
royalty
zesty

-y
anybody
apathy
busybody
happy
lazy
pygmy
sassy
spunky

In VCy words, *y* makes the /ē/ sound.
any
icy
ivy

-ry
accessory
artery
binary
category Sp
cemetery Sp
ferry/fairy
itinerary Sp
laundry Sp
library Sp
jewelry Sp
mercury
necessary Sp
quarry
rivalry
savory
secretary Sp
slavery

-ey
cagey
donkey
honey
kidney
medley *
monkey
motley *
osprey
paisley
pulley
surrey
trolley
turkey
valley
volley

-try
ancestry
bigotry
carpentry
entry
geometry
industry
ministry
poetry
sentry
symmetry
wintry

-phy
Words of Greek origin have /f/ spelled *ph*.
biography
geography
photography
trophy

-gy
archaeology
biology
cardiology
energy
geology
paleontology
psychology Sp
synergy
zoology

Words with both long vowel sounds: /ē/ and /ī/.

crybaby cryosurgery dryly dynasty
hydrology hyperactivity
lyingly phytochemistry
pryingly psychology Sp shyly wryly

-y

-fy
acidify
beautify
certify
clarify
diversify
fortify
glorify
intensify
magnify
modify *
notify
pacify *
simplify
unify

Medial
asylum
bye H
byte H
cycle
cypress
dye H
gyrate
hydra
hyena
hyphen
lying
myopia
nylon
python
rhyme Sp

Final -ny
When an *n* precedes a *y*, the *y* usually has a /ē/ sound.
botany
mutiny zany

Exception:
deny

Final -ly
ally
apply
comply
rely
reply
supply

-ry
Usually, the *y* in the spelling *-ry* sounds like /ē/. (See list, above.)

Exceptions:
awry
cry
decry
dry
fry H
pry H
try
wry

Three-letter words
In CCy words, *y* makes the /ī/ sound.
fly H
ply H
shy
sky
sly
sty
why

Bigrams
Two-letter CC words *y* always sounds like /ī/.
by H
my

See page 359, Vowels, for more on -y used as a vowel.

Consonant *y* sounds like a long vowel.

-y = /ī/

Two-Pocket Foldable®: Find words that begin and end with consonant blends or digraphs, write them on eighth- or quarter-sheet papers, and store them in the appropriate pockets of a Foldable.

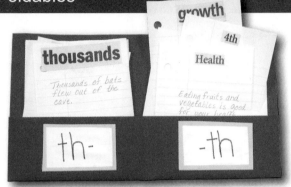

Foldable® Pocket Book (right): As pictured, when multiple Two-Pocket Foldables are glued together side by side, they form a Multi-Pocket Book that can be used to collect digraph word cards and VKVs. See page 28 for instructions on how to glue Foldables side by side to bind them into a book.

Two- or Three-Tab Foldables™ or Two- or Three-Column Foldable™ Charts: Make Foldables with two or three sections (tabs or columns) to feature three words beginning with the same blend or words that begin with three different blends—*gr, fr, pr*. Draw or glue a picture of each word on the front tabs of the Foldable. Write or glue examples of other words that begin with the same blend, and write sentences or a short paragraph using the words under the tabs.

Pyramid Foldable (below): Make a pyramid following the instructions on page 407. Use the three sides of the pyramid to record three things. In the example pictured below, students found examples of RWP for initial and medial /j/ spelled as *g*, and initial /j/ spelled *j*.

> **Time Management:**
> A class Foldable can be photocopied for each student. Students continue to add information and examples.

Bound Book Foldable® Journal: Use four sheets of paper to make a Bound Book Journal and use it to collect s clusters—sc, scr, sk, sl, sm, sn, sp, spl, spr, squ, st, str, sw.

Variation: Use seven sheets of paper to make a Foldable book with 14 pockets. Use the pockets to collect word cards and VKVs for the clusters listed.

Use two sheets of paper to make a Bound Book Journal and use it to collect l clusters—bl, cl, gl, pl, sl.
Variation: Use two sheets of paper to make a Foldable book with four pockets.

Use three sheets of paper to make a Bound Book Journal and use it to collect r clusters—br, cr, dr, fr, gr, pr, tr, wr.
Variation: Use four sheets of paper to make a Foldable book with eight pockets.

bl-
Initial Blend
blanch *
bleak *
blight *
blintze/blintz
bliss *
blizzard
bloc * H
blouse
bludgeon *
blunder
blunt *
bluster *

br-
Initial Blend
brash *
brave
brawn *
brazen *
breach *
brevity *
brigand *
brine *
brink *
bristle *
broach *
broccoli Sp
bronchitis
brusque *

ch-
Initial Digraph
chafe *
chandler *
changeable Sp
channel *
charade *
charge *
chariot
chastise *
chatter *
chauvinism *
chide *
chortle *
churlish *

ch-
Hard c Sound
chameleon *
chaos *
charisma *
chasm *
chronicle *
chronology *
chrysalis

cl-
Initial Blend
clandestine *
clarify *
class H
cleave *
clemency
clench *
cliche *
climactic *
climatic
clique *
cloister *
clone *
close H

cr-
Initial Blend
cranium *
crater
craze *
crease
creditable *
creditor *
credulous *
crescendo *
crescent
crest
crevice *
cringe *
criteria *
critique *
croissant *
crony *
crux *
cryptic *

dw-
Only four common words.
dwarf
dweeb (slang)
dwell *
dwindle *

dr-
Initial Blend
draconian *
dragoon *
drainage
drawl *
dredge
dregs *
drench
dresser
drinkable
drizzle
droll *
dromedary *
drone * H
dross *
drudgery *
drunkenness Sp

fl-
Initial Blend
flab
flaccid
flagella
flagrant *
flake
flawless
flaxen *
fledgling *
fleece *
fling
float
flora
floss
flotilla *
flotsam
flout *
fluency *
fluorescent Sp

fr-
Initial Blend
fracas *
fractious *
fragmentary *
frail *
franchise
frank *
frantic
fraternal *
fraud
fray * H
friction *
frivolous *
frugal *
fruitful *
fruition *
frustration *

gh-
Initial Digraph:
gh sounds like /g/.
Few common words.
ghastly *
ghee
gherkin
ghetto
ghost
ghostwriter
ghoul

gl-
Initial Blend
glassy
glaucoma *
glaze
gleam
glean *
glib *
glisten
gloat *
globular *
glove
glow
glower *
glut *
glutton

gr-
Initial Blend
gracious
grackle
gradient *
gradual
graduation
graffiti
graft *
grandiose *
grandparent
grandstand
grapple *
grateful Sp
gratuity *
gravity *
grease
gregarious *
grill * H
grimace *
grizzly *
grotesque *
groundwater
grovel *
grower

kr-
Initial Blend
Not common; usually spelled cr- in English.
krill
krypton

-lm
Final Blend
balm
calm
elm
film
helm
overwhelm
palm
psalm
qualm
realm
whelm

-nc(e)
Final sound;
-ance and -ence words are common; also see -nse list below.
chance
dance
fence
glance
lance
mince
occurrence Sp
perseverance Sp
prance
presence Sp
since
trance

-nch
Final Blend
bench
bunch
cinch
clench
drench
finch
flinch
hunch
inch
lunch
munch
pinch
stench
trench
wrench

-ns(e)
-nse spelling is not common for this sound. See -nc(e) list, above.
defense
dense
expense
immense
intense
license Sp
offense
tense

ph-
Initial Digraph *ph* sounds like /f/. Usually words of Greek origin.

phantom
pharmacy
pharynx
phase
pheasant
phenomenon *
philosophy
phlegm
phlegmatic *
phobic *
phone
phonetic *
phony
phosphorous
photocopy
photogenic *
photon
photosphere
photosynthesis *
phrase
phraseology *
phylum
physical
physician
physics
physiology
physique
phytoplankton

pl-
Initial Digraph

placard *
placate *
placid *
plagiarism *
plague
plaintiff *
planetary
plasma
plateau Sp
platinum
platitude *
platonic *
platoon
plausible *
plesiosaur
pliable *
plumb * H
plume
plunder
plurality *

pr-
Initial Blend

pragmatic *
prairie Sp
prawn
precede Sp
precedent * Sp
precious
precipitation *
predator
presence Sp
pressure
pretzel
price
primal *
principal Sp
principle Sp
printable
pristine *
privilege Sp
prize
pronunciation Sp

qu-
Initial Digraph

quadrangle
quadrant
quadrilateral
quadrillion
quadruped
quaff
quagmire
quaint
quake
qualify
quality
quantity
quarrel
quarter
quartet
quartile
quartz
queasy
queen
quench
questionnaire Sp
queue Sp (Note different *qu-* sound.)
quintet
quiver H
quota
quote
quotient

qu-
Medial Blend

acquaint
acquire Sp
acquit Sp
banquet
bequest
conquest
earthquake
equality
equilateral
equipment Sp
inquire
inquisition
requisition
tranquil

sc-
Initial Blend, hard sound.

scaffold
scald
scale H
scalene
scallion
scallop
scalp
scalpel
scar
scarab
scarcity *
scarlet
scathing *
scatology *
scatter
scavenger
scoff *
sconce
scone
scope
scornful *
scout
scowl
scuba
scuff
sculpt
scum

sc-
Initial Blend, /s/ sound; few common words.

scene H
scent H
science
scissel
scissors Sp

sc- /sh/
A few words spell /sh/ as *sc* after *con-*.

conscience Sp
conscientious Sp
conscionable
conscious Sp

sh-
Digraph, also commonly spelled -*ti*- as in -*tion* or -*ci*- as in -*cion* in a medial or final spelling.

shackle *
shadow
shah
shake H
shale
shallow
shaman
shambles *
shanty
shear * H
sheer * H
sheik Sp H
shepherd Sp
shrewd *
shun *

sh-
In a few words, *c*, *s*, and *x* can sound like *sh*.

anxious Sp
noxious
obnoxious
ocean
sugar

sk-
Initial Blend

skate *
skeletal
skeptical *
sketched
sketchy
skewer
skid
skiff *
skiing Sp
skillful Sp
skimp
skink
skirmish *
skittish *

sl-
Initial Blend
slack
slag
slake *
slander *
slant
slash
slate H
slavery
slew H
slight * H
slime
slink
slither
slogan
sloth * H
slovenly *
sludge
sluggish *
sly

sm-
Initial Blend
smack
smallpox
smarmy *
smash
smatter
smear
smelt
smidgen
(smidgin,
smidgeon)
smirk
smite
smog
smoke
smudge
smug
smuggle

sn-
Initial Blend
snafu *
snare H
snarl
snatch
snazzy
sneer
sneeze
snicker
snide
snit *
snitch
snobbery
snub
snuff
snug

sp-
Initial Blend
spa
spacious *
spam
span
sparkle
spate *
spawn *
specialize
species *
specimen
spectacle *
spectrum
speculate *
spelunk
spent
spew *
spice
splinter
spontaneous *
spoof *
sporadic *
spurious *
spurn *
spurtle *
spy

st-
Initial Blend
stagnate *
stamen
static * H
stationary * Sp H
stationery Sp H
statue
steppe Sp
stereotype *
sterile *
stigma *
stimulus
stint *
stoic *
stolid *
stout *

sw-
Initial Blend
swab
swaddling
swagger *
swallow
swam
swamp
swan
swanky
swap
swarm
swashbuckle
swatch
sway
sweat
sweep *
sweetbreads
swell
swelter *
swerve
swill
swindle *
switch
swivel *
swoon *
sword
swung

th-
Digraph; voiceless as in thin.
thank
thatch
thaw
theater
theme
theocracy
theory
thermostat
thick
thin
thing
think
third
thirty
thorax
thorough Sp
thought
thousand
threshold Sp
thumb
thwart

th-
Digraph; voiced as in that.
than
that
their H
them
then
there H
therefore
these
they
they're H
this
thou
though
thus

tr-
Initial Blend
traction
traitor
traits
transient *
translucent
transparent
transportation
trapezoid
travesty *
treachery *
treasury
trespass *
triad
tributary
trillion
triple
trite *
triumph
trivial *
trooper *
tropical
truculent *
truly Sp
truncate *

tw-
Initial Blend
tweed
tweezers
twelfth Sp
twilight *
twill
twine
twinge
twister
twitch

wh-
Digraph /hw/
whale
wham
wharp
wheedle *
wheeze
whelk
whelp *
whence
wherever Sp
whet *
whether
whicker
whim *
whimper
whimsical *
whinny
whisk
whisper
whiten
whittle *

wh-
Digraph /h/
who
wholesome
whoop H
whooping cough
whooping crane

wr-
/r/ Sound

wrangler
wrath *
wreath
wreckage
wren
wrench
wrest * H
wrestle
wretched
wring H
wrinkle
wrist
writhe *
wrong
wrought *
wry H

sch-
Initial Blend:
Hard Sound /sk/.

schedule Sp
schema
schematic *
scheme
schism * (also pronounced siz•uhm)
schizoid
schizophrenia
scholar
scholarship
scholastic
school

Soft Sound /sh/:
schist
schlep
schnapps
schwa

scr-
Initial Blend

scram
scrape
scratch
scrawl
scream
screech
screen
screw
scribble
scribe
scrimmage
scrimp
script
scroll
scrub
scrupulous *
scrutinize *

shr-
Initial Blend

shrank
shred
shrew *
shrewd *
shriek
shrill
shrimp
shrine *
shrink
shrivel
shroud
shrub
shrubbery
shrug
shrunk
shrunken

sph-
Initial Blend

sphagnum
sphere
sphincter
sphinx

spl-
Initial Blend

splash
splay
spleen
splendid
splendor
splice
splint
splinter *
splurge

spr-
Initial Blend

sprain
sprawl
spray H
spread
spree
sprig
sprinkler
sprint
sprite
spritz
sprout
spruce
spry

Multi-Layered (above) **and Multi-Tabbed Foldables** (right): Use to focus attention on either the initial or final spelling of words beginning and/or ending in blends and digraphs.

squ-
Initial Blend
- squabble
- squadron
- squalid *
- squall *
- squander *
- square
- squash H
- squatter
- squaw
- squeamish *
- squeeze
- squelch
- squid
- squire
- squirmy
- squirrel
- squish

str-
Initial Blend
- straddle
- straggle
- straight H
- strait H
- strangle
- strategic *
- strategy *
- stratosphere
- stratus
- straw
- strawberry
- strenuous
- stress
- strident *
- strife *
- structure
- struggle

thr-
Initial Blend
- thrash
- thread
- three
- threshold * Sp
- threw H
- thrice
- thrifty
- thrill
- thrive *
- throat
- throb
- throne H
- throng *
- throttle *
- through H
- throughout
- thrown H
- thrush
- thrust

Foldables (right): Two-column chart used to collect words and photographs of signs with words that feature triple letter consonant blends.

Below: Layered Foldable made using seven sheets of paper.

Folded Book Spelling Practice (below): Use one sheet of paper to make a four-section Foldable and use it to collect examples of words that begin with four blends or digraphs.

Writing Extension: On the back of the Foldable, have students write a paragraph that uses a given number of words from their Foldable.

Think-Fast Extension: As a fun class activity, randomly select a word from the Foldable and have a student use it orally in a sentence within five seconds of being given the word. To heighten suspense, quietly count to five or signal five seconds by moving your fingers while the student is thinking of a sentence.

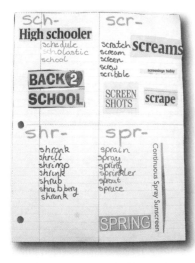

Same Word, But Different:
When using RWP (real world print), ESL/ELL students are encouraged to find the same word written in different fonts and in uppercase and lowercase letters. For example, the word *spring* was found in all capital letters and also in lowercase letters with a capital *S*. Students seem to relate to a word faster and remember it longer and if they can view it and use it in different ways. See page 32 of the Introduction.

Contractions VKVs®

Slang contractions like those pictured on some of the flashcards below are common in advertisements and headlines. See a list on page 170.

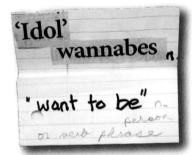

Students write or glue a slang contraction on the front of a Double Flashcard. Cut the top card to indicate the number of words represented, and write the words under the tabs.

Glue or write a contraction on the inside top of the Triple Flashcard. Write the meaning on the lower tab as illustrated; and with all tabs open, write sentences using the contractions to the inside.

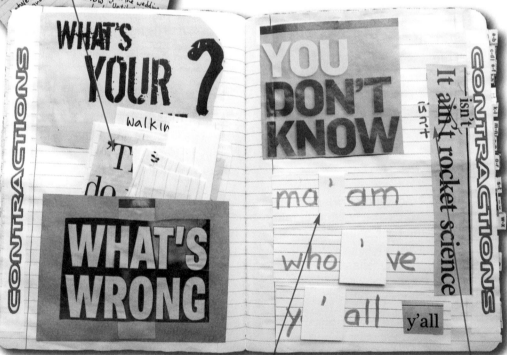

Colloquial contractions and terms like *ma'am* are frequently seen in literature, movies, and plays. In the southern U.S., *ma'am* is used to address a respected woman. In Britain, *ma'am* is used to address the queen. It can be fun to collect examples of these terms and relate them to the region of their origin.

Word Study: History
Even though *ain't* is nonstandard, it is sometimes used to mean
either,
am not,
are not, or
is not.
It was originally used during 1770-1780 as a variation of *amn't* (am not), which was usually pronounced the same as *ant*.

  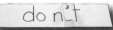

1. Write two words that form a contraction under the tab of a Double VKV Flashcard.

2. With the card open, draw lines to indicate which letters will be omitted. Above, draw width of the *o*.

3. Cut the top strip away to expose the letters that will remain in the contraction. Keep the section above the *o*.

4. Fold the tab down to cover letter/letters that will not remain in the contraction, and draw an apostrophe on top of the tab.

Contractions are frequently used in headlines and advertisements. Cut them out and glue them into a notebook to form tabs. Students use the word featured on the top—either as a contraction or two separate words—in sentences under the tab.

Word Study: Contractions can be Homophones

he'd	heed
he'll	heal, heel
I'll	aisle, isle
they're	their, there
we'd	weed
we've	weave
who's	whose
y'all	yawl
you'll	yule
you're	your

Two Two-Tab notebook Foldables were used to collect contractions formed by *have*, *not*, *would*, and *will*. Students find examples of words in RWP, or write words that they are familiar with, and then use them in sentences under the tabs.

VKV (right): Write terms along the left side of a quarter-sheet flashcard. Make cuts along the right side between the words so tabs can be folded over to cover the part of the word omitted to form a contraction.

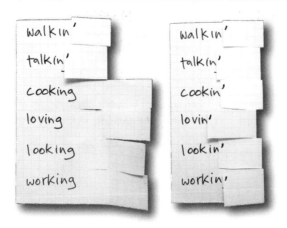

Slang Contractions

ain't	is not, am not, are not sometimes a double negative
'em	them
gonna	going to
gimme	give me
-in'	-ing workin'/working
ma'am	madam
o'	of
o'clock	of the clock
she'd've	she would have
'til	till, until
'twas	it was
'tweens	betweens between child and teen (age)
wanna	want to
y'all	you all

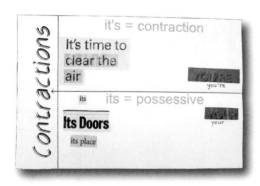

Left: Use a Foldable Chart to compare contractions and possessive pronouns. *Note that possessive pronouns are never spelled with apostrophes.*

Poss. Pronoun	Contraction
its	it's
their	they're
whose	who's
your	you're

Become a Word Collector (below right):
Ask students and parents to find and collect contractions they encounter in RWP. Store the words until needed. (See storage ideas, pages 28 and 30.) When you are ready to use the words, carefully place them onto a piece of posterboard to make access and selection easier. Remind students that it is important to keep the words turned so that the RWP side (in this example, contractions) is easily read and identified. Remind parents and students who collect RWP to always arrange and store the cut words so that they face upwards and can be read.

Foldable® Contractions Table (left):
This folded table can be made out of butcher paper and used to illustrate how word pairs are written as contractions. Encourage students to collect examples of contractions they encounter in RWP and glue them onto the table. See page 415.

Contractions

Contractions

Not

are not	aren't
cannot	can't [H]
can not	can't [H]
could not	couldn't
did not	didn't
do not	don't
does not	doesn't
had not	hadn't
has not	hasn't
have not	haven't
is not	isn't
might not	mightn't
must not	mustn't
need not	needn't
should not	shouldn't
was not	wasn't
were not	weren't
will not	won't
would not	wouldn't

Be

I am	I'm
you are	you're [H]
he is	he's
she is	she's
it is	it's [H]
we are	we're
they are	they're [H]

Have

I have	I've
you have	you've
we have	we've [H]
they have	they've
could have	could've
might have	might've
should have	should've
there have	there've
who have	who've
would have	would've

Would

I would	I'd
you would	you'd
he would	he'd [H]
she would	she'd
it would	it'd
we would	we'd [H]
they would	they'd
that would	that'd
there would	there'd
what would	what'd
who would	who'd

Will

I will	I'll [H]
you will	you'll [H]
he will	he'll [H]
she will	she'll
it will	it'll
we will	we'll
they will	they'll
who will	who'll

Other Contractions

I had	I'd
I would	I'd
he had	he'd [H]
he would	he'd [H]
he has	he's
let us	let's [H]
she has	she's
there is	there's
that is	that's
that has	that's
what is	what's
what has	what's
where is	where's
where has	where's
who is	who's [H]
who has	who's [H]

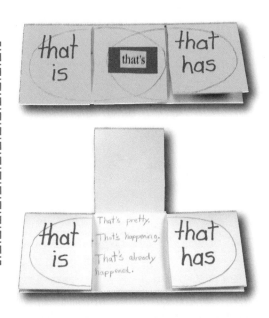

Word Study: Venn Diagram

Make a Venn Diagram Foldable for contractions that are written the same but have different meanings:

that's: that is and that has
who's: who is and who has
where's: where is and where has
what's: what is and what has
I'd: I had and I would
he'd: he had and he would.

Contronyms

Contronyms are words that can be their own antonyms. They present a contradiction either in terms or ideas (*antilogy*). The term *contronyms* was first coined by Richard Lederer in <u>Crazy English</u> (Pocket Books, 1989). They are also called *antagonyms*, *autoantonyms*, *contranyms*, and *enantiodromes*. Contronyms are homographs that have the same spelling and pronunciation, but opposite, or contradictory, meanings.

Word Study: Homophone Contronyms

Have students design Foldables or VKVs featuring contronyms. Review homophones, page 189, and make some of the activities based upon homophone contronyms.

aural:	heard
oral:	spoken
erupt:	to burst out
irrupt:	to burst in
petalless:	lacking petals
petalous:	having petals
raise:	to grow or erect
raze:	to tear down

Single VKV Flashcards (left):
Dollop = small amount
I'll have just a dollop of sour cream.
Dollop = large amount
Dollop the sour cream over the entire potato.
See Antonyms, page 76.
See VKV instructions, page 376.

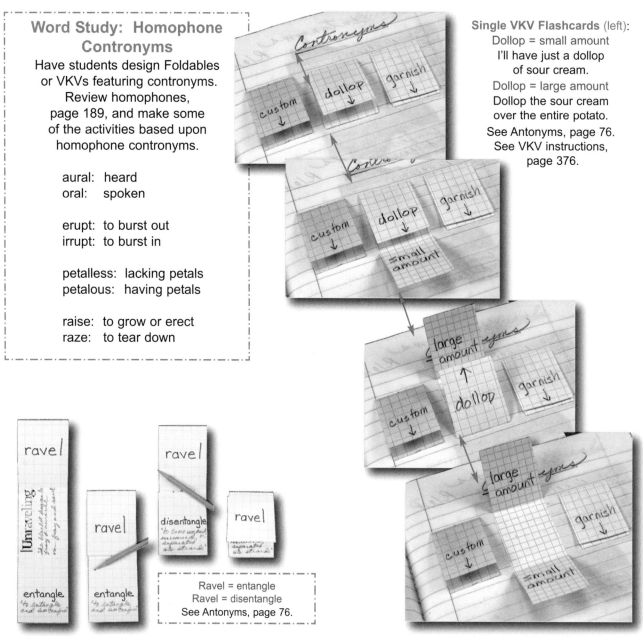

Ravel = entangle
Ravel = disentangle
See Antonyms, page 76.

Contronym Phrases:

all downhill from here   easier going, now that this point has been reached
vs. going to get worse or more difficult now that this point has been reached
tell me about it   asking for information from someone
vs. "I already know something (or a lot) about what you are talking about."

Contronyms

Contronyms

apology: expression of regret, fault
apology: defense or justification

aught: anything, any part
aught: zero, nothing

bolt: to fasten, secure
bolt: to escape

bound: moving toward
bound: unable to move

cleave: to adhere
cleave: to split

clip: to cut something
clip: a device that grips or holds tightly

consult: to seek advice or help
consult: to give advice; be a consultant

custom: usual or conventional practice
custom: created specially

deposition: removal from office or position
deposition: the process of depositing

dollop: a large lump or portion
dollop: small quantity

dust: to cover with fine particles
dust: to remove dust particles

fast: moving quickly
fast: unmoving (held fast)

garnish: to add to, adorn
garnish: to hold or take away (garnish wages)

give out: to tire, be unable to continue
give out: to distribute

grade: a slope
grade: to cut down (grade a road)

handicap: an advantage
handicap: a challenge, disadvantage

left: remaining (left over)
left: went away

overlook: to look over
overlook: to fail to see, ignore

patronize: to support
patronize: to act condescendingly toward

peer: a person of nobility
peer: an equal

ravel: to disentangle
ravel: to entangle

rent: pay for use of (I rent an apartment.)
rent: sell use of (The landlord rents an apartment to me.)

scan: to examine closely, scrutinize
scan: to review or look over quickly

screen: to show or view
screen: to hide from view

seed: to remove seeds from a fruit
seed: to scatter seeds, plant
        to seed a cloud (sow particles to induce precipitation)

stain: to color on purpose
stain: to discolor

variety: one of a type (this variety); a category within
          a species
variety: many types, a diverseness

vital: lively
vital: deadly (a vital wound)

weather: to break down
weather: to withstand

wind up: start (wind up the toy)
wind up: end (wind up at the finish line)

Double Letters Geminating

Many spelling mistakes are made over whether a word is spelled with a double or a single consonant. Some words have two or more sets of double letters, as in *co**mm**i**tt**ee*. Other words have only one set of double letters but are frequently misspelled with two. *Necessary* and *recommend* are words that are sometimes misspelled by doubling the *c*. Review the lists on pages 176 to 179 and observe how some rules apply to doubling letters.

Some compound words have double letters. See the list on page 121.

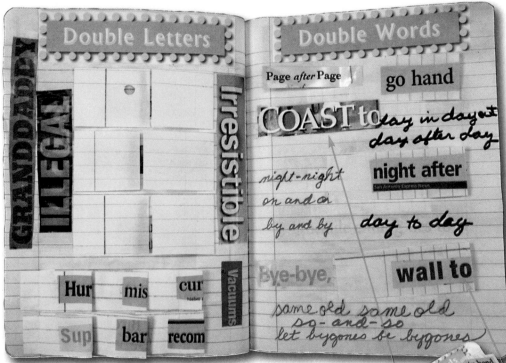

Hinged VKVs

Left and Above: Fold a Single Flashcard in half. Glue or write a word with double letters in the middle of the flashcard so that the double letters are on either side of the fold line. Fold equal-sized, wing-like tabs on the two ends of the flashcard and glue the "wings" into a notebook as pictured left. Students read the words as they flip the tabs. Since doubling occurs when the consonant at the end of one syllable is the same as the consonant at the beginning of another, this VKV is used to separate consonants. See page 369.

NOTE: Many two-syllable nouns, adjectives, and adverbs are stressed on the first syllable, and most two-syllable verbs on the second. The activity to the left is perfect for illustrating this.

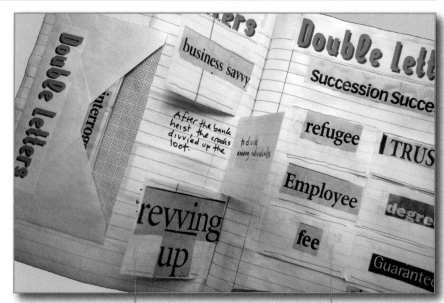

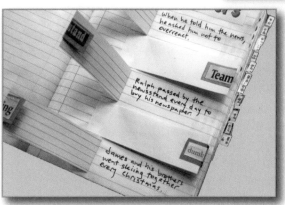

Compound Words with Double Letters
(above): There is a limited number of double-letter compound words. See the list on page 121. A compound word with double letters was glued (or written) on the right side of a Single Flashcard, then folded back to expose only half of the word at a time. When the Flashcard is open, the entire word is visible.

Doubling to Protect a Short Vowel:
Doubling most commonly occurs to ensure that a vowel is kept short. For example, the *ss* in *unnecessary* ensures that the second *e* has a short *e* sound. As usual, there are many exceptions. The word *dissect* can be pronounced with a long *i* sound (and also a short *i* sound), and the related word *bisect* has only one *s*. Also, doubling would seem necessary to keep the *o* short in *proper*, but it is spelled without doubling and has a short *o* anyway.

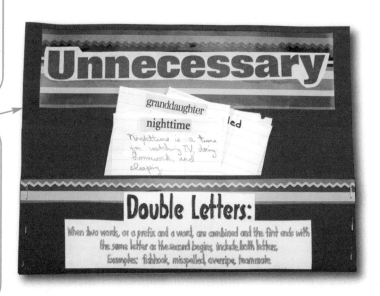

Double Letters Geminating

To *geminate* means to double or pair something or to become doubled or paired. Look at the double-letter words on this page. English words do not double the consonants j, k, v, w, and x.

Also see double letters with *Syllables*, page 310.
Also see double letters when forming *Compound Words*, page 121.
Also see double letters throughout the *Vowel* pages, 334 to 366.

aa

Only doubled in adopted words or in words that spell sounds.

<u>aa</u>, a'a Hawaiian lava

<u>aa</u>h Int oohed and

aahed

<u>aa</u>rdvark

<u>aa</u>rgh Int

Just for fun!

A<u>aa</u>donta genus of slugs

Digraph -ee

See *Vowels*: /ē/, page 347.

b<u>ee</u>tle

command<u>ee</u>r *

d<u>ee</u>m *

discr<u>ee</u>t *

<u>ee</u>l

exc<u>ee</u>d Sp

filigr<u>ee</u>

fores<u>ee</u> *

guarant<u>ee</u> Sp

h<u>ee</u>d *

lev<u>ee</u> *

pedigr<u>ee</u> *

p<u>ee</u>r * H

p<u>ee</u>rless *

s<u>ee</u>the *

sp<u>ee</u>ch

squ<u>ee</u>gee

st<u>ee</u>p *

t<u>ee</u>m * H

w<u>ee</u>vil

wh<u>ee</u>dle *

wildeb<u>ee</u>st

-ii

In Latin, *-ii* forms the plural of *-us* words.

gen<u>ii</u> pl. of *genius*; L

rad<u>ii</u> pl. of *radius*; L

Only two common words.

Digraph

-oo-

Long Sound
See page 357.

al<u>oo</u>f *

bamb<u>oo</u>zle

baz<u>oo</u>ka

beh<u>oo</u>ve *

cab<u>oo</u>se

cr<u>oo</u>n *

g<u>oo</u>se

igl<u>oo</u>

lamp<u>oo</u>n *

l<u>oo</u>se Sp

m<u>oo</u>t *

<u>oo</u>dles

pr<u>oo</u>f *

repr<u>oo</u>f *

sh<u>oo</u>t H

sp<u>oo</u>f *

sp<u>oo</u>n

t<u>oo</u>th

Digraph

-oo-

Short Sound
See page 358.

b<u>oo</u>k

br<u>oo</u>k *

l<u>oo</u>k

n<u>oo</u>k

sh<u>oo</u>k

t<u>oo</u>k

Long /oo/

b<u>oo</u>r *

b<u>oo</u>rish *

<u>oo</u>h Int

-uu

Only three common words:

contin<u>uu</u>m

m<u>uu</u>m<u>uu</u>

vac<u>uu</u>m Sp

-bb

a<u>bb</u>ey

a<u>bb</u>reviate *

ba<u>bb</u>le

blu<u>bb</u>er

bu<u>bb</u>le

co<u>bb</u>ler

dri<u>bb</u>le

e<u>bb</u>

go<u>bb</u>ler

ho<u>bb</u>y

lo<u>bb</u>yist *

pe<u>bb</u>le

qui<u>bb</u>le *

ra<u>bb</u>i

ru<u>bb</u>ish

sca<u>bb</u>ard *

scri<u>bb</u>le

stu<u>bb</u>orn

-cc

a<u>cc</u>elerate

a<u>cc</u>ent

a<u>cc</u>eptable Sp

a<u>cc</u>identally Sp

a<u>cc</u>ommodate Sp

e<u>cc</u>entric *

fla<u>cc</u>id *

hi<u>cc</u>up

impe<u>cc</u>able

mo<u>cc</u>asin Sp

o<u>cc</u>luded *

o<u>cc</u>urrence Sp

pe<u>cc</u>ary

preo<u>cc</u>upation *

ra<u>cc</u>oon

sa<u>cc</u>harin *

su<u>cc</u>essive *

su<u>cc</u>inct *

su<u>cc</u>or *

su<u>cc</u>umb *

-dd

a<u>dd</u>end

befu<u>dd</u>le

bla<u>dd</u>er

bu<u>dd</u>ing

co<u>dd</u>le *

cu<u>dd</u>le

e<u>dd</u>y *

embe<u>dd</u>ed

fa<u>dd</u>ish *

fi<u>dd</u>le

forbi<u>dd</u>ing

gi<u>dd</u>y

go<u>dd</u>ess

gri<u>dd</u>le

la<u>dd</u>er

ma<u>dd</u>en

mu<u>dd</u>le *

o<u>dd</u>

sa<u>dd</u>en

sa<u>dd</u>le

sho<u>dd</u>y *

sle<u>dd</u>ing

tro<u>dd</u>en

we<u>dd</u>ing

-ff

Often doubled at the end of a word, as in *doff*.
Exceptions: *clef, if.*

ba<u>ff</u>le *

cha<u>ff</u> *

di<u>ff</u>erence

di<u>ff</u>use *

do<u>ff</u> *

cont. next column

-ff (cont.)

e<u>ff</u>igy *

e<u>ff</u>usive *

ga<u>ff</u>e *

gira<u>ff</u>e

gu<u>ff</u>aw *

midri<u>ff</u> *

plainti<u>ff</u> *

ponti<u>ff</u> *

qua<u>ff</u> *

rebu<u>ff</u> *

sco<u>ff</u> *

ski<u>ff</u> *

su<u>ff</u>icient *

wa<u>ff</u>le *

-gg

a<u>gg</u>ravate

a<u>gg</u>regate

a<u>gg</u>ressive

ba<u>gg</u>age

be<u>gg</u>ar

bra<u>gg</u>art

bu<u>gg</u>y

chi<u>gg</u>er

da<u>gg</u>er

gi<u>gg</u>le

ha<u>gg</u>le

ja<u>gg</u>ed

lu<u>gg</u>age

ma<u>gg</u>ot

skuldu<u>gg</u>ery

smu<u>gg</u>le

ve<u>gg</u>ie

zi<u>gg</u>urat

-hh

beac<u>hh</u>ead

fis<u>hh</u>ook

hig<u>hh</u>anded

hitc<u>hh</u>iked

roug<u>hh</u>ouse

sleut<u>hh</u>ound

wit<u>hh</u>eld Sp

wit<u>hh</u>old Sp

wit<u>hh</u>oldment

-jj

Only doubled in adopted words.

ha<u>jj</u> pilgrimage; hadj=Western spelling

-kk

boo<u>kk</u>eeper Sp

jac<u>kk</u>nifed

knic<u>kk</u>nack

tre<u>kk</u>ed

176   Dinah Zike's *Foldables*, *Notebook Foldables* and *VKVs* for Spelling and Vocabulary

Double Letters Geminating

When a single short-vowel word ends in *f*, *l*, *s*, or *z*, the final consonant is doubled to retain the short vowel sound.   Examples: mi<u>ff</u>, te<u>ll</u>, hi<u>ss</u>, ja<u>zz</u>.

-ll
Doubled at the end of a word with a stressed syllable: *foretell*. Exception: *until*.

a<u>ll</u>ude *
a<u>ll</u>ure *
be<u>ll</u>icose *
be<u>ll</u>igerent *
ca<u>ll</u>ow *
co<u>ll</u>age *
co<u>ll</u>ate *
co<u>ll</u>ection *
co<u>ll</u>oquial *
co<u>ll</u>usion *
cu<u>ll</u> *
da<u>ll</u>y *
de<u>ll</u> *
e<u>ll</u>ipsis *
fa<u>ll</u>acy *
fa<u>ll</u>ow *
forete<u>ll</u>
ga<u>ll</u> *
ga<u>ll</u>eon *
gri<u>ll</u> *
gu<u>ll</u>ible *
ha<u>ll</u>ow *
idy<u>ll</u>ic *
jo<u>ll</u>ity *
<u>ll</u>ama
<u>ll</u>ano
L<u>l</u>oyd
lo<u>ll</u> *
mo<u>ll</u>ify *
osci<u>ll</u>ate
pa<u>ll</u>id *
que<u>ll</u> *
reca<u>ll</u>

-mm
a<u>cc</u>o<u>mm</u>odate Sp
co<u>mm</u>a
co<u>mm</u>ercial
co<u>mm</u>itted Sp
co<u>mm</u>ittee
dile<u>mm</u>a
gi<u>mm</u>ick
gli<u>mm</u>er
gra<u>mm</u>ar
ha<u>mm</u>ock
hu<u>mm</u>us
i<u>mm</u>aculate *
i<u>mm</u>ature
i<u>mm</u>ediate Sp
i<u>mm</u>inent *
ma<u>mm</u>al
pu<u>mm</u>el *
reco<u>mm</u>end Sp
sy<u>mm</u>etry *

-nn
Only one common noun spelled with -nn at the end of the word: *inn*.

a<u>nn</u>ex
a<u>nn</u>iversary Sp
a<u>nn</u>ual
ca<u>nn</u>ibal
ca<u>nn</u>on
ci<u>nn</u>amon
co<u>nn</u>iving *
fla<u>nn</u>el
i<u>nn</u> H
i<u>nn</u>ate *
i<u>nn</u>ing
i<u>nn</u>ocuous *
legio<u>nn</u>aire
ma<u>nn</u>er
mille<u>nn</u>ium Sp
pere<u>nn</u>ial *
perso<u>nn</u>el Sp
questio<u>nn</u>aire Sp
tyra<u>nn</u>y Sp

-oo
micr<u>oo</u>rganism

-pp
a<u>pp</u>arent Sp
a<u>pp</u>le
fli<u>pp</u>ant *
fo<u>pp</u>ish *
hi<u>pp</u>opotamus
ina<u>pp</u>ropriate *
sti<u>pp</u>le *
su<u>pp</u>lant *
su<u>pp</u>ress *

-qq
Not doubled in any English words.

-rr
abe<u>rr</u>ation *
ba<u>rr</u>acks
ba<u>rr</u>age *
biza<u>rr</u>e *
ca<u>rr</u>ion *
co<u>rr</u>espondence*
co<u>rr</u>oborate * Sp
co<u>rr</u>ugated *
dete<u>rr</u>ent *
emba<u>rr</u>ass Sp
e<u>rr</u> *
e<u>rr</u>ant *
e<u>rr</u>atic *
e<u>rr</u>oneous *
fe<u>rr</u>et *
fu<u>rr</u>ow *
i<u>rr</u>ational *
na<u>rr</u>ative
o<u>cc</u>u<u>rr</u>ence Sp
refe<u>rr</u>ed Sp
se<u>rr</u>ation *
su<u>rr</u>ender *
su<u>rr</u>eptitious *
te<u>rr</u>estrial *
to<u>rr</u>id *

-ss
The letter *s* is often doubled at the end of a word with a stressed syllable, as in *undress*.

Final -s sounded as /z/ isn't doubled: *as, is, has, his, was*.

aby<u>ss</u>al *
a<u>ss</u>e<u>ss</u>
blo<u>ss</u>om
compa<u>ss</u>ion *
connoi<u>ss</u>eur *Sp
cra<u>ss</u> *
di<u>ss</u>ension *
di<u>ss</u>onant *
di<u>ss</u>uade *
dure<u>ss</u> *
egre<u>ss</u> *
engro<u>ss</u> *
e<u>ss</u>ential *
exce<u>ss</u> *
fi<u>ss</u>ure *
ga<u>ss</u>es * gases
gro<u>ss</u> *
hara<u>ss</u> Sp
mora<u>ss</u> *
o<u>ss</u>ified *
po<u>ss</u>e<u>ss</u>ion Sp
po<u>ss</u>um opossum
prowe<u>ss</u> *
renai<u>ss</u>ance Sp
succe<u>ss</u>ive *
tu<u>ss</u>le *

Words with the suffixes -less and -ness have double final letters.

-le<u>ss</u>
-ne<u>ss</u>

-tt
The letter *t* is infrequently doubled at the end of a word.

boyco<u>tt</u> *
bu<u>tt</u> H
mi<u>tt</u>
wa<u>tt</u>

The letter *t* is frequently doubled in the middle of a word.

beli<u>tt</u>le *
cha<u>tt</u>er *
di<u>tt</u>o
fe<u>tt</u>er *
glu<u>tt</u>on
intermi<u>tt</u>ent *
ma<u>tt</u>e
ne<u>tt</u>le *
o<u>tt</u>er
pra<u>tt</u>le *
rebu<u>tt</u>al *
thro<u>tt</u>le
vigne<u>tt</u>e *
whi<u>tt</u>le *

-vv
Only doubled in adopted or clipped words.

be<u>vv</u>y also bevy
bo<u>vv</u>er British slang: troublemaking
ci<u>vv</u>y civilian + y
di<u>vv</u>y divide + y
lu<u>vv</u>y actor/actress w/an affected manner
re<u>vv</u>ed CI revolution of an engine
sa<u>vv</u>y Spanish: to know or understand

English words do not end with the letter *v*. A final /v/ is always spelled -ve, no matter what the preceding vowel sound: *have, love, move, prove.* Exception: clipped words like *rev*.

-ww
Doubled in a few adopted words and compound words.

arro<u>ww</u>ood
bo<u>ww</u>ow
   rhyming compound; onomatopoeic
po<u>ww</u>ow
   Native American
scre<u>ww</u>orm
swallo<u>ww</u>ort
   plant
willo<u>ww</u>are
yello<u>ww</u>are

-xx
Not doubled in any English words.

-yy
Not doubled in any English words.

sa<u>yy</u>id *Arabic*

-zz
The letter *z* is often doubled at the end of a word *buzz*.

bli<u>zz</u>ard
bu<u>zz</u>
bu<u>zz</u>ard
da<u>zz</u>le
di<u>zz</u>y
fi<u>zz</u>
fra<u>zz</u>le
fri<u>zz</u>
fu<u>zz</u>
ja<u>zz</u>
piza<u>zz</u>
pi<u>zz</u>a
ra<u>zz</u>le-da<u>zz</u>le
ra<u>zz</u>mata<u>zz</u>
whi<u>zz</u>ing

Just for Fun!
Zy<u>zz</u>yxdonta
a genus containing a species of land snail

Double Letters Geminating

Compound Words

When two words are combined and the first ends with the same letter with which the last begins, include both letters.

arrowwood
barroom
bathhouse
beachhead
birddog
bookkeeper Sp
cannot
cattail
coattail
cutthroat
dumbbell Sp
earring
filmmaker
fishhook
glowworm
granddaughter
headdress
highhanded
hitchhike
holddown
jackknife
knickknack
lamppost
nighttime
overrate
override
overripe
overrule
overrun Sp
roommate
roughhouse
sleuthhound
teammate
underrate
withheld Sp
withhold Sp

Syllables

Words have double letters when a syllable ends in a consonant and the next syllable starts with the same consonant.

accurate
approximately
borrow
common
commutative
corresponding
dally *
diffuse *
eccentric *
ellipse
fissure *
flippant *
gallon
immaculate *
innate *
nettle *
parallel
scribble
scrimmage
shoddy *
supplementary
tally
terrestrial *

roommate

Prefixes

collinear
connotation *
cooperative
correspond
immaculate *
immature *
innate *
innocent *
innocuous *
innumerate
irrational
irrefutable *
irregular
irritable *
irritate *
misshapen *
misspell Sp
nonnarcotic
nonnative
nonnegotiable
preeminent *
reelect
reentry
reescalation
reestablish
reevaluate
reexamine
reexperience
reexport
symmetry
unnamed
unnatural
unnavigable
unnecessary
unneeded
unnerve
unnoticed
unnumbered

See Prefixes,
pages 225-243.

Words that have a stressed last syllable with a short vowel sound, and ending in a single consonant, have that consonant doubled when the suffix begins with a vowel. Example: *occur* becomes *occurred* or *occurring*. But when the suffix begins with a consonant, there is no doubling. Example: *occurs*

Doubling occurs to prevent the short vowel from becoming a long vowel.

occur	occurred Sp
omit	omitted Sp
permit	permitted
recur	recurring
remit	remitted

Suffixes

Double letters result when a suffix starts with the letter that the word ends with, as in green**ness**.

accidental	accidentally
annual	annually
brazen	brazenness
broken	brokenness
brown	brownness
common	commonness
cool	coolly
driven	drivenness
drunken	drunkenness
general	generally
golden	goldenness
green	greenness
hidden	hiddenness
incidental	incidentally
keen	keenness
mean	meanness
mistaken	mistakenness
northern	northernness
solemn	solemnness
stubborn	stubbornness
wheel	wheelless

Words ending in two or more consonants in a blend (such as *lk*) or digraph (such as *ck*), do not have doubling. Thus *silk* becomes *silken*, *fast* becomes *fastest*, *kick* becomes *kicking*, and *wash* becomes *washed*.

Word Study:
Do Not Double

a lot ^{Sp} Common   allot Less comon; means to divide, distribute.

fulfill ^{Sp} Etymology is *full-* + *fill*, but *full* is spelled with only one *-l*.

pastime ^{Sp} No double *-t* nor double *-s*.

until ^{Sp} Etymology is *un-* + *till*, but *-till* is spelled with only one *-l*.

Other words likely to be misspelled by doubling include:

anoint ^{Sp}   biased

apartment   omit ^{Sp}

The compound word *withhold* has a double *h*,
but the word *threshold* has only one *h*.

withhold ^{Sp}   threshold ^{Sp}

USA Geography
Double Letters

Begin a list of city, state, country, and world locations with double letters in their names.

Appalachian Mountains
Chattahoochee River
Chattanooga, Tennessee
Tallahassee, Florida

Nine States of the United States have double letters in their names.

Connecticut
Hawaii
Illinois
Massachusetts
Minnesota
Mississippi
Missouri
Pennsylvania
Tennessee

Spelling Gremlins
Triple Sets of
Double Letters

This list includes root words with double letters, sufffixes with double letters, and prefixes or suffixes that resulted in the doubling of letters.

addressee
bookkeeper ^{Sp}
committee
commonness
heedlessness
pennilessness
rottenness
successfully
successiveness
tattooless
wheelless
woolliness

Spelling Gremlins
Double Sets of
Double Letters

This list includes some words with prefixes and suffixes that resulted in the doubling of letters.

accessory ^{Sp}
accidentally ^{Sp}
accommodate ^{Sp}
address ^{Sp}
aggression ^{Sp}
annually
arrowwood
assassinated
assess
balloon ^{Sp}
beekeeper
birddogged
boondoggle
bootlegged
buccaneer
bulldogging
butterball
commandeer *
committed ^{Sp}
connoisseur * ^{Sp}
embarrass ^{Sp}
footdragging
gallbladder
grasshoppers
greediness
greenkeeper
grubbiness

heartbrokenness
hoggishness
hootenanny
lollygagging
millennium ^{Sp}
misspelled ^{Sp}
mollycoddle
muggee
occurrence ^{Sp}
oddball
outspokenness
paddleball
piggishness
possession ^{Sp}
raccoon
reddishness
restlessness
riffraff
ruddiness
skiddoo
sleeveless
snobbishness
succeed
success *
suppress
unnecessary ^{Sp}
unneeded

Two-Tab Foldable (above):
comparing a word with and without double letters.

Note From Dinah
(right): Using RWP in all forms turns students into word detectives, both in and out of the class-room. When working with ESL/ELL students, I have found that using RWP in combination with photographs of signs and print from their own environment helps students to learn and use English as their second language more quickly.

Heteronyms

Words that have the same spelling but different meanings and pronunciations are called heteronyms. Example: *desert* (arid land) and *desert* (to leave).

Top Pocket Foldable Example #1 (below): Label and illustrate a pair of heteronyms on the two front tabs of the Foldable. The word *graduate* is written across both tabs. A picture of a *graduate* was placed on the left front tab, and a picture of a ceremony where students will *graduate* is on the right. Under the tabs, pictures and/or written dictionary definitions and pronunciations of the words are given. Look at the detailed information on what goes on the inside and outside of a Top Pocket, below.

Quarter Sheets: Use quarter sheets and/or VKVs to collect examples of heteronyms. Store them in the top pocket.

Central Production: The inside center section of a Top Pocket Foldable is perfect for student writing, to illustrate concepts mastered.

A person observes the arid land, or *desert*.

A penguin has been *deserted* by its companions.

To the inside left, people are picking vegetables from a *row.*

To the right, there is a big commotion or a *row.*

To the inside left, a *pencil lead* and the symbol for the element *lead*.

To the right, a guide is *lead*ing a camel.

To the inside left, students are following a code of *conduct*.

To the right, a man *conducts* an orchestra or a choir.

Heteronyms

Both Pages: The Top Pockets featured on these pages were made using 11" x 17" index paper or white copy paper. This size paper makes a functional individual project for students. A half sheet of notebook paper (or multiple half sheets) can be used for writing activities and can be glued or stapled to the middle inside section, or stored in the top pocket. Folded worksheets, VKVs, student note cards, index cards, and more can be stored in the pocket.

Top Pocket Example #2 (right): Label and illustrate a pair of heteronyms on the two front tabs of the Foldable—*present*, *present*.

Write four heteronyms on the four inside front tabs—*bass*, *content*, *wound*, and *read*. Under the tabs, have students compose and write sentences using the featured heteronyms, define each one, and include dictionary pronunciation guides to help differentiate between the terms. ESL/ELL learners might choose to find pictures to illustrate the terms, as shown on these pages.

Right:
Four-Tab Foldable used for
bow arrow, *bow* present,
bow bend, *bough* tree branch.

Four-Tab Foldable® Bound Books (above): See page 28 for instructions and photographs. These books were made using 11" x 17" paper folded like *hotdogs*, folded in half, and cut to form either two large tabs or four quarter-sized tabs. Multiple sections were glued side by side to form the number of pages required, and then a spine was added to strengthen and finish the books. The book to the left is used with students. The center book was part of a final project at the Dinah Zike Academy. Thanks go to Nancy Wisker from Maury County, Tennessee.

Heteronyms

Homographs that are spelled the same but have different pronunciations and meanings are called *heteronyms*. See homographs, page 183.

address	address	entrance	entrance	raven	raven
August	august	escort	escort	read	read
axes	axes	evening	evening	rebel	rebel
bass	bass	excise	excise	record	record
bow	bow	excuse	excuse	recount	recount
close	close	forte	forte	recreation	recreation
closer	closer	graduate	graduate	refuse	refuse
combine	combine	house	house	relay	relay
conduct	conduct	incense	incense	repeat	repeat
conflict	conflict	intern	intern	rerun	rerun
commune	commune	intimate	intimate	resign	resign
compact	compact	invalid	invalid	resume	resume
console	console	laminate	laminate	row	row
consort	consort	lead	lead	sake	sake
construct	construct	live	live	secreted	secreted
content	content	minute	minute	separate	separate
contest	contest	object	object	sewer	sewer
contract	contract	overhead	overhead	slough	slough
converse	converse	pate	pate	sow	sow
convert	convert	peaked	peaked	subject	subject
convict	convict	perfect	perfect	tarry	tarry
crooked	crooked	permit	permit	tear	tear
desert	desert	present (give)	present (gift)	uplift	uplift
digest	digest		present (time)	wind	wind
do	do (music)	primer	primer	wound	wound
does	does	produce	produce		
dove	dove	project	project		
drawer	drawer	protest	protest		

Test-Prep Heteronyms:
- affect * Sp
- buffet *
- conflict *
- content *
- deliberate *
- duplicate *

VKV Bound Flashcard Books:
See page 378 for instructions.

Word Study: Capitonym

A *capitonym* is a word that changes its meaning and sometimes its pronunciation when capitalized. The examples below all change pronunciation when capitalized.

August	august
Concord town	concord
Job	job
Lima Peru	lima
Natal S. Africa	natal
Nice France	nice
Polish	polish
Reading town	reading
Rodeo town	rodeo
Tangier Morocco	tangier

Homographs Written the Same (*homo-* = same; *-graph* = writing)

Homographs are words that have the same spelling, but differ in meaning and usually origin. They may or may not be pronounced the same. When homographs are spelled the same but pronounced differently, they are called heteronyms. Sow (seeds) and sow (female swine) are heteronyms; they are spelled the same but have different meanings and pronunciations.

Activity: Make a large chart and use it to collect examples of homographs that are commonly used in content subject areas: math, geography, science, and social sciences. Make a Foldable Chart like the one pictured bottom right and use it to compare and contrast homographs and homophones.

Activities:
Write homographs for the following math terms:

base	line	mean
point	pound	ruler
scale	set	

Write homographs for the following geography terms:

bay	gulf	ice
land	lock	pole
scale	vent	

Write homographs for the following science terms:

bark tree	cast fossil	egg
fall season	fathom	float
hatch	iron	rock
scale	sink	space
spring season	tick	
vent	wave	

Write homographs for the following social science terms:

arms	bank	bill
fleet	major	ruler
sage	steep	yen

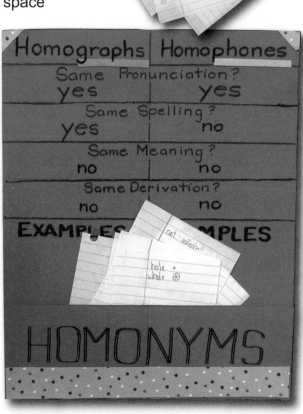

Homographs Written the Same (*homo-* = same; *-graph* = writing)

Homographs are words that have the same spelling, but differ in meaning and usually origin. They may or may not be pronounced the same. When homographs are spelled the same but pronounced differently, they are called heteronyms. Sow (seeds) and sow (female swine) are heteronyms; they are spelled the same but have different meanings and pronunciations.

arms	-upper body appendages -weapons		flounder	-a saltwater fish with a flat body -to struggle, have difficulty
bail	-a semicircular handle on a bucket -to use something to remove water -money deposited for release		forge	-to proceed, move ahead -a furnace for heating metals, as in a blacksmith shop
bark	-outer tree covering -a sound a dog makes -a sailing vessel		fray	-to become ragged -a ruckus or fight
baste	-a long sewing stitch -to put liquid on while roasting		fuse	-a slow-burning wick -to mesh, put together
bear	-a large mammal -to support, carry weight		gore	-"blood and guts" -to pierce with a horn or tusk
blaze	-to burn brightly -to mark a path to show the way -to proclaim, make known		grave	-a burial spot -very serious
bowl	-to play the game of bowling -a dish with a rounded bottom		haze	-to bully -misty, smoky air
brush	-thick vegetation -a tool for sweeping and cleaning		junk	-trash -a Chinese ship with square sails
clove	-a type of spice -a section of a bulb		loaf	-to be lazy or idle -a shaped mass of food
colon	-a punctuation mark -part of the large intestine		lock	-a device to secure something -a device to admit or release water -a curl of hair
counter	-a long table in a store or cafe -one who counts -to oppose something		loom	-a frame for weaving -to threaten
cue	-a signal -a long stick used to play pool		lumber	-to move slowly -timber that has been cut
dock	-to deduct, to cut off -a wharf, a place for boats		mail	-posted letters; to post letters -flexible metal armor
dub	-to give a descriptive nickname or title -to add a soundtrack		maroon	-a brownish-red color -to abandon, leave helpless
duck	-a waterfowl -to dodge or bend suddenly -a type of cotton cloth		mean	-the opposite of kind -an average -to intend to
			mold	-to form or shape something -a fungus

Homographs Written the Same (*homo-* = same; *-graph* = writing)

mole	-a dark growth on skin -a small, burrowing mammal
nap	-a short rest -the fuzzy ends of fibers on fabric
net	-a mesh bag used for fishing or for holding things -what remains after costs
pawn	-a chess piece -to deposit on security or loan
pile	-a stack -a strand of fabric with upright yarn, as on carpet
pitcher	-container for holding and pouring liquids -a baseball player
pole	-a long stick; a fishing pole -one end of a magnet, a pole of the earth
prune	-a dried plum -to cut or trim
punch	-to hit -a beverage made of fruit juices
pupil	-dark opening in the iris of the eye -a student
quack	-a fake or phony person -a sound that a duck makes
quail	-a bird -to be afraid, to lose courage
rail	-a metal or wooden bar for support -to complain
rare	-under-cooked -unusual, unique
rash	-thoughtless, hasty -red bumps on skin
ream	-500 sheets of paper -to form, shape, or enlarge a hole
sap	-fluid in a plant or tree -to take away energy, to weaken
scale	-a covering on reptiles and fish -musical notes, steps, or degrees -a balancing tool -to climb up or over

shed	-a small building for storage or shelter -to get rid of or remove
sock	-a covering for one's foot -to hit hard
squash	-a fruit that is often called a vegetable -to crush or flatten
stake	-a stick or post placed in the ground -to risk something for a prize
steer	-to drive or guide -a male bovine
story	-a tale or account -a set of rooms on the same level of a building
strip	-a narrow piece of something -to remove, to clean
stroke	-to hit or strike -to pet or caress -a blood vessel blockage
stunt	-a feat of skill or dexterity -to stop the growth of something
suit	-a set of clothing -a court case -a set or group of playing cards
swallow	-to ingest, to take in -a small, insect-eating bird
tap	-to lightly strike or hit something -a faucet
tart	-sour tasting -a fruit-filled pie
tip	-the point or end of something -to slant something -to leave money for services
tire	-to become weary -a bend of rubber covering a wheel
toast	-heated, browned bread -words of good luck or congratulations
troll	-a giant or dwarf living in a cave or underground -to fish by trolling

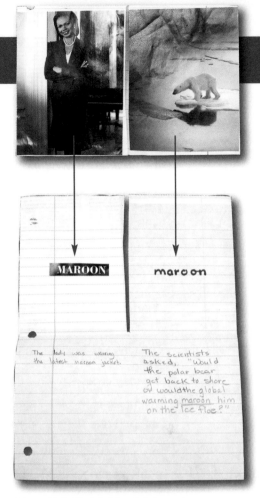

vault   -a safe place to keep valuables
           -to leap over, to jump

wake   -to be roused from sleep
           -a trail left by a ship in water

wax   -to grow bigger (waxing moon)
           -candle wax, beeswax
           -a substance made by trees
           -to apply as a polish

well   -a hole dug to obtain groundwater
           -satisfactory, pleasing

yak   -a large, shaggy-haired ox
           -to chatter

yard   -the ground around a house
           -a measurement of 36 inches

yen   -a strong desire
           -a unit of Japanese currency

vent   -an opening
           -to freely express emotional opinions

zest   -great enjoyment; gusto
           -the skin or rind of a fruit or vegetable

MAROON   maroon

The lady was wearing the latest maroon jacket.

The scientists asked, "Would the polar bear get back to shore or would the global warming maroon him on the Ice floe?"

Two-Tab Foldables® (above):
Homographs or Homophones
Make Two-Tab Foldables and use them to collect examples of homographs or homophones found in RWP, encountered while reading literature and short stories, and used in writing. Write sentences or paragraphs using the homographs or homophones under the tabs. See page 396.

Side-By-Side Bound Books:
Glue multiple sections of Two-Tab Foldables side by side to make Bound Books to be used by the class, cooperative learning groups, or individual students. See page 28 for instructions and other examples.

Display, Collect, and Store (left):
Use a sheet of posterboard to make a large Pocket Chart to display information on homographs and to collect Foldables, VKVs, and quarter-sheet cards relating to homographs. Note that metal nuts (as in "nuts and bolts") have been glued to the Pocket Chart. See page 416.

Homographs

pen

nuts

fence

Homographs are words that have the same spelling, but different meanings.

Homographs Written the Same (homo- = same; -graph = writing)

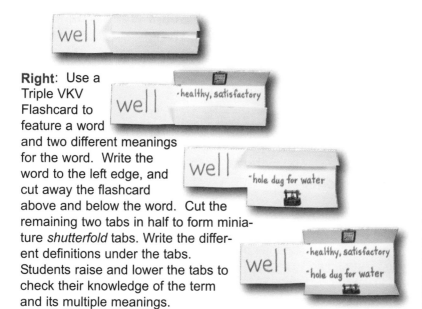

Right: Use a Triple VKV Flashcard to feature a word and two different meanings for the word. Write the word to the left edge, and cut away the flashcard above and below the word. Cut the remaining two tabs in half to form miniature *shutterfold* tabs. Write the different definitions under the tabs. Students raise and lower the tabs to check their knowledge of the term and its multiple meanings.

Word Study: well
Idioms and Homographs
As an exercise, have students find idioms based upon a word that is a homograph and use the idioms to define the different meanings of the word.

First Definition:
alive and *well*
come out *well*
get *well*
go *well* with
leave *well* alone
mean *well*
think *well* of
well and good
well done
Second Definition:
You never miss the water until the *well* runs dry.

VKV Triple Flashcards for Homographs

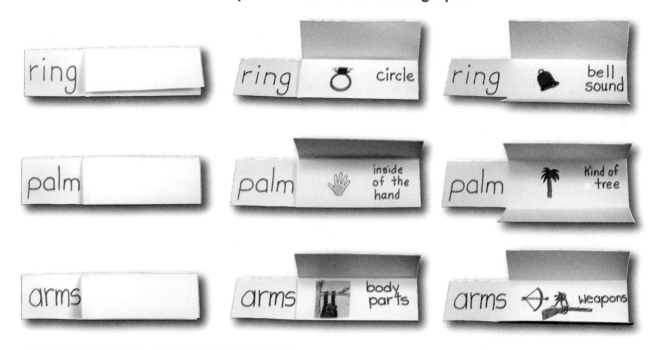

Above: Use Triple VKV Flashcards to make homograph flashcards that give two or three meanings for each term. Keeping the right tabs closed, students read the word and think of multiple meanings. They then check their answers by opening the tab to reveal the meanings. See page 386 for instructions.

Homographs — Written the Same (*homo-* = same; *-graph* = writing)

Animals

bat	bat
bear	bear
buck	buck
carp	carp
crow	crow
dove	dove
duck	duck
fawn	fawn
flounder	flounder
fluke	fluke
fly	fly
fry	fry
grouse	grouse
gull	gull
hawk	hawk
husky	husky
lark	lark
mole	mole
mule	mule
nag	nag
school	school
seal	seal
shark	shark
slug	slug
sole	sole
sow	sow
steer	steer
tick	tick
whale	whale
yak	yak

Plants

bark	bark
brush	brush
clove	clove
date	date
gum	gum
lime	lime
lumber	lumber
nut	nut
palm	palm
pine	pine
prune	prune
root	root
sage	sage
sap	sap
soil	soil
sow	sow
spray	spray
spruce	spruce
squash	squash
stalk	stalk
stem	stem

Competitors *bark* at heels of

Word Study: Idioms

Bark: First Definition
bark at the heels of...
*bark*ing up the wrong tree
someone's *bark* is worse than their bite
Bark: Second Definition
not covered in *bark* (coined by students)

VKVs on this Page: Use a Double VKV Flashcard to feature a word and two different meanings for the word. Write the word to the inside left edge, and cut away the flashcard above the word. Cut the remaining top tab into two tabs. Write the different definitions under the tabs. Students raise and lower the tabs to check their knowledge of the term and its homographs. On the back of each flashcard, have students write idioms using each definition of the term.

Word Study (Left):

Buck: Idioms (first definition)
buck stops here
make a quick *buck*
pass the *buck*
bang for the *buck*
Buck: Idioms (second definition)
buck up
buck the system

Word Study

Palm: Idioms (first definition)
in the *palm* of your hand
grease someone's *palm*
palm off something
Palm: Proverbs (second definition)
A righteous man like the palm tree shall flourish...
Psalms 92:12

It is good to know the truth, but it is better to speak of palm trees. Arab Proverb

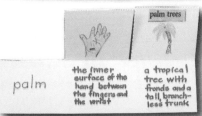

VKV Bound Flashcard Books (left):
See page 378 for instructions.

Homophones Sound Alike (*homo-* = same; *-phone* = sound)

Homophones are words that sound the same but differ in meaning, and sometimes differ in spelling. Some homophones are also *homographs* (*bear*) and *heteronyms* (*lead*).

Sixty-three of the Most Common Homophones

ad	close	hymn	night	pole	role	soar	team
add	clothes	him	knight	poll	roll	sore	teem
bail	die	in	none	rain	rose	stair	their
bale	dye	inn	nun	rein	rows	stare	there
				reign			they're
beat	eye	knot	one		rote	stake	
beet	I	not	won	rap	wrote	steak	threw
				wrap			through
berry	fir	leak	our		sail	steal	
bury	fur	leek	hour	read	sale	steel	to
				reed			too
blue	flower	led	pail		sea	sum	two
blew	flour	lead	pale	read	see	some	
				red			toe
board	hall	made	pain		seam	sun	tow
bored	haul	maid	pane	right	seem	son	
				rite			vary
brake	hear	mail	peace	write	sew	to	very
break	here	male	piece		so	two	
				road	sow	too	you
buy	hi	meat	peal	rode			ewe
by	high	meet	peel	rowed	sight	tea	
bye					site	tee	would
							wood

Matchbook Homophone Concentration:
Use strips of paper to make an even number of small matchbooks. See page 400. Write or glue sets of homophones under the tabs. When gluing the tabs to a board, be sure to separate the homophones so they will be more difficult to find and match once all tabs are closed. Students take turns opening a tab, saying the revealed word, defining it, and trying to match it with the correct corresponding word. The tabs are opened and closed until students are able to match a word to its homophone. Points are given and the correctly matched words are left uncovered as play continues.

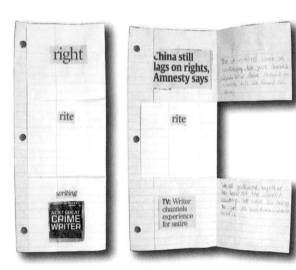

Three-Tab Foldables (above): Use either a sheet of notebook paper or photocopy paper to make the Foldables pictured.

Above Left: The words *write*, *rite*, and *right* were featured on the front tabs, and students defined and used the homophones in sentences under the tabs.

Above Right: The words *pare*, *pair*, and *pear* were featured on the front tabs, and students defined and used the homophones in sentences under the tabs.

Word Study: Determine the Part of Speech

When deciding the meaning or spelling of a homophone, remember that usage determines which word is correct. For example, the words *mist* and *missed* sound alike, but one is a noun and one is a past-tense verb ending in the *-ed* suffix.

	Verbs		Verbs
band	banned	past	passed
bard	barred	road	rode, rowed
brood	brewed	side	sighed
gourd	gored	toad	towed
least	leased	trust	trussed
mist	missed	wade	weighed

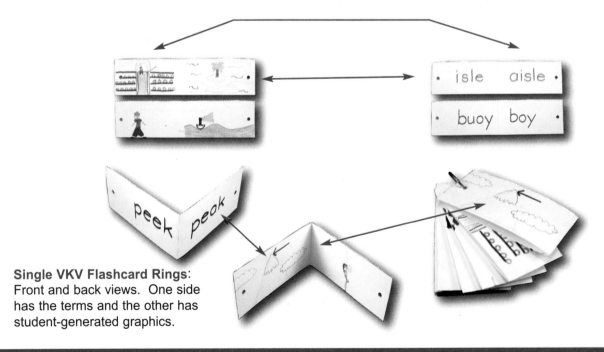

Single VKV Flashcard Rings: Front and back views. One side has the terms and the other has student-generated graphics.

Contractions can be Homophones:
Make a book like the ones featured on this page to collect examples of contraction homophones. See page 28.

he'd	heed
he'll	heal, heel
I'll	aisle, isle
they're	there, their
we'd	weed
we'll	wheel
we've	weave
who's	whose
you'll	yule
you're	your

Past and Present (above and below): This Two-Tab Foldable book was made using 11" x 17" paper folded like a *hotdog* and cut to form two large tabs per spread. The photo above shows what the book looked like two weeks after it was made by the class. The photo below was taken months later. Notice how students continued to find words—**rain** and **reign** and **see** and **sea**—in RWP and add them to the class homophone book.

Two-Tab Foldable® Books: Homographs or Homophones
Use a *hamburger* fold to make Two-Tab Foldables with 11" x 17" paper. Make multiple sections, depending on the number of homophones or homophones to be featured. Always provide extra pages for future additions to the booklet.

Fold the Two-Tab Foldables in half and glue them side by side to make Bound Books. Clothespins can be used to hold the sections together while the glue dries.

Use the book to collect examples of homographs or homophones found in RWP or encountered while reading literature, singing songs, reading signs, or completing worksheets on homographs or homophones.

Write sentences or paragraphs using the homographs or homophones under the tabs. See page 181 for other examples.

Homophones Sound Alike

Double VKV Flashcards (right): Fold the flashcard in half and cut to form two tabs. Write homographs or homophones on the front tabs. Define the terms under the tabs. Use this VKV with any of the words featured in this section or with any words listed in this book and marked H.

Rime and Rhyme (below): The homophones *rime* and *rhyme* do not have the same meaning, but they are related. If two words have identical *rime* (or the same word family), such as *r-eel* and *f-eel*, then they also rhyme, or sound the same. And if two words have rimes that are pronounced the same but spelled differently, such as *r-eal* and *r-eel*, they also rhyme, but have different rimes. See Phonograms, page 203.

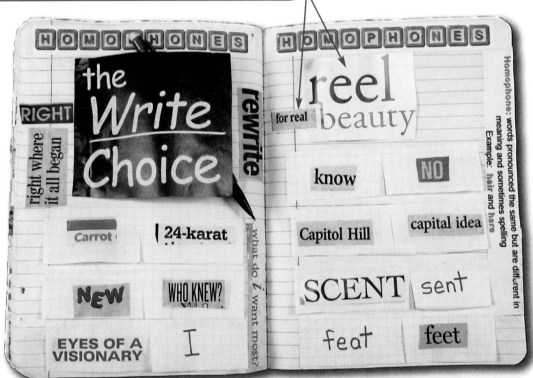

Double VKV Flashcards (above and right): This composition book has more examples of Double Flashcards used to feature homophones. Notice that a picture of *carrots* was glued under the *carrot* tab.

ESL/ELL students benefit from visual aids when working with homophones.

Homophones Sound Alike (*homo-* = same; *-phone* = sound)

Homophones are words that sound the same but differ in meaning and sometimes differ in spelling. Some homophones are also *homographs* (*bear*) and *heteronyms* (*lead*).

Zigzag VKV: Use a Single VKV Flashcard and fold it into thirds. Glue the right tab into a notebook and refold so that the tabs zigzag. On the top tab, write one of a pair of homophones. On the glued base, write the second word. In the middle write a sentence using one or both of the terms, and/or define the terms. Read the word on the front, determine its homophone, and open and close the Zigzag to check answers.

Above & Left: Zigzag open. Under the homophones, students might be asked to write dictionary pronunciations to emphasize common pronunciations.

Below: Zigzag closed.

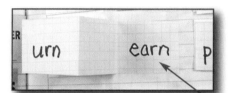

Never Finished: Students might be asked to write immediate responses under tabs, but they are also reminded to continue to look for examples in RWP. When words are found, they should be added to the composition book even if it has been months since the original words were written. This keeps students actively involved in past and present vocabulary studies, while reinforcing terms and skills.

RWP Notebook Tabs (above): Use RWP words or phrases as tabs in a notebook. Glue one edge into the notebook to form the tab. Write or glue examples of homophones under the tabs.

Homophones Sound Alike (*homo-* = same; *-phone* = sound)

Homophones are words that sound the same but differ in meaning and sometimes differ in spelling.
Some homophones are also *homographs* (*bear*) and *heteronyms* (*lead*).

Math

add	ad
arc	ark
ball	bawl
base	bass
bases	basis
bloc	block
byte	bite
cash	cache
cent scent	sent
complement	compliment
cord	chord
dual	duel
eight	ate
feet	feat
four fore	for
fourth	forth
halve	have
hour	our
least	leased
mean	mien
one	won
pair pare	pear
pi	pie
plane	plain
rows	rose
side	sighed
sine	sign
straight	strait
symbol	cymbal
sum	some
time	thyme
two to	too
vary	very
week	weak
weigh Sp way	whey
weighed	wade
weight	wait
whole	hole

Animals

ant		aunt
bear		bare
boar		bore
bee		be
burro		burrow
		borough
deer		dear
doe		dough
ewe	you	yew
flea		flee
fowl		foul
gnu		knew
gorilla		guerrilla
grizzly		grisly
hare		hair
herd		heard
horse		hoarse
lamb		lam
lox		locks
lynx		links
mane		main
mite		might
moose		mousse
mussel		muscle
paws		pause
prey		pray
tapir		taper
tern		turn
tick		tic
toad		towed
whale		wail

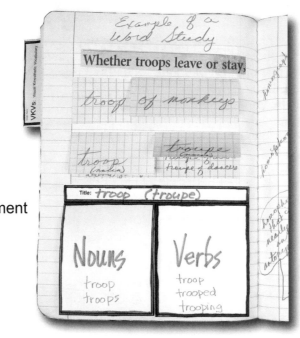

Above:
A Two-Tab Foldable template from Dinah Zike's *Notebook Foldables* was used to compare the word *troop* used as a noun and a verb.

Below:
A Two-Tab Foldable was made using notebook paper and used to compare and define the homophones *tail* and *tale*.

Homophones Sound Alike (*homo-* = same; *-phone* = sound)

Science

air	heir
base (acid, base)	bass
birth	berth
blew	blue
brood	brewed
bruise	brews
buoy	boy
cell	sell
coral	choral
core	corps
current	currant
dew do	due
die	dye
epoch	epic
eye aye	I
feet	feat
flare	flair
floe	flow
freeze	frieze
fur	fir
gene	jean
hail	hale
hair	hare
hear	here
heart	hart
herd	heard
hertz	hurts
hue	hew
lead	led
lichen	liken
lightning	lighten-ing
lode	load
mantle Sp	mantel Sp
metal medal	mettle
mist	missed
mite	might
muscle	mussel
oral	aural
ore oar	or
palate	pallett
phase	faze

pore		pour
prey		pray
rain	rein	reign
rays	raise	raze
sea		see
scent	cent	sent
sense		cents
sight	site	cite
skull		scull
steel		steal
sun		son
tail		tale
tide		tied
toad		towed
toe		tow
vein	vane	vain
waste		waist
watt		what
wave		waive
weather		whether
wet		whet
wood		would
yolk		yoke

Plants

beet		beat
berry		bury
carrot caret		carat
cherry		chary
currant		current
fir		fur
flower		flour
gourd		gored
grown		groan
hay		hey
maize		maze
pear		pair
plum		plumb
reed		read
root		route
seed		cede
vein	vane	vain
yew	ewe	you
weed		we'd

Health

(Also see science homophones.)

ail		ale
die		dye
flu	flue	flew
heal	heel	he'll
pain		pane
patients		patience

> **Double VKV Flashcards:**
> See page 379.

Above:
Double VKV Flashcard used to differentiate between *flower* and *flour*.

Below:
Double VKV Flashcard used to differentiate between *beet* and *beat*.

Word Study:
Select examples of homophones to include in science and health units. As illustrated in the examples below, sometimes a word and its homophone apply to different branches of science.

Examples:
sun, son
sun = astronomy
son = heredity

muscle, mussel
muscle = health/fitness
mussel = biology/invertebrate

blew, blue
blew = meteorology, weather
blue = physical science, light

Homophones Sound Alike (*homo-* = same; *-phone* = sound)

Homophones are words that sound the same but differ in meaning and sometimes differ in spelling. Some homophones are also *homographs* (*bear*) and *heteronyms* (*lead*).

Social Studies Homophones

acts	ax, axe	hostile	hostel
adz	ads	isle aisle	I'll
aid	aide	knight	night
ante	anti-	loot	lute
awl	all	maize	maze
banned	band	manor	manner
bard	barred	marshal ^Sp	martial ^Sp
baron	barren	miner	minor
barque	bark	naval	navel
Basque	bask	past	passed
bazaar ^Sp	bizarre ^Sp	peace	piece
beach	beech	peddle	pedal
belle	bell	pier	peer
berth	birth	poll	pole
border	boarder	principle	principal
borough	burro	profit	prophet
	burrow	rack	wrack
bullion	bouillon	raze raise	rays
bury	berry	reign rain	rein
cache	cash	right	write
cannon	canon	sail	sale
canvass	canvas	seer	sear
capital	capitol	serf	surf
caste	cast	session	cession
censor	censer	sheik	chic
	sensor	sow so	sew
chants	chance	tax	tacks
colonel	kernel	tea	tee
corps	core	throne	thrown
council	counsel	tool	tulle
desert	dessert	troop	troupe
disperse	disburse	trust	trussed
duel	dual	urn	earn
fort	forte	weave	we've
franc	frank	wheel weal	we'll
friar	fryer	witch	which
guerrilla	gorilla	won	one
hall	haul	yoke	yolk
hew	hue		
horde	hoard		

Geography

beach	beech
bight byte	bite
border	boarder
buoy	boy
capital	capitol
clime	climb
course	coarse
creek	creak
dam	damn
desert	dessert
isle I'll	aisle
islet	eyelet
high	hi
loch	lock
Maine mane	main
overseas	oversees
peak	peek
plain	plane
road rowed	rode
sea	see
steppe	step
strait	straight
surge	serge
tide	tied
vale	veil
wave	waive
weir	we're
wet	whet
where wear	ware

Above: Double VKV Flashcard used to differentiate between *knight* and *night*. Graphics can be helpful for ESL/ELL students. See page 378.

Idioms

Idioms are expressions that cannot be understood from the combined meanings of the words that form them. Idioms are usually distinctive to a language and can be colorful when used by native speakers, but they can provide challenges for those learning a language.

Many idioms have multiple meanings that are confusing for English language learners. For example, *throw* may mean to toss a ball, to give a party (*throw* a party), to give the wrong impression (*throw* someone off, *throw* a curve), to vomit (*throw* up), to toss something (*throw* out), or to exert influence (*throw* weight around).

Common Idioms

all	break	call	come	get
all along	break a heart	call a strike	come about	get ahead
all at once	break a leg	call attention to	come across	get a life
all ears	break a neck	call for	come again	get around to
all eyes	break down	call in	come alive	get away with
all hours	break even	call it a day	come around	get back at
all out	break ground	call it quits	come back	get cold feet
all over	break in	call names	come by	get even
all set	break out	call on	come clean	get into
all there	break the ice	call out	come into	get lost
all thumbs	break the news	call the shots	come off it	get on with
all wet	break through	call to order	come out	get out
	break up		come up to	get out of
				get over it
				get the ball rolling
				get up
				get up and go
				get your feet wet

Idioms
Slow and steady wins the race.
A drop in the bucket.
A chip on your shoulder.
A dime a dozen.
Definition of Idiom

Layered Foldable (left): Made using three sheets of paper. See page 382.

Triple VKV Flashcard (right): Tabs form four idioms. See page 388.

back	hit	make	run
back and forth	hit bottom	make a move	run away
back down	hit it off	make a play	run away from/with
back off	hit the books	make a point	run down
back on track	hit the bull's-eye	make believe ᔆᵖ	run in
back yonder	hit the gym	make certain	run into
back to back	hit the hay	make ends meet	run out of
black	hit the high points	make friends	run over
black and blue	hit the jackpot	make fun of	run short
black and white	hit the nail on the head	make good	run the risk of
black day	hit the road	make heads or tails	run through
black mark	hit the roof	make over	run wild
black sheep	hit the spot	make up	running neck and neck

Idioms

bend
bend over backwards
bend someone's ear
bend/stretch the rules
round the bend

catch
catch a break
catch a cold
catch a ride
catch sight
catch some Z's
catch someone's eye
catch someone off guard
catch someone red-handed
catch up on something
catch your breath

crack
crack a book
crack a smile
crack down
crack of dawn
crack the whip
fall through the cracks

dead
dead as a doornail
dead loss
dead on your feet
dead to the world
half dead

down
down and out
down in the dumps
down in the mouth
down on your luck
down the drain
down the hatch
down the road

drop
drop a bombshell
drop a hint
drop a line
drop everything
drop in
drop off
drop out

fall
fall apart
fall by the wayside
fall down on the job
fall flat on your face
fall into place
fall head over heels
fall on hard times

feel
feel honor-bound
feel it in my bones
feel like a million bucks/dollars
feel the pinch
feel under the weather

fly
fly by night
fly in the ointment
fly off the handle
fly on the wall
fly the coop
go fly a kite

hang
hang by a thread
hang in the balance
hang in there
hang on
hang tough
hang your hat (on something)

look
don't look back
look before you leap
look down your nose at
look for trouble
look forward to something
look the other way
look the part
look someone/something up

pay
pay a call on
pay the piper
pay through the nose
pay top dollar
pay your dues
pay your way

sight
catch sight of
have someone in your sights
lost sight of
lower your sights
out of sight, out of mind
sight for sore eyes
sights set on something

stick
stick in the mud
stick in your mind
stick it out
stick out your neck
stick together
stick to something
stick to your ribs

take
take a back seat
take a bath
take a break
take after
take aim
take a rain check
take a stand
take back something
take care
take each day as it comes
take heart
take hold
take it easy
take it hard
take it or leave it
take no prisoners
take note of
take root
take someone at their word
take the brunt of something
take the cake
take the plunge
take the rap
take your eye off the ball
take your time

Heart

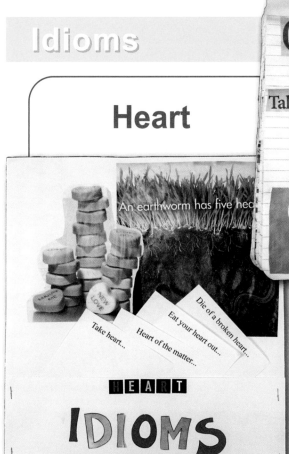

a heart of gold
a heart of stone
a man/woman after
        your own heart
at heart
bleeding heart
bless your heart
break a heart
by heart
change of heart
close to your heart
cross your heart
eat your heart out

from the bottom of
        your heart
half-hearted
harden your heart
have a heart
heart isn't in it
heart sinks
heart skips a beat
heart-to-heart
in your heart of hearts
lose heart
melt my heart
open your heart
pour your heart out
put your heart into
        something
set your heart on
        something
sick at heart
straight from the heart
take heart
take something to heart
tear your heart out
wear your heart on
        your sleeve

talk
talk a blue streak
talk big
talked to death
talk in riddles
talk out of both sides
        of your mouth
talk sense
talk shop
talk turkey
turn
turn a blind eye
turn back the clock
turn for the worse
turn on a dime
turn the other cheek
turn up the heat
turn your back on someone
turn your head/turn heads
turn your stomach

Right: Triple VKV Flashcards used to form three idioms that begin with the same word. See page 386.

The top VKV card illustrates the following collective nouns:
-*army* of ants
-*army* of frogs
-*army* of soldiers.

Above and Right:
Triple VKVs show three to four idioms based upon one similar word.
See list, page 198.
See VKVs, page 386.

once in a Blue Moon!

Idiom: blue moon
A blue moon is the second of two full moons occurring in the same month. Since this doesn't happen frequently, the idiom refers to a long period of time.

An opportunity like this comes once in a blue moon.

I haven't seen you in a blue moon.

stars in your eyes

Idiom: stars in your eyes
It refers to someone who is excited and hopeful about the future; often their optimism relates to the hope that they will be successful future and someone famous.

He had stars in his eyes when it came to a...

She went to Hollywood with stars in her eye...

On the Ball
Idioms

SEEING THE LIGHT

Idiom: see the light
To understand something clearly after having been confused or bewildered. To start believing in religion, sometimes suddenly.

Reading that book made her see the light.
Other Idioms:
see the light of day
(something is brought out so people can see it)

not counting chickens

Idiom: don't count your chickens
Said to warn someone to wait until a good thing they are expecting has already happened before they make any plans relating to it.

Don't count your chickens before they hatch.

Other Idioms:
no spring chicken
a chicken and an egg situation
chicken feed
chickens come home to roost
...ing around like a chicken with its head cut off

go fly a kite

Idiom: go fly a kite
Said to someone who is annoying to make them go away.

What are you talking about? Go fly a kite.
Other Idioms:
as high as a kite
fly off the handle
fly blind
feathers fly
sparks fly

Idioms: nose...
follow your nose
won by a nose
can't see past the end of your nose
have a nose for something
have your nose in a book
have your nose in the air
no skin off my nose
keep your nose clean
pay through the nose
poke your nose into something
under someone's nose

go nose to nose
with

spin good yarn

Idiom: spin a good yarn
The ability to tell a good tale or to invent a tale that is supposed to be a truth.

He spins a good yarn.
Other Idioms:
spin your wheels
spin doctor

Putting a Spin On It

Chinks in the Armor

Idiom: a chink in someone's armor
Something or someone who seems strong/perfect, but they seem to have a small fault which may cause them problems.

She is a good student, but her lack of turning in homework may be a chink in her armor.

Other Idioms:
knight in shining armor

Right: Bound Two-Tab Foldables used to form a book of common idioms. See pages 28.

Cartoon Speech Bubbles:
Collect examples of onomatopoeia words used in cartoons. Glue one edge of the cartoon into the notebook to form a tab. Under the tab, explain the purpose and use of the "sound" word in the cartoon. Remember to give credit to the cartoonist by including his/her name and/or logo.

Post-It Notes™ and Gummed Stickers (right):
Use Sticky Notes™ to make Notebook Foldable tabs.

Speech Bubbles: The speech bubbles pictured on the tabs are gummed stickers. **Inexpensive Alternatives**: Have students design and draw unique speech bubbles on small sections of paper. Collect selected examples, arrange them on a single sheet of copy paper, tape them in place, make numerous photocopies, and have them available for students to cut and use on tabs.

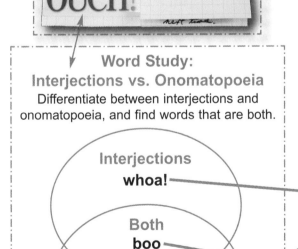

Word Study:
Interjections vs. Onomatopoeia
Differentiate between interjections and onomatopoeia, and find words that are both.

- **Interjections**
  - **whoa!**
- **Both**
  - **boo**
  - **shh**
- **Onomatopoeia**
  - **buzz**

Onomatopoeia Spelling Sound Words

Onomatopoeia is the naming of a thing or action by a vocal imitation of the sound associated with it, and the formation of words to express those sounds. Example: *buzz* imitates the sound of a bee, a fly, a saw, or a low-flying airplane. Note that interjections can be, but are not necessarily, onomatopoeia.

Not all of these words may be found in a dictionary. Example: *"Tlot-tlot, tlot-tlot!* Had they heard it? The horse-hoofs ringing clear..."—*The Highwayman,* by Alfred Noyes

aargh	choo-choo	growl	ooze	slop	tweet
achoo Int	chug	grrrr Int	ouch Int	slurp	twitter
ahchoo	clack	grunt	patter	slush	varoom vroom
hachoo	clang	guffaw	peal H	smack	whack
kerchoo	clank	gurgle	peep	smash	wham
arf (dog bark)	clap	gush	ping	snap	wheeze
baa	clash	ha-ha Int	pitter-patter	sniff	whew
bam	clatter	hee-haw	plink	sniffle	whimper
bang	click	hiccup	plop	snort	whine
bark H	clickety-clack	hiss	pop	splash	whir whirr
bash	clink	hmm, h'm Int	pow	splatter	whish
bawl	clip-clop	ho-hum Int	puff	splish-splash	whiz
bay H	clippety-clop	honk	purr	sputter	whoohoo
beep	clomp	hoot	putt-putt	squeak	whoop
belch	cluck	howl	quack	squeal	whoopee
blab	conk	huff	rat-a-tat-tat	squish	whoosh woosh
blare	coo	huff and puff	rattle	stomp	whop
blast	crack	hum	ring H (a bell)	swish	woof
blather	crackle	hurrah hurray	ring-a-ling	swoosh	yip
bleat	crash	hooray	rip	thud	yuck
bleep	creak	hoorah	roar	thump	yum-yum
bling	crinkle	hush Int	rumble	thwap	zap
blink	croak	jabber	rustle	ticktock	zing
blob	crunch	jangle	screech	tinkle	zip
blubber	cuckoo	jingle	shh Int	tom-tom	zonk
blurt	ding-a-ling	ka-ching	shriek	toot	zoom
bong	ding-dong	kerplunk	sigh	twang	zzz
bonk	drip	knock	sizzle		
boo	drone	lisp			
boohoo	drop	meow			
boom	eek Int	mew			
bow-wow	fizz	moan			
bray	flap	moo			
brr Int	flutter	mumble			
bump	giggle	murmur			
burp	gobble	neigh			
burr	gong	oink			
buzz	grate	ooh-lah-lah Int			
caw	grind	oompah-pah			
chirp	groan	oops Int			
chomp					

Two-Tab Bound Book: This Two-Tab book is a collection of Foldables made during a training session at the Dinah Zike Academy. See page 28.

Phonograms contain a vowel grapheme followed by a consonant grapheme.
Examples of *phonograms* include *-an, -ay, -ill, -ip, -ot,* and *-un.*
Most words that have the same phonogram rhyme with each other.
Rime and *rhyme*: If two words have identical *rime* (the same word family), such as b-est and w-est, then they also *rhyme*. Two words that are pronounced the same but spelled differently, such as *r-eal* and *r-eel*, rhyme, but have different rimes. Also see homophones, page 189.

To Rhyme, Words Must ...
... end in the same or nearly the same sounding syllable.
... have the same stress pattern.

beet	beat
feet	feat
flee	flea
heel	heal
leek	leak
meet	meat
need	knead
peel	peal
seem	seam
steel	steal
tee	tea
teem *	team
week	weak

One Triple VKV Flashcard forms three words (above):
See page 386.

Four Double VKV Flashcards feature eight words (right):
See page 379.

No Rhyme or Reason?
A few monosyllabic words and numerous polysyllabic words have no rhyme.

The color words *orange*, **purple**, and **silver** are examples of poly- and monosyllabic words that do not have common word rhymes.

Monosyllabic Examples
angst
breadth
depth
fifth
gulf
ninth
twelfth
wolf

Polysyllabic Examples
Words with the stress toward the beginning of the word are less likely to have perfect rhymes.
No common word rhymes:
almond
bulb
circle
month
olive
penguin
rhythm Sp
sanction
vacuum Sp
width

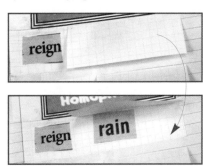

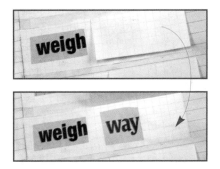

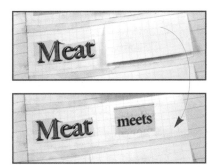

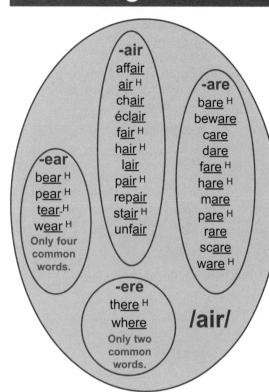

/air/

-air
aff<u>air</u>
<u>air</u> H
ch<u>air</u>
écl<u>air</u>
f<u>air</u> H
h<u>air</u> H
l<u>air</u>
p<u>air</u> H
rep<u>air</u>
st<u>air</u> H
unf<u>air</u>

-are
b<u>are</u> H
bew<u>are</u>
c<u>are</u>
d<u>are</u>
f<u>are</u> H
h<u>are</u> H
m<u>are</u>
p<u>are</u> H
r<u>are</u>
sc<u>are</u>
w<u>are</u> H

-ear
b<u>ear</u> H
p<u>ear</u> H
t<u>ear</u> H
w<u>ear</u> H
Only four common words.

-ere
th<u>ere</u> H
wh<u>ere</u>
Only two common words.

-ame
bl<u>ame</u>
c<u>ame</u>
d<u>ame</u>
f<u>ame</u>
g<u>ame</u>
l<u>ame</u>
n<u>ame</u>
s<u>ame</u>
t<u>ame</u>

/eym/

-aim
<u>aim</u>
cl<u>aim</u>
m<u>aim</u>
Only three common words.

/eyl/

-ale
<u>ale</u> H
b<u>ale</u> H
d<u>ale</u>
fem<u>ale</u>
g<u>ale</u> H
h<u>ale</u> H
imp<u>ale</u>
k<u>ale</u>
m<u>ale</u> H
p<u>ale</u> H
res<u>ale</u>
s<u>ale</u> H
sc<u>ale</u>
t<u>ale</u> H
v<u>ale</u> H
wh<u>ale</u>

-ail
<u>ail</u> H
av<u>ail</u>
b<u>ail</u> H
f<u>ail</u>
fl<u>ail</u>
h<u>ail</u> H
j<u>ail</u>
m<u>ail</u> H
n<u>ail</u>
p<u>ail</u> H
r<u>ail</u>
ret<u>ail</u>
s<u>ail</u> H
sn<u>ail</u>
t<u>ail</u> H
tr<u>ail</u>
w<u>ail</u>

-eil
v<u>eil</u> H
Only one common word.

Word Study:
No Rhyme This Time

/air/	no rhyme
b<u>are</u>	are
b<u>ear</u>	clear
wh<u>ere</u>	were
/eyl/	**no rhyme**
ass<u>ail</u>	wassail
g<u>ale</u>	locale
v<u>eil</u>ing	ceiling
/eym/	**no rhyme**
c<u>ame</u>	madame
s<u>ame</u>	sesame

Word Study: /eyl/
Homophones:

<u>ail</u>	<u>ale</u>
b<u>ail</u>	b<u>ale</u>
h<u>ail</u>	h<u>ale</u>
m<u>ail</u>	m<u>ale</u>
p<u>ail</u>	p<u>ale</u>
s<u>ail</u>	s<u>ale</u>
t<u>ail</u>	t<u>ale</u>
w<u>ail</u>	wh<u>ale</u>

See page 189.

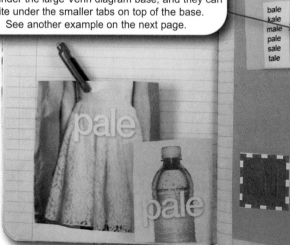

Venn Diagram Tabs (below): Fold a tab on one edge of a half sheet of colored paper and use the tab to glue the paper into a notebook. This paper forms the base of a rectangular Venn diagram. Cut smaller sections of paper, fold a tab on each, and glue the tabs on top of the colored paper. Students can write in the notebook under the large Venn diagram base, and they can write under the smaller tabs on top of the base. See another example on the next page.

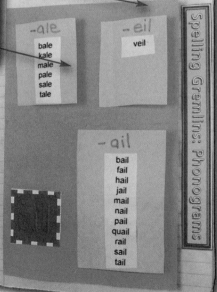

Most words with the same phonogram rhyme with each other.
If two words have identical *rime* (the same word family), such as *l-ane* and *p-ane*,
then they also *rhyme*.

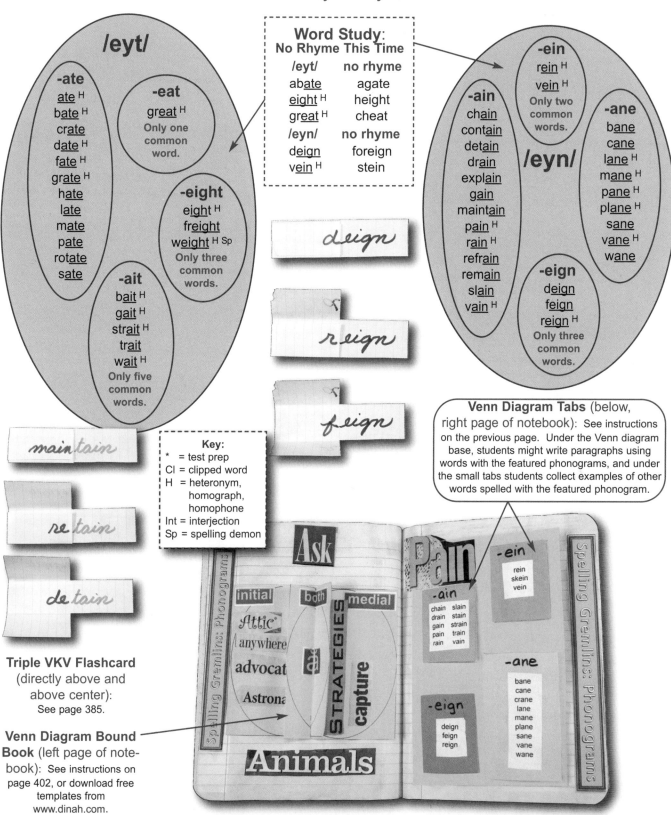

/eyt/

-ate
ate H
bate H
crate
date H
fate H
grate H
hate
late
mate
pate
rotate
sate

-eat
great H
Only one common word.

-eight
eight H
freight
weight H Sp
Only three common words.

-ait
bait H
gait H
strait H
trait
wait H
Only five common words.

Word Study:
No Rhyme This Time

/eyt/	no rhyme
abate	agate
eight H	height
great H	cheat
/eyn/	**no rhyme**
deign	foreign
vein H	stein

/eyn/

-ein
rein H
vein H
Only two common words.

-ain
chain
contain
detain
drain
explain
gain
maintain
pain H
rain H
refrain
remain
slain
vain H

-ane
bane
cane
lane H
mane H
pane H
plane H
sane
vane H
wane

-eign
deign
feign
reign H
Only three common words.

deign

reign

feign

maintain

retain

detain

Key:
* = test prep
Cl = clipped word
H = heteronym, homograph, homophone
Int = interjection
Sp = spelling demon

Venn Diagram Tabs (below, right page of notebook): See instructions on the previous page. Under the Venn diagram base, students might write paragraphs using words with the featured phonograms, and under the small tabs students collect examples of other words spelled with the featured phonogram.

Triple VKV Flashcard
(directly above and above center):
See page 385.

Venn Diagram Bound Book (left page of notebook): See instructions on page 402, or download free templates from www.dinah.com.

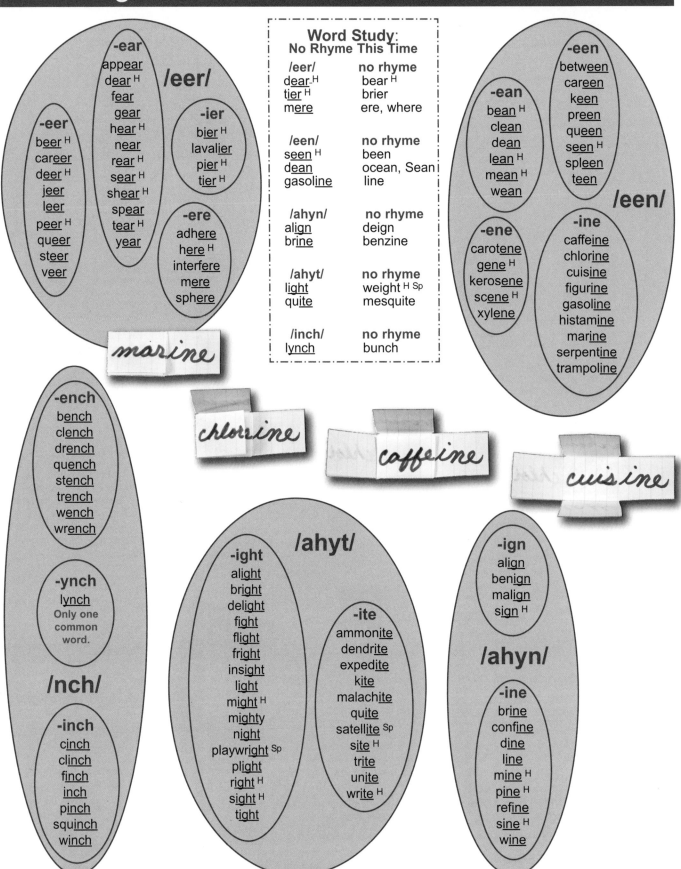

/eer/

-ear
appear
dear H
fear
gear
hear H
near
rear H
sear H
shear H
spear
tear H
year

-eer
beer H
career
deer H
jeer
leer
peer H
queer
steer
veer

-ier
bier H
lavalier
pier H
tier H

-ere
adhere
here H
interfere
mere
sphere

Word Study:
No Rhyme This Time

/eer/	no rhyme
dear H	bear H
tier H	brier
mere	ere, where

/een/	no rhyme
seen H	been
dean	ocean, Sean
gasoline	line

/ahyn/	no rhyme
align	deign
brine	benzine

/ahyt/	no rhyme
light	weight H Sp
quite	mesquite

/inch/	no rhyme
lynch	bunch

-een
between
careen
keen
preen
queen
seen H
spleen
teen

/een/

-ean
bean H
clean
dean
lean H
mean H
wean

-ene
carotene
gene H
kerosene
scene H
xylene

-ine
caffeine
chlorine
cuisine
figurine
gasoline
histamine
marine
serpentine
trampoline

marine

chlorine

caffeine

cuisine

-ench
bench
clench
drench
quench
stench
trench
wench
wrench

-ynch
lynch
Only one
common
word.

/nch/

-inch
cinch
clinch
finch
inch
pinch
squinch
winch

/ahyt/

-ight
alight
bright
delight
fight
flight
fright
insight
light
might H
mighty
night
playwright Sp
plight
right
sight H
tight

-ite
ammonite
dendrite
expedite
kite
malachite
quite
satellite Sp
site H
trite
unite
write H

-ign
align
benign
malign
sign H

/ahyn/

-ine
brine
confine
dine
line
mine H
pine H
refine
sine H
wine

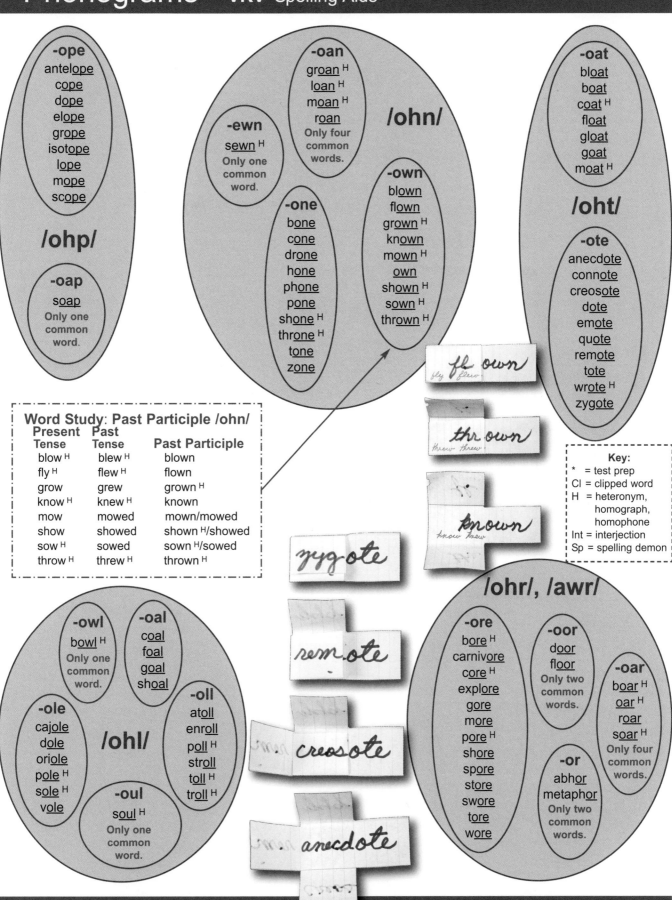

-ope
antelope
cope
dope
elope
grope
isotope
lope
mope
scope

/ohp/

-oap
soap
Only one common word.

-ewn
sewn H
Only one common word.

-oan
groan H
loan H
moan H
roan
Only four common words.

/ohn/

-one
bone
cone
drone
hone
phone
pone
shone H
throne H
tone
zone

-own
blown
flown
grown H
known
mown H
own
shown H
sown H
thrown H

-oat
bloat
boat
coat H
float
gloat
goat
moat H

/oht/

-ote
anecdote
connote
creosote
dote
emote
quote
remote
tote
wrote H
zygote

Word Study: Past Participle /ohn/

Present Tense	Past Tense	Past Participle
blow H	blew H	blown
fly H	flew H	flown
grow	grew	grown H
know H	knew H	known
mow	mowed	mown/mowed
show	showed	shown H/showed
sow H	sowed	sown H/sowed
throw H	threw H	thrown H

Key:
* = test prep
Cl = clipped word
H = heteronym, homograph, homophone
Int = interjection
Sp = spelling demon

-owl
bowl H
Only one common word.

-oal
coal
foal
goal
shoal

-ole
cajole
dole
oriole
pole H
sole H
vole

/ohl/

-oll
atoll
enroll
poll H
stroll
toll H
troll H

-oul
soul H
Only one common word.

/ohr/, /awr/

-ore
bore H
carnivore
core H
explore
gore
more
pore H
shore
spore
store
swore
tore
wore

-oor
door
floor
Only two common words.

-oar
boar H
oar H
roar
soar H
Only four common words.

-or
abhor
metaphor
Only two common words.

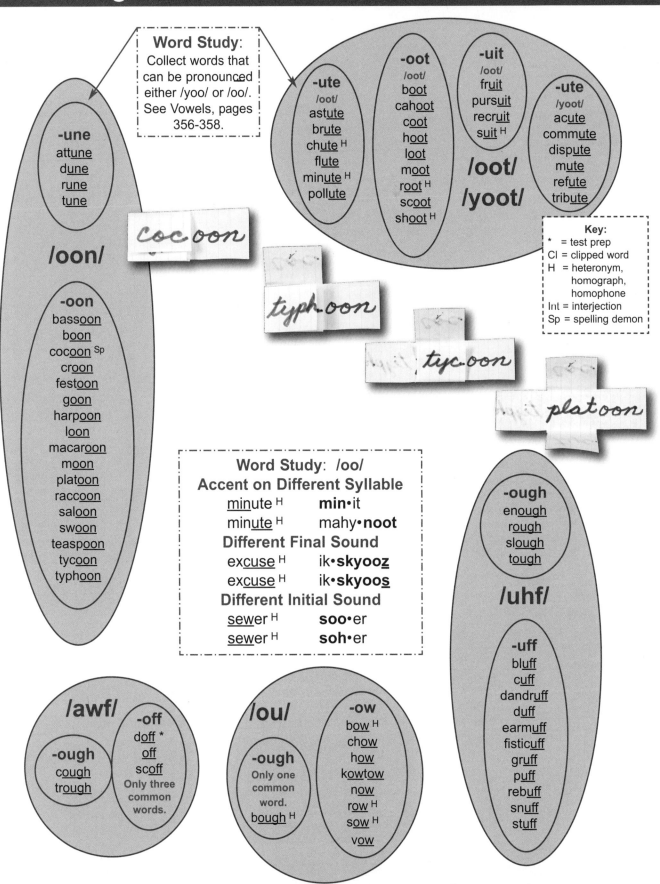

Word Study:
Collect words that can be pronounced either /yoo/ or /oo/. See Vowels, pages 356-358.

/oon/

-une
attune
dune
rune
tune

-oon
bassoon
boon
cocoon Sp
croon
festoon
goon
harpoon
loon
macaroon
moon
platoon
raccoon
saloon
swoon
teaspoon
tycoon
typhoon

-ute
/oot/
astute
brute
chute H
flute
minute H
pollute

-oot
/oot/
boot
cahoot
coot
hoot
loot
moot
root H
scoot
shoot H

-uit
/oot/
fruit
pursuit
recruit
suit H

**/oot/
/yoot/**

-ute
/yoot/
acute
commute
dispute
mute
refute
tribute

cocoon

typh·oon

tyc·oon

platoon

Key:
* = test prep
Cl = clipped word
H = heteronym, homograph, homophone
Int = interjection
Sp = spelling demon

Word Study: /oo/
Accent on Different Syllable
minute H   **min•it**
minute H   mahy•**noot**
Different Final Sound
excuse H   ik•**skyooz**
excuse H   ik•**skyoos**
Different Initial Sound
sewer H   **soo•**er
sewer H   **soh•**er

-ough
enough
rough
slough
tough

/uhf/

-uff
bluff
cuff
dandruff
duff
earmuff
fisticuff
gruff
puff
rebuff
snuff
stuff

/awf/

-ough
cough
trough

-off
doff *
off
scoff
Only three common words.

/ou/

-ough
Only one common word.
bough H

-ow
bow H
chow
how
kowtow
now
row H
sow H
vow

Venn Diagram:
The Venn diagram was made using the CD template from Dinah Zike's *Notebook Foldables* book. The center section is labeled with the sound that the two phonograms share. The phonograms and examples of words containing them are written on the front tabs. Under the tabs, students either write sentences using the terms or do a specific word study of an example word from each list. See page 245 for more information on word studies.

Accordion VKVs®:
The pocket in this notebook is filled with accordion VKVs like those pictured to the right. Each half sheet of notebook paper (cut on the vertical axis) makes a five-word study aid based upon the same phonogram. See folding instructions on page 392.

Plurals

A *plural* is a form of a word that indicates more than one. A plural subject requires that the corresponding verb agree in number. Most plurals include a base word and a plural suffix. Sometimes, making a word plural changes the spelling of the base word. Infrequently, the plural word is spelled the same as the base word.

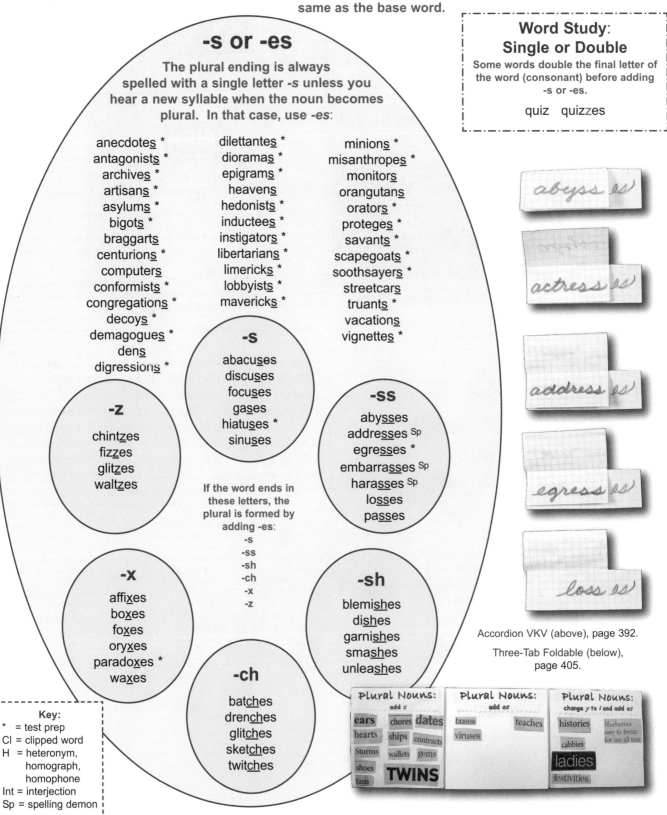

-s or -es

The plural ending is always spelled with a single letter -s unless you hear a new syllable when the noun becomes plural. In that case, use -es:

anecdote<u>s</u> *
antagonist<u>s</u> *
archive<u>s</u> *
artisan<u>s</u> *
asylum<u>s</u> *
bigot<u>s</u> *
braggart<u>s</u>
centurion<u>s</u> *
computer<u>s</u>
conformist<u>s</u> *
congregation<u>s</u> *
decoy<u>s</u> *
demagogue<u>s</u> *
den<u>s</u>
digression<u>s</u> *

dilettante<u>s</u> *
diorama<u>s</u> *
epigram<u>s</u> *
heaven<u>s</u>
hedonist<u>s</u> *
inductee<u>s</u> *
instigator<u>s</u> *
libertarian<u>s</u> *
limerick<u>s</u> *
lobbyist<u>s</u> *
maverick<u>s</u> *

minion<u>s</u> *
misanthrope<u>s</u> *
monitor<u>s</u>
orangutan<u>s</u>
orator<u>s</u> *
protege<u>s</u> *
savant<u>s</u> *
scapegoat<u>s</u> *
soothsayer<u>s</u> *
streetcar<u>s</u>
truant<u>s</u> *
vacation<u>s</u>
vignette<u>s</u> *

-s
abacu<u>ses</u>
discu<u>ses</u>
focu<u>ses</u>
ga<u>ses</u>
hiatu<u>ses</u> *
sinu<u>ses</u>

If the word ends in these letters, the plural is formed by adding -es:
-s
-ss
-sh
-ch
-x
-z

-z
chint<u>zes</u>
fiz<u>zes</u>
glit<u>zes</u>
walt<u>zes</u>

-ss
aby<u>sses</u>
add<u>resses</u> Sp
eg<u>resses</u> *
embarra<u>sses</u> Sp
hara<u>sses</u> Sp
lo<u>sses</u>
pa<u>sses</u>

-sh
blemi<u>shes</u>
di<u>shes</u>
garni<u>shes</u>
sma<u>shes</u>
unlea<u>shes</u>

-x
affi<u>xes</u>
bo<u>xes</u>
fo<u>xes</u>
ory<u>xes</u>
parado<u>xes</u> *
wa<u>xes</u>

-ch
bat<u>ches</u>
dren<u>ches</u>
glit<u>ches</u>
sket<u>ches</u>
twit<u>ches</u>

Word Study: Single or Double

Some words double the final letter of the word (consonant) before adding -s or -es.

quiz   quizzes

Accordion VKV (above), page 392.

Three-Tab Foldable (below), page 405.

Plural Nouns: add s
ears chores dates
hearts ships contracts
Storms wallets gems
shoes
fans TWINS

Plural Nouns: add es
buses teaches
viruses

Plural Nouns: change y to i and add es
histories Blueberries easy to freeze for use all year
cabbies
ladies
festivities

Plurals

Single and Plural VKVs® (right):
The plural form of a noun is written or glued onto the center of a Single VKV Flashcard, and the right tab is folded over to cover the plural ending. The singlular noun is visible when the tab is closed, and the plural when the tab is open.

Eight-Word VKVs® (below):
A Triple VKV Flashcard was used to make these singular/plural VKV flashcards for irregular nouns.
Follow the instructions on page 389 to make this VKV by using either a sheet of 8½" x 11" paper for a class display or a quarter-sheet paper for a VKV that can be glued into a notebook or stored in a pocket.
See page 389.

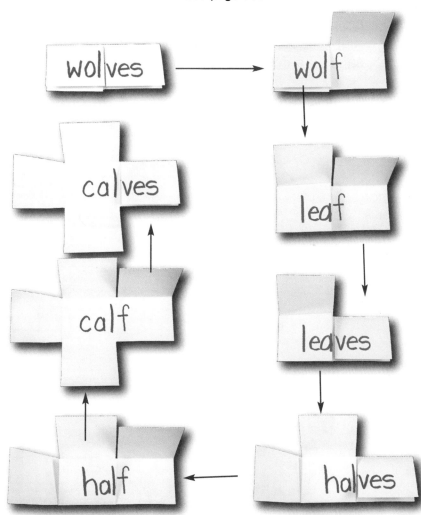

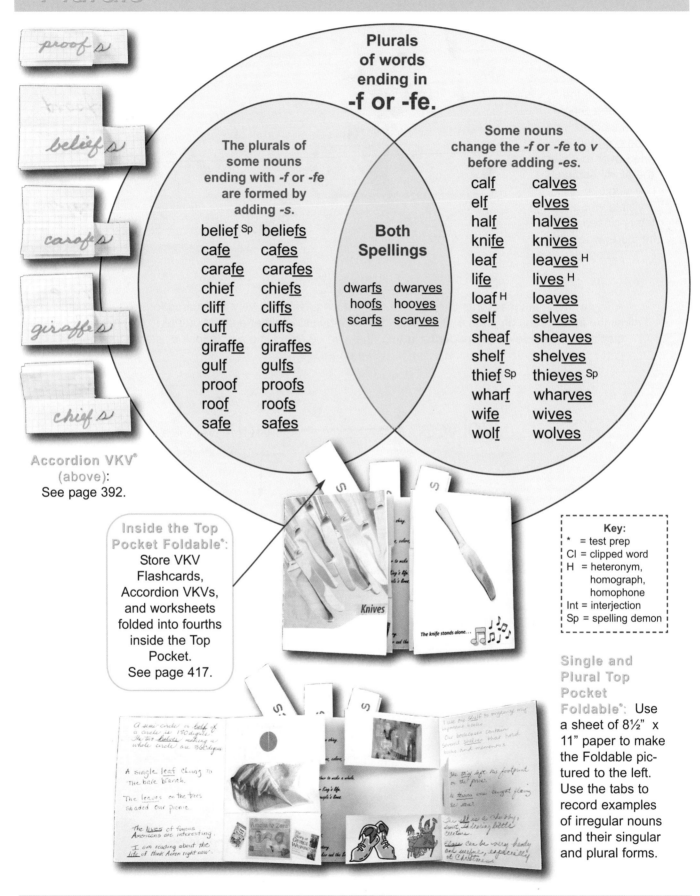

Plurals of words ending in -f or -fe.

The plurals of some nouns ending with *-f* or *-fe* are formed by adding *-s*.

belief Sp	beliefs
cafe	cafes
carafe	carafes
chief	chiefs
cliff	cliffs
cuff	cuffs
giraffe	giraffes
gulf	gulfs
proof	proofs
roof	roofs
safe	safes

Both Spellings

dwarfs	dwarves
hoofs	hooves
scarfs	scarves

Some nouns change the *-f* or *-fe* to *v* before adding *-es*.

calf	calves
elf	elves
half	halves
knife	knives
leaf	leaves H
life	lives H
loaf H	loaves
self	selves
sheaf	sheaves
shelf	shelves
thief Sp	thieves Sp
wharf	wharves
wife	wives
wolf	wolves

Accordion VKV® (above): See page 392.

Inside the Top Pocket Foldable®: Store VKV Flashcards, Accordion VKVs, and worksheets folded into fourths inside the Top Pocket. See page 417.

Knives

The knife stands alone...

Key:
* = test prep
Cl = clipped word
H = heteronym, homograph, homophone
Int = interjection
Sp = spelling demon

Single and Plural Top Pocket Foldable®: Use a sheet of 8½" x 11" paper to make the Foldable pictured to the left. Use the tabs to record examples of irregular nouns and their singular and plural forms.

Four-Tab Foldable, page 398.

Word Study Time Line: Disney vs. Tolkien

Dwarf, before 900 AD: ME *dwerf,* from OE *dweorh*

1900's: Dwarfs is the common spelling of the plural of the word *dwarf,* as illustrated in fairy tales and astronomy throughout the 19th century.

1910: An "unusual faintness" was documented by astronomers.

1922: This faintness was named *white dwarf* by Willem Luyten. Since that time, astronomers have learned more about white dwarfs, also called degenerate dwarfs, or stars that have exhausted their nuclear fuel supply.

1934: Walt Disney produced the first animated feature film, *Snow White and the Seven Dwarfs.* Dwarfs were pictured as cute "little people."

1937-1949: J. R. R. Tolkien wrote about beings inhabiting Middle-earth that he called Dwarves. It is said he changed the spelling of the plural to differentiate the fantasy race of *dwarves* he created in his novels from the *dwarfs* of fairy tales.

Single and Plural Fold-Over VKVs® (below):

Plural forms of nouns collected from RWP can be glued onto single strips of notebook paper. Fold the paper over to cover the plural suffix, then write the singular suffix on the front of the single strip. These small Fold-Over VKV Flashcards can be glued into a notebook or stored in pockets or envelopes that have been glued into notebooks.

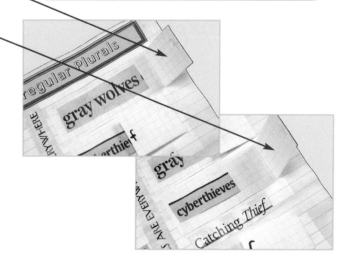

-y to -i and add -es:
Use Triple Flashcards to illustrate the *-y to -i and add -es* rule. The Triple Flashcard will have three tabs to the left and two tabs to the right. Three words are written to the left so that the consonant preceding the *-y* in each word is along the right edge of the left tabs. The final *-y* is written on the first right tab, and *-ies* is written on the second. When the left tabs are flipped, the right tabs are also moved to form the singular and plural of each word.

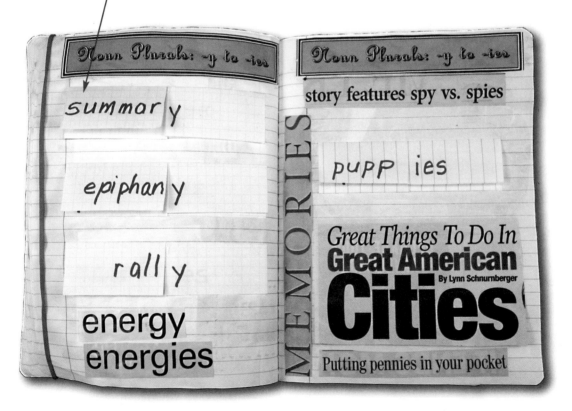

When *y* is preceded by a consonant, the plural is formed by changing the -*y* to -*i* and adding -*es*.

adversi**ty** *	adversi**ties**
anoma**ly** *	anoma**lies**
cacopho**ny** *	cacopho**nies**
can**dy**	can**dies**
ci**ty**	ci**ties**
colo**ny**	colo**nies**
come**dy**	come**dies**
effi**gy** *	effi**gies**
epipha**ny** *	epipha**nies**
levi**ty** *	levi**ties**
perju**ry** *	perju**ries**
prosperi**ty** *	prosperi**ties**
spontanei**ty** *	spontanei**ties**
stu**dy**	stu**dies**
summa**ry**	summa**ries**

Words ending in -y

When *y* is preceded by a vowel, the plural is formed by adding -*s*.

all**ey**	all**eys**
b**ay** H	b**ays** H
conv**ey**	conv**eys**
del**ay**	del**ays**
ess**ay**	ess**ays**
highw**ay**	highw**ays**
monk**ey**	monk**eys**
pl**ay** H	pl**ays** H
str**ay**	str**ays**
turk**ey**	turk**eys**

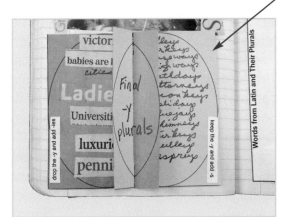

Venn Diagram Bound Book (left):
This Foldable was used to collect examples of nouns that end in -*y*.
To the left are examples of words that change the *y* to *i* before adding a plural suffix, and the words to the right retain the -*y* and add -*s* to form the plural. Compare and contrast the two lists to determine when and why a -*y* changes. The rules for forming these plurals are written in the diagrams above.
Below: Comparing words that end in -*ey* and -*y*. Both have the /e/ sound. See folding instructions, page 402.

Free Template:
Go to www.dinah.com to download the template for this Bound Foldable Venn Diagram book.

Word Study: Proper Nouns That End in -y
Proper nouns ending in a -*y* preceded by a consonant usually do not change the -*y* to *i*, but add -*s* instead.
Emm**y**, Emm**ys** - That TV show won several *Emmys*.
German**y**, German**ys** - In 1990, the two *Germanys* were unified.
Gramm**y**, Gramm**ys** - His song won two *Grammys*.
Tomm**y**, Tomm**ys** - There are two *Tommys* in our class.
The rule does not apply to words that are merely capitalized common nouns.
Twin Ci**ties**

Plurals Mass Nouns, Countable Nouns, and Plurals

Mass nouns (uncountable nouns) do not have a plural form: *air, soap, sand, water.*
Countable nouns do have plural forms: *apples, cars, rivers, tables.*

Some words can be both a *mass* noun and a *countable* noun:

Uncountable (Mass) Example: *Cake* is good.

Countable Example: Two *cakes* are better.

Collective nouns are countable nouns that name groups composed of members: *herd* of cattle, *group* of people.

Tests for Identifying Mass Nouns

1. Mass nouns cannot be used with the articles *a* or *an*.
2. The words *much* and *little* can be used only with mass nouns.

Mass (Uncountable) examples using *much* and *little*:

Little cash is left in the bank. (Correct.)   Much cash is left in the bank. (Correct.)

Countable examples using *few* and *many*:

Few cars are left in the garage. (Correct; *little is incorrect.*)

Many cars are left in the garage. (Correct; *much is incorrect.*)

Liquids:	Gases:	Small Units:	Collections or Groups:	Abstract Concepts:	Others:
blood	air [H]	barley	aircraft	advice [Sp]	arms [H]
coffee	carbon dioxide	corn	baggage	anger	barracks
cream	carbon monoxide	dirt	bread	applause	chess
gasoline	ether	flour [H]	British	beauty	communication
gravy	hydrogen	grass	cash	chaos	dregs
juice	neon	gravel	citrus	courage	goods
lemonade	nitrogen	hay	clergy	dissent	help
milk	oxygen	oatmeal	clothing	fun	homework
oil	pollution	pollen	corps [Sp] [H]	good	housework
paint	smog	rice	equipment	happiness	information
shampoo	smoke	rye	food	honesty	momentum
soup	steam	salt	furniture	intelligence	music
syrup	tear gas	sand	garbage	knowledge	mustard
water	vapor	sugar	gross	literacy	news
wine		tapioca	hardware	love	outskirts
	Fields:	water	jelly	majority	remains
Solids:	astronomy	wheat	jewelry	means	research
butter	biology		luggage	peace [H]	scenery
cloth	civics		lumber	sadness	slang
cotton	English		machinery	strength	weather
gold	geology		mail [H]	stuff	
land	history		money	wealth	
rayon	music		paper		
silver	poetry		people		
soap	politics		police		
toast [H]	physics		silverware		
tooth-paste	psychology		software		
			Swiss		
			traffic		
			troops		

These words can also be countable:

bonsai	haiku
chamois	series

> ### Word Study: Are They Game?
> When discussed in a preservation or sporting context, groups of game and wild animals are sometimes referred to in the singular:
>
> There were nine lion in the pride.
> The villages killed three tiger last year.

Plurals of a few nouns are the same as the singular. These are called *invariable nouns*.

Word Study: Fish or Fishes?

Most names of fish have no separate plural form, though there are exceptions—*lampreys, rays, sharks*. The word *fish* is usually used as a plural in the context of food, but *fishes* is used to describe individual fishes of different species.

Examples:
There are five *fish* in the aquarium.
Buy three plates of *fish and chips*.
List some of the various *fishes* of the Colorado River.

bass

carp

cod

fish

-jellyfish
-lungfish
-sawfish
-sunfish

grouper

mackerel

perch

pike

salmon

shrimp

squid

trout

tuna

The King James Version of the Bible tells of the miracle of the *loaves and fishes*, but newer versions speak of *loaves and fish*.

Animals:

Some of these terms are used in their "singular" form in the collective sense, but with a plural ending in a counting sense (*chicken* for dinner; three *chickens* in the yard).

beef/beeves

bison

cattle

chicken/chickens

deer/deers

fish/fishes

fowl/fowls

grouse

head
(of cattle, sheep, horses)

killdeer

moose

offspring

poultry

quail/quails

sheep

silverfish/-es

snipe/snipes

springbok/-s

swine

vermin

walrus/walruses

wapiti/wapitis

waterfowl/-s

Binary Nouns:

Binary nouns refer to objects that have two parts, or are perceived to have two parts. Although the noun takes a plural form, it refers to only one thing. Binary nouns name types of:
1. tools and instruments
2. clothing
3. optical lenses.

biceps

binoculars

forceps

glasses

goggles

jeans [H]

leggings

overalls

pants [H]

pantyhose

pliers

scissors

shorts [H]

sunglasses

tights

tongs

tweezers

Below: Multi-Tab Notebook Foldables can be used to collect examples of binary nouns.

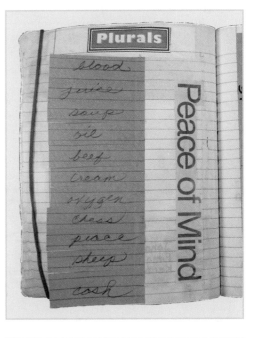

Mongooses:

The plural of *goose* is *geese*, but the plural of mongoose is *mongooses* (not *mongeese*).
DZ Note: I found the cartoon pictured to the right in a travel magazine I received when conducting a workshop in the Virgin Islands. This cartoon is a great teaching aid. It says, "Mongooses need love, too." The little guy at the bottom says "No, it's not mongeese!" Remember, RWP can be made into a notebook by folding a tab and gluing the tab into a notebook. Under this tab is expository writing about mongooses.

Irregular Plural Forms:

A few nouns change the spelling of the vowel sound to form the plural.

Plural	Singular
dice	die
feet	foot
geese	goose
lice	louse
men	man
mice	mouse
parentheses	parenthesis
teeth	tooth
women	woman

Mouses or Mice

The plural of *mouse*, an object used to move the cursor on a computer monitor, is sometimes written *mouses*.
But the plural of *mouse*, a rodent, is always *mice*.

zucchini

Italian singular: *zucchino*
Italian plural: *zucchini*

The Americanization of this word uses *zucchini* as both singular and plural (although some dictionaries list *zucchinis* as a plural option).

Adding -en and -im:

A few words form the plural by adding *-en*. These words come to us from Old English.

brother	brothers
	brethren
	(archaic plural)
child	children
ox	oxen

A few Hebrew loanwords form the plural by adding *-im*.

cherub	cherubim
seraph	seraphim

Fold-Over VKVs®:

A Fold-Over VKV was used to illustrate the singular and plural forms of the word *child*. The word *children* was placed on the left side of a single flashcard, and the tab was folded over to cover *-ren* —*child, children*.

Fold-Back VKVs®:

The left edge of a single tab was glued into the notebook. The word *tooth* was written to the left. The tab was folded in half, and the word *teeth* was written on the back.

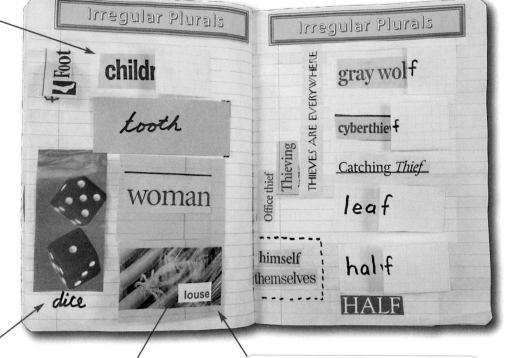

Tabbed Notebook Foldables®:

A quarter sheet of paper was used to make a small Two-Tab Foldable. A tab was folded along the right edge and glued into the notebook before the tabs were cut.

A magazine picture was used to make the tab for *dice* and *die*. A picture of a *die* was glued under the tab, with a picture of *dice* on the front.

If a word ends in o...

Words that end in -o that form the plural by adding -s.

auto	aut<u>os</u>
kilo	kil<u>os</u>
patio	pati<u>os</u>
photo	phot<u>os</u>
piano	pian<u>os</u>
radio	radi<u>os</u>
solo	sol<u>os</u>
studio	studi<u>os</u>
video	vide<u>os</u>

Both Spellings

buffal<u>os</u>	buffal<u>oes</u>
carg<u>os</u>	carg<u>oes</u>
grott<u>os</u>	grott<u>oes</u>
hal<u>os</u>	hal<u>oes</u>
mang<u>os</u>	mang<u>oes</u>
mosquit<u>os</u>	mosquit<u>oes</u>
mott<u>os</u>	mott<u>oes</u>
n<u>os</u>	n<u>oes</u>
placeb<u>os</u>	placeb<u>oes</u>
tornad<u>os</u>	tornad<u>oes</u>
volcan<u>os</u>	volcan<u>oes</u>
zer<u>os</u>	zer<u>oes</u>

Words that end in -o that form the plural by adding -es.

cargo	carg<u>oes</u>
domino	domin<u>oes</u>
echo	ech<u>oes</u>
embargo	embarg<u>oes</u>
hero	her<u>oes</u>
potato Sp	potat<u>oes</u> Sp
tomato Sp	tomat<u>oes</u> Sp
torpedo	torped<u>oes</u>
vertigo *	vertig<u>oes</u>
veto	vet<u>oes</u>

Key:
* = test prep
Cl = clipped word
H = heteronym, homograph, homophone
Int = interjection
Sp = spelling demon

Word Study: Loanword Study
Many nouns of foreign origin, including almost all Italian loanwords, add only -s (not -es) to form the plural:

	Singular	Plural
It	canto	cantos
Japn	kimono	kimonos
It	libretto	libretti
It	piano	pianos Cl pianoforte
It	portico	porticos, porti-coes
L	pro	pros
It	tempo	tempi, tempos

Venn Diagram: This Notebook Foldable was made using a half sheet of notebook paper trimmed to fit into a composition book. Fold a tab along the left edge, glue the tab into the notebook, and cut tabs to form a three-tab Venn diagram. Use the Foldable to collect examples of *-o words* that form their plurals by adding *-es*, *-o words* that add *-s*, and *-o words* that can be written either way.

English has many words of Latin and Greek origin that maintain their original Latin and Greek spellings when forming the plurals—schema, schemata. However, some Latin and Greek nouns have been modernized, or made to conform to American English spellings. For plurals of some words, either the original Latin or Greek spelling or the modern spelling can be used, depending on the context.

Examples: radios have antennas; insects have antennae;
research libraries use appendices; human bodies have vermiform appendixes;
media refers to channels of communication; artists work with various mediums like watercolor.

Nouns ending in -on form the plural with -a:

	Singular	Plural
Gk	automaton	automata
Gk	criterion	criteria
Gk	phenomenon	phenomena
Gk	polyhedron	polyhedra

Nouns ending in -a form the plural with -ta, or add -s:

Gk	dogma	dogmata, dogmas
Gk	lemma	lemmata, lemmas
Gk	schema	schemata, schemas
Gk	stigma	stigmata, stigmas
Gk	stoma	stomata, stomas

Nouns ending in -ies remain the same in plural:

	Singular	Plural
L	series	series
L	species	species

Nouns ending in -um form the plural with -a, or add -s:

	Singular	Original Plural, Modernized Plural
L	addendum	addenda
L< Gk	bacterium	bacteria
L	corrigendum	corrigenda
L	curriculum	curricula, curriculums
L	datum	data
L	dictum	dicta
L	erratum	errata
L	forum	fora, forums
L	medium	media, mediums
L	memorandum	memoranda, memorandums
L	ovum	ova
L	spectrum	spectra, spectrums
L	stratum	strata
Gk	symposium	symposia, symposiums

Spelling: Latin Origin

STIMULATE YOUR STIMULUS.

SLIPPERY WHEN AQUEOUS

STIMULUS PACKAGE
Stimulus plan

Duo tries out 'vox populi' approach

Singular and Plural Forms

alumnus	alumni
bacillus	bacilli
cactus	cacti, cactuses
census	censi
focus	foci, focuses
fungus	fungi, funguses
genus	genera
nucleus	nuclei
radius	radii
stimulus	stimuli
syllabus	syllabi, syllabuses
terminus	termini

Nouns ending in -is change to -es in plural:

	Singular	Plural
Gk	analysis	analyses
L	axis	axes [H]
Gk	basis	bases
Gk	crisis	crises
Gk	diagnosis	diagnoses
Gk	emphasis	emphases
Gk	hypothesis	hypotheses
L	neurosis	neuroses
Gk	oasis	oases
Gk	parenthesis	parentheses
Gk	synopsis	synopses
L	testis	testes
Gk	thesis	theses

Note: The plural of axis (axes; ak-seez) is a homograph—but not a homophone—for the plural of ax (axes; ak-siz).

Multi-Tab Template (above) from Dinah Zike's *Notebook Foldables* book and CD.

Plurals Greek and Latin Words

Many science terms have retained their their original plurals, but a few have been adapted to more modern spellings.
Latin nouns ending in *-a* form the plural with *-ae*, or *-s*.

	Singular	Original Plural	Modernized Plural
L	alg**a**	alg**ae**	
L	alumn**a**	alumn**ae**	
L<Gk	amoeb**a**	amoeb**ae**	amoeba**s**
L	antenn**a**	antenn**ae**	antenna**s**
L	formul**a**	formul**ae**	formula**s**
L	larv**a**	larv**ae**	
L	nebul**a**	nebul**ae**	nebula**s**
L	vertebr**a**	vertebr**ae**	vertebra**s**

Latin nouns ending in *-us* form the plural with *-i* or *-era /-ora*:
Example: *hippopotamus, hippopotami* or *hippopotamuses* (modern plural).
Note also that some definitions of a word require the original plural form,
while other definitions require the modernized form. (Consult a dictionary.)

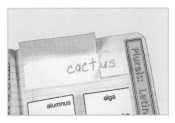

	Singular	Original Plural	Modernized Plural
L	alumn**us**	alumn**i**	
L	bacill**us**	bacill**i**	
Gk	cact**us**	cact**i**	cactus**es**
L	cens**us**		census**es**
L	corp**us**	corp**ora**	corpus**es**
L	foc**us**	foc**i**	focus**es**
L	fung**us**	fung**i**	fungus**es**
L	gen**us**	gen**era**	genus**es**
L	nucle**us**	nucle**i**	nucleus**es**
Gk	octop**us**	octop**i**	octopus**es**
Gk	platyp**us**	platyp**i**	platypus**es**

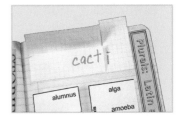

Note: *Octopodes* and *platypodes* are rarely used as the plurals of these words, but they are technically correct plural forms since the original words are directly from Greek and not Latin.

L	rad**ius**	rad**ii**	radius**es**
L	stimul**us**	stimul**i**	
L	syllab**us**	syllab**i**	syllabus**es**
L	termin**us**	termin**i**	terminus**es**
L	uter**us**	uter**i**	uterus**es**
L	vir**us**	(no Latin plural)	virus**es**
L	visc**us**	visc**era**	

Latin nouns ending in *-ex* or *-ix* form the plural with *-ices*:

	Singular	Plural	Modernized Plural
L	ap**ex**	ap**ices**	apex**es**
L	append**ix**	append**ices**	appendix**es**
L	ind**ex**	ind**ices**	indexes
L	matr**ix**	matr**ices**	matrix**es**
L	vert**ex**	vert**ices**	vertex**es**
L	vort**ex**	vort**ices**	vortex**es**

Six-Word VKV®:
Fold and cut a Triple VKV Flashcard so that it has three tabs to the left and two tabs to the right. Use this VKV to kinesthetically show the formation of singular and plural forms of Latin nouns. See VKV variation on page 389.

radius radii
cactus cacti
alumnus alumni

Portmanteau Words

Portmanteau words are formed by blending two or more words and combining their meanings. Lewis Carroll first described these types of words in *Through the Looking-Glass* (1871). There, Humpty-Dumpty explains that the word *mimsy* is a combination of *miserable* and *flimsy*. On a very personal note, during chemotherapy treatments, one becomes terribly *exhausted* and *constipated*. My portmanteau word for this condition was *exhaustipated*. I hope you are never exhaustipated.—dz

alpha + beta	alphabet	International + network	Internet
animate + electronics	animatronics	McDonald's + mansion	McMansion
automobile + memorabilia	automobilia	malicious + software	malware
beef + buffalo	beefalo	modulator + demodulator	modem
biology + electronic	bionic	motor + pedal	moped
binary + digit	bit	motor + hotel	motel
Web + log	blog	motorcycle + cross country	motocross
blot + botch	blotch	motor + cavalcade	motorcade
breath + analyser	breathalyser	motor + town	Motown
breakfast + lunch	brunch	Internet + etiquette	netiquette
bungle + stumble	bumble	pal + alimony	palimony
camera + recorder	camcorder	parachute + troopers	paratroopers
celebrity + debutante	celebutante	petroleum + chemical	petrochemical
cheese + hamburger	cheeseburger	picture + dictionary	pictionary
Chinese + English	Chinglish	picture+ x + element	pixel
chocolate + alcoholic	chocoholic	ipod + broadcasting	podcasting
chunk + lump	chump	precede + sequel	prequel
cinema + complex	cineplex	prim + sissy	prissy
clap + dash	clash	pulsating + star	pulsar
condensation + trail	contrail	Reagan + economics	Reaganomics
cybernetic + organism	cyborg	sprawl + crawl	scrawl
documentary + drama	docudrama	sea + landscape	seascape
educational + games	edugames	share + software	shareware
electronic + execute	electrocute	sheep + people	sheeple
electronic + mail	email, e-mail	simultaneous + broadcast	simulcast
escalade + elevator	escalator	skirt + shorts	skort
electronic + magazine	e-zine	sky + highjack	skyjack
fare + ye + well	farewell	smoke + fog	smog
flounce + founder	flounder	sound + landscape	soundscape
flinch + funk	flunk	spoon + fork	spork
fourteen + nights	fortnight	sports + broadcast	sportscast
free + software	freeware	tangerine + pomelo	tangelo
glitter + ritz	glitz	television + marathon	telethon
globe + blob	glob	television + evangelist	televangelist
God+ o + be (with) + ye	goodbye	Texas + Oklahoma	Texoma
guess + estimate	guestimate	travel + monologue	travelogue
hazardous + materials	hazmat	volcanic + smog	vog
high + fidelity	hi-fi	wiki + encyclopedia	Wikipedia
information + commercial	infomercial	work + alcoholic	workaholic

Portmanteau Words

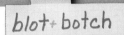

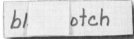

Double VKV® Flashcards (above and below): This one-tab omission VKV is perfect for portmanteau words that are formed from the beginning letters of the first word and the ending letters of the second. See page 382.

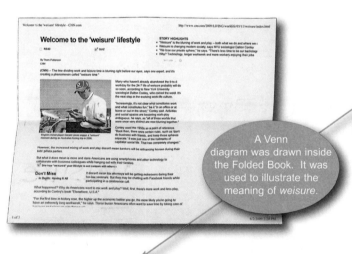

A Venn diagram was drawn inside the Folded Book. It was used to illustrate the meaning of *weisure*.

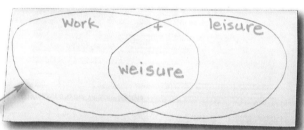

Variation: Inside the Folded Book, draw a Venn diagram based on the new portmanteau word *weisure*, coined by New York University sociologist Dalton Conley and described in the folded CNN news article. Since this Venn diagram is inside the Folded Book made from the article pictured left, there are no cuts. See page 395.

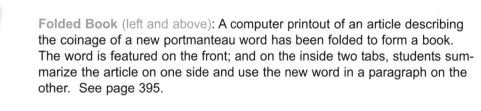

Folded Book (left and above): A computer printout of an article describing the coinage of a new portmanteau word has been folded to form a book. The word is featured on the front; and on the inside two tabs, students summarize the article on one side and use the new word in a paragraph on the other. See page 395.

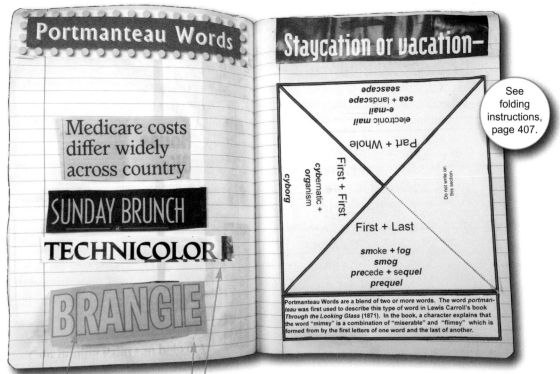

Portmanteau Words

Medicare costs differ widely across country

SUNDAY BRUNCH

TECHNICOLOR

BRANGIE

Staycation or vacation—

seascape
sea + landscape
e-mail
electronic mail

Part + Whole

First + First

cybernatic + organism

cyborg

Do not write on this section

First + Last

smoke + fog
smog
precede + sequel
prequel

Portmanteau Words are a blend of two or more words. The word *portmanteau* was first used to describe this type of word in Lewis Carroll's book *Through the Looking Glass* (1871). In the book, a character explains that the word "mimsy" is a combination of "miserable" and "flimsy" which is formed from by the first letters of one word and the last of another.

See folding instructions, page 407.

SUNDAY BRUNCH
TECHNICOLOR
Brad & Angelina

Notebook Foldable® Pyramid (above): This Pyramid Foldable was made using the CD template from Dinah Zike's *Notebook Foldables* book. Notice how the copy on this Pyramid differs from the computer-generated copy on the prefixes Pyramid pictured on the next page. This 3-D Foldable lies flat, forms a three-sided pyramid shape, and flips back to allow students to write or glue examples of words, sentences, quotes, definitions, etc., on the inside of the Pyramid.

Notebook Foldable® Tabs (above): Titles and headlines (RWP) can be turned into Notebook Foldables by gluing one edge of the cutout into a notebook and leaving the rest of it free to move as a tab.

Glue Left, Glue Right: If the RWP is to be glued on the left page of a spiral or composition book, glue the tab down on the right side. (The opposite is true if the tab is glued to the right page.) This prevents the loose edges of the tabs from getting bent when the notebooks are opened and closed.

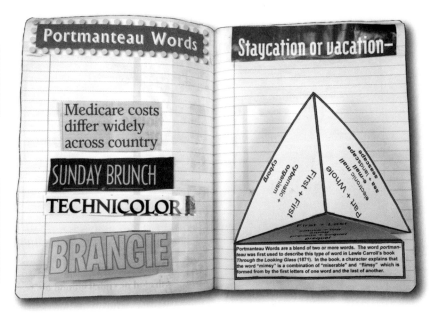

Portmanteau Words

Medicare costs differ widely across country

SUNDAY BRUNCH

TECHNICOLOR

BRANGIE

Staycation or vacation—

seascape
sea + landscape
electronic mail

cyborg

cybernatic + organism

First + First

Part + Whole

First + Last

Portmanteau Words are a blend of two or more words. The word *portmanteau* was first used to describe this type of word in Lewis Carroll's book *Through the Looking Glass* (1871). In the book, a character explains that the word "mimsy" is a combination of "miserable" and "flimsy" which is formed from by the first letters of one word and the last of another.

Fold-Over VKV: See pages 370 and 373.

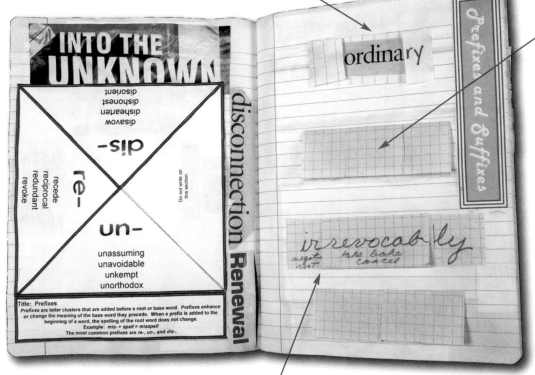

Double VKV® Flashcard (above): Examine the root *onerate*, the prefix *ex-*, and the suffix *-ed*. See page 378. Cut three tabs instead of two.

Triple VKV Flashcard: See page 388.

Notebook Foldable® Pyramid (above left): This Pyramid Foldable was made using the CD template from Dinah Zike's *Notebook Foldables* book. This 3-D Foldable lies flat, forms a Pyramid (below left), and flips back (below right) to allow students to write or glue examples of words, sentences, quotes, definitions, etc., to the inside of the Pyramid.

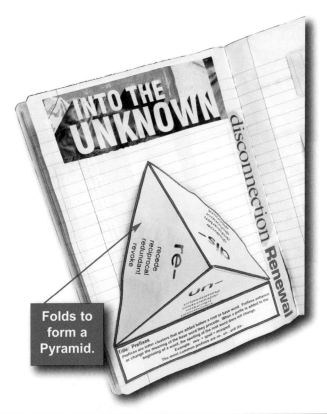

Folds to form a Pyramid.

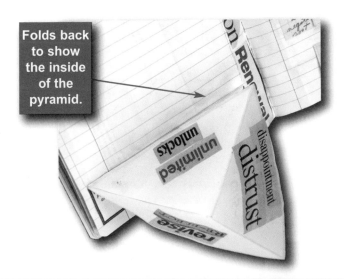

Folds back to show the inside of the pyramid.

Prefixes VKVs®

Prefixes are letter clusters that are added to the beginning of a root or base word. Prefixes enhance or change the meaning of the base word they precede. When a prefix is added to the beginning of a word, the spelling of the root word does not change. **Example:** *mis-* + *spell* = **misspell.**
The most common prefixes are *re-*, *un-*, and *dis-*.

 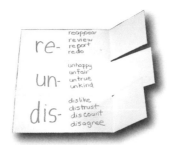

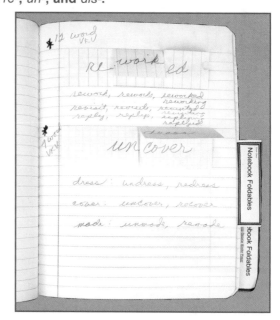

Foldables® and VKVs® (above and below): There are many ways Foldables and VKVs can be used to teach and rein-force the use of prefixes. **Above**, a half sheet of copy paper was used to make a Three-Tab Fold-Over VKV. Multiple words for each of the three most common prefixes were recorded under the tabs. **Below**, Single VKV Flashcards were used to add or delete prefixes. See pages 370-373.

Word Study: Not a Prefix
Students might notice that sometimes the letters *un-* at the beginning of a word are either part of the root word and not a prefix, or they are part of the combining form *uni-*, meaning *one.*
Examples: *unary, uncle, under, uniform, unit*

Prefixes Can Change the Meanings of Words and Form Antonyms

Triple VKV Flashcards, **see** page 385.

Triple VKV Flashcards can be used for the following: *cover, discover, recover*
like, dislike, unlike
cooked, uncooked, precooked
told, retold, untold

Test Prep Examples:

abridged	*unabridged*
credit	*discredit*
aesthetic	*unaesthetic*
pretentious	*unpretentious*
rational	*nonrational*
subtle	*unsubtle*

Three- and Four-Word VKVs® (above):
Fold and cut a Triple VKV Flashcard so that it has a single central tab to the left. A prefix will be written on this extended tab. Cut the right side so that either three or four roots can be added after the prefix. The notebook above has five different VKVs that expose students to the formation of 18 words. Other similar words found in RWP are glued onto the page, increasing the number of terms to 30.
See VKV instructions on pages 368 to 392.

Notebook Exchange: Have students exchange notebooks with three other students. This will allow them to read, kinesthetically manipulate, and be immersed in nearly 100 related terms in a very short period of time.

Word Study: Redundancies
Unnecessary Prefixes

irregardless: The word *irregardless* is a redundancy since the prefix *ir-* is negative and the suffix *-less* is negative. It is incorrect to add the ir- prefix; use *regardless* instead.
You must take the test regardless of what your friends say.

debone: *Bone* is nearly a contronym, as it refers to skeletal bone and it is a verb meaning to remove bones. There is no need to add *de-* before **bone**, but it is not incorrect to do so.
He will bone the fish before cooking it.
He will debone the fish before cooking it.

unravel: *Ravel* is a contronym meaning both *entangle* and *disentangle*. It is unnecessary, but not incorrect, to add the *un-*. The term **unravel** has been used since the late 1500's.
The rug was raveling along the edge.
The rug was unraveling along the edge.

Lesson Plan Notebook (below): The teacher-made composition book featured on this page is used as a lesson plan book.
The teacher's lesson plan notebook might include the following:
• VKVs students will make
• Foldables students will make
• teacher notes and reminders
• test prep terms that relate to skills studied
• extension and application of skills

Test Prep: The teacher plans to use VKV Flashcards as a study aid to feature affixes being studied and reviewed in class. The note indicates that the words will be selected from SAT word lists.

Notebook Foldables® Templates (below): This example came from Dinah Zike's *Notebook Foldables for Spirals, Binders, and Composition Books: Strategies for All Subjects, 4th-College.*

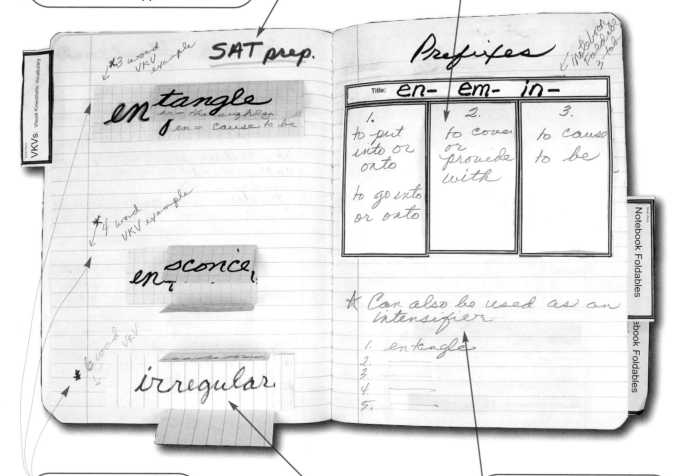

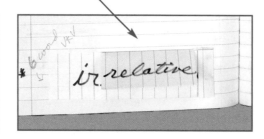

Triple VKV® Flashcards (above): The three VKVs pictured in the notebook form 13 words. The VKVs could have been placed closer together to provide room for two or three more VKVs made using quarter sheets of notebook paper.

The Teacher's Plan: The teacher has made notes on what students will be asked to write on, under, and around the notebook Foldables and VKVs. For example, at the bottom of this page, students would be asked to explain how these prefixes alter the meanings of words.

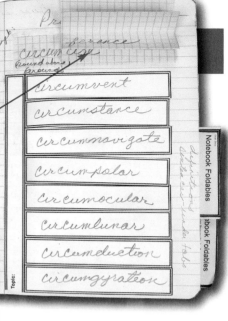

VKVs® (above and below): VKVs can be used in many ways to teach and reinforce the use of prefixes. Above, a half sheet of copy paper was used to make an Accordion VKV featuring *circum-*.
Left: Single VKV Flashcards were used as Fold-Over VKVs. Triple VKV Flaschards are seen below.

Multi-Tab Foldable® (above): Make from a half sheet of copy paper or with a template from Dinah's *Notebook Foldables* book and CD.

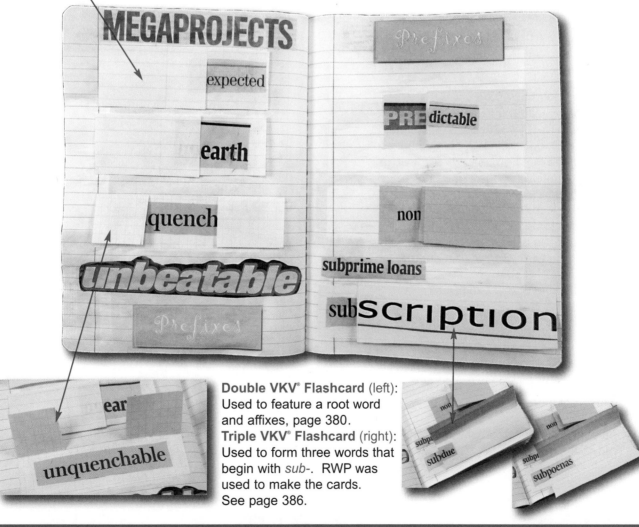

Double VKV® Flashcard (left): Used to feature a root word and affixes, page 380.
Triple VKV® Flashcard (right): Used to form three words that begin with *sub-*. RWP was used to make the cards. See page 386.

(closed)

Foldable® Pocket Chart (left and right): A sheet of posterboard was used to make this giant bulletin board pocket chart. Students from mulitple classes found examples of words beginning with *con-* and *com-* and wrote or glued the examples to the top chart. Words that they were required to know were recorded on flashcards and stored in the pocket. Students put envelope pockets in their notebooks to collect their personal flashcards of *con-* and *com-* words that they needed to learn to spell and use comfortably in spoken language.

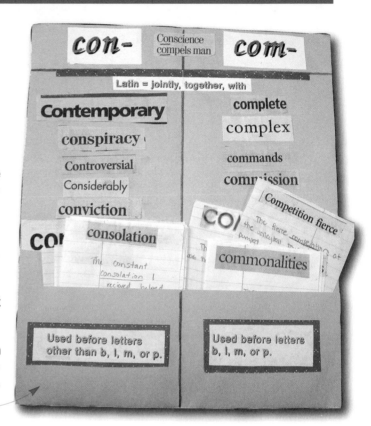

Foldable® Bound Book (right):

Use a *hotdog* fold to make Two-Tab Foldables with 11" x 17" paper. Make multiple sections, depending on the number of prefixes to be featured. Always allow extra pages for future additions to the booklet.

Fold the two-tab sections in half and glue them side by side to make bound books. Clothespins can be used to hold the sections together while the glue dries.

Use the book to collect examples of prefixes found in RWP and encountered while reading literature, poems, short stories, or completing worksheets on prefixes.

Under the tabs, write sentences or paragraphs using the words collected on the front tabs.

See page 28 for photographs and instructions on binding a Foldable book.

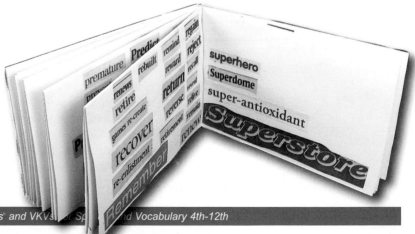

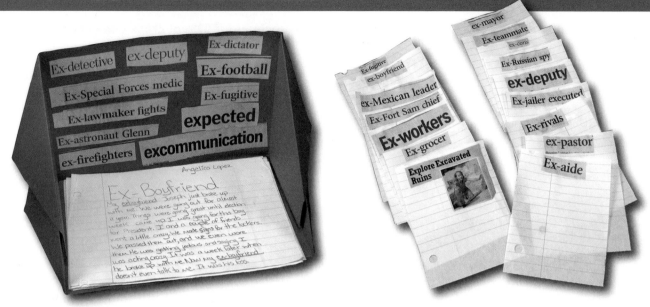

Four-Door Foldable® Display Case (above left): When a sheet of 11" x 17" paper is used to make this display case, half sheets of paper from the classroom publishing center can be collected within the display (as seen above), or they can be glued to the inside back of the display and physical objects can be displayed in front of the writing. Compare the scale of the half-sheet pages of paragraphs and the quarter-sheet flashcards. Both sizes can be used with this display. See page 410.

Single VKV® Flashcards (below): These notebook VKVs were made using RWP glued onto a Single VKV Flashcard made from a quarter sheet of notebook paper. The featured prefix *un-* can be covered and *un*covered by the left tab to form a word with and without an affix. See page 370.

Accordion VKV® Flashcard (left): The prefix *un-* and five words that have *un-* as an affix are on this small VKV. Because a half sheet of notebook paper was used to make this Flashcard, it can be glued into a composition book or spiral notebook or stored in a pocket. See page 392 for photos and step-by-step instructions.

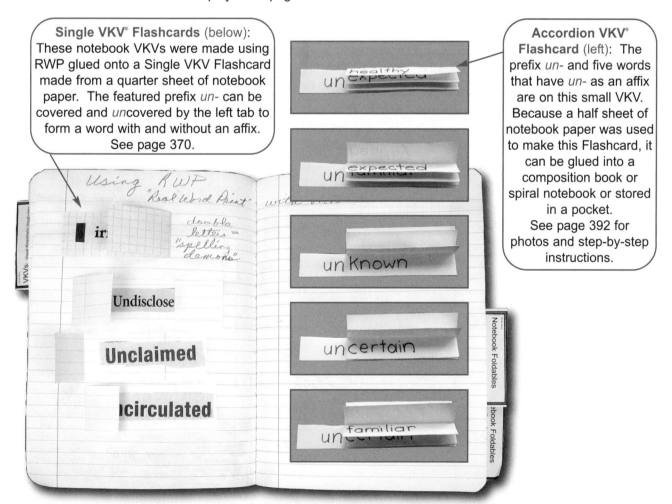

Prefixes Twenty Most Common

The twenty prefixes listed below have been found to account for 93% of prefix use in common language. Select ability-appropriate words for student use.

1. un-
ME prefix; not, negative, opposite

unaffected *
unassailable *
unassuming *
unauthentic *
unavoidable *
uncanny *
uncomfortable
uncouth *
undemonstrative *
undeniable *
unequal
unexpected
unfair
unforgettable
unharmed
unhurt
unkempt *
unkind
unload
unlucky
unmitigated *
unopened
unorthodox *
unpretentious *
unseasonable
untrue
unusual
unwrap

2. re-
L prefix; again, back

readmit
reappear
reattach
rebate
rebound
recede *
receipt Sp
reciprocal *
record
recreation *
recurrent *
recycle
redecorate
reduce *
redundant *
refinement *
reflect
refrain *
refute *
regurgitated *
rehearse
relinquish *
remainder *
renounce *
reproach *
retract *
review
revoke *

3. il-, im-, in-, ir-
L prefixes similar to -un; not, opposed to; without, from; used to form adjectives and nouns
il- used before l

illegal
illiterate
illogical
illusion

im- used before b, m, p

imbalance
immeasurable
impermanent *
impolite
impossible

in-

inaccurate
inalienable *
inappropriate *
incomprehensible *
incorrect
incredible * Sp
independent Sp
indignant *
indispensable Sp
inexpensive
inoculate Sp
inorganic
invisible

ir- used before r

irrefutable *
irregular
irreparable
irreplaceable
irresponsible

4. dis-
L prefix; lack of, not, opposite, away, free from, apart

disable
disagree
disappear
disappoint Sp
disapprove
disavow *
discontinue
discount
discourse*
discover
disdain *
dishearten *
dishonest *
disinfect
disingenuous *
disloyal *
disorient *
disown *
dispel *
displace *
disprove *
dissimilar *
dissolve
dissuade *
distaste *
distraction *
distrust

5. em-, en-
L prefixes; variations of im- and in-; put into, within, cover, cause to be
em- used before b, p

embargo *
embark
embarrass Sp
embassy
embedded *
embellish
embody *
embryo
empathetic *
enable
encase
enchanted
encircle
enclose
encounter
encourage
endanger
endemic *
enduring *
engulf *
enhance
enquire
enrage
ensuing *
enthusiastic *
entomb
entrap *
envision

Accordion Foldables® fold flat. They can be "read" like a book by turning the "pages," or displayed extended like the one pictured at the bottom of the next page. See page 403.

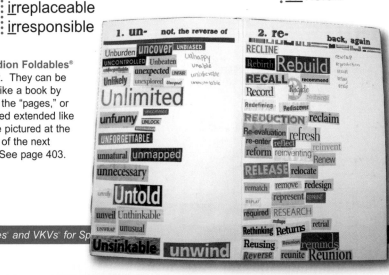

Source: White, T.G.I., Sowell, V., and Yanagihara, A. (1999). Teaching elementary students to use word-part clues. *The Reading Teacher*, 42, 302-308.

6. non-

L prefix; not, opposite of

nonalcoholic
nonaquatic
nonchalant *
noncombatant
nonconformist *
nondairy
nondescript
nonfat
nonfiction
nonjudgmental *
nonliving
nonpoisonous
nonprofit
nonsense
nonsmoking
nonstop
nonuniform *
nonviolent

7. in-, im-

E prefixes; variations of em- and en-; put into, within, cover, cause to be

im- before b, m, p

imbalance
immediate Sp
immerse
immigrate
impassioned *
impetus *
implant

in-

incision
include
income
indispensable Sp
induce
infect
inhale
inland
inside
intelligent Sp

8. over-

ME prefixal use of the word *over*; too much, excess, over the limit

overdue
overflow
overgrown
overhead
overland
overlap
overload
overnight
overpass
overreaction
overrun Sp
overshoe *
overshot *
overstatement *
overtake
overtime
overwhelm
overwork

9. mis-

OE prefix: wrong, not, mistaken

misanthrope *
misbehave
miscarry
miscellaneous *
mischievous Sp
miscount
misdeed
misfit
misfortune *
mislay
mislead
misprint
misshapen *
misspell Sp
mistake
mistreat
mistrust
misunderstand

10. sub-

L prefix; under, less, below, beneath

subatomic
subcutaneous
subdivision
subdue
sublet
sublime
submarine
submerge
subscribe
subsequent *
subsoil
substantiate *
subterranean *
subtract
subtropical
suburb
subversive *
subway

11. pre-
L prefix; before, early, prior to

preamble *
precaution
preconceived
predictable *
prefix
preheat
prejudice * Sp
premolar
preoccupation *
prepared
preschool
prescription *
presell
preside
pretense *
pretext *

12. inter-
L prefix; between, among

interact
intercept
intercity
intercoastal
interlocking
intermediate
intermission
intermittent *
international
Internet
interrupt
intersection *
interstate
intervention
interview
interwoven

13. fore-
ME<OE prefix; before, in front, superior

forearms
forebear
foreboding *
forecast
foreclosure
forefathers
foreground
forehand
forehead
forerunner
foresee *
foreseeable *
foreshadow
foretell *
foretokening *
forewarn

14. de-
L prefix; down, away from, removal, separation, reverse

debone
debug
debus
decaffeinated
deception *
declaw
decomposition *
defend
deficiency *
deflate
dehydrate *
demagnetize
deplane
depose
depreciate *
deride *
descent H

15. trans-
L prefix; across, beyond, through

transaction
transantarctic
transarctic
transatlantic
transceiver
transcontinental
transferable
transfiguration
transform
transient *
transitionary
transitive verb
transitory *
transpiration
transport
transportation
transverse

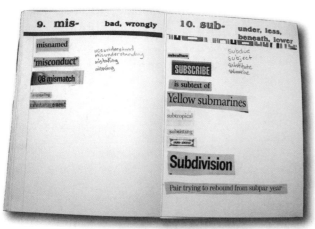

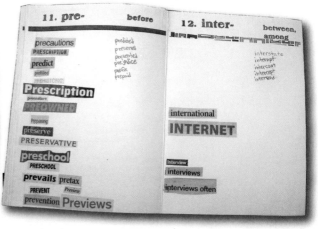

Twenty-Page Accordion Foldable®:
See page 403.

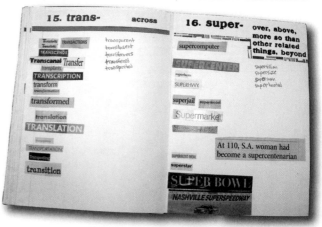

16. super-
L prefix; above, over, more so than other related things, beyond

superabundant
supercenter
supercharge
supercluster
supercollider
superconductor
supercontinent
superfluity *
superfluous *
superglue
superhero
superhighway
superhuman
superimpose
superior
superman
supermarket
supermodel
supernatural
supernova
superpower
supersede * Sp
supersize
superstore
superstructure
superwoman

17. semi-
L combining form; half, partial, incompletely

semiarid
semiautomatic
semicircle
semicolon
semiconscious
semidarkness
semifinal
semiformal
semigloss
semihard
semiliterate
semimoist
seminomadic
semipermanent
semipermeable
semiprecious
semiprivate
semiprofessional
semisoft
semisweet
semitrailer

semi- same as bi- L prefix; half, two over time

semiannually
semiweekly
semiyearly

18. ant-, anti-
Gk prefix; against, opposite of

antacid
antagonist
antarctic
antibacterial
antibiotic
anticlimactic *
anticline
anticoagulant
antidepressant
antidote
antifreeze
antilock
antimatter
antioxidant
antipathy *
antiperspirant
antiquity *
antiseptic
antislavery
antismoking
antisocial *
antithesis *
antitoxin

19. mid-
ME < OE combining form of the word *mid*; near the middle point or place

midafternoon
midair
midcourse
midday
midfield
midlevel
midlife
midline
midnight
midpoint
midrange
midriff
midsemester
midship
midshipman
midsize
midstream
midsummer
midterm
midtown
midweek
midwife
midyear

20. under-
ME prefixal use of the word *under*; too little, beneath or below

underachieve
underage
underbelly
underbite
underclothes
undercook
undercover
undercurrent
underdog
underestimate
underfed
underfoot
undergo
underground
undergrowth
underline
undermine *
underneath
underpass
underscore
undersea
understand
understate
understudy
undertake
underwater

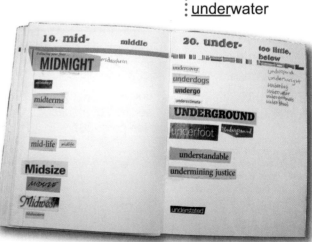

Twenty-Page Accordion Foldable®:
See page 403.

Often, letters are doubled when prefixes are added to root or stem words that begin with the same letter with which a prefix ends. Failure to double these letters is a common spelling mistake.

ac-
L variation of *ad-* before *c* and *qu*
accede
accept
acquire

ad-
L prefix; toward, near
address Sp

al-
L variation of *ad-* before *l*
allow
allure

ap-
L variation of *ad-* before *p*
appear

co-
L variation of *com-* before a vowel, the consonant *h*, and *gn-*
cooperative *
coordinates

col-
L variation of *com-* before *l*
collateral
collinear

com-
L prefix; with, together
command
commemorate
commendable *
commerce
commingle
commitment
committee Sp
commune

con-
L variation of *com-* before consonants other than b, h, l, p, r; by assimilation before n
connect
connotation *

cor-
L variation of *com-* before *r*
correlate
correspond

mobile

immobile

immortal

immortal

immodest

immodest

Triple VKV® Flashcard (above): This six-word flashcard illustrates how letters can be doubled with the addition of a suffix. See page 387.

dis-
L prefix; apart, away, reverse force
dissatifactory
dissatisfied
dissension
dissenter
dissimilar
dissuade

il-
L variation of *in-* before *l*
illation
illegal
illegible
illegitimate
illicit *
illiteracy
illogical
illusion

im-
L variation of *in-* before b, m, p
imbibe
immaculate *
immanent
immaterial *
immature *
immediate Sp
immemorial
immense
immerse
immigrate
imminent
immiscible
immobile
immodest
immoral
immortal
immure
impecunious
impure

in-
E prefix; within, inclusion
innate *
innocent *
innocuous
innominate *
innumerate *

inter-
L prefix; among, between, together
interracial
interrelate
interrupt

ir-
L variation of *in-* used before *r*
irradiate
irrational
irreconcilable
irrefutable *
irregular
irrelevant *
irreparable
irreproachable
irresistible
irresolvable
irrespective
irresponsible
irrevocable *
irritable *
irritate *

micro-
Gk combining form; small, short
microorganism

mis-
OE prefix; wrong, not, mistaken
misshapen *
misspeak
misspell Sp
misspend
misstate
misstep

Double Letters

Adding a prefix rarely changes the spelling of a word, so the added letters can result in doubling:

satisfied	*dis*satisfied
necessary	*un*necessary
mode	*com*mode

non-
L prefix; not
nonnarcotic
nonnative
nonnegotiable

o-
L variation of *ob-* before *m*
omission

ob-
L prefix; to, on, over, against
object
obligate

oc-
L variation of *ob-* before *c*
occasion Sp
occident
occlude

of-
L variation of *ob-* before *f*
offend
offense

op-
L variation of *ob-* before *p*
opposite
opposition

over-
ME prefixal use of the word *over*; too much, excess, over the limit
overran Sp
overrate
overreach
overreact
override
overripe
overrule

post-
L prefix; behind, after, later
posttest
posttranscriptional
posttransfusion
posttranslational

pre-
L prefix; before, early, prior to
preelection
preeminent *
preempt
preengineered
preestablished
preexist

re-
L prefix; again
reelect
reembrace
reenact
reenter
reentry
reescalation
reestablish
reevaluate
reexamine
reexperience
reexport

sub-
L prefix; under, below, beneath
subbase
subbranch

sym-
Gk variation of *syn-* before *b, m, p*
symbiosis
symmetry
symphony

un-
ME prefix meaning *not*
unnamed
unnatural
unnavigable
unnecessary
unneeded
unnerve
unnoticed
unnumbered

under-
ME prefixal use of the word *under*; beneath or below
underrated
underreport
underrepresent
underrun

> **Word Study: To Use or Not to Use?**
> When prefixes like *co-*, *micro-*, and *pre-* are used before words beginning with a vowel, a hyphen can be used to make the pronunciation clearer.
>
> ## Examples:
> | | |
> |---|---|
> | co-ordinate | coordinate |
> | micro-organism | microorganism |
> | pre-empt | preempt |

> **Word Study:**
> Latin prefixes can result in doubling.
> Examples:
> ab - abbreviation
> ac - accept
> ad- address Sp
> al - allow
> ap - appoint
> com - commit
> con - connect
> im - immediately Sp
> in - innate
> ir - irresistible
> oc - occasion Sp
> op - opposite

Prefixes and Combining Forms

a, ab-
L prefix; away from
abbreviate *
abdicate
abduct
abhor *
abject *
abjure
abnegate *
abnormal
abolition
aboriginal *
abrasion
abridge *
abscess Sp
abscond *
absent
absentee
absolute *
absolve *
absorb
absorption
abstain *
abstract *
absurd *
abyss *

ac-
L variation of prefix ad-; used before c- and qu-; toward, near
accede
accelerate
accent
accept
accession
accident
acclimate
accommodate Sp
accompany
accountable
acquaint
acquire
acquisition
acquit Sp

ad-
L prefix; toward, near
adaptable
addicted *
addiction
address * Sp
adept
adequate
adhere *
adhesive *
adjacent *
adjoin
adjourn *
adjunct *
administer
admiration *
admonish *
adoration *
advance
advantage *
advent
adversity *
advocate *
advise Sp

ant-, anti-
Gk prefix; against, opposite of
See 20 Most Common Prefixes list, page 235.

ante-
L prefix; before
antebellum *
antecedent *
antediluvial *

aut-
Gk prefix; variation of auto- ; used before vowels; same, spontaneous
autarchy
autarky
autecology
autism

auto-
Gk combining form; self, someone
autobahn
autobiography
autoclave
autocrat
autocratic
autodestructs
autodial
autofocus
autogenesis
autograph
autoimmune
automaker
automate
automatic
automobile
autonomous
autopilot
autopsy

be-
E prefix; thoroughly, intensive, surround with
bedazzle
befriend
behalf
behave
belabor
belated
belittling *
beloved
bemoan *
beneath
bequest
beseech
besiege Sp
bestow *
betrayal *
bewail *
bewilder *
bewitch

bi-
L prefix; two, both, twice, two at a time
bicarbonate
biceps
bicuspid
bicycle
biennial *
bifocal
bigamy
bimonthly
binary
binocular
binomial
biopsy
bipartisan
biped
bipedal
bisect
bivalve
biweekly

bio-
Gk combining form of bios; life, course or way of living
bioactivity
biochemist
bioconversion
biodegradable
biodiversity
bioengineer
bioethics
biofeedback
biogenetic
biography
biohazard
biological
biology
bioluminescence
biomass
bionic
biopsy
biorythmic
biosphere
biotechnology
biotype

Double VKV® Flashcard (above): See page 379.

Single VKV® Flashcard Fold-Over (right): See page 372.

Two-Tab Foldable (right) made using a quarter sheet of notebook paper. See page 396.

Prefixes and Combining Forms

co-
L - also col-, com-, con-, cor-; with, together, to same degree

coauthor
cogent *
cohere
cohort *
cooperate
cooperation
copilot
copious *
cotangent
covert *

col-
L - also col-, com-, con-, cor-; col- is used before the letter *l*; with, together, to same degree

collaborate *
collateral *
collation *
collision
collusion *

com-
L - also col-, com-, con-, cor-; com- is used with b, m, or p; with, together, to same degree

combine
combustible *
commiserate
compassion *
compound
compress
compromise *

con-
L - also col-, com-, con-, cor-; with, together, to the same degree

concave
concentric *
condescending *
conditional *
confer *
configuration *
conformist *
confound *
confrontational *
congregate *
congregation *
conjecture *
conjunction *
conscience Sp
consensus * Sp
considerate *
construction *
contempt *
contender *
contraction
contrive
convene *
convention
convergence *
convex

cor-
L - also col-, com-, con-, cor-; cor- used before r; with, together, to same degree

correct
correlate
correspond
corridor
corrigible
corroborate Sp
corrosion
corrugated
corrupted

contra-
L prefix; against, opposite, contrasting

contraband
contrabass
contradict
contradiction
contraflow
contraindicate
contralateral
contraposition
contrapositive
contrary
contravention

de-
L prefix; down, away from, removal, separation, reversal
See 20 Most Common Prefixes list, page 234.

dis-
L prefix; lack of, not, opposite, away, free from, apart
See 20 Most Common Prefixes list, page 232.

e-
Modern shortening of the word electronic

e-commerce
e-mail, email

en-, em-
L prefixes; variations of im- and in-; put into, within, cover, cause to be
See 20 Most Common Prefixes list, page 232.

epi-
Gk prefix found in loan-words; upon, near, over, before/after, at

epicenter
epicure *
epicycle
epidemic *
epidermal
epidermis
epidural
epifauna
epiglottis
epigram
epigraph *
epilepsy
epilogue
epipelagic
epiphenomenon
epiphyte
episodic *
epistle
epitaph *

Four-Door Display Foldable® (right): Use a piece of 11" x 17" index-weight (80#) or cover stock paper (100#) to make this collapsible display case. Make one for each prefix studied and use them to collect examples of words formed with each prefix. Words collected on quarter sheets and student writing on half sheets of lined paper can also be stored in the display. After using the displays for as long as needed, collapse them and store them in a "Prefixes" cereal storage box. See folding instructions, page 410.

Note From Dinah: Use the displays again later in the year as a review. I have found that students like to see work they have done in the past and how much easier it looks now, due to their academic growth. This process not only functions as a review, but also builds student confidence.

Four-Word Triple VKV® Flashcard (left): See page 388.

Prefixes and Combining Forms

ex-
L prefix; from, out of, former, completely without

ex<u>ag</u>geration *
ex<u>ca</u>vate
ex<u>cel</u> Sp
ex<u>cep</u>tional *
ex<u>change</u>
ex<u>claim</u>
ex<u>clave</u>
ex-convict
ex<u>ha</u>lation *
ex<u>plant</u>
ex<u>port</u>
ex<u>pound</u>
ex<u>press</u>
ex<u>tant</u> *
ex<u>tinct</u>

extra-
L prefix; from, outside, beyond

extra<u>curricular</u>
extra<u>judicial</u>
extra<u>legal</u>
extra<u>ordinary</u> Sp
extra<u>polate</u>
extra<u>sensory</u>
extra<u>terrestrial</u>
extra<u>vagant</u> *

fore-
ME<OE prefix; before, in front, superior
See 20 Most Common Prefixes list, page 234.

homo-
Gk prefix; common, like, same, one and the same

<u>homo</u>geneous
<u>homo</u>genize
<u>homo</u>geny
<u>homo</u>graph
<u>homo</u>logize
<u>homo</u>logous
<u>homo</u>logy
<u>homo</u>nym
<u>homo</u>phile
<u>homo</u>phobic
<u>homo</u>phone
<u>homo</u>phony
<u>homo</u>polar
<u>Homo</u> sapiens
<u>homo</u>taxis

hyper-
Gk prefix; over, above, beyond, exaggeration

<u>hyper</u>active
<u>hyper</u>bole *
<u>hyper</u>sensitive
<u>hyper</u>tension
<u>hyper</u>thermia *
<u>hyper</u>ventilate

hypo-
Gk prefix; under, below, less, sub

<u>hypo</u>chondria
<u>hypo</u>cotyl
<u>hypo</u>crisy * Sp
<u>hypo</u>derma
<u>hypo</u>dermic
<u>hypo</u>thesis *
<u>hypo</u>thetical *

in-, im-, ir-, il-
L prefixes similar to -un; not, opposed to. without, from; used to form adjectives and nouns
See 20 Most Common Prefixes list, page 232.

in-, im-
E prefixes; variations of em- and en; put into, within, cover, cause to be
See 20 Most Common Prefixes list, page 233.

inter-
ME < L prefix; between, among
See 20 Most Common Prefixes list, page 234.

magni-
L combining form; large, great

<u>magni</u>ficence *
<u>magni</u>ficent *
<u>magni</u>fy *
<u>magni</u>tude

mal-
ME < F < L combining form; bad, badly, evil

<u>mal</u>adjusted
<u>mal</u>adroit *
<u>mal</u>ady *
<u>mal</u>aria
<u>mal</u>content *
<u>mal</u>eficent
<u>mal</u>feasance
<u>mal</u>formation
<u>mal</u>function
<u>mal</u>ice
<u>mal</u>icious *
<u>mal</u>ignant *
<u>mal</u>leable *
<u>mal</u>nutrition *
<u>mal</u>practice

mid-
ME< OE combining form of the word mid; near the middle point or place
See 20 Most Common Prefixes list, page 235.

mini-
L combining form: a shortening of the word miniature

<u>mini</u>ature Sp
<u>mini</u>bar
<u>mini</u>blinds
<u>mini</u>car
<u>mini</u>course
<u>mini</u>dress
<u>mini</u>fy
<u>mini</u>mal
<u>mini</u>max
<u>mini</u>mum
<u>mini</u>series

mis-
OE prefix: wrong, not, mistaken
See 20 Most Common Prefixes list, page 233.

mon-, mono-
Gk combining forms; alone, single, one

<u>mon</u>arch
<u>mon</u>archy *
<u>mon</u>astery
<u>mon</u>etary
<u>mon</u>iker *
<u>mon</u>itor Sp
<u>mono</u>chromatic
<u>mono</u>chrome
<u>mono</u>cle
<u>mono</u>cycle
<u>mono</u>gamy
<u>mono</u>lithic *
<u>mono</u>logue
<u>mono</u>polize *
<u>mono</u>tonous *
<u>mono</u>tony *

non-
L prefix; not, opposite of
See 20 Most Common Prefixes list, page 233.

over-
ME prefixal use of the word over; too much, excess, over the limit
See 20 Most Common Prefixes list, page 233.

per-
L prefix; through, complete, very

<u>per</u> annum
<u>per</u> capita
<u>per</u>ceive * Sp
<u>per</u>centage
<u>per</u>colate *
<u>per</u>cussion
<u>per</u>ennial *
<u>per</u>fect
<u>per</u>fidious *
<u>per</u>forated *
<u>per</u>jury *
<u>per</u>missive *
<u>per</u>mutation
<u>per</u>plex *
<u>per</u>secute
<u>per</u>severe *
<u>per</u>sistent *
<u>per</u>tinent *
<u>per</u>turb *
<u>per</u>use *

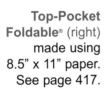

Top-Pocket Foldable® (right) made using 8.5" x 11" paper. See page 417.

(closed)

(open)

Prefixes and Combining Forms

poly-
Gk combining form; much, many; in chemistry, it means polymeric

polychromatic
polydactyl
polyester
polygamy
polygon
polymer
polynomial
polypod
polystyrene
polysyllabic
polyunsaturated

post-
L prefix; behind, later, after something

postdated
postelection
postfix
postglacial
postgraduate
posthumous
postindustrial
postmeridian
postmodern
postmortem
postnasal
postorbital
postpone *
postproduc-tion
postscript
postviolent
postwar

pre-
L prefix; before, early, prior to
See 20 Most Common Prefixes list, page 234.

pro-
L prefix; before, in favor of

proboscis
proceed Sp
proclaim *
procure *
produce
profess *
profile
profuse *
progress
prohibition *
prolific *
pronoun
propel
proportion
propulsion *
protest
protrude
provide
provoke

re-
L prefix; again, back
See 20 Most Common Prefixes list, page 232.

semi-
L combining form; half, partial, incompletely
See 20 Most Common Prefixes list, page 235.

sub-
L prefix; under, less, below, beneath
See 20 Most Common Prefixes list, page 233.

super-
L prefix; above, over, more so than other related things, beyond
See 20 Most Common Prefixes list, page 235.

syl-, sym-
Gk prefixes; together, with; sym- is used before b, m, p

syllable
symbolism *
symmetry *
sympathetic *
symphony
symptomatic *

syn-
Gk prefix found in loanwords; same function as, with, together

synchronize *
syncopation
syndicate
syndrome
synonym
synthesis *
synthetic

tele-
Gk combining form; distant, far

telecast
teleconference
telegraph
telemarketing
telepathic
telephone
telephoto
telescope
televangelist
television

trans-
L prefix; across, beyond, through
See 20 Most Common Prefixes list, page 234.

ultra-
L prefix; beyond, exceed-ing, on the far side of

ultraconservative
ultraliberal
ultralight
ultraluxurious
ultramarine
ultramodern
ultrasonic
ultrasound
ultraviolet

un-
ME One of twenty most common prefixes. See 20 Most Common Prefixes list, page 232.

under-
ME prefixal use of the word under; too little, beneath or below
See 20 Most Common Prefixes list, page 235.

up-
OE combining form; up, upward

upbeat
upbraid *
upbringing
upchuck
upcoming
upcountry
update
updraft
upend
upfield
upgrade
upheaval *
upheld
uphill
uphold *
upkeep
uplift
uplight
upraise
upright *
uprise
upriver
uproar *
uproot
upscale
upset
upshot
upstage
upstairs
upstream
upsurge
uptake
uptight
upturn
upward
upwind

Three-Tab Foldable® (above) made using a sheet of 11" x 17" photocopy paper. See page 397.

macro- Gk large, long

- macrobiotic
- macrocephaly
- macroclimate
- macrocosm
- macrocyte
- macroevolution
- macrofossil
- macro lens
- macromolecule
- macronutrient
- macrophysics
- macrophyte
- macroscopic

magni- L large, great

- magnification
- magnificent
- magnify
- magnitude

mega- Gk large, million

- megabar
  - one million bars, pressure
- megabucks
- megabyte one million bytes
- megadose
- megafauna
- megahertz one million hertz
- megalosaur
- megaparsec
  - 3.262×10^6 light-years
- megaphone
- megatons one million tons
- megavitamin
- megavolts one million volts
- megawatts one million watts

Science: Four M's of Measurement

micro- Gk small, short, millionth

- microaerophile
- microampere one millionth of an ampere
- microaneurysm
- microbar one millionth of a bar
- microbial
- microbiology
- microbrewery
- microcapsule
- microcephaly
- microchemistry
- microclimate
- micrococcus
- microcosm
- microcrystal
- microcyte
- microelements trace elements
- microevolution
- microfiber
- microfilament
- microflora
- microfossil
- micrograph
- microgravity zero gravity
- microhabitat
- microinch one millionth of an inch
- micrometeorite
- micronutrient
- microorganism
- micropaleontology
- microphone
- microphyte
- micropipette
- microscope
- microsecond one millionth of a second
- microspore
- microsurgery
- microvessels
- microvolt one millionth volts
- microwatt one millionth watts
- microwave

Large Two-Tab Foldable® (above): Prefixes can be written on front tabs of a Foldable. Then, over a period of several weeks, students from one class or several classes write or glue examples of words beginning with the featured prefixes. See page 396.

In this example, *macro-* and *micro-* were written on front tabs, and words were collected under the tabs.

Two-Pyramid Diorama (above): Two sheets of 11" x 17" paper (100#) were used to make this dual display. See page 407.

Combining Forms That Denote Numbers

One

mono-
Gk combining form; one, single
monocle
monomial
monosyllable

uni-
L combining form; one
unicameral
unicellular
unicolor
unicorn
unicycle
unidirectional
unification
uniform
unify
unilateral
unilingual
unitarian
univalve
universe

Two

bi- Gk combining form; two
bicycle
binary
binocular
binomial
bisect

di-
Gk combining form; two
dicephalous
dichromatic
dicot
dicotomy
dicotyledon
digraph
dioxide
diphthong

du-, duo-
Gk combining form; two, double
duet
duologue
duplicate

Three

tri-
L combining form; three
triangle
Triassic Period
triceps
tricycle
trillion
triplet

Four

quadr-, quadri-
L combining form; four
quadrangle
quadrant
quadriceps
quadrilateral
quadrille
quadruple

tetra-
Gk combining form; four
tetradactyl
tetragram
tetrahedron
tetrameter
tetrapod
tetrasyllable

Five

pent-, penta-
Gk combining form;; five
pentacle
pentadactyl
pentagon
pentagram
pentangle
pentarchy
pentasyllabic
pentathlon

quint-
L combining form; five
quintessence
quintet
quintile
quintillion
quintuplets

Six

hex-, hexa-
Gk combining form; six
hexagon
hexagram
hexahedra
hexameter
hexangular
hexahedron
hexapod
hexarchy

sex-, sexi-
L combining form; six
sexagenarian
sexcentenary
sexdigitism
sexennial
sexivalent
sextant
sextet
sextillion
sextuplet

Seven

hept-, hepta-
Gk combining form; seven
heptachord
heptagon
heptahedron
heptameter
heptarchy
heptasyllable
heptathlon
heptatonic

sept-
L combining form; seven
Roman 7th month = Septembre
September
septenary
septennial
septet
septillion
septuagenarian
septuplets

Eight

oct-, octa-, octo-
Gk combining form; eight
octagon
octane
octarchy
octave
octet
October
octocentenary
octogenarian
octohedron
octopod
octopus
octosyllabic
octuplets

Nine

ennea-
Gk combining form; *ennea* = nine
ennead
enneagon
enneahedron
enneandrian
enneastyle

nona-
L originally *nonus*; ninth
nonagenarian
nonagon

nove-
L *novem* = nine
November
novena

Ten

dec-, deca-
Gk combining form; ten
December
decade
decameter
decathlon
decimal

A *root word* is a word that has meaning and stands alone without anything added at its beginning or end.   When affixes are added, new words are formed that alter the original meaning of the root.
Affixes can be added in any of the following ways:

• a prefix before the root	color	use
• a suffix after the root	colorful	using
• affixes before and after the root	coloring	usable
• two or more affixes	colorfully	uselessness

Reading and writing experience, as well as spelling rules, help us to know how to add suffixes and prefixes to root words.   See prefixes, page 225, and suffixes, page 270.

Understanding the origins of words helps students understand why words are spelled the way they are, and enables them to spell related words. With root word practice, students begin to identify patterns within words. This pattern identification helps students read and spell unknown words and provides tools for determining word meanings. Dictionaries, thesauruses, and other reference books and on-line resources can be used for word studies like the one illustrated on the next page. This level of word study prepares students for standardized tests, and all or part of it is appropriate for students in grades four through college.

www.dictionary.com
www.etymonline.com
www.thesaurus.com

Triple VKV® Flashcards (left):
The inside left of the Triple VKV Flashcard was used to define and focus attention on the root word exposed on the right tab. As the left tabs are closed, two new words are formed. Students write the meaning of the *bi-* and *tri-* prefixes under them or on the back of the Flashcard.

Double VKV® Flashcard (right):
The root word is exposed in the middle of this card, and affixes can be added or deleted by raising or lowering the top tabs. This Flashcard forms four words: *call, calling, recall, recalling*.

Variation: Cut off the first tab when the root/stem word is at the beginning of a word.

Examples:			
mean	thought	hope	kind
mean**ing**	thought**ful**	hope**ful**	kind**ness**
mean**ingful**	thought**fulness**	hope**fully**	kind**nesses**

Above: *Meaningful* is the only common word with *-ingful* as a double suffix.

Examples:			
like	fold	read	dial
un**like**	re**fold**	re**read**	re**dial**
un**like**ly	re**fold**ing	re**read**ing	re**dial**ing

Word Study Guide:
How Students Use VKVs for Word Studies

Depending on the level of the students, word studies might include all or part of the following:

- word
- part of speech
- definition
- meaning of root
- country or language of origin of the root
- a list of related words
- meanings of suffixes, if applicable
- meanings of prefixes, if applicable
- how the root changes with the addition of affixes
- determining if the meaning, spelling, or pronunciation of the word has changed over time
- using a reverse dictionary to translate the word into another language and determine if the words are cognates
- antonyms
- synonyms
- sentences using the word
- quotes using the word
- When applicable, include the following: abbreviation, clipped word, homographs, homophones, compound words that include the term.

See the VKV® examples above, and an example of a word study based upon the VKVs® to the right.

Word Study: *Affirm*, vb.

Verb: *affirm*
to state positively, confirm as truth

af- L prefix meaning *toward*;
variation of *ad*-; *af*- is used instead of *ad*-
before a root word beginning with the letter *-f*
Examples: *affect, affront, affiliate*
-firm L, *to make firm, solid, hard, rigid*

Antonym for *affirm*: deny
Synonyms for *affirm*: aver, declare, maintain

Transitive Verbs:
reaffirm: to affirm again
reaffirmed
reaffirming
disaffirm: to deny or repudiate
disaffirmed
disaffirming

Cognate: English to Spanish

| affirm | *afirmar* |
| to affirm that | *afirmar que* |

Root Words   Foldables®

Side-by-Side Foldable® Book:
Five sheets of 11" x 17" paper (80#) were folded in half along the long axis (like a *hamburger*) to form an 8½" x 11" Half Book, then folded in half again like a *hamburger* to form two 4¼" x 8½" sections. With the booklet slightly open, the inside top section was cut along the valley fold line to form two tabs. The five two-tab sections were glued side by side to make this ten-page book. See page 28.

Variation: Compare this book to the one pictured on page 230. We chose to do this one on the longer axis so we would have room to write the titles "Root" and "Meaning" in large letters across the top of each tab.

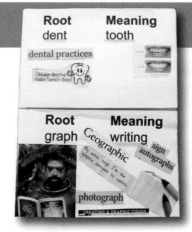

(cover)

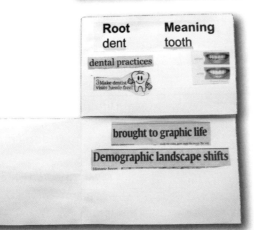

Four-Word Triple VKV® Flashcard (below):
Cut four tabs to the left and leave one extended
tab to the right. See page 388.

- otoscope
- periscope
- microscope
- telescope

Three-Word Triple VKV® Flashcard
(below): When words of Greek origin
begin with *ps-*, the *p-* is often silent.
See page 386.

tele scope

micro scope

peri scope

SCOPES

psyllium

Psychic

PSORIASIS

STETHOSCOPES

oto scope

HEMISPHERES

← hydro sphere

photography

DICTIONARY

photo copy

GREEK

PSYCH

psyche

PSORIASIS

psychology

Myth

MYTHS BUSTED

ROOT WORDS

Myths—

**Triple VKV
Flashcard:**
See page 388.

-sphere
atmo<u>sphere</u>
bio<u>sphere</u>
hydro<u>sphere</u>
litho<u>sphere</u>

**Two-Word Triple VKV®
Flashcard:**
This VKV Flashcard
was made using RWP
and hand-lettering. The
top tab of the three
right tabs was left blank. This blank tab
draws attention to the root before affixes
are added. See page 386.

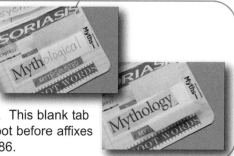

PSORIASIS

Mythological

Myths—

Mythology

Recognize *stem* or *root words* changed by added affixes.

Example: joy joyful, enjoyed, enjoyment

Latin	annus (year)	annual, perennial, anniversary
Greek	aster (star)	aster, astronomy, asterisk
Latin	aqua (water)	aqueduct, aquaplane, aquarium
Latin	audio (hearing)	auditorium, audible, audition
Latin	avis (bird)	aviary, aviation, aviator
Greek	cycle (ring or circus)	bicycle, motorcycle, cyclone
Latin	ducere (to lead)	conduct, educate, aqueduct
Greek	graph (to write)	autograph, telegraph, graph
Greek	logos (word, speech, discourse, ratio, reason)	catalog, dialogue, logic
Greek	metron (measure)	meter, thermometer, speedometer
Greek	phone (sound)	phonics, telephone, phonograph
Latin	via (way, road)	viaduct, trivial, deviate

Brainstorm and list as many words as you can for given root words. Consult a dictionary to check the etymologies of the words.

Activity:

Root	Meaning	Math	Geography	Health	Science	Social Sciences
acu-	sharp	acute angle		acupuncture		
aqu-	water		aquifer		aquarium	aqueduct
ca-	hollow	concave	caverns	cavity	cave	excavate
grap-	write	graph	geography	electroencephalograph		telegraph

Activity:

Root	Meaning	Science Related Vocabulary	General
ast(r)	star	astronaut	asterisk
		astronomy	disaster
		astrophysics	

Example: gram diagram, grammar, telegram

The explorer was shocked to discover pictographs along the river's rocky ledge. He carefully drew a *diagram* of what he observed and used his best *grammar* to describe it. When he reached a town, he sent a *telegram* informing the world of his discovery.

Nine-Word VKV®
(left and right):
Note that the meaning of the Latin root word is written in pencil under the word. The prefixes and suffixes are also defined. See all nine words pictured on page 245.

Geography Root Words

aqu- water
aquamarine
aquarium
aquatic
aquatint
aqueduct
aquifer

caput head, cap
capital * H
capitol * H
captain
decapitate

cavus hollow
cave
cavern
cavity

cittade city
civitas city, state
citadel *
citizen
city
civilian

colonia settled land
colonial *
colonization
colony

communis common
communal
commune
communication
communism
community

cover hide
covert *
discover
discoveries
uncover

geo- earth
geocentric
geochemistry
geographer
geography
geology
geothermal

gorg- throat
gorge
gorget

hemi- half
hemianopia
hemisect
hemisphere
hemithorax

insul- island
insular *
insulate
peninsula

locus place
local
locale
locate
location
relocation

pax peace
pacificus peace-making
Pacific Ocean
pacify

polaris a pole
polar
polarity
polarization *

populus people
popular
populate
population

posit- place, put
depose
deposit
deposition
opposition
position
positive

tangere to touch
contiguous *
contingent
tangent

terra land, earth
terrace
terra firma
terrain
terrestrial *
territorial
territory

topos place
topography
topology
topotype

tribuere pay, grant
tributary
tribute

tropicos pertaining to the solstice; pertaining to a turn
tropical
tropics

summus highest
summation
summit

Accordion VKV Flashcard (above): This VKV forms five words based upon the same rood word: *terra*. See page 392 for folding instructions.

Root Words and Combining Forms

Health and Life Science

arthr- joint, -s, -ed
arthritis
arthropod

audire to hear
audible
auditorium
auditory

bakterion a staff
bacteria, -um (sing.)
bacterial

bronchos windpipe
bronchia
bronchial
bronchitis
bronchus, -i

calc- limestone, pebble
calcareous
calcium

calor heat
caloric
calorie

cardia- heart
cardiac *
cardiology
cardiovascular

cavus hollow
cave
cavern
cavity

cephal- about the head
cephalad
cephalothorax
encephalitis

cerebrum brain
cerebellum *
cerebral *
cerebrospinal

-cide killer
genocide *
homicide
patricide
pesticide
suicide

corpus body
corporeal *
corpse
corpulent *
corpuscle

cyt-, cyto- about cells
cytoblast
cytoplasm
cytostasis

-derm- skin
dermatitis
epidermis
mesoderm

-emia blood
anemia
leukemia
uremia

epi- on, over, around
epidermis
epidural

febris, fev- fever
fever
feverish
feverroot

flexus bend
flexibility
inflexible
reflex

gastro- stomach
gastric
gastrointestinal
gastronomic *

germen seed, sprout
germ
germicide

glotta tongue
epiglottis
glottal

halare breathe
exhale
halitosis
inhale

hem-, hemo- blood
hematology
hemocyte
hemoglobin
hemophilia
hemorrhage
hemorrhoids

-iatry medical, healing
pediatrician
podiatrist
psychiatry

intes- inside
intestinal
intestine

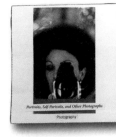

Three-Tab Foldable® (right): This large Foldable was made using a sheet of 11" x 17" paper (#80). It examines the roots *photo-*, *audio-*, and *val-*. Under these larger tabs there is room for students to write fairly detailed paragraphs. See page 397.

Helpful Hint: If students make mistakes in their writing or want to start over, have them glue a quarter sheet of paper under the tab and use it for revisions. Quarter sheets can be stapled under the tabs to provide extra writing space or to collect multiple examples of words.

Health and Life Science

-join-, junctum join
conjoin
joint
junction

lact-, lacto- milk
galactic
lactate
lactose

ligare bind, tie
ligament
ligature
religion

-logy, -ology science, theory, study of
archaeology
biology
psychology

neur-, neuro- nerve
neurological
neuron
neurosis

nutr- nourish
nutrient
nutrition

-odont- tooth
odontoid
odontology
orthodontist

odor smell, scent
odiferous
odoriferous
odorous

opticus pertaining to sight or vision
myopic
optic nerve
optician

optimus the best
optimism
optimize
optimum

org- instrument, pertaining to an organ of the body
organ
organic
organize

ov-, ovum egg
ova, ovum
ovarian
oviparous
ovulation

oste-, osteo- bone
osteoarthritis
osteoporosis *

palatum roof of the mouth, sense of taste
palatable *
palate

-ped-, -pod- foot
biped
pedestrian
podiatrist
quadruped
tripod

rhin-, rhino- nose
rhinoceros
rhinoplasty

spirare breathe
perspire
respiration

-tact- touch
contact
tactile
tactless

-tast- taste
distaste
foretaste
taste
tasteful

-tend- stretch
attend
contend
tendency
tendon

-therm- heat
biotherm
thermal
thermometer

-tom- cut
anatomy
atom

tundere, tus- to beat, make dull
contusion
obtuse

ulc- a sore, wound
ulcer
ulceration

vocem voice, speech, utterance
vocal chords
vocalization
vociferous

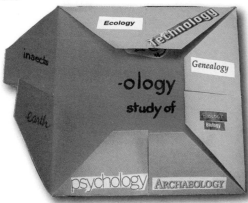

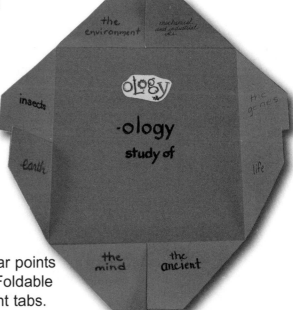

Envelope Foldable®: Cut away the triangular points of the four tabs to form a window. Use the Foldable with four tabs or cut them in half to form eight tabs. See page 404.

Math and Science

acu- sharp, needle
acuity *
acupuncture
acute *

alle-, allo- other, else
allegory *
parallel Sp

angulus corner, bend
angle
angular
quadrangle
rectangle
triangle

annus year
anniversary
annual

arcus arch, bow
arc, arch
archery

axioma authoriy, worthy
axiom *
axiomatic

basis base, foundation
base
basement
basic

bi-, bin- two, twice
biennial *
binocular
bisect

calc- limestone, pebble
calcium
calculate
calculus

capere take, hold
capacity
capsule
captivate

cavus hollow
cave
concave

centum hundred
cent
centenarian
centennial

circ(um) around
circuitous *
circumference
circumspect *
circumvent *

circ(us) ring, circle
circle
semicircle

clinare lean, bend
decline
inclination *
incline
recline

conter reckon, count
account
accountable
count
discount
recount
uncounted

cubitum elbow, bend
cubical
cubit

deci-, deca- ten
decade
decimal

dek- ten
dekagram
dekaliter
dekameter

digitus finger, toe
digit
digital

dividere divide
divide
dividend
division

equ- equal
equal
equality
equation/s
equator

esti- value, esteem
estimable
estimate
estimation

ext- outer, outward
exterior
external
extreme

fig- form, figure
configuration
figure
refigure

fract- to break-
fraction
fractious
fracture

frequ- often, repeated
frequency
frequent

geo- earth
geography
geology
geometry

gonia angle
diagonal
pentagon
trigonometry

gram write, letter
diagram
grammar
telegram

-gru- agree, fit in
congruent
incongruent

hepta seven
heptagon

hex six
hexagon

inter- within, among
interior
internal

iso- equal
isosceles
isotope

kilo- thousand
kilogram
kiloliter
kilometer

latus side
equilateral
multilateral

linea line
delineate
lineal
linear

longus long
oblong
prolong

meter measure
centimeter
diameter
thermometer

metric measure
geometric
logometric
metric

-metry process of measuring
geometry
symmetry
trigonometry

micro- small
micrometer
microscope

milli- thousand
millennium
milligram
millimeter

min- less, smaller
minimum
minus

mult-, multi- many, much
multiple
multiplication
multitude

neg- deny, not
negation
negative

nomen name
binomial
monomial
nominal
trinomial

numer number, count
enumerate
numeral
numerous

opera work
operations

ordo, ord- order, rank, arrange
coordinate
order
of operations
ordinal numbers
ordinate
superorder

pandere spread, stretch
expand
expanded
notation

par equal
compare
par

penta- five
pentagon
pentathlon

ply bend, fold
apply
multiply

poly- many
polygon
polygraph *

-portio- part
portion
proportion

positus to place, put
position
positive

primus first
primary
prime

prop(er) one's own, particular to itself
improper
proper

prove prove, test
approve
disprove
prove

-prox- near
approximate
proximate
proximity

Math and Science

quant-
how much
quantity
quantum

quart one fourth
quart
quarter
quartile

quint five
quintet
quintuplet

quot- how many
quota
quote
quotient

radius ray,
spoke
radial
radius
ray
rayon

ratus think, rea-
son
ratify *
ratio
rational

rect(us) right
rectangle

scala ladder,
climb
escalator
scale

-scend- climb
ascending
descending

semi- half
semiannual
semicircle

septem seven
September

**sequi-
(secut-)
xequ-** follow
consecutive
execute
execution
prosecute
sequence

sextus six, sixth
sextant
sextuplets

-spher-
ball, globe
sphere
spherical
spheroid

struct- build
construct
structure

sum- highest,
whole
sum
summary
summit

sym-, syn-
with, together
symbiotic *
symbol

tal- that kind
tally
talus
retaliate

**tangere
(tang-, teg-)**
to touch
integer
integrate
tangent
tangible

temper regulate
temperate
temperature

terminus end
terminal *
terminating *

tetra- four
tetrahedron
tetrameter

theoria
observe, look at
theorem
theoretical *
theory

totalis entire
total
totalitarian *

tract pull, draw
protractor
subtract
subtraction

tri- three
triangle
tripod
trisect

**tundere,
tus-** to beat,
make dull
obtuse
contusion

two, twi- two
twenty
twice
twins
two

uni- one
uniform
unique

valere be
strong, be able
evaluate *
validate *
value

vect- carry
convection
vector

vers-, vert-
turn
adverse *
converse
convert
reverse

void empty
avoid
void *
voided

volut-
(L volvere) turn, roll
convolute
involute
revolve

Three-Tab Foldable® (above):
Notice that the notebook holes are uncovered to allow storage in a three-hole binder. See page 397.

Word Study (above):

-vore Latin combining form meaning *one that eats*

L *carni-* "flesh" + **-vore** = carnivore, n. - *one that eats flesh/meat* (carnivorous, adj.)

L *frugi-* "fruit" + **-vore** = frugivore, n. - *one that eats fruit* (frugivorous, adj.)

L *herbi-* "plant" + **-vore** = herbivore, n. - *one that eats plants* (herbivorous, adj.)

L *insectum* "divided body" + **-vore** = insectivore, n. - *one that eats insects* (insectivorous, adj.)

L *omni-* "all" + **-vore** = omnivore, n.- *one that eats both meat and plants* (omnivorous, adj.)

Root Words and Combining Forms

Earth, Life, and Physical Science

(See also "Root Words: Health and Life Science" on pages 250-251.)

acid- sour, sharp
acid
acidic
acidity

acoust- hearing
acoustic, -s
acoustical
acoustically

aero- air
aerobic, -s
aerodynamic
aeronautics

alb- white
albino
albumen egg

allo- other
allotrope
allosaurus

altus high
altitude
altocumulus

ampl- large, wide
amplify *
amplitude

-anim- living, breathing
animal
inanimate

aqua-, aqui- water
aquarium
aquatic
aquifer

arbor- grass, herb, tree
arbor
arboretum

arthr- joint, -s, -ed
arthritis
arthropod

-astr- star
astronaut
astronomy
disaster

atmos- vapor
atmosphere
atmospheric

audire to hear
audible
audiovisual
auditory

avi- bird
aviary
aviator

bakterion- a staff
bacteria
bacterial

baro- weight
barometer *
baroscope

batho- depth
batholith
bathysphere

bio- life
biology
biopsy *

botan- of herbs, plants
botanical
botany

bryo- moss
bryology
bryophyte

calc- limestone, pebble
calcium
calculate

calor heat
caloric
calorie

cardia- heart
cardiac *
cardiologist
cardiology

cavus hollow
cave
cavern
cavity

cephal- about the head
cephalopod
cephalothorax

cerebrum brain
cerebellum *
cerebral *
cerebrospinal

chloro- (1) green
chlorophyll
chloroplast

chloro- (2) presence of chlorine
chloroform

chrom- color
chromatic
chrome
chromosome

cipit-, caput head, cap
precipitate *
precipitation

class- rank, class
class
classify

com- with, with intensive force, completely
combustible *
compound *
comprehend *

cur- run
current
curriculum *

-dens- thick
condensation
density

dorm- sleep
dormant *
dormitory

electr- electric
electricity
electrode
electrolyte
electron, -ic

elem- first, main
element
elemental
elementary

exper- try, test
experience
experiment

fissi- cleft, split
fission
fissure

flect- bend
deflect
reflect
reflection

flor- flower
flora
florid

foli- leaf
defoliate
exfoliate
foliage *

frig- cold
fridge (slang)
frigid
refrigeration

front forepart
front
frontier

fru- fruit, enjoy the produce of
fructose
frugivorous
fruit
fruitless

germen seed, sprout
germ
germinate

Earth, Life, and Physical Science

(See also "Root Words: Health and Life Science" on pages 250-251.)

grav- heavy, weighty
grave
gravitate
gravity *

hab- have, hold
habit
habitat *

helio- sun
heliocentric
heliotrope

herb grass, herbs
herbaceous
herbal
herbicide

-hes- stick, cling
adhesion
adhesive
cohesion

heter- different, other
heterogeneous *
heterosexual

hydr- water
hydra
hydraulic
hydroelectric
hydrogen

ign- fire
igneous
ignite

insul- island
insulate
insulation
insulator
isolated (from Latin
insula)

iso- equal
isotherm
isotope

-it (from Latin -ire)
to go
circuit
exit

-lev- raise, lift
elevator
levee
lever

liqu- liquid, fluid
liquefy
liquidity

-lum- light, shining
illuminate
luminous *

luna moon
lunacy
lunar

lus-, lustr-
light, brilliancy
luster
lustrous

magn- large, great
magnify

mar- of the sea
marine
submarine

meso- middle
mesoderm
mesosphere
mesozoic

meter measure
barometer
hydrometer
thermometer

mole- mass, barrier
(some other forms of *mole*
have different etymologies)
molecule

morph- form, shape
metamorphosis *
morph

mut- change
mutation

noct- night
nocturnal

ornith- of birds
ornithology

pan- all
pandemic
panoply

pandere
spread, stretch
expand

pend- hang
pendulum

petr- rock, stone
petrify *
petroleum

phyto- of plants
phytoplasm

pred- plunder
predator
predatory *

proto- first
protoplast
protozoa

rodere (ros-)
to gnaw
corrosion
erosion

-saur- lizard
dinosaur
sauropod
tyrannosaur

-scop-, scope
seeing, viewing
microscope
periscope
telescope

sed- to settle, sit
sediment
sedimentary
supersede Sp

serv- keep, save,
preserve, protect
conserve
reservoir

sol- sun
insulate
solar
solstice *

sonus sound
sonar
sonic

sorb- drink, suck in
absorb
absorption

stella star
constellation
stellar

tele- far, distant
telephone
telescope

temper regulate
temperate *
temperature

therm heat
biotherm
thermal
thermometer

tomos a cutting
anatomy
atom
diatom

umbra shadow
penumbra
umbra

vac- empty, void
vacuous *
vacuum Sp

valv- revolving
bivalve
valve

vapor steam
evaporate
vaporize

Root Words and Combining Forms

Social Sciences

agere set in motion, drive, conduct
agency
agenda *
agent

-agogue leader
demagogue *
pedagogue *

agro- field, soil, crop production
agriculture
agrobiology
agroeconomics

ante- before
antebellum

anthropo- man, human being
anthropologist
philanthropist

anti- against, opposite of
antisocial
antiwar

antiqu- ancient
antique
antiquity *

arbitrari to judge, give a decision
arbitration
arbitrator

aristos best
aristocracy
aristocratic *

arkhein to rule
matriarchal
monarchy *

arm- weapon
armada *
armistice *
armory, arms

barbar- foreign, strange, savage
barbarian
barbarous

bark (Latin *barca*) ship
debark
disembark
embark

-bat- beat, strike
battlefield
combat

bellum war
antebellum
belligerent *

camp- field, open space
camp
campaign

-cand- shining, white
candidate
candle
incandescent

-cap-, -capit- head
capital * H
capitol * H
captain
decapitate

caval- to ride on horseback
cavalcade
cavalier
cavalry

chef head, ruler, chief
chef
chief, -tain

chron- time
chronicle
chronology

cit-, civ- citizen, town
citizen
civic
civil, -ization

col-, -cul- tend, till, cultivate, inhabit
agriculture
colonial
colony, -ization
cultivate*
culture

coron- crown
coronation
coroner

-crat-, -cracy power, rule(r)
aristocratic *
democracy
theocracy

crypt hidden
crypt, -ic *
cryptogram

deus god
deify
deity *

demos peple
democracy
demagogue
demographics *

dogma opinion, tenet
doggerel
dogmatic *

domus house
domestic *
domicile *

edi- to build
edifice *
edify *

emp- command, rule
emperor
empire

ethn- nation, people
ethnic, -al
ethnology

ev- (Latin *aevum*) age, lifetime
longevity *
medieval
primeval

exequi- to follow out
execute
execution
executive

factor maker, doer
benefactor *
factory
manufacture

fames hunger
famine

-fed- league
confederation
federal

finis end, payment in settlement
finance
financial

fort strong
fortify
fortress

-fug- flee
fugitive
refugee

govern rule, ommand
government
governor

-grapher one who writes, records, describes
geographer
oceanographer
photographer
stenographer

-graphy process of writing, recording, describing
cartography *
geography
oceanography
photography

-gri- land, country
peregrine
pilgrim

heir heir
heir-apparent
heiress
heirloom*

Social Sciences

-holo- whole
catholic
holocaust

host guest, host; enemy
hostage
hostile, -ility *

jud-, jur-, jus-
law, right, judge
judge
judicial
judicious *
jury
justice

legis law
illegal
legal
legislature

liber- free
liberal
liberate
liberty

lith- stone
lithograph
monolith *
neolithic
paleolithic

maj- great
majesty
major
majority

-mand- order
command
mandate *
mandatory

merc- trade
mercantile
mercenary
merchant

-migr- move, change, depart
emigrate
emigration
immigrant
immigration
migrate

-minis- serve
administrate
administration
minister

mun- (Latin *munus, -ia*)
office, duty, work
municipal
municipality

pluto- wealth
plutocracy
plutocrat

populus people
populace
popular election
population

-port- carry
export
import
porter
transportation

-pov- poor
impoverished
poverty

rit- ceremony, custom
rite of passage
ritual
ritualistic

-roy- royal, to lead
royalist
royalty
viceroy

rur-, rus- country
rural
rustic *

script writing
inscription
script
scripted
scripture
transcript
transcription

-serv- serve, preserve, protect
conservative
preserve
reservation
servant

-sid- to sit in front of, superintend
preside
president
presidio

solidus firm, entire
solidarity *
soldier

stat- standing, position
station, -ary * Sp
statue
status quo *

-struc- building
construction
destruction
instruction
structure

surgere rise
insurgency
resurgent

**-temp-,
tempo** time
contemporary
temperate

terr- earth, land
terrace
terrain
territory

theos god
atheism
pantheon
theocracy
theology *

thronos high seat, throne
dethrone
enthrone
throne

tyra- ruler, master, tyrant
tyranny *
tyrant

uni- one
uniform
unify
union
unity

venire to come
convene
convention

-vet- old
veteran
inveterate

-vict-
conquer, overcome
convict
conviction
victory

-vol- will, free will
benevolent
voluntary
volunteer

volut- (Latin *volvere*)
turn, roll
evolution
revolution

votum vow
devoted
vote
voter

xequi to follow out
execute
execution
executive

zeal ardor
zealot *
zealous *

Spelling Gremlins: Silent letters can cause words to be difficult to spell. Some commonly paired letters, one of which is silent, can be easily recognized.

Examples: gn, pn, kn = /n/
    gnome
    pneumonia
    knife

Examples: rh, wr = /r/
    rhyme Sp
    wrestle

Examples: pt, ght = /t/
    height
    ptarmigan
    pterodactyl
    pterosaur
    ptomain

Examples: ps, sc = /s/
    psalm
    pseudo
    psittacosis
    psoriasis
    psyche
    psyllium
    science

Example: wh = /h/
    whole

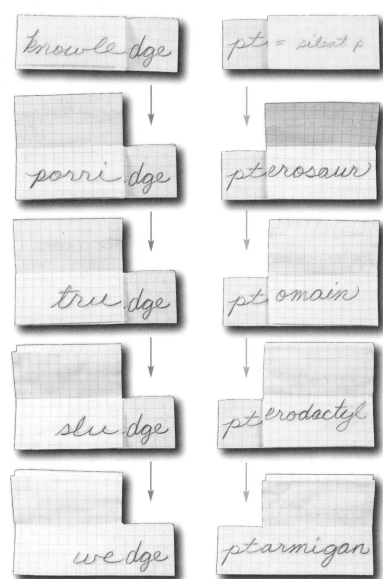

Accordion VKV Flashcards (above left and right):
See page 392 for folding instructions.

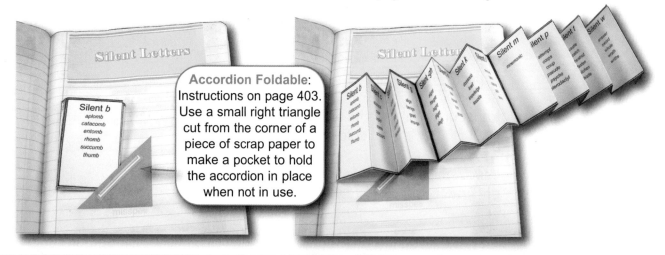

Accordion Foldable: Instructions on page 403. Use a small right triangle cut from the corner of a piece of scrap paper to make a pocket to hold the accordion in place when not in use.

Silent Letters in RWP Words (left and right): RWP examples of silent letters can form Foldable tabs within a notebook.
Two Eight-Tab Notebook Foldables® (below) were used to record initial silent letters and final silent letters.

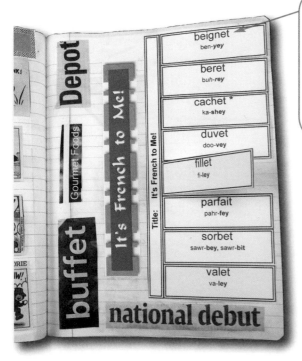

Silent Letters in Adopted Words (left): An Eight-Tab Notebook Foldable was used to record French loanwords that have silent final letters. The edge of each tab could be folded over the silent letter to illustrate that it is not sounded when the word is spoken but must be included when the word is written.

Multi-Tab Foldable® (right): Eight tabs were cut and used to feature words that begin with *gn-*. Since the initial *g* is silent, the tabs can be folded over the *g* to illustrate that it is not sounded when the word is spoken but must be included when the word is written.

Compare the independent Foldable (right) to the Eight-Tab Notebook Foldables pictured left and above.

Silent b

Silent *b* as in *debt*, and silent *b* when following an *m* as in la*mb*.

aplomb *
bomb
catacomb
climb H
comb
crumb
dumb
dumbfounded *
entomb *
lamb
limb
numb
plumb * H
plumber
rhomb
rhumb H
subpoena
subtle Sp
succumb *
thumb
tomb
womb

Only two common words end in *-bt*.

debt
doubt

Word Study: Patterns

Make Foldables to illustrate these patterns.

gn-, kn-, pn- = /n/
gnaw
knight H
pneumonia

-ght, -pt = /t/
weight H Sp
pterodactyl

sc-, ps- = /s/
science
psyche *

rh-, wr = /r/
rhyme Sp
wreath

Silent c

abscess Sp
ascend
ascent H
Connecticut
czar
descend
indict Sp
scene H
scenery
scenic
scent H
sciatica
science
scimitar
scissors Sp
scythe

Silent *c* before *k* or *q*.

acknowledge
acquaint
acquire Sp
acquit Sp

c is not pronounced in the ending *-scle*.

corpuscle
muscle

Words ending in the following have a silent *c*:

-esce
acquiesce
coalesce
effervesce
incandesce

-escent
adolescent
candescent
convalescent
crescent
effervescent
incandescent
luminescent

-escence
acquiescence
fluorescence Sp
iridescence

Silent c

Silent *c* in *-ck* words.

buck H
clock
cluck
crack H
dock H
duck H
flock
knack
lack
lick
lock
luck
mock
shack
shock
stack
stick H
stuck
tick H
track
trick
truck
wick

Silent -ch

Only one common word.

yacht

Silent d

handkerchief
sandwich (can also be pronounced with the *-d* sound)
Wednesday

Silent d

Found in *-dge*.

abridge
badge
begrudge
bludgeon *
bridge
budge
budget
cartridge
dodge
drudgery
edge
fledgling
fudge
grudge
hedge
judge Sp (no *e* after *-dg* in judgment Sp)
knowledge
ledge
nudge
pledge
porridge
ridge
sludge
smudge
trudge
wedge

Silent d

Silent *d* before *j*.

adjacent
adjourn
adjudicate
adjunct
adjust

Silent g

Silent *g* before *n*.

align
alignment
arraignment
assignment
benign *
campaign
consignment
cosign H
deign *
design
ensign *
feign *
foreign Sp
gnarl
gnash *
gnat
gnaw
gneiss H
gnetophyte
gnocchi
gnome
gnostic
gnu H
impugn *
malign *
poignant *
reign H
resign
sign H

Silent *g* before *-m*.

diaphragm
epiphragm
paradigm *
phlegm

Silent -gh

alight *
blight *
bought
bright
brought
caught
daughter
delight
drought
eight H
fight
flight
fought
fraught *
freight
fright
haughty
height Sp
high H
light
might H
naughty
neighbor Sp
night H
ought H
plight *
right H
sigh
sight H
slaughter
sleigh H
slight H
sought
straight H
taught H
thigh
thought
through H
tight
twilight *
weight H Sp

Silent Letters Spelling Aids

In a group of three consonants, the middle consonant is often silent:

attem**p**t

cas**t**le

ches**t**nut

Chris**t**mas

door**k**nob

han**d**kerchief

mor**t**gage

mus**t**n't

temp**t**ation

this**t**le

Exceptions are found when there is an /s/ on both sides of a consonant. The middle consonant has to be heard to separate the s sounds. Examples: *asks, fasts, lists, wasps,* and *texts.*

When three consonants, the middle one being *t,* are found at the end of a word (or at the end of one word and the beginning of another), the middle *t* is silent:

ac**t**s

duc**t** tape

Small Matchbook Foldables® (below): One sheet of white photocopy paper was used to make twelve small matchbooks, which were then glued onto a colored sheet of paper. See page 400.

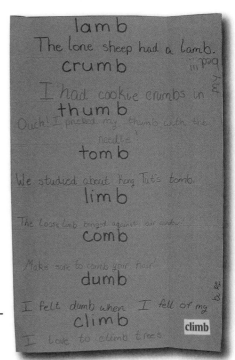

Three-Tab Foldable® (left): Notice that the notebook holes are uncovered to allow storage in a three-hole binder. See page 397.
Eight-Row Fold (right): A sheet of paper was folded to define space for eight examples of words with silent letters, sentences using the words, and RWP (if found).

Silent Letters Spelling Aids

Silent h

H is not pronounced in the following words. Use the article *an* before an unvoiced *h* that is the first letter of a word.

heir [H]
herb (The *h* is pronounced in British English.)
honest
honor
hour [H]

The *h* is not pronounced when it follows a hard *c* sound.

bronchitis
chord [H]
loch [H]
saccharine
schedule
scheme
scholar
school [H]

Words of Greek origin often have a silent *h* after an *r*.

diarrhea [Sp]
hemorrhage
rhombus/-i
rhonchus/-i
rhyme [Sp]
rhythm [Sp]

Other silent *h* words:

exhaust [Sp]
exhibit
ghetto
ghost
ghoul
myrrh
shepherd
silhouette [Sp]
spaghetti
thyme [H]

Silent k

Silent *k* in consonant diagraph kn-

doorknob
knack
knapsack
knave [H]
knead [H]
knee
kneel
knell *
knelt
knew [H]
knife
knight [H]
knit [H]
knives
knob
knock
knoll
knotty *
know [H]
knowledge
known
knuckle
knurl

Silent l

A silent *l* is often found before the letters *d, f, k,* or *m*. For example, silent *l* is found in the consonant diagraphs -lk and -lf.

almond
alms
balk
balm
calf
calm
chalk
colonel [H] [Sp]
could [H]
folk
folklore
half
palm
psalm
salmon
salve
should
stalk
talk
walk
would [H]
yolk [H]

Silent m

Both of these silent *m* words are of Greek origin. Notice that in words that end in -mn, the *m* is silent and the *n* is voiced.

Mnemosyne
(Greek goddess)
mnemonic

Silent n

The letter *n* is silent when preceded by *m*.

autumn
column [Sp]
columnist (This *n* can be also be voiced.)
condemn *
contemn
damn [H]
hymn [H]
solemn

Silent o

country

Silent p

cupboard
pneumonia
raspberry

Words often have a silent *p* when it is followed by an *s* or *t*. Many of these words are of Greek origin.

attempt
corps [H]
coup * [H]
empty
psalm
pseudo
pseudonym *
psittacosis
psoriasis
psyche *
psychedelic
psychiatry
psychology [Sp]
psychosis
psyllium
ptarmigan
pterodactyl
ptomain
receipt [Sp]
temptation

Silent s

In a few words, the letter *s* is not pronounced before *l*. Some French loanwords have a silent *s*, often as the final letter.

aisle [H]
Arkansas
apropos *
corps [H]
debris *
Illinois
island
isle [H]
Louisville

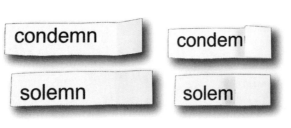

Silent Initial or Final Consonants Fold-Overs (above): Write or glue a word onto the right end of a Single VKV Flashcard. Fold the left edge of the strip over to cover silent initial consonants. Write or glue a word with a silent final consonant to the left edge. See pages 370-373.

Silent Letters Spelling Aids

Silent t
ballet
beignet
(also silent g)
beret *
bouquet
buffet *
cabaret
cachet *
castle
chalet
chestnut
Christmas
crochet *
croquet
debut
depot
duvet
fasten
fillet
listen
mortgage Sp
mustn't
often
parfait
rapport
sachet
soften
sorbet
thistle
tsar
tsarevna
tsunami
valet
whistle
wrestle

Silent t in -tch words
batch
blotch
botch
catch
ditch
glitch
hatch H
hatchet
hitch
kitchen
latch
match H
notch
patch
pitch H
ratchet
snatch
stitch
stretch
watch H
witch

Silent -th
asthma
isthmus

Silent u
built
circuit
silhouette Sp
The letter g can be followed by a silent u.
beleaguered
bodyguard
guarantee
guard
guess
guest
guidance
guide
guild * H
guile *
guise *
league
lifeguard

Silent w
Silent w, and silent w before r.
answer
sword
two H
who
whole H
whom
whose H
wrap H
wrath *
wreath
wrestle
wrist
write H
writhe *
wrong
wrought *

Silent x
faux *

Silent y
vinyl

Silent z
rendezvous * Sp

Sorting RWP (below right): Eight display boxes were glued together to make this RWP collection tray. Notice that the word list on this page was photocopied, cut, and placed in the boxes to guide students in their word search.

rules right
wr
bazaar wrongly
plan riles some 'everything has to go wrong
movie ratings

Two-Tab Foldable®:
See page 396.

Silent Medial or Ending Consonants (left and right): Glue or write a word with silent letters inside a Double VKV Flashcard. Cut the top section of the card so that silent letters in the word will be hidden under the remaining tab. Cut the cards to graphically demonstrate how some letters used to spell a word are not heard when the word is read or spoken. See Contractions, page 168, for cutting suggestions.

mortgage

mor gage

mustn't

mus n't

Frequently Misspelled Words

abscess
acceptable
accidentally
accommodate
accordion
acquire
acquit
address H
advice/advise
aggression
a lot/allot
amateur
angel/angle
annual
anoint
anxious
apologize
apparent
appoint
archaeology
argument
balloon
banana
basically
battalion
bazaar
beautiful
beginning
belief/believe
benefited/-fiting
bizarre
bologna
bookkeeper
broccoli
burglar
calendar
category
cemetery
challenge
changeable
chauffeur
chile H, chili H
cocoon
collectible
colonel H
column
committee
completely

connoisseur
corroborate
conscience
conscientious
conscious
consensus
corps H
deceive
decide
definite/-ly
desperate
diarrhea
dilemma
difference
dining
disappoint
discipline
dumbbell
easily
ecstasy
embarrass
enervate
equipment
espresso
exceed
excel/excellent
exhaust
exhilarate
existence
extraordinary
extreme
fiery
finally
fluorescent/-ence
forty
fulfill
grateful
guarantee
hamster
harass
height
hierarchy
hors d'oeuvre
hypocrite/-crisy
humorous
iceberg
icicle
idiosyncrasy

ignorance
imitate/imitation
immediate
incredible
independent/-ence
indict
indispensable
inoculate
impugn
installment
intelligence/-ent
itinerary
jewelry
judge/judgment
kernel H
laundry
leisure
liaison
library
license
lieutenant
lightning
loose/lose
maintenance
maneuver
mantle/mantel
marshal
marshmallow
memento
miniature
minuscule
mischievous
misspell
moccasin
monitor
mortgage
naive
nauseous
necessary
negligible
neighbor
niece
ninety
noticeable
occasion/-ally
occur/-urred/-urring
occurrence
omit/omitted

once
original
outrageous
overran/overrun
parallel
pastime
pavilion
perceive
perseverance
personnel
picnicking
pigeon
plateau
possession
potato/potatoes
practice
precede/precedent
prejudice
presence H
principal H
principle H
privilege
proceed/procedure
professor
pronunciation
psychology
publicly
questionnaire
queue H
raspberry
really
receipt
receive
recommend
reference
referred
regimen
relevant
relief/relieve
renaissance
rendezvous
restaurant
rhyme
rhythm
sacrilegious
sandal
satellite
schedule

scissors
secretary
seize/seizure
sentence
separate
sergeant
several
scary
sheik H
shepherd
siege/besiege
silhouette
skied/skiing
skillful
soliloquy
sophomore/-oric
stationary H
stationery H
subtle
succeed
success/-essor
superintendent
supersede
suppress
symptom
temporarily
thief/thieves
thorough
threshold
tired
together
tomato/-oes
tomorrow
truly
twelfth
unfortunately
until
vacuum
vegetarian
vehicle
Wednesday
weigh/weight
weird
wherever
withheld/withhold
yield

Two-Tab Notebook Foldables® (above): At top right, piece of blue scrap paper was used to make this Notebook Foldable for comparing *lose* and *loose*. At bottom right, a Sticky Note® was used to make a Foldable to compare *receipt* and *recipe*. Bottom left, notice that the tab of this Two-Tab Foldable was glued to the right with the tabs extending to the left. This is to prevent the tabs from getting crushed when the book is closed.

Concentric-Circle Venn Diagram (above): Four circles were cut so that the second circle was ½" smaller in diameter than the first, and the third was ½" smaller in diameter than the second, and the fourth was ½" smaller in diameter than the third. All circles were stacked, a tab was folded, and the circles were glued on top of each other by gluing the tabs together. The Venn diagram can be used independently, or it can be glued into a composition book or spiral.

When planning how many circles will be needed, count the top circle as a title page. It will cover the writing and RWP collected on the second circle.

Social Sciences, Geography	Science	Math	Language Arts
Antarctic	accelerate	across	address H
apartheid	aluminum	adjacent	author
Arctic	amplitude	angle not angel	beginning
bourgeois	antenna	approximately	category
boycott	axle	average	column
business	buoyancy	cardinal H	comedy
capital H	camouflage	circumference	humor/humorous
capitol H	category	column	library
Caribbean	Celsius	complementary H	literacy
coliseum	describe	congruent	misspell
colonel H	disease	coordinate	omit/omitted
committee	eclipse	decimal	playwright
descendant	empirical	denominator	predicate
discrimination	environment	difference	pronunciation
enemy	equipment	divisible	punctuation
foreign	Fahrenheit	eighth	reference
government	fluorescent	equivalent	rhyme
governor	frequency	finite, infinite	sentence
Hawaii	gauge	forty no u	soliloquy
indigenous	genus	fourth H	tragedy
island	gravity	height	
judge, judgment	hurricane	hour H	
legion	hygiene	inequalities	
lieutenant	hypothesis	kilogram	
medieval	lightning	length	
Mediterranean	liquefy	mathematics	
millennium	metalloid	negative	
missile	mirror	ninety keeps the e	
neighbor	molecule/-lar	numerator	
official	mosquito	occurrence	
peace H, piece H	organelle	ordinal	
peninsula	photosynthesis	parallel	
pharaoh	respiration	positive	
prairie	satellite	principle H	
senator	seismic	quantity	
sergeant	species	quartile	
sheriff	spectrum/-tra	similarity	
Spain, Spanish	temperature	simplifying	
tariff	theories	symmetry	
tyranny	tissue	tangent	
village	vacuum	tessellations	
violence	vision	thirteen	
	volume	twelfth	
	weather	twentieth	

Triple VKV Flashcard (above):
See page 385.

Frequently Misspelled Words on Blogs
1. your H - you're H
2. then - than
3. its H - it's H
4. to H - too H - two H
5. were - where - we're
6. there H - their H - they're H
7. a - an - and
8. off - of
9. here H - hear H
10. lose - loose

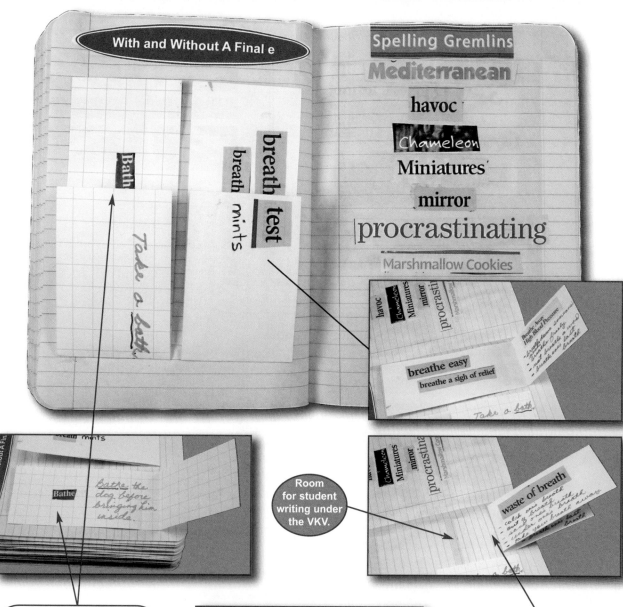

With and Without A Final e

Spelling Gremlins

Mediterranean

havoc

Chameleon

Miniatures

mirror

procrastinating

Marshmallow Cookies

breathe easy
breathe a sigh of relief

Room for student writing under the VKV.

waste of breath

Spell and Pronounce These With and Without -e:

bathe	bath
breathe	breath
clothe	cloth
lathe	lath
loathe	loath
sheathe	sheath
teethe	teeth
unite	unit
wreathe	wreath

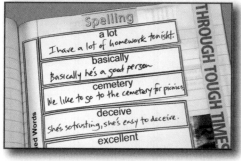

Spelling

a lot
I have a lot of homework tonight.

basically
Basically he's a good person

cemetery
We like to go to the cemetery for picnics

deceive
She's so trusting, she's easy to deceive.

excellent

THROUGH TOUGH TIMES

Multi-Tab Notebook Foldable® (above): Frequently misspelled words were typed into the template found in Dinah Zike's *Notebook Foldables* book and CD.

How to Glue Large VKVs® into a Notebook: The VKV Flashcards used in the composition book above are large, and they take up a lot of notebook space. Instead of gluing the entire back of the card, place glue along the back fold edge only, allow it to dry, and then fold the card back along the glue line to make a large tab.

-er
center
theater

-or
Usually spelled -or.
color
humor

-ize
recognize
Usually spelled -ize.
Many words are always spelled -ize,
and others spelled *-ise*.
Examples: *advertise, exercise, excise*

-re
centre
theatre

-our
colour
humour

-ise or -ize
Can be spelled either way.
recognise, recognize

Theaters preview
theater

Live
life in
full
color.

Autumn's True Colors

Two-Tab Foldable
Illustrating
Different Spellings:

American	British
theater	theatre
color	colour

-yze
analyze

vowel + l
Verbs ending in a vowel plus *l*
usually do not double the *l* when adding suffixes.
travel, traveled, traveler

-e- only
archeology *also archaeology*
maneuver

-ense
license
defense

-og
catalog
dialog
Catalogue and *dialogue* also acceptable.
Catalogue, in particular, seems to be falling out of use.

-yse
analyse

vowel + l
Verbs ending in a vowel plus *l*
double the *l* when adding suffixes.
travel, travelled, traveller

-ae- or -oe-
archaeology
manoeuvre

-ence
licence
defence

-ogue
catalogue
dialogue

Spelling American vs. British

Two-Tab Foldables® (above) can be used to compare and contrast different words used in different languages to name the same thing. In America, the words "boot" and "bonnet" are not used to name parts of a car, as they are in England.

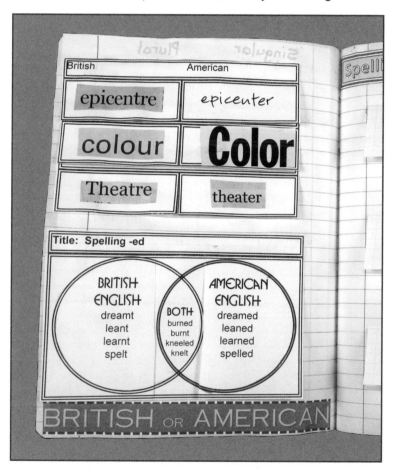

Notebook Foldables® (above): At the top of the composition book page are three Two-Tab Notebook Foldables glued over each other to form six tabs. At the bottom of the page, a Venn diagram template was used to compare and contrast the spelling of -ed in British English and American English.

American vs. British English: Different Terms for the Same Things

American	British
apartment	flat
argument	row
backpack	rucksack
bar ᴴ	pub
bathroom	loo, lavatory
cafeteria	refectory/canteen
can ᴴ	tin
chips	crisps
closet	wardrobe
clothespin	clothes-peg
cookie	biscuit
diaper	nappy
elevator	lift
faucet	tap
flashlight	torch
fries	chips
garbage can	dustbin
gas	petrol
gas station	garage
lawyer	solicitor
line	queue
living room	lounge
mail ᴴ	post
movie	film
movie theater	cinema
oatmeal	porridge
package	parcel
pants ᴴ	trousers
pharmacist	chemist
plastic wrap	cling film
potato chips	crisps
principal ᴴ	headmaster/ headmistress
raincoat	mackintosh/mac
rent	hire
sausage	banger
sidewalk	pavement
soccer	football
subway	underground, tube
truck	lorry
vacation	holiday

Suffixes General Review

A *suffix* is a letter or letter cluster that is added to the end of a root or base word.
Sometimes a suffix is added directly to a word.
For example, *-s* is added directly to *boy* to form the word *boys*.
Examples: talk, talk**s**, talk**ed**, talk**ing**

Sometimes adding a suffix changes the spelling of a word.
Examples: cry, cri**ed** (*-y* changed to *-i* before suffix is added)
sip, sipp**ed**, sipp**ing** (the final consonant is doubled to maintain the short vowel sound)

Sometimes suffixes change the tense or meaning of a word.
Examples: I look at books. (present tense)
I look**ed** at books. (past tense)

A word that ends in silent **e** usually keeps the **e** when adding a suffix beginning with a consonant.

Examples:
awe	awesome
care	careful
nine	ninety

A word that ends in silent **e** usually drops the **e** when adding a suffix beginning with a vowel.
See word lists on the next page.

Examples:
explore	explor**ed**	explor**ing**
fine	finer	finest
tire	tired	tiring

A word ending in a **y** that follows a consonant usually changes the **y** to **i** before a suffix is added, unless the suffix begins with **i**. A word ending in **y** following a vowel usually keeps the **y** before adding a suffix.

Examples:
carry	carried	carrying
bray	brays	braying

When a word ends in *ie* in which the **e** is silent, change the *ie* to **y** before adding *-ing*.

Examples: die dying   lie lying

The letter **k** is usually added to words ending in **c** before a suffix beginning with **e**, **i**, or **y**.

Examples: mimic   mimicking   picnic   picnicking

When adding a suffix to a one-syllable word ending with a single vowel and consonant, double the final consonant before adding a suffix that begins with a vowel.

Examples: chop chopped chopping   drop dropped dropping

A word having more than one syllable, ending in one consonant that follows one short vowel, usually doubles the final consonant before a suffix beginning with a vowel, provided the accent is on the last syllable.

Examples: forget forgetting   commit committed committing
BUT benefit benefiting Sp (accent on the first syllable, so the final consonant is not doubled)

In words ending in a final consonant preceded by two vowels, do not double the final consonant when adding a suffix beginning with a vowel.

Examples: beat, beaten   need, needed   seed, seeded

Suffixes General Review

Stressed Syllables

Some languages, like Finnish and Hungarian, have fixed stress (always on the first syllable). Others have regular rules for syllable stress. But in some languages, including English and Russian, stress is often unpredictable.

Some words change syllable stress according to their parts of speech. For example:

ob·**ject** v.   **ob**·ject n.
pre·**sent** v.   **pres**·ent n.
re·**cord** v.   **re**·cord n.

Word Study: Suffixes That Differ by One Vowel Can Contribute to Spelling Errors

-able   **-ible**

-able - most common spelling of the two
-ible is used with words borrowed from Latin
Spelling Hint: *-ible* is never used after a vowel

-ant   **-ent**

Nouns: confid**a**nt and depend**a**nt
Adjectives: confid**e**nt, depend**e**nt,
Adjective and noun the same: dissident, adolescent

-ance   **-ence**

Nouns ending in *-ance* or *-ence* usually
can also form adjectives ending in *-ant* or *-ent*.
Example: independence, n.; independent, adj.

-ancy   **-ency**

Nouns ending in *-ancy* or *-ency* usually
can form adjectives ending in *-ant* or *-ent*.
Example: dependency, n.; dependent, adj.

-ary   **-ery**

The spelling *-ary* is the most common suffix and can
form adjectives or nouns. The suffix
-ery usually forms nouns. Example: bakery
Homophones: stationary, adj.; stationery, n.

-er   **-or**

Both suffixes can be used to form nouns or action
verbs. When used to form nouns, they refer to a person
or thing that does something—baker, actor.

-ist   **-est**

When trying to decide which spelling to use, remember,
the suffix *-ist* means someone who does something, and
the suffix *-est* is usually used to form superlative
adjectives. Examples: activist, greatest

-ous   **-eous, -ious**

All of these suffixes are used to form adjectives
that mean full of, possessing, or relating to.
Examples: lumin**ous**, vorac**ious**

Word Study: Two Groups

Suffixes can be divided into two groups based upon their beginning letter— vowel or consonant.

Vowel Suffixes	Consonant Suffixes
-able, -ible	-dom
-age	-hood
-ance, -ence	-less
-ed	-ly
-est	-ment
-ing	-ness
-ism	-ward
-ous	-wise

Spelling challenges occur more frequently with the addition of vowel suffixes.

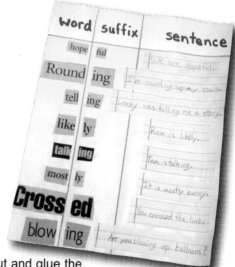

Variation Using RWP (right): The folded chart to the right was made using 8½" x 11" paper. In RWP, find words with suffixes. Cut and glue the base word in the first column and the suffix in the second column. Use the word in a sentence in the last, largest column. Use several of the words to write a simple paragraph on the back, or use the words to write a poem or short story.

Variation: Make a chart with an extra column to collect examples of words with two suffixes. Example: exceedingly.

A word ending in a *y* following a consonant usually changes the *y* to *i* before a suffix
is added, unless the suffix begins with *i*. Example: *cry, cries*
A word ending in *y* following a vowel usually keeps the *y* before a suffix is added. Example: *key, keys*

Test Prep Practice
Final -y Words:

alchemy *
anomaly *
cacophony *
chary *
cursory *
dally *
decry *
depravity *
dichotomy *
doughty *
dowdy *
earthy *
epiphany *
etymology *
fidelity *
fluency *
frugality *
humility *
impiety *
indemnify *
latency *
levity *
magnanimity *
ossify *
parity *
paucity *
perjury *
posterity *
privy *
propinquity *
putrefy *
sundry *
usury *
vagary *
verity *
vilify *

Basic Vocabulary
Final -y Examples:

berry
bunny
bury
carry
comedy
cry
curry
fly
funny
happy
humidity
hungry
hurry
jury
marry
money
party
pry
sunny
try
windy

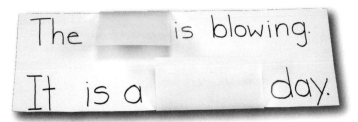

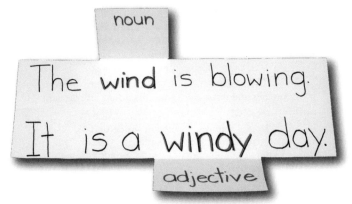

Shutterfold VKV® (above): Make a shutterfold using a
sheet of 11" x 17" photocopy paper. Write a simple sentence under the top shutter using a noun that can be
turned into an adjective by adding *-y*. Write a simple
sentence under the bottom shutter using the adjective.
Cut the top and bottom shutters away so that only a
small section is left to cover the featured noun and
adjective. Close the tabs and see if students can complete the sentences. Open the tabs to check responses.

Word Study:
Words that Look "Funny"
with Suffixes
Make a three-column chart
and collect examples:

see sees
shy shied shying
ski skied skiing

Final -y (left): The suffix *-y* is one
of the twenty most common
suffixes. It has either an /ē/ or an
/ī/ vowel sound.

A word that ends in silent *e* usually keeps the *e* when adding a suffix beginning with a consonant.
A word that ends in silent *e* usually drops the *e* when adding a suffix beginning with a vowel.
The final *e* is not needed to give the preceding vowel a long sound, as the vowel on the suffix will
serve the same purpose. Examples: fam*e*, fam*ous*; pol*e*, pol*ar*; ros*e*, ros*y*

Test-Prep Practice
Drop the -e Example Words:

abase *   v. -ed, -ing; n. -ment, -er
abjure *   v. -ed, -ing; n. -er; adj. -atory
allocate *   v. -ed, -ing; n. -or
amalgamate *   v. -ed, -ing; n. -or; adj. -ble, -ive
articulate *   v. -ed, -ing; adv. -ly; n. -ness, -cy
condone *   v. -ed, -ing; n. -er; adj. -able
consecrate *   v. -ed, -ing; n. -ness; adj. -ive
denigrate *   v. -ed, -ing; n. -ion, -or; adj. -ive
deride *   v. -ed, -ing; n. -er; adv. -ingly
efface *   v. -ed, -ing; n. -ment, -er; adj. -able
emanate *   v. -ed, -ing; n. -or; adj. -ive
evoke *   v. -ed, -ing; n. -er
execute*   v. -ed, -ing; n. -er; adj. -able
exhume *   v. -ed, -ing; n. -er, -ation
expunge *   v. -ed, -ing; n. -er
fortitude *   adj. -inous
germane *   adv. -ly, n. -ness
innate *   adv. -ly; n. -ness
lambaste *   v. -ed, -ing
modulate *   v. -ed, -ing; adj. -ive, -ory
nettle *   n. -s, -er; v. -ed, -ing; adj. -like, -ly
oscillate *   v. -ed, -ing; n. -ion
prattle *   .v -ed, -ing; n. -er; adv. -ingly
propagate*   v. -ed, -ing; n. -or; adj. -ive, -ory
reiterate *   v. -ed, -ing; n. -ion; adj. -able
relegate *   v. -ed, -ing; n. -ion; adj. releg-able
repudiate *   v. -ed, -ing; n. -or; adj. -ble, -ive
revile *   v. -ed, -ing; n. -er, -ment; adv. -ingly
seethe *   v. -ed, -ing; n. -s; adv. -ingly
subjugate *   v. -ed, -ing; n. -or, -ion; adj. -ble
subsume *   v. -ed, -ing; adj. -able
traduce *   v. -ed, -ing; n. -er, -ment; adv. -ingly
undermine   v. -ed, -ing; n. -er; adv. -ingly
vindicate *   v. -ed, -ing; n. -or
wane *   v. -ed, -ing

Basic Vocabulary
Drop the -e Example Words:

advise Sp v.	advised	advising
breeze n.	breezes	
explore v.	explored	exploring
fade v.	faded	fading
false adj.	falser	falsest
fine H adj.	finer	finest
freeze v.	frozen	freezing
hate v.	hated	hating
haze H n.	hazed	hazy adj.
hope v./n.	hoped v.	hoping v.
ice n.	icy adj.	
image n.	images	imaging
impose v.	imposed	imposing
incline v.	inclined	inclining
live H v.	living	livable adj.
move v.	moving	movable adj.
prove v.	proven	proving
race H v.	raced	racing
save v.	saved	saving
time H n.	timed	timing
zone v./n.	zoned	zoning

Word Study: Drop Silent -e or Keep It?
A silent e is usually dropped
before adding a vowel suffix:
bandage bandaging
cruise cruising
determine determined
However, if the word ends in -ce or -ge and the vowel
suffix begins with an a, o, or u, the silent e
is needed to keep the soft sound in the root.
change   changeable
courage   courageous
knowledge   knowledgeable
manage   manageable
notice   noticeable Sp
outrage   outrageous
peace   peaceable
revenge   vengeance

A one-syllable word that ends in one consonant following a short vowel usually doubles the consonant before a suffix that begins with a vowel.

abut *v.*	abutted	abutting
confer	conferred	conferring
deter	deterred	deterring
drop *v.*	dropped	dropping
flag *v.*	flagged	flagging
flat *adj.*	flatter	flattest
fog *v.*	fogged	fogging
glad *adj.*	gladder	gladdest
grab *v.*	grabbed	grabbing
knit *v.*	knitted	knitting
knot *v.*	knotted	knotting
jar *v.*	jarred	jarring
lag *v.*	lagged	lagging
lap *v.*	lapped	lapping
log *v.*	logged	logging
map *v.*	mapped	mapping
mat *v.*	matted	matting
occur *v.*	occurred Sp	occurring Sp
plan *v.*	planned	planning
plot *v.*	plotted	plotting
swim *v.*	swimmer *n.*	swimming
trot *v.*	trotted	trotting
zip *v.*	zipper *n.*	zipped

A word of more than one syllable that ends in one consonant following one short vowel usually doubles the final consonant before a suffix beginning with a vowel, provided the accent is on the last syllable.

be•**gin**	beginning	
com•**mit**	committed	committing
e•**quip**	equipped	equipping
ex•**cel**	excellent	excellence
for•**get**	forgot	forgetting
per•**mit** *v.*	permitted	permitting
re•**fer**	referred Sp	referring

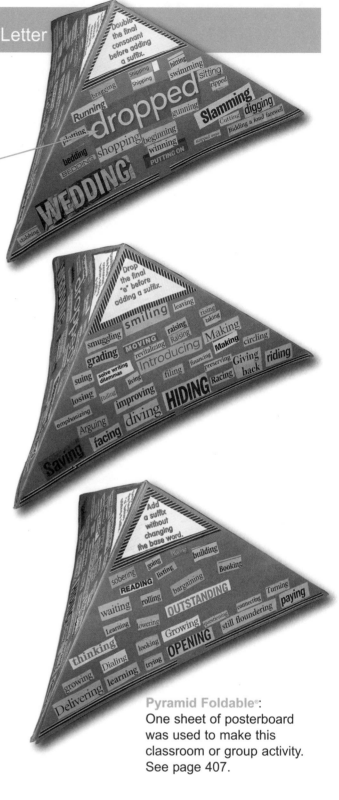

Pyramid Foldable®:
One sheet of posterboard was used to make this classroom or group activity. See page 407.

/sh/

When this sound occurs before a vowel suffix, it is spelled -ci, -si, or -ti.

cautious	inertia	patient	special
deficient	musician	pension	statistician
delicious	nutrition	physician	suction
electrician	optician	quotient	suspicion
expulsion	partial	revulsion	vacation

But how do you know which spelling to use?

1. -cian always refers to a person, and...

beautician	magician
clinician	musician
cosmetician	physician
diagnostician	politician
dietician	technician
electrician	

...-tion and -sion are never used for people.

abbreviation	allusion
absorption	collision
combination	comprehension
definition	decision
elevation	diffusion
graduation	division
isolation	erosion
legislation	intermission
navigation	obsession
perspiration	recession
rotation	seclusion
salvation	session
vacation	vision

Three-Pocket Trifold (above): Made using 11" x 17" coverstock paper (100#) and used by cooperative learning groups. Quarter-Sheet VKV Flashcards fit inside the pockets.
See pages 397 and 416 .

Three-Tab Foldable® (below): Notice that the notebook holes are uncovered to allow storage in a three-hole binder. See page 397.

2. If the root word ends in /t/, use -tion:
hibernate, hibernation
illustrate, illustration

3. If the root word ends in /s/ or /d/, use -sion:
occlude, occlusion
transcend, transcension

possess, possession
profess, profession

4. If the word ends is /zhun/ instead of /shun/, use -sion:
aversion
confusion

5. The ending -mit becomes -mission:
commit, commission
permit, permission
submit, submission

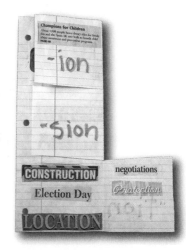

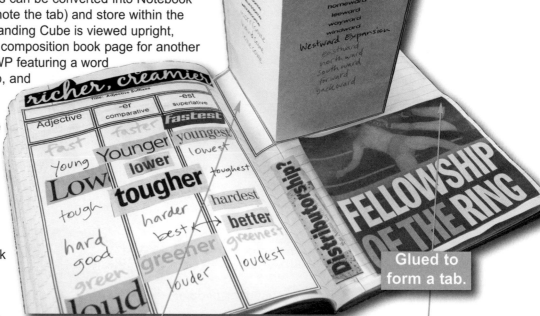

Notebook Foldables® Standing Cube Project (right, standing): Dinah's 3-D Foldables can be converted into Notebook Foldables. They fold flat (note the tab) and store within the notebook. Because the Standing Cube is viewed upright, there is room on the same composition book page for another activity. Notice that the RWP featuring a word with the suffix *-ship* is a tab, and students collected other *-ship* words underneath. See the Independent Cube Project on page 289 and instructions on how to make it on page 418.

Three-Column Notebook Chart (right): Glue was placed behind the title bar of a three-column Notebook Foldable, and the bar was glued to the top of a page in a composition book. When dry, the title bar acts as a tab, allowing the body of the chart to be raised and lowered. Students can write under the chart.

Cube closed flat for storage

Glued to form a tab.

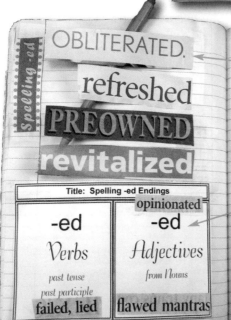

Combination of Suffix Activities:

1. Tabbed RWP.

2. Two-Tab Notebook Foldable.

3. VKVs with kinesthetic suffix tabs.

Nouns
Double Suffixes
bashfulness
blissfulness
boastfulness
carefulness
cheerfulness
fearfulness
forcefulness
hatefulness
joyfulness
lawfulness
resentfulness
sinfulness
skillfulness
thankfulness
thoughtfulness
ungratefulness
youthfulness

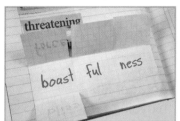

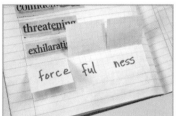

Far Right: Words, pictures, graphs, charts, and diagrams can be turned into Notebook Foldables by gluing one edge into a notebook so the rest of the graphic forms a tab. **Note**: Since these tabs were placed on the **right page**, they were glued along the **left edge**. The tabs open from the right. This prevents the tabs from being crushed when the notebook is opened and closed. See page 265 for examples of tabs glued on their right edges.

The twenty suffixes listed below have been found to account for 93% of suffix use in common language. Select ability-appropriate words for student use.

1. -s, -es
E suffix forming plurals

acres
antagonists *
bicycles
caldrons *
calves
cities
compromises *
conformists *
congregations *
daughters
diaries
enemies
graphs
hedonists *
highways
knights H
knives
leaves H
lobbyists *
memories
novices *
palisades *
pillows
precepts *
precipices *
syllables
symphonies
textbooks
transients

2. -ed
E suffix forming past tense of verbs

abbreviated
amazed
annoyed
burgeoned *
buried
covered
dejected *
delayed
dilapidated
extended
extolled *
finished
forced
grasped
hackneyed *
hampered *
motivated
parched *
remained
restrained *
resulted
rounded
shortened
truncated *
undecided
voiced
withered *
worried

3. -ing
E suffix forming present participles of verbs; adj.

abstaining *
billowing *
collaborating *
enervating *
enhancing *
exasperating *
extenuating *
fetching
freezing
imposing
knowing
laughing
manufacturing
meandering
reconciling *
renovating *
rising
scrutinizing *
stopping
talking
vindicating *
working

> Many words are spelled with the double suffixes **-ingly** and **-fully**: **willingly**, **wrongfully**. See page 289.

4. -ly
E suffix forming adverbs from adjectives; like, characteristic of
E suffix forming adjectives meaning like

accidentally Sp
anonymously *
benevolently *
compassionately *
conditionally *
consequentially *
covertly *
diligently *
frugally *
ghostly
happily
leisurely Sp
loosely
nonchalantly *
peacefully
primarily
prudently *
quietly
saintly
sincerely
surreptitiously *
tactfully *
tentatively *
timely
unfriendly
womanly

5. -er, -or
E suffixes forming nouns; person connected with

buyer
cartographer *
lawyer
painter
seller
teacher
treasurer

-or nouns are not as common as -er nouns

actor
author
conductor
counselor
dictator
director
distributor
doctor
editor
elevator
escalator
exhibitor
governor
inventor
irrigator
orator *
professor Sp
predecessor *
prospector
regulator
senator
suitor
survivor
visitor

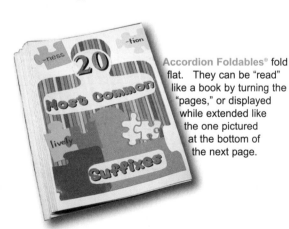

Accordion Foldables® fold flat. They can be "read" like a book by turning the "pages," or displayed while extended like the one pictured at the bottom of the next page.

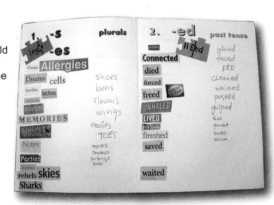

Source: White, T.G.I., Sowell, V., and Yanagihara, A. (1999). Teaching elementary students to use word-part clues. *The Reading Teacher*, 42, 302-308.

6. -ion, -tion, -ation, -ition
L suffixes forming nouns: action, condition

- addit**ion**
- attent**ion**
- celebrat**ion**
- enunciat**ion** *
- expedit**ion**
- intent**ion**
- jubilat**ion** *
- lacerat**ion** *
- protect**ion**
- reconciliat**ion** *
- remunerat**ion** *
- renovat**ion** *
- resignat**ion** *
- resolut**ion** *
- separat**ion**
- starvat**ion**
- vacat**ion**

-cion is a variation of -tion. Only two common words are spelled with -cion— coercion and suspicion.

7. -able, -ible
L suffixes forming adj.: can be done, capable of

- amic**able** *
- change**able** Sp
- collect**ible** Sp
- combust**ible**
- comfort**able**
- do**able**
- gull**ible**
- incompat**ible** *
- inevit**able***
- laugh**able**
- malle**able** *
- notice**able** Sp
- plaus**ible** *
- pli**able** *
- poss**ible**
- read**able**
- reprehens**ible** *
- suit**able**
- terr**ible**
- vener**able** *

8. -al, -ial
L suffixes forming adj.: having characteristics of

- chemic**al**
- commerc**ial**
- condition**al** *
- ephemer**al** *
- financ**ial**
- frug**al**
- inconsequent**ial** *
- logic**al**
- magic**al**
- mechanic**al**
- music**al**
- mystic**al**
- physic**al**
- spheric**al**
- superfic**ial** *

9. -y
Gk suffix forming adj.; characterized by

- brawn**y** *
- cage**y**
- cursor**y** *
- drear**y**
- earth**y**
- fish**y**
- flight**y**
- foolhard**y**
- haught**y** *
- health**y**
- thrift**y** *
- trust**y**
- unwield**y** *
- war**y** *
- wil**y** *
- wind**y**
- zan**y** *

10. -ness
E suffix attached to adj. to form nouns; state of, condition of

- bitter**ness**
- clean**liness**
- close**ness**
- discursive**ness** *
- fit**ness**
- forgive**ness**
- haught**iness** *
- helpless**ness**
- hoarse**ness**
- idle**ness**
- inevitable**ness** *
- like**ness**
- listless**ness**
- lush**ness**
- ornate**ness** *
- shrewd**ness**
- soft**ness**
- subtle**ness** *
- tight**ness**
- vacuous**ness** *
- weak**ness**
- wear**iness**
- wilder**ness**
- willing**ness**

Accordion Foldable®: Ten sheets of 11" x 17" paper were used to make this accordion. Each page features one of the 20 most common suffixes. See page 403.

The twenty prefixes listed below have been found to account for 93% of suffix use in common language. Select ability-appropriate words for student use.

11. -ity, -ty

L suffiesx use to form abstract nouns; state of, condition

activ**ity**
acu**ity** *
advers**ity** *
animos**ity** *
brev**ity** *
civil**ity**
creativ**ity**
debil**ity** *
hones**ty**
individual**ity** *
integr**ity** *
lev**ity** *
longev**ity** *
loyal**ty**
pover**ty**
procliv**ity** *
profan**ity** *
prosper**ity** *
sagac**ity** *
serendip**ity** *
spontane**ity** *

12. -ment

L suffix of nouns; denoting an action, process, state

abase**ment** *
achieve**ment**
amend**ment**
amuse**ment**
argu**ment** Sp
assign**ment**
battle**ment**
bewilder**ment**
compli**ment** H
depart**ment**
disagree**ment**
entertain**ment**
experi**ment**
frag**ment**
govern**ment**
impeach**ment**
install**ment** Sp
move**ment**
orna**ment**
predica**ment** *
punish**ment**
refresh**ment**
require**ment**
resent**ment**
sedi**ment**
settle**ment**
state**ment**
treat**ment**

13. -ic

L suffix forming adj.; having characteristics of Gk noun suffix found in loanwords such as *music*

aesthet**ic** *
anachronist**ic** *
angel**ic**
apathet**ic** *
bucol**ic** *
caust**ic** *
choler**ic** *
com**ic**
crit**ic**
dogmat**ic** *
eccentr**ic** *
eclect**ic** *
endem**ic** *
esoter**ic** *
fantast**ic**
histor**ic**
impolit**ic** *
letharg**ic**
mag**ic**
mus**ic**
poet**ic**
pragmat**ic** *
problemat**ic** *
prolif**ic** *
prosa**ic** *
sardon**ic** *
terrif**ic**
top**ic**
trag**ic**

14. -ous, -eous, -ious

L suffixes forming adj.; possessing the qualities of, full of

amorph**ous** *
anonym**ous** *
assidu**ous** *
atroci**ous**
circuit**ous** *
covet**ous** *
curi**ous**
deleteri**ous** *
dubi**ous** *
extran**eous** *
fastidi**ous** *
fortuit**ous** *
hilari**ous**
impetu**ous** *
ostentati**ous** *
pretenti**ous** *
prodigi**ous**
querul**ous** *
rancor**ous** *
scrupul**ous** *
seri**ous**
superflu**ous** *
surreptiti**ous** *
tedi**ous** *
tenaci**ous** *
voraci**ous** *
wondr**ous**

15. -en

E suffix used to form verb forms; used to form adj. from nouns

barr**en** *
black**en**
bright**en**
dark**en**
earth**en**
eat**en**
flax**en**
fright**en**
froz**en**
hast**en** *
light**en**
oak**en**
quick**en**
shak**en**
slack**en**
straight**en**
strength**en**
swoll**en**
thick**en**
weak**en**

used to form some irregular noun plurals

breth**ren**
child**ren**
ox**en**

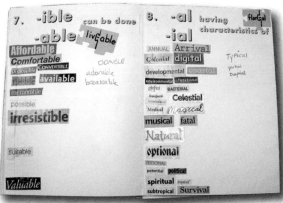

Accordion Foldables® fold flat. See pages 278 and 279 for photographs of other pages in this book.

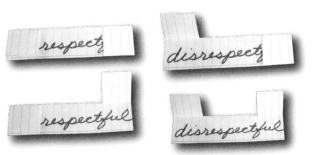

Double VKV Flashcard (above) used to form four words with a focus on a root word, a prefix, and a suffix. See page 380.

Source: White, T.G.I., Sowell, V., and Yanagihara, A. (1999). Teaching elementary students to use word-part clues. *The Reading Teacher*, 42, 302-308.

16. -er
E suffix used to form comparative degree of adj. and adv.; also a noun suffix

bigger
brighter
colder
drier, dryer
faster
flier, flyer
farther, further
harbinger *
heavier
higher
hotter
lighter
lower
newer
nicer
older
quicker
quieter
shorter
slower
smaller
smarter
softer
taller

17. -ive, -ative, -itive
L adj. suffixes, also used to form nouns from adj.; tendency, disposition, function

active
attentive
corrective
creative
definitive
destructive
detective
exhaustive *
fugitive
instructive
lucrative
palliative *
passive
restorative *
talkative
tentative *

18. -ful
E adj. suffix; full of, characterized by

bashful
beautiful
careful
faithful
forceful
forgetful
graceful
harmful
healthful
helpful
hopeful
painful
peaceful
restful
stressful
successful
tactful *
willful

E noun suffix; a quantity that fills

armful
cupful
mouthful
teaspoonful

19. -less
E adj. suffix; without

aimless *
blameless
childless
doubtless
fearless
fruitless *
harmless
helpless
homeless
hopeless
mindless
penniless
scoreless
senseless *
thankless
thoughtless
timeless
tireless
waterless

20. -est
ME suffix; superlative degree of adj. and adv.

ablest
austerest *
biggest
boldest
busiest
clearest
cloudiest
drollest *
dullest
earliest
finest
frailest
greediest
hottest
meanest
nearest
oldest
quaintest *
quirkiest *
sparsest *
wisest
youngest

Note: *-st* is a variation of *-est*. Example: *least*

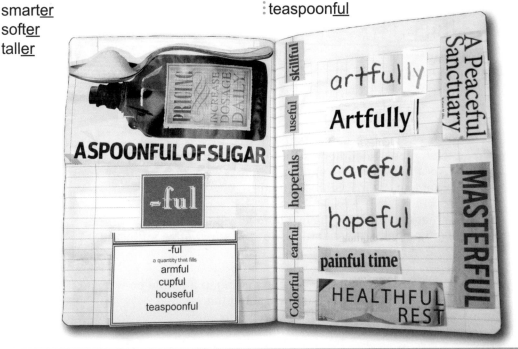

Note the variety of ways in which the suffix *-ful* is featured in the composition notebook to the left.

• RWP tabs
• RWP words
• Half-Book Foldable
• Double VKV Flashcards forming adjectives and adverbs with the suffixes *-ful* and *-ly*.

Adjectives modify nouns and pronouns and tell *which one*, *what kind*, *how many*, and *whose*.
Adjectives have positive, comparative, and superlative forms.
The comparative and superlative forms can show degrees by adding suffixes.
See page 270, Suffixes: Instructor Review.

<u>Positive</u>:
beautiful, calm, handsome
• describes one thing or a group of things that will not be compared
• root form of adjective

<u>Comparative</u>:
more beautiful than, calmer than, more handsome than
• usually compares two things
• usually formed by adding -er
• adjectives of more than one syllable usualy use *more* + the root form: *more capable*
(exceptions: *prettier, funnier*)
• are often followed by the word *than*

<u>Superlative</u>:
the prettiest, the most beautiful, the most handsome
• usually compares three or more things
• usually preceded by the word *the*
• usually formed by adding -est
• adjectives of more than one syllable usually use *most* + the root form: *most capable*

Pocket Chart Foldable (left): A sheet of 11" x 17" paper (100#) was used to make this combination Foldable:

Chart

Pocket

Display Strip

Sentence Strip (above): Use half sheets of 8½" x 11" paper to make the Foldable pictured above. See page 413.

Three Exceptions:
1. **Adjectives ending in a consonant followed by a -y, change the -y to an -i before adding the comparative ending -er or the superlative ending -est.**
Example: funny, funnier, funniest

2. **One-syllable adjectives that end in -e and have a long vowel sound (CVCe words) drop the -e before adding the comparative suffix -er or the superlative suffix -est.**
Example: cute, cuter, cutest

3. **One-syllable adjectives with a short vowel sound and ending in a single consonant double the final consonant before adding the comparative suffix -er or the superlative suffix -est.**
Example: sad, sadder, saddest

Suffixes Adjectives

> Some suffixes are used with more than one part of speech.

-able, -ble, -ible

Suffixes; capable of, fit for, tending to

- ami**able** *
- culp**able** *
- estim**able** *
- extric**able** *
- fall**ible***
- formid**able***
- igno**ble** *
- immut**able** *
- imperturb**able** *
- implac**able** *
- incorrig**ible** *
- indomit**able** *
- ineluct**able** *
- intract**able** *
- iras**cible** *
- malle**able** *
- ostens**ible** *
- palp**able** *
- pot**able** *
- reprehens**ible** *
- ris**ible** *
- tract**able** *
- vi**able** *
- volu**ble** *

-al, -ial, ical

Suffixes; of the kind of, pertaining to

- aborigin**al**
- abysm**al**
- artifici**al**
- benefici**al**
- bienni**al** *
- celesti**al** *
- commerci**al**
- condition**al** *
- continent**al**
- custodi**al**
- detriment**al** *
- dimension**al**
- economic**al** *
- ephemer**al** *
- elliptic**al** *
- fanatic**al**

-al, -ial, ical

(cont.)

- feud**al**
- fiction**al**
- financi**al**
- fraction**al**
- grammatic**al**
- historic**al**
- horizont**al**
- hypothetic**al**
- inconsequenti**al** *
- logic**al**
- monument**al**
- music**al**
- potenti**al**
- practic**al**
- profession**al**
- radic**al**
- remedi**al**
- residenti**al**
- rhetoric**al**
- senatori**al**
- sensation**al**
- spheric**al**
- superfici**al** *
- tradition**al**
- unethic**al** *
- univers**al**
- upheav**al** *
- vertic**al**
- whims**ical**

Note: The addition of the suffix -al forms an adjective, and the addition of -ally forms an adverb. **Example:** univers**al** adj. univers**ally** adv.

Double Suffixes: -al can be added after the suffixes -ic, -tion, -sion. **Examples:** magic magical tradition traditional dimension dimensional

-an, -ian

Suffixes; related to, belonging to, resembling

- come**dian**
- histor**ian**
- urb**an**

-ant

Suffix forming n. and adj. from verbs; characterized by, inclined to

- arrog**ant**
- buoy**ant**
- clairvoy**ant** *
- compli**ant** *
- disson**ant** *
- domin**ant**
- exorbit**ant** *
- exuber**ant**
- flagr**ant***
- flamboy**ant** *
- nonchal**ant** *
- pleas**ant**
- recus**ant** *
- redund**ant** *
- repugn**ant** *
- reson**ant** *
- supplic**ant** * adj.
- vac**ant** *
- vari**ant** *
- vigil**ant** *

-ar

Variation of -al; pertaining to, characterized by

- angul**ar**
- circul**ar**
- lun**ar**
- singul**ar**

-ary

Suffix; pertaining to, connected with

- arbitr**ary**
- auxili**ary**
- custom**ary**
- exempl**ary** *
- fragment**ary**
- heredit**ary**
- honor**ary**
- imagin**ary**
- involunt**ary**
- legend**ary**
- liter**ary**
- milit**ary**
- moment**ary**
- pecuni**ary**
- planet**ary**
- pulmon**ary**
- reaction**ary**
- revolution**ary**
- sanit**ary**
- second**ary**
- solit**ary**
- tempor**ary**
- vision**ary**
- volunt**ary**

-ate

Suffix occurring in L loanwords: originally -atus, -ata, -atum

- illiter**ate**
- inconsider**ate**
- liter**ate**
- moder**ate**
- passion**ate**
- temper**ate**

-ed

Suffix used to form adj. from nouns (also verb forms)

- abbreviat**ed** *
- dejec**ted** *
- dela**yed**
- dilapidat**ed**
- motivat**ed**
- rag**ged**
- round**ed**
- shorten**ed**
- undecid**ed**
- voic**ed**
- wither**ed** *

-en

Suffix used to form adj. of source material ("made of") from n.

- ash**en**
- earth**en**
- flax**en**
- gold**en**
- wood**en**

Trifold Chart (above): See page 399.

Dinah Zike's *Foldables*, Notebook Foldables* and VKVs* for Spelling and Vocabulary 4th-12th   283

Suffixes Adjectives

Some suffixes are used with more than one part of speech.

-ent, -lent -ulent

Suffixes similar to -ant; characterized by, inclined to, in the capacity of

antecedent
benevolent *
coherent *
complacent *
despondent *
divergent *
fraudulent
imminent *
impudent *
inconvenient
independent
indolent *
inherent *
insolvent *
intermittent *
malevolent *
munificent *
omniscient *
opulent *
persistent
recumbent *
resplendent *
resurgent *
reverent
salient *

-ent, -ulent, cont.

subservient
transient *
truculent *
turbulent

-eous

Suffix; composed of

courteous
gaseous
hideous
igneous
instantaneous
spontaneous

-er

Comparative degree of adjectives

bigger
brighter
cooler
drier
farther
faster
heavier
higher

-er, cont.

hotter
lower
meaner
nicer
older
quicker
quieter
shorter
smaller
smarter
softer
taller

-est

Superlative degree of adj.

angriest
baldest
beefiest
blousiest
bubbliest
chewiest
craggiest
creamiest
dizziest
filthiest
greediest
haughtiest *
mousiest

-est, cont.

numbest
obscurest *
poshest
quirkiest
saltiest
securest
tiniest
untimeliest
vainest
wisest

-ferous

Combining form; bearing, producing, containing

aquiferous
carboniferous
crystalliferous
pestiferous

-fic

Combining form; producing, causing

beatific * no -u-
horrific
prolific
scientific
terrific

-fold

E suffix; of so many parts

fourfold
fivefold
manifold
tenfold
twentyfold

-genous

Suffix -ous used with nouns ending in -gen to form adjectives

androgenous
endogenous
hydrogenous
indigenous

-ic

L suffix forming adjectives; having characteristics of Gk n. suffix found in loanwords such as music

aesthetic *
aseptic *
caustic *
eccentric *
eclectic *
egocentric *
erratic *
esoteric *
ethnic *
exotic *

-ic, cont.

fanatic *
forensic *
frenetic *
impolitic *
laconic *
pontific
pragmatic *
problematic *
prolific *
quixotic *
sardonic *
static *
stoic *
vitriolic *

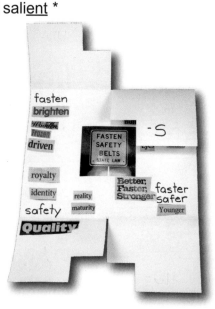

Four-Door Foldable® (left and right): This example was made using a sheet of 11" x 17" copy paper. Trace a square or a circle in the middle of the closed Foldable and cut away the traced shape to form a window. Use the window to draw attention to a picture, word, or phrase. The street sign featured to the left has three suffixes. Students collect examples of RWP and write their own examples under the tabs. See page 401

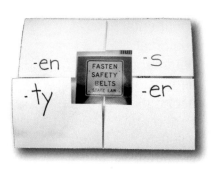

Suffixes Adjectives

Some suffixes are used with more than one part of speech.

-il, -ile
Suffix; capability, susceptibility

agile
civil
docile
ductile
fertile
fragile
imbecile adj.
immobile
infantile
juvenile
mercantile
mobile
prehensile
retractile
senile
versatile
volatile

-ing
Common suffix used to form adj. and v.

adjoining
diminishing
enduring
fetching
imposing
knowing
meandering
outstanding
pleasing
shocking
working

Only one common word is spelled with the double suffix *-ingful* – meaningful.

It is common for words to be spelled with the double suffix *-ingly* – daunt*ing*-*ly*. The addition of *-ly* usually changes a word to an adverb.

-ish
ME>OE suffix; forms adj. from n. and other adj. (also occurs in v. from French: *ravish*); belonging to, like, near or about

amateurish
babyish
blackish
bleakish
boorish *
boyish
brackish
childish
churlish
devilish
dullish
feverish
foolish
fortyish Sp
garish
girlish
grayish
impish
outlandish
peevish
reddish
selfish
sheepish
sluggish
snobbish
stylish
ticklish
unselfish
waspish
whitish

-ive, -ative, -itive
Suffixes; tendency, disposition, function

adaptive
addictive
affirmative
aggressive
allusive
attentive
competitive
conclusive
cooperative
creative
decisive
definitive
demonstrative
destructive
detective adj.
diminutive
elusive *
exhaustive *
fugitive
furtive *
illusive
impulsive
informative
inquisitive
instinctive
intuitive *
inventive
lucrative
massive
offensive
palliative *
passive
possessive
productive
reflective
restorative *
sensitive
submissive *
talkative
tentative *

-less
ageless
aimless *
airless
artless
baseless
blameless
careless
childless
colorless
countless
doubtless
dreamless
endless
fearless
feckless *
flightless
fruitless *
graceless
groundless
guiltless
harmless
helpless
homeless
lawless
lifeless
mindless
peerless
penniless
scoreless
senseless *
sleeveless
tactless
thankless
timeless
tireless
useless
waterless
weightless Sp
wireless

-like
Combining form using the word *like* as a suffix to form an adjective.

catlike
childlike
dreamlike
earthlike
lifelike
weblike

-ly
Suffix forming an adj. or adv.; like, characteristic of

ghostly
hourly
leisurely
lowly
manly
monthly
saintly
timely
unfriendly
womanly

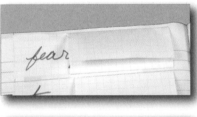

Triple VKV® Flashcard (above):
Sometimes adjective suffixes can be used to form antonyms.
See page 386.

Six-Tab Foldable (above):
See page 397.

Some suffixes are used with more than one part of speech.

-most

Combining form using the word *most* to form superlatives.

eastern<u>most</u>
fore<u>most</u>
further<u>most</u>
inner<u>most</u>
northern<u>most</u>
outer<u>most</u>
southern<u>most</u>
upper<u>most</u>
ut<u>most</u>
western<u>most</u>

-ory, -tory

Suffixes from Latin

accusa<u>tory</u>
advis<u>ory</u>
celebra<u>tory</u>
concilia<u>tory</u> *
deroga<u>tory</u> *
desul<u>tory</u> *
excre<u>tory</u>
inhibi<u>tory</u>
manda<u>tory</u>
obliga<u>tory</u> *
sens<u>ory</u>
statu<u>tory</u>

-ous, ious

Suffix; possessing, full of a quality

anonym<u>ous</u> *
anx<u>ious</u>
ard<u>uous</u> *
assid<u>uous</u> *
bil<u>ious</u> *
ceremon<u>ious</u>
circuit<u>ous</u> *
coni<u>ferous</u>
contig<u>uous</u> *
contin<u>uous</u>
danger<u>ous</u>
decid<u>uous</u> *
dev<u>ious</u> *
disingen<u>uous</u> *

-ous (cont.)

fabul<u>ous</u>
fortuit<u>ous</u> *
fur<u>ious</u>
harmon<u>ious</u> *
heterogene<u>ous</u>
homogene<u>ous</u>
humor<u>ous</u>
impet<u>uous</u> *
inconspic<u>uous</u>
incredul<u>ous</u>
indigen<u>ous</u> *
innoc<u>uous</u> *
judic<u>ious</u>
lumin<u>ous</u>
luxur<u>ious</u>
magnanim<u>ous</u>
marvel<u>ous</u>
miracul<u>ous</u>
monstr<u>ous</u>
murder<u>ous</u>
nause<u>ous</u>
nutrit<u>ious</u>
obsequi<u>ous</u>
omin<u>ous</u>
perfid<u>ious</u> *
precoc<u>ious</u>
pomp<u>ous</u>
precipit<u>ous</u>
preposter<u>ous</u>

-ous (cont.)

querul<u>ous</u> *
ridicul<u>ous</u>
tortur<u>ous</u>
venom<u>ous</u>
rebell<u>ious</u>
stud<u>ious</u>
sumptu<u>ous</u> *
superflu<u>ous</u> *
suspic<u>ious</u>
ted<u>ious</u>
tempestu<u>ous</u> *
tort<u>uous</u> *
vivac<u>ious</u>

-ious

deleter<u>ious</u> *
hilar<u>ious</u>
infect<u>ious</u>
labor<u>ious</u>
obnox<u>ious</u>
ostentat<u>ious</u> *
pretent<u>ious</u> *

-ose

Suffix occurring in adj. borrowed from Latin; full of, given to

bellic<u>ose</u>
comat<u>ose</u>
grandi<u>ose</u>
mor<u>ose</u>
verb<u>ose</u> *

-some

ME Suffix; characterized by a quality, action, condition

adventure<u>some</u>
awe<u>some</u>
bother<u>some</u>
burden<u>some</u>
cumber<u>some</u>
fear<u>some</u>
grue<u>some</u>
hand<u>some</u>
irk<u>some</u>
loath<u>some</u>
lone<u>some</u>
meddle<u>some</u>
play<u>some</u>
quarrel<u>some</u>
tire<u>some</u>
trouble<u>some</u>
two<u>some</u>
unwhole<u>some</u>
venture<u>some</u>
weari<u>some</u>
whole<u>some</u>
win<u>some</u>
worri<u>some</u>

-sy

Suffix used to form adj. (and nouns)

ant<u>sy</u>
art<u>sy</u>
bos<u>sy</u>
clas<u>sy</u>
clum<u>sy</u>
cute<u>sy</u>
dres<u>sy</u>
flim<u>sy</u>
folk<u>sy</u>

-vorous

Combining form; eating, feeding on

carni<u>vorous</u>
herbi<u>vorous</u>
omnii<u>vorous</u>

Two-Column Pocket Chart: Use a sheet of 11" x 17" (80#) paper to make this indivdual, group, or class VKV Pocket Chart. Notice how quarter-sheet flashcards fit in the pockets. The Chart can be folded in half for storing. See page 415.

Variation: Multiple Two-Column VKV Charts can be glued side by side to make a booklet of Charts with or without pockets.

Some suffixes are used with more than one part of speech.

-y

Suffix used to form adjectives; characterized by or inclined to

balmy
bosky *
brawny *
cagey
cursory *
dreary
earthy
fishy
fleshy
flighty
foamy
foolhardy *
frisky
frosty
fruity
glassy
greedy
guilty
hardy
healthy
itchy
jaunty
leathery
lengthy
moody
mossy
oily
pearly
savory
scratchy
shadowy
squeaky
thirsty
thrifty *
trusty
unwieldy *
waxy
windy
wordy
zany *

Sentence Strip Foldable® Pocket Chart (right): Use a sheet of posterboard to make a large classroom VKV Pocket Chart. Collect examples of words found in RWP, literature, and oral communication. Glue or write them into the appropriate column, and use them to make quarter-sheet flashcards. Display sentences, phrases, quotes, and/or word flashcards in the sentence strip along the bottom of the chart.

Notebook Foldables® (above): The templates for the Notebook Foldables pictured above were taken from Dinah Zike's *Notebook Foldables* book and CD.
Above Left: A pocket full of Eighth-Sheet VKV Flashcards used to find examples of **noun** + **-y suffix** = **adjective**.
Above Right: A Shutterfold used to compare and contrast adjectives and nouns formed by adding **-y**.

Suffixes Adverbs

Some suffixes are used with more than one part of speech.

An adverb is a word used to modify (describe, or qualify) a verb, an adjective, or another adverb. Adverbs answer the following questions: *How? When? Where? Why? How much?* and variations such as *How often?* and *To what extent?*

• Over 99% of all adverbs end in -ly, and the rest are words like *afterward* and *likewise*.
• Adverbs are formed by adding -ly to an adjective, but some adjectives end in -ly, too.
Exceptions add and delete the letter -y. Words ending in -ll add -y to form an adverb—*full, fully*.
• Words of two or more syllables that end in -y have the -y replaced by -i before adding -ly.
Example: *merry, merrily*
Only two common single-syllable words ending in -y form adverbs this way:
day, daily and *gay, gaily*.
• Non -ly adverbs answer the same questions as above, and include words like *well* and *very* (which can also be adjectives, depending on how they are used).

Adverbs Ending in -ly:

Answer Questions
How? How often? When? To what extent?

abjectly	forthrightly	roughly
abrasively	fully	skillfully
absently	gaily	sleepily
absolutely	generally	slowly
absurdly	gently	speedily
accidentally	gloomily	precipitately
actively	harshly	scarcely
adeptly	humbly	severely
angrily	independently	sickly
briefly	indirectly	slightly
capably	initially	slovenly *
cheerfully	largely	softly
clearly	lastly	temporarily
completely	meekly	terribly
constantly	momentarily	totally
continuously	mostly	transitorily
delicately	newly	unhappily
deviously	nightly	warmly
diagonally	originally	wholly
dismally	overtly	willingly
drowsily	personally	
eagerly	potentially	
earnestly	primarily	
easily	promptly	
finally	properly	
firmly	publicly Sp	
firstly	purposely	
fleetingly	quickly	

Many words that are spelled with these double suffixes form adverbs: -ingly, willingly; -fully, wrongfully. See page 289.

Adverbs With Other Suffixes:

Most of these words can also function as other parts of speech.

-fold	-ward	-ways
fourfold	afterward	always
tenfold	backward	crossways
twofold	downward	longways
	eastward	sideways
	forward	
	homeward	
	landward	**-wise**
	leeward	clockwise
	northward	crosswise
	seaward	lengthwise
	southward	likewise
	upward	longwise
	westward	timewise
	windward	widthwise

Word Study: Adverbs Without Suffixes

Most of these adverbs can also function as other parts of speech—nouns, adjectives, prepositions, or interjections: *Why,* you're early! *Good!*

afoot	over	too
fast	piecemeal	toward
good	rather	verbatim
inchmeal	seldom	very
just	sometimes	well
never	soon	westward
nowhere	still	why
often	today	worse
outright	tomorrow	yesterday

Suffixes Adverbs

Some suffixes are used with more than one part of speech.

One function of the suffix -al is to form adjectives: nature (n.), natural (adj.)
Sometimes the -al suffix is added to words that already end in a suffix.
The suffixes -al and -ally can be added to words ending in -ic, -tion, and -sion.

-ical, -ically
-tional, -tionally
-sional, -sionally

When -ly is added to the adjective suffix -al, an adverb is formed: partial (adj.), partially (adv.).
This double suffix can sometimes result in spelling errors.
VKVs can help students understand how and why these suffixes are added.

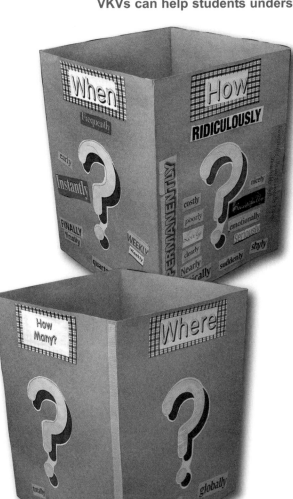

Double Suffixes

-ed + -ly	-ful + -ly	-ing + -ly
admittedly	artfully	amusingly
allegedly	beautifully	annoyingly
bigheartedly	cheerfully	blisteringly
broadmindedly	colorfully	broodingly
brokenheartedly	delightfully	challengingly
decidedly	doubtfully	condescendingly
devotedly	dreadfully	decreasingly
disgustedly	gratefully	depressingly
hotheadedly	joyfully	doubtfully
limitedly	peacefully	fleetingly
notedly	playfully	forgivingly
offhandedly	regretfully	hauntingly
purportedly	rightfully	irritatingly
relatedly	truthfully	knowingly
repeatedly	unlawfully	provokingly
ruggedly	unsuccessfully	ravishingly
secludedly	watchfully	scrutinizingly
subduedly	wrongfully	seemingly
unbiasedly		staggeringly
undeservedly		swimmingly
wickedly		teasingly

Display Cube Foldable® (above):
Use a sheet of posterboard cut in half to form the two sections used to make this large classroom display. Collect examples of words found in RWP, literature, and oral communication, and glue or write them onto the appropriate side. See page 418.

Word Study: VKV®

Verb: di *vide*
Noun: di *vi* sion
Adjective: di *vi* sion al
Adverb: di *vi* sion al ly

Many two-syllable words are stressed on the second syllable. Study what happens to the stressed syllable when suffixes are added.

Word Study: Three Suffixes

Only one common word ends in the three suffixes -*inglessly*:
meaning**lessly**.

Find examples of other words with three suffixes:
alphabet**ically**
organ**ically**
urbanist**ically**

Some suffixes are used with more than one part of speech.

-ability
-ibility

Double Suffixes; combination of -ible + -ity; -able + -ity

cap**ability**
feas**ibility**
in**ability**
invis**ibility**
poss**ibility**
reli**ability**
respons**ibility**
vi**ability** *

-acy

L suffix of nouns of office, quality, state

accur**acy**
inaccur**acy**
intim**acy**
leg**acy**
liter**acy**
pir**acy**
suprem**acy**

-ad

Gk suffix denoting a unit comprising a certain number

chili**ad** goup of 1000
dy**ad**
tri**ad**

-ade

Suffix; action, process

block**ade**
char**ade**
crus**ade**
pali**ade**
stock**ade**

Also as in -ad

dec**ade**

Sweetened beverage

lime**ade**
orange**ade**

-age

Suffix extension of -ate; forms mass or abstract nouns

break**age**
cour**age**

-age (cont.)

drain**age**
mile**age**
patron**age**
percent**age**
pilgrim**age**
plum**age**
post**age**
rough**age**
sew**age**
short**age**
shrink**age**
spoil**age**
stor**age**
tonn**age**
wreck**age**

-al, ial

Suffixes forming n. from v.; pertaining to

infomerc**ial**
marsup**ial**
rehears**al**
renew**al**
upheav**al**

Suffix indicating that a compound contains an aldehyde group

chlor**al**
citronell**al**

-ana, -iana

Suffix; assembly of items

Americ**ana**
Edward**iana**
Shakespear**eana**
Victor**iana**

-ance

Suffix forming n. from adj. or v.; action, state, condition (equiv. to -ence)

abey**ance**
accept**ance**
accord**ance**
allow**ance**
annoy**ance**
assur**ance**
cogniz**ance**
dist**ance**
disturb**ance**
endur**ance**
extravag**ance**
griev**ance**
hindr**ance**
import**ance**
insur**ance**
luxuri**ance**
proven**ance**
radi**ance**
repugn**ance**
resist**ance**
reson**ance**

-ancy, -ency

Suffixes combination: -ance + -y; -ence + -y; state or quality

buoy**ancy**
curr**ency**
delinqu**ency**
hesit**ancy**
indec**ency**
presid**ency**
tend**ency**
transpar**ency**
vac**ancy**

Multi-Tab Shutterfold:
See page 384.

-ant, -ent

Suffixes added to words of L origin; characterized by, serving as

account**ant**
adher**ent**
adolesc**ent**
clairvoy**ant** *
descend**ant**
immigr**ant**
nutri**ent**
oppon**ent** *
pati**ent**
pollut**ant**
resid**ent**
rumin**ant**
transi**ent** *

-archy

Dk>L suffix; rule, government

an**archy**
hier**archy**
matri**archy**
mon**archy**
olig**archy**
patri**archy**
the**archy**

-ard, -art

Suffix; persons who, characterized by

bragg**art** *
cow**ard**
drunk**ard**
dull**ard**
slugg**ard**
wiz**ard**

-arium

Suffix from L words; location or receptacle

aqu**arium**
insect**arium**
sol**arium**
terr**arium**

-ary

L suffix; pertaining to, connected with

avi**ary**
capill**ary**
diction**ary**
document**ary**
gloss**ary**
infirm**ary**
libr**ary**
mercen**ary** *
mission**ary**
obitu**ary**
sanctu**ary**
secret**ary**
summ**ary**

-ate

Suffix; forms nouns from verbs

acet**ate**
conglomer**ate**
expatri**ate**

a salt of an acid ending in -ic

nitr**ate**
sulf**ate**

offices, functions, institutions, bodies, individuals

consul**ate**
elector**ate**
magistr**ate**
sen**ate**

-ation, -fication

Suffixes; -ate + -ion; -fy + -tion

adapt**ation**
administr**ation**
ador**ation**
classi**fication**
comput**ation**
dramatiz**ation**
emancip**ation**
narr**ation**
specifi**cation**

Suffixes Nouns

Some suffixes are used with more than one part of speech.

-cide
L>ME suffix; killer, act of killing

fratri**cide**
fungi**cide**
geno**cide**
germi**cide**
herbi**cide**
homi**cide**
infanti**cide**
insecti**cide**
matri**cide**
patri**cide**
pesti**cide**

-cle
Suffix found in French loanwords of Latin origin

corpus**cle**
cubi**cle**
mana**cle**
ora**cle**
parti**cle**
specta**cle**

-cracy
Gk suffix; rule, power, government

aristo**cracy**
bureau**cracy** *
demo**cracy**
mono**cracy**
pluto**cracy**
theo**cracy**

-crat
Gk suffix; ruler, member of a ruling body, advocate of a form of rule

aristo**crat**
auto**crat**
bureau**crat**
demo**crat**
theo**crat**

-cy, -acy
Suffixes; rank, quality, state, office

clemen**cy** *
fluen**cy**
inaccura**cy**
lega**cy**
obstina**cy**
secre**cy**

-cycle
Suffix; wheel, cycle, period of time

bi**cycle**
motor**cycle**
re**cycle**
tri**cycle**

-dom
Suffix; domain, collection of persons, rank, condition

bore**dom**
chief**dom**
duke**dom**
fief**dom**
free**dom**
king**dom**
martyr**dom**
star**dom**
wis**dom**

-eer
Fr. suffix; persons associated with, engaged in, concerned wtih

auction**eer**
ballad**eer**
buccan**eer**
chariot**eer**
engin**eer**
mountain**eer**
mutin**eer**
pion**eer**
privat**eer**
puppet**eer**
racket**eer**
rocket**eer**
volunt**eer**
weapon**eer**

-ence
Suffix forming n. from adj.; action, state, condition (equiv. to -ance)

abhorr**ence**
abstin**ence** *
benevol**ence**
convalesc**ence**
dilig**ence**
evid**ence**
impertin**ence**
inconveni**ence**
independ**ence** Sp
indiffer**ence**
infer**ence**
intellig**ence**
neglig**ence**
obedi**ence**
occurr**ence** Sp
perman**ence**
pestil**ence**
refer**ence**
viol**ence**

-er, -ier, -yer
Suffixes; one who, that which; occupations; action or process
-ier denotes trades [clothier]
-yer var. of -er after w-

batt**er**
explor**er**
follow**er**
glaz**ier**
law**yer**
paint**er**
perform**er**
play**er**
runn**er**
teach**er**
vot**er**
work**er**

-ery (also see -ry)
Suffix denoting occupation, business, condition, etc.

artill**ery**
batt**ery**
brav**ery**
chican**ery** *

-ery (cont.)
distill**ery**
hatch**ery**
jewel**ry** Sp
mock**ery**
refin**ery**
robb**ery**
scen**ery**
shrubb**ery**
slav**ery**
treach**ery**
trick**ery**

-ess
Suffix forming feminine n. (many denoting occupation are falling out of use)

actr**ess**
baron**ess**
count**ess**
duch**ess**
empr**ess**
enchantr**ess**
godd**ess**
govern**ess**
headmistr**ess**
heir**ess**
host**ess**
laundr**ess**
leopard**ess**
lion**ess**
mistr**ess**
priest**ess**
princ**ess**
seamstr**ess**
sorcer**ess**
steward**ess**
temptr**ess**
waitr**ess**
webmistr**ess**

-et, -ette
Suffixes, ME from OF; indicates diminutive

ank**let**
bar**rette**
bri**quette**
din**ette**
disk**ette**
doub**let**
falcon**et**
hatch**et**
is**let**
kitchen**ette**
major**ette**
midg**et**
pack**et**
pip**ette**
sonn**et**
tab**let**
ush**erette**

-ful
Suffix; full of, characterized by (also an adj. suffix)

cup**ful**(s)
hand**ful**
mouth**ful**
spoon**ful**

-ian, -an
Suffixes formed from n.; membership, part of, contemporary with

Americ**an**
amphibi**an**
barbari**an**
Christi**an**
comedi**an**
custodi**an**
electrici**an**
Elizabeth**an**
histori**an**
musici**an**
pedestri**an**
republic**an**
totalitari**an**
veter**an**

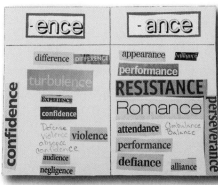

Two-Column Foldable Chart
See page 415.

Some suffixes are used with more than one part of speech.

When trying to determine whether to spell a word with *-tion* or *-sion*, look at the root word.
If the root ends in /t/, spell the word with *-tion*. Example: obstruct, obstruction
If the root word ends in /s/ or /d/, use *-sion*: extend, extension; regress, regression
If the last sound of the root is a /zh/ sound, use *-sion*: adhesion, compassion.

-iatry
Suffix; healing, medical treatment
podiatry
psychiatry

-ic
N. suffix; chiefly in loanwords from Gk
comic
heretic *
magic
music
Hispanic

-ics
N. suffix denoting facts, knowledge, principles
economics
graphics
physics
tactics
thermodynamics

-ide
Suffix forming names of chemical compounds
phosphatide
sodium chloride
trisaccharide

Word Study: Your "Mission"
Verbs ending in *-mit* change the *-mit* to *-mis* when adding the noun suffix *-sion* and when adding the adjective suffix *-ive*.

admit	admission
commit	commission
omit	omission
permit	permission
	permissive
remit	remission
submit	submission
	submissive *
transmit	transmission

See adjective suffixes, page 282.
See noun suffixes, page 290.

-ing
Suffix of n. formed from v.
bedding
bowling
building
clothing
dwelling
filling
flavoring
flooring
housing
learning
meaning
molding
offering
opening
painting
schooling
scouting
seasoning
singing
swelling
trucking

-ion, incl. -ation, -cion, -sion, -tion, -xion
Suffixes forming n. from other words; action, state
contagion
legion
region
religion

-cion
coercion
suspicion

-sion
accession
adhesion
admission
aggression
allusion *
aspersion *
cohesion *
collusion *
compassion *
compulsion
contusion *
decision
derision *
discussion
diversion
emulsion
erosion
evasion *
excursion
expansion
fusion
illusion
incursion *
obsession
oppression
permission
procession
profession

-ion (cont.)
-sion (cont.)
profusion *
progression
propulsion
provision
revision
revulsion
seclusion
suspension
transmission

-tion
abbreviation
absorption
abstention
accretion
acculturation
administration
affection
ambition
association
attention
cessation *
collection
combination
condensation
construction
convention
declaration
definition
denomination
elevation
evaporation
examination
exception
formation
illustration
investigation
legislation
migration

-ion (cont.)
-tion (cont.)
motivation
navigation
observation
obstruction
participation
perspiration
population
preposition
pronunciation
punctuation
radiation
registration
relaxation
reservation
retraction *
revelation
revolution
secretion
starvation
tradition
translation
trepidation *
vacation
vaccination
vocation

-xion [more often used in Brit. E.]:
complexion
crucifixion
flexion
transfixion

-ish
ME suffix; inclined to (See Adj. Suffixes)
gibberish
rubbish

-ism
Gk suffix; action, process, practice, trait
activism
alcoholism
altruism *
anachronism *
antagonism *
baptism
communism
criticism
despotism *
elitism
escapism
euphemism *
extremism
fanaticism
fascism
feudalism
heroism
hypnotism
imperialism
individualism
journalism
magnetism
mannerism
metabolism
nihilism *
optimism
organism
purism
racism
sexism
syllogism *
terrorism
vandalism
witticism *

Some suffixes are used with more than one part of speech.

-ist, -yst

Suffixes; one who practices or is concerned with something

- abolition**ist**
- anal**yst**
- anarch**ist** *
- antagon**ist** *
- capital**ist**
- catal**yst**
- chem**ist**
- column**ist**
- conform**ist** *
- drugg**ist**
- essay**ist**
- evangel**ist**
- flor**ist**
- hygien**ist**
- industrial**ist**
- manicur**ist**
- minimal**ist**
- motor**ist**
- natural**ist**
- nonconform**ist** *
- optim**ist**
- optometr**ist**
- pacif**ist** *
- pessim**ist**
- pharmac**ist**
- pian**ist**
- pragmat**ist** *
- real**ist**
- reception**ist**
- royal**ist**
- scient**ist**
- soph**ist** *
- special**ist**
- styl**ist**
- typ**ist**
- violin**ist**
- vocal**ist**
- zoolog**ist**

Small Suffix RWP Ring (above): Cut a quarter sheet of paper into fourths to make the single small suffix cards pictured. Fold them in half and position RWP across the fold so that the base word is on one side and the suffix on the other. Punch holes and store the cards on rings. Read the words on the ring with and without suffixes. See page 368.

Two-Column Chart Foldable® (left): Use a sheet of posterboard to make a large classroom chart. Collect examples of words found in RWP, literature, and oral communication, and glue or write them into the appropriate column. See page 415.

-ite

Suffix forming n.

- ammon**ite**
- anthrac**ite**
- calc**ite**
- compos**ite**
- dendr**ite**
- dynam**ite**
- gran**ite**
- graph**ite**
- meteor**ite**
- vulcan**ite**

-itis

Suffix; inflammation of, preoccupation with

- arthr**itis**
- bronch**itis**
- gastr**itis**
- laryng**itis**
- neur**itis**
- phleb**itis**

-ity (also see -ty)

Suffix used to form abstract nouns; condition or state of

- abil**ity**
- advers**ity** *
- brev**ity** *
- creativ**ity**
- festiv**ity**
- formal**ity**
- generos**ity**
- humid**ity**
- ident**ity**
- immens**ity**
- inferior**ity**
- inhuman**ity**
- integr**ity**
- legal**ity**
- local**ity**
- longev**ity** *
- major**ity**
- minor**ity**
- necess**ity**
- neutral**ity**
- nobil**ity**
- obscur**ity**
- odd**ity**
- possibil**ity**
- practical**ity**
- probabil**ity**
- prosper**ity** *
- qual**ity**
- radioactiv**ity**
- real**ity**
- regular**ity**
- san**ity**
- scarc**ity**
- secur**ity**
- sensibil**ity**
- serendip**ity** *
- sever**ity**
- un**ity**

Suffixes Nouns

Some suffixes are used with more than one part of speech.

-ium
Suffix of n. from Latin

auditor<u>ium</u>
colloqu<u>ium</u>
delir<u>ium</u>
equlibr<u>ium</u>
millenn<u>ium</u> Sp
morator<u>ium</u>
ted<u>ium</u>

Names of metallic elements

bar<u>ium</u>
calc<u>ium</u>
titan<u>ium</u>

-let
ME n.suffix; small one; something worn on

ank<u>let</u>
arm<u>let</u>
book<u>let</u>
brace<u>let</u>
cover<u>let</u>
drop<u>let</u>
lance<u>let</u>
leaf<u>let</u>
pamph<u>let</u>
pig<u>let</u>
ring<u>let</u>
wave<u>let</u>

-ling
OE>ME n. suffix; connected with; having a specified quality; young, small, inferior

duck<u>ling</u>
finger<u>ling</u>
fledg<u>ling</u>
hatch<u>ling</u>
hire<u>ling</u>
prince<u>ling</u>
spider<u>ling</u>
under<u>ling</u>
year<u>ling</u>

-logy, -ology
ME suffix; science, theory, study, expression

archaeo<u>logy</u>
astro<u>logy</u>
bio<u>logy</u>
chrono<u>logy</u> *
ideo<u>logy</u> *
paleonto<u>logy</u>
psycho<u>logy</u> Sp
termino<u>logy</u>

This **Triple VKV Flashcard** has three tabs to the left and a long fold-over tab to the right. Folding the right tab changes the word from English to Spanish.

-ment
N. suffix; denotes an action or resulting state

achieve<u>ment</u>
advertise<u>ment</u>
agree<u>ment</u>
amuse<u>ment</u>
announce<u>ment</u>
apart<u>ment</u>
arg<u>ument</u>
assign<u>ment</u>
base<u>ment</u>
bewilder<u>ment</u>
compli<u>ment</u> H
depart<u>ment</u>
disagree<u>ment</u>
doc<u>ument</u>
entertain<u>ment</u>
equip<u>ment</u>
experi<u>ment</u>
frag<u>ment</u>
fulfill<u>ment</u>
govern<u>ment</u>
impeach<u>ment</u>
imple<u>ment</u>
instr<u>ument</u>
invest<u>ment</u>
move<u>ment</u>
orna<u>ment</u>
pay<u>ment</u>
punish<u>ment</u>
refresh<u>ment</u>
replace<u>ment</u>
require<u>ment</u>
retire<u>ment</u>
sed<u>iment</u>
seg<u>ment</u>
settle<u>ment</u>
ship<u>ment</u>
state<u>ment</u>
treat<u>ment</u>

-mony
Suffix found in abstract n. denoting status, role, function, personal quality

acri<u>mony</u>
matri<u>mony</u>
patri<u>mony</u>
testi<u>mony</u>

-ness
OE>ME suffix attached to adj. and participles; qualiity or state

bitter<u>ness</u>
cleanli<u>ness</u>
dreadful<u>ness</u>
fit<u>ness</u>
forgive<u>ness</u>
happi<u>ness</u>
helpless<u>ness</u>
idle<u>ness</u>
ill<u>ness</u>
kind<u>ness</u>
like<u>ness</u>
listlessn<u>ness</u>
lush<u>ness</u>
numb<u>ness</u>
pure<u>ness</u>
short<u>ness</u>
shrewd<u>ness</u>
sick<u>ness</u>
slim<u>ness</u>
sudden<u>ness</u>
tasti<u>ness</u>
tight<u>ness</u>
weak<u>ness</u>
weari<u>ness</u>
wilder<u>ness</u>
willing<u>ness</u>
wit<u>ness</u>

-nomy
Gk suffix; distribution, arrangement, management

agro<u>nomy</u>
astro<u>nomy</u>
eco<u>nomy</u>
gastro<u>nomy</u>
taxo<u>nomy</u>

-oid
N. suffix; resembling, like (also an adj. suffix)

aster<u>oid</u>
human<u>oid</u>
paran<u>oid</u>
planet<u>oid</u>

-ol
Suffix representing "alcohol," used in the names of chemical derivatives

erythrit<u>ol</u>
glyc<u>ol</u>
menth<u>ol</u>
xylit<u>ol</u>

-or, -tor
ME, L suffixes; one who performs an action; state, quality, activity

abduc<u>tor</u>
agita<u>tor</u>
doc<u>tor</u>
eleva<u>tor</u>
escala<u>tor</u>
govern<u>or</u>
illustra<u>tor</u>
legisla<u>tor</u>
libera<u>tor</u>

Suffixes Nouns

Some suffixes are used with more than one part of speech.

-ory, -tory
L>ME suffixes; place or receptacle

access<u>ory</u>
conservat<u>ory</u>
invent<u>ory</u>
laborat<u>ory</u>
lavat<u>ory</u>
purgat<u>ory</u>
supervis<u>ory</u>
territ<u>ory</u>
traject<u>ory</u>

-ose
Suffix used in terminology for naming carbohydrates, etc.

cellul<u>ose</u>
gluc<u>ose</u>
lact<u>ose</u>

-phobia
L>Gk suffix; fear, dread of

acro<u>phobia</u>
arachno<u>phobia</u>
claustro<u>phobia</u>
hydro<u>phobia</u>
pyro<u>phobia</u>
triskaideka-
    <u>phobia</u>

-ry (also see -ery)
Suffix denoting occupation, business, condition, etc.

dentist<u>ry</u>
herald<u>ry</u>
husband<u>ry</u>
mason<u>ry</u>
revel<u>ry</u>
rival<u>ry</u>
savage<u>ry</u>
tenant<u>ry</u>

-ship
E suffix denoting condition, character, state, office, skill

apprentice-
<u>ship</u>
citizen<u>ship</u>
companion-
<u>ship</u>
dictator<u>ship</u>
fellow<u>ship</u>
friend<u>ship</u>
governor<u>ship</u>
guardian<u>ship</u>
hard<u>ship</u>
kin<u>ship</u>
intern<u>ship</u>
lady<u>ship</u>
leader<u>ship</u>
lord<u>ship</u>
member<u>ship</u>
musician<u>ship</u>
partner<u>ship</u>
penman<u>ship</u>
relation<u>ship</u>
scholar<u>ship</u>
showman<u>ship</u>
town<u>ship</u>

-ster
OE>ME suffix; one who does or is associated with (often derogatory)

game<u>ster</u>
gang<u>ster</u>
mob<u>ster</u>
prank<u>ster</u>
song<u>ster</u>
trick<u>ster</u>
young<u>ster</u>

-stress
(also see -ess)
Suffix; feminine equivalent of -ster

huck<u>stress</u>
song<u>stress</u>

-th
Suffix forming nouns of action and abstract nouns

ber<u>th</u> H
dep<u>th</u>
fil<u>th</u>
leng<u>th</u>
streng<u>th</u>
warm<u>th</u>
wid<u>th</u>

Note: *height* has no -h at the end.
Suffix used in the formation of ordinal numbers

billion<u>th</u>
dozen<u>th</u>
fif<u>th</u>
ten<u>th</u>
twelf<u>th</u>

-ty (also see -ity)
Suffix that forms n. denoting quality, state

certain<u>ty</u>
gaie<u>ty</u>
humili<u>ty</u>
loyal<u>ty</u>
pover<u>ty</u>
sagaci<u>ty</u> *
simplici<u>ty</u>

Suffix of numerals denoting multiples of ten

for<u>ty</u> Sp
thir<u>ty</u>
twen<u>ty</u>
nine<u>ty</u> Sp

-ure
Suffix forming abstract n.; shows action, result

architect<u>ure</u>
cens<u>ure</u>
depart<u>ure</u>
fail<u>ure</u>
lect<u>ure</u>
legislat<u>ure</u>
literat<u>ure</u>
pict<u>ure</u>
press<u>ure</u>
script<u>ure</u>
sculpt<u>ure</u>
struct<u>ure</u>

-y, -ie
Suffixes that form action n. from v., also found in abstract n.

archer<u>y</u>
autonom<u>y</u>
diplomac<u>y</u>
epiphan<u>y</u>
factor<u>y</u>
felon<u>y</u>
infam<u>y</u>
inquir<u>y</u>
iron<u>y</u>
jealous<u>y</u>
larcen<u>y</u> *
pharmac<u>y</u>

Suffixes that create (usually) informal n., that show extreme qualities, or that indicate endearment

cabb<u>ie</u>
cheap<u>ie</u>
junk<u>y</u>
sweet<u>ie</u>

Display Cube Foldable® (above): When this Foldable is made using 11" x 17" or 12" x 18" paper, it folds flat to make a four-page 8½" x 11" booklet. See page 418.

Some suffixes are used with more than one part of speech.

-er, -or

Add *-er or -or* to a verb to change the meaning to one who or that which.

actor
adviser
announcer
attacker
backer
baker
banker
batter [H]
bearer
believer [Sp]
bidder
blender
boarder [H]
boaster
boater
boiler
bomber
booster
bowler
builder
bumper
burner
buyer
calculator
caller
camper
carrier
catcher
checker
chopper
cleaner
climber
coaster
comforter
commuter
computer
conductor
consumer
cooker
counselor
crawler

crier
cruiser
cutter
deserter
designer
developer
dicer
dictator
digger
dinner
director
discounter
distractor
distributor
doer
doubter
dreamer
dresser
drinker
driver
dropper
drummer
earner
editor
elevator
enabler
energizer
enforcer
error
escalator
exchanger
exhibitor
explorer
farmer
fastener
feeder
fighter
finder
finisher
flier, flyer
floater
follower

forecaster
gardener
giver
golfer
governor
grader
grinder
grower
gunner
hanger [H]
harvester
healer
helper
hiker
hitter
hopper
hugger
hunter
inquirer
inspector
investigator
investor
ironer
irrigator
jailer
jogger
jumper
kicker
kidnapper
kisser
laborer
leader
learner
lifter
lighter
liner
loader
locker
lover
listener
mailer

maker
miner [H]
mixer
mover
mower
navigator
nurturer
observer
opener
orbiter
owner
painter
performer
picker
pitcher [H]
planner
planter
player
porter
preacher
predictor
presenter
printer
professor [Sp]
programmer
promoter
prospector
protector
protester
provider
pumper
rafter [H]
reader
rebuilder
recliner
recorder
reformer
regulator
reminder
reporter
rescuer

researcher
rider
riser
roaster
rocker
roller
runner
sailor
sander
schemer
screamer
seller
sender
server
shaker
shooter
shopper
sifter
sinker
sitter
sketcher
skier
skinner
skipper
sleeper
slicer
smiler
snorer
speaker
speller
spinner
sprayer
sprinkler
sprinter
starter
sticker
stinker
streamer
stroller

stunner
suitor
supporter
surfer
survivor
sweeper
swimmer
taker
talker
teacher
teller [H]
terminator
thinker
thriller
tiller
timer
tracker
trader
trainer
traveler
trimmer
trucker
turner
vacationer
viewer
visitor
waiter
walker
washer
waterer
weaver
whaler
winner
wiper
worker
wrapper [H]
writer
zapper
zipper

-ee

Add *-ee* to some transitive verbs to change the meaning to denote a person who is the object or beneficiary of the *verb*.

Three-Column Chart Foldable®:

Make a three-column chart and write/place a word in the left column. Record as many new words as possible by adding endings to the given word in the second column. Use the new words in sentences in the third column. Try using all the words in sentences to form a paragraph.

Example of new words:

Given Word: employ

New Words: employs, employing, employed, employer, employee

Sentences: The department store employs many people.
My mother is employed there.
They will be employing students during the summer months.
Everyone says they are a good employer if one is a good employee.

-ee	
absent<u>ee</u>	grant<u>ee</u>
address<u>ee</u>	honor<u>ee</u>
attend<u>ee</u>	invit<u>ee</u>
boot<u>ee</u>	nomin<u>ee</u>
deport<u>ee</u>	refug<u>ee</u>
draft<u>ee</u>	return<u>ee</u>
employ<u>ee</u>	stand<u>ee</u>
escap<u>ee</u>	train<u>ee</u>

Variation: Make a Four-Column Foldable Chart with the following column titles: *adjective*, *adverb*, *noun*, *verb*. Students list words according to their parts of speech while noting which suffixes are related to particular parts of speech.

verbs: employ, employed, employing
nouns: employer, employee, employment, employability
adjectives: employable

Multi-Tab Fold-Over (left and below): This computer-generated Foldable had six words with lots of space left between them. After gluing the left tab into a notebook, students cut between the words to form tabs.

Forming Plurals (above): To form the plural of an *-ee* word, add the suffix *-s*.

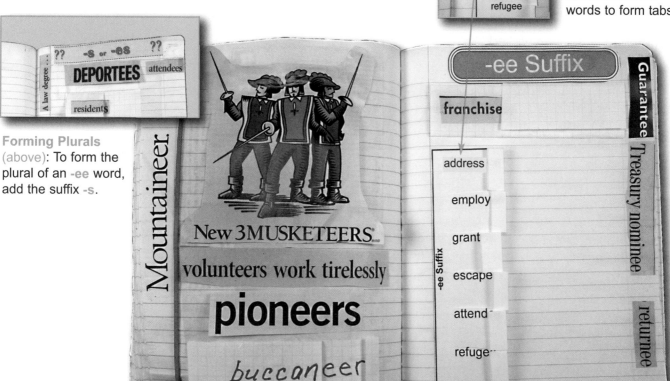

Suffixes Verbs

Some suffixes are used with more than one part of speech.

-ade

Suffix forming n. that can also be used as v.; action, process, a person acting

blockade
cascade
crusade
escalade
masquerade
parade
promenade

-ate

L suffix: to have, be characterized by, or resemble

abbreviate *
abdicate *
accelerate
accommodate Sp
activate
collaborate *
contemplate
cooperate
defoliate *
demonstrate
duplicate
emigrate
emulate *
evaluate
fumigate *
humiliate
illuminate *
imitate
liberate
negotiate
obliterate
proliferate
recapitulate *
regulate
saturate
speculate
substantiate *
terminate
tolerate
vindicate *

-ed

OE>ME suffix; forms past tense and past participal of verbs

abandoned
accepted
assisted
calculated
campaigned
cleared
destroyed
determined
dictated
discovered
discussed
exasperated *
experimented
explored
lived
moved
respected
rushed
sailed
talked
walked
yelled

-en

OE>ME suffix; forms verbs from adj. or n.; to make, make happen

blacken
broaden
fasten
freshen
frighten
lengthen
shorten
slacken
soften
strengthen
sweeten
threaten
toughen
waken
widen

OE>ME suffix; forms past participle of v.

eaten
gotten
shaken
stolen
taken

-er

OE>ME suffix of v. showing repetition of an action

clatter
flicker
flutter
shiver
shudder

-fer

L suffix: *ferre*; to bear, carry

confer
infer
prefer
refer
suffer
transfer

-ify, -fy

OF>ME suffixes; cause to become, to make happen

beautify
clarify
classify
codify *
edify *
falsify
humidify
identify
indemnify *
justify
modify
mollify *
mystify
ossify *
purify
qualify
rectify
sanctify
satisfy
simplify
solidify
specify
terrify

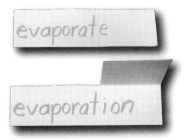

Double VKV® Flashcards (above and below): See page 379.
Note: Use this Flashcard with the word study to the right.

Word Study:
root + suffix =
On the back of VKV Flashcards, have students write a word equation that illustrates the etymology of the word featured on the front of the card.

Examples (left):
e- + vapor + -ate = evaporate
evaporate + -ion = evaporation

liberal + -ate = liberate
liberate + -ion = liberation

Suffixes Verbs

-ing
ME suffix; forms present participle of verbs

- call<u>ing</u>
- clean<u>ing</u>
- comput<u>ing</u>
- destroy<u>ing</u>
- discuss<u>ing</u>
- experiment<u>ing</u>
- feel<u>ing</u>
- grow<u>ing</u>
- growl<u>ing</u>
- hir<u>ing</u>
- idoliz<u>ing</u>
- jump<u>ing</u>
- look<u>ing</u>
- observ<u>ing</u>
- read<u>ing</u>
- runn<u>ing</u>
- shoot<u>ing</u>
- snor<u>ing</u>
- splash<u>ing</u>
- stor<u>ing</u>
- swimm<u>ing</u>
- talk<u>ing</u>
- walk<u>ing</u>
- watch<u>ing</u>

-ish
Suffix occurring in i-stem borrowed from French

- accompl<u>ish</u>
- brand<u>ish</u>
- burn<u>ish</u> *
- cher<u>ish</u>
- distingu<u>ish</u>
- embell<u>ish</u> *
- impover<u>ish</u>
- langu<u>ish</u> *
- nour<u>ish</u>
- outland<u>ish</u>
- rav<u>ish</u>
- tarn<u>ish</u>

-ize
Suffix; forms v. from adj. and n.; to cause, to make

- aggrand<u>ize</u> *
- agon<u>ize</u>
- amort<u>ize</u> *
- antagon<u>ize</u>
- capital<u>ize</u>
- caramel<u>ize</u>
- central<u>ize</u>
- civil<u>ize</u>
- compartmental<u>ize</u>
- computer<u>ize</u>
- critic<u>ize</u>
- crystall<u>ize</u>
- dramat<u>ize</u>
- familiar<u>ize</u>
- fantas<u>ize</u>
- fertil<u>ize</u>
- final<u>ize</u>
- general<u>ize</u>
- harmon<u>ize</u>
- hospital<u>ize</u>
- hypnot<u>ize</u>
- hypothes<u>ize</u>
- idol<u>ize</u>
- immun<u>ize</u>
- industrial<u>ize</u>
- item<u>ize</u>
- legal<u>ize</u>
- legitim<u>ize</u>
- local<u>ize</u>
- magnet<u>ize</u>
- material<u>ize</u>
- memor<u>ize</u>

-ize, cont.

- minim<u>ize</u>
- mobil<u>ize</u>
- modern<u>ize</u>
- monopol<u>ize</u>
- natural<u>ize</u>
- notar<u>ize</u>
- organ<u>ize</u>
- ostrac<u>ize</u> *
- oxid<u>ize</u>
- pasteur<u>ize</u>
- penal<u>ize</u>
- plagiar<u>ize</u>
- plural<u>ize</u>
- popular<u>ize</u>
- public<u>ize</u>
- pulver<u>ize</u>
- real<u>ize</u>
- recogn<u>ize</u>
- romantic<u>ize</u>
- scrutin<u>ize</u> *
- special<u>ize</u>
- stabil<u>ize</u>
- steril<u>ize</u>
- stigmat<u>ize</u> *
- summar<u>ize</u>
- sympath<u>ize</u>
- synthes<u>ize</u>
- tantal<u>ize</u>
- terror<u>ize</u>
- vapor<u>ize</u>
- visual<u>ize</u>
- vital<u>ize</u>
- vulcan<u>ize</u>

Multi-Tab Bound Book (above): See book binding instructions, page 28. See Multi-Tab Foldables, page 415.

-le
Suffix; frequentative force, repetitive

- crumb<u>le</u>
- dazz<u>le</u>
- mumb<u>le</u>
- tumb<u>le</u>
- twink<u>le</u>

Triple VKV Flashcard (below): See page 386 for instructions.

Suffix Fold-Over VKVs (right): Glue a word with a suffix to the left edge of a two-inch strip of paper or index card. This is a good size for individual student cards using RWP. Fold the right edge over to cover the suffix. Open and close the tab to read the word with and without the suffix. See page 370.

Syllables Review

**Words have one or more parts, called *syllables*, that we can hear as we say them. We can tap a finger or clap our hands to the single or multiple syllable sounds of a word.
Try to determine the longest one-syllable English word. Two fairly common eight-letter one-syllable words are *squirrel* and *strength*.   A nine-letter one-syllable word is *scrunched*.**

All words have syllables.

There is one vowel sound in every syllable.
    Examples: Jan·u·ar·y, hel·lo, sum·mer

Two vowels can make one sound:
    Examples: thir·teen, rai·sin.

Some vowels are silent. A word with two vowels, one voiced and one silent, can have one syllable.
    Examples: bike, joke, like, wake

Sometimes *y* functions like a vowel in a syllable.
    Examples: cy·cle, hap·py

Prefixes and suffixes are usually separate syllables.
    Examples: re·lax, walk·ing
Exceptions: Often, the suffix *-s*, and sometimes the suffix *-ed*, do not form separate syllables: *dogs, walked*.

When there are two consonants in the middle of a word, the syllables are divided between the consonants...
    Examples: dad·dy, mat·ter

...unless the double consonants are part of the root word; then they are not divided.
    Examples: will·ing, miss·ing

When a syllable ends with a vowel, the vowel usually has a long sound.
    Examples: ho·tel, hip·po

When a syllable ends with a consonant, the vowel in the syllable is short.
    Example: mag·net

Consonant blends and digraphs usually stay together in a syllable.
    Examples: with·out, fish·er·man

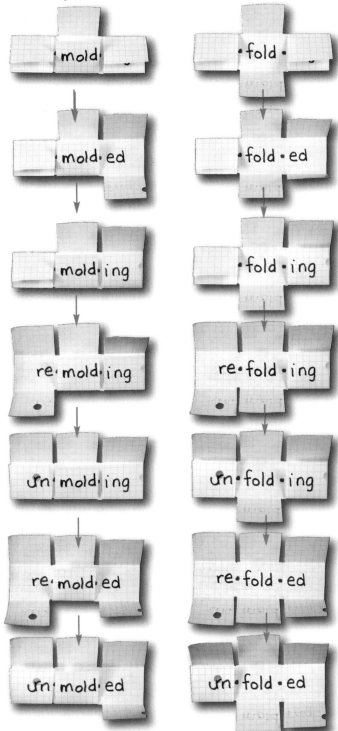

Fourteen-Word VKV (above right): A quarter sheet of grid paper was used to make a Triple VKV Flashcard. Extra space was cut between the three tabs at the top and bottom to leave room for the dots used to divide the word into syllables. This VKV illustrates that prefixes and suffixes often form separate syllables when added to a root word.

Six Types of Syllables

1. **A closed syllable has one short vowel and ends in a consonant.**
   Examples: bet   mat   win   one-syllable examples
            bet·ter   mat·ter win·ning   two-syllable examples

2. **An open syllable ends in a long vowel sound.**
   Examples: o·pen   re·o·pen

3. **A Vowel-Consonant-e syllable (VCe Syllable) is usually found at the end of a word. This follows the silent e rule, so the vowel will be long.**
   Examples: name   re·name   re·nam·ing

4. **A vowel-digraph/diphthong syllable (Vowel Teams) has two vowels that jointly form a new sound.**
   Closed Examples: mouth   booth
   Open Examples: paw   win·dow   cau·tion   law·less

5. **An *r*-controlled syllable contains any vowel followed by the letter *r*. The *r* controls the sound the vowel makes.**
   Examples: farm   stir   whirl

6. **A consonant/-le syllable is found in words like *mantle* Sp, *puzzle, tangle*.**
   Examples: fiddle   maple   wiggle

7. **Prefix and Suffix syllables are found at the beginnings and endings of base words.**
   Examples: re·dis·cov·er   dis·crep·an·cy   dis·pos·a·ble

Dictionary Integration:
Observe how syllables of words are indicated within the dictionary pronunciation guide. Note the dots dividing the syllables and relate them to the dots used on the folds of the VKV syllable cards.

Accordion VKV Flashcards: To study words with more than one syllable, fold the Single Flashcard so only the first syllable shows. Slowly unfold the flashcard to sequentially reveal the next syllables. See page 375.

On the Back:
• Write a pronunciation guide for the word.
• Write a sentence using the word.
• Write a sentence and leave a blank for students to fill in the word mentally or orally.

Word Study:
English and Russian from Greek
astro-   a Greek combining form; pertaining to stars or space
cosmo-   a Greek combining form; universe, world
nautes   Greek, sailor; related word = *nautical*
        Explain why *astronaut* and *cosmonaut* are synonyms.

Syllables

Foldable® Syllable Charts: Fold a sheet of copy paper or chart paper into fourths along the vertical axis. Fold the same sheet of paper into multiple rows along the horizontal axis. Use the table to record a one-, two-, or three-syllable word and show two- or three-syllable words divided into syllables.

Variation: Label the columns to indicate a given number of syllables. Students write words or glue examples of words found in RWP that have the number of syllables indicated at the top of each column.

Lined Paper Charts (left): When sheets of notebook paper are used to make charts, horizontal lines do not have to be folded to form rows. See page 415.

Note: The photocopy chart (far left) was folded into a Trifold and then folded in half again to form nine rows.

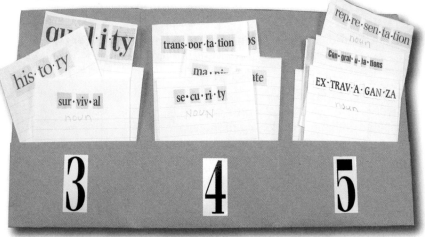

Three-Pocket Foldable® (right): Make a Three-Pocket Foldable using 11" x 17" paper and use it to collect word cards with examples of three-, four-, and five-syllable words. See page 399.

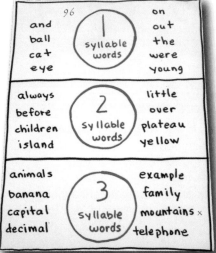

Trifold Foldable® (left): Make and use a Trifold to collect examples of one-, two-, and three-syllable words. Have students select a given number of words and use them to write a short story on the back of the Foldable, or use the words to write an expository or narrative paragraph. See page 399.

Note: Two grades were taken—front and back.

Word Study:
Really Big One-Syllable Words

The longest one-syllable words are spelled with nine letters. Examples include *screeched*, *scratched*, and *stretched*. Encourage students to search for other long one-syllable words and record them in their journals.

Syllables

Cube Project (right): Use two sheets of 11" x 17" or 12" x 18" paper to make this freestanding, collapsible display. Write or glue examples of three-, four-, five-, and six-syllable words onto the sides. See page 418.

3-D Variation Pictured: Cut small index cards into strips. Write or glue words from RWP on the strips. Accordion-fold the words between syllables. Glue the first or last syllable section onto the appropriate side of a labeled cube project, and leave the other folded syllable sections extended and dimensional.

Reinforce RWP (below): Clear tape can be used to reinforce words from RWP that have been folded to indicate syllables.

First, glue the word to the project. Second, place tape on the back of the extended syllable and then onto the display cube to make the fold strong and to keep the tab three-dimensional.

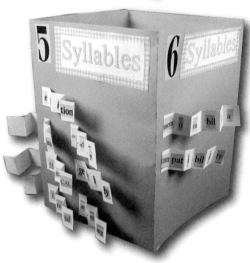

Layered Notebook Foldable® Tabs:
Eight quarter-sheets of paper were glued into this notebook to form seven tabbed sections for recording information with a title tab on top. Examples of one- to seven-syllable words were recorded on the appropriate tabs. See under the tabs on page 309. You can also use Layered Foldables, page 402.

Monosyllabic Words

* Words with an asterisk have been found on advanced tests such as SAT, ACT, and state exit exams.

ace	cache * H	dearth *	flout *	guy	muse* H	sane	spew *	trail
ache	cane H	deem *	fluke *	hail * H	nest *	scale *	spur *	trait *
ad H	carve	deft *	fob *	hale * H	next	scan	spurn *	tray
ail H	cast H	deign *	ford	harp *	once H	scant *	squall *	treat
aim	cede * H	dell *	forge *	hawk	oust *	scoff *	square	tribe
air	chafe *	delve *	fort	heed * H	pact *	scorn *	staid * H	trite *
aisle H	chaff *	din*	frail *	herb	paid	sear * H	stark *	trunk *
ale H	chaste *	dire *	frank * H	hoard * H	pall *	sect *	staunch *	trust
alms *	check * H	doff *	fray *	hone *	pan *	seethe *	steep *	tryst *
angst *	chide *	dolt *	freeze H	horde * H	pause H	sense H	still	turn
apt *	chord * H	don*	frost	jaunt *	paws H	serve	stint *	twelve
awe *	churl *	dose	fuel *	jaw	pearl	shade	stir	twin
balk *	cite * H	doubt	fun	jazz	phone	shall	stoke *	twist
bane *	claim	dour *	gaff *	jilt *	pied*	shark	stole	veer *
bask *	clamp	dove H	gaunt *	join	pole H	shear * H	stout *	vein H
beat H	cleave *	drawl *	ghost	kin *	poll H	sheep	strife *	vent *
bilge *	clench *	dream	gild * H	knell *	preen*	sheer *	style	verse
bilk *	clerk	dregs *	gird	laud *	prose*	shun *	sure	vest
blanch *	clique * H	drew	girth *	lax * H	purge*	seize Sp	svelte *	vex *
bland *	clone *	droll *	gist *	lead H	quaff *	siege Sp	taint *	view
bliss *	clout *	drone *	glean *	leaf	quail *	sign H	taunt *	voice
blithe *	cloy *	dross *	glib *	lieu *	quaint *	site H	team * H	void *
bloc * H	club H	due H	gloat *	limb	quay * H	skiff *	teem * H	wage
blood	code	dumb	glut *	loaf	quell *	skit	terse *	wake *
blunt *	coil	dupe *	gnash *	loan H	quick	skulk *	tier * H	wane *
board H	come	dwell *	gnaw	loath *	quip *	skull	tint *	weigh Sp
boon *	cone	earth	goad *	loathe *	quirk *	sky	toast	weird
boor *	cost	ebb *	gouge *	loll *	rail * H	slake *	toil *	woe *
bore H	coup *	egg *	grasp	lope*	rash *	sloth *	toll	yen *
botch *	cove	eye H	grease	lout*	raze * H	sneeze	tour	zest *
brain	coy *	fair H	greet	lure*	realm *	snit *		
brake H	crass *	farce *	grill * H	lush*	rend *	spate *		
brash *	cringe *	fault	ground H	maim*	rife *	spiel *		
brawn *	cruise H	faux *	growl	main H	rift *			
breach *	crux *	fawn *	grown H	male H	rind *			
breadth *	cull *	feign *	guard	mar*	rogue *			
breath	curb *	feint * H	guess	mean* H	rote * H			
brink *	cusp *	fiat *	guest	mince*	rout * H			
broach *	dare	fjord *	guide	mire*	rue			
brook *	dash	flak*	guild *	moist	sage*			
brusque *	daub *	flay *	guile *	mode*				
butte *	daunt *	floe * H	guise * H	molt*				

Monosyllabic Words

Because one-syllable words look simple, we tend to think students in upper elementary, middle school, and high school will be able to easily read and spell them and understand their meanings. As the words on the previous page illlustrate, though, this is not always the case. The five words with the longest definition entries in the Oxford English Dictionary are all one-syllable words—*make, set, run, take, go*.

Tabbed Cover-up Foldable (below): Students begin with all tabs open. As a word is called, students cover the number that tells how many syllables they hear, and they write the word in their journals. The first student to cover all numbers "wins." See page 406.

Above: A Tabbed Cover-up Foldable might have two or more of the same numbers to make the cards vary. Numerous three-syllable words might be called. This activity can be used with spelling words, content vocabulary terms, and test-prep vocabulary.

> **Word Study: *Up***
> Even a word as "simple" as *up* can be difficult to define. Determine how many definitions there are for the word *up*. How many idioms use the word *up*?
>
> | | |
> |---|---|
> | wake **up** | build **up** muscle |
> | get **up** | build **up** skills |
> | | build **up** a following |
> | the topic came **up** | build **up** the walls |
> | the wind came **up** | |
> | the seeds came **up** | take **up** time |
> | | take **up** money |
> | move **up** | |
> | stand **up** | give **up** trying |
> | rise **up** | give **up** the ghost |
> | | |
> | **up** for election | wrap **up** a present |
> | **up** for the trip | wrap **up** a meeting |
> | **up** for the challenge | |
> | | stir **up** trouble |
> | what happens is **up** to the principal | stir **up** a hornet's nest |
> | | stir **up** the pot |
> | call **up** your mom | polish **up** your shoes |
> | warm **up** dinner | polish **up** the silver |
> | clean **up** your room | polish **up** your English |
> | lock **up** the car | |
> | fix **up** the house | move **up** in line |
> | speak **up** | move **up** in the world |
> | line **up** to go outside | |
> | work **up** an appetite | look **up** at the sky |
> | think **up** excuses | look **up** the word |
> | dress **up** special | look **up** his friend |
> | open **up** the window | |
> | the papers are mixed **up** | |

> Note that in informal speech, people often add the word *up* to phrases where it is not required (as in *open up the window*).

Accordion Pocket Foldable® (above): Use 11" x 17" index-weight paper to make this classroom Pocket Accordion Foldable. Fold Single VKV Flashcards into eighths. Write words divided into syllables (or glue words from RWP that have been cut into syllables) on the sections of the sentence strip. Cut off any extra sections and save them for future use. See Accordion VKVs on page 301 and 303.

Disyllabic Words

* Words with an asterisk have been found on advanced tests such as SAT, ACT, and state exit exams.
Many two-syllable nouns, adjectives, and adverbs are stressed on the first syllable, and many verbs on the second.

abduct *	candy	galore *	nation	quickly	taboo *
abet *	carpet	gaudy *	navy	refute *	tactile *
abhor *	carry	glutton *	neglect	retract *	tempo *
abide *	caucus *	grapple *	neutral *	revel *	tepid *
absent	cavort *	grotesque *	nomad *	revere	thorny *
abut *	cement	guru *	novel *	revile *	tirade *
acid *	censor * H	haggle *	novice *	river	tonic * H
acme *	center	hamster Sp	obese *	science	torpid *
acrid *	channel *	harangue *	obtuse *	secede *	torque *
action	cipher *	heirloom *	ocean	seizure Sp	torrid *
active	circa *	hovel *	octave *	seven	totem *
acute *	circle	iceberg Sp	opaque *	skirmish *	toxic *
alloy *	civil *	impeach *	orange	slander *	tumor *
allude *	clamor *	implore *	oval	solid	tundra *
alter H	coddle *	incite *	over	solstice *	under
amass *	codger *	inept *	paper	solvent *	urbane *
amend *	coerce *	influx *	pencil	spatial *	usurp *
amid *	construe *	insect	perplex *	spectrum *	venom *
angel Sp	content * II	island	peruse *	static *	vial *
angle Sp	contest H	isthmus *	pigment *	stoic *	viscous *
answer	convince	jargon *	pinion *	subdue *	vivid *
apex *	cosmic *	jetsam *	planet	sublime *	vortex *
applaud	country	journey	plasma	subtle * Sp	water
appraise *	cricket H	July	plastic	summer	winter
April	danger	karma *	plateau	surly *	woman
ardent	decrease	kayak	pompous *	surmise *	
arid *	decree *	kingdom	porous *	suspend	
army	deduce *	kiosk *	portal *	syntax *	
August H	destroy	lambaste *	posture *		
balloon Sp	dirty	latent *	potent *		
bazaar Sp	dwelling	libel *	pretext *		
bedlam	embrace	liquid	pretzel		
belief Sp	emit *	malice *	primal *		
believe Sp	engulf *	malign *	pumice *		
bemoan	extol *	mammoth *	purple		
bemuse	facet *	mantle Sp			
between	fauna *	marker			
bias	femur *	marshal * Sp			
bizarre Sp	flounder * H	martyr *			
bovine	forage *	mores *			
brigand		mountain			

Check student-made VKVs® before
including them in study aids:
VKV® Incorrect:
Should be Math•e•mat•ics
VKV® Correct:
Sat•ur•day

Trisyllabic Words

* Words with an asterisk have been found on advanced tests such as SAT, ACT, and state exit exams.

abacus *
abdicate *
aesthetic *
amplify *
animal
another
appendage *
armada *
astonished
banana Sp
battery *
beautiful Sp
beginning Sp
bicycle
bodyguard
boisterous
burgundy
canopy
capital H
capitol H
catacomb *
chloroform *
chocolate
chromosome
chronicle *
cognizant *
collusion *
complacent*
computer
conductor
contraband*
crustacean
cucumber
December
decimal
decorous*
delinquent*
diagram
difference Sp
different

director
discovered
ecstasy Sp
effigy *
elusive *
embargo *
enervate Sp
estimate
exercise
fantastic
federal
fiasco *
following
galvanize *
generic *
genocide *
government
gullible *
handwriting
haphazard *
hemisphere
herbicide *
hospital
hydraulic *
impromptu *
incessant *
indulgent *
infamous *
insular *
interlude *
janitor
jeopardize *
juggernaut *
juvenile
juxtapose *
kinetic *
latitude *
laudable *
leverage *
liberal *
lineage *

logistics *
luminous *
maritime *
memento * Sp
meteor *
migratory *
national
nautical *
nebulous *
newspaper
nocturnal *
November
nullify *
objective *
October
odyssey *
officer
osmosis *
ossify *
pacifist *
palisade *
parallel *
paraphrase *
patriarch *
pedagogue *
perjury *
photograph
pinnacle *
polygraph *
prehensile *
primary
prisoner
propagate *
prosthesis *
pseudonym *

quarantine *
rambunctious *
rectangle
regimen * Sp
remember
repugnant *
retrospect *
rhapsody *
rhetoric *
salient *
satellite Sp
scientists
scrupulous *
seasonal *
secular *
segregate *
semantic *
September
sequential *
serrated *
stigmatize *
subjugate *
suffragist *
surrogate *
surrounded
surveillance *
syllables
symmetry *
synonym *
synopsis *

tantamount *
telephone
temperate *
terminal *
titanic *
together
tolerate *
transient *
transparent *
treachery *
triangle
tyranny *
verbatim *
vertical
vertigo
vindictive
vocation
volatile
understand
wilderness

Folded Syllables: See page 303. Notice the use of ½" clear tape to reinforce this word taken from flimsy newsprint, in order to keep it dimensional on a Foldable or in a notebook.

Polysyllabic Words: Tetrasyllabic Words

* Words with an asterisk have been found on advanced tests such as SAT, ACT, and state exit exams.

abbreviate *
accommodate * Sp
accouterment *
acquisitive *
adrenaline *
adventitious *
alternative
ambiguous *
American
amphibian
available
benefactor *
beneficial
benevolent *
biennial *
capillary
carnivorous *
cerebellum
chameleon *
chicanery *
circumference
combustible *
commemorate *
compatible *
comprehensive *
contemptuous *
contiguous *
corresponding
corroborate *
cumulative *
curriculum *
deciduous
dehydration
detrimental *
developing
diarrhea Sp
diameter
dictionary
discovery
distributive

egocentric *
elliptical *
engineering
entrepreneur *
equivalent
experience
experiment
filibuster *
fortuitous *
fragmentary *
gastronomy *
generalize *
geography
geometry
gratuitous *
harmonious *
horizontal
hypothesis *
iconoclast *
impeccable *
imperial *
impervious *
indigenous *
indoctrinate *
information
insurrection *
intersection
invalidate *
irrigation
irritation
jubilation *
liquidation *
lugubrious *
magnanimous *
malnutrition *

manifesto *
melancholy *
mercenary *
millennium *
monotonous *
municipal *
necessary Sp
nonpartisan *
obliterate *
obsequious *
olfactory *
omnipotent *
omnivorous *
opposition *
oxymoron *
parabola *
parameter *
particular
pedestrian *
perennial *
perfunctory *
philanthropic *
pontificate *
precarious *
precipitous *
predatory *
predicament *
preponderant *
prohibition *
propensity *
protagonist *
provocation *
pulmonary
quotidian *

rationalize *
reciprocal *
reparation *
reproduction
resignation *
respiration
reverberate *
rigidity *
salubrious *
sanctuary *
secondary
sedentary *
segregation
soliloquy * Sp
spontaneous *
subservient *
superlative *
supervising
symbolism *
symmetrical
taxonomy
television
temperature
terrestrial *
traditional *
trajectory *
trepidation *
unethical *
usually
vaccination
viscosity *
voluntary *
vulnerable *
witticism *

Accordion Single VKV® Flashcards: See page 375.

Polysyllabic Words: Pentasyllabic and Hexasyllabic Words
* Words with an asterisk have been found on advanced tests such as SAT, ACT, and state exit exams.

Pentasyllabic Words

acrimonious *
administration
alliteration
alliterative *
ambulatory *
anachronism *
anonymity *
antagonism *
anthropology
approximately
archaeology Sp
archipelago *
aristocratic *
auditorium
bicentennial
capitalism
carcinogenic *
categorical *
ceremonial
chemotherapy *
choreography
chromatography
circumnavigate *
civilization
classification
configuration *
conservatory *
constitutional
cornucopia *
cosmopolitan *
curvilinear *
decontaminate
denominator
denunciation *
departmentalize
derogatory *
diametrical
dilapidated *
discrimination
disingenuous *

electricity
elementary
emancipation
entomology
etymology
evaporation
hippopotamus
homogeneous
hydroelectric
hypocritical *
hypothetical *
imperceptible *
imperturbable *
inequality
innumerable *
intermediate
international
investigation
lexicography *
mathematical
metamorphosis *
monosyllabic *
multiplication
nationalism
nonrenewable
oceanography
pandemonium *
pecuniary *
peregrination *
perpendicular
photosynthesis
precipitation
premeditated *
prepositional
probability
ramification *
reactionary *
recapitulate *
refrigeration

reprehensible *
representatives
retaliation *
sociopathic *
supercilious *
superintendent Sp
technicality
testimonial
thermodynamic *
transcontinental
unilateral *

> **Layered Notebook Foldable®**
> (below):
> Under the tabs, students collect examples of words with different numbers of syllables, and show how they are divided.
> See page 303.
> **Vairation:** Students might be asked to mark stressed syllables.

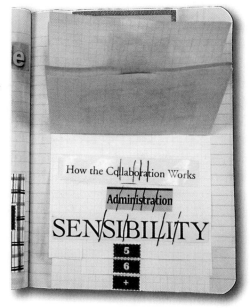

Hexasyllabic Words

authoritarian *
autobiography
cinematographer *
conviviality *
ecclesiastical *
egalitarian *
egomaniacal *
electromagnetic
encyclopedia
ethnocentricity *
extraterrestrial
geomorphology
heterosexual *
humanitarian
hypoglycemia
idiosyncrasy * Sp
inalienable *
incontrovertible *
indefatigable *
octogenarian *
onomatopoeia
osteoporosis *
overpopulation
paleontology
paraphernalia *
phantasmagoria *
reorganization
totalitarian *
unconstitutional
utilitarian *

Words with double letters are usually divided between the letters. Exceptions include some words in which the double letters are part of the base word, such as *bee·tle*, *call·ing*, *grass·y*, or *moo·ing*.

abbess *	babble *	cotton	glossary	parry *	summit
abbey	ballad*	croissant *	glutton *	passe *	summons *
accede *	ballet	daddy	gorilla H	pebble	supper
accent	balloon Sp	dessert H	grapple *	pellet	supplant *
acclaim *	ballistic *	differ	guffaw *	pepper	suppress * Sp
accord *	barren	difficult	haggle *	planner	surreal *
accost *	beggar	dilemma * Sp	hammer	potter	surrogate *
account	berry H	dinner	happen	prattle*	swagger *
accrue *	biennial	dissent * H	happy	preempt*	swimmer
accuse	biggest	dollar	lessen H	pretty	symmetry *
address Sp H	bitter	hobby	lesser *	puppy	tally *
adduce *	blossom	horrific	letter	puzzle	tattoo
affect *	bookkeeper Sp	imminent *	lettuce	quarry *	territory
affirm *	brilliant	intermittent *	litter H	quizzical *	terror
allay *	bunny	jelly	little	rabbit	torrid *
allege *	button	jiffy	lobby *	rabble *	traffic
allot * Sp	buttress *	jolly	lummox *	raccoon	tussle *
allow	cannon H	juggle	mammal	raffish *	tyrannosaur
annals *	cannot	kettle	mammoth *	rapport *	tyranny *
annex *	carrot H	kidding	marriage	rattle	udder
annual Sp	carry	kitten	marrow *	reappear	umbrella
appear	cattle	effect	matter H	reelection	upper
appraise *	cellar H	errand	message	ruffle *	utter *
array *	coffee	error *	motto	rugged	vaccine
arrow	college	essay	middle	sally *	valley
assay *	comma	essential	million	scallop H	vanilla
assert *	command	fallow *	missile H	scissors Sp	vessel
assess *	commend	fattest	misspell Sp	scrabble	villa
attorney	common	fellow	mitten	sniffle	village
	connect	ferret *	muffin	sparrow	villain *
	correct	fiddle	nanny	stopped	volley
	corrupt *	fluffy	narrate	stubborn	waffle *
	cottage	fodder *	narrow	succor *	wallow
		follow	occupy	succulent *	warrant *
		giggle	occur Sp	succumb *	wedding
			offer	suffice *	whittle *
			office	suffrage *	wiggle
			pallet H	sufficient	winnow *
			pallid *	suffuse *	winner
			parrot	suggest	ziggurat *
				summer	zucchini

Single VKV
Flashcards (left):
See page 368.

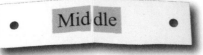

Word Study: Unstressed Syllables

The syllabic stress pattern of some words can make them challenging to pronounce and spell. For example, look at the spelling of the vowels *a* and *e* in the unstressed syllables of the following words. Note the spelling of the vowels and compare the spelling to the pronunciation of the words.

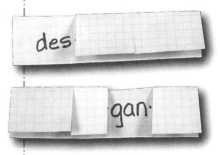

-ate sounds like -it
desper<u>ate</u>   **des•per•<u>it</u>**
separ<u>ate</u> (adj.)   **sep•er•<u>it</u>** Sp

-e- sounds like /i/
cat<u>e</u>gory   **kat•<u>i</u>•gohr•ee**
<u>e</u>licit   <u>i</u>•**lis**•it
(elicit also sounds like illicit)

-ar sounds like -er
circul<u>ar</u>   **sur**•kyuh•**<u>ler</u>**
pol<u>ar</u>   **poh**•<u>ler</u>
gramm<u>ar</u>   **gram**•<u>er</u>
vineg<u>ar</u>   **vin**•i•<u>ger</u>

Double VKV Flashcards (above and below): Write the dictionary pronunciation of a word under the tabs. Cut the top tabs to illustrate syllables. Cut away the stressed syllable tab so the stressed syllable is constantly visible.

When *a* and *e* sound like /uh/ in unstressed syllables, it can be difficult to determine which vowel should be used to spell the word.

<u>a</u>ffect   <u>uh</u>•**fekt**
<u>a</u>llude   <u>uh</u>•**lood**
ben<u>e</u>fit   **ben**•<u>uh</u>•fit Sp
liqu<u>e</u>fy   **lik**•<u>wuh</u>•fahy
propag<u>a</u>nda   prop•-<u>uh</u>•**gan**•-duh
propag<u>a</u>te   **prop**•<u>uh</u>•geyt

Procedure: With all tabs closed, say the stressed syllable. Gradually open the tabs, saying each syllable, and remembering to stress the exposed syllable.

See *corroborate* below.

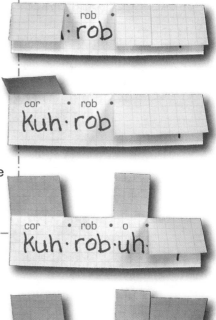

Unstressed *e* is sometimes misspelled as -er. The following words have the same Latin combining form, -teg-, which comes from *tangere*, to touch.

int<u>e</u>ger   **in**•ti•jer (**NOT** int<u>er</u>ger)
int<u>e</u>gral   **in**•ti•gruhl (**NOT** int<u>er</u>gral)
int<u>e</u>grate   **in**•ti•greyt (**NOT** int<u>er</u>grate)

Unstressed *o* can be misspelled as *a* or *e* when it sounds like /uh/ in unstressed syllables.
corrob<u>o</u>rate   kuh•**rob**•<u>uh</u>•reyt ⟶

CCVCe Words

syllables

Consonant Blends/Digraphs and Phonograms vs. Syllables (left): Differentiate between the way graphemes form syllables and words (as in CCVCe words, pictured top left), and syllables as units of speech (pictured lower left). CCVCe words are always one syllable. Remind students that there has to be a vowel in every syllable. See rules, page 300.

Synonyms

Synonyms are words that have the same or almost the same meaning:
repair - mend, restore - fix, commotion - ruckus

**Double VKV®
Flashcards (right):**
Use these flashcards
to practice finding
synonyms for
vocabulary terms.
Students can raise
and lower tabs to
check their answers.
Alternative
synonyms can be
written under the
tabs or in
the margins of the
notebook
surrounding the
flashcards.

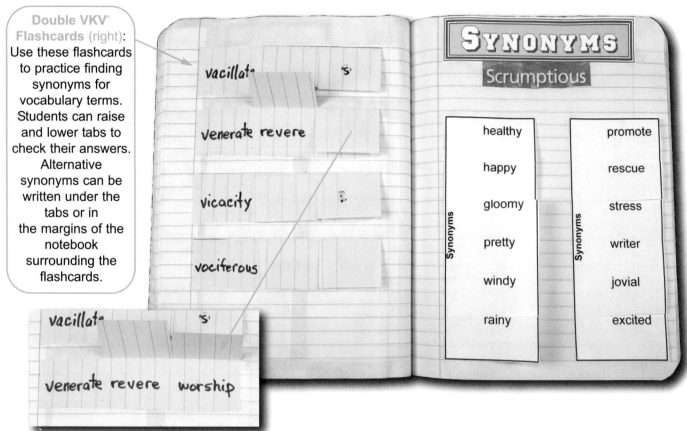

SYNONYMS

Scrumptious

Synonyms		Synonyms	
healthy		promote	
happy		rescue	
gloomy		stress	
pretty		writer	
windy		jovial	
rainy		excited	

vacillat⁻   's'

venerate revere   worship

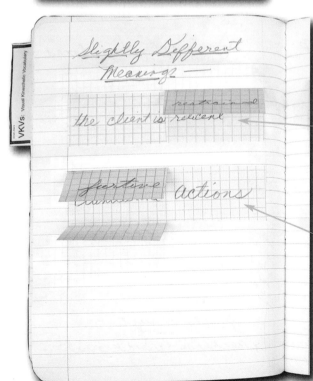

Word Study:
Slightly Different, But the Same?

restrained calm, quiet

the client is restrained
the client is reticent
the client is uncommunicative

Other synonyms for *restrained*:
cool, under control, withdrawn

furtive sneaky, secretive

furtive actions
clandestine actions
covert actions

Other synonyms for *furtive*:
artful, calculating, cautious, evasive, foxy, scheming, surreptitious, underhanded, wily

Synonyms

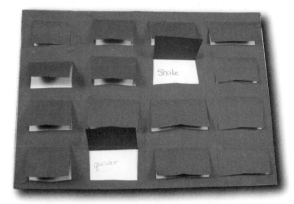

Multi-Tab Concentration: Make sixteen small matchbooks and glue them onto a sheet of paper to make a synonym concentration board. Write eight terms at random under the tabs and write eight synonyms, one for each of the eight terms, under the remaining tabs. Two students use one game board. Students take turns opening tabs to try to match a word and its synonym. Students get one point for each pair they match. See page 400.

Variation (above): Small tabs were cut in a single sheet of paper to form a similar game board. See page 412.

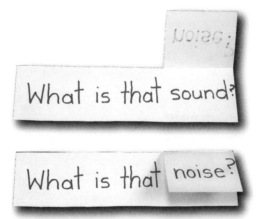

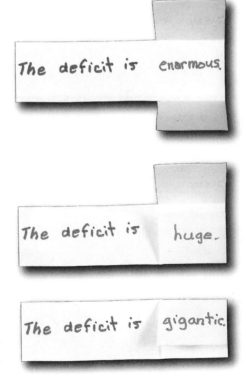

Double and Triple VKV® Flashcards (above and right): Write a sentence or phrase on the inside section of a Double (above left) or Triple (right) VKV Flashcard. Use a thesaurus to find synonyms for one of the words in the phrase or sentence. Cut away the top and bottom tabs of the VKV to expose the words not featured as a synonym. Leave the upper and/or lower VKV Flashcard sections in place above and below the selected word. As the tabs are opened and closed, write synonyms on the front of them and read the sentence with the different synonyms. Have students write sentences in their notebooks or journals using the original word and its synonyms. Do some of the synonyms slightly change the meaning of the sentence or phrase?

Synonyms

A *synonym* has the same meaning, or nearly the same meaning, as another word.

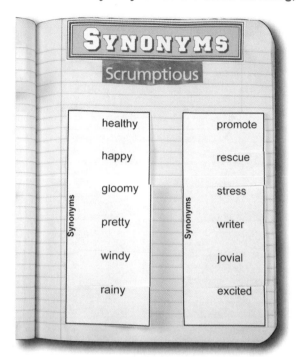

Multi-Tab Foldable® (above): Write words on the front tabs of a Multi-Tab Foldable, and write synonyms for the words under the tabs. Students might write synonyms on one side of the inside tab and use one of the synonyms in a sentence on the other side. See page 415.

Above Left: A computer was used to type six words on a piece of paper, leaving three or more blank lines after each typed word. The words were printed, and the paper was cut into rectangular shapes. Students glue the left edge of the rectangle into their notebooks, cut between the words, and write synonyms under the tabs.

Left: Double VKV Flashcards can be used to make synonym cards. Definitions, pronunciation guides, and other synonyms can be included on the flashcards.

Single Flashcards: Make and use as folded, ringed flashcards. Students read the flashcards forward and backward and give synonyms for the terms as quickly as possible. Great vocabulary enrichment for ESL/ELL students. See page 368.

Sentence Strip Synonyms: Sentence Strip Holders can be used to sort, match, and display synonym flashcards. See page 413.

Synonyms

Green Knowledge Pays Off, Literally
ENVIRONMENTAL AWARENESS IS PROFITABLE
vanishing coasts
disappearing   shorelines
raze [reyz]

Synonyms for RWP Titles or Phrases:
Have students select and glue RWP titles or phrases into their notebooks and write synonyms for the terms. Determine whether the meanings are exactly the same or slightly different. Investigate the importance of word selection when writing.

Note Academic Vocabulary:
Students will hear, read, and use the terms *cyclone* and *hurricane* in science classes, and the terms *ally* and *enemy* in social sciences classes.

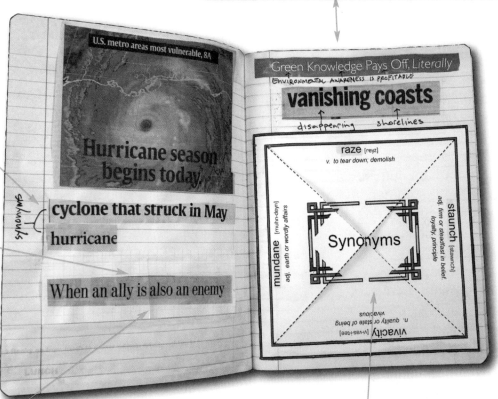

Write Synonyms for Antonyms:
Students find antonyms in RWP and glue them onto the front tabs of a Two-Tab Notebook Foldable, or they write antonyms on the tabs. Under the tabs, students write synonyms for the featured words.

Envelope Notebook Foldable (above):
Use the templates in Dinah Zike's *Notebook Foldables* book and CD to make this example, or have students use a paper square measuring no larger than 5" to make this four-tab activity. Glue the outer edges only. Write words on the front tabs, and write synonyms for the words under the tabs.

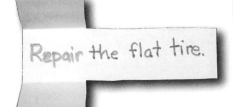

Repair the flat tire.   Fix the flat tire.   Mend the flat tire.

The Same, but Different (variation of above): Make a Three-Tab Foldable and write the words *repair*, *fix*, and *mend* on the front of the three tabs. Under the tabs, use the words in sentences that illustrate how you hear them used in daily life. For example, we would not normally say "Mend the flat tire," but we might say, "Mend the torn shirt."

Common Synonyms

after, following, behind
anger, rage, fury
answer, response, reply
appreciative, thankful, grateful Sp
aroma, smell
ask, inquire, question
baby, infant
bad, naughty, delinquent
barren, bare H, sterile
before, prior to, in front of
begin, start, initiate
below, under, beneath
boy, lad, youth
brave, courageous, daring
bright, radiant, luminous
call, shout, summon, yell
calm, tranquil, serene, placid
car, automobile, vehicle
carry, tote, lug
clear, transparent
close H, shut, seal H
come, arrive, reach
conclusion, close H, ending
contaminate, taint, pollute
dangerous, hazardous, risky
day, date, occasion Sp
decay, decompose, rot, spoil
declare, proclaim, advertise
decrease, diminish, lessen H
delay, postpone, wait H
dialect, vernacular, lingo, jargon
different, varied, unique, diverse
dislike, hate, detest
dormant, latent
during, throughout, while
eat, devour, dine, consume
end, finish, complete
enough, sufficient, ample
equal, same, matching
error, mistake, blunder

expand, swell, inflate, dilate
expression, phrase
fat, obese, overweight
feel, touch, sense H
fictitious, legendary, mythical
figure, form, shape
find, locate, discover
fix, mend, repair
elevation, height Sp
food, nourishment, meal
form, shape, makeup H
get, obtain, fetch, retrieve
give, donate, present H, bestow
go, leave, depart
good, suitable, just
grow, increase, accumulate, develop
guide, lead H, direct, steer
happy, joyful, glad
hard, difficult, troublesome
have, own, possess
help, aid H, assist
heroism, valor, prowess, gallantry
high H, tall, lofty
huge, giant, enormous, vast
hurry, hasten, rush
idea, thought, concept
imaginary, fanciful, visionary
important, needed, necessary
job, occupation, vocation
just, fair H, reasonable, unbiased
keep, hold, retain, save
kind, humane, considerate
large, big, huge, enormous, spacious
late, tardy
learn, acquire, understand
like, enjoy, relish H, savor
little, tiny, small, wee H
long, lengthy, drawn-out
lucky, fortunate, blessed

The fair judge...

The unbiased judge...

The reasonable judge...

Triple VKV® Flashcard:
See page 388.

Common Synonyms

make, build [H], construct, manufacture

many, numerous, several

might [H], may [H], perhaps

move, transport, budge

name, title, designation

near, close by, convenient

need, require, want

odd, unusual, peculiar

often, frequent, regular, habitual

old, aged, ancient

one, single, unit

open, unlock, unseal

part, portion, piece, division

place, put, arrange

play, frolic, romp, participate

point, peak [H], apex

present [H], gift, offering, donation

rear, back, bottom

right [H], correct, proper

salary, pay, wage

say, state, remark

show, demonstrate, display, exhibit

start, begin, commence

still, unmoving, silent

stop, halt, end

structure, anatomy

study, consider, reflect

take, grab, remove

tall, lofty, high [H]

think, consider, believe [Sp]

time [H], period, season

try, attempt, endeavor

turn, revolve, twist

walk, stroll, saunter

want, desire, crave

while, during, throughout

word, term, expression

write [H], compose, record [H]

wrong, incorrect, mistaken

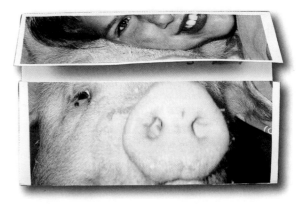

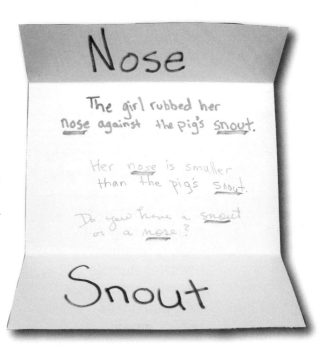

Shutterfold (right): Students found this picture, cut it so the girl's nose and the pig's snout were in separate sections, and then folded a *shutterfold* to the size of the pictures. The pictures were glued onto the front tabs, synonyms were recorded on outer inside tabs, and sentences were written in the center section. See page 400.

ambiguity *	uncertainty, vagueness	garble *	distort, confuse
amiable *	friendly, affable	garish *	gaudy, tasteless
amity *	friendship, harmony	garner *	gather, collect
analogous *	comparable, similar	garrulous *	talkative, loquacious
artisan *	craftsman, composer	gaunt *	emaciated, thin
augment *	increase, intensify	gravity *	seriousness, importance
auspicious *	favorable, advantageous	indolence *	laziness, sloth
begrudge *	resent, covet	intermittent *	sporadic, irregular
belittle *	demean, undervalue	intrepid *	brave, undaunted
benevolent *	kindly, charitable	ire *	anger, fury, rage
boorish *	ill-mannered, impolite	irksome *	annoying, irritating
burgeon *	grow, flourish	irrational *	unreasonable, illogical
burnish *	polish, shine	jaded *	tired, bored
buttress *	fortify, strengthen	jubilant	ecstatic, delighted
capacious *	spacious, roomy	lucid *	clear, explicit
circuitous *	indirect, roundabout	malady *	illness, affliction
circumscribe *	limit, restrict	malleable *	flexible, moldable
clemency *	mercy, forgiveness	mire *	swamp, bog, quagmire
clientele *	customers, patronage	misnomer *	wrong, misapplied name
coalesce *	merge, come together	monotonous *	dull, unvarying
coddle *	pamper, indulge	mundane *	ordinary, banal, routine
coercion *	force, duress	nefarious *	wicked, immoral
confound *	confuse, astonish	negligence *	carelessness, disregard
congeal *	solidify, coagulate	nettle *	annoy, provoke
consensus * Sp	agreement, concurrence	novel *	new H, unique
contrite *	sorry, remorseful	orthodox *	conventional, traditional
corpulent *	fat, overweight	pallid *	pale H, colorless
deteriorate *	decline, worsen	parched *	dried, dehydrated
discord *	disagreement, tumult	parity *	equality, balance
dubious *	doubtful, suspicious	paucity *	shortage, scarcity
disparage *	criticize, belittle	penury *	poverty, indigence
dynamic *	lively, vibrant	perceptive *	observant, astute
edifice *	building, structure	perfidy *	treachery, faithlessness
effusive *	demonstrative, gushing	persnickety *	fastidious, fussy
egress *	exit, departure, escape	pertinent *	relevant, applicable
emerge *	appear, emanate	placate *	pacify, calm
enduring *	lasting, permanent	potent *	powerful, efficacious
expatriate *	refugee, emigrant	pristine *	unspoiled, pure
extol *	praise, comment	procrastinate *	delay, put off
falter *	hesitate, stumble	prosaic *	dull, boring
fervor *	passion, enthusiasm	quagmire *	bog, marsh
finesse *	skill, adroitness	quaint *	picturesque, antique
flamboyant *	showy, ornate	quandary *	dilemma Sp, puzzle
furtive *	hidden, secret	quirk *	oddity, peculiarity
futile *	hopeless, useless		

rancor *	resentment, bitterness
raze * H	destroy, demolish
receptacle *	container, vessel
remorse *	regret, contrition
replete *	full, overflowing
respite *	break, intermission
resplendent *	shining, glowing
retraction *	withdrawal, removal
revere *	worship, honor
serrated *	jagged, saw-like
sophomoric * Sp	juvenile, immature
sporadic *	intermittent, infrequent
staid * H	dull, sober, serious
staunch *	loyal, faithful, dependable
stifle *	suppress, extinguish
stratagem *	plot, plan, trick
succinct *	concise, brief, pithy
surly *	grumpy, churlish, cross H
suspect *	doubt, distrust
thwart *	prevent, frustrate
timorous *	cowardly, fearful
truant *	deserter, runaway
tumult *	uproar, commotion
urbane *	sophisticated, suave
utilitarian *	useful, functional
vacillate *	waver, hesitate
vehement *	forceful, passionate
venerate *	revere, worship
veracity *	truthfulness, accuracy
verbose *	talkative, garrulous
vertigo *	dizziness, disequilibrium
vivacity *	liveliness, animation
vivify *	enliven, activate
vitriolic *	corrosive, scathing
vociferous *	loud, boisterous
voluminous *	spacious, expansive
waive * H	abandon, surrender, renounce
waylay *	accost, stop, approach
weighty *	serious, heavy, important
willful *	stubborn, obstinate
wily *	cunning, crafty
zealot *	fanatic, enthusiast
zenith *	summit, peak H, pinnacle

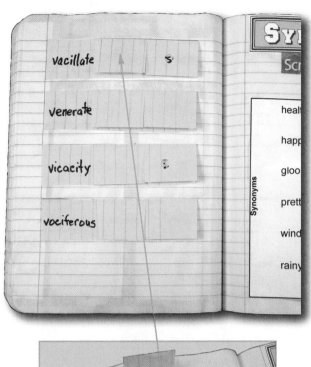

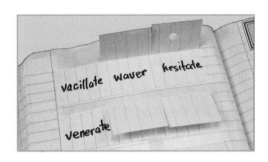

Double VKV Flashcard (above): This is a variation of the Double Flashcard activity pictured on page 314, featuring the words *make* and *build*. For this VKV, the Double Flashcard was folded into thirds, the top left tab was cut away to reveal the key term, and the remaining top tab was cut along the fold line to form two tabs to cover two synonyms written under the tabs. See page 380.

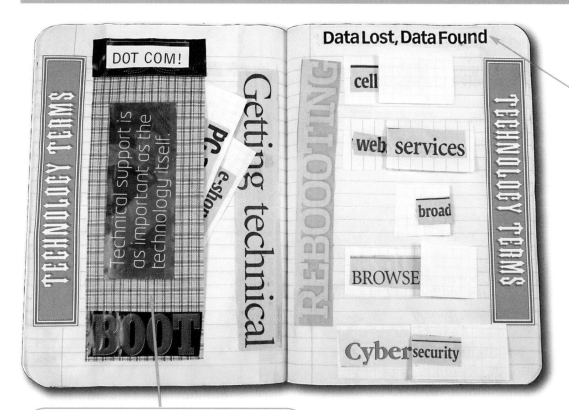

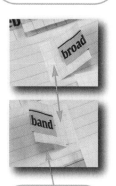

Titles that Teach: Titles of articles in technology magazines often provide examples of antonyms and idioms.

Single VKV Flashcard: Used with compound words. See page 369.

Hi-Tech VKVs®: Use a scrap of decorative paper to make a vertical pocket that will fit on a notebook page. Glue the pocket so that the opening is facing the inside fold. This will help prevent flashcards from falling out of the pocket.

Single VKVs® (above right): Look at the word *cell.* The word *cellular* was glued to the left edge of a Single VKV Flashcard, and the right edge was folded over to cover the ending *-ular* (of or relating to, resembling). The same procedure was used with the words *browse* and *browser*.
Extension: Find other *-ular* words: *circular, modular, singular, tubular.*

Tech Abbreviations:

Alt	alternate
Caps	capital letters
Ctrl	control
Del	delete
Esc	escape
GB	gigabyte
KB	kilobyte
MB	megabyte
txt	text file without programing or graphics

Acronyms and Initializations:

CAD	Computer Aided Design
CAM	Computer Aided Manufacturing
CD	Compact Disk
CD-ROM	Compact Disk-Read Only Memory
CPU	Central Processing Unit
CSS	Cascading Style Sheet
DOS	Disk Operating System
DVD	Digital Video Disk, Digital Versatile Disk
ESC	Escape (key on keyboard)
FTP	File Transfer Protocol
GIF	Graphics Interchange Format
HTML	HyperText Markup Language
HTTP	HyperText Transfer Protocol
JPEG	Joint Photographic Experts Group
LAN	Local Area Network
MP3	MPEG-1 Audio Layer 3
MPEG	Moving Pictures Experts Group
PC	Personal Computer
PDA	Personal Data Assistant, Personal Digital Assistant
PDF	Portable Document Format
RAM	Random-Access Memory
ROM	Read-Only Memory
TCP/IP	Transmission Control Protocol/Internet Protocol
URL	Uniform Resource Locator
USB	Universal Serial Bus
WWW	World Wide Web

Technology Terms

Common Terms

abort
back up v., backup n.
binary
bit
blog
blogosphere
Bluetooth
bookmark
boot, reboot
broadband
browse, browser
bug, debug
byte
cable
CC (carbon copy)
cell, cellular
cell phone
chat, chat room
chip
click on
computer
cookie
crash
cursor
cyber-
cyberbullying
cybermarket
cybersecurity
cyberspace
data
database
default
desktop
digitalize
disk drive
diskette
domain name
dot com   .com
dot net   .net
download
drag
e-commerce
e-mail, email

field
firewall
floppy disk
freeware
hard disk
hard drive
hardware
hit
home page
host
hyperlink
hypermedia
hypertext
icon
inbox
initialize
instant messaging (IM)
internet
IP address
keyword, keyword search
kilobyte (K)
laptop
link
log on, log off
mainframe
megabyte (MB)
memory
microprocessor
modem
monitor
mouse
navigation
netiquette
network
notebook
on line/online/on-line
off line/offline/off-line
operating system
outbox
output
password
peripherals

phishing
pixel
plug-ins
podcast
processor
program
protocol
purge
query
record
save
scanner
screen
screen saver
search, search engine
server
software
spam
spreadsheet
streaming
surf, surfing
tablet
technical support
texting
trojan
user
user name
videocast
virus
web
web host
webmaster
web page
web searches
web services
websites
wiki
wireless
word processor
worm
zip drive

Above:
Technology terms found in RWP (Real World Print.)

Above: Triple VKV Flashcard used to form three technology compound words that begin with *cyber-*, a combining form meaning *computer, computer network, virtual reality.*

Spelling Rules for Verbs:

Verbs ending in a double consonant keep both consonants when adding a suffix.
    Example: distress, distressed, distressing

One-syllable verbs with a short vowel double the final consonant when adding a suffix.
    Example: grin, grinned, grinning

Two-syllable verbs that stress the second syllable, double the final consonant when adding a suffix.
    Examples: acquit Sp, acquitted, acquitting
                 occur Sp, occurred Sp, occurring Sp
                 prefer, preferred, preferring
                 submit, submitted, submitting

Two-syllable verbs that stress the first syllable do not double the final consonant when adding a suffix.
    Examples: credit, credited, crediting
                 budget, budgeted, budgeting
                 focus, focused, focusing
                 profit, profited, profiting

Three-or-more-syllable verbs whose final syllable is not stressed do not double the final consonant when adding a suffix.
    Examples: benefit, benefited Sp, benefiting Sp
                 develop, developed, developing

Verbs that end in e drop the e and add -ed to form the past tense.
See VKV® example below based upon the word *criticize*.
    Examples: improve, improved
                 rescue, rescued

Most verbs drop the e before adding -ing.
See VKV® example below based upon the word *criticize*.
    Examples: gape, gaping (vs. gap, gapping)
                 rake, raking
                 tame, taming

    Exceptions: ageing, aging (both spellings are correct)
                  singe, singeing (if the e is dropped, it becomes *singing*)

Nine Words:
research
researched
researching

criticize
criticized
criticizing

abbreviate
abbreviated
abbreviating

Triple VKV® Flashcards: This small flashcard forms nine words.
When a verb ends in a silent -e which is dropped before adding a verb suffix,
draw a line through the -e with a different color of ink to indicate that
it is not needed with the suffix. See Variation, page 390.

Multi-Tab Foldable®
Book: 8½" x 11" paper was used to make this booklet. The paper was folded in half along the long axis to make *hamburgers*. The *hamburgers* were folded in half. Cuts were made along the inside fold line to form two tabs.

Each of the two tabs was cut into three tabs, forming six small tabs on each spread of the book. Students wrote verbs on the front tabs, wrote definitions on the inside back of the tabs, and used the words in sentences on the uncut base of the Foldable under the tabs. Sections were glued together side by side, a cover was glued around the bound pages, and a spine was attached.

See book binding photographs on page 28.

See page 394, Book Spine for Foldables.

Word Study:
The Same Ol', Same Ol'
Some verbs are the same in these three tenses.

Base Form	Simple Past Tense	Past Participle
(I *hit* the ball.)	(I *hit* it yesterday.)	(I had *hit* the ball before.)
bet	bet	bet
burst	burst	burst
bust	bust	bust
cast	cast	cast
cost	cost	cost
cut	cut	cut
fit	fit	fit
hit	hit	hit
hurt	hurt	hurt
knit	knit	knit
let	let	let
preset	preset	preset
put	put	put
quit	quit	quit
read	read	read
rid	rid	rid
set	set	set
shed	shed	shed
shut	shut	shut
slit	slit	slit
split	split	split
spread	spread	spread
sublet	sublet	sublet
thrust	thrust	thrust
upset	upset	upset
wed	wed	wed

Verbs Irregular Verbs

Base Form	Past Simple	Past Participle (have, has, had (been))	3rd Person Singular (he, she, it)	Gerund (noun from verb) Present Participle
awake	awoke	awoken	awakes	awakening
be H	was, were	been	is	being
bear H	bore H	born H	bears H	bearing H
become	became	become	becomes	becoming
begin	began	begun	begins	beginning
bite H	bit H	bitten	bites H	biting
bleed	bled	bled	bleeds	bleeding
blow	blew H	blown	blows	blowing
break H	broke	broken	breaks H	breaking H
bring	brought	brought	brings	bringing
build	built	built	builds	building
buy H	bought	bought	buys	buying
catch	caught	caught	catches	catching
choose	chose	chosen	chooses	choosing
come	came	come	comes	coming
creep	crept	crept	creeps	creeping
deal	dealt	dealt	deals	dealing
dive	dived/dove	dived	dives	diving
do H	did	done	does H	doing
draw	drew	drawn	draws	drawing
drive	drove	driven	drives	driving
drink	drank	drunk	drinks	drinking
eat	ate H	eaten	eats	eating
fall H	fell	fallen	falls	falling
feed	fed	fed	feeds	feeding
feel	felt	felt H	feels	feeling
fight	fought	fought	fights	fighting
find H	found	found	finds	finding
flee H	fled	fled	flees H	fleeing
fling	flung	flung	flings	flinging
fly	flew H	flown	flies	flying
forget	forgot	forgotten	forgets	forgetting
forgive	forgave	forgiven	forgives	forgiving
forsake	forsook	forsaken	forsakes	forsaking
freeze H	froze	frozen	freezes	freezing
give	gave	given	gives	giving
go	went	gone	goes	going
grind	ground H	ground H	grinds	grinding
grow	grew	grown H	grows	growing
hang	hung/hanged	hung/hanged	hangs	hanging
hear H	heard H	heard H	hears	hearing
hide	hid	hidden	hides	hiding
hold	held	held	holds	holding

Verbs Irregular Verbs

Base Form	Past Simple	Past Participle (have, has, had (been))	3rd Person Singular (he, she, it)	Gerund (noun from verb) Present Participle
keep	kept	kept	keeps	keeping
know H	knew H	known	knows H	knowing
lay	laid	laid	lays	laying
lead H	led H	led H	leads H	leading
leap	leaped	leaped	leaps	leaping
learn	learned	learned	learns	learning
leave	left	left	leaves H	leaving
lend	lent H	lent H	lends	lending
lie H	lay	lain	lies H	lying
light	lighted/lit	lighted/lit	lights	lighting
lose Sp	lost	lost	loses	losing
make	made	made	makes	making
mean H	meant	meant	means	meaning
meet H	met	met	meets H	meeting
mow	mowed	mowed/mown	mows	mowing
pay	paid	paid	pays	paying
prove	proved	proved/proven	proves	proving
ride	rode	ridden	rides	riding
ring H	rang	rung H	rings H	ringing H
rise	rose H	risen	rises	rising
run	ran	run	runs	running
say	said	said	says	saying
see	saw	seen H	sees H	seeing
seek	sought	sought	seeks	seeking
sell H	sold	sold	sells H	selling
send	sent	sent	sends	sending
shake	shook	shaken	shakes	shaking
shrink	shrank	shrunk	shrinks	shrinking
slay	slew	slain	slays	slaying
sleep	slept	slept	sleeps	sleeping
slide	slid	slid/slidden	slides	sliding
speak	spoke H	spoken	speaks	speaking
spring H	sprang	sprung	springs	springing
steal H	stole H	stolen	steals	stealing
stink	stank	stunk	stinks	stinking
strive	strove	striven	strives	striving
swim	swam	swum	swims	swimming
take	took	taken	takes	taking
tear	tore	torn	tears	tearing
throw	threw H	thrown H	throws	throwing
wake H	woke	woken	wakes	waking
write H	wrote	written	writes H	writing

Word Study:
Add Prefixes or Suffixes to Irregular Verbs, or Use Them to Form Compound Words

Base Word	Past Simple	Past Participle	Present Participle
come	came	come	coming
become	became	become	becoming
overcome	overcame	overcome	overcoming
do	did	done	doing
overdo	overdid	overdone	overdoing
redo	redid	redone	redoing
undo	undid	undone	undoing
set	set	set	setting
reset	reset	reset	resetting
upset	upset	upset	upsetting
take	took	taken	taking
mistake	mistook	mistaken	mistaking
overtake	overtook	overtaken	overtaking
retake	retook	retaken	retaking
undertake	undertook	undertaken	undertaking
throw	threw	throw	throwing
overthrow	overthrew	overthrow	overthrowing

Verb Phrases with VKVs®: A Triple VKV Flashcard was used to make four simple verb phrases. Note that short, different-colored lines were drawn across the center cut to show correct phrases. For example, the orange line indicates that *I will come* is correct, and the red line for *I come* and *I came* indicates that those are correct

I come

I will come

I came   I am coming

Half-Book Foldable Portfolio (above): Made using a sheet of 11" x 17" paper covered with tissue paper. See page 395.

Word Study: Verb Prefixes
The prefixes *be-*, *de-*, and *en-* can be clues that a word is a verb.

bedazzle	design	enable
befall	detain	enclose
begrudge	dethrone	entangle
bestow	devise	entrap

This entire book is filled with vocabulary-enriching Foldables® and VKVs®.

Design Contest for a Logo to Denote Test Prep Words: Have students design a logo to be used in notebooks to denote test prep words. The logo can be duplicated, placing as many as possible on one sheet of paper. The paper is duplicated, and logos are cut apart and made available for students to glue or staple into notebooks near special words. Logos help students focus on and review terms that have previously been featured in tests.

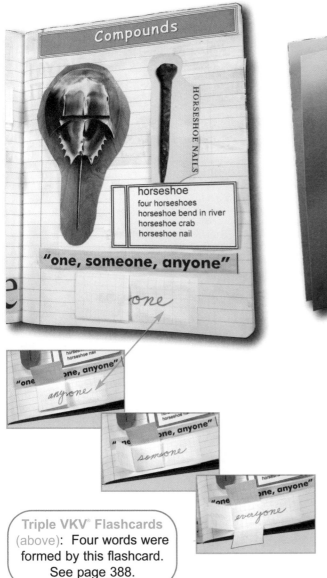

Triple VKV® Flashcards (above): Four words were formed by this flashcard. See page 388.

Tabbed Project Foldable (above): Pictures from RWP, maps, graphics on worksheets, or student-generated photographs can become basic vocabulary activities for ESL/ELL learners, or they can be used for content vocabulary extension by all students. See page 412 for instructions on how to cut the tabs.

Bigger is Better (variation): This same procedure can be used to make tabs in giant butcher paper murals, poster-board projects, bulletin boards, and more.

Bound Book Foldable: The Foldable that the Tabbed Projects are featured in was made using two sheets of 11" x 17" paper and bound using Dinah's "cut-up and cut-out" method of book binding. See page 401.

Two-Pocket Foldable® for Know/Learned: Make a Two-Pocket Foldable. Label one pocket *Terms I Know* and label the other pocket *Terms I Need to Know*. Students move vocabulary cards from the "Need to Know" pocket to the "Know" pocket as the words are mastered.

Right: Two-Pocket Foldables were made for each unit in a textbook and glued side by side to collect and organize academic vocabulary terms.

Notebook Pockets: Two pockets can be glued into a composition book and used to collect vocabulary flashcards made using quarter or eighth sheets of paper. Pockets can be made using scraps of paper, letter envelopes, small manila envelopes, and CD sleeves. See Introduction.

Two-Pocket Academic Vocabulary® (right): Use pockets glued side by side to collect vocabulary terms that relate to different topics, concepts, lessons of a chapter, or any other method of organizing information.

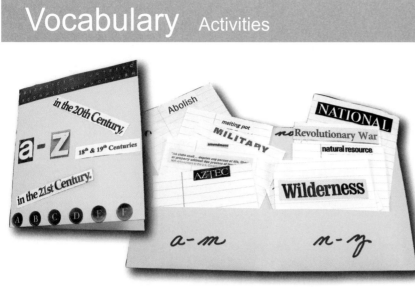

Two-Pocket Foldable® Sorting (above): Use a sheet of 8½" x 11" paper to make Two-Pocket Foldables for collecting content vocabulary terms. In the example above, social studies terms were collected from RWP or written on flashcards. The terms were sorted and stored in pockets labled with the letters from the first and second halves of the alphabet.

Alphabetize Vocabulary with Foldable Pocketbooks (above): Use 13 sheets of paper to make this 26-Pocket Foldable. Label each pocket with a letter of the alphabet.

Right: Use the pockets to sort and store 1/8-sheet flashcards of vocabulary terms studied throughout the year.

Other Foldable Vocabulary Aids:
Sentence Strip Holders, page 413.
Sentence Strips, page 413.

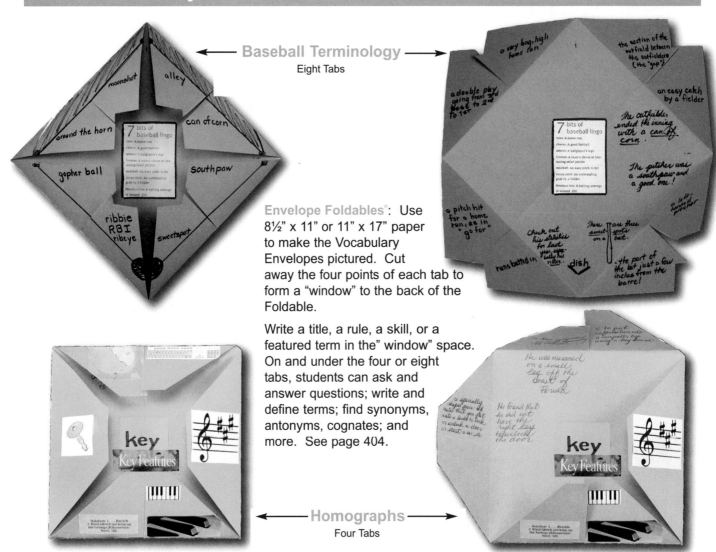

Baseball Terminology — Eight Tabs

Homographs — Four Tabs

Envelope Foldables®: Use 8½" x 11" or 11" x 17" paper to make the Vocabulary Envelopes pictured. Cut away the four points of each tab to form a "window" to the back of the Foldable.

Write a title, a rule, a skill, or a featured term in the" window" space. On and under the four or eight tabs, students can ask and answer questions; write and define terms; find synonyms, antonyms, cognates; and more. See page 404.

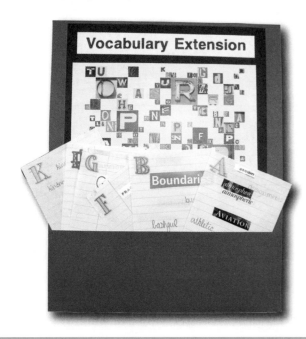

Pocket Chart Extension: A sheet of 11" x 17" cover stock paper was used to make the Single Pocket Chart pictured left. Students make flashcards of terms that they find challenging and/or terms they feel might be challenging to their classmates. These flashcards are stored in the Pocket Chart. Once or twice a week, the teacher or a student removes some of the cards and quizzes the class to see who can define and/or spell the terms. Certain terms might be added to required spelling lists or written in student notebooks, or students might be asked to use them in their writing. This word search activity is designed to actively involve students in a process that will help expand their oral and written vocabulary.

Vocabulary Foldables

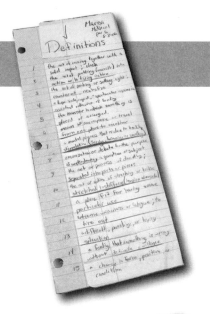

Multi-Tab Vocabulary Foldables®:

1. Make a Foldable with tabs. See pages 415.
2. On the front tabs, do any of the following:
   - Write a vocabulary term.
   - Glue terms cut from RWP.
   - Glue a picture representation of the term.
   - Glue a photograph of something representing the term.
3. Depending on what was placed on the front tabs, place any of the following under the word tabs:
   - Glue or draw a picture of the word.
   - Write the definition of the word.
   - Use a dictionary to determine and write the part of speech, the proper pronunciation, or multiple definitions.
   - Use the word in a sentence.
   - Write a synonym or an antonym for the term.
   - If the term is a noun, write the singular and plural forms of the word.
   - If the word is a verb, write the present and/or past tense forms of the word.
4. The backs of Independent Foldables can have an extension activity and/or an application of skills learned.

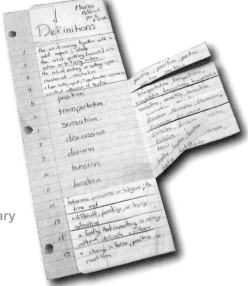

Hints for Using Notebook Paper to Make Multi-Tab Vocabulary Foldables® (right):

When using wide-ruled paper, if every third line is cut, about ten tabs will be formed, including the heading space.
If the Multi-Tab Foldable is to be glued inside a Shutterfold or other large project, fold the paper so the three holes are covered.
Leave the holes exposed for storing the Vocabulary Foldable in a three-ring binder or pocket folder.

Variation: Use three binder rings to form a booklet composed of examples of student/class Foldables made using notebook paper.

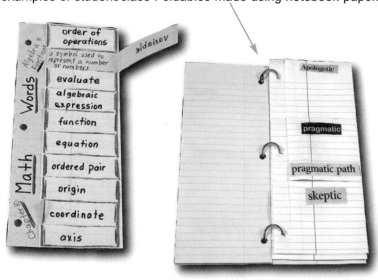

Tabbed Cover-Up (left):
Use 12" x 12" scrapbook paper, or cut a sheet of 12" x 17" paper, to form a 12" square. See photographs and instructions on page 406. Write 12 vocabulary words under the tabs. Begin the activity by opening all tabs. When students hear a word that they have on their card, they cover the word by closing the tab over the word. The students try to cover all words on their vocabulary cards. See instructions on page 406 for a more advanced example.

Four-Tab Foldable® Vocabulary Books (below and right):
Make Four-Tab Foldables as needed. Write a vocabulary word on each tab. Under the tab, define the word, place a picture of the word, and/or use the word in a sentence. As more Four-Tab Foldables are made, glue them side by side to make a Multi-Tab Vocabulary Booklet that contains new terms and terms for review.

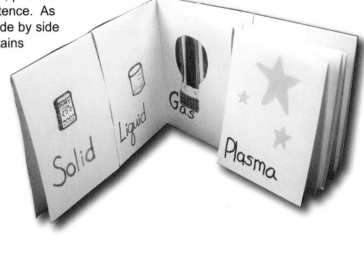

Definitions with Matchbook Foldables® (right):
Use a sheet of 8½" x 11" paper to make the base of this study aid. (Index-weight paper or card stock makes a sturdier study board.) Make and glue 12 to 18 small matchbooks on the base, as seen in the photograph. Write vocabulary terms on the front tabs and definitions under the tabs. Students select terms, define them, and then open and close the tabs to check their definitions.

Jeopardy® Variation: Students write definitions on the front tabs and questions under the tabs. Students read the answers, form questions, and open the tabs to check their responses. See page 400.

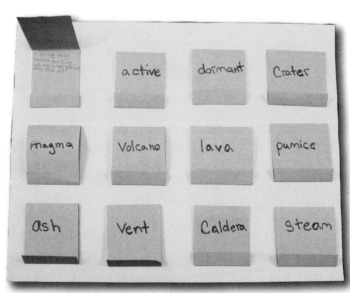

Instant Words for ESL/ELL

Based on a five-million-word count done by Carroll et al. (1971) and modified by Sakiey (1977) and Fry (1998, 2000).

a	come	going	land H	north	remember	then	was
about	complete	good	large	not H	right H	them	water
after	covered	got	last	notice	rock	there H	waves H
all	could H	great H	left	now	room	these	way H
also	cried	green	let	number	run	they	we H
am	dad	ground H	light H	numeral	said	thing	well H
an	day	had	like	of	same	think	went
and	did	happened	line	off	sat	this	were
any	didn't	has	listen	oil	saw H	three	what
are	do	have	little	old	say	through H	when
area	dog	he	live H	on	school H	time	where
around	doll	heard H	long	one H	see H	to H	which
as	door	help	look	only	seen H	today	while
ask	down H	her	low	open	sentence	told	white
at	draw H	here H	made	or H	several	too H	who
away	during	him	make	orange	she	top	whole H
baby	each	himself	man	order	show H	toward	why
back	early	his	many	other	side H	town	will H
ball	easy	hold	map	our H	since H	travel	wind H
bat	eat	home	mark	out	ship	true	with
be H	ever	horse H	may H	over	short	two H	wood H
been	fall H	hours H	me	paper	sing	under	word
before	farm	house	mean H	part	sit	unit	work
best	fast H	how	measure	passed H	slowly	up	would H
better	field	however	men	pattern	small	upon	write H
big	figure	hundred	money	people	so H	us	year
birds	find	I H	more	piece H	some H	use	yellow
blue H	fire H	if	morning H	place	sound	usually	yes
black	first	I'll H	most	plan	south	very	you H
body	fish	I'm	mother	plants	space	voice	your H
book	five	in H	move	play	stand	vowel	zero
boy	follow	into	much	pretty	stop	want	zoo
brown	food	is	music	problem	story	war	
but H	for	it	must	products	sun H		
by H	four	its H	my	pulled	sure		
call	friends	jump	name	put	table		
came	from	just	near	question	take		
can	fun	keep	need H	quiet	tell		
can't	get	kind	never	quick	than		
certain	girl	king	new H	quit	that		
cold	give	knew H	next	reached	the		
color	go	know H	no H	red H	their H		

The five *vowels* are **a**, **e**, **i**, **o**, and **u**.
Vowels usually make two sounds—*long* and *short*.

The letter *y* sometimes acts as a long vowel (*by*, *cry*) or a short vowel (*myth*, *symbol*).

Some clusters of vowels and vowels combined with consonants can make vowel sounds.
The following clusters make long vowel sounds:

/ā/ =   -ai- in *maid*, -ay in *may*
/ē/ =   -ea- in *meat*
/ī/ =   -igh in *light*, -ie in *pie*
/ō/ =   -oa- in *boat*
/ū/ =   -ue in *cue*

The following letters or letter clusters make short vowel sounds:

/e/ =   -ea- in *bread*
/i/ =   -y- in *myth*
/u/ =   -ou- in *rough*, *tough*, *trouble*

There are many vowel rules and exceptions to these rules, but two of the most common rules are listed below.

When a four-letter word (CVC*e*) ends in *e*, the *e* is silent and the vowel says its name—*cake*, *kite*, *late*, *note*.
When two vowels "go walking" the first "does the talking." This means the first vowel says its name, or is long—*m**ea**n*, *l**oa**n*, *p**ai**n*.

Vowel diphthongs, written as two vowels or one vowel and a consonant, make a unique sound. Common diphthongs include the following: -oi, -oy, -ow, -ou, -aw.
See pages 364-366.
When vowels are grouped with an **r**, the vowel sound is changed and the new sound is said to be *r-controlled*—*star*, *her*, *hire*, *horse*, *turn*.

Look for the following complex vowel patterns and note how they relate to the letters surrounding them:

-ai- in *aid*, *hair*, *wait*
-ay in *day*, *may*, *spray*
-ea- in *read* and *read*, or *meat* and *bread*
-ee- in *feel*, *green*, *sweet*, *week*
-ei- in *eight* and *receive*, or *neighbor* and *ceiling*
-ie in *pie* and *piece*, or *lie* and *thief*
-oa- in *coat*, *goat*, *float*
-oo- in *book* and *soon*, or *cook* and *balloon*
-ow in *slow* and *cow*, or *know* and *now*

See Silent Letters, page 258.

ESL/ELL students need lots of experience with short words that contain complex vowel patterns to help them think about letter/sound relationships while looking at each word as a whole, and then applying what they have learned to more complex words.

With and Without Air: Vowels and Consonants

Vowels are speech sounds made without constriction of the air that flows from the lungs. *Consonants* are speech sounds made by varying degrees of obstruction of the air flowing through the vocal tract. Partial to complete obstruction causes friction, resulting in different sounds.

No *a*, *e*, *i*, *o*, or *u*

Longest common word without a, e, i, o, u:

rhythms Sp

Also:

myrrh

One Vowel

Longest common word with only one vowel:

strengths

Other common words with only one vowel:

twelfths

schmaltz

schnapps

Vowels Only

Longest common words:

a	an indefinite article
aa, a'a	a type of lava
ai	a three-toed sloth
Eiao	a Marquesas island
I	first person pronoun
Io	a moon of Jupiter
Iouea	a genus of sea sponges
O	an interjection (also spelled *oh*)

All Five Vowels

sequoia

Every Syllable

Every syllable of a word has a vowel sound. A single vowel can be a syllable.

tax

tax•a•tion

Long or Short

Vowels make long or short sounds. Only one vowel is needed to form a short vowel sound:

bled

Two vowels—VV, CVVC, or CVCe—are needed to form a long vowel sound:

easy, bleed, cave

Two Vowels Together

In the -VVC pattern, the second vowel is next to the first:

beast

Two Vowels Separated

In the CVCV pattern, the second vowel may be separated from the first by one consonant. When this happens, the first vowel sound changes from short to long.

rave

Two Vowels Separated by 2+ Consonants

In the VCCV pattern, the second vowel may be separated from the first by two consonants. When this happens, the first vowel is *not* changed, but remains short.

ballet short *a*

but CVCV: bale long *a*

Spelling Note

Doubling a consonant can *protect* or *maintain* a short vowel. The extra consonant/s prevent an added vowel from getting close enough to the first vowel to change its sound from short to long.

beat	beating	/ē/ - no doubling with vowel suffix
bet	better	/e/ - double to protect first vowel sound when adding vowel sufix
diner /ī/	dinner /i/	

Common Vowel Prefixes

A vowel prefix begins with a vowel:

a-
a-, ab-, ac-, ad-, af-, ag-, al-, an-, ap-, as-, at-

e-
e-, ec-, ef-, em-, en-, ex-

i-
im-, in-

o-
ob-, oc-, of-, op-, over-

u-
un-, uni-

Common Vowel Suffixes

A vowel suffix begins with a vowel:

-a
-able, -age, -al, -ance, -ancy, -ant, -ar, -ary, -ate, ation

-e
-ed, -en, -eous, -er, -es, -est

-i
-ic, -ify, -ing, -ious, -ish, -ism, -ist, -ive, -ize

-o
-o, -on, -or, -ory, -ose, -ous

-u
-ure

a and u

Spelling challenge: *a* comes before *u*...

gauge

...and after *u*

guard

u before o

Spelling challenge: *u* comes before *o*:

buoy

buoyant

Half-Book Foldable made using 11" x 17" paper. The left side of the Half-Book was cut 1" shorter than the right side. When closed, the taller back tab sticks above the cover. The title of the project is written on the tab. Students collect examples of words, and glue or write them inside. See page 395.

Word Study: Regional Use of Vowels in Hawaiian

a'a	[**ah**·ah] - rough lava
aalii	[ah·**lee**·ee] - shrub
Hawaii	[huh·**wahy**·ee] - 50th state of USA
iiwi	[ee·**ee**·wee] - bird, honeycreeper
muumuu	[**moo**·moo] - loose dress
pahoehoe	[pah·**hoh**·ee·hoh·ee] - smooth lava

Compare and contrast how vowels are used to spell words in different languages. Notice that in Hawaiian, words have lots of vowel sounds and nearly every vowel has a sound.

Word Study: One or Two Vowels Determines Short or Long Sound:

Two vowels are needed to make a long vowel sound.

b**ea**d, bed, bad
b**ea**n, Ben, ban
b**ea**t, bet, bat
c**oa**t, cot, cat
l**ai**d, lad, lid
l**ea**d ᴴ, led ᴴ, lad
m**ea**n ᴴ, men, man
m**ea**t ᴴ, met, mat
p**ai**n ᴴ, pan, pin
p**ea**t, pet, pat
m**ai**d ᴴ, mad, mid
s**ea**t, set, sat
s**oa**p, sop, sap

Double VKV Flashcard/ Two Medial Vowels (below): Write *m* as the initial consonant and *d* as the final consonant. Write *a* under the first medial tab and *i* under the second. Alternate raising the tabs to read *mad* and *mid*. Raise both medial tabs to read *maid*. See page 386.

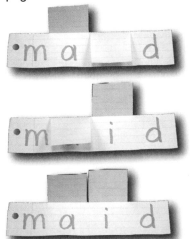

Word Study: *either* Pronounce with /ī/ or /ē/.

The /ē/ pronunciation is more common in American English, but the /ī/ pronunciation can often be heard on broadcast news and in speeches. Since the 1800s, the /ī/ has been the more common pronunciation in British English, and the trend toward this pronunciation in America is a borrowing of the British pronunciation.

Adjective:
As an adjective, *either* refers to two things: *either* hand, *either* riverbank, *either* bike tire.

Pronoun:
As a pronoun, *either* can be the subject of a sentence.
Either can be used.

Conjunctions:
either...or
The paper was written by *either* the student *or* his parent.

Adverb:
If you don't go swimming, I won't *either*.

Word Study Extension:

not + either = neither
Neither is also pronounced with /ī/ or /ē/.

neither...nor

Neither the doctor *nor* the nurse heard the patient cough.

Bound Four-Tab Foldable® Book
(right and below): Use 11" x 17"
paper to make Four-Tab Foldables
folded in half along the short axis
(like a *hotdog*). Glue them side by
side and bind them as a book.
See page 28 for photographic instructions.

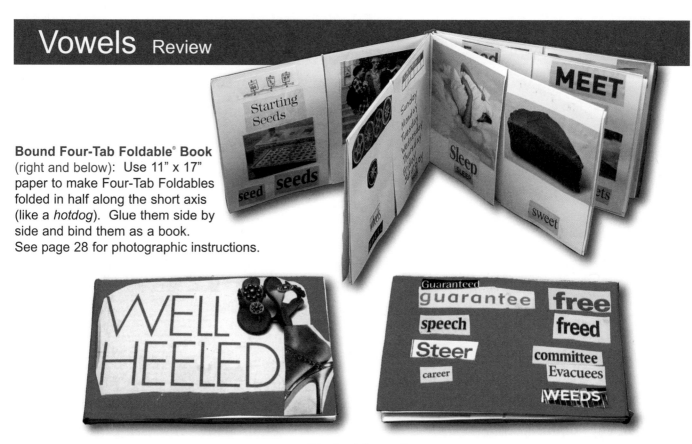

Twin Vowels

**Double *ee* and *oo* are common spellings in American English, but double *aa*, *ii*, and *uu*
are uncommon and usually occur in loanwords from other languages.
See page 347 for lists of *ee* words, and page 351 for lists of *oo* words.**

aa

a'a
a type of lava

aardvark
aardwolf
marsupial animals

aargh Int
baa
sounds; omomatopoeia

bazaar Sp
marketplace; Middle East

haaf
deep-sea fishing grounds off
Shetland and Orkney Islands

laager
camp encircled by wagons

maar
volcanic land form

naan
Indian bread

quaalude
drug; methaqualone

ii

**A plural ending
for words of Latin origin, and
found in loanwords from other
languages such as Japanese and
Hawaiian. See page 336.**

congius   congii pl.
0.8 US gallon

genius   genii pl.

Hawaii
50th state of U.S.A

medius   medii pl.

radius   radii pl.
also radius*es*

senarius   senarii pl.

shiitake mushroom
Japanese; shee•ee•-**tah**•key

ski   skiing suffix

splenius   splenii pl.

torii
gateway, portal
Japanese; **tawr**•ee•ee

uu

**is found in only a
few common
words.**

continuum
continua pl.

residuum
residua pl.

triduum
three-day religious
observances (Roman
Catholic Church)

vacuum Sp
vacuums pl.
vacua pl.

Adding Vowel Suffixes to Long-Vowel Words by Dropping a Silent *e*

Silent *e Rule*

When adding a vowel suffix to a long-vowel word that ends in a silent *e*, the *e* is nearly always dropped.

Examples: create, creator
hype, hyped, hyping
late, later, latest
like, likable
machine, machinist
lose, losing
use, usable, used, using

No Silent *e*

When adding a vowel suffix to a word that does not end in a silent *e*, no letters are omitted.

Examples: last, lasted, lasting
real, realist, realistic
work, worked, worker, working

Exceptions to the Silent e Rule

There are a few exceptions to the silent *e* rule. These words keep the silent *e* at the end when a vowel suffix is added. Words that end in *-ee* have one voiced *e* and one silent *e*. These words keep the silent *e* when adding suffixes.

Examples: agree, agreeable
degree, degrees
see, seeing, sees

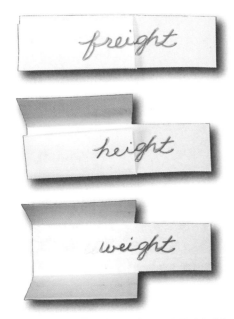

Triple VKV Flashcards and Foldable Pocket Chart: See rules for spelling *-ie-* or *-ei-* words on the next page.

Vowels Spelling -ie- and -ei-

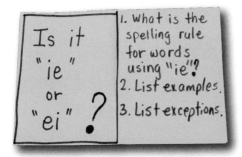

Spelling: -ie- and -ei-
Put i before e

achieve	lieutenant Sp
alien	mien H
ancient	mischief
anxiety	niece Sp
belief Sp	piece H
believe Sp	pierce
besiege Sp	priest
brief	quiet
chief	relief Sp
die H	riel H
diesel	Cambodian currency
fief	shield
field	shriek
fiend	siege Sp
fierce	sieve
frieze H	thief
grief	tie
hierarchy *	tier H
lie	wield
lien H	yield Sp
lieu	

Except after c
ceiling H
conceit
conceive
deceit
deceive
perceive
receipt Sp
receive Sp

Or when sounded as /ā/
As in neighbor and weigh.
beige
deign *
eight H
feign *
feint * H
freight
heinous *
neigh H
neighbor
obeisance *
reign * H
rein H
seine H
sleigh H
surveillance
veil H
vein H
weigh H Sp

Double VKV Flashcard (above): Use this VKV Flashcard for spelling an -ie- word, for test prep vocabulary extension, and for root word analysis. See page 378.

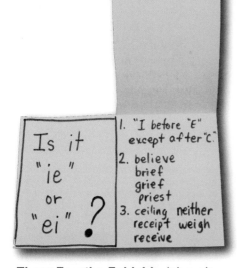

Three-Fourths Foldable (above): The main idea—or, in this example, a question—is written on the left side of a Three-Fourths Foldable, and related questions are on the front of the right tab. Answers to the questions on the right are under the tabs and are numbered to correspond to the questions on the front. This is a great Foldable to teach students how to write test-like questions that can be shared with and answered by classmates. Students might include an answer key on the back of their Foldable. See page 397.

Direct ei Loanwords:
lei /ā/ Hawaiian
sheik /ē/ or /ā/ Arabic
stein /ī/ German

Word Study: Exceptions to i before e Rule:
caffeine
codeine
counterfeit
deity
eiderdown
either
feisty
foreign
forfeit
heifer
height
heir H
heirloom
heist
kaleidoscope
leisure Sp
meiosis
neither
protein
seismic
seize Sp
seizure Sp
sovereign
their H
weird Sp

British Version of Rule:
When the sound is ee it's i before e except after c.

Add a Silent e

Adding a silent e to some short-vowel words forms long-vowel words. Many students will need to review and practice this basic skill. Select words from the list on the next page.

Single VKV Flashcards Illustrate How Short Vowels Become Long:

1. Use a Single VKV Flashcard or half of a sentence strip.
2. Select a word pair from the list on the next page.
3. Write a CVC word on the left side of the flashcard. Illustrate the word to the far right if possible.
4. Bend the right edge of the flashcard over to cover the e and form a CVC word. Fold it in place.
5. Write an e on the top of this right tab. Write the e close to the edge of the tab.
6. Open and close the tab, alternately adding and removing the e, and read the short CVC word and the long vowel word which has a silent e.

Variation: Write a CVCe word on the left side. Fold the right edge over to cover the letter e.

Multi-Word Variation (right and below):

Fold a Triple VKV Flashcard into fifths. Cut off the right top and bottom four sections. Write three initial consonants on and under the three left tabs. Write a -VCe phonogram on the sections after the consonants. The far right tab will be blank.

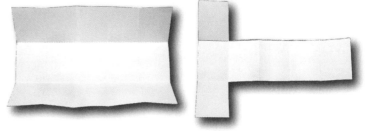

With the far right tab folded over to cover the e, three CVC words with short medial vowel sounds are formed.

With the far right tab open, three CVCe words are formed. Students experience how the silent e changes the medial vowel to a long sound.

CVC/CVCe and CCVC/CCVCe Examples:

The CVCe pattern illlustrates how the addition of a second vowel to the end of a CVC word changes the vowel sound from short to long. Use these one-syllable words to form, read, and spell multisyllabic words, many of which are compound words.

bad	bade	forbade
ban	bane	urbane
bar H	bare	threadbare
bid	bide	abide
bit H	bite	frostbite, trilobite
can	cane	arcane, hurricane
cap	cape H	scape, cityscape
cop	cope	scope, stethoscope
cub	cube	cubed, ice cube
cut	cute	acute
dim	dime	
din	dine	
dot	dote	anecdote, antidote
dud	dude	dude ranch duds = suit of clothes
fad	fade	prefaded
far	fare H	airfare, fanfare, welfare
fat	fate H	sulfate
fin	fine H	confine, define, refine
fir H	fire	backfire, bonfire, crossfire
gap	gape	agape
glad	glade	everglade
glob	globe	
grim	grime	begrime
grip	gripe	
hat	hate	
hid	hide	rawhide
hop	hope	
hug	huge	
kit	kite	
mad	made	handmade, readymade
man	mane H	germane, humane
mar	mare	nightmare
mat	mate	acclimate, automate, decimate, primate
mop	mope	

nap	nape	
not H	note	connote, denote, keynote
pan H	pane H	propane, windowpane
par	pare H	compare, prepare
past H	paste	toothpaste
pin H	pine	alpine, spine, porcupine
pip	pipe	drainpipe, tailpipe, windpipe
plan	plane H	biplane, deplane, hydroplane
plat	plate	copperplate, electroplate
pop H	pope	antipope
rag H	rage	enrage, outrage
rat	rate	accelerate, berate, celebrate, serrate
rid	ride	astride, bride, chloride, deride, joyride, override
rip	ripe	gripe, overripe, stripe
rob	robe	aerobe, microbe, wardrobe
rot	rote	garote, rewrote, underwrote
sag	sage	
scrap	scrape	
sham	shame	ashamed
shin	shine	earthshine, outshine, shoeshine
sit	site H	campsite, marcasite, parasite, website
slid	slide	backslide, landslide, mudslide
slop	slope	aslope, downslope
snip	snipe	guttersnipe derogatory
spin	spine	vespine
stag	stage	backstage, offstage, upstage
star	stare H	outstare
strip H	stripe	pinstripe
tap H	tape	audiotape, pretape, videotape
tot	tote	
trip H	tripe	stripe, penstripe
tub	tube	protuberant, tuberous, tubeworms
twin	twine	entwine
van	vane H	weathervane
wag	wage	
war	ware H	aware, beware, glassware, hardware
win	wine	swine

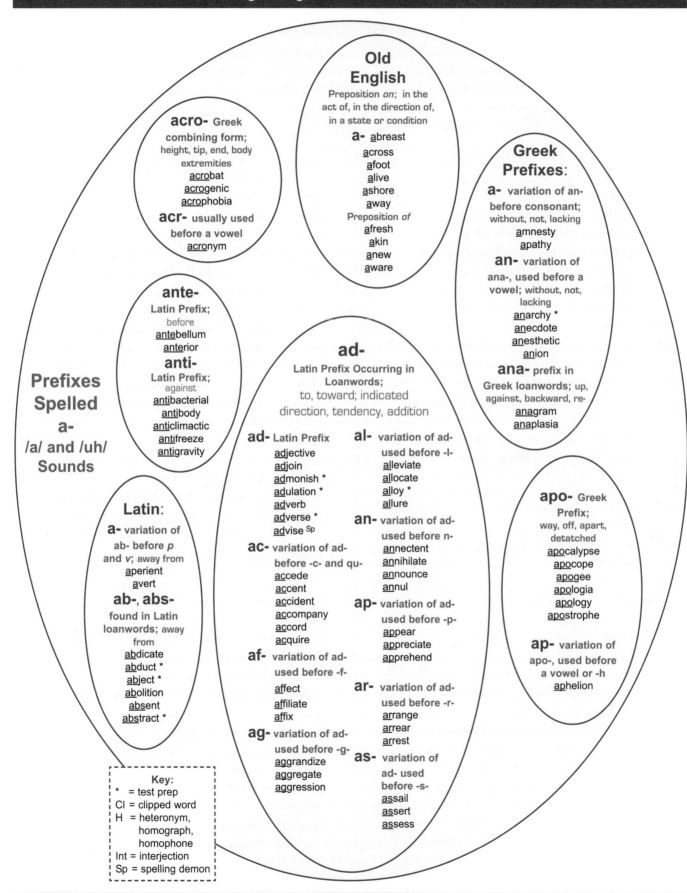

acro- Greek
combining form;
height, tip, end, body
extremities
acrobat
acrogenic
acrophobia

acr- usually used
before a vowel
acronym

Old English
Preposition *on*; in the
act of, in the direction of,
in a state or condition

a- abreast
across
afoot
alive
ashore
away
Preposition *of*
afresh
akin
anew
aware

Greek Prefixes:

a- variation of an-
before consonant;
without, not, lacking
amnesty
apathy

an- variation of
ana-, used before a
vowel; without, not,
lacking
anarchy *
anecdote
anesthetic
anion

ana- prefix in
Greek loanwords; up,
against, backward, re-
anagram
anaplasia

ante-
Latin Prefix;
before
antebellum
anterior
anti-
Latin Prefix;
against
antibacterial
antibody
anticlimactic
antifreeze
antigravity

**Prefixes
Spelled
a-
/a/ and /uh/
Sounds**

ad-
Latin Prefix Occurring in
Loanwords;
to, toward; indicated
direction, tendency, addition

ad- Latin Prefix
adjective
adjoin
admonish *
adulation *
adverb
adverse *
advise Sp

ac- variation of ad-
before -c- and qu-
accede
accent
accident
accompany
accord
acquire

af- variation of ad-
used before -f-
affect
affiliate
affix

ag- variation of ad-
used before -g-
aggrandize
aggregate
aggression

al- variation of ad-
used before -l-
alleviate
allocate
alloy *
allure

an- variation of ad-
used before n-
annectent
annihilate
announce
annul

ap- variation of ad-
used before -p-
appear
appreciate
apprehend

ar- variation of ad-
used before -r-
arrange
arrear
arrest

as- variation of
ad- used
before -s-
assail
assert
assess

Latin:
a- variation of
ab- before *p*
and *v*; away from
aperient
avert

ab-, abs-
found in Latin
loanwords; away
from
abdicate
abduct *
abject *
abolition
absent
abstract *

apo- Greek
Prefix;
way, off, apart,
detached
apocalypse
apocope
apogee
apologia
apology
apostrophe

ap- variation of
apo-, used before
a vowel or -h
aphelion

Key:
* = test prep
Cl = clipped word
H = heteronym,
   homograph,
   homophone
Int = interjection
Sp = spelling demon

a
Indefinite Article
When unstressed, it is pronounced *uh*.

When stressed, it is pronounced /ā/.

Initial ă

abdomen	agony	ancestor
acid	album	animal
acme *	algebra	answer
acrid *	allergy	antelope
action	amber	aquifer
after	amity *	asset *
		asthma
		athlete
		avid *

Key:
* = test prep
Cl = clipped word
H = heteronym, homograph, homophone
Int = interjection
Sp = spelling demon

Both
If a word is spelled with more than one letter *a*, and it begins with the short *a* sound, the other *a* will not be short, but will sound like /uh/ or /ā/, or will be r-controlled.
/uh/: animal
/ā/: ablate
r-controlled: anarchy *
Exceptions:
abstract, amtrac (military vehicle)

Root Words

annus Latin; circuit of the sun, year
anniversary
anno Domini (A.D.)
annual

altus Latin; high
altimeter
altitude
altocumulus

aster Greek; star
asterisk
asteroid
astrology
astronaut
astronomy

Medial
Phonograms

Spelling /a/ Sounds

-ab
cab Cl
scab
slab

-aft
craft H
draft H
graft

-and
grand
stand
strand

-ask
flask
mask
task

-ack
lack
sack
track H

-ag
brag
shag
swag

-ang
clang
sprang
twang

-asm
chasm
cytoplasm
spasm

-act
distract
pact H
tact H

-am
cram
gram
sham

-ank
blank
shrank
stank

-asp
clasp
gasp
grasp

a-e
Silent Final e *(Usually results in a long vowel sound: stave.)*
chance
dance
enhance
glance
have
lance
prance
stance

-ad
fad
grad Cl
triad

-amp
champ Cl
clamp
stamp H

-ant
recant
scant
supplant

-ass
bass
brass
mass H

-aff
chaff
gaff H
staff H

-an
ban
bran
clan

-ap
scrap
strap
wrap SL

-ast
blast
mast
vast

-ance
glance
stance
trance

-as
alas Int
gas Cl

-at
gnat SL
slat
spat H

-anch
blanch
branch

ash
flash
slash
trash

-ax
ax
fax Cl
relax
tax

Final
Vowel Suffixes begin with -a but can have the /uh/ sound.

-an, -ian
artisan
guardian
historian
mathematician

-ance, -ence
abundance
extravagance
resistance
subservience

-ant noun
contestant
disinfectant
fragrant
tenant

-ant adj.
constant
pleasant

Spelling /ā/ Sound

-ea-
break H
steak H
yea

a-e
Silent -e Rule Phonograms

-ace
ace
brace
cyberspace
embrace
grace
misplace
pace
race H

-ade
accolade
arcade
bade
evade *
glade

-age
rage
sage *
wage

-ake
brake H
forsake
quake Cl
shake H

-ale
ale H
scale H
hale * H
whale * H

-ame
blame
frame H
shame
surname

-ane
bane *
cane * H
inane *
sane H

-ape
ape
drape
escape
gape
misshape
scrape

-ase
abase
base H
chase
database
phase H
phrase
trace

-ate
grate H
innate *
plate
rate
state H

-ave
grave
knave SL
shave
slave
stave

-aze
blaze
crave
daze H
haze H
raze * H

/ā/ Suffixes

-ade noun;
denotes action or process of acting
blockade
cannonade
masquerade
renegade

-ade noun;
indicating a drink made from fruit
lemonade
limeade
orangeade

-ate noun;
state, office, function
candidate
delegate
invertebrate

-ate verb
accelerate
calibrate
designate
differentiate
litigate
primate

-ation noun;
action, resulting state
aggravation
revelation
specialization

a
Indefinite Article
When unstressed, it is pronounced *uh*.

When stressed, it is pronounced /ā/.

-ay
allay *
array *
assay *
crayfish
day
decay
delay
dismay *
flay *
foray *
fray *
gray
pray
relay
slay
spray
stray
tray
way H

-eigh
Only three common words.
neigh SL
sleigh H
weigh H Sp

-ai
-aid
braid H
staid H

-ail
bail H
fail
hail H
mail H
pail H
quail *
rail H
sail H
tail H
wail H

-aint
faint H
quaint
saint
taint

-aise
braise
chaise
praise H
raise H

-ait
bait H
gait H
strait H
trait
wait H

-et
Words of French origin. See Silent Letters, page 258.
ballet
fillet

-ei-
beige /j/
deign * SL
eight SL
feign * SL
feint * H
freight SL
heinous *
lei flowers
neighbor SL
reign * H
rein H
reindeer
sei H whale
seine H
veil H
vein H
weigh H Sp

Initial Long Vowel:
ache
acre
agency
aid H
ail H
aim
alias
alien
anal
ancient
angel Sp
ape
apex
aphid
asymmetric
AWOL

-ee
Words of French origin.
entree
matinee
melee *
nee
toupee
Different from -ee suffix. See page 297.
absentee
escapee

-ey
convey *
grey
hey Int
heyday
whey

Word Study
Make a Two-Tab Foldable and use it to differentiate between the articles *a* and *an*.

Key:
* = test prep
Cl = clipped word
H = heteronym, homograph, homophone
Int = interjection
Sp = spelling demon

(outside)

(inside)

Accordion Foldable® (above): Use three sheets of 8½" x 11" paper to make the Accordion Foldable pictured at the bottom of this page. Leave the tab on the last section so more pages can be added in the future. See page 403.

Book Jacket (left): Students were given ten minutes to find 20 words spelled with a given vowel sound and write them in their book jackets. Students then sorted the words into groups according to what letters formed the sound. Students exchanged book jackets and asked each other to spell the words they collected. See page 414.

Matchbook Foldable® (below): Use one sheet of 11" x 17" paper for the base of the Foldable pictured below. Glue 18 small matchbooks onto the base. Use to collect words with a specified vowel sound. Put pictures, definitions, or simple sentences under the tabs. See page 400.

Triple VKV Flashcard (below): This Triple VKV Flashcard forms six words—three plural nouns and three singular nouns. Notice that the singular word are formed by folding the end of the flashcard over to cover the **-s**.

Variation: Write singular nouns on the VKV and fold the right edge over with an **-s** written on the back to form the plural.

Note: Use giant rubber bands to keep completed notebook pages closed and to mark the page currently being used.

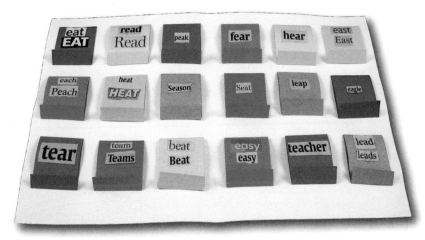

Word Study:
Add the suffix **-ee** to verbs to form nouns.
Example: *offeree*
See list, page 297.

-ea
already
breath
deaf
dread
feather
head
heaven
heavy
leather
meadow
measure
pleasant
ready
spread
steady
swear
sweat
thread
threat
treasure
wealth
weapon
wear [H]
weather

/e/ or /i/
Spelled e
Prefixes and Combining Forms

Spelling /e/

Latin:

en-, em-
embolden
empathy *
empower
enamor
enhance *
enslave

equi- equilateral
equilibrium
equinox

ex- exacerbate
exasperate *
exempt
expedite *
extant *
extenuate *

ec- eccentric
eclectic
eclipse
ecstasy
eczema

ef- effective
efficient
effort

e- enervate [Sp]
emit
erase
eternal

ex- ex-president
ex-girlfriend
ex-sheriff

extra-, extro-
extrajudicial
extralimital
extraterrestrial
extrovert

Greek:

eco-
ecology
ecosystem *
ecotourism

ect-, ecto-
ectal
ectoderm
ectoplasm
ectotherm

ep-, eph-, epi-
ephedrine
epidermis
epicenter
epigram
epilogue *
epiphyte
epoch *

ex-, exo-, ecto-
ectoplasm
exocentric
exoskeleton
exosphere
extradition

Both
exempt
exasperate
exacerbate

Medial
/e/ Phonograms

-ealth
health
wealth
stealth
-ed
bled
fled
shred
-edge
hedge
ledge
pledge
-eft
bereft
cleft
theft
-eg
dregs
leg
nutmeg
-eld
beheld
meld
weld [H]
-ell
dwell
quell
swell
-elp
help
kelp
whelp [SL]
yelp
-elt
dwelt
knelt [SL]
pelt [H]
smelt

-em
ahem [Int]
gem
stem
them
-en
yen [H]
glen
wren [SL]
-ence
fence
hence
whence
-ench
clench
drench
quench
stench
trench
wrench [H]
-empt
attempt
comtempt
preempt
unkempt
-end
blend
spend
trendy
-ense
dense
sense [H]
tense
-ent
scent [H]
sent [H]
spent
vent

-ep
rep [Cl]
pep
step [H]
steppe [H]
-ept
crept
inept
slept
wept
-esh
enmesh
flesh
fresh
-ess
chess
dutchess
stress
tress
-est
crest
quest
wrest [H]
zest [H]
-et
abet
amulet
asset
beset
fret [H]
whet [SL]

Initial
e-
echo
eddy *
edge
edit
education
egg
elbow
elephant
elevator
else
empty
enemy

energy
engine
enjoy
enter
entrance
enzyme
epic *
epicure *
essay
estimate
etching *
extra

-e Suffixes
Some Do Not Have /e/ Sound

-ed v./adj.
censured *
enhanced *
parched *
-en v.
embolden
lengthen
whiten

-ence n.
abstinence *
convergence *
independence
reference
-ent n./adj.
benevolent *
divergent *
resilient *
superintendent [Sp]
-es, -ies pl.

-ess n.
countess
hieress
seamstress
-est adj.
astutest
choicest
dreariest
healthiest
sightest

Spelling ē Sound

Word Study: ennui
[ahn•wee]
French loanword; utter weariness, boredom

Initial
each
eager
eagle
eaglet
earring
ease
easel
east
easy
eat
eaves
edict *
eon *
equal
eve
even
evening
evil

-eer
Noun Suffix; originally in Fr. loanwords; persons who
auctioneer
buccaneer
engineer
mountaineer
mutineer
pioneer

-ee-
beetle
between
breeze
creek H
creep
discreet * H
eel
esteem
fleece *
fleet
freeze H
genteel *
heed * H
indeed
kneel
leech
leeward
needle
peerless *
preen *
redeem *
screen H
seethe *
sheer * H
sleek
sleet
sneeze
steep *
sweeping
vaneer *
veer *
wheedle *
wheel

-ea Phonograms

-ea
flea H
pea H
plea
sea H
tea H

-each
bleach
breach *
impeach *
peach
preach

-ead
bead
knead H
lead H
plead
read H

-eak
bleak *
freak
streak
tweak

-eal
congeal *
squeal
steal H
surreal *
veal
zeal

-eam
gleam
ream
stream

-ean
demeanor *
mean * H
glean

-eap
cheap
heap
leap
reap

-ease
appease *
disease
please
tease

-east
beast
feast
least
yeast

-eave
bereave *
cleave
upheaval *

-eat
entreat *
pleat

-ee Final
agree
apogee *
coffee
decree *
degree
emcee
filigree *
guarantee Sp
jubilee
levee H
pedigree
toffee

-ee Noun Suffix denotes people
absentee
devotee
employee
escapee
grantee
invitee
referee
refugee
trustee

-oe
amoeba

-eCe
Long e, silent e.
complete
concrete
discrete H
replete
scheme
secede
secrete
sleeve
theme

e- Technology Prefix
e-book
e-business
e-cash
e-commerce
e-group
e-mail, email
e-store

-ey
medley *
monkey *
motley *
trolley
turkey
valley

-ei
ceiling
conceit
deceit *
deceive Sp
leisure Sp
protein
receive Sp
seize Sp
seizure Sp
sheik Sp
weird Sp

-y Adjective Suffix
blurry
dreary
grouchy
juicy
zany
Word list on page 287.

-ear
endear *
fear
gear
sear * H
shear * H
year

-ia Noun Suffix
anemia
bacteria
malaria
phobia

-ie
achieve
aggrieve *
alien
believe Sp
besiege * Sp
brie
brief
chief
fief
fiend
mien * H
niece Sp
piece H
relief Sp
relieve Sp
shriek
spiel *
thief Sp
unwieldy *
yield Sp

ier- eir-
coheir
fierce
pierce
See page 339.

-e
abalone

-i
broccoli Sp
confetti
daiquiri
hibachi
Nazi
quasi
spaghetti
taxi

Suffixes
See page 278.
-ly
defiantly
fluently

-ium Latin, Noun Suffix
consortium
delirium
odium
tedium

Vowels Spelling /i/

Spelling Ĭ Sound

Prefixes

in-
English; in
- income
- ingrown
- inland

il-, im-, in-, ir-
Latin origin; in
- illegal
- immigrate
- impair *
- impeach *
- imperative
- imperial *   import *
- incarcerate
- innate   inquire
- inside   intrusive
- invade   inverse
- investigate
- irrigate

il-, im-, in-, ir-
Latin origin; negative, similar to *un-*
- illiterate
- immeasurable
- impartial *
- inattention
- indefensible
- inexpensive
- inexperienced
- irregular

inter- Latin origin; between, among, mutually, during, together
- intercept
- intercom
- interdepartmental
- interdependent
- interest
- interior
- intermission
- intermittent
- interview

intra- Latin origin; within, on the inside
- intramural
- intrastate
- intravenous

intro- Latin origin; to the inside
- introjection
- introspection
- introverted

Suffixes

-ic, -ics
- mathematics

-ice
- malice

-ile
- projectile also /ī/

-ing adj.
- cohering

-ing noun
- building

-ing verb
- designing

-ish
- bluish

-ism
- commercialism

-ist
- pharmacist

-ity
- nativity

-ive, -itive
adj.
- sensitive

-ive n.
- native

> The pronunciation of an **-i** that precedes /ŋ/ (*-ing* as in *sing* and *-ink* as in *sink*) often sounds similar to /ē/. This might be confusing for ESL/ELL students since the *-ing* and *-ink* rimes are sometimes included in the teaching of /i/ words.

i-e
- give
- live

Medial
Phonograms

-ib
- crib
- fib
- gib

-ick
- flick
- slick
- thick
- trick

-id
- grid
- quid
- skid
- slid

-iff
- midriff
- skiff
- tiff
- whiff

-ift
- drift
- rift
- shift
- swift
- thrift

-ig
- brig
- jig
- sprig
- swig
- twig

-ild
- build
- guild

-ilk
- bilk
- milk
- silk

-ill
- krill
- shrill
- swill
- twill

-ilt
- hilt
- kilt
- quilt
- stilt
- wilt

-im
- brim
- prim
- vim
- whim

-imp
- blimp
- crimp
- limp
- skimp

-in
- chin
- shin
- tin
- twin

-ince
- mince
- since
- wince
- prince

-inch
- cinch
- clinch
- finch
- winch

-ing
- cling
- string
- wring

-inge
- binge
- cringe
- fringe
- hinge
- singe
- tinge
- twinge

-ink
- bring
- chink
- shrink
- slink

-int
- lint
- glint
- splint
- sprint
- squint
- stint

-ip
- blip
- quip
- snip
- strip

-ish
- dish
- fish
- swish
- wish

-isk
- disk
- frisk
- risk
- whisk

-isp
- crisp
- lisp
- wisp

-iss
- bliss
- dismiss
- hiss

-ist
- mist
- grist
- twist
- wrist

-it
- knit
- grit
- quit
- slit
- split

-ix
- fix
- mix
- six

-y-
- crypt
- crystal
- cystic
- dyslexic
- gym
- hymn
- krypt
- mystic
- myth
- platypus
- symbol
- tryst

e-
- efface
- effect
- effeminate
- effusive

-age
- acreage
- carriage
- cartilage
- hermitage
- language
- marriage
- pillage
- suffrage
- village
- voyage

Initial
- idiom *
- idiosyncrasy Sp
- igloo
- igneous
- ignore
- inalienable *
- inane *
- inch
- incite *
- inept *
- infer *
- inimitable
- iniquity
- initial
- insect
- intrigue *
- issue
- isthmus *
- italic

ie-, ei-
- forfeit
- friend
- mischief
- sieve

See page 347 for examples of the /ē/ sound.

Key:
- * = test prep
- Cl = clipped word
- H = heteronym, homograph, homophone
- Int = interjection
- Sp = spelling demon

Spelling ī Sound

Medial

Phonograms

-ibe
bribe
jibe
scribe
tribe

-ice
slice
splice
thrice
twice
vice H

-ide
chide
pride
snide
stride

-ife
fife
knife
rife
strife

-ike
pike H
spike
strike

-ile
bile
pile H
vile
while

-ime
clime H
grime
mime
prime H

-ine
brine
shrine
swine
tine
whine

-ipe
gripe
snipe
swipe
tripe

-ire
hire
spire
tire H
wire

-ise
guise H
rise
wise

-ite
mite H
quite
rite H
sprite

-ive
chive
drive
rive
strive
thrive

Silent Final e

-ier -ies
brier
crier, cries
drier, dries
flier, flies
skies
tries

Final
alibi
alumni
cacti
gemini
hi H
magi
pi H
stimuli

Phonograms
These phonograms can make the long and short sound. See page 203.

-ild
child
mild
wild

-ind
hind
rind
wind H

Test Prep
abide *
ascribe *
aspire *
chide *
concise *
contrite *
demise *
deride *
despite
divine *
entice *
excise *
imbibe *
inspire *
ire *
knife
mire *
quite
reside *
revile *
revive *
rife *
strife *
sublime *
subside *
thrive *
vile

Initial
ibex
Iberian
iceberg Sp
icing H
icicle
icon
idea
ideal
identify
idol * H
idyllic *
iodine
iota *
I'm
irate *
ironic *
irony
island *
isolated *
isosceles
isotherm
isotope
item
ivory
ivy

-y
vowel
ally
asylum *
awry *
byte H
certify *
clarify *
comply *
cycle
cypress
decry *
deny
diversify *
dynasty
gyrate *
hydra
hyena
hype
hyphen
lying
modify *
myopia
pacify *
ply
pry
python
rely
reply
rhyme Sp
spry

-igh
-ight silent gh
blight
bright
fight
flight
high H
light
might H
nigh
night H
right H
sight H
slight
thigh
tight

-ie -ied
belie *
cried
die H
fie
lie H
lied
pie H
pied
plied
relied
vie

Suffix
-ite noun
ammonite
graphite
Israelite
malachite

-ye
aye H
dye H
eye H
lye H
rye

Suffixes
-iatry noun
podiatry
psychiatry
-ile adjective
infantile
-phile noun
bibliophile
-ize verb
hypothesize

-ei
feisty
Geiger
counter
height
heist
neither (also pronounced /ē/)
seism, seismic
stein

Medial
giant
lion
pilot
spider
title
trifle

Prefixes
bi-
bipedal
bivalve
biweekly
di-
didactyl
digest
diglycerides
divergent
dia-
diagonal
diameter
tri-
triad
triangle
tripod

-ai
bonsai
chai H
(pronounced chī and shē)
haikai
nilgai
shanghai

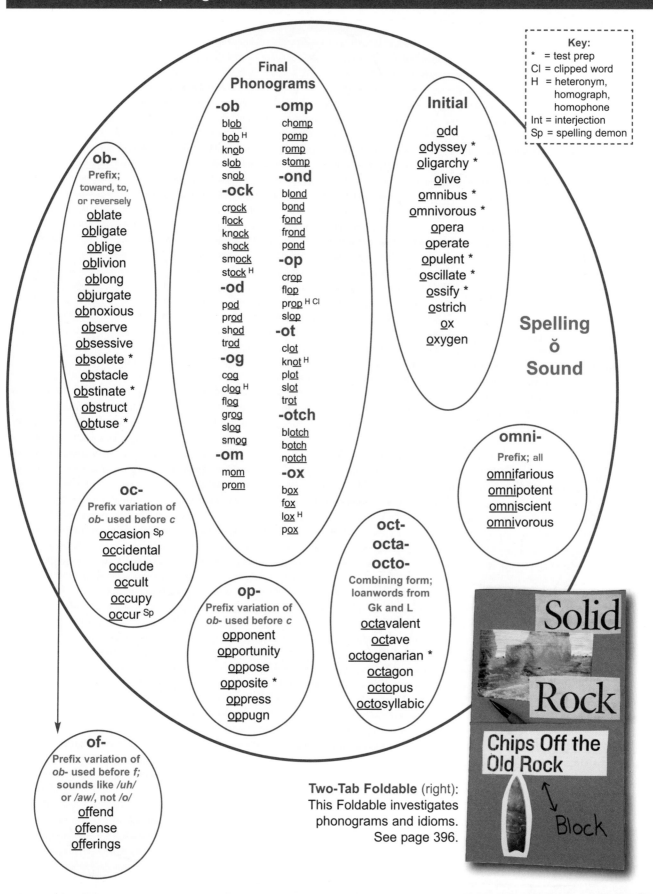

Key:
* = test prep
Cl = clipped word
H = heteronym, homograph, homophone
Int = interjection
Sp = spelling demon

Final Phonograms

-ob
blob
bob H
knob
slob
snob

-ock
crock
flock
knock
shock
smock
stock H

-od
pod
prod
shod
trod

-og
cog
clog H
flog
grog
slog
smog

-om
mom
prom

-omp
chomp
pomp
romp
stomp

-ond
blond
bond
fond
frond
pond

-op
crop
flop
prop H Cl
slop

-ot
clot
knot H
plot
slot
trot

-otch
blotch
botch
notch

-ox
box
fox
lox H
pox

Initial
odd
odyssey *
oligarchy *
olive
omnibus *
omnivorous *
opera
operate
opulent *
oscillate *
ossify *
ostrich
ox
oxygen

Spelling ŏ Sound

ob-
Prefix; toward, to, or reversely
oblate
obligate
oblige
oblivion
oblong
objurgate
obnoxious
observe
obsessive
obsolete *
obstacle
obstinate *
obstruct
obtuse *

oc-
Prefix variation of *ob-* used before *c*
occasion Sp
occidental
occlude
occult
occupy
occur Sp

op-
Prefix variation of *ob-* used before *c*
opponent
opportunity
oppose
opposite *
oppress
oppugn

**oct-
octa-
octo-**
Combining form; loanwords from Gk and L
octavalent
octave
octogenarian *
octagon
octopus
octosyllabic

omni-
Prefix; all
omnifarious
omnipotent
omniscient
omnivorous

of-
Prefix variation of *ob-* used before *f*; sounds like /uh/ or /aw/, not /o/
offend
offense
offerings

Two-Tab Foldable (right): This Foldable investigates phonograms and idioms. See page 396.

Solid
Rock
Chips Off the Old Rock
Block

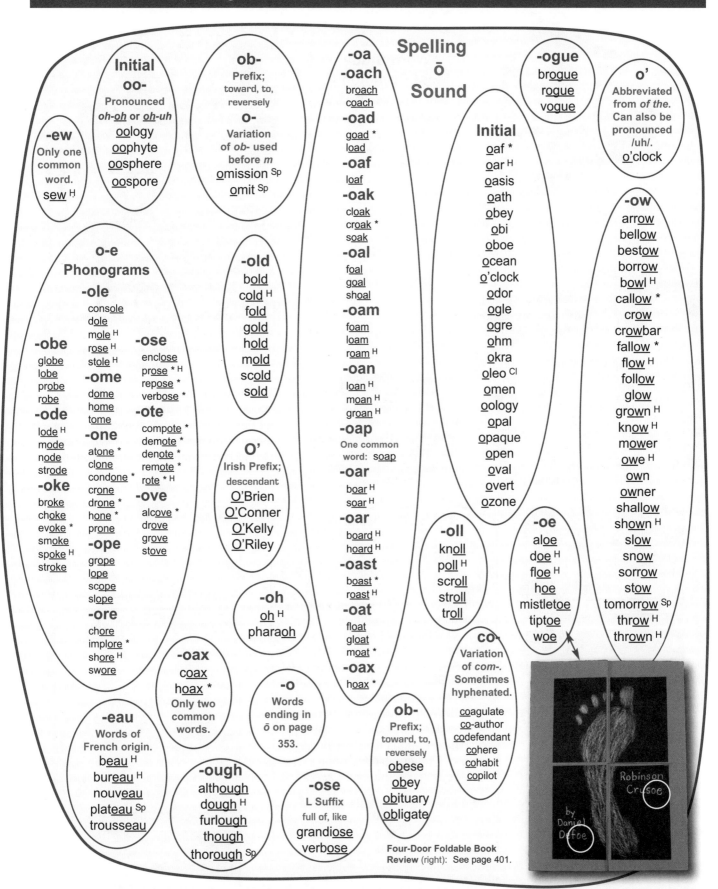

Spelling ō Sound

-ew
Only one common word.
s<u>ew</u> ᴴ

Initial oo-
Pronounced oh-<u>oh</u> or <u>oh</u>-uh
<u>oo</u>logy
<u>oo</u>phyte
<u>oo</u>sphere
<u>oo</u>spore

ob-
Prefix; toward, to, reversely
o-
Variation of ob- used before m
<u>o</u>mission ˢᵖ
<u>o</u>mit ˢᵖ

-oa -oach
br<u>oa</u>ch
c<u>oa</u>ch
-oad
g<u>oa</u>d *
l<u>oa</u>d
-oaf
l<u>oa</u>f
-oak
cl<u>oa</u>k
cr<u>oa</u>k *
s<u>oa</u>k
-oal
f<u>oa</u>l
g<u>oa</u>l
sh<u>oa</u>l
-oam
f<u>oa</u>m
l<u>oa</u>m
r<u>oa</u>m ᴴ
-oan
l<u>oa</u>n ᴴ
m<u>oa</u>n ᴴ
gr<u>oa</u>n ᴴ
-oap
One common word: s<u>oa</u>p
-oar
b<u>oa</u>r ᴴ
s<u>oa</u>r ᴴ
-oar
b<u>oar</u>d ᴴ
h<u>oar</u>d ᴴ
-oast
b<u>oa</u>st *
r<u>oa</u>st ᴴ
-oat
fl<u>oa</u>t
gl<u>oa</u>t *
m<u>oa</u>t *
-oax
h<u>oa</u>x *

-ogue
br<u>ogue</u>
r<u>ogue</u>
v<u>ogue</u>

o'
Abbreviated from of the. Can also be pronounced /uh/.
<u>o</u>'clock

Initial
<u>o</u>af *
<u>o</u>ar ᴴ
<u>o</u>asis
<u>o</u>ath
<u>o</u>bey
<u>o</u>bi
<u>o</u>boe
<u>o</u>cean
<u>o</u>'clock
<u>o</u>dor
<u>o</u>gle
<u>o</u>gre
<u>o</u>hm
<u>o</u>kra
<u>o</u>leo ᶜˡ
<u>o</u>men
<u>o</u>ology
<u>o</u>pal
<u>o</u>paque
<u>o</u>pen
<u>o</u>val
<u>o</u>vert
<u>o</u>zone

-ow
arr<u>ow</u>
bell<u>ow</u>
best<u>ow</u>
borr<u>ow</u>
b<u>ow</u>l ᴴ
call<u>ow</u> *
cr<u>ow</u>
cr<u>ow</u>bar
fall<u>ow</u> *
fl<u>ow</u> ᴴ
foll<u>ow</u>
gl<u>ow</u>
gr<u>ow</u>n ᴴ
kn<u>ow</u> ᴴ
m<u>ow</u>er
<u>ow</u>e ᴴ
<u>ow</u>n
<u>ow</u>ner
shall<u>ow</u>
sh<u>ow</u>n ᴴ
sl<u>ow</u>
sn<u>ow</u>
sorr<u>ow</u>
st<u>ow</u>
tomorr<u>ow</u> ˢᵖ
thr<u>ow</u> ᴴ
thr<u>ow</u>n ᴴ

o-e Phonograms

-ole
cons<u>ole</u>
d<u>ole</u>
m<u>ole</u> ᴴ
r<u>ose</u> ᴴ
st<u>ole</u> ᴴ

-obe
gl<u>obe</u>
l<u>obe</u>
pr<u>obe</u>
r<u>obe</u>
-ode
l<u>ode</u> ᴴ
m<u>ode</u>
n<u>ode</u>
str<u>ode</u>
-oke
br<u>oke</u>
ch<u>oke</u>
ev<u>oke</u> *
sm<u>oke</u>
sp<u>oke</u> ᴴ
str<u>oke</u>

-ose
encl<u>ose</u>
pr<u>ose</u> * ᴴ
rep<u>ose</u> *
verb<u>ose</u> *
-ome
d<u>ome</u>
h<u>ome</u>
t<u>ome</u>
-ote
comp<u>ote</u> *
dem<u>ote</u> *
den<u>ote</u> *
rem<u>ote</u> *
r<u>ote</u> * ᴴ
-one
at<u>one</u> *
cl<u>one</u>
cond<u>one</u> *
cr<u>one</u>
dr<u>one</u> *
h<u>one</u> *
pr<u>one</u>
-ove
alc<u>ove</u> *
dr<u>ove</u>
gr<u>ove</u>
st<u>ove</u>
-ope
gr<u>ope</u>
l<u>ope</u>
sc<u>ope</u>
sl<u>ope</u>
-ore
ch<u>ore</u>
impl<u>ore</u> *
sh<u>ore</u> ᴴ
sw<u>ore</u>

-old
b<u>old</u>
c<u>old</u> ᴴ
f<u>old</u>
g<u>old</u>
h<u>old</u>
m<u>old</u>
sc<u>old</u>
s<u>old</u>

O'
Irish Prefix; descendant
<u>O</u>'Brien
<u>O</u>'Conner
<u>O</u>'Kelly
<u>O</u>'Riley

-oh
<u>oh</u> ᴴ
phara<u>oh</u>

-oax
c<u>oa</u>x
h<u>oa</u>x *
Only two common words.

-o
Words ending in ō on page 353.

-oll
kn<u>oll</u>
p<u>oll</u> ᴴ
scr<u>oll</u>
str<u>oll</u>
tr<u>oll</u>

-oe
al<u>oe</u>
d<u>oe</u> ᴴ
fl<u>oe</u> ᴴ
h<u>oe</u>
mistlet<u>oe</u>
tipt<u>oe</u>
w<u>oe</u>

co-
Variation of com-. Sometimes hyphenated.
<u>co</u>agulate
<u>co</u>-author
<u>co</u>defendant
<u>co</u>here
<u>co</u>habit
<u>co</u>pilot

-eau
Words of French origin.
b<u>eau</u> ᴴ
bur<u>eau</u> ᴴ
nouv<u>eau</u>
plat<u>eau</u> ˢᵖ
trouss<u>eau</u>

-ough
alth<u>ough</u>
d<u>ough</u> ᴴ
furl<u>ough</u>
th<u>ough</u>
thor<u>ough</u> ˢᵖ

-ose
L Suffix full of, like
grandi<u>ose</u>
verb<u>ose</u>

ob-
Prefix; toward, to, reversely
<u>ob</u>ese
<u>ob</u>ey
<u>ob</u>ituary
<u>ob</u>ligate

Four-Door Foldable Book Review (right): See page 401.

Robinson Crusoe
by Daniel Defoe

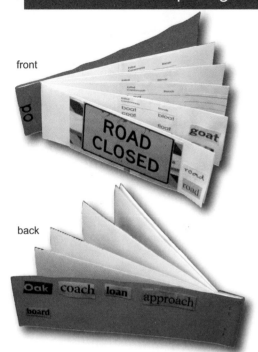

front

back

Sentence Strip Foldable (above):
Six half-sheets of paper were used
to make this vowel-based vocabulary
teaching aid. ESL/ELL students
collected terms from RWP, examples
of other terms with the same phonograms, and graphics to illustrate
some of the terms. See page 413.

Word Study:
**Most Common *O*-
Surnames In U.S.**

(in alphabetical order):

O'Brian
Ochoa
O'Connor
Odom
O'Neal
O'Nell
Orr
Ortega
Ortiz
Osborn, Osborne
Owen, Owens

Source: 1990 U.S. Census
Bureau; www.mongabay.com

**Plurals of
Words Ending
in -o**:
See page 219.

Mr. PRESIDENT
Obama landslide signals new era for America

Shutterfold Project: U.S. President
Barack Obama [ō•bä•mə] has a name
that begins with the /ō/ sound; but, unlike
names of Irish origin like O'Kelly, it does
not have punctuation after the first letter.

Triple VKV Flashcards:
The three-word VKV Flashcard (left)
was made using words found in RWP.
It focuses on the combining form *eco-*.
(See the Word Study below.) The four-
word Triple VKV Flashcard (right)
focuses on the phonogram *-ote*, and
the *silent -e rule*.

Word Study: **Combining Forms**
Define and collect examples of
combining forms ending in *-o*.
Compare and contrast final *-o*
combining forms, affixes, and clipped
words. Find combining forms in the
word list on the next page.

Examples of Combining Forms:
biblio-
bio-
eco-

Final -o

Open syllable rule: An open syllable has only one vowel that occurs at the end of the syllable.

afficionado	commando	grandioso	manifesto *	pompano	tangelo
ago	Congo	gringo	matzo, -ah	poncho	tango
Alamo	credo	grotto	memento * Sp	portabello	Tejano
Alfredo	crescendo *	guano	memo CI	portfolio	tempo *
alfresco	de facto	gumbo	metro CI	portico	terrazzo
Afro	demo CI	gusto	Mexico	potato	tobacco
allegro	desperado	gyro	micro-	presidio	Tokyo
also	disco CI	hallo Int	milo	presto	Toledo
alto	ditto	hello Int	mono-	primero	tomatillo
amigo	dodo	hero	Morocco	primo	tomato
amino acid	domino H	hidalgo	mosquito	pronto	tornado
Apollo	dynamo	hobo	motto	proviso *	toro
archipelago *	echo	honcho	mucho slang	pseudo-	Toronto
arroyo	ego	hydro-	mumbo jumbo	Pueblo	torpedo
audio	electro-	Idaho	narco-	pueblo	torso
auto CI	Elmo	impresario	Navajo	queso	tostado, -da
bambino	embargo *	incognito	Negro	radio	trio
banjo	embryo	indigo	neutrino	ratio	turbo
basso	enviro-	inferno	nitro-	repo CI	typo CI
beefalo	ergo	info CI	no H	risotto	vaquero
bingo	Eskimo	innuendo *	Ohio	rodeo	Velcro®
bongo	espresso	intro CI	oleo CI	romeo	vertigo *
bravado	Euro, euro	jalapeno	oregano	sago	veto
bravo	expo CI	Jell-O®	Oreo®	saguaro	vibrato
bronco	falsetto *	jumbo	Pacino, Al	salvo	video
buffalo	farrago *	kilo CI	paisano	San Antonio	volcano
burrito	fiasco *	kimono	palmetto	scenario	weirdo
burro	flamenco	largo	palomino	serrano	yo Int
cacao	flamingo	lasso	patio	sicko slang	yo-yo
Cairo	folio	Latino	peccadillo *	silo	zero
cajunto music	forego	libido	peso	so H	
calico	forgo * H	libretto	pesto	solo *	
cameo	fresco	limbo	petro-	soprano	
cappuccino	garbanzo	limo CI	photo CI	staccato	
cargo	gauchos	lobo	phyllo, filo	steno CI	
casino	gazebo	loco slang	piano	stereo	
Castro, Fidel	gecko	lotto	Picasso, Pablo	stiletto	
cello	gelato	lumbago	pimiento	stucco	
chemo CI	geo-	macho	pinto	studio	
Chicago	gesso	macro-	placebo	sub-zero	
Chicano	ghetto	mako	Pluto	sumo	
Colorado	gismo	mambo	polio	synchro-	
combo	go	mango	polo	taco	

Word Study: /u/ Spelling Gremlins

Find examples of words spelled with the vowels a, e, i, and o, but that have the /uh/ sound.

a-

Prefix a- can sound like /uh/. See other examples of /uh/ spelled a on page 366.

ab<u>a</u>te
<u>a</u>bout
<u>a</u>ffront
<u>a</u>go
<u>a</u>ppalled
<u>a</u>ppear
<u>a</u>scend

-e-

anth<u>e</u>m
probl<u>e</u>m
strat<u>e</u>gem
syst<u>e</u>m
theor<u>e</u>m
xyl<u>e</u>m

-i-

an<u>i</u>mal
an<u>i</u>mate
an<u>i</u>mus
unan<u>i</u>mous

-o-

c<u>o</u>ndemn
n<u>o</u>ne [H]
<u>o</u>bjection
<u>o</u>ther
sm<u>o</u>ther
s<u>o</u>n [H]
t<u>o</u>n
w<u>o</u>n [H]

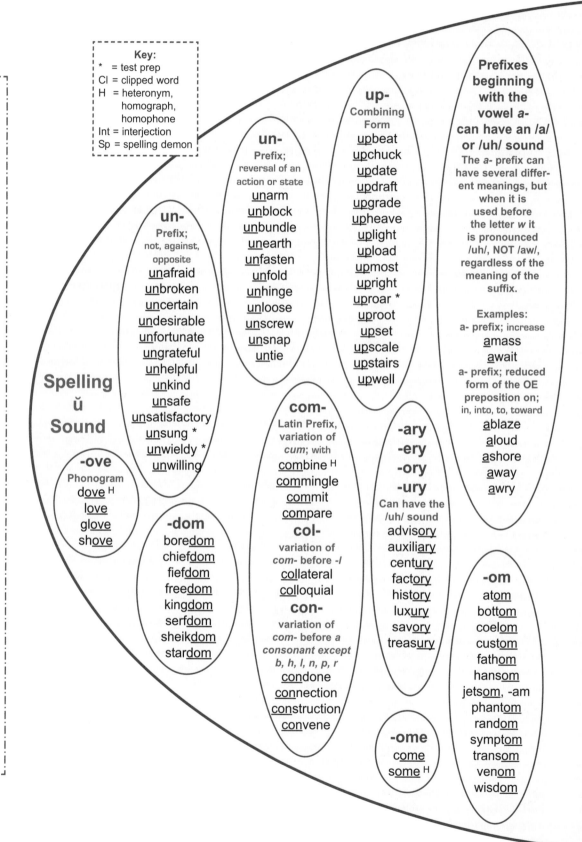

Key:
* = test prep
Cl = clipped word
H = heteronym, homograph, homophone
Int = interjection
Sp = spelling demon

Spelling ŭ Sound

un-
Prefix; not, against, opposite
<u>un</u>afraid
<u>un</u>broken
<u>un</u>certain
<u>un</u>desirable
<u>un</u>fortunate
<u>un</u>grateful
<u>un</u>helpful
<u>un</u>kind
<u>un</u>safe
<u>un</u>satisfactory
<u>un</u>sung *
<u>un</u>wieldy *
<u>un</u>willing

-ove
Phonogram
d<u>ove</u> [H]
l<u>ove</u>
gl<u>ove</u>
sh<u>ove</u>

-dom
bore<u>dom</u>
chief<u>dom</u>
fief<u>dom</u>
free<u>dom</u>
king<u>dom</u>
serf<u>dom</u>
sheik<u>dom</u>
star<u>dom</u>

un-
Prefix; reversal of an action or state
<u>un</u>arm
<u>un</u>block
<u>un</u>bundle
<u>un</u>earth
<u>un</u>fasten
<u>un</u>fold
<u>un</u>hinge
<u>un</u>loose
<u>un</u>screw
<u>un</u>snap
<u>un</u>tie

up-
Combining Form
<u>up</u>beat
<u>up</u>chuck
<u>up</u>date
<u>up</u>draft
<u>up</u>grade
<u>up</u>heave
<u>up</u>light
<u>up</u>load
<u>up</u>most
<u>up</u>right
<u>up</u>roar *
<u>up</u>root
<u>up</u>set
<u>up</u>scale
<u>up</u>stairs
<u>up</u>well

com-
Latin Prefix, variation of *cum*; with
<u>com</u>bine [H]
<u>com</u>mingle
<u>com</u>mit
<u>com</u>pare

col-
variation of *com-* before -l
<u>col</u>lateral
<u>col</u>loquial

con-
variation of *com-* before a consonant except b, h, l, n, p, r
<u>con</u>done
<u>con</u>nection
<u>con</u>struction
<u>con</u>vene

-ary
-ery
-ory
-ury
Can have the /uh/ sound
advis<u>ory</u>
auxili<u>ary</u>
cent<u>ury</u>
fact<u>ory</u>
hist<u>ory</u>
lux<u>ury</u>
sav<u>ory</u>
treas<u>ury</u>

-ome
c<u>ome</u>
s<u>ome</u> [H]

-om
at<u>om</u>
bott<u>om</u>
coel<u>om</u>
cust<u>om</u>
fath<u>om</u>
hans<u>om</u>
jets<u>om</u>, -am
phant<u>om</u>
rand<u>om</u>
sympt<u>om</u>
trans<u>om</u>
ven<u>om</u>
wisd<u>om</u>

Prefixes beginning with the vowel a- can have an /a/ or /uh/ sound

The a- prefix can have several different meanings, but when it is used before the letter w it is pronounced /uh/, NOT /aw/, regardless of the meaning of the suffix.

Examples:
a- prefix; increase
<u>a</u>mass
<u>a</u>wait
a- prefix; reduced form of the OE preposition on; in, into, to, toward
<u>a</u>blaze
<u>a</u>loud
<u>a</u>shore
<u>a</u>way
<u>a</u>wry

n. vb.
tr j ust

j ust

n.
crust

vb.
Base
Past Tense
Past Part.

Phonograms

-ud	-ulk	-un	-up
bud	bulk	shun	cup
cud	hulk	spun	pup
dud	sulk	stun	sup
spud	**-ull**	**-unch**	**-us**
stud	bull H	brunch	bus
thud	full	crunch	plus

-ub
grub H
hub
nub
scrub
shrub
snub
stub

-uck
muck
pluck
puck
shuck
struck
yuck

-udge
budge
fudge H
grudge
nudge
sludge
smudge
trudge

-uff
bluff
buff
gruff
scuff

-ug
mug
pug
slug
smug
thug

pull
-um
chum
glum
scum
slum
strum
swum

-umb
crumb
dumb
numb
plumb H
thumb

-ump
chump
clump
plump
slump
stump
trump

hunch
munch
punch

-ung
clung
dung
flung
sprung
wrung H

-unk
punk
shrunk
skunk
spunk
trunk

-unt
blunt
bunt
punt
runt
shunt
stunt

pus
thus

-ush
blush
crush
gush
hush
plush
thrush H

-uss
cuss
fuss
muss
truss

-ust
crust
gust
just
rust
trust

-ut
glut
gut
hut
jut
rut
shut
strut

-utch
clutch
crutch
hutch

-utt
butt H
mutt
putt

Final -a
/uh/ sound
alfalfa
algebra
aqua
aroma
balsa
cola
comma
dogma
enigma
henna
iguana
kiva
lava
mantra
opera
polka
rutabaga
salsa
scuba
terra
tundra
umbra
vista
yoga
zebra

o'
Abbreviated
from of the. Also
pronounced /ō/.
o'clock

Spelling ŭ Sound

-er-
Medial
Before -ate
accelerate
exaggerate
generate
operate
proliferate
tolerate
venerate
Final
When -y is
added after -er
battery
discovery
flattery
jittery
lottery
pottery

-ough
Phonogram
enough
rough
tough
slough

Initial
udder
ugly
ulcer
ultra
umbel
umber
umbra
umbrage *
umbrella
umpire
uncle
unctuous *
uneven
ugly
unguent *
usher
utter

-um -ium
L Suffix
colloquium
consortium
delirium
equilibrium
millennium
Metals
aluminum
barium
beryllium
cadmium
titanium

-ence
benevolence
condolence
indolence
insolence
malevolence
redolence
somnolence
violence

-ou
country
couple
double
enough
rough
slough
tough
trouble

thr ust

vb.
Base
Past Tense
Past Part.

Four-Word Triple VKV Flashcard (above):
See page 388.

Vowels Spelling ū, /yoo/

Yellow /ū/, /yoo/
Violet /oo/

Spelling ū /yoo/ Sound

-ou
Final
you [H]
See Word Study, next page.

BOTH: Words with two pronunciations -- /yoo/ and /oo/.

/yoo/ Phonograms

-ube
cube
tube

-uge
centrifuge
huge

-uke
puke

-ule
mule
pule
yule [H]

-ume
costume
fume
legume
perfume
spume
volume

-une
tune

-ure
cure
demure

-use
abuse
accuse
excuse
fuse
muse

-ute
cute
mute

/yoo/ Initial Including the prefix *uni-*

ubiquitous *
unicellular
unicorn
unicycle
uniform
unify
unilateral *
unique
unit

unitarian
united
universe
university
urea
urine
usage
use
useful
usual
usurp *

usury *
utensil
utilitarian *
utility
utilize *
utopia
utopian *

/yoo/ -u-, -ue
argue
avenue
barbecue
continue
cue
hue
menu
value

BOTH due impromptu

/oo/ -u-, -ue
blue [H]
clue
cruel
flue [H]
glue
pursue
rumor
sue
sumo
tissue
true

/yoo/ spelled ew
askew
curfew
ewe [H]
few
hew [H]
nephew
newbie
mew [H]
pew [H]
preview
review
skewer
view
yew [H]

BOTH
dew [H]
knew [H]
new [H]
newt
stew
steward

/oo/ spelled -ew
blew [H]
brew
cashew
drew
flew [H]
grew
jewel
screw
slew [H]
strew
threw [H]

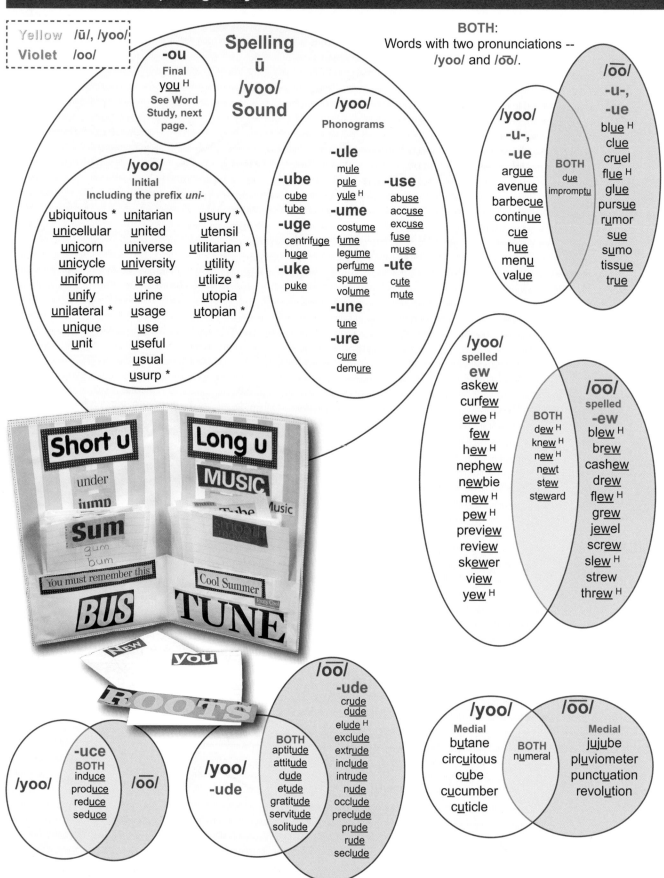

/yoo/   **-uce** BOTH
induce
produce
reduce
seduce   **/oo/**

/yoo/ -ude

BOTH
aptitude
attitude
dude
etude
gratitude
servitude
solitude

/oo/ -ude
crude
dude
elude [H]
exclude
extrude
include
intrude
nude
occlude
preclude
prude
rude
seclude

/yoo/ Medial
butane
circuitous
cube
cucumber
cuticle

BOTH numeral

/oo/ Medial
jujube
pluviometer
punctuation
revolution

Word Study: Regional

you /yoo/

y'all = you-all

you-uns *you + ones*
Another usage of *ones*:
young + ones = young'uns

yous *you + plural s*

you guys *you + guys*

-ough
Only one common word.
thr**ough** [H]

-o
Final
d**o** [H]
t**o** [H]
tw**o** [H]
wh**o**

Yellow   ū, /yoo/
Violet   /oo/

-oe
Final
can**oe**
sh**oe** [H]

-ook
baz**oo**ka
k**oo**k
sp**oo**k

-u
Final
Open Syllable
Spelled *-u*
ecr**u**
em**u**
fl**u** [H]
gn**u** [H]
gur**u**
haik**u**
kud**u**
kudz**u**
lul**u** *slang*
muum**u**u, mum**u**
rak**u**
snaf**u**
tut**u**
ul**u**
Zul**u**

-oo
Final
ach**oo** [Int]
bamb**oo**
b**oo**
boob**oo**
cockat**oo**
c**oo** [H]
g**oo**
igl**oo**
kangar**oo**
m**oo**
peekab**oo**
shamp**oo**
sh**oo**
tab**oo**
tatt**oo**
t**oo** [H]
vood**oo**
w**oo**
yah**oo**
z**oo**

/oo/
Phonograms
-oom
bl**oom**
d**oom**
gl**oom**
gr**oom** [H]
l**oom**
r**oom**
z**oom**
-oon
bab**oon**
ball**oon**
cart**oon**
coc**oon** [Sp]
cr**oon**
harp**oon**
lag**oon**
lamp**oon**
l**oon**
mons**oon**
n**oon**
s**oon**
sp**oon**
sw**oon**
-oop
c**oop** [H]
dr**oop**
h**oop**
l**oop**
sc**oop**
sn**oop**
st**oop**
sw**oop**
tr**oop** [H]

-ood
br**ood** [H]
f**ood**
m**ood**
-oodle
d**oodle**
n**oodle**
p**oodle**
-oof
al**oof** *
g**oof**
repr**oof** *
r**oof**
sp**oof** *
-ool
c**ool**
dr**ool**
f**ool**
p**ool**
sch**ool**
sp**ool**
st**ool**
t**ool**

-oose
cab**oose**
ch**oose**
g**oose**
l**oose** [Sp]
m**oose**
n**oose**
-oost
b**oost**
r**oost**
-oot
b**oot**
h**oot**
l**oot**
m**oot** *
r**oot** [H]
t**oot**
sc**oot**
sh**oot**
-oup
cr**oup**
gr**oup**
s**oup**
st**oup** [H]

-eu
French origin
li**eu**
man**eu**ver [Sp]

oo-
Initial
oodles
ooh [Int]
oolong
oompah
oomph
oops [Int]
ooze

Spelling /o͞o/ Sound

Compare these /o͞o/ phonograms to the /yoo/ phonograms on the previous page. Find examples of words spelled the same that use both sounds:
d**uke**: dook, dyook

-ume
ass**ume**
cons**ume**r
fl**ume**
pl**ume**
pres**ume**
res**ume**

-uke
fl**uke**

-ule
r**ule**

-une
J**une**
pr**une**

-use
r**use**

-ute
br**ute**
ch**ute** [H]
fl**ute**
j**ute**
l**ute**

-ui
br**ui**se
cr**ui**se
fr**ui**t
j**ui**ce
recr**ui**t
s**ui**t
s**ui**tcase

-ou,
c**ou**p [H]
gr**ou**p
gr**ou**per
gr**ou**pie
r**ou**te [H]
s**ou**p
tr**ou**pe

o-e
CVCe
appr**o**v**e**
l**o**s**e**
m**o**v**e**
gr**o**ov**e**
pr**o**v**e**
rem**o**v**e**

Key:
* = test prep
Cl = clipped word
H = heteronym, homograph, homophone
Int = interjection
Sp = spelling demon

kangaroo

MOOSE   food   moon

Vowels Spelling /oo/

/oo/
Phonograms

Spelling /oo/ Sound

-ood
good
hood
stood
wood H

-oof
hoof

-ook
book
brook *
cook
cookie
crook
hook
look
nook
rook
rookie
shook
snook
took

-ool
wool

-oot
afoot
foot
soot

-u
bull
bullet
bush
full
pull
push
put
sugar

-ou,
could H
should
would H

-olf
One common word.
wolf

Bound Four-Tab Foldables® (above and below): Fold multiple Four-Tab Foldables in half and glue them side by side to make a Bound Book. See page 28.

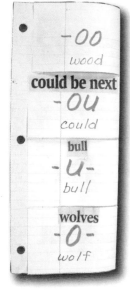

(outside tabs)

(student work under the tabs)

Four-Tab Foldable (above): See page 398.

Word Study: -ood Words
Design a Venn diagram to collect words with the same -ood phonogram but two different oo sounds.

hood	food
good	brood
wood	mood

Word Study: Venn Diagram

Have students make a Venn Diagram Foldable and use it to find words ending in *-y* with two different vowel sounds— /ē/ and /ī/. On the back, sort words by their spelling of the different final vowel sounds.

/ē/ smelly   Final -y Acts as a Vowel   /ī/ putrify

Notebook Foldable Shutterfolds (above): Two sections of paper can be glued along outer edges to form a Notebook Foldable Shutterfold. Templates for the *shutterfold* and the pocket (above left) are from Dinah Zike's *Notebook Foldables* book and CD.

Venn Diagram Bound Book (above): This Venn diagram book is made using Dinah's "cut up and cut out" method of book binding. See instructions on page 402 or go to the internet to download a free template (www.dinah.com).

Test Prep Words

alchemy *	earthy *	magnanimity *
anomaly *	epiphany *	ossify *
anxiety *	fidelity *	parity *
cacophony *	fluency *	paucity *
cursory *	frugality *	perjury *
dally *	homily *	privy *
decry *	humility *	propinquity *
depravity *	impiety *	putrefy *
dichotomy *	indemnify *	sundry *
doughty *	latency *	usury *
dowdy *	levity *	vilify *

When a vowel is combined with an *r*, the vowel sound changes.
Sometimes these vowels are referred to as being *r-controlled*.

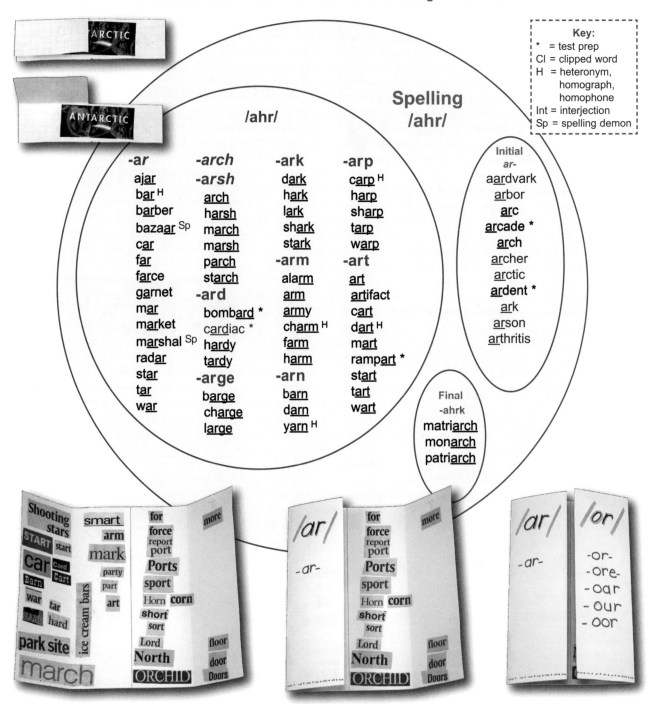

Key:
* = test prep
Cl = clipped word
H = heteronym, homograph, homophone
Int = interjection
Sp = spelling demon

ARCTIC

ANTARCTIC

/ahr/

Spelling /ahr/

-ar
ajar
bar ᴴ
barber
bazaar ˢᵖ
car
far
farce
garnet
mar
market
marshal ˢᵖ
radar
star
tar
war

-arch
-arsh
arch
harsh
march
marsh
parch
starch
-ard
bombard *
cardiac *
hardy
tardy
-arge
barge
charge
large

-ark
dark
hark
lark
shark
stark
-arm
alarm
arm
army
charm ᴴ
farm
harm
-arn
barn
darn
yarn ᴴ

-arp
carp ᴴ
harp
sharp
tarp
warp
-art
art
artifact
cart
dart ᴴ
mart
rampart *
start
tart
wart

Initial *ar-*
aardvark
arbor
arc
arcade *
arch
archer
arctic
ardent *
ark
arson
arthritis

Final -ahrk
matriarch
monarch
patriarch

Shutterfold (above): Use a Shutterfold made from 8½" x 11" paper to collect examples of words containing *r-controlled* vowels. Note the use of RWP. See page 400.

When a vowel is combined with an *r*, the vowel sound changes.
Sometimes these vowels are referred to as being *r*-controlled.

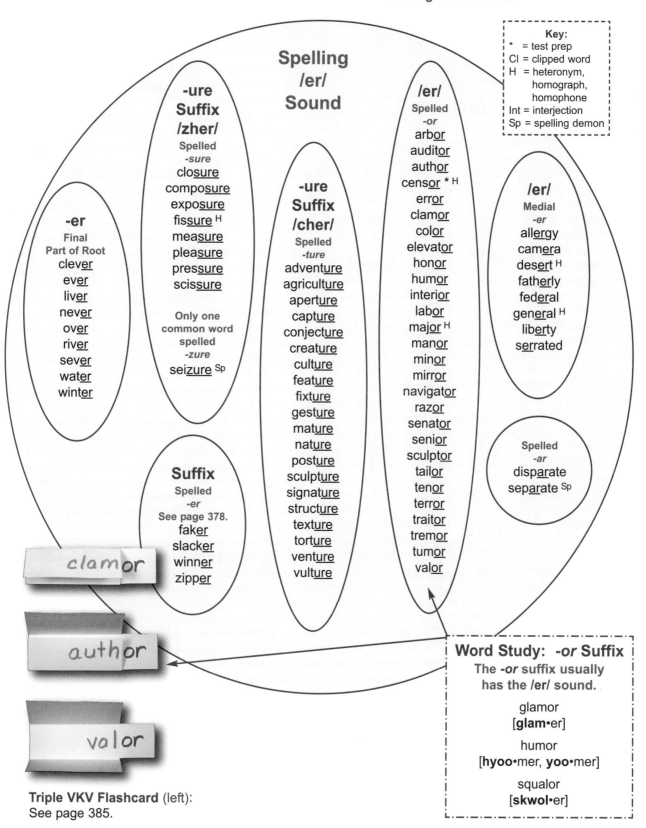

Spelling /er/ Sound

Key:
* = test prep
Cl = clipped word
H = heteronym, homograph, homophone
Int = interjection
Sp = spelling demon

-er
Final Part of Root
clev**er**
ev**er**
liv**er**
nev**er**
ov**er**
riv**er**
sev**er**
wat**er**
wint**er**

-ure Suffix /zher/
Spelled *-sure*
clo**sure**
compo**sure**
expo**sure**
fis**sure** H
mea**sure**
plea**sure**
pres**sure**
scis**sure**

Only one common word spelled *-zure*
sei**zure** Sp

Suffix
Spelled *-er*
See page 378.
fak**er**
slack**er**
winn**er**
zipp**er**

-ure Suffix /cher/
Spelled *-ture*
adven**ture**
agricul**ture**
aper**ture**
cap**ture**
conjec**ture**
crea**ture**
cul**ture**
fea**ture**
fix**ture**
ges**ture**
ma**ture**
na**ture**
pos**ture**
sculp**ture**
signa**ture**
struc**ture**
tex**ture**
tor**ture**
ven**ture**
vul**ture**

/er/
Spelled *-or*
arb**or**
audit**or**
auth**or**
cens**or** * H
err**or**
clam**or**
col**or**
elevat**or**
hon**or**
hum**or**
interi**or**
lab**or**
maj**or** H
man**or**
min**or**
mirr**or**
navigat**or**
raz**or**
senat**or**
seni**or**
sculpt**or**
tail**or**
ten**or**
terr**or**
trait**or**
trem**or**
tum**or**
val**or**

/er/
Medial *-er*
all**er**gy
cam**er**a
des**er**t H
fath**er**ly
fed**er**al
gen**er**al H
lib**er**ty
s**er**rated

Spelled *-ar*
disp**ar**ate
sep**ar**ate Sp

clamor

author

valor

Triple VKV Flashcard (left):
See page 385.

Word Study: -or Suffix
The *-or* suffix usually has the /er/ sound.

glamor
[**glam**•er]

humor
[**hyoo**•mer, **yoo**•mer]

squalor
[**skwol**•er]

When a vowel is combined with an *r*, the vowel sound changes.
Sometimes these vowels are referred to as being *r*-controlled.

Key:
* = test prep
Cl = clipped word
H = heteronym,
    homograph,
    homophone
Int = interjection
Sp = spelling demon

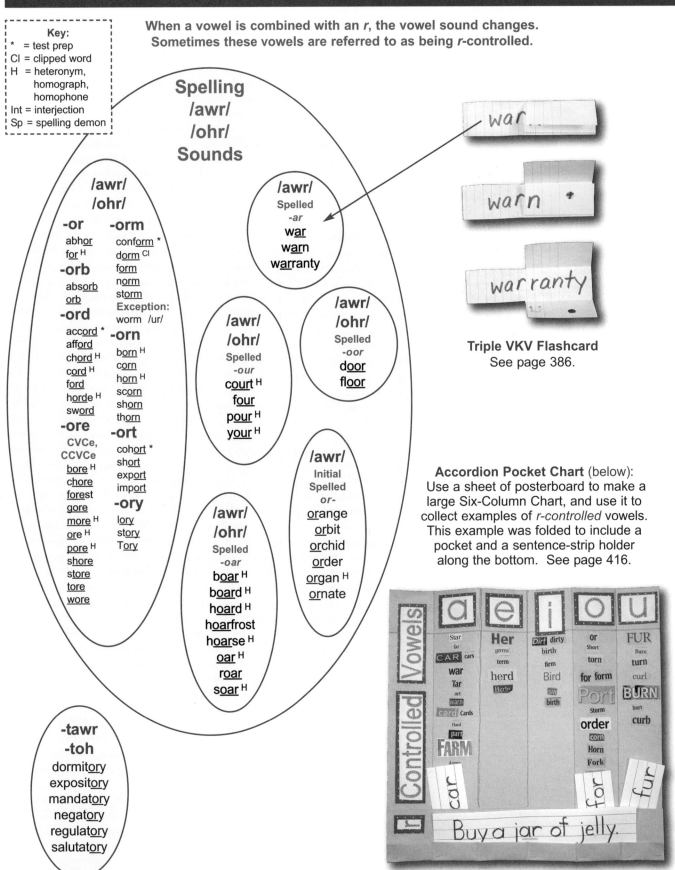

Spelling /awr/ /ohr/ Sounds

/awr/ /ohr/

-or
abhor
for H
-orb
absorb
orb
-ord
accord *
afford
chord H
cord H
ford
horde H
sword
-ore
CVCe,
CCVCe
bore H
chore
forest
gore
more H
ore H
pore H
shore
store
tore
wore

-orm
conform *
dorm Cl
form
norm
storm
Exception:
worm /ur/
-orn
born H
corn
horn H
scorn
shorn
thorn
-ort
cohort *
short
export
import
-ory
lory
story
Tory

/awr/ Spelled -ar
war
warn
warranty

/awr/ /ohr/ Spelled -our
court H
four
pour H
your H

/awr/ /ohr/ Spelled -oor
door
floor

/awr/ /ohr/ Spelled -oar
boar H
board H
hoard H
hoarfrost
hoarse H
oar H
roar
soar H

/awr/ Initial Spelled or-
orange
orbit
orchid
order
organ H
ornate

-tawr -toh
dormitory
expository
mandatory
negatory
regulatory
salutatory

Triple VKV Flashcard
See page 386.

Accordion Pocket Chart (below):
Use a sheet of posterboard to make a
large Six-Column Chart, and use it to
collect examples of *r-controlled* vowels.
This example was folded to include a
pocket and a sentence-strip holder
along the bottom. See page 416.

When a vowel is combined with an *r*, the vowel sound changes. Sometimes these vowels are referred to as being *r*-controlled.

covert operations

desert operations

expert operations

Spelling /ur/ Sound

-ur
-urb
curb
disturb
-urd
absurd
curd
-urf
surf H
turf
-urk
lurk
murk
-url
churl *
curl
-urn
burn
burned
turn
urn H
-urp
burp
-ur
blur
burden
burl
burr
burro
concur *
cur
occur Sp
spur
-urt
curt
curtsy
hurt

-ur
-er
Phonograms

-erb
adverb
herb
verb
-erd
herd H
nerd
-erm
berm
germ
perm Cl
term
-ern
fern
-er
confer *
her
infer
-erse
verse
-erve
conserve *
nerve
serve
-ert
convert
desert H
dessert H
expert
invert *

-ur
First
Syllable
Spelled
-ur
curse
cursory *
curtain
furrow
hurry
nurse
purchase
purple
purse
surly
survey
turkey
turtle

Spelled
-our
journal
courtesy

Spelled
er-
ergate a
worker ant
ergo
ermine

-ir
Medial
Spelled
-ir
circle
circus
first
third
thirsty
thirteen
thirty

-ur
Medial
Spelled
-er
certain
fertile *
person
serpent
invertebrate *

ur-
Initial
Spelled
ur-
urban
urbane
urchin
urge
urp

Spelled
-ear
early
earn H
earnest
earth
heard H
learn
pearl H
search

-ir
astir
fir H
sir
stir
tapir H
-ird
bird H
gird
-irk
quirk
shirk
smirk
-irl
girl
swirl
whirl
-irm
affirm *
firm
infirm *
-irp
chirp
twirp slang
-irst
first
thirst
-irt
dirt
flirt
shirt
skirt
smirk
squirt
-irth
birth H
girth

Spelled
-ere
were

Spelled
-or
word
world
worm
worse
worst
worth

Spelled
-ar
collar
dollar

Two-Tab Foldable
(above): See page 396.

DESERT

Desserts

Key:
* = test prep
Cl = clipped word
H = heteronym,
homograph,
homophone
Int = interjection
Sp = spelling demon

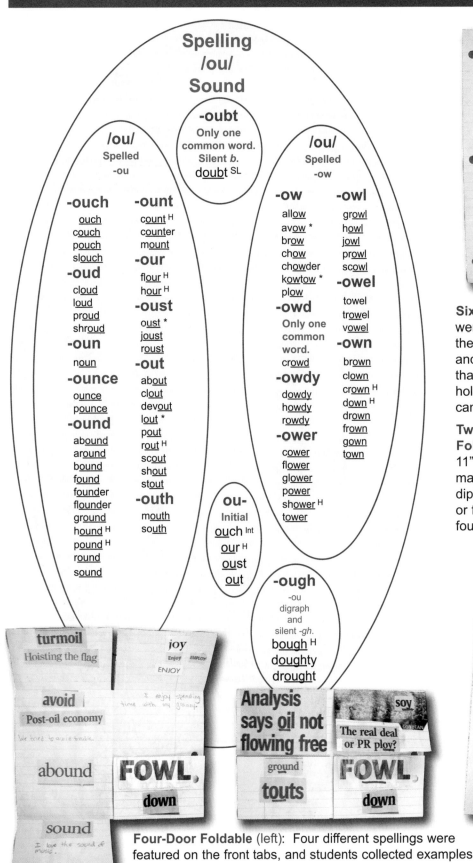

Spelling /ou/ Sound

-oubt
Only one common word. Silent *b*.
<u>doubt</u> SL

/ou/ Spelled -ou

-ouch
<u>ouch</u>
c<u>ouch</u>
p<u>ouch</u>
sl<u>ouch</u>

-oud
cl<u>oud</u>
l<u>oud</u>
pr<u>oud</u>
shr<u>oud</u>

-oun
n<u>oun</u>

-ounce
<u>ounce</u>
p<u>ounce</u>

-ound
ab<u>ound</u>
ar<u>ound</u>
b<u>ound</u>
f<u>ound</u>
f<u>ound</u>er
fl<u>ound</u>er
gr<u>ound</u>
h<u>ound</u> H
p<u>ound</u> H
r<u>ound</u>
s<u>ound</u>

-ount
c<u>ount</u> H
c<u>ount</u>er
m<u>ount</u>

-our
fl<u>our</u> H
h<u>our</u> H

-oust
<u>oust</u> *
j<u>oust</u>
r<u>oust</u>

-out
ab<u>out</u>
cl<u>out</u>
dev<u>out</u>
l<u>out</u> *
p<u>out</u>
r<u>out</u> H
sc<u>out</u>
sh<u>out</u>
st<u>out</u>

-outh
m<u>outh</u>
s<u>outh</u>

ou-
Initial
<u>ouch</u> Int
<u>our</u> H
<u>oust</u>
<u>out</u>

/ou/ Spelled -ow

-ow
all<u>ow</u>
av<u>ow</u> *
br<u>ow</u>
ch<u>ow</u>
ch<u>ow</u>der
k<u>ow</u>t<u>ow</u> *
pl<u>ow</u>

-owd
Only one common word.
cr<u>owd</u>

-owdy
d<u>owdy</u>
h<u>owdy</u>
r<u>owdy</u>

-ower
c<u>ower</u>
fl<u>ower</u>
gl<u>ower</u>
p<u>ower</u>
sh<u>ower</u> H
t<u>ower</u>

-owl
gr<u>owl</u>
h<u>owl</u>
j<u>owl</u>
pr<u>owl</u>
sc<u>owl</u>

-owel
t<u>owel</u>
tr<u>owel</u>
v<u>owel</u>

-own
br<u>own</u>
cl<u>own</u>
cr<u>own</u> H
d<u>own</u> H
dr<u>own</u>
fr<u>own</u>
g<u>own</u>
t<u>own</u>

-ough
-ou digraph and silent -gh.
b<u>ough</u> H
d<u>ough</u>ty
dr<u>ough</u>t

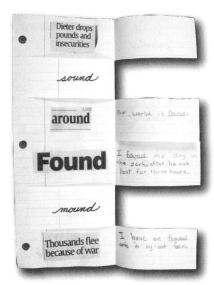

Six-Tab Foldable (above): Six words were featured on this study aid. Under the tabs, students defined the words and used them in sentences. Notice that notebook paper was folded so the holes are exposed and the Foldable can be stored in a three-ring binder.

Two-Column and Three-Column Foldable® Charts (below): Use 11" x 17" paper or posterboard to make charts for students to record diphthongs they encounter in reading, or for students to glue diphthongs found in RWP. See page 415.

Four-Door Foldable (left): Four different spellings were featured on the front tabs, and students collected examples of words under the tabs: *-oi, -oy, -ou, -ow*. See page 410.

Two-Pocket Foldable® (above): Collect and store diphthong word cards in the pockets. See page 399.

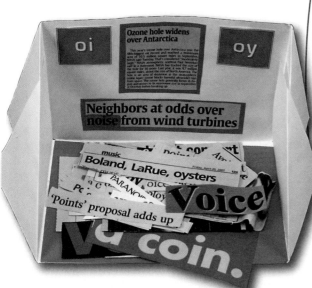

Four-Door Foldable Display Case (above): Use display cases to collect RWP, flashcards, half-page student reports, VKVs, and more. See page 410.

Word Study: noisome
annoy + some
The word *noisome* is an example of an *aphesis*, or a word that has lost an unstressed initial vowel or syllable.
Find other examples:
cute acute
slant aslant
squire esquire

Spelling /oi/ Sound

/oi/ Spelled -oi

-oi
foible *
koi *
noisome *
poi
poignant SL
poinsettia
poise
poison

-oice
choice
rejoice
voice

-oid
avoid
devoid *
void

-oil
boil
broil
coil
despoil *
doily
foil
oil
oily
soil
toil
toilet

-oin
coin
join
loin
sirloin

-oint
appoint
joint
ointment
point

-oise
noise
poise
turquoise

-oist
foist *
hoist
joist
moist
moisten

-oit
adroit *
loiter *
maladroit *

/oi/ Spelled -oy

alloy *
annoy
boy
boysenberry
cloying *
convoy
corduroy
coy *
coypu nutria
cowboy
decoy
destroy
employ
employer
enjoy
flamboyant *
foyer
joy
loyal
oyster
ploy
royal
soy
toy
viceroy *
voyage
zoysia

Special Six-Tab Foldable (above): Students folded a tab along the bottom of each of the large tabs, and they cut window-like tabs to feature the *oi* in the middle of each word. This ESL/ELL Foldable could also be used for spelling review.

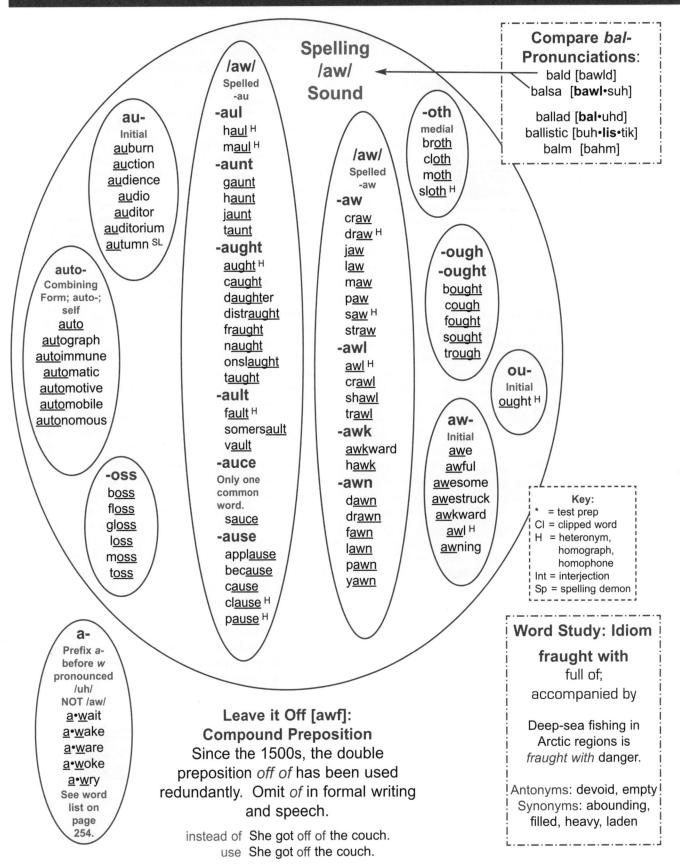

Spelling /aw/ Sound

Compare *bal*- Pronunciations:
bald [bawld]
balsa [**bawl**•suh]

ballad [**bal**•uhd]
ballistic [buh•**lis**•tik]
balm [bahm]

au-
Initial
auburn
auction
audience
audio
auditor
auditorium
autumn SL

auto-
Combining Form; auto-; self
auto
autograph
autoimmune
automatic
automotive
automobile
autonomous

-oss
boss
floss
gloss
loss
moss
toss

/aw/
Spelled -au
-aul
haul H
maul H
-aunt
gaunt
haunt
jaunt
taunt
-aught
aught H
caught
daughter
distraught
fraught
naught
onslaught
taught
-ault
fault H
somersault
vault
-auce
Only one common word.
sauce
-ause
applause
because
cause
clause H
pause H

/aw/
Spelled -aw
-aw
craw
draw H
jaw
law
maw
paw
saw H
straw
-awl
awl H
crawl
shawl
trawl
-awk
awkward
hawk
-awn
dawn
drawn
fawn
lawn
pawn
yawn

-oth
medial
broth
cloth
moth
sloth H

-ough
-ought
bought
cough
fought
sought
trough

ou-
Initial
ought H

aw-
Initial
awe
awful
awesome
awestruck
awkward
awl H
awning

Key:
* = test prep
Cl = clipped word
H = heteronym, homograph, homophone
Int = interjection
Sp = spelling demon

a-
Prefix *a-* before *w* pronounced /uh/ NOT /aw/
a•wait
a•wake
a•ware
a•woke
a•wry
See word list on page 254.

Leave it Off [awf]: Compound Preposition
Since the 1500s, the double preposition *off of* has been used redundantly. Omit *of* in formal writing and speech.

instead of She got off of the couch.
use She got off the couch.

Word Study: Idiom

fraught with
full of; accompanied by

Deep-sea fishing in Arctic regions is *fraught with* danger.

Antonyms: devoid, empty
Synonyms: abounding, filled, heavy, laden

Appendix One

Dinah Zike's

Visual Kinesthetic Vocabulary®

VKV®
Flashcard
Instructions

Classroom or Group: Use 8½" x 11" paper to cut Single VKV Flashcards. See page 16.
Individual Student: Use quarter sheets of paper to cut Single VKV Flashcards. See page 18.

Single VKV® Flashcards: VKV® Rings

1. Fold a Single VKV Flashcard in half.
2. Write a word or word pair on one side of the fold and another word or word pair on the other.
3. Punch a hole along the short edge of the folded card and store the VKV flashcards on a metal ring, bag tie, or cord.
4. "Read" the ring of cards like a book. Analyze the first word and try to predict the second word. To check answers, turn the card or open the cards to view both sides at once.

ESL/ELL or **Foreign Language Variations**
Variation: Use one language on one side of the fold and a second language on the other.
Variation: Use one language on both sides of the fold and a second language on the back. Cards can be placed on the ring to feature either language.

Use For:
- antonyms
- before and after
- cause and effect
- compound words
- double letters
- heteronyms
- homographs
- homophones
- past and present
- pros and cons
- spelling
- syllables
- synonyms

Single VKV® Flashcard: VKV® Books

1. Fold a Single VKV Flashcard in half so that the left side is ½" longer than the right side. Fold the extended section to form a ½" tab.
2. On one side of the card, write a word/word pair/phrase or glue RWP, and write or place another word/word pair/phrase on the other side of the card. Leave the ½" tab blank.
3. Staple multiple cards together along the ½" tab to form a VKV word booklet.
4. View the cards open to compare and contrast both sides of each card at the same time.
5. Close the cards, read the first word, and try to predict the second word. To check answers, turn the cards as if reading a book or open the cards to view both sides at once.
6. A piece of scrap paper could be glued around the stapled end to form a spine.

ESL/ELL or **Foreign Language**
Variation: Use one language on one side of the fold and a second language on the other.

Variation: Use one language on both sides of the fold and a second language on the back. Cards can be folded and placed in position on the ring to feature either language.

Classroom or Group: Use 8½" x 11" paper to cut Single VKV Flashcards. See page 16.
Individual Student: Use quarter sheets of paper to cut Single VKV Flashcards. See page 18.

Single VKV® Flashcards: Use In a Notebook

1. Fold a Single VKV Flashcard in half so that the left side is ½" longer than the right side. Fold to form a ½" tab.
2. Glue the ½" tab onto a page in a composition book or spiral notebook.
3. Glue other tabs on top of the first ½" tab, or glue other tabs onto the page separately, to make columns of Single VKV Flashcards.

VKVs® on Foldables: Large VKVs can be attached to a bulletin board or to a large posterboard Foldable by this method.

ESL/ELL or Foreign Language
Variation: Use one language on one side of the fold and a second language on the other.
Variation: Use one language on both sides of the fold and a second language on the back.

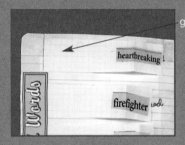
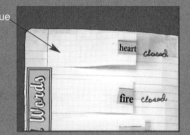

glue

Use for:
- antonyms
- before and after
- cause and effect
- compound words
- double letters
- homographs
- homophones
- past and present
- pros and cons
- syllables
- synonyms

Single VKV® Flashcards: Hinged VKVs®

1. Fold a Single VKV Flashcard in half.
2. Fold a ½" tab along the short edge of both sides.
3. Write on both sides of the center fold line.
4. Splay the ½" tabs and glue them into a composition book or a spiral notebook as illustrated below. When glued, the tabs act as hinges.
5. Analyze the word on the visible side of the tab and try to determine what will be found on the side that is not visible. Turn the tab to check your response.

Use for:
- antonyms
- before and after
- cause and effect
- compound words
- double letters
- homographs
- homophones
- past and present
- pros and cons
- spelling
- syllables
- synonyms

glue

Classroom or Group: Use 8½" x 11" paper to cut Single VKV Flashcards. See page 16.
Individual Student: Use quarter sheets of paper to cut Single VKV Flashcards. See page 18.

Single VKV® Flashcard: Fold-Over Cover-Ups

1. Write a word or glue RWP on a Single VKV Flashcard. Position the word on the left half of the card to cover a spelling at the end of a word, or the right half to cover a spelling at the beginning of a word.
2. Roll the edge opposite of the writing over to cover everything except the part of the word that is the focus of the lesson. Fold.
3. If needed, add punctuation or letters on the back of the folded section of the card.

Use for:
- abbreviations
- clipped words
- plurals
- possessives
- root words
- silent letters
- suffixes

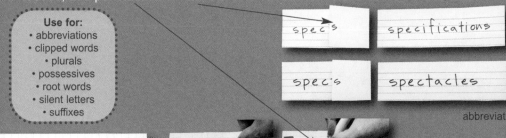

abbreviations

Single VKV® Flashcards: Fold-Overs Used In a Notebook

1. Glue the back of a folded Single VKV Flashcard into a composition book or spiral notebook.
2. Do not glue the fold-over tab.

silent letters

condemn   condem

solemn   solem

irregular plurals

Single VKV® Flashcards: Fold-Over Rings

1. To feature a spelling at the beginning of a word, write a term or glue RWP near the left edge of a Single VKV Flashcard.
2. Roll the right edge over to cover everything except the first part of the word that is the focus of the lesson. Fold.
3. Add graphics to illustrate the meaning of the word, when needed.

Variation: To feature a spelling at the end of a word, write a term or glue RWP near the right edge and roll the left edge over.

Use for:
- abbreviations
- clipped words
- plurals
- possessives
- root words
- suffixes

Classroom or Group: Use 8½" x 11" paper to cut Single VKV Flashcards. See page 16.
Individual Student: Use quarter sheets of paper to cut Single VKV Flashcards. See page 18.

Single VKV® Flashcard: Fold-Over Cover-Ups

1. Write or glue a word with a prefix and a suffix in the middle of a Single VKV Flashcard.
2. Roll the left edge over to cover the prefix. Fold.
3. Roll the right edge over to cover the suffix. Fold.
4. Read the stem/root word without affixes.

Alternate opening and closing the tabs to read the word with and without affixes.

foreshadowing

foreshadow

shadowing

shadow

Use for:
• prefixes
• root words
• syllables
• suffixes
• key word in a phrase

unlikeable

unlike

likeable

like

Notebook VKV® Flashcards

1. Glue the center section of the Single VKV Flashcard onto a page in a composition book or a spiral notebook.
2. Manipulate the tabs and read the different words formed. Write the words in the notebook and use them for spelling and vocabulary activities.

Single VKV® Flashcards: Binding Double Fold-Overs

1. Cut paper sections from scrap paper. The sections should be about one-third the size of the Single VKV Flashcards.
2. Glue one edge of the paper under the left edge of a closed flashcard. Glue paper sections on all flashcards.
3. Stack the cards and staple the flashcards together along the left edge through the extended paper tabs.
4. Glue or staple a piece of decorative scrap paper around the stapled edge to form a spine.

4.

(Back of flashcard.)

1.

2.

3.

Single, Double, and Triple VKVs can be bound using this procedure.

Classroom or Group: Use 8½" x 11" paper to cut Single VKV Flashcards. See page 16.
Individual Student: Use quarter sheets of paper to cut Single VKV Flashcards. See page 18.

Single VKV® Flashcards: Half-and-Half Flashcards

1. Write or glue a word in the center of a Single VKV Flashcard.
2. Roll the left edge over to cover the initial part of the word or phrase. Fold.
3. Roll the right edge over to cover the final part of the word or phrase. Fold.
4. Manipulate the tabs and read the different words or phrases formed.
Or, after observing what is under the first tab, try to predict what will be under the second.

Use for:
- antonyms
- compound words
- double letters
- homographs
- homophones
- idioms
- matching activities
- synonyms

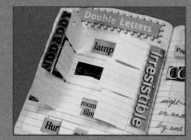  

Single VKV® Flashcard: Fold-Over Omissions

1. Write or glue a word, title, or phrase on the left half of a Single VKV Flashcard.
2. Fold the right edge of the flashcard backward so only the first letter or part of the abbreviation is showing.
3. Continue folding the card in an accordion manner, omitting letters not needed to form the abbreviation.
4. If needed, use paper clips to hold the folds in place.
5. Open and close the flashcard to read and study the word and its abbreviation.

Use for omitted letters:
- abbreviations
- acronyms
- clipped words
- contractions
- initializations
- portmanteau words
- symbols (chemistry)

Fort Davis

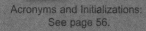

Acronyms and Initializations:
See page 56.

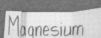

Magnesium
Mag
Ma

Chemical Element Symbols:
See page 49.

Fort
Ft
Ft.

Abbreviations:
See page 44.

When necessary, fold
the right edge over
to add a period
at the end.

miss
misspell
misspell

Adding Prefixes:
See pages 225-243.

Classroom or Group: Use 8½" x 11" paper to cut Single VKV Flashcards. See page 16.
Individual Student: Use quarter sheets of paper to cut Single VKV Flashcards. See page 18.

Single VKV® Flashcard: Fold-Over Add-Ons

1. Write or glue a root word to the left side of a Single VKV Flashcard.
2. Roll the right edge over to touch the end of the word. Fold.
3. Write or glue a suffix on the top of the folded tab.
4. Alternate opening and closing the right tab to read the word with and without the suffix.

Variation: Write the meaning of the suffix under the tab.

Variation: Reverse the fold for prefixes. Write the meaning of the prefix under the tab.

Use for:
- compound words
- prefixes
- suffixes
- plurals
- possessives
- root word study

Single VKV® Flashcard: Fold-Back

1. Write or glue a word or phrase near the right edge of a Single VKV Flashcard.
2. Roll the right edge back, leaving only the desired portion of the word or phrase exposed.
3. Glue the left edge of the flashcard into a notebook or onto a Foldable Project. Define the word and use it in a sentence under the tab.

Use for:
- initial consonants, blends, digraphs
- prefixes
- suffixes
- plurals
- possessives
- root word study
- two terms

Variation: Reverse the process to make a Fold-Back VKV Flashcard that folds back the beginning of a word. The word will be written near the left edge of the paper and the right edge of the Single Flashcard is glued into a notebook.

Classroom or Group: Use 8½" x 11" paper to cut Single VKV Flashcards. See page 16.
Individual Student: Use quarter sheets of paper to cut Single VKV Flashcards. See page 18.

Multi-Tab VKV® Flashcard: Cut-and-Fold

1. Write or glue root words along the left side of a quarter sheet or half sheet of paper. Make short cuts between the words along the right side.
2. Roll the right edges over to cover the suffixes. Fold.
3. Open to expose the entire word.
4. Alternate opening and closing the tabs to read the words with and without suffixes. Read the stem/root word without an affix.

Prefix Variation: Reverse the procedure by writing the word to the right side of the paper.

No-Cut Variation: Students align the prefixes or suffixes so they are exposed when the card is folded and root words are covered.

Root Word Variation: Glue or write words in the center of the paper. Make cuts between the words on both the left and right sides. Fold tabs, leaving only the root word exposed.

Use for:
- clipped words
- cognates
- final blends/digraphs
- initial blends/digraphs
- final double letters
- plurals
- possessives
- prefixes
- root words
- suffixes

Classroom or Group: Use 8½" x 11" paper to cut Single VKV Flashcards. See page 16.
Individual Student: Use quarter sheets of paper to cut Single VKV Flashcards. See page 18.

Single VKV® Flashcard: Three-Section Accordion

1. Fold a Single VKV Flashcard into thirds.
2. Refold the tabs to form a zigzag or accordion fold.
3. Write a word on the top section of the folded accordion.
4. Open the accordion and write a second word on the last section.
5. Open and close the accordion to read the two terms. Predict the second word before pulling the accordion open.

Notebook VKV® (right): Glue the back of the bottom section into a notebook.

Use for:
- antonyms
- cognates
- dual languages
- homographs
- homophones
- synonyms

Single VKV® Flashcard: Multi-Section Accordion

Fold a Single VKV Flashcard into the required number of sections to illustrate parts or pieces of a whole. The example pictured right was folded into six sections to illustrate a word with six syllables.

Project or Bulletin Board Display: Glue the back of the first section of an accordion VKV onto a project or bulletin board to emphasize parts or sections of something. See the Syllabication Project Cube pictured below.

Other Examples: See Syllables, pages 300-311.

Use for:
- pronunciation aids
- stressed syllables
- syllabication

Classroom or Group: Use 8½" x 11" paper to cut Single VKV Flashcards. See page 16.
Individual Student: Use quarter sheets of paper to cut Single VKV Flashcards. See page 18.

Single VKV® Flashcard: Flip-Flops

1. Fold a Single VKV Flashcard into thirds.
2. On the top and bottom sections inside the open strip, draw or use pictures of antonyms as seen in the example. In the middle of the strip, write a sentence using the antonyms.
3. Raise the bottom tab so you can write the word that is illustrated on the top section with the *interior* picture of planet Earth. Write the word *interior*.
4. Fold the top and bottom tabs down and write the word that is illustrated on the lower tab with the *exterior of the planet* picture. Write the word *exterior*.
5. Open and close the tabs to view antonyms, words, and matching pictures.

1.

2.

3.

4.

5.

With or Without Graphics (left):

a. Open the Single Flashcard and read the antonyms written on the top and bottom sections— *Federalists* and *Antifederalists*.

b. Raise the bottom tab and read the word *Federalist* while reading the definition of Federalist on the tab above.

c. Lower the bottom tab and the top tab and read the word *Antifederalist* while reading the definition of Antifederalist on the tab below the term.

d. Teach students how to self-question as they use the cards, and demonstrate how students can manipulate the VKV to answer their own questions.

When students see a term, idea, opinion, or action labeled on one tab, they should try to predict what will be on the second tab. Students then flip the tabs to check their response/s.

Use for:
- antonyms
- before and after
- cause and effect
- cognates
- dual languages
- homographs
- homophones
- past and present
- pros and cons
- synonyms

Classroom or Group: Use 8½" x 11" paper to cut Single VKV Flashcards. See page 16.
Individual Student: Use quarter sheets of paper to cut Single VKV Flashcards. See page 18.

Single VKV® Flashcard: Zigzag Accordion

1. Fold a Single VKV Flashcard like a *shutterfold*.
2. Refold the tabs to form a zigzag or accordion-like fold. The center section will be twice the size of the outer tabs.
3. On one side of the closed flashcard, write a term under the small tab to the left, and draw a graphic or write a definition to the right.
4. Turn the card over and repeat the process.

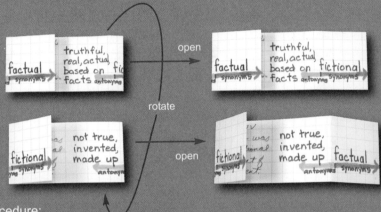

Use for:
- antonyms
- cognates
- dual languages
- homographs
- homophones
- synonyms

Procedure:

1. View one side of a closed flashcard at a time. Read the term and its definition to the right. **Rotate**, or flip the card over, and do the same to the other side. Determine the relationship between the words on the front and back. Are they antonyms? homographs? the same word in two different languages?
2. View one side of a closed flashcard. Read the word to the left and its definition to the right. **Move** the tab out from under the right end (definition end) of the card. View the words on the small tabs to the left and right. Note the relationship between the two words and the definition of one of the words in the middle.

On the flashcards pictured above and below, the orange arrows indicate synonyms and green indicate antonyms. Students devise their own methods for marking relationships between words.

Zigzag **Flashcard** **Key** :
   antonyms: green
   synonyms: orange

Note arrows illustrating the meaning of the terms *climax* and *anticlimax*. Use graphics if they help define a term.

Classroom or Group: Use 8½" x 11" paper to cut Double VKV Flashcards. See page 16.
Individual Student: Use quarter sheets of paper to cut Double VKV Flashcards. See page 18.

Double VKV® Flashcard: Two-Tab VKV®

1. Fold a Double VKV Flashcard in half.
2. Cut along the fold line of one side to form two tabs. Do NOT cut the back tab.
3. Write half of a compound word under the first tab and the other half under the second tab. The first word should stop at the cut line, and the second word should begin at the cut line. When both tabs are open, the word appears as a closed compound word.
4. Open and close the tabs to view the words separately or joined to form a compound word.

   Examples: *look, out*   or   *lookout*

Use for:
- antonyms
- cognates
- compound words
- confusing words
- contractions
- dual languages
- homographs
- homophones
- two syllable words
(show accented syllable)

Variation
Three or More Top Tabs:
Cut three or more tabs on the top half of the VKV. Do NOT cut the back tab. See an example of a Three-Tab VKV on page 225.

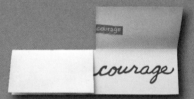

Double VKV® Flashcard: Side-by-Side VKV® Book

1. Fold two or more Double VKV Flashcards in half.
2. Glue the folded sections side by side to form a booklet.
   See page 28, book binding instructions.
3. Make sure the side and top folds are aligned before gluing.
4. Continue to add flashcards as new terms are studied.
5. When the final flashcard has been added, fold a spine and glue it around the multiple center folds.
6. Write a title on the booklet and use it for review.

NOTE: This binding method can be used with any Single, Double, or Triple VKV Flashcards that are made by folding the flashcard in half. This does not bind VKV flashcards folded into thirds.

Classroom or Group: Use 8½" x 11" paper to cut Double VKV Flashcards. See page 16.
Individual Student: Use quarter sheets of paper to cut Double VKV Flashcards. See page 18.

Double VKV® Flashcard: One-Tab VKV®

1. Fold a Double VKV Flashcard in half.
2. Cut along the fold line of one side to form two tabs. Do NOT cut the back tab.
3. Cut away the top left rectangle.
4. Write a word on the remaining single tab to the left.
5. Write a synonym or multiple synonyms for the word under the right tab.
6. Students look at the left word, independently try to determine a synonym for the word, and then look under the right tab to view synonyms and see if their word is listed. Explain that the word or words under the tab might not be the only synonyms for the given word. For English Language Learners, use only the most common synonyms.

Use for:
- antonyms
- antonyms formed by adding a prefix
  responsive/unresponsive
- antonyms formed by adding a suffix
  fear/fearless
- clipped words
- cognates
- dual languages
- synonyms

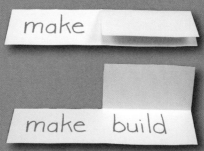

Other synonyms that could have been written under the right tab:
- construct
- produce
- assemble
- manufacture

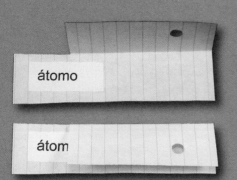

English/Spanish Cognates:
atom - English
atomo - Spanish

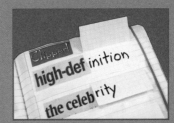

Clipped Words:
- high-def
- celeb

Antonyms formed by adding either a prefix or a suffix (right):
sini**s**tral • dextral
orthodox • **un**orthodox
abridged • **un**abridged
accelerate • **de**celerate

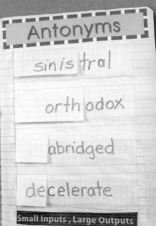

Classroom or Group: Use 8½" x 11" paper to cut Double VKV Flashcards. See page 16.
Individual Student: Use quarter sheets of paper to cut Double VKV Flashcards. See page 18.

Double VKV® Flashcard: Finding Alternatives

1. Fold a Double VKV Flashcard into thirds.
2. Cut along the fold lines on top side only. Do NOT cut the bottom section.
3. Cut off the top left tab.
4. Write a word on the left tab.
5. Write and/or illustrate homographs for the word under the two remaining tabs.
6. Check your knowledge of homographs by trying to name the homographs before opening and closing the tabs.

Use for:
• antonyms
• homographs
• homophones
• synonyms

Double VKV® Flashcard: Medial View

1. Fold a Double VKV Flashcard into thirds.
2. Cut along the fold lines of the top strip. Do NOT cut the bottom strip.
3. Cut off the top middle tab.
4. Write a root word in the middle, exposed, center section.
5. Write a prefix under the left tab. Write a suffix under the right tab.
6. Read the words formed. Determine how many words can be formed.

Examples:

joy	school	cover
en joy	pre school	dis cover
en joy ment	pre school er	dis cover ing
		cover ing

Use for:
• antonyms
formed by adding a prefix
• prefixes
• root words
• suffixes

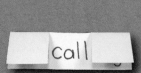  

Variation: Use this VKV flashcard to review affixes. The example pictured features prefixes that form antonyms.

Classroom or Group: Use 8½" x 11" paper to cut Double VKV Flashcards. See page 16.
Individual Student: Use quarter sheets of paper to cut Double VKV Flashcards. See page 18.

Double VKV® Flashcard: Spelling Rings

Base of the VKV® Flashcard
1. Write final double letters on the inside right end of a Double VKV Flashcard.
2. Cut away the top tab, but do not cut the tab section that covers the final letters.
3. Cut the remaining tab in half so that each of the final letters is covered by a separate tab.

Word Cards
4. Measure the distance from the left edge of the Base Flashcard to the inside edge of the first tab.
5. Cut word card sections slightly shorter than the measured length.
6. Write terms on the word cards that end in either one or both of the final letters featured on the Base Flashcard, but do not write the final letters that spell the word.
7. Punch a hole in the center of the left edge of the Base Flashcard and each of the Word Cards.
8. Place the Word Cards on top of the base card and connect them with a metal binder ring.
9. Flip the Word Cards and spell the word using either one or both of the double final letters.
Write the correct spelling on the back of each Word Card so students can self-check their responses. See examples, page 132.

Use for:
• final double letters
  -e or -ee
  -f or -ff
  -l or -ll
• spelling final consonant sounds
  -ck or -ic
  -n or -gn, others.

See Consonants pages 129-167.

Variation (below): Use a Triple VKV Flashcard to make the base. Note how the three tabs to the right can be raised or lowered to spell a word with a single or double final letter.

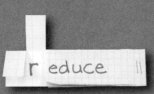

Student-Sized Variation (left): Follow the steps above, using Double and Single VKV Flashcards cut from a quarter sheet of paper.

Do not punch holes for a binder ring. Instead, staple the flashcards together as indicated in the top photograph to the left.

The base of the flashcard can be glued into a notebook or the stapled set of terms can be stored in a pocket.

Classroom or Group: Use 8½" x 11" paper to cut Double VKV Flashcards. See page 16.
Individual Student: Use quarter sheets of paper to cut Double VKV Flashcards. See page 18.

Double VKV® Flashcard: One-Tab Omission

1. Write two words that form a contraction under the tab of a Double VKV Flashcard.
2. With the card open, draw lines to indicate which letters will be omitted. In the example below left, draw lines on the tab above the word that indicate the width of the **o** in *not*. Use a ruler to help align and sketch these cutting lines.
3. Cut the top strip away to expose the letters that will remain in the contraction. Leave the top strip intact over the letter/s that are to be omitted.
4. Fold the tab down, covering the letter/s to be omitted, and draw an apostrophe on the front of the tab.
5. Open and close the tab to see the two words become a contraction, and the contraction revert back to two words.

Use for:
• clipped words
• contractions
• portmanteau words

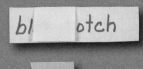

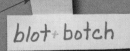

Portmanteau Words

Tabs will vary in size and position, and must be cut based upon the words written inside the Double VKV Flashcard.

Double VKV® Flashcard: One-Tab Replacement

1. Write a sentence under the tab of a Double VKV Flashcard, as seen in the photographs below.
2. Select a word whose synonym/s you will name. On the top tab, mark the location of the word that will have a synonym. (See first photograph below.)
3. Cut away the top tab, leaving the small, marked tab to cover the word that will have a synonym.
4. Close the tab and write a synonym for the word on the top of the tab.
5. Read the sentence with one word and then the other. Explain how they are alike.
List other synonyms on the back of the flashcard.

Variation: This could have been made using a Triple VKV Flashcard, and a bottom tab could have been cut to allow another synonym to be featured.

Use for:
• adjectives
• antonyms
• synonyms

The small boy ran home.   The small boy ran home.   The little boy ran home.

Classroom or Group: Use 8½" x 11" paper to cut Double VKV Flashcards. See page 16.
Individual Student: Use quarter sheets of paper to cut Double VKV Flashcards. See page 18.

Double VKV® Flashcard: Medial Changes

1. Fold a Double VKV Flashcard into fourths.
2. Cut along the fold lines of the top strip. Do NOT cut the bottom strip.
3. Cut off the top left and the top right tabs.
4. Write each letter of a four-letter CVVC word under the four tabs.
See word list, page 335.
5. Raise and lower the medial tabs to form three words.

Use for:
• medial spelling
• simple sentences
• CVVC words

Variation: Do not cut these medial tabs apart.
1. Write initial and ending consonants to the left and right of the large medial tab.
2. Write two vowels under the medial tab.
3. Cover the vowels with the medial tab, then raise it to observe the "two vowels walking."
4. Read the word by sounding the initial consonant, the single vowel sound, and the final consonant.
5. What can happen when two vowels "go walking"? See Vowels, pages 334-366.

Double VKV® Flashcard: Analogies

1. Fold a Double VKV Flashcard into fourths.
2. Write an analogy under the tab so that the symbols : and :: are on the three fold lines in the appropriate order for an analogy (:, ::, :), and the four words or phrases of the analogy are in each of the four sections.
3. Cut the top tab along the fold lines so that each of the four sections of the analogy can be viewed separately.
4. Raise and lower the tabs to view what the two sides have in common.

a. Raise the first and third tabs and analyze the words/phrases in these sections.
b. Predict what might be found on the second and fourth tabs. Raise the tabs and check responses.
c. In student notebooks, write alternative terms/phrases that would make the analogy correct.
d. Have students design their own analogy VKVs and trade them with classmates.

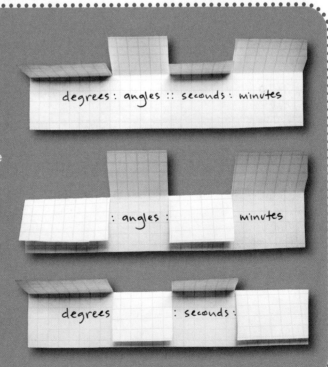

Classroom or Group: Use 8½" x 11" paper to fold Triple VKV Flashcards. See page 16.
Individual Student: Use quarter sheets of paper to fold Triple VKV Flashcards. See page 18.

Triple VKV® Flashcard: Shutterfold

1. Fold a Triple VKV Flashcard like a Shutterfold. See Foldables, page 400.
2. Select a pair of confusing words and write one of each of the terms on the front of each of the two tabs.
3. Under the tabs, use the words in sentences or glue examples of the words found in RWP.

Use for:
• cognates
• confusing words

| atomic number |
| numero atómico |

| chemical formula |
| fórmula química |

| chemical reaction |
| reacción química |

Variation (below):

1. Fold a Triple VKV Flashcard like a Shutterfold. See Foldables, page 399.
2. Write a word inside the *shutterfold*, near the left edge.
3. Cut the top and bottom tabs away to expose the word.
4. Under the tabs, explain two meanings of the word.

Use for:
• antonyms/synonyms
• comparing two words
• definitions
• homographs
• homophones

well

well   -healthy, satisfactory

well   -hole dug for water

well   -healthy, satisfactory   -hole dug for water

Use for:
• affixes
• compound words
• double letters

surfer
Bus driver
worker
Bowler

Variation (left):

1. Fold a Triple VKV Flashcard like a Shutterfold. See Foldables, page 400.
2. Write a word or glue RWP across the front of the *shutterfold* so that it is divided at the point where the two tabs come together.
3. Define and use the word in sentences under the tabs.

 The _____ is blowing. It is a _____ day.

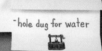 *noun* The wind is blowing. It is a windy day. *adjective*

Variation (left):

1. Fold a Triple VKV Flashcard like a Shutterfold.

Use for:
• affixes
• antonyms
• cognates
• singular/plural
• synonyms
• verb tenses

See Foldables, page 400.
2. Write a sentence or phrase under each of the two tabs.
3. Cut away sections of the top and bottom tab, leaving part of each tab intact to cover one or more words in each of the sentences or phrases.

Example Above: wind, n.
windy, adj.

Classroom or Group: Use 8½" x 11" paper to fold Triple VKV Flashcards. See page 16.
Individual Student: Use quarter sheets of paper to fold Triple VKV Flashcards. See page 18.

Triple VKV® Flashcard: Trifold

1. Write an initialization on the front of a Triple VKV Flashcard.
2. Inside, write the initialization in the top section, use it in a sentence in the center section, and write the words it stands for in the bottom section.
3. Cut between the words on the last section.

Use for:
- acronyms
- initializations

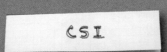

Use for:
- antonyms
- cognates
- confusing words
- dual languages
- synonyms

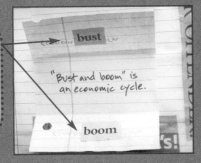

Procedure:
1. Open the top tab and identify the initialization.
2. Open and close the bottom tabs to self-check.
3. When reading the sentence, read the initialization as words instead of an abbreviation.

Variation (left): Use the top and bottom tabs to compare and contrast two terms. See the example left—bust, boom.

Triple VKV® Flashcards: Initial Tabs

1. Fold a Triple VKV Flashcard in half.
2. Cut off the top and bottom sections of one half of the card. Do NOT cut the middle section.
3. Turn the single tab to the right to focus on different initial spellings and a common spelling at the end of a word.
4. Open and close the left tabs to form three words with the same final spelling.

Variation: Reverse the procedure for three words with the same initial spelling but different final spellings.
See instructions on the next page.

Use for:
- blends/digraphs
- phonograms
- prefixes
- root words
- suffixes

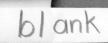

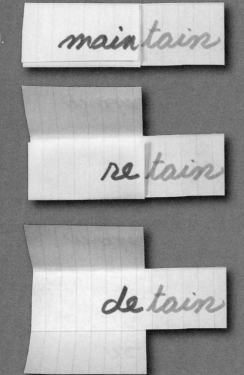

Classroom or Group: Use 8½" x 11" paper to fold Triple VKV Flashcards. See page 16.
Individual Student: Use quarter sheets of paper to fold Triple VKV Flashcards. See page 18.

Triple VKV® Flashcard: Final Tabs

1. Fold a Triple VKV Flashcard in half.
2. Cut off the upper left and bottom left sections of one half of the card.
3. Turn the single middle remaining tab to the right to focus on a common spelling at the beginning of a word and different final spellings.
4. Write the first half of a compound word on the single extended tab.
   Example: *blue*
5. Write nouns on the three flashcard sections to the right that will combine with the first word to form three compound words.
   Examples: *bird, berry, bell*
6. Open and close the two right tabs to form three compound words.
   Examples: *bluebird*
                    blueberry
                    bluebell

Use for:
- antonyms
- cognates
- compound words
- dual languages
- idioms
- phrases
- prefixes
- root words
- synonyms
- suffixes

Send in the sub*stitute*

Send in the sub*marine*

Send in the subs!

See examples on page 134.

Classroom or Group: Use 8½" x 11" paper to fold Triple VKV Flashcards. See page 16.
Individual Student: Use quarter sheets of paper to fold Triple VKV Flashcards. See page 18.

Triple VKV® Flashcard: Initial Changes

1. Cut off the top and bottom sections of one half of a Triple VKV Flashcard. Do NOT cut the middle section.
2. Turn the single middle remaining tab to the left to focus on an initial spelling.
3. Write an initial spelling on the single flashcard section so that it is close to the middle.
4. Write three *word families (rimes) or other spellings* to form words on the three sections to the right. Open and close the right tabs and read the three words formed.

Variation: Reverse the procedure to cover or add a final spelling. See Cognates, page 95.

Variation Pictured Below: Fold the left tab over the initial spelling and write the sound heard— *photo, phrase, phone.*

Use for spelling:
- gh- words
- gn- words
- kn- words
- ph- words
- pn- words
- rh- words
- wr- words
- others

Six-Word Variation Pictured Below:
Fold the left tab over the initial spelling to feature base/root words. Example:
mobile, immobile
mortal, immortal
modest, immodest

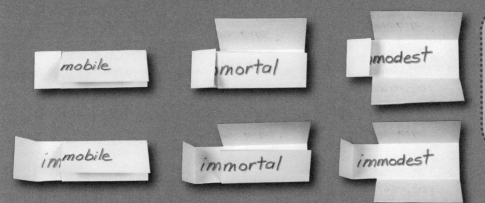

Depending on the direction of the Fold-Over Tab, use to form words with and without:
- plurals
- prefixes
- suffixes

Classroom or Group: Use 8½" x 11" paper to fold Triple VKV Flashcards. See page 16.
Individual Student: Use quarter sheets of paper to fold Triple VKV Flashcards. See page 18.

Triple VKV® Flashcard: Four-Word Initial

1. Fold a Triple VKV Flashcard into thirds.
2. Cut off the top left and top right sections. Cut off the bottom left and bottom right sections.
3. Write a final spelling on the far right tab.
4. Write an initial consonant, blend, or digraph (so that it will be completely covered by the other three tabs) before the phonogram in order to form a word.
5. Fold the other three tabs over and write consonants, blends, or digraphs on these tabs to form three more words. Open and close the tabs and read the four words formed.

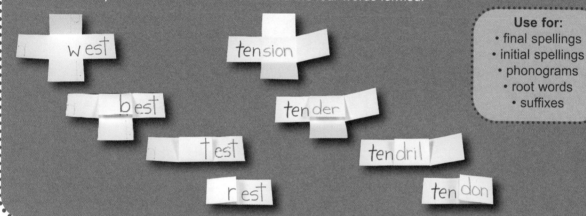

Use for:
- final spellings
- initial spellings
- phonograms
- root words
- suffixes

Triple VKV® Flashcard: Medial Changes

1. Fold a Triple Flashcard into thirds.
2. Cut along the fold lines of the top and bottom sections. Do NOT cut the middle section.
3. Cut off the top left and bottom left sections.
4. Cut off the top right and bottom right sections.
5. Write an initial consonant on the left tab, close to the middle section, and write a final consonant on the right tab, close to the middle section.
6. Write a vowel pair on the inside center section of the flashcard. Close one tab and write another vowel pair. You can leave one tab blank, as illustrated below, or write another vowel pair on this tab to form three different words.

Procedure: With the blank medial tab in position, observe and sound the initial and final consonants. Raise the tab and read the CVVC word formed. Change the medial tab so the second word is formed, and repeat the process. After all tabs are opened, close the tabs and read the words again. In their notebooks, students record the words formed.

Use for:
- base/root words
- initial and final spellings
- medial spellings
- "two vowels walking"

Classroom or Group: Use 8½" x 11" paper to fold Triple VKV Flashcards. See page 16.
Individual Student: Use quarter sheets of paper to fold Triple VKV Flashcards. See page 18.

Triple VKV® Flashcard: Eight-Word VKV®

1. Fold a Triple Flashcard into thirds.
2. Cut along the fold lines of the top and bottom sections. Do NOT cut the middle section.
3. Cut off the top left and the bottom left sections.
4. Cut off the bottom right section only.
5. Write two different final spellings on the two right tabs.
6. Write four different initial spellings on the left tabs.
7. Open and close the tabs to read the eight words formed. See the example Eight-Word VKV below.

Variation in Notebook (right): Fold the Triple Flashcard in half. Cut along the fold lines of the top and bottom sections. This will form three tabs to the left. Cut off the bottom right section, forming two tabs to the right. Write two different final spellings on the two right tabs. Write three different initial spellings on the left tabs. Open and close the tabs to read the six words formed.

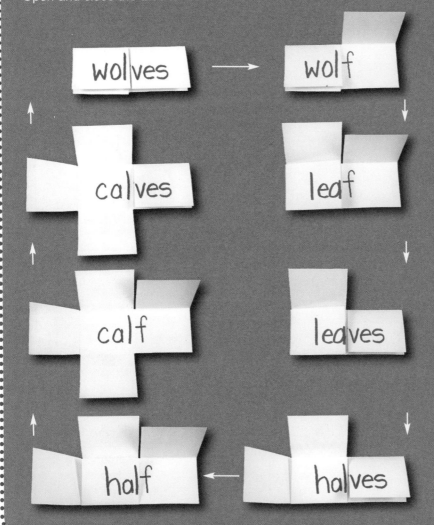

Use for:
- blends, digraphs
- phonograms
- rhyming words
- singular/plural nouns
- suffixes
  adjective suffixes
  verb suffixes

Classroom or Group: Use 8½" x 11" paper to fold Triple VKV Flashcards, see page 16.
Individual Student: Use quarter sheets of paper to fold Triple VKV Flashcards, see page 18.

Triple VKV® Flashcard, Nine-Word VKV®
Example: Double Suffixes VKV®

1. Fold a Triple Flashcard into thirds.
2. Cut along the fold lines of the top and bottom sections. Do NOT cut the middle section.
3. Write three different root words on the first (left) section of tabs.
4. Write two different suffixes on the middle tabs, leaving the top tab blank.
5. Write two different suffixes on the last (right) section of tabs, leaving the top tab blank.
6. Open and close the tabs to read the three root words. Open and close the middle tabs and read the three root words with each of the two suffixes. Open and close the last tabs and read the root words with double suffixes. See the photographs below.

Twelve-Word Variations

Variation: Write three root words in the middle section, three prefixes in the first section, and three suffixes in the last section. Read the twelve words formed.

 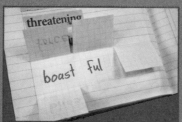 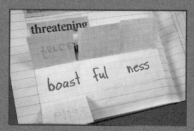

 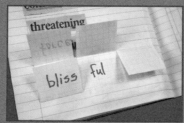 

Note: Some VKVs, including the one pictured on this page, have to be opened in sequential order to make true words.

Use for:
- phrases
- prefixes
- root words
- simple sentences
- suffixes
- syllabication

Classroom or Group: Use 8½" x 11" paper to fold Triple VKV Flashcards, see page 16.
Individual Student: Use quarter sheets of paper to fold Triple VKV Flashcards, see page 18.

Triple VKV® Flashcard: Nine-Word VKV®

1. Fold a Triple Flashcard into thirds.
2. Cut along the fold lines of the top and bottom sections. Do NOT cut the middle section.
3. Cut off the middle top and bottom sections only.
4. Write a root word in the remaining middle section.
5. Write two or three different initial spellings on the left sections, and write two or three different final spellings on the last section. (If only two are written, leaving one tab blank, focus is placed on the root word, but fewer words are formed. In the example below, one of the first section tabs and one of the last section tabs was left blank to draw attention to the word *affirm*.)
6. Open and close the tabs to read the nine words formed.

Use for:
- phrases
- prefixes
- root words
- simple sentences
- suffixes

Classroom or Group: Use a whole sheet of 8½" x 11" paper.
Individual Student: Use half sheets of photocopy paper or notebook paper.

Accordion VKV® Flashcard

1. Fold a half sheet of copy paper into an eight-section accordion book. See photographs below.
2. Cut a 1" strip off the right side of the top seven sections, leaving the bottom, eighth, section, whole.
3. Glue the accordion sections together, using clothespins to hold them in place until the glue dries.
4. Write a suffix on the extended tab so that the first letter is next to the accordion fold.
5. Select and write five words on the accordion strips, aligning the last letter of each word next to the edge of each accordion section as illustrated in the photographs.
6. Fold and flip the accordion section to add the suffix to each of the words listed.

Ten-Word VKV® Variation:
7. Fold the affix tab to the back and read the words without an affix. Fold the affix tab so that it shows, and read the words with the affix.

Twenty-Word VKV® Variation: Make the extended tab longer so a tab can be folded over on the right end. Write a second suffix under the folded tab. Read the word without a suffix, with one suffix, and with two suffixes.

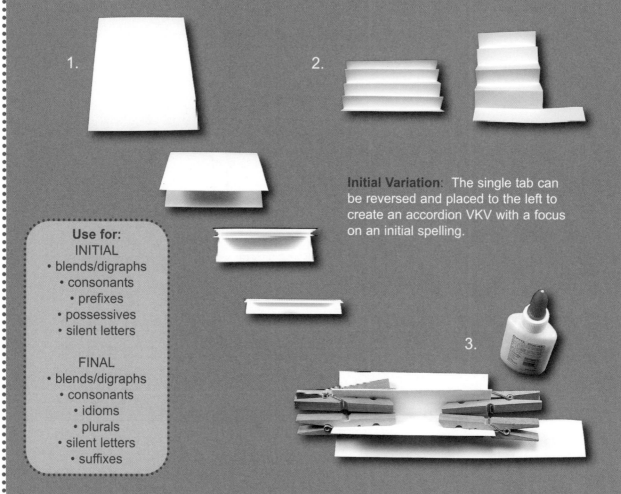

1.

2.

Initial Variation: The single tab can be reversed and placed to the left to create an accordion VKV with a focus on an initial spelling.

3.

Use for:
INITIAL
• blends/digraphs
• consonants
• prefixes
• possessives
• silent letters

FINAL
• blends/digraphs
• consonants
• idioms
• plurals
• silent letters
• suffixes

Examples of Accordion VKVs®

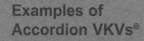

Half Sheets of Photocopy Paper (4¼" x 11") or Notebook Paper (4" x10½") can be used to make small Accordion VKVs to be used as flashcards or glued into student notebooks.

Independent Accordion VKV® Flashcard (above right): This multi-word VKV can be stored in a pocket or envelope. Students might be asked to make one flashcard and then to exchange their cards with other students. In their spelling or vocabulary journals, students record the words they encounter.

Dependent Accordion VKV® Flashcard, also called **Notebook VKV®** (left): This multi-word VKV is like the Independent VKV discussed above, but it is dependent upon the composition book page. It takes up a small amount of space but kinesthetically forms five words, as illustrated in the photographs to the left. Students could make and glue several Accordion VKVs onto one notebook page.

Multi-Tab Accordion (right): Fold a sheet of paper as described in #1. Skip #2. Glue the Accordion sections together. Cut tabs to form two or three sections that flip independently. Do NOT cut through the base. Glue the base into a notebook, or store the VKV in a pocket. Flip the tabs to form words, phrases, idioms, simple sentences, and more.

Appendix Two

Dinah Zike's

Foldables®
Instructions

How to Fold a Book Spine for Foldable Books or Bound VKVs® By Dinah Zike

1. Cut a strip of paper the length of the spine and about one-third the width of the cover. I use scraps of paper to make spines.
   - colored copy paper
   - salvaged wrapping paper
   - scrapbooking paper
   - old maps, pamphlets, advertising flyers
   - colored index cards
   - pictures from magazines
2. Fold one side over leaving a ½" extension.
3. Roll the long, extended side over to cover the short side, but leave ½" of the edge of the short side exposed. Fold. This will form a central spine ½" in width.

Note: Vary the width of the spine by adjusting the amount of space that is left on each side when the paper is folded. To make a thin spine, leave a ¼" space. To make a wider spine leave a 1" space. Observe the width of a Foldable Book or a Bound VKV Book and fold the spine to match this width.

1   2   3

Half-Book Foldable® By Dinah Zike

Fold a sheet of paper or posterboard in half. Label the exterior tab and use the inside space to write information.

1. This Foldable can be folded vertically like a *hotdog*, or...

2. ...it can be folded horizontally like a *hamburger*.

Use this Foldable for descriptive, expository, persuasive, or narrative writing, as well as graphs, diagrams, or charts.

Variation: Half Books can be folded so that one side is ½" wider than the other side. A title or question can be written on the extended tab.

Worksheet or Folded Book Foldable® By Dinah Zike

Make a Half Book (see above) using worksheets, internet printouts, and student-drawn diagrams or maps.

1. Fold it in half again like a *hamburger*. This makes a small book with a cover and two small pages inside for taking notes, comparing and contrasting, exploring cause and effect, and other skills.

2. The Foldable book can be expanded by making several of these folds and gluing them side by side. Glue a cover around the multi-paged pocketbook.

Variation (right): When open, one sheet of paper becomes two activities—one inside and one outside—for two grades. When open, the four quadrants can be used collectively or separately to show sequences or steps.

Two-Tab Foldable® By Dinah Zike

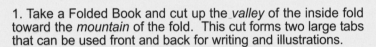

1. Take a Folded Book and cut up the _valley_ of the inside fold toward the _mountain_ of the fold. This cut forms two large tabs that can be used front and back for writing and illustrations.

2. The Foldable book can be expanded by making several of these folds and gluing them side by side. Glue a cover around the multi-paged pocketbook.

Use this Foldable with data occurring in twos. For example, use it for comparing and contrasting, determining cause and effect, finding similarities and differences, and more.

Variation (below left): Concept maps can be made by leaving a 1/2" tab at the top when folding the paper in half. Use arrows and labels to relate topics to the primary concept.

hamburger
version

hotdog
version

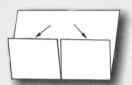

Two-Tab Matching Foldable® By Dinah Zike

1. Fold a sheet of 11" x 17" or 12" x 18" paper so that one third is left uncovered.
2. Fold the paper in half along the long axis to form two columns. Cut along the fold line of the inside small section to form two tabs. Make a fold about ½" above the bottom fold. Label the tabs.
3. Place an equal number of quarter sheets of paper on the inside of both sides.
4. Staple along the ½" fold line to hold the papers in place.

Write or glue a word on a quarter sheet of paper under the left tab of the Foldable, and write or glue its antonym on a random sheet under the right tab.

When the Foldable is complete, students select a word card from the left section and search to find its antonym on the right. See page 81.

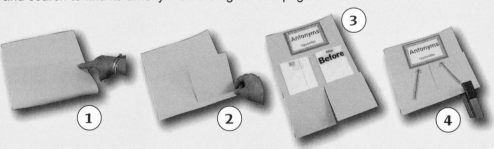

Three-Fourths Foldable® By Dinah Zike

1. Make a Two-Tab Foldable. Raise the left-hand tab.

2. Cut the tab off at the top fold line.

A larger book of information can be made by gluing several Three-Quarter Foldables side by side. Glue a cover around the multi-paged pocketbook.

Use this Foldable to sketch or glue a graphic to the left, write one or more questions on the right, and record answers and information under the right tab.

Variation: Compose a self-test using multiple choice answers for your questions. Include the correct answer and three wrong responses. The correct answers can be written on the back of the Foldable or upside down on the bottom of the inside page.

Three-Tab Foldable® By Dinah Zike

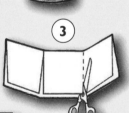

1. Fold a sheet of paper or posterboard like a *hotdog*.

2. With the paper horizontal and the fold of the *hotdog* up, fold into thirds.

Note: If you fold the right edge over first, the final graphic organizer will open and close like a book.

3. Open the Foldable. Placing one hand between the two thicknesses of paper, cut up the two *valleys* on one side only. This will create three tabs.

Use this Foldable to record data occurring in threes.

Variation: Before cutting the three tabs, draw a two-part Venn diagram across the top flap. See page 398.

Variation (right): Make a space to use for titles or concept maps by leaving a ½" tab at the top when folding the paper in half.

Three-Tab Venn Diagram Foldable® By Dinah Zike

1. Fold a sheet of paper like a Three-Tab Foldable (previous page).

2. Before cutting, draw a Venn diagram on the top flap, as shown.

3. Cut the top flap along the folds like a Three-Tab Foldable (previous page).

 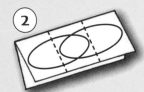 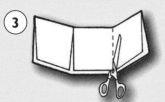

Four-Tab Foldable® By Dinah Zike

1. Fold a sheet of paper or posterboard in half like a *hotdog*.

2. Fold this long rectangle in half like a *hamburger*.

3. Fold both ends back to touch the *mountain* of the fold, or fold it like an accordion.

4. On the side with two *valleys* and one *mountain*, cut along the three folds of the top sheet only, forming four tabs (illus. #5).

Variation: Make a space to use for titles or concept maps by leaving a 1/2" tab at the top when folding the paper in half.

Variation (right): Use the Foldable on the vertical axis, with or without an extended tab.

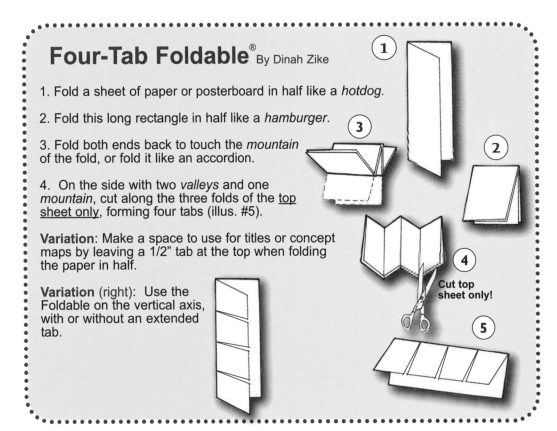

Cut top sheet only!

Trifold Foldable® By Dinah Zike

1. Fold a sheet of paper or posterboard into thirds.

2. Use this Foldable as is, or cut into shapes. If cutting, leave plenty of fold on both sides of the designed shape so the Foldable will still open and close into three sections.

Variation: Use this Foldable to make charts with three columns or rows, large Venn diagrams, and reports on data occurring in threes; or to show and write about the outside and inside of something.

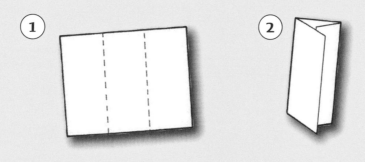

Pocket Foldable® By Dinah Zike

1. Fold a sheet of paper or posterboard in half like a *hamburger*.
2. Open the fold and make a 2"-wide fold along the long side to form a long pocket.
3. Glue the outer edges of the 2" fold with a small amount of glue.
4. Make a multi-paged booklet by gluing several pockets side by side. Glue a cover around the multi-paged pocketbook.

Use 3" x 5" index cards inside the pockets, or use quarter sheets of notebook paper as note cards in the pockets. Store student-made books, such as Two-Tab Foldables and Folded Books, in the pockets, too.

Variation: Make a Three-Pocket Foldable by using a *trifold*. (See top of page.)

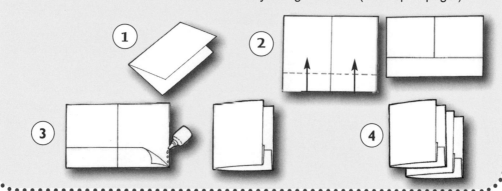

Matchbook Foldable® By Dinah Zike

1. Fold a sheet of paper (8½" x 11") in half like a *hamburger*, but fold it so that one side is 1" longer than the other side.

2. Fold the 1" tab over the short side to form an envelope-like fold.

3. **Variations**: Cut the front flap in half toward the *mountain* to create a Two-Tab Matchbook, or cut the Matchbook in half to create two smaller One-Tab Matchbooks.

Use this Foldable to report on one thing, such as one person, place, or thing; or use the two-tab version for reporting on two things such as causes and effects.

Variation: Mini-Matchbooks can be made using 2½" x 4" sections of paper. See page 189.

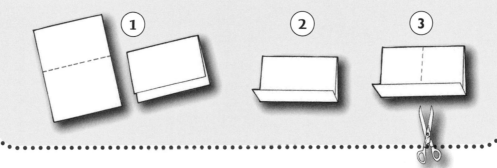

Shutterfold Foldable® By Dinah Zike

1. Begin as if you were going to make a *hamburger*, but instead of folding the paper or posterboard, pinch it to define the midpoint.

2. Fold the outer edges of the paper around to meet at the pinch, or midpoint, forming a *shutterfold*.

Use this Foldable for data occurring in twos, or make this fold using 11" x 17" paper and glue smaller books—such as a Bound Book Journal or Two-Tab Foldable—inside to create a large project full of student work. See example, pages 64-65.

Variation: Use the *shutterfold* on the horizontal axis. Create a center tab by leaving a 3/4" gap between the folded flaps in Step 2.

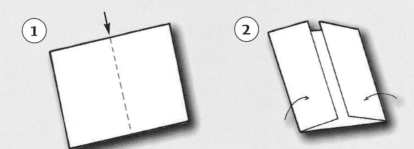

Four-Door Foldable® By Dinah Zike

1. Make a *shutterfold* using paper or posterboard.
2. Fold the *shutterfold* in half like a *hamburger*. Crease well.
3. Open the project and cut along the two inside *valley* folds.
4. These cuts will form four doors on the inside of the project.

Use this fold for data occurring in fours. See example, page 113.

Variation: When folded in half like a *hamburger*, a finished Four-Door Foldable can be glued inside a large (11" x 17") Shutterfold as part of a larger project.

Variation: Create a center tab by leaving a 3/4" gap between the folded flaps in Step 2.

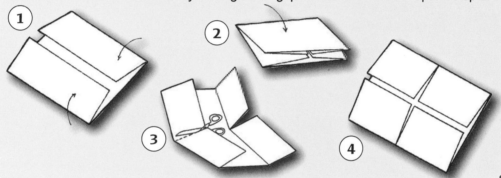

Bound Book Foldable® By Dinah Zike

1. Take two sheets of paper or posterboard and separately fold them like *hamburgers*. Place the papers on top of each other, leaving 1/16" between the *mountains*.

2. Mark both folds 1" from the outer edges.

3. Cut one sheet 1" along the fold at each end to the marked spots.

4. On the second folded sheet, start at one of the marked spots and cut the fold (or "shave it off") between the two marks.

5. Take the cut sheet from Step 3 and fold it like a *burrito*. Place the *burrito* through the other sheet, and then open the *burrito*. Fold the bound pages in half to form an eight-page Foldable book. You can add more pages by inserting more sheets like the ones from Step 3. See page 191.

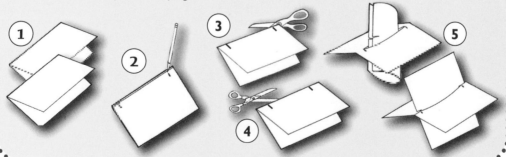

Venn Diagram Bound Book Foldable® By Dinah Zike

1. Stack two sheets of paper, aligning the edges. Fold a tab one-fourth the width of the paper along one of the long sides. Separate the papers.
2. Place the papers on top of each other, leaving 1/8" between the *mountains*. Mark both folds 1" from the outer edges, as illustrated in the second photo.
3. Cut one sheet 1" along the fold at each end, up to the marked spots. On the second folded sheet, start at one of the marked spots and cut the fold (or "shave it off") between the two marks.
4. Place the "cut up" sheet through the "cut out" sheet, and open it to form the overlapping section of this kinesthetic Venn Diagram Bound Book. See page 135.
Note: Two different colors of paper illustrate two different sets. What the sets have in common, or their relationship, is illustrated by the overlap in the middle. Students write on the left side, on the right side, and in the overlapping middle section.

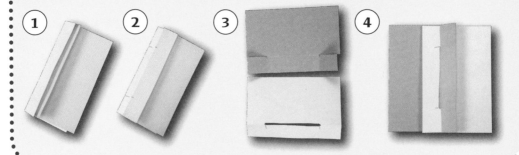

Layered Foldable® By Dinah Zike

1. Stack two sheets of paper or posterboard so that the bottom sheet is 1" (or more when using posterboard or chart paper) higher than the top sheet.

2. Bring the bottom of both sheets upward and align the edges so that all of the layers or tabs are the same distance apart. When all tabs are an equal distance apart, fold the papers and crease well.

3. Open the papers and glue them together along the *valley*, or inner center fold, or staple them along the *mountain*. See examples, page 166 and 167.

4. Finished Foldable.

Variation: Expand the Foldable by adding more pages.

Variation: Rotate the Foldable so the fold is at the top or to the side.

Accordion Foldable® By Dinah Zike

1. Fold two sheets of paper into *hamburgers*.

2. Cut each sheet in half along the fold lines.
(To make a large accordion, omit this step. Use whole sheets of paper.)

3. Fold each half sheet into *hamburgers*, making sure to fold one side 1" shorter than the other side. This will form a tab that is 1" tall.

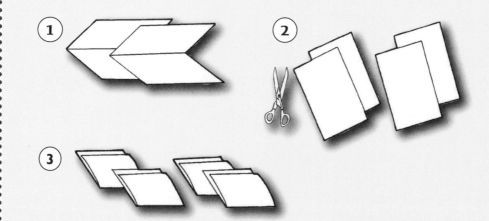

4. Fold this tab forward over the shorter side, then fold it back the other way.

5. To form an accordion, glue a straight edge of one section into the *valley* of another section's tab. See page 279.

NOTE: Before gluing, stand the sections on end to form an accordion. This will help students visualize how to glue the sections together. (See illustration #5.) Always place the extra tab at the end of the Foldable book so you can add more pages later.

Use this Foldable for time lines, student projects that grow, sequencing events or data, and biographies.

Variations: Use whole sheets of paper to make a large Accordion Foldable. Use sheets of posterboard to make a giant Accordion Foldable.

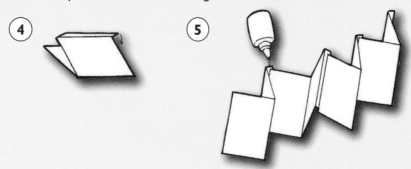

Envelope Foldable® By Dinah Zike

1. Fold a sheet of paper (8½" x 11") into a *taco*. Cut off the excess strip of paper.

2. Open the folded *taco* and refold it the opposite way, forming another *taco* and creating an X-fold pattern on the sheet of paper.

3. Open the *taco* fold and fold each corner toward the center point of the X to create a small, square envelope (illustration #4).

Cut to fit a map, a photo from a magazine, a piece of paper with four words written on it, etc., and place it to the inside of the envelope, under the tabs. Pictures can be placed under or on top of the tabs, or the tabs can be used to teach fractional parts. Use this Envelope Foldable for data occurring in fours.

Variation: For ESL/ELL students, envelope folds can be used for a "hidden picture" vocabulary activity. Have students select or create a picture that fits inside the finished envelope fold. Students can number the tabs in the order in which they are to be opened, then have a friend guess the contents of the picture, raising one tab with each guess.

Variation: Use 11" x 17" or 12" x 18" sheets of paper to make a large Envelope Foldable.

Variation: Cut off the points of the four tabs to create a "window" in the middle of the Foldable.

See examples, pages 315 and 330.

Top-Tab Foldable® By Dinah Zike

1. Fold a sheet of paper or posterboard in half like a *hamburger*. Cut along the center fold, forming two half-sheets.

2. Fold one of the half sheets four times, each time folding in half like a *hamburger*. This folding forms a pattern of four rows and four columns, or 16 small squares.

3. Fold two more sheets of paper or posterboard in half like a *hamburger*. Cut along the folds, forming four half-sheets.

4. Hold the pattern horizontally, and place a half sheet of paper under the pattern. Cut the top right-hand square out of both sheets. Set this first page aside.

5. Take a second half-sheet of paper and place it under the pattern. Cut the first and second upper right squares out of both sheets. Place the second page on top of the first page.

6. Take a third half-sheet of paper and place it under the pattern. Cut the first, second, and third upper right squares out of both sheets. Place this third page on top of the second page.

7. Place the fourth, uncut half-sheet of paper under the three cut-out sheets, leaving four aligned tabs across the top of the Foldable. On top of this stack you can place a full half-sheet of paper (no tabs) to form a cover.

8. Staple several times on the left side. You can also glue along the left paper edges and stack them together. The glued spine is very strong.

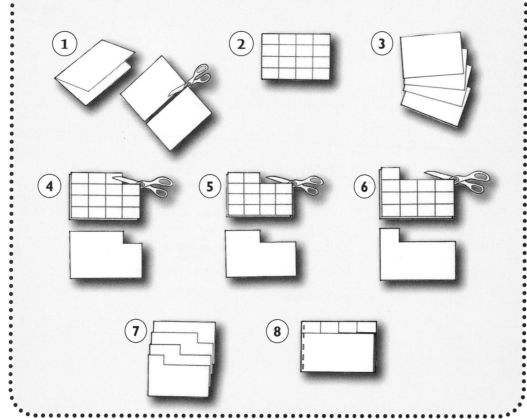

Tabbed Cover-Up Foldable® By Dinah Zike

Use a square of scrapbook paper (12" x 12") or cut a square from a sheet of 11" x 17" photocopy paper or 12" x 18" art paper. This activity works best when the paper used is opaque so students can't see what is written under the tabs.

1. Fold the square into thirds and then sixths along one axis.
2. Fold the square into thirds and then sixths along the second axis.
      This will form 36 square sections.
3. Cut away two sections from each of the four corners. See photo #3.
4. The remaining tabs can be folded forward and backward to expose or
      cover what is written in the sections under the twelve tabs.
5. Have each student make one Tabbed Cover-Up and write examples from a given list of skill-based responses under the tabs. Note: The same response might be written more than once. Not all responses will be on every card. Cards should vary as much as possible. Have students exchange Cover-Ups for exposure to different examples.

Procedure: This board is used in the same manner as a bingo card. Students begin the activity with all tabs open. Something is "called," and if students find it on their card they cover it with the adjacent tab. The first student to cover all the writing on their card "wins."

① ② ③ ④

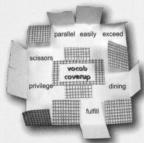

Observing Frequently Misspelled Words (left): Examples of words from the lists on pages 264-269 were written under the tabs. Definitions were "called," and if students found the words that corresponded to the definitions, they covered the words with tabs.
Extension: Students exchange Cover-Ups and quiz each other on how to spell the words on the cards. Words spelled correctly are covered.

Skill	Under the Tabs	What is "Called"
abbreviations, initializations	See page 43.	words that can be abbreviated
antonyms	See page 76.	antonyms of words under the tabs
clipped words	See page 90.	
consonant spellings	blends/digraphs See page 129.	words spelled with blends/digraphs
vowels/diphthongs	See page 334.	words spelled with diphthongs
syllables	See example, page 305.	words with different numbers of syllables
synonyms	See page 312.	synonyms of words under the tabs
vowel spellings	Examples: ea, ie, ei See page 334.	words spelled with different vowel pairs

Pyramid Foldable® By Dinah Zike

1. Fold a sheet of paper or posterboard into a *taco*. Cut off the excess rectangular tab formed by the fold.

2. Open the folded *taco* and refold it like a *taco* the opposite way to create an X-fold pattern.

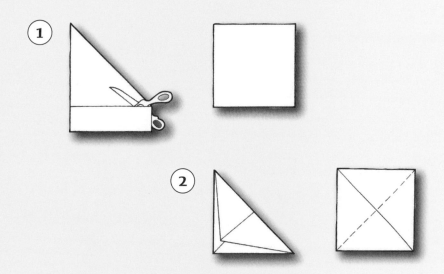

3. Cut one of the folds to the center of the X, or the midpoint, and stop.

4. Glue one of the flaps under the other, forming a 3-sided pyramid, or use a paper clip to hold the tab in place.

5. Label the bottom of each triangular section and write information, notes, thoughts, and questions inside each triangular section.
See examples, pages 162 and 274.

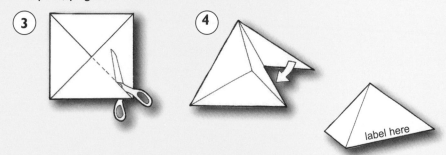

label here

Use the Pyramid Foldable with data occurring in threes.

Variation: Don't cut off the tab in Step 1. Use it to title the Pyramid. Also use it to glue the Pyramid into a notebook (pages 224-225). Unfold the Pyramid and lay the sheet inside the notebook so it fits, and glue the tab to the notebook. That leaves the triangular sections free to fold back into a Pyramid when the notebook is open to that page. The same applies for a project.

Folding Fifths

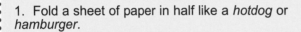
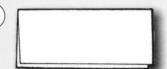

1. Fold a sheet of paper in half like a *hotdog* or *hamburger*.

2. Fold the paper so that one third is exposed and two thirds are covered.

3. Fold the two-thirds section in half.

4. Fold the one-third section backward to form a fold line.

5. Leave open for a five-part folded table or chart, or cut along each fold to create a Five-Tab Foldable.

Variations:
• Unfold and cut along the fold lines to form five tabs (right).
• Make a Five-Tab Foldable with a ½" tab at the top (below).
• Use 11" x 17" paper and fold into fifths to make a five-section chart or table.

Folding a Circle into Tenths

1. Fold a paper circle in half.

2. Fold the half circle so that one third of it is exposed and two thirds are covered.

NOTE: *Paper squares and rectangles are folded into tenths the same way. Fold them so that one third is exposed and two thirds are covered. Continue with steps 3 and 4.*

3. Fold the one-third section backward to form a fold line.

4. Fold the two-thirds section in half.

5. The half circle will be divided into fifths. When opened, the circle will be divided into tenths.

Circle Graph By Dinah Zike

1. Cut out two circles using a pattern.

2. Fold each of the circles in half on each axis, forming fourths. Cut along one of the fold lines (the radius) to the middle of each circle. Flatten the circles.

3. Slip the two circles together along the cuts until they overlap completely.

4. Spin one of the circles while holding the other stationary. Estimate how much of each of the two (or more) circles should be exposed to illustrate given percentages or fractional parts of data. Add circles to represent more than two percentages.

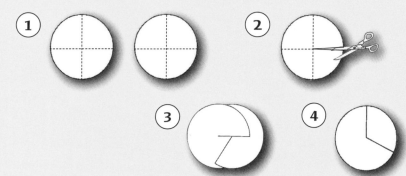

Concept Map Foldable® By Dinah Zike

1. Fold a sheet of paper along the long (*hotdog*) or short (*hamburger*) axis, leaving a 2" tab uncovered along the top.

2. Fold in half or in thirds.

3. Unfold and cut along the two or three inside fold lines. Write a title or main idea on the long top tab, and connect the title with arrows to the supporting information on the tabs.

Four-Door Foldable® Diorama By Dinah Zike

1. Make a four-door Foldable out of a *shutterfold*. Fold it in half along the short axis (*hamburger* fold), then unfold it. You will use this fold in Step 3.

2. Fold the two inside top corners back to the outer edges (*mountains*) of the *shutterfold*. This will result in two *tacos* that will make the Four-Door Foldable look like it has a shirt collar. Do the same thing to the bottom of the Four-Door Foldable. When finished, four small triangular *tacos* will have been made.

3. Fold the *shutterfold* to a 90-degree angle, and overlap the folded triangles to make a diorama display that doesn't use staples or glue. (It can be collapsed for storage.) See examples, pages 137 and 231.

4. **Variation**: For a more permanent diorama, you can cut off all four triangles, or *tacos*, and staple or glue the sides to create the diorama display.

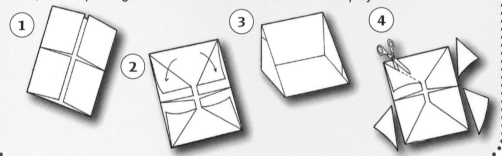

Picture Frame Foldable® By Dinah Zike

1. Fold a sheet of paper or posterboard in half like a *hamburger*.

2. Open the *hamburger* and gently roll one side of the *hamburger* toward the *valley*. Try not to crease the roll.

3. Cut a rectangle out of the middle of the rolled side of the paper to leave a ½" border and form a frame.

4. Fold another sheet of paper (the same size) in half like a *hamburger*. Apply glue to the inside border of the picture frame and place the folded, uncut sheet of paper inside.

Use this Foldable to feature a person, place, or thing. Inside the picture frame glue photographs, magazine pictures, computer-generated graphs, or pictures sketched by students. The Picture Frame Foldable has four inside pages for writing and recording notes.

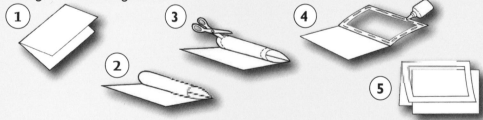

Display Box

1. Make a *taco* fold and cut off the rectangular tab formed. This will result in a square sheet of paper.

2. Fold the square into a *shutterfold*.

3. Unfold and fold the square into another *shutterfold* perpendicular to the direction of the first. This will form a small square at each of the four corners of the sheet of paper (illustration #4).

5. Cut along two fold lines on opposite sides of the large square.

6. Collapse in and glue the cut tabs to form an open box. See page 263.

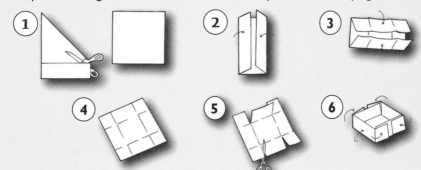

Display Box Lid

1. Fold another open-sided box using a square of paper half an inch larger than the square used to make the first box. Example: If the base is made out of an 8½" paper square, then make the top out of a 9" square. This will make a lid that fits snugly over the Display Box.

2. Turn the box over. Cut a square hole out of the top and cover the opening with a piece of acetate used for overhead projectors. Cut the clear plastic 1" larger than the opening, and glue or tape it to the inside of the lid. Heavy, clear plastic wrap or scraps from a laminating machine would also work.

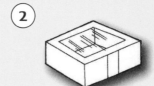

Tabbed Project Foldable® By Dinah Zike

1. Draw a large illustration or a series of small illustrations, or write on the front of a sheet of selected-size paper. You will be forming tabs at each small illustration or forming tabs on one large illustration.

2. To form a tab, pinch and slightly fold the paper at the point where a tab is desired on the illustrated project board. Cut into the paper on the fold. This allows the scissors inside the sheet. Cut a "U"-shaped tab and fold it upward. Fold it back down, flat, to form a tab with an illustration on the front.

3. After all tabs have been cut, glue this front sheet onto a blank sheet of paper of the same size. Place glue around all four edges and in the middle, away from the tabs.

4. Write or draw on the exposed blank paper under the tabs.
See pages 313 and 327.

Billboard Foldable® By Dinah Zike

1. Fold various sheets of same-sized paper in half like *hamburgers*.

2. Place a line of glue at the top and bottom of one side of each folded Billboard section and glue them edge to edge on a background paper or project board. If glued correctly, all doors will open from right to left.

3. Pictures, dates, words, etc., go on the front of each Billboard section. When opened, writing or drawings can be seen on the inside left of each section. The base, or the part glued to the background, is perfect for recording more in-depth information or definitions.

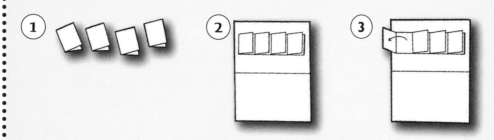

Sentence Strip Foldable® By Dinah Zike

1. Take two sheets of paper (8½" x 11") and fold into *hamburgers*. Cut along the fold lines to make four half-sheets. (Use as many half sheets as necessary for additional pages to your Foldable book.)

2. Fold each half sheet in half like a *hotdog*.

3. Place the folds side by side and staple them together on the left side.

4. One inch from the stapled edge, cut the front page of each folded section up to the *mountain* fold. These cuts form flaps that can be raised and lowered. See example, page 352.

NOTE: To make a half cover, use a sheet of construction paper 1" longer than the book. Glue the back of the last sheet to the construction paper strip, leaving 1" on the left side to fold over and cover the original staples. Staple or glue this half cover in place.

 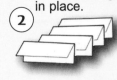  

Variation: Expand the book by adding more pages. Use whole sheets of paper to make a larger Sentence Strip Foldable.

Sentence Strip Holder By Dinah Zike

1. Fold a sheet of paper (8½" x 11") in half like a *hamburger*.

2. Open the *hamburger* and fold the two outer edges toward the *valley*.

3. Fold one of the inside edges back to the outside fold, or *mountain*. This fold forms a floppy "L-tab."

4. Glue the floppy L-tab down to the base so that it forms a strong, straight L-tab.

5. Glue the large unfolded side to the front of the L-tab. This forms a tent that is the backboard for the flashcards or student work to be displayed.

6. Fold the outer edge of the L-tab up ¼" to ½" to form a lip that will keep the student work from slipping off the holder. See example, page 116.

Book Jacket Foldable® By Dinah Zike

1. Fold a sheet of paper (8½" x 11") in half like a *hamburger*, leaving one side ¼" shorter than the other side, then crease.

2. Move the short side up, making it ½" longer than the long side, and crease. This forms the ½" spine of the Foldable book.

3. Fold the outer edges toward the spine, forming two flaps 1½" wide.

4. With the Book Jacket open flat, fold it in half like a *hotdog* and cut along this fold to create two mini Book Jackets.

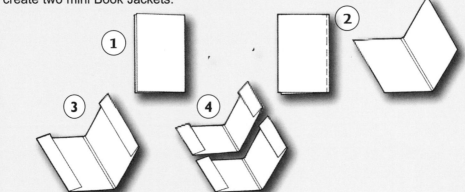

Mini-Book Foldable® By Dinah Zike

1. Fold a sheet of paper (8½" x 11") in half like a *hotdog*.

2. Fold it in half again like a *hamburger*.

3. Fold it in half again, forming eight sections on the page.

4. Open the fold and cut the eight sections apart.

5. Stack the eight sections, and then fold the stack in half like a *hamburger*.

6. Staple along the center fold line. Glue the front and back sheets onto a construction paper cover.

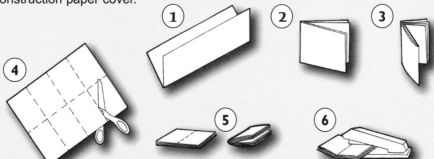

Folded Table or Chart

1. Fold the number of vertical columns needed to make the table or chart.

2. Fold the horizontal rows needed to make the table or chart.

3. Label the rows and columns.

Remember: Tables are organized along vertical axes and horizontal axes, while charts tend to be organized along one axis, either vertical or horizontal.

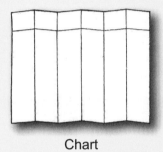

Chart

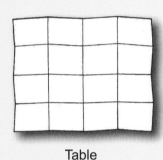

Table

Multi-Tab Foldable® By Dinah Zike

1. Fold a sheet of notebook paper in half like a *hotdog*.

2. On one side, cut every third line. This results in ten tabs on wide-ruled notebook paper and twelve tabs on college-ruled paper.

3. Label the tabs on the outside, and use the inside space for definitions or other information.

Variation: Make a tab for a title by folding the paper so the holes remain uncovered. This also allows the Foldable to be stored in a three-hole binder.

Pocket Chart Foldable® By Dinah Zike
Optional Sentence Strip Holder

Help students create this large Pocket Chart Foldable and use it to collect examples of student work, student art and illustrations, digital photographs, current events, and other items that help students visualize things past and present.

1. Fold a sheet of posterboard in half or into thirds.

2. Fold a 5" tab along the bottom of the posterboard to form a pocket.

3. As an option, you can make a sentence strip holder at the bottom of the Pocket Chart. Make a 1" tab along the bottom of the poster pocket to make a sentence strip holder. Staple ¼" along the ends of the folded pocket and sentence strip holder.

4. Label the tops of the three columns with titles.

Student work and art can be stored in the three pockets, and sentence strips and vocabulary cards can be displayed along the bottom of the Foldable, as illustrated.

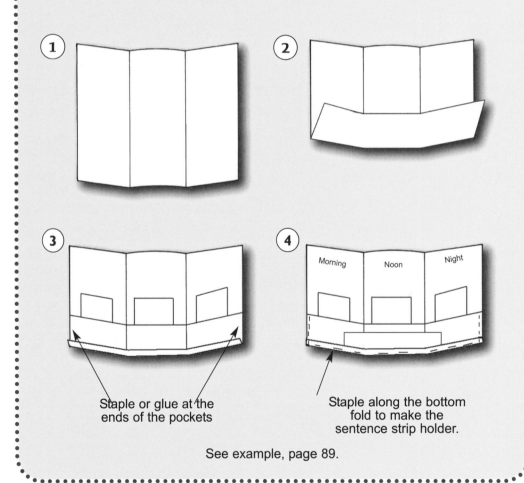

Staple or glue at the ends of the pockets

Staple along the bottom fold to make the sentence strip holder.

See example, page 89.

Top Pocket Foldable® By Dinah Zike

1. Hold a sheet of posterboard with the long edge held horizontally and fold in half like a *hamburger*, but instead of creasing the paper, pinch it to show the midpoint.

2. Fold the outer edges of the paper to meet at the pinch, or midpoint, forming a *shutterfold*. Write the unit title on the front of the *shutterfold*.

3. Crease the folds well, and then open the *shutterfold*.

4. Fold the posterboard upward like a *hotdog* so that the two edges meet.

5. Use the left and right creases to fold the edges of the *hotdog* inward, which will create a large central pocket that can hold student work. Glue or staple the left and right creases to reinforce the pocket.

6. Cut off the bottom fold line of the right and left tabs, allowing them to open and close.

7. Label the front of the Foldable and the four inside tabs.

Write terms and definitions, as well as student-dictated information and thoughts, under the tabs. Collect pictures, illustrations, student worksheets, photographs, and current events, and store them in the top pocket. See examples, page 180 and 181.

Variations: Make small Top-Pocket Foldables using 8½" x 11" paper, and store quarter-sheet flashcards in the top pocket. Or make the Foldables using 11" x 17" paper, and store half-sheet flashcards in the top pocket.

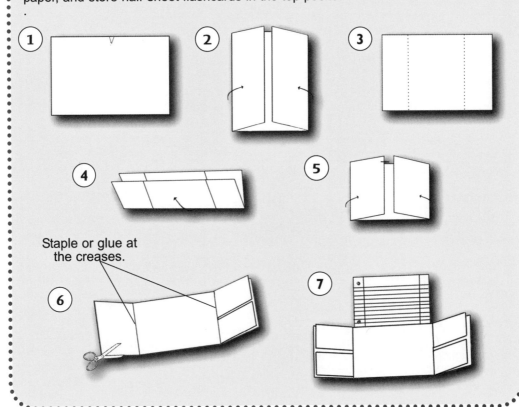

Staple or glue at the creases.

Standing Cube Foldable® By Dinah Zike

1. Use two sheets of the same size paper or posterboard. Fold each like a *hamburger*, making sure to fold one side ½" shorter than the other side.

2. Fold the long side over the short side on both sheets of paper, making tabs.

3. On one of the folded papers, place a small amount of glue along the tab, next to the *valley* but not in it.

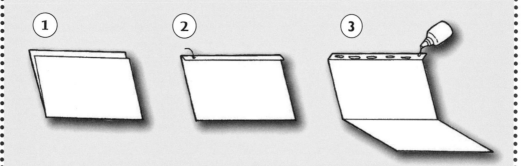

4. Place the non-folded edge of the second sheet of paper squarely into the *valley*, and fold the glue-covered tab over this sheet of paper. Press flat until the glue holds. Repeat with the other side.

5. Allow the glue to dry completely before continuing. After the glue has dried, the cube can be collapsed flat to allow students to work at their desks. The cube can also be folded into fourths for easier storage or for moving it to a display area.

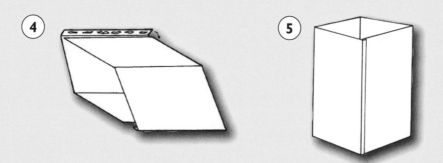

Use with data occurring in fours, or make it into a project. See pages 303 and 329.

Variations:
• Make a small display Cube using 8½" x 11" paper.
• Use 11" x 17" paper to make large project Cubes onto which you can glue other Foldables for display. Notebook paper, photocopied sheets, magazine pictures, and current events can also be displayed on the large cube.
• Cut 1" off the bottom of three of the four sides. One side will have a 1" extension. Fold this back and forth to form a 1" tab.
Use this tab to glue the Cube into a Foldable project or notebook.
See 275 for a photograph of a Cube in a composition book.

Pop-Up Book

1. Fold a sheet of paper (8½" x 11") in half like a *hamburger*.

2. Beginning at the fold, or *mountain*, cut one or more tabs.

3. Fold the tabs back and forth several times to make good fold lines.

4. Partially open the *hamburger* fold and push the tabs through to the inside.

5. With one small dot of glue, glue figures for the Pop-Up Book to the front of each tab. Allow the glue to dry before proceeding to the next step.

6. Make a cover for the Foldable book by folding another sheet of paper in half like a *hamburger*. Place glue around the outside edges of the Pop-Up Book and firmly press inside the *hamburger* cover.

Appendix Three

Research Citations

Evidence-Based Resources
to Support Twelve Common
Instructional Skills & Tools
Used with
Foldables® and VKVs®

Evidence-Based Resources to Support Twelve Common Instructional Skills & Tools Used with Foldables® and VKVs®

Cause and Effect

- Williams, J. P.; Nubla-Kung, A.M; Pollini, S.; Stafford, K. B.; Garcia, A.; Snyder, A. E. 2007. Teaching cause-effect text structure through social studies content to at-risk second graders. *Journal of Learning Disabilities*, 40. 111-120.
- "Cause & Effect." www.literacymatters.org/content/text/cause.htm
- "Cause and Effect Reading Lesson Plan." An introduction for science teachers to the concept of cause & effect. Offers a chart, chain of events, problem/solution diagram, and Venn diagram to analyze different aspects of cause and effect. www.everestquest.com/read2.htm

Compare and Contrast

- Hall, K.M.; Sabey, B. L.; and McClessan, M. 2005. Expository text comprehension: helping primary-grade teachers use expository texts to full advantage. *Reading Psychology*, 26. 211-234.
- Marzano, R.J.; Pickering, D.J.; and Pollock., J.E. 2001. Classroom Instruction That Works. Identifying similarities & differences is the #1 way to raise student achievement. Representing similarities & differences in graphic or symbolic form enhances learners' understanding of and ability to use knowledge.
- Chen, 1999; Cole & McLeod, 1999; Glynn & Takahashi, 1998, Lin, 1996. Combining the instructional strategies of asking students to construct their own means for comparing similarities and differences with the use of nonlinguistic representation significantly enhances student achievement.

Concept Maps & Webs

- Horten et al. 1993. Meta-analysis of studies using concept mapping as a learning strategy showed that concept mapping raised student achievement on average 0.46 standard deviations and contributed to strong improvement in student attitude.
- Novak & Gowan. 1984. In addition to a key role as assessment tools (consider differences before, during and after instruction), concept maps offer a useful way to help students learn how to learn.
- Readence, J. E., Moore, D. W., and Rickelman, R. J. 2000. Pre-reading Activities for Content Area Reading and Learning. 62-81. Describes seven graphic representation strategies.
- Constructing concept maps is a demanding cognitive task that requires training. www.flaguide.org/cat/minutepapers/conmap4.php
- Concept maps, used for over 25 years, help students focus on the "big picture," enabling them to devote more time to conceptual understanding versus rote learning. www.flaguide.org/cat/minutepapers/conmap7.php

Graphs and Diagrams

- Disess, Hammer, Sherin & Kopakowski. 1991. One of the difficulties with conventional instruction is that students' meta-knowledge is often not engaged, so they come to know "how to graph" without understanding what graphs are for or why the conventions make sense.
- Friel, S.N., Curcio, F.R, Bright, G. W. 2001. *Journal for Research in Math. Education*, 32, 2, 124-158. Four critical factors influence graph comprehension: purposes for using graphs, task characteristics (visual decoding, judgment, tasks, and the context or semantic content of a graph), discipline character istics, and reader characteristics . . . Graph sense or comprehension develops gradually as one creates graphs and uses already-designed graphs in a variety of problem-solving contexts that involve the use of data" . . . Consider using a constructivist perspective to enable students to organize and make sense of information before introducing formal work with the traditional types of graphs.
- Pressley et. al, 1988; Woloshy et al., 1990. Non-linguistic representations are important for engaging students in elaborative thinking in two ways. When students elaborate on knowledge, they not only understand it in greater depth, but also recall it much more easily.

Journaling and Bookmaking

- Fordham, N.W., Wellman, D. & Sandman, A. 2002. Taming the text. The Social Studies. 93. 149-158. Writing to learn in all content areas is vital, because considering a topic under study and then writing requires more extensive processing than reading alone entails.
- NWP & Nagin. 2003. Writing to Learn (WTL) advocates encouraging writing to help students discover new knowledge--to sort through previous understandings, draw connections, and uncover new ideas as they write. WTL activities can also encourage reflection on learning strategies and thereby increase students' meta-cognitive skills. (exs: journals, learning logs, exit slips)
- Sprenger, M. 2005. Students reinforce their learning when they communicate and especially write about "their content, be it concepts, facts or procedures."

KWL and Variations

- Eshelman, John W., Ed.D. 2001. Commentary on Behavior and Instruction: Ausubel, Advance Organizers, and Replicable Research. www.members.aol.com;johneshleman/comment12.html
- Frey, N. and Fisher, D.B. 2006. 19-20. *Language Arts Workshop: Purposeful Reading and Writing Instruction.*
- Merkley, D.M. and Jeffries, D. 2001. Guidelines for Implementing a Graphic Organizer. *The Reading Teacher* 54 (4), 538-540.
- Ogle, D. M. *The Reading Teacher*, 39, 564-570. KWL: A teaching model developed by Ogle in 1986 that develops active reading of expository text.
- Readence, J.E., Bean, T.W., & Baldwin, R. S. 1998. Teachers can vary the way to expose students to information before they "learn" it. KWL is a good, logical graphic application.

Main Idea & Supportive Facts

- Barton, J. and Sawyer, D. 2004. Our students are ready for this: Comprehension instruction in the elementary school. *The Reading Teacher*, 57, 334-347.
- Just, M. and Carpenter, P. 1992. A capacity theory of comprehension: Individual differences in working memory. *Psychological Review*, 1992, 122-149. In most reading situations we read for the main points, in part, due to memory constraints. We can't process every line in the text at the same level if our working memory is overloaded with too much information. Part of the information then is displaced or 'forgotten.'
- Tomitch. L.M.B. 2000. Teaching main ideas -- Are we really teaching? *Linguagem & Ensino*, 45-53. Main idea identification is one of the most important literacy comprehension skills. Textbooks typically provide tasks or practice involving the main ideas, but do not actually provide explicit procedures and instruction in main idea identification and formulation.

Opposites (Pairing of Antonyms)

- Heidenheimer, P. 1978. Logical relations in the semantic processing of children between six and ten: emergence of antonym and synonym categorization. *Child Development*. 49. 1243-1246.
- Jones, Steven. 2007. "Opposites" in discourse: a comparison on antonym use across four domains. *Journal of Pragmatics*. 39. 1105-1119.
- Jones, S. and Murphy, M. L. Antonymy in childhood: a corpus-based approach to acquisition.
- McKeown,M. G. 1993. Creating effective definitions for young word learners. *Reading Research Quarterly*, 27, 16-31.

Questioning

- Cotton, K. Teaching questioning skills: Franklin Elementary School. *School Improvement Research Series*. http://www.nwrel.org/scpd/sirs/4/snap13.html. Research on questioning reveals among other findings that teaching students how to respond to and how to frame higher-level questions is positively related to their voluntary participation in such higher cognitive processes in classroom discussions.
- McKenzie, Jamie. 2005. Learning to Question to Wonder to Learn.
- Raphael, T. E., 1986. Promotes replacing traditional cognitive hierarchies of questions relative to text and graphics with classifications that identify the kinds of transactions that learners/readers use with the text to answer questions. One way to teach these important QAR strategies is with the help of graphic organizers.

Sequencing Events/Cycles/Ordering

- Cusimano, A., M.Ed. 2006. Auditory Sequential Memory Instructional Workbook.   Within the area of the brain controlling the processing of information presented in isolation or sequential order, each aspect (numbers, letters and words) is specific unto itself. Students who have mastered the skill of number memory may not have developed the skill of remembering letters and words, or vice versa. Thus, we must consider the development of all numbers, letters, and words separately.
- Frey, N.and Fisher, D. B. 2006. 337-340. *Language Arts Workshop: Purposeful Reading and Writing Instruction*. Focus on temporal or sequential text structure and signal words in expository text with explicit instruction on structure and styles used in content area texts and informational trade books.

Tables and Charts

- Bruning, Schraw, Norby & Roning. 2003. Research on the effects of students self-generating material that involves recoding, as is built into interactive graphic organizers, shows that students consistently do better.
- Katayama & Robinson, 2000. Evidence suggests that blank or partially completed graphic organizers promote greater text comprehension than those completed in advance for students.
- Graphic displays outside of text, such as pictures, geographic and concept maps, tables and charts, and the like promote recall of text when used in concert with each other. The belief is that such displays are effective because they provide the learner with two avenues to memory: verbal (text) and spatial (the placement of information in relation to other facts), and that the spatial and verbal work in concert with one another (Kulhavy, Lee, & Caterino, 1985 as cited in Fischer et. al., 2007, *50 Content Area Strategies for Adolescent Literacy*. p. 3). "For real learning to occur, students must use the graphic organizer to transform information. The goal . . . is not to fill it out; that's a worksheet." The graphic organizer "is an external storage device for information" and to be useful, it "should be used to transform information into verbal or written form" so that students can make the information their own. Fischer et. al., 2007. *50 Content Area Strategies for Adolescent Literacy*. p. 3.

Vocabulary Development

- Baumann, F.F. and Kame'enui, E.J. 2004. *Vocabulary Instruction: Research to Practice*. Three of four research-based modes for teaching vocabulary: wide reading, explicit teaching of specific words, teaching of word-learning strategies, and development of word consciousness can be well supported by interactive graphic organizers. Marzano's vision for direct vocabulary instruction aims for a top-level linguistic understanding of words accompanied by visual representation of terms that students encounter in their academic reading.
- Beck, I. L, McKeown, M. G, & Kucan, L. 2002. *Bringing Words to Life: Robust Vocabulary Instruction*.
- Dolch, E. W. Problems in Reading, 1948. First publication of the Dolch high frequency list.
- Fry, E. B. 2004. The Vocabulary Teacher's Book of Lists.
- Fry, E. B. and Kress, J. E. 2006. The Reading Teacher's Book of Lists, 5th Edition.
- Moore, D. W. and Readence, J. 1984 . A qualitative and quantitative review of graphic organizer research. Journal of Educational Research. 78. 11-17. Meta-analysis of 24 studies suggests that vocabulary knowledge gains following graphic organizer use may be even greater than comprehension gains.
- Sakiey, E. and Fry, E. B. 1979. 3000 Instant Words. Presents the 3,000 most frequently used words in rank and alphabetical orders. ERIC ID169516
- White T.G., Sowell, V., and Yanagihara, A. 1989. Teaching elementary students to use word-part clues. *The Reading Teacher*. 42. 302-309. Includes list of 20 most common prefixes and suffixes.

Dinah Zike Academy   www.dzacademy.com

Dinah Zike is proud to introduce the Dinah Zike Academy, a teacher training institute outside of San Antonio in the beautiful and historic Texas Hill Country.

Dinah: *It has always been my dream to have a location for teachers to immerse themselves in a fully developed, hands-on lab setting that will provide strategies to address diverse learners, meet state and national benchmarks, and build student learning skills for life. I also want to provide the opportunity for teachers to become Dinah Zike Certified trainers for their district, state, or nationwide, because I can't physically reach all the teachers who want to learn more about Foldables®, VKVs,® and my other teaching strategies.*

In three-day, jam-packed sessions at the Academy, Dinah and/or DZA's pro facilitators will engage and immerse you in the power and potential of 3-D interactive graphic organizers, dynamic and efficient classroom organization, and effective teaching strategies across age-grade levels and content areas. Research grounding, implementation for a variety of learners, and practicality are built in. A session maximum of 24 participants allows for hands-on individual and small-group work, technology use, and direct application to participants' teaching practices. Some seminars are cross-curricular and targeted to either elementary or secondary levels. Others are focused on specific content/subject areas, such as science, mathematics, social studies, and reading/language arts.

The expansive Academy is well-equipped with group and individual classrooms, high-speed Internet access, computer work stations, working design areas and tools, easily replicable supply stations, displays and publishing centers plus resources including artifacts, a research and reference library, and the list goes on.

The Academy is located in the heart of the historic and charming village of Comfort, Texas, in the beautiful Texas Hill country, 45 minutes from San Antonio and 1½ hours from Austin. Most convenient airport is San Antonio. Antiquing, shopping, golfing, fishing, bicycling, sightseeing, caving, natural and historic-site adventuring are popular area pursuits. Or just relaxing on the porch of your B&B!

Testimonial: "*I just returned from the Dinah Zike Academy, and I'm overwhelmed with the vast amount of information provided. This is my 37th year in education, and I've never enjoyed a course of study as much as the Academy.*"

For More Information, or to reserve your spot:

WEBSITE: www.dzacademy.com
PHONE: 830-995-3800
FAX: 830-995-5205
EMAIL: dzi@hctc.net
DZ Academy, P. O. Box 340, Comfort TX 78013

Other Language Arts Materials by Dinah Zike
To see all of Dinah's books and materials visit www.dinah.com
or call 800-99DINAH for a color catalog

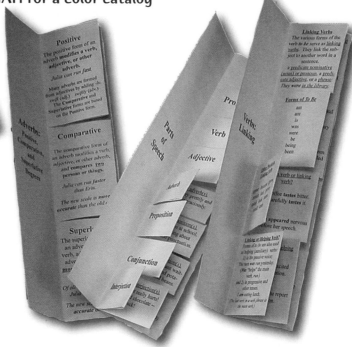

NEW ELEMENTARY BOOK
Foldables and VKVs for Phonics, Spelling and Vocabulary PreK - 3rd

New Folds & 1000 Color Photos!
Dinah has compiled her best phonics, vocabulary, and spelling Foldables®, word lists, and Visual Kinesthetic Vocabulary (VKV®) flashcards into this 350-page illustrated teaching manual with over 1000 full-color photographs. The book is arranged in alphabetical order to quickly find activities and word lists for teaching consonants, vowels, antonyms, synonyms, homographs, homophones, prefixes, suffixes, and more!
CCC112...$34.95

STUDY FLIPS™
NEW for Middle School, High School and College Review:
Packet includes the following:
- **One set of 20 color-coded Study Flips™ printed on heavy 67# Vellum Bristol paper.** These sturdy, colorful Study Flips™ are to be made into a classroom set for use in class discussions and by students as a manipulative review or writing aid.
- **One master set of 20 Study Flips™ printed on 20# white paper.** This set can be kept on file to make photocopies for student use as study guides, homework papers, note-taking devices, and tools for strengthening writing skills. **Study Flips Grammar SF101....$20.00**

Academic Vocabulary Pocketbooks™

Each packet contains an instruction sheet and a master set of pocketbooks (**A**) to be duplicated for individual students to make and use. Students write or collect "real world print" examples onto the pockets (**B**) or analyze new terms by researching word etymology and meaning and make flashcards for those terms (**C**) and sort the flashcards into the 27 titled pockets (**D**) such as *Clipped Words, Syllabication, Root Words, Prefixes, Suffixes, Homophones, Acronyms,* etc.). Great review of word rules for beginning and advanced students (and teachers)!
U.S. History PB101....$9.95
Reading, Writing & Literature PB102....$9.95
Science PB103....$9.95   Math PB104....$9.95

Finished Pocketbooks

To order call 1-800-99DINAH or visit www.dinah.com

Dinah Zike's
Academic Vocabulary Pocketbooks™

Reading, Writing, Literature

Each packet includes a master set of pocketbooks printed on 20-pound paper to be duplicated for individual student use. Students make small flashcards for new terms, analyze and research the etymologies and meanings of the terms using their text and computer dictionaries, and sort the flashcards into the pockets of their booklets. Students are encouraged to collect and include words found in "real world print."

Photos: An example of a finished book

Dinah Zike's Academic Vocabulary Pocketbooks™ consist of 28 pages of pockets for collecting terms presented in literature, language arts textbooks, or independent units of study. Words are analyzed using books or on-line dictionaries, thesauri, and etymology aids and then sorted into any of the following pockets:

-Abbreviations
-Acronyms and Initializations
-Analogies
-Antonyms
-Borrowed Words (Loan Words)
-Clipped Words
-Compound Words
-Consonants (spelling gremlins)
-Double Letters
-Heteronyms
-Homographs
-Homophones
-Idioms

-Plurals
-Prefixes
-Proper Nouns (Person)
-Proper Nouns (Place)
-Proper Nouns (Thing, Idea)
-Root Words
-Silent Letters
-Suffixes
-Syllabication
-Synonyms
-Vowels (spelling gremlins)
-Know
-Need to Know

Example page before folding

Big Book Series
Middle School & High School
Foldables® for Every Subject

You've attended a Dinah Zike workshop at your school or at a teacher's conference and are ready to start using 3-D graphic organizers in the classroom, but you need help generating those great ideas. Now Dinah has combined instructions for her most popular folds, full-color photographs of examples, and lists of thousands of ideas she has collected over her thirty years of inventing and teaching using graphic organizers. The lists of ideas are divided by the skill being taught, an activity to teach the subject or concept, and how many foldable parts so you can quickly choose an appropriate graphic organizer. Books are subject specific and geared towards elementary level or middle school/high school level.

Big Book Series, Middle School & High School

Big Book of Science (6-12) CCC102..$19.95
Big Book of Math (6-12) CCC104..$19.95
Big Book of Texas History (Perfect for 7th Grade Texas History Teachers) CCC105..$19.95
Big Book of United States History (5-12) CCC107..$19.95
Big Book of World History (6-12) CCC108..$19.95

The Earth Science Book overflows with dozens of easy-to-do activities that explain basic Earth science facts and important environmental issues. Using simple materials you can find around the classroom or home, these activities show you all about the planet Earth, its composition and atmosphere, life on Earth, and much more. ***CCC92..$12.95***

Classroom Periodic Table of Elements

Make an interactive **Giant Classroom Periodic Table of Elements** (60"W x 40"H), or reduce the size of these reproducible patterns to make individual element flashcards. Under each tab, students are prompted to fill in the atomic number, atomic weight, melting point, boiling point, properties, and history of the element. Packet includes 112 elements. **CCC79..$10.00**

To order call 1-800-99DINAH or visit www.dinah.com

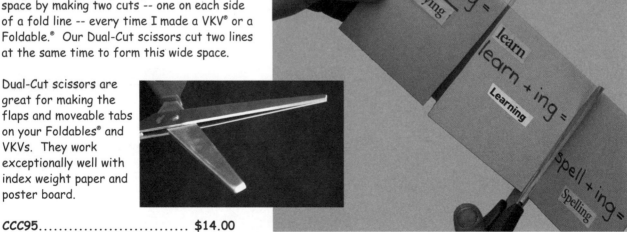

Notebook Foldables®
For Spirals, Binders, & Composition Books

Strategies for all Subjects 4th-College

Dinah's latest book features adaptations of her Foldables® specially designed to fit in composition books, spiral notebooks, binders, and even exam books. Notebook Foldables® work well in any subject area to stimulate ideas and represent information in a format more familiar and useful to more advanced/upper level students. Reproducible Notebook Foldable® templates are supplied in the book, as well as instructions on how to create these modified Foldables® using regular paper. This 129-page book contains over 400 full-color photos of examples of Notebook Foldables®! **CCC 113....$24.95**

Dinah Zike's
Notebook Foldables®
For Spirals, Binders, & Composition Books
Strategies for All Subjects 4th Grade - College

Fast becoming a bestseller!

ALSO RECOMMENDED FOR **ESL/ELL**

Dinah Zike, M.Ed.

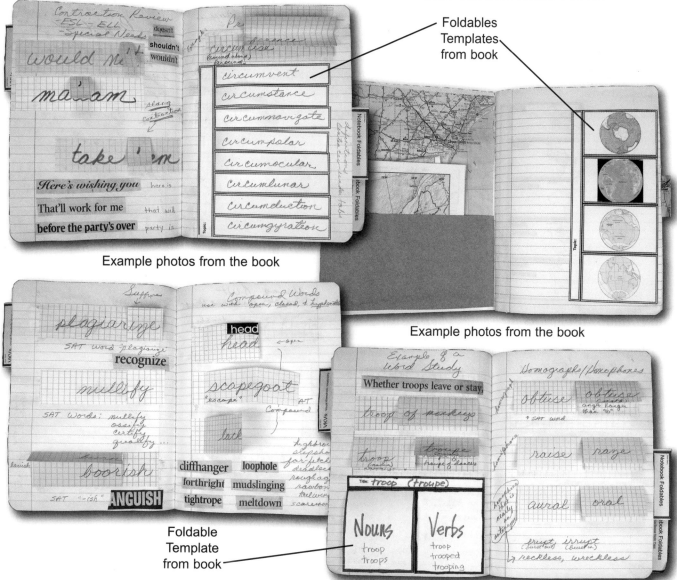

Foldables Templates from book

Example photos from the book

Example photos from the book

Foldable Template from book